I & II PETER
I, II, & III JOHN
JUDE

VOLUME 12

THE
PREACHER'S
OUTLINE & SERMON
BIBLE®

I & II PETER
I, II, & III JOHN
JUDE

VOLUME 12

THE
PREACHER'S
OUTLINE & SERMON
BIBLE®

NEW TESTAMENT

NEW INTERNATIONAL VERSION

Leadership Ministries Worldwide
PO Box 21310
Chattanooga, TN 37424-0310

Publisher & Distributor

DEDICATED:

To all the men and women of the world
who preach and teach the Gospel of our
Lord Jesus Christ and
To the Mercy and Grace of God.

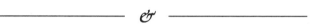

- Demonstrated to us in Christ Jesus our Lord.

  "In him we have redemption through his blood, the forgiveness
  of sins, in accordance with the riches of God's grace." (Eph. 1:7 NIV)

- Out of the mercy and grace of God His Word has flowed.
  Let every person know that God will have mercy upon him,
  forgiving and using him to fulfill His glorious plan of salvation.

  "For God so loved the world, that he gave his one and only Son, that
  whosoever believes in him shall not perish, but have eternal life. For
  God did not send his Son into the world to condemn the world, but to
  save the world through him." (Jn 3:16-17 NIV)

  "This is good and pleases God our Saviour; who wants all men to be
  saved and to come to the knowledge of the truth." (I Tim. 2:3-4 NIV)

_____ & _____

The Preacher's Outline and Study Bible®-NIV
is written for God's servants to use in their
study, teaching, and preaching of God's Holy Word.

OUR VISION - PASSION - PURPOSE

- To share the Word of God with the world.
- To help the believer, both minister and layman alike, in his understanding,
  preaching, and teaching of God's Word.
- To do everything we possibly can to lead men, women, boys, and girls to
  give their hearts and lives to Jesus Christ and to secure the eternal life
  which He offers.
- To do all we can to minister to the needy of the world.
- To give Jesus Christ His proper place, the place which the Word gives Him.
  Therefore — No work of Leadership Ministries Worldwide will ever be
  personalized.

12/98

HOW TO USE... The Preacher's Outline & Sermon Bible®

A	Your **Scripture Passage** always printed out
B	Your **Sermon Outline** located next to each verse
C	A Wealth of **Practical Commentary** Material
D	**Illustrations** and **Applications** for every audience
E	**Support Scripture** thoroughly researched & written out

First: Glance at the **Subject Heading**. Think about it for a moment. *Then*: Glance at the **Subject Heading** & the **Major Points** together.

Now: Glance at both the **Major Points** & **Subpoints** while reading the Scripture. Note how the points are beside the applicable verse—simply stating what the Scripture is saying—in Outline form.

Finally: Read the **Commentary**. KEY: Note that the *major point numbers* in the *outline* match those in the *commentary*.

MATTHEW 6:1-4

CHAPTER 6

K. The Right Motive for Giving, psi 6:1-4

1 Acts of righteousness—doing good & giving
   a. Warning: Do not seek recognition
   b. The reason: God will not reward
2 The wrong motive
   a. Giving for recognition

"Be careful not to do your 'acts of righteousness' before men, to be seen by them. If you [A], you will have no rew[A]rom your Father in heaven.
2 "So when you give to the needy, do not announce it with trumpets, as the hy-pocrites do in the syna-gogues and on the streets, to be honored by men. I tell you the truth, they have received their reward in full.
3 But when you give to the needy, do not let your left hand know what your right hand is doing,
4 So that your giving may be in secret. Then your Father, who sees what is done in se-cret, will reward you.

   b. Characteristic of hypocrites
   c. Reward: Recognition by men only
   [B]
3 The right motive
   a. Giving unconsciously
   b. Giving quietly—privately—secretly
4 The reasons
   a. Father sees in secret
   b. Father rewards openly

DIVISION IV

THE TEACHINGS OF THE MESSIAH TO HIS DISCIPLES: THE GREAT SERMON ON THE MOUNT, 5:1-7:29

K. The Right Motive for Giving, 6:1-4

(6:1-4) **Introduction—Motive**: what a man does matters greatly to God. God expects men to be kind and to do good in the world: to help others both through personal involvement and through giving generously and sacrificially.

But there is something else that God expects, something of critical importance: God expects a man to have *the right motive*. Just why [C] man does good and shows kindness matters greatly to God. It matters so much that a person's eternal fate is determined by his motive. Because of this, Christ warns us about right and wrong motives.
1. Acts of righteousness—doing good and giving (v.1).
2. The wrong motive (v.2).
3. The right motive (v.3-4).
4. The reasons (v.4).

1 (6:1) **Righteous Acts—Service—Giving**: there are acts of righteousness—doing good and giving to others. The phrase "acts of righteousness" means giving in order to meet the needs of the poor. To the Jew, acts of righteousness and righteousness meant the same thing. Doing righteous acts was the greatest thing a Jew could do; it was the first act of religion. It was considered to be the very embodiment of righteousness, so much so that the two words began to be used synonymously. Giving acts of righteousness merited and assured one of righteousness and salvation. (See note 5—Mt.5:6.) Christ warned there is great danger in giving and doing acts of righteousness. Take heed and guard yourself. Do not give for recognition, or you will lose your reward.

Thought 1. There are two important lessons in this verse.
1) Man must guard and be alert to the deception of giving and doing good before men. A person's heart can be deceived. The sin creeps up on man; it is insidious and [D]tle. It will keep a person from receiving anything from God.
2) A person must do righteous acts, do good. It is a duty of the Christian. In this passage alone Christ says four times, "Do your acts of righteousness."

2 (6:2) **Motive**: there is the wrong motive for doing good. Christ takes for granted that the believer gives and does good. What Christ strikes at is the motive of the human heart for giving and doing good.

1. Giving for recognition is the wrong motive for giving. Recognition is said to be sought by blowing one's own horn in two places: (a) in the synagogue before religious people, and (b) in the streets before the public.

[E] **"Everything they do is done for men to see: They make their phylacteries wide and the tassels on their garments long; (Mat 23:5)**

"Beware of the teachers of the law. They like to walk around in flowing robes and love to be greeted in the marketplaces and have the most important seats in the synagogues and the places of honor at banquets. (Luke 20:46)

OUTLINE BIBLE RESOURCES

This material, like similar works, has come from imperfect man and is thus susceptible to human error. We are nevertheless grateful to God for both calling us and empowering us through His Holy Spirit to undertake this task. Because of His goodness and grace **The Preacher's Outline & Sermon Bible®** - New Testament is complete in 14 volumes, and the Old Testament volumes release periodically. **The Minister's Handbook** is available and *OUTLINE* Bible materials are releasing electonically on **POSB-CD** and our **Web site**.

God has given the strength and stamina to bring us this far. Our confidence is that, as we keep our eyes on Him and grounded in the undeniable truths of the Word, we will continue working through the Old Testament volumes and the second series known as **The Teacher's Outline & Study Bible.** The future includes helpful *Outline Bible* books and **Handbook** materials for God's dear servants.

To everyone everywhere who preaches and teaches the Word, we offer this material firstly to Him in whose name we labor and serve, and for whose glory it has been produced.

Our daily prayer is that each volume will lead thousands, millions, yes even billions, into a better understanding of the Holy Scriptures and a fuller knowledge of Jesus Christ the incarnate Word, of whom the Scriptures so faithfully testify.

> As you have purchased this volume, you will be pleased to know that a small portion of the price you have paid has gone to underwrite and provide similar volumes in other languages (Russian, Korean, Spanish and others yet to come) — To a preacher, pastor, lay leader, or Bible student somewhere around the world, who will present God's message with clarity, authority, and understanding beyond their own. *Amen.*

For information and prices, kindly contact your *OUTLINE* Bible bookseller or:

LEADERSHIP
MINISTRIES
WORLDWIDE

P.O. Box 21310, 515 Airport Road, Suite 107
Chattanooga, TN 37424-0310
(423) 855-2181 FAX (423) 855-8616
E-Mail - outlinebible@compuserve.com
www.outlinebible.org — *FREE* download materials

9/98

PUBLISHER & DISTRIBUTOR OF OUTLINE BIBLE MATERIALS

Currently Available Materials, with New Volumes Releasing Regularly

- **THE PREACHER'S OUTLINE & SERMON BIBLE® — DELUXE EDITION**

  3-Ring, looseleaf binder

- **THE PREACHER'S OUTLINE & SERMON BIBLE® — OLD TESTAMENT**

  New volumes release periodically

- **THE PREACHER'S OUTLINE & SERMON BIBLE® — SOFTBOUND EDITION**
  Identical content as Deluxe above. Lightweight, compact, and affordable for overseas & traveling

- **THE PREACHER'S OUTLINE & SERMON BIBLE® — 3 VOL HARDCOVER w/CD**

- **THE PREACHER'S OUTLINE & SERMON BIBLE® — NIV SOFTBOUND EDITION**

- **The Minister's Personal Handbook - What the Bible Says...to the Minister**
  12 Chapters - 127 Subjects - 400 Verses *OUTLINED* - Paperback, Leatherette, 3-ring

- **THE TEACHER'S OUTLINE & STUDY BIBLE™ • New Testament Books •**
  Complete 45 minute lessons - 4 months of studies/book; 200± pages - Student Journal Guides

- **OUTLINE Bible Studies series: 10 Commandments - The Tabernacle**

- **Practical Word Studies: New Testament - 2,000 Key Words Made Easy**

- **CD-ROM: Preacher, Teacher, and Handbook-** (Windows/STEP) - WORD*Search*

- **Translations of Preacher, Teacher, and Minister's Handbook: <u>Limited Quantities</u>**
  Russian — Spanish — Korean Future: *French, Portuguese, Hindi, Chinese*
  — Contact us for Specific Language Availability and Prices —

For quantity orders and information, please contact either:

LEADERSHIP MINISTRIES WORLDWIDE   *Your OUTLINE Bible Bookseller*
PO Box 21310
Chattanooga, TN 37424-0310
(423) 855-2181 (9am - 5pm Eastern) • FAX (423) 855-8616 (24 hours)
E•Mail - outlinebible@compuserve.com.
→ FREE Download Sample Pages — www.outlinebible.org

• *Equipping God's Servants Worldwide with OUTLINE Bible Materials* •
LMW is a nonprofit, international, nondenominational mission agency   9/98

ACKNOWLEDGMENTS

Every child of God is precious to the Lord and deeply loved. And every child as a servant of the Lord touches the lives of those who come in contact with him or his ministry. The writing ministry of the following servants have touched this work, and we are grateful that God brought their writings our way. We hereby acknowledge their ministry to us, being fully aware that there are so many others down through the years whose writings have touched our lives and who deserve mention, but the weaknesses of our minds have caused them to fade from memory. May our wonderful Lord continue to bless the ministry of these dear servants, and the ministry of us all as we diligently labor to reach the world for Christ and to meet the desperate needs of those who suffer so much.

THE GREEK SOURCES

1. Expositor's Greek Testament, Edited by W. Robertson Nicoll. Grand Rapids, MI: Eerdmans Publishing Co., 1970

2. Robertson, A.T. Word Pictures in the New Testament. Nashville, TN: Broadman Press, 1930.

3. Thayer, Joseph Henry. Greek-English Lexicon of the New Testament. New York: American Book Co, No date listed.

4. Vincent, Marvin R. Word Studies in the New Testament. Grand Rapids, MI: Eerdmans Publishing Co., 1969.

5. Vine, W.E. Expository Dictionary of New Testament Words. Old Tappan, NJ: Fleming H. Revell Co. No date listed.

6. Wuest, Kenneth S. Word Studies in the Greek New Testament. Grand Rapids, MI: Eerdmans Publishing Co., 1966.

THE REFERENCE WORKS

7. Cruden's Complete Concordance of the Old & New Testament. Philadelphia, PA: The John C. Winston Co., 1930.

8. Josephus' Complete Works. Grand Rapids, MI: Kregel Publications, 1981.

9. Lockyer, Herbert. Series of Books, including his Books on All the Men, Women, Miracles, and Parables of the Bible. Grand Rapids, MI: Zondervan Publishing House, 1958-1967.

10. -Nave's Topical Bible. Nashville, TN: The Southwestern Co., No date listed.

11. The Amplified New Testament. (Scripture Quotations are from the Amplified New Testament, Copyright 1954, 1958, 1987 by the Lockman Foundation. Used by permission.)

12. The Four Translation New Testament (Including King James, New American Standard, Williams - New Testament In the Language of the People, Beck - New Testament In the Language of Today.) Minneapolis, MN: World Wide Publications.

13. The New Compact Bible Dictionary, Edited by T. Alton Bryant. Grand Rapids, MI: Zondervan Publishing House, 1967.

14. The New Thompson Chain Reference Bible. Indianapolis, IN: B.B. Kirkbride Bible Co., 1964,

THE COMMENTARIES

15. Barclay, William. Daily Study Bible Series. Philadelphia, PA: Westminster Press, Began in 1953.

16. Bruce, F.F. The Epistle to the Ephesians. Westwood, NJ: Fleming H. Revell Co., 1968.

17. Bruce, F.F. Epistle to the Hebrews. Grand Rapids, MI: Eerdmans Publishing Co., 1964.

18. Bruce, F.F. The Epistles of John. Old Tappan, NJ: Fleming H. Revell Co., 1970.

19. Criswell, W.A. Expository Sermons on Revelation. Grand Rapids, MI: Zondervan Publishing House, 1962-66.

20. Greene, Oliver. The Epistles of John. Greenville, SC: The Gospel Hour, Inc., 1966.

21. Greene, Oliver. The Epistles of Paul the Apostle to the Hebrews. Greenville, SC: The Gospel Hour, Inc., 1965.

22. Greene, Oliver. The Epistles of Paul the Apostle to Timothy & Titus. Greenville, SC: The Gospel Hour, Inc., 1964.

23. Greene, Oliver. The Revelation Verse by Verse Study. Greenville, SC: The Gospel Hour, Inc., 1963.

24. Henry, Matthew. Commentary on the Whole Bible. Old Tappan, NJ: Fleming H. Revell Co.

25. Hodge, Charles. Exposition on Romans & on Corinthians. Grand Rapids, MI: Eerdmans Publishing Co., 1972-1973.

26. Ladd, George Eldon. A Commentary On the Revelation of John. Grand Rapids, MI: Eerdmans Publishing Co., 1972-1973.

27. Leupold, H.C.   Exposition of Daniel. Grand Rapids, MI: Baker Book House, 1969.

28. Morris, Leon.   The Gospel According to John. Grand Rapids, MI: Eerdmans Publishing Co., 1971.

29. Newell, William R.   Hebrews, Verse by Verse. Chicago, IL: Moody Press, 1947.

30. Strauss, Lehman. Devotional Studies in Galatians & Ephesians. Neptune, NJ: Loizeaux Brothers, 1957.

31. Strauss, Lehman.   Devotional Studies in Philippians.   Neptune,   NJ: Loizeaux   Brothers, 1959.

32. Strauss, Lehman. James, Your Brother. Neptune, NJ: Loizeaux Brothers, 1956.

33. Strauss, Lehman.   The Book of the Revelation. Neptune, NJ: Loizeaux Brothers, 1964.

34. The New Testament & Wycliffe Bible Commentary, Edited by Charles F. Pfeiffer & Everett F. Harrison. New York: The Iverson Associates, 1971. Produced for Moody Monthly. Chicago Moody Press, 1962.

35. The Pulpit Commentary, Edited by H.D.M. Spence & Joseph S. Exell. Grand Rapids, MI: Eerdmans Publishing Co., 1950.

36. Thomas, W.H. Griffith.   Hebrews, A Devotional Commentary. Grand Rapids, MI: Eerdmans Publishing Co., 1970.

37. Thomas, W.H. Griffith.   Outline Studies in the Acts of the Apostles. Grand Rapids, MI: Eerdmans Publishing Co., 1956.

38. Thomas, W.H. Griffith.   St. Paul's Epistle to the Romans. Grand Rapids, MI: Eerdmans Publishing Co., 1946.

39. Thomas, W.H. Griffith.   Studies in Colossians & Philemon. Grand Rapids, MI: Baker Book House, 1973.

40. Tyndale New Testament Commentaries. Grand Rapids, MI: Eerdmans Publishing Co., Began in 1958.

41. Walker, Thomas.   Acts of the Apostles. Chicago, IL: Moody Press, 1965.

42. Walvoord, John.   The Thessalonian Epistles. Grand Rapids, MI: Zondervan Publishing House, 1973.

MISCELLANEOUS ABBREVIATIONS

&	=	And
Arg.	=	Argument
Bckgrd.	=	Background
Bc.	=	Because
Circ.	=	Circumstance
Concl.	=	Conclusion
Cp.	=	Compare
Ct.	=	Contrast
Dif.	=	Different
e.g.	=	For example
Et.	=	Eternal
F.	=	Following
Govt.	=	Government
Id.	=	Identity or Identification
Illust.	=	Illustration
K.	=	Kingdom, K. of God, K. of Heaven, etc.
No.	=	Number
N.T.	=	New Testament
O.T.	=	Old Testament
Pt.	=	Point
Quest.	=	Question
Rel.	=	Religion
Resp.	=	Responsibility
Rev.	=	Revelation
Rgt.	=	Righteousness
Thru	=	Through
V.	=	Verse
Vs.	=	Verses
Vs.	=	Versus

The Preacher's
Outline
&
Sermon
Bible®

"

Woe to me if I do not
preach the gospel!

"   *(I Cor. 9:16 NIV)*

---

1 PETER

INTRODUCTION

AUTHOR: Simon Peter, the Apostle (1 Pt.1:1).

The author claims to be an eyewitness of Christ's sufferings (1 Pt.5:1). Peter was an apostle of the Lord Jesus and he witnessed the sufferings of Christ. He is the best known among the apostles.

1. He was a businessman, a fisherman (Mk.1:16-20).

2. He became a disciple through the witness of his own brother (Jn.1:40-42).

3. He was given the name of Peter by the Lord Himself (Jn.1:41-42; cp. Mt.16:16-18).

4. He was one of three men who were apparently closer to the Lord than others who followed the Lord—one of three who formed an inner circle around Christ. James and John were the other two (Mt.17:1-2; Mk.5:37; 9:2; 14:23).

5. He was a natural born leader and became the leader of the twelve apostles (Mt.19:27; Mk.8:29; Jn.6:67-68; Acts 1:15; 2:14; 4:8-12; 15:7).

6. He publicly denied Christ at the crucifixion, but he later repented rather bitterly (Mt.26:69-75).

7. He had a private interview with the *risen* Lord which deeply affected him (1 Cor.15:5; cp. Jn.21:7, 15-21).

8. He was filled with God's Spirit on the day of Pentecost and immediately became the leader of the early church (Acts 2:1f).

9. He was chosen by God to become the missionary apostle to the circumcision, the Jews of the dispersion (Gal.2:7-8, 11-21). Eventually, he travelled further and further afield (see outline—Acts 9:32-12:25).

10. He was martyred by crucifixion in Rome under Nero (around AD 68), according to tradition. It is said that he felt so unworthy to be crucified like his Lord that he begged to be crucified upside down. Interestingly, tradition also says that Peter's wife served with him in the ministry. William Barclay quotes a touching picture by Clement of Alexandria who said that she was martyred with Peter: "On seeing his wife led to death, Peter rejoiced on account of her call and her conveyance home, and called very encouragingly and comfortingly, addressing her by name: 'Remember thou the Lord'" (Stromateis 7:6). (*The Gospel of Matthew.* "The Daily Study Bible." Philadelphia, PA: The Westminster Press, 1956, p. 313).

DATE: Uncertain. Probably A.D. 63-67. The early date is indicated by the following facts.

1. The organization of the church seems to be in its primitive form. Only elders are mentioned. Deacons are not mentioned (cp. 1 Pt.5:1).

2. The theology of the epistle is stated in the purest and simplest form possible.

3. The scribe, Silas, was the one to whom Peter actually dictated the epistle. He could possibly be the missionary associate of Paul who is also known as Silas (1 Pt.5:12).

4. The epistle was written after some of Paul's letters were penned. Peter knew of Paul's writings (2 Pt.3:15).

The first three facts point toward an early dating; the last fact would place the writing after Paul's epistles. If tradition is correct, the writing would be before Nero's death. It was probably written A.D. 63-67.

TO WHOM WRITTEN: "To God's elect, strangers in the world scattered throughout" five Roman provinces (1 Pt.1:1).

These strangers or pilgrims of the Lord included both Jewish and Gentile believers. It is definitely clear that some Gentiles, probably many, had been reached for the Lord (1 Pt.1:14; 4:3-4).

Peter wrote the epistle from Babylon (1 Pt.5:13). There were three Babylons.

1. The historical Babylon in Mesopotamia. However, the church in this Babylon was scattered under severe persecution by Caligula (about A.D. 41).

2. The Babylon of Egypt. There is nothing known about Peter ever being there.

3. The symbolic Babylon, Rome itself. Throughout history the name of Babylon has stood for evil; therefore, when Rome began its harassment and persecution of the church, Christians began to refer to Rome as Babylon (see Rev.17:18). Peter was probably in Rome when he wrote the epistle.

PURPOSE: There are at least two reasons for Peter writing this letter.

1. To challenge and strengthen believers to stand against the onslaught of persecution being levelled against them. This is Peter's primary purpose. (See Special Feature, point 3.)

2. To reinforce the glorious truth that the believer is only a stranger and an alien upon the earth (1 Pt.1:1-4; 2:11; cp. Heb.11:13). Peter sensed that the message of holiness and dedication was especially needed during this period of persecution. There was a strong temptation to return to the world in order to save one's life and property.

SPECIAL FEATURES:

1. I Peter is "A General Epistle." That is, it is not written to a specific church or individual, but rather, it is written to all Christian believers.

2. I Peter is "An Epistle of Pastoral Warmth." It bristles with tenderness, love, understanding, and encouragement. It is a warm epistle, flowing from the depth and richness of a pastor's heart (see 1 Pt.1:8, 17, 19, 22; 2:2-4, 7, 11, 25; etc.)

3. I Peter is "The Epistle for the Suffering Church." The church was being severely persecuted, suffering "in all kinds of trials" (1 Pt.1:6) They were suffering "unjustly" (1 Pt.2:19), suffering *for righteousness' sake*, that is, having to suffer for standing up for the name of Christ. Malicious charges were made against them (1 Pt.2:12, 15; 3:16; 4:14). Their suffering is mentioned at least sixteen times.

4. I Peter is "An Epistle of the True Grace of God" (1 Pt.5:12). Peter reveals that the *true grace of God* involves three stages.

    a. There is the grace of salvation (1 Pt.1:10).

    b. There is the grace of redemption, that is, the end of one's salvation (1 Pt.1:13).

    c. There is the grace that carries one through life day by day (1 Pt.1:2; 3:7; 4:10; 5:5).

5. I Peter is "An Epistle Emphasizing the Second Coming." The coming again of Jesus Christ is mentioned around eight times (1 Pt.1:5, 7, 13; 2:12; 4:13, 17; 5:1-4). It is a dominant theme upon Peter's mind.

6. I Peter is "An Alien's Epistle." It is written to the strangers and aliens whose home is in heaven, but who are presently plowing their way through this life (1 Pt.1:1-4; 2:11; cp. Heb.11:13).

7. I Peter is "The Epistle of the Missionary Apostle to the Jews." Peter was given the primary responsibility of reaching the Jews throughout the world. He was the apostle to the Jews (Gal.2:7-8, 11-21). (See Author, point 10.)

OUTLINE OF 1 PETER

THE PREACHER'S OUTLINE & SERMON BIBLE® is *unique*. It differs from all other Study Bibles & Sermon Resource Materials in that every Passage and Subject is outlined right beside the Scripture. When you choose any *Subject* below and turn to the reference, you have not only the Scripture, but you discover the Scripture and Subject *already outlined for you—verse by verse.*

For a quick example, choose one of the subjects below and turn over to the Scripture, and you will find this marvelous help for faster, easier, and more accurate use.

In addition, every point of the Scripture and Subject is *fully developed in a Commentary with supporting Scripture* at the bottom of the page. Again, this arrangement makes sermon preparation much easier and faster.

Note something else: The Subjects of FIRST PETER have titles that are both Biblical and *practical*. The practical titles sometimes have more appeal to people. This *benefit* is clearly seen for use on billboards, bulletins, church newsletters, etc.

A suggestion: For the quickest overview of FIRST PETER, first read *all the major titles* (I, II, III, etc.), then come back and read the subtitles.

OUTLINE OF 1 PETER

I. **HOW TO BE SECURE THROUGH SUFFERING: KNOW THAT YOU ARE SAVED, 1:1-12**
   A. Know that You Are the Chosen of God, 1:1-2
   B. Know the Believer's Living Hope, 1:3-5
   C. Know the Truth About Trials and Temptations, 1:6-9
   D. Know the Wonder and Greatness of Salvation, 1:10-12

II. **HOW TO LIVE THROUGH SUFFERING: GIVE YOUR LIFE TO GOD, 1:13-3:12**
   A. Get Your Mind Ready, 1:13-16
   B. Live on Earth in the Fear and Reverence of God, 1:17-21
   C. Love One Another Fervently, 1:22-25
   D. Strip Off Some Things and Crave the Word of God, 2:1-3
   E. Come to Christ, the Living Stone, 2:4-8
   F. Know Who You Are: The People of God, 2:9-10
   G. Abstain from Fleshly Lusts, 2:11-12
   H. Submit to the State, 2:13-17
   I. Submit to Masters or Employers, 2:18-20
   J. Follow Christ's Great Suffering, 2:21-25
   K. Submit to One's Own Husband, 3:1-6
   L. Understand One's Wife, 3:7
   M. Live at Peace with Others, 3:8-9
   N. Love and Enjoy Life, 3:10-12

III. **HOW TO HANDLE AND CONQUER SUFFERING: LIVE FOR RIGHTEOUSNESS AND NOT FOR EVIL, 3:13-4:19**
   A. Stand Up For Christ: Suffer for Righteousness' Sake, 3:13-17
   B. Understand the Death and Triumph of Christ, 3:18-22
   C. Arm Yourself with the Mind of Christ, 4:1-6
   D. Live Under the Shadow of History's Climax, 4:7-11
   E. Stand Up Under the Fiery Trial of Persecution, 4:12-19

IV. **HOW THE CHURCH IS TO FUNCTION UNDER SUFFERING: BE FAITHFUL, 5:1-14**
   A. The Duties of the Elder or Minister, 5:1-4
   B. The Duties of the Believer (Part I): Humility and Subjection, 5:5-7
   C. The Duties of the Believer (Part II): Vigilance and Resistance Against the Devil, 5:8-9
   D. The Suffering of the Believer and God, 5:10-14

CHAPTER 1

I. HOW TO BE SECURE THROUGH SUFFERING: KNOW THAT YOU ARE SAVED, 1:1-12

A. Know That You Are the Chosen of God, 1:1-2

1 They are believers, believers who are only strangers scattered over the earth	Peter, an apostle of Jesus Christ, To God's elect, strangers in the world, scattered throughout Pontus, Galatia, Cappadocia, Asia and Bithynia,
2 They are people elected (chosen) by God^DS1	2 Who have been chosen according to the foreknowledge of God the Father, through the sanctifying work of the Spirit, for obedience to Jesus Christ and sprinkling by his blood: Grace and peace be yours in abundance.
3 They are people set apart to God & covered by the blood of Christ^DS2	
4 They are people who obey God	
5 They are people who experience grace & peace	

DIVISION I

HOW TO BE SECURE THROUGH SUFFERING: KNOW THAT YOU ARE SAVED, 1:1-12

A. Know that You Are the Chosen of God, 1:1-2

(1:1-2) **Introduction**: Peter is writing to people who were hurting and suffering, people who were being ridiculed and persecuted because they lived for Jesus Christ. Throughout the Roman Empire believers had been attacked and were being savagely persecuted—so much so that they had been forced to flee for their lives. They had been forced to leave everything behind: homes, property, estates, businesses, jobs, money, church, friends, and fellow believers. Believers had apparently taken their families and what belongings they could carry and fled for their lives. Peter is writing to five Roman provinces where most of the believers had apparently tried to hide and find safety. But note how the church is continuing on as an underground church.

Imagine the fear, uncertainty, and insecurity; the wandering about and the searching for a safe place and for a way to earn a living. In some cases, the believers did not even know where their next meal would come from. The church and its dear believers were fleeing for their lives. All the feelings that attack human emotions when a person is being hunted down for brutal slaughter were attacking these believers: fear, concern, restlessness, sleeplessness, anxiety, stress, uncertainty, insecurity, and a pounding heart at the slightest shadow or noise.

The believers desperately needed strong encouragement. But how? How do you shore up and strengthen a person who is suffering and hurting so much? How can a person be secure through suffering and persecution? There is one way and only one way: he must know that he is saved and be absolutely sure that he is under the care and love of God. This is the discussion of the first section of First Peter. It clearly tells us how to be secure through suffering. Our security is this: knowing that we are saved, that we belong to God and are looked after by God.

The first thing to know about our salvation is this: *know that you are the chosen of God.*

1. They are believers who are only strangers or aliens scattered over the earth (v.1).
2. They are people elected (chosen) by God (v.2).
3. They are people set apart to God and covered by the blood of Christ (v.2).
4. They are people who obey God (v.2).
5. They are people who experience grace and peace (v.2).

1 (1:1) **Believers—Chosen, The**: the chosen are believers, believers who are only strangers scattered over the earth. This is the descriptive picture being painted in verse one. Believers are only strangers (parepidemois) on earth. The word means alien, pilgrim, sojourner, visitor, or exile. The idea is that of a person visiting a place for a while, but he is not a permanent resident. Believers are citizens of heaven; their home is in heaven *with* God, not on earth with the rulers of this world. The rulers and people of this earth may persecute believers, but believers are here on earth only temporarily—only as strangers, aliens, pilgrims, sojourners, and exiles. This is significant; it means two things:

1. It means that where we live on this earth does not matter all that much. No matter where we live, it is not our permanent home. Our home is in heaven. We may be forced to leave our homes and countries because of trouble and persecution—we may be poor and suffer great hardship in this life, but it is only for a brief time. We are only strangers and pilgrims on earth. We shall soon be called to go home—to go to our permanent home in heaven and be there forever and ever. And there shall be no hunger or poverty or suffering or hardship in heaven.

2. It means that we should keep our eyes and minds...
   - focused upon heaven as our permanent home.

- focused upon how short life is.
- focused upon how uncertain, insecure, and short-term all things upon earth really are.

> **All these people were still living by faith when they died. They did not receive the things promised; they only saw them and welcomed them from a distance. And they admitted that they were aliens and strangers on earth. (Heb 11:13)**

> **For here we do not have an enduring city, but we are looking for the city that is to come. (Heb 13:14)**

> **Dear friends, I urge you, as aliens and strangers in the world, to abstain from sinful desires, which war against your soul. (1 Pet 2:11)**

> **And Jacob said to Pharaoh, "The years of my pilgrimage are a hundred and thirty. My years have been few and difficult, and they do not equal the years of the pilgrimage of my fathers." (Gen 47:9)**

> **We are aliens and strangers in your sight, as were all our forefathers. Our days on earth are like a shadow, without hope. (1 Chr 29:15)**

> **"Hear my prayer, O LORD, listen to my cry for help; be not deaf to my weeping. For I dwell with you as an alien, a stranger, as all my fathers were. (Psa 39:12)**

> **I am a stranger on earth; do not hide your commands from me. (Psa 119:19)**

2 (1:2) **Chosen, of God—Election—Foreknowledge—God**: the chosen are elected by God. They are actually called the elect, a people who had been elected or chosen by God. This means a most wonderful thing. It means that believers have the highest position in all the world, the position of being *God's own holy and dearly loved people* (cp. Col.3:12).

⇒ Believers have been chosen to be *holy*. The word "holy" (hagios) means separated or set apart. God called believers out of the world and away from the old life it offered, the old life of sin and death. He called believers to be separated and set apart unto Himself and the new life He offers, the new life of righteousness and eternity.

⇒ Believers have been chosen to be the dearly loved of God. God has called believers to turn away from the old life that showed hatred toward God, the old life that rejected, rebelled, ignored, denied, and was constantly cursing in the face of God. God has called believers to be the dearly loved of God, the persons who receive His love in Christ Jesus and who allow Him to shower His love upon them.

If God loves believers this much, enough to actually choose and elect them to be His very own holy and dearly loved people, then God will look after and take care of them. No matter how ridiculed, abused, and persecuted—no matter how poor, hungry, troubled, and distressed—no matter how great the hardship, God will meet the need of the dear believer, the one whom He has elected to be His own. (See note, *Chosen*—2 Th.2:13 for more discussion. Remember that the Thessalonian believers were suffering trouble and persecution even as these believers were. The truths of election and predestination were used by both Paul

and Peter to encourage believers when they were suffering great trouble and hardship. These are wonderful truths to encourage us when we have to face the great trials of this world.)

Note one other point: how believers are chosen. They are chosen by the *foreknowledge of God*. What does this mean? Foreknowledge can mean two things.

First, foreknowledge means that God sees the future. No matter how far a person looks into the future, God has already seen it. God knows...

- exactly what will happen, every single event and consequence.
- exactly what could happen (but will not), every single possibility and its consequences.

Foreknowledge means that God knows exactly what all men will do, every single act and consequence. God has one supreme overall view of all things—all things past, present, and future. But note: in this meaning foreknowledge does not determine anything; it only faces and forecasts what shall be. It is somewhat like an astronomer who can foresee the exact position and size of the moon on the first day of the month. He knows the future because He foresees the events that will take place with the moon between now and then. God has one supreme panoramic view of all things past, present, and future.

Second, foreknowledge means to foreordain, determine, appoint, and predestine. This is definitely the meaning in Acts 2:23:

> **This man was handed over to you by God's set purpose and foreknowledge; and you, with the help of wicked men, put him to death by nailing him to the cross. (Acts 2:23)**

God did not just foresee the death of Christ, He foreordained it. Peter himself makes this point:

> **He [Christ] was chosen before the creation of the world, but was revealed in these last times for your sake. (1 Pet 1:20)**

The foreknowledge of God is a most wonderful truth for the believer. God is in total control. He not only can foresee all events, He can foreordain and control them—work them all out for good. Just imagine! Every single event on earth is worked out for good by God. He works the events out for His people. No matter how much trouble and hardship we suffer, no matter how little we may understand, God knows and will work it all out for our good. Why? Because we are His elect, His holy and dearly loved people. The chosen of God are those who are elected according to the foreknowledge of God: elected because He foresaw them and ordained them to be His holy and dearly loved people. (See note, *Foreknowledge*—1 Pt.1:2 for more discussion and verses.)

DEEPER STUDY # 1

(1:2) **Foreknowledge—Chosen**: the word "foreknowledge" (prognosis) means to see before; to know beforehand; to see and know the future; to foreordain.

God is God; therefore He sees the future. No matter how far a person looks into the future, God sees it. God knows...

- exactly what *will* happen, every single event and its consequences.
- exactly what *could* happen (but will not), every single possibility and its consequences.

Therefore God knows...
- exactly what man *will* do, every single act and its consequences.
- exactly what man *could* do (but will not), every single possibility and its consequences.

God is God. He is eternal and omniscient (knowing all). He knows the past, the present, and the future. And note: He knows it all eternally, forever. God knew...
- every event of world history before the *creation of the world*.
- every event of a person's life before the *creation of the world* (cp. Eph.1:4).

Now in light of this, a question arises that is extremely important. If God knew all the terrible consequences of evil and death that would enter and overtake the world, if He knew the world would even kill His Son, why did He go ahead and create the world? Why did He not choose another way to do things? In the simplest terms possible, there are at least two reasons.

1. God wanted a creature, a being with free will. God created man because God willed to have the *presence* of a being who could *freely choose*...
- to love and worship Him.
- to obey and fellowship with Him.
- to serve and reign with Him.

In His foreknowledge, God knew that some would choose Him and some would reject Him. But He was willing to face...
- the pain and hurt to His heart,
- the abuse and shame to His person,
- the rejection and rebellion against His will,

...in order that some might know His glorious mercy and grace and experience all the glory of Himself and of heaven. (See outline and note—Ro.9:22-24; Eph.1:5-6; 2:7 for more discussion.)

2. God did not choose another way to create and deal with man...
- because the way God created man was the best way: perfect, in a perfect environment, with free choice and will, and in perfect fellowship with God (cp. Gen.2:16-17).
- because the way God deals with man is the best way: in love, in the mercy and grace of His Son. Love is the greatest force on earth. It is the very nature of God Himself (1 Jn.4:8). Love will change and transform, help and give, win and conquer when nothing else will. Love will cause a person to reach out and help another and even cause a person to sacrifice his life quicker than any other force on earth (Jn.3:16; 15:13; Ro.5:8).

Note one other point that is critical, a point that stresses the glorious love and care of God: it is God's set purpose (Acts 2:23)

The word "set" (horismenei) means predetermined, appointed, decreed, ordained, planned, purposed. It is a plan set within bounds, within a certain boundary. It is a purpose that is set, marked out, determined, decreed to happen.

The word "purpose" (boulei) means to advise, design, will; to give a piece of advice. It carries the force of being willed and determined. Since God knows exactly what *would* happen in every situation, He plans for the best thing to happen. God takes counsel, puts all things under advisement and chooses the best way.

We may not understand some things that happen nor why they happen the way they do. We may think some-

thing else or some other way would have been better. But we must remember two things.

1. We cannot see into the future. No man can. We cannot know what would have happened if another way had been chosen. We cannot know what would have happened...
- to us
- to others
- to the world

In every situation or event there are many other things that could have taken place. This is true of every situation, whether we call it *good or bad*. Think for a moment.
⇒ What would have taken place if the situation had been replaced by some other happening?
⇒ What would have taken place if another way had been chosen?
⇒ What and how much would be changed for the worse eventually, if not now?

We cannot know. But we can know this: God knows, for He deals with the future as well as the present. God deals with eternity, with the whole view. Therefore another situation, another way could have changed things for the worse. Simply stated...
- God knows the future, everything that could happen as well as what is best and should happen.
- God takes counsel, purposes, determines, plans and chooses the best thing to happen.

2. We who love God and are called according to His purpose know that all things work together for good. How do we know? Because we *do* love God and *are called* according to His purpose.

God knew that we would say "Yes" to Jesus, that we would love and follow Him. Therefore, God called us.

For those God foreknew he also predestined to be conformed to the likeness of his Son, that he might be the firstborn among many brothers. (Rom 8:29)

Note why we are predestinated. This is the key: "that he [God's Son] might be the firstborn among many brothers." God has determined that Jesus might have many brothers, many who will live and fellowship with Him as the first Person, the preeminent Person throughout the universe.

This is the reason God chooses the very best events and the very best way for us. It is the reason He works all things out for good for believers. God knows all the possibilities; therefore, He is able to take counsel and determine, to plan the very best for us. *Believe and trust this glorious truth.*

However, as it is written: "No eye has seen, no ear has heard, no mind has conceived what God has prepared for those who love him"— (1 Cor 2:9)

Oh, the depth of the riches of the wisdom and knowledge of God! How unsearchable his judgments, and his paths beyond tracing out! "Who has known the mind of the Lord? Or who has been his counselor?" "Who has ever given to God, that God should repay him?" For from him and through him and to him are all things. To him be the glory forever! Amen. (Rom 11:33-36)

Now to him who is able to do immeasurably more than all we ask or imagine, ac-

cording to his power that is at work within us, (Eph 3:20)

Being confident of this, that he who began a good work in you will carry it on to completion until the day of Christ Jesus. (Phil 1:6)

How great is your goodness, which you have stored up for those who fear you, which you bestow in the sight of men on those who take refuge in you. (Psa 31:19)

A STUDY OF SOME SCRIPTURES DEALING WITH GOD'S FOREKNOWLEDGE AND SET PURPOSE

(A study giving comfort and security—God is in control.)

1. The Scripture dealing with God's foreknowledge.
   a. God's foreknowledge concerns Christ.

This man was handed over to you by God's set purpose and foreknowledge; and you, with the help of wicked men, put him to death by nailing him to the cross. (Acts 2:23)

He was chosen before the creation of the world, but was revealed in these last times for your sake. (1 Pet 1:20)

   b. God's foreknowledge concerns believers.

Who have been chosen according to the foreknowledge of God the Father, through the sanctifying work of the Spirit, for obedience to Jesus Christ and sprinkling by his blood: Grace and peace be yours in abundance. (1 Pet 1:2)

And we know that in all things God works for the good of those who love him, who have been called according to his purpose. For those God foreknew he also predestined to be conformed to the likeness of his Son, that he might be the firstborn among many brothers. (Rom 8:28-29)

(Note. These two verses actually show that God acts or predestines on the basis of His foreknowledge, of His counsel.)
   c. God's foreknowledge concerns Israel.

God did not reject his people, whom he foreknew. Don't you know what the Scripture says in the passage about Elijah—how he appealed to God against Israel: (Rom 11:2)

2. The Scripture dealing with God's purpose and will. (See Subject Index *Predestination* for more discussion.)
   a. God's purpose and will concerns Christ.

They did what your power and will had decided beforehand should happen. (Acts 4:28)

The Son of Man will go as it has been decreed, but woe to that man who betrays him." (Luke 22:22)

This man was handed over to you by God's set purpose and foreknowledge; and you, with the help of wicked men, put him

to death by nailing him to the cross. (Acts 2:23)

And who through the Spirit of holiness was declared with power to be the Son of God by his resurrection from the dead: Jesus Christ our Lord. (Rom 1:4)

He commanded us to preach to the people and to testify that he is the one whom God appointed as judge of the living and the dead. (Acts 10:42)

For he has set a day when he will judge the world with justice by the man he has appointed. He has given proof of this to all men by raising him from the dead." (Acts 17:31)

   b. God's purpose and will concerns salvation and security for believers.

Therefore God again set [determines, appoints, plans] a certain day, calling it Today, when a long time later he spoke through David, as was said before: "Today, if you hear his voice, do not harden your hearts." (Heb 4:7; cp. 2 Tim.1:9; Heb.13:8).)

   c. God's purpose and will concerns believers and salvation.

"For when David had served God's purpose in his own generation, he fell asleep; he was buried with his fathers and his body decayed. (Acts 13:36)

In him we were also chosen, having been predestined according to the plan of him who works out everything in conformity with the purpose of his will, (Eph 1:11)

Because God wanted to make the unchanging nature of his purpose very clear to the heirs of what was promised, he confirmed it with an oath. (Heb 6:17)

   d. God's purpose and will concerns God's plan for the world.

For I have not hesitated to proclaim to you the whole will of God. (Acts 20:27)

   e. God's purpose and will concerns those who reject Him.

But the Pharisees and experts in the law rejected God's purpose for themselves, because they had not been baptized by John). (Luke 7:30)

3 (1:2) **Sanctification—Holy Spirit, Work**: the chosen are sanctified by the Holy Spirit and covered by the blood of Christ. What does this mean? It means that a person cannot be saved anytime he wants and any way he wants. It means that a person cannot just choose some religion and some particular time of life to come to God. Two things are absolutely necessary for a person to be saved and to receive eternal life.

1. First, a person must be sanctified by the Holy Spirit of God (see DEEPER STUDY # 1, *Sanctification*—1 Pt.1:15-16 for more discussion). To be *sanctified* means to be set apart

unto God; to be *made holy, pure and righteous* unto God. Before a person can come to God, he must be attracted and pulled to God—convicted that he should turn to God. He must be convicted that he needs the forgiveness and acceptance of God. This is the work of the Holy Spirit. And this is the reason a man must turn to God when he feels the conviction of sin and his great need for God. This conviction is the Holy Spirit working within him, struggling to set the man's life apart unto God—to save him and to give him eternal life. The Holy Spirit wants *every one of us* to be God's; to be set apart unto God, living holy, righteous, and pure lives; and He wants us living with God forever and ever—throughout all eternity. But remember what is stated above: a person cannot just turn to God by himself, by following some earthly religion or some earthly way to God. The only way a person can turn to God and be acceptable to God is by the Holy Spirit. The person must respond to the conviction of the Holy Spirit when the Holy Spirit draws and convicts him: he must be sanctified, set apart unto God to live a holy, righteous, and pure life.

Thought 1. This stresses the utter necessity of responding to the Spirit of God when we feel Him working within our hearts. All of us have sensed Him convicting us and we have delayed making a decision. Remember what happened? His conviction left us. He spoke to us, convicted and pulled us to make the decision, but we pushed it aside and said, "Later." And He left us. The conviction and desire to make the decision was soon gone. The point is forceful: we must respond and *respond immediately* when the Spirit of God works within us. We must make the decision...

- to be set apart unto God for salvation and eternal life.
- to be set apart unto God to live a life that is totally different from the life we have been living, a life that is more holy, righteous, and pure.

Note the end or purpose of sanctification: that we might be obedient to God. The one thing God wants is the same thing that any good father wants: obedient children. God wants us to love, fellowship, and commune with Him day by day and to follow His instructions. God knows and understands life, for He created life. Therefore, He wants the very best for all of us. This is the reason He has done so much to save us. His whole purpose—the very end toward which He has done all—is to lead us to a life of obedience. Obeying God is the only way we can know a full and complete life. Therefore, obedience is the purpose and end of sanctification.

> It is because of him that you are in Christ Jesus, who has become for us wisdom from God—that is, our righteousness, holiness and redemption. (1 Cor 1:30)
> Since we have these promises, dear friends, let us purify ourselves from everything that contaminates body and spirit, perfecting holiness out of reverence for God. (2 Cor 7:1)
> To make her holy, cleansing her by the washing with water through the word, (Eph 5:26)
> If a man cleanses himself from the latter, he will be an instrument for noble purposes, made holy, useful to the Master and prepared to do any good work. (2 Tim 2:21)
> Make every effort to live in peace with all men and to be holy; without holiness no one will see the Lord. (Heb 12:14)
> And so Jesus also suffered outside the city gate to make the people holy through his own blood. Let us, then, go to him outside the camp, bearing the disgrace he bore. For here we do not have an enduring city, but we are looking for the city that is to come. Through Jesus, therefore, let us continually offer to God a sacrifice of praise—the fruit of lips that confess his name. (Heb 13:12-15)
> Who have been chosen according to the foreknowledge of God the Father, through the sanctifying work of the Spirit, for obedience to Jesus Christ and sprinkling by his blood: Grace and peace be yours in abundance. (1 Pet 1:2)
> For it is written: "Be holy, because I am holy." (1 Pet 1:16)
> Since everything will be destroyed in this way, what kind of people ought you to be? You ought to live holy and godly lives as you look forward to the day of God and speed its coming. That day will bring about the destruction of the heavens by fire, and the elements will melt in the heat. But in keeping with his promise we are looking forward to a new heaven and a new earth, the home of righteousness. So then, dear friends, since you are looking forward to this, make every effort to be found spotless, blameless and at peace with him. (2 Pet 3:11-14)

2. Second, a person must be sprinkled or covered by the blood of Jesus Christ. What does this mean? It means to be justified by His blood.

> Since we have now been justified by his blood, how much more shall we be saved from God's wrath through him! (Rom 5:9; see note, Justification—Ro.5:1 for more discussion)

We have broken the law of God. We have neglected God, ignored God, cursed God, rebelled against God, and rejected God. We have chosen to live like we want, to do our own thing, and we have refused to live like God says. Therefore, we stand before the law of God guilty. As with all law, we must bear...

- the penalty of the law
- the judgment of the law
- the condemnation of the law
- the punishment of the law
- the wrath of the law

We stand before the wrath of God—His law, His justice—and there is no escape. We have broken the law of God; therefore, the penalty has to be paid. *But this is the glorious gospel*: Jesus Christ has paid the penalty for us. He has stepped forth and offered His life as a substitute and sacrifice for us. He has borne the judgment and condemnation of our transgression. How could He do this? Because He was the Son of God and He lived a perfect and sinless life when He was upon earth. He stood before God as the Perfect and Ideal Man, as the Ideal Righteousness that could cover all men. Consequently, when He died on the cross, His death was the perfect and ideal sacrifice for sins. His blood—the blood He shed for us—was the perfect and ideal sacrifice for transgressions. Therefore, His blood can cover us and all of our transgressions.

This is the way we are saved and the way we receive eternal life; this is the way we are made acceptable to God: by being sprinkled or covered by the blood of Jesus Christ. The blood of Jesus Christ covers all our transgressions and makes us guiltless before God—perfect and acceptable to Him.

This is the chosen of God—a people chosen to come to God by being sprinkled with the blood of Jesus Christ, God's dear Son.

> **Since we have now been justified by his blood, how much more shall we be saved from God's wrath through him! (Rom 5:9)**
>
> **How much more, then, will the blood of Christ, who through the eternal Spirit offered himself unblemished to God, cleanse our consciences from acts that lead to death, so that we may serve the living God! (Heb 9:14)**
>
> **For you know that it was not with perishable things such as silver or gold that you were redeemed from the empty way of life handed down to you from your forefathers, but with the precious blood of Christ, a lamb without blemish or defect. (1 Pet 1:18-19)**
>
> **But if we walk in the light, as he is in the light, we have fellowship with one another, and the blood of Jesus, his Son, purifies us from all sin. (1 John 1:7)**
>
> **And from Jesus Christ, who is the faithful witness, the firstborn from the dead, and the ruler of the kings of the earth. To him who loves us and has freed us from our sins by his blood, (Rev 1:5)**

DEEPER STUDY # 2

(1:2) **Jesus' Blood—Death**: Peter says the blood of Jesus Christ was symbolized in the Old Testament. There are three references to the sprinkling of the blood, and all three references have meaning for the believer.

1. The blood symbolized cleansing from sin. A believer was looked upon as becoming defiled while he walked throughout the world. Thus, he was occasionally to make sacrifice and be sprinkled with the blood of the sacrifice (Num.19:9; Heb.9:13). A man who was cleansed from leprosy was also sprinkled with blood—the blood of a bird (Lev.14:1-7).

2. The blood symbolized obedience to God. God made several great promises to Israel. But the promises were conditional; Israel had to obey the law of God. If Israel obeyed, God promised to bless the nation beyond imagination. This is what is meant by *God's covenant relationship* with Israel. God made a covenant with Israel, but the covenant was conditional upon their obedience.

The symbol of God's covenant relationship, of His promises, was blood. There was a ceremony in which the people surrounded the tabernacle and promised to obey God, and then Moses took an animal sacrifice and sprinkled half the blood on the altar and half the blood on the people (Ex.24:3-8; Heb.12:24). Note that the Lord Himself called the sprinkled blood, "My blood of the new covenant" (Mt.26:28; Mk.14:24).

4 (1:2) **Obedience—Chosen, The**: the chosen are the people who obey God. The only kind of faith that really saves a person is the kind of faith that is obedient, that diligently seeks God. Believing faith is obedient faith. A person who really believes in Christ, who really trusts the blood of Christ to cover his transgressions, obeys Christ. This is exactly what Scripture says.

> **And without faith it is impossible to please God, because anyone who comes to him must believe that he exists and that he rewards those who earnestly seek him. (Heb 11:6)**
>
> **And, once made perfect, he became the source of eternal salvation for all who obey him (Heb 5:9)**

Now, note the verse: the very end or purpose of sanctification is that we might be obedient to God. The one thing God wants is obedience—obedient children—the very same thing that any good father wants. God wants us to follow His Word and its instructions. Why? Because God knows and understands life. God created and made life; therefore, He knows exactly how life has to be lived in order to get the most out of it. God is God and He is a God of love; consequently He wants the very best for us. This is the reason He has done so much to save us; this is the reason He has given us His Word and its instructions. His whole purpose—the very end toward which He has done all—is to lead us to a life of obedience. Obeying God is the only way we can know a full and complete life.

> **Thought 1.** This means a most significant thing: the persons who are truly chosen by God are those who are obeying God. It does not matter what a person may be professing; it does not matter to which church or religion a person may belong. What matters is obedience: is the person obeying God? Is he truthfully believing and trusting, surrendering and casting his life upon the Lord Jesus Christ and His blood to cleanse him from all transgressions?

> **"Not everyone who says to me, 'Lord, Lord,' will enter the kingdom of heaven, but only he who does the will of my Father who is in heaven. (Mat 7:21)**
>
> **Since they did not know the righteousness that comes from God and sought to establish their own, they did not submit to God's righteousness. Christ is the end of the law so that there may be righteousness for everyone who believes. (Rom 10:3-4)**
>
> **Who gave himself for us to redeem us from all wickedness and to purify for himself a people that are his very own, eager to do what is good. (Titus 2:14)**
>
> **And, once made perfect, he became the source of eternal salvation for all who obey him (Heb 5:9)**
>
> **And without faith it is impossible to please God, because anyone who comes to him must believe that he exists and that he rewards those who earnestly seek him. (Heb 11:6)**
>
> **But if we walk in the light, as he is in the light, we have fellowship with one another, and the blood of Jesus, his Son, purifies us from all sin. (1 John 1:7)**

And this is his command: to believe in the name of his Son, Jesus Christ, and to love one another as he commanded us. (1 John 3:23)

"Blessed are those who wash their robes, that they may have the right to the tree of life and may go through the gates into the city. (Rev 22:14)

5 (1:2) **Grace—Peace—Chosen, The**: the chosen people who experience grace and peace.

1. Grace (charis) means the *undeserved favor and blessings* of God. (See notes—Ro.4:16; DEEPER STUDY # 1— 1 Cor.1:4; DEEPER STUDY # 1—Tit.2:11-15.) The word *undeserved* is the key to understanding grace. Man does not deserve God's favor; he cannot earn God's approval and blessings. God is too high and man is too low for man to deserve anything from God. Man is imperfect and God is perfect; therefore, man cannot expect anything from God. (See DEEPER STUDY # 1, *Justification*—Gal.2:15-16 for more discussion.) Man has reacted against God too much. Man has...

- rejected God
- rebelled against God
- ignored God
- neglected God
- cursed God
- sinned against God
- disobeyed God
- denied God
- questioned God

Man deserves nothing from God except judgment, condemnation, and punishment. But God is love—perfect and absolute love. Therefore, God makes it possible for man to experience His grace, in particular the favor and blessing of salvation which is in His Son, Jesus Christ. (See DEEPER STUDY # 1, *Grace*—1 Cor.1:4 for more discussion.)

And are justified freely by his grace through the redemption that came by Christ Jesus. (Rom 3:24)

For you know the grace of our Lord Jesus Christ, that though he was rich, yet for your sakes he became poor, so that you through his poverty might become rich. (2 Cor 8:9)

In him we have redemption through his blood, the forgiveness of sins, in accordance with the riches of God's grace (Eph 1:7)

In order that in the coming ages he might show the incomparable riches of his grace, expressed in his kindness to us in Christ Jesus. (Eph 2:7)

And my God will meet all your needs according to his glorious riches in Christ Jesus. (Phil 4:19)

The grace of our Lord was poured out on me abundantly, along with the faith and love that are in Christ Jesus. (1 Tim 1:14)

2. Peace (eirene) means to be bound, joined, and woven together. It means to be assured, confident, and secure in the love and care of God. It means to have a sense, a consciousness, a knowledge that God will...

- provide
- guide
- strengthen
- sustain
- deliver
- encourage
- save
- give life, real life both now and forever

A person can experience true peace only as he comes to know Jesus Christ. Only Christ can bring peace to the human heart, the kind of peace that brings deliverance and assurance to the human soul.

Peace I leave with you; my peace I give you. I do not give to you as the world gives. Do not let your hearts be troubled and do not be afraid. (John 14:27)

"I have told you these things, so that in me you may have peace. In this world you will have trouble. But take heart! I have overcome the world." (John 16:33)

Therefore, since we have been justified through faith, we have peace with God through our Lord Jesus Christ, (Rom 5:1)

The mind of sinful man is death, but the mind controlled by the Spirit is life and peace; (Rom 8:6)

But the fruit of the Spirit is love, joy, peace, patience, kindness, goodness, faithfulness, gentleness and self-control. Against such things there is no law. (Gal 5:22-23)

I will lie down and sleep in peace, for you alone, O LORD, make me dwell in safety. (Psa 4:8)

	B. Know the Believer's Living Hope, 1:3-5
1 The source of the hope: The God & Father of our Lord Jesus Christ a. By the mercy of God b. By the new birth c. By the resurrection of Christ	3 Praise be to the God and Father of our Lord Jesus Christ! In his great mercy he has given us new birth into a living hope through the resurrection of Jesus Christ from the dead,
2 The inheritance of the hope a. Never perishes or spoils b. Never fades away c. Is kept in heaven	4 And into an inheritance that can never perish, spoil or fade—kept in heaven for you,
3 The assurance of the hope a. Shielded by God's power b. Guarded by faith	5 Who through faith are shielded by God's power until the coming of the salvation that is ready to be revealed in the last time.

DIVISION I

HOW TO BE SECURE THROUGH SUFFERING: KNOW THAT YOU ARE SAVED, 1:1-12

B. Know the Believer's Living Hope, 1:3-5

(1:3-5) **Introduction—Hope**: this is a rich, rich passage of Scripture. It is one of those passages that is so rich that it would take an eternity to grasp all that is taught herein. And note the most wonderful thing: it has to do with the believer's glorious hope. What is the great hope of the believer? It is eternal life—the glorious privilege of living forever with God. Just imagine living face to face with God forever! No greater privilege could ever be given man. Note that our hope is said to be a *living hope*.

⇒ A living hope means that it is not a dead, lifeless hope. It is not the kind of hope that we use to stir positive thinking for the moment but does nothing for us beyond the grave; not the kind of hope that gives us meaning and motivation for life but is dead and lifeless beyond this life. Despite all the earthly benefit we get from positive thinking and motivational hope, these have no meaning beyond this life and the grave.

⇒ A living hope means that it is not a *probable hope*; it is not the kind of hope that may or may not come to pass.

The hope that God gives is a *living hope*, a hope that is real and true, that actually exists. A *living hope* is active and functioning; it acts and works both within the heart of the believer and within heaven apart from the believer. Eternal life is a *living hope* because it is reality; it is a life that really exists in another world, the spiritual world, that is more real than the world in which we live. The believer's hope for eternal life lives, acts, and works within the believer now, even while he is on earth. It is not that the believer is going to receive eternal life; he has already received eternal life. His hope for eternal life is living, acting, and working within him right now. This is the glorious hope of the believer, the living hope of living forever with God face to face.

1. The source of the hope: the God and Father of our Lord Jesus Christ (v.3).
2. The inheritance of the hope (v.4).
3. The assurance of the hope (v.5).

1 (1:3) **Hope, Believer's—Mercy**: there is the source of the hope. The source is the God and Father of our Lord Jesus Christ. Note who our Lord Jesus Christ is.

⇒ He is *our Lord*, the One to whom we have surrendered and subjected our lives; the One who sits in the spiritual and heavenly world at the right hand of God the Father.

⇒ He is *Jesus*, the carpenter from Nazareth, the Man who claimed to be the Son of God and who was sent into the world as the Savior of men.

⇒ He is *Christ* the Messiah who was promised by God to save men.

This means a most wonderful thing: if we follow the Lord Jesus Christ, then the God and Father of Jesus Christ becomes our God and Father. And note: He is the God who gives eternal life. This too means a most wonderful thing: God is not off in outer space someplace, far removed from us, a god with little or no interest in our welfare. God is near at hand, all about us, living within the spiritual world and dimension, longing to relate to us and to look after and care for us, and to give us eternal life. Jesus Christ shows us this. This was the way His Father took care of Him; and if we follow Christ, it is the way God, *even our Father*, takes care of us. He gives us the most wonderful of gifts: eternal life—the *living hope* of living forever with Him even as Christ our Lord is now living with Him in heaven.

Thought 1. Note: eternal life exists nowhere else. Only the God and Father of our Lord Jesus Christ possesses eternal life. Therefore, if a person wants to know God and to receive eternal life, he has to come to the Lord Jesus Christ. The person has to trust Christ if he wants the God and Father of Christ to give him eternal life. And we must always remember: only the God and Father of the Lord Jesus Christ can give a person the living hope of living forever.

Now, how does God go about giving us the living hope of eternal life? This is a critical question, for when we look around our world all we see is corruption and death. We are born and then before we know it, it is time to die. There is so little time in between birth and death. And even while we are here on earth there is sin, shame, accident, disease, suffering, evil, cursing, lying, stealing, deception, assaults, murders, wars—so much corruption that death just seems to engulf the earth. The thinking and honest person knows that he and everything else including the world itself are dying. How then does God stop this process of corruption and death? How does God go about giving us the living hope of eternal life?

1. The living hope comes by the mercy of God. This is the basis of our hope; it could be no other way. Man is just so sinful he has only one hope: the hope that *God will have mercy upon him*. Just think how we have treated God. We have…

- ignored Him
- neglected Him
- failed Him
- rebelled against Him
- rejected Him
- cursed Him
- disobeyed Him
- sinned against Him
- disbelieved Him
- turned away from Him

The list could go on and on, but the point is clearly seen. Our only hope is the mercy of God. If we are going to ever be accepted and given the living hope of living forever and ever, then God has to be merciful. He has to have mercy upon us.

The word "mercy" (eleos) means feelings of pity, compassion, affection, and kindness. It is a desire to succor; to tenderly draw unto oneself and to care for. Two things are essential in order to have mercy: seeing a need and being able to meet that need. God sees our need and feels for us (Eph.2:1-3). Therefore, He acts; He has mercy upon us. How? By doing two things:

⇒ God withholds His judgment.
⇒ God provides a way for us to be saved.

And note that God is said to have great mercy (overflowing, abundant, endless, boundless mercy). His mercy just flows on and on; it is ever covering us and creating the living hope and presence of eternal life within our hearts.

> **For God has bound all men over to disobedience so that he may have mercy on them all. (Rom 11:32)**
>
> **But because of his great love for us, God, who is rich in mercy, made us alive with Christ even when we were dead in transgressions—it is by grace you have been saved. (Eph 2:4-5)**
>
> **He saved us, not because of righteous things we had done, but because of his mercy. He saved us through the washing of rebirth and renewal by the Holy Spirit, (Titus 3:5)**
>
> **But from everlasting to everlasting the Lord's love is with those who fear him, and his righteousness with their children's children— (Psa 103:17)**
>
> **Because of the Lord's great love we are not consumed, for his compassions never fail. (Lam 3:22)**
>
> **Who is a God like you, who pardons sin and forgives the transgression of the remnant of his inheritance? You do not stay angry forever but delight to show mercy. (Micah 7:18)**

2. The living hope comes by the new birth. Note the words *new birth* or *born again*. There is no hope for eternal life unless a person is *born again* by the Spirit of God. A person has to be regenerated and made into a *new* person, a new self before he can ever live forever.

> **In reply Jesus declared, "I tell you the truth, no one can see the kingdom of God unless he is born again." (John 3:3)**
>
> **Jesus answered, "I tell you the truth, no one can enter the kingdom of God unless he is born of water and the Spirit. Flesh gives birth to flesh, but the Spirit gives birth to spirit. You should not be surprised at my saying, 'You must be born again.' (John 3:5-7)**
>
> **Therefore, if anyone is in Christ, he is a new creation; the old has gone, the new has come! (2 Cor 5:17)**
>
> **And to put on the new self, created to be like God in true righteousness and holiness. (Eph 4:24)**
>
> **And have put on the new self, which is being renewed in knowledge in the image of its Creator. (Col 3:10)**
>
> **For you have been born again, not of perishable seed, but of imperishable, through the living and enduring word of God. (1 Pet 1:23)**
>
> **Everyone who believes that Jesus is the Christ is born of God, and everyone who loves the father loves his child as well. (1 John 5:1)**

3. The living hope comes by the resurrection of Jesus Christ from the dead. Jesus Christ was raised from the dead to live forever in heaven with His Father. How does His resurrection give us the hope of living forever? By three things.

a. First, God has proven that He has the power to raise the dead. There should never be any question about this; for God, if He is truly God, has unlimited power to do anything. But His power to raise the dead and to keep them from ever dying again is now proven beyond all question: it is proven by the fact that He has raised Jesus Christ from the dead and exalted Him into heaven never again to die.

b. Second, the fact that God raised Jesus Christ from the dead proves that Jesus Christ is exactly who He claimed to be: the Son of God who came into the world to save men. God would have never raised Christ if He had been a liar and deceiver. Jesus Christ is the Savior of the world; therefore, God raised Him from the dead.

c. Third, Jesus Christ is the Son of God, the Perfect and Ideal Man who lived a sinless life when He was upon earth. Therefore, He stands before God as the Perfect and Ideal Man. What this means is most significant. Being the Perfect and Ideal Man, whatever He does is acceptable to God. When He arose from the dead, His resurrection was the perfect and ideal resurrection. Therefore, it can stand for and cover every man's resurrection. If we are *in Christ*—if we really *believe in Christ*—then God can *count us* in the ideal resurrection of Christ. God can raise us up to live with Him forever and ever just as He did with Christ. Remember why—because Jesus Christ arose and has given us the ideal and perfect resurrection, and the Ideal can stand for and cover the resurrection of all others.

He was delivered over to death for our sins and was raised to life for our justification. (Rom 4:25)
That if you confess with your mouth, "Jesus is Lord," and believe in your heart that God raised him from the dead, you will be saved. For it is with your heart that you believe and are justified, and it is with your mouth that you confess and are saved. (Rom 10:9-10)
Now, brothers, I want to remind you of the gospel I preached to you, which you received and on which you have taken your stand. By this gospel you are saved, if you hold firmly to the word I preached to you. Otherwise, you have believed in vain. For what I received I passed on to you as of first importance : that Christ died for our sins according to the Scriptures, that he was buried, that he was raised on the third day according to the Scriptures, (1 Cor 15:1-4)
And his incomparably great power for us who believe. That power is like the working of his mighty strength, which he exerted in Christ when he raised him from the dead and seated him at his right hand in the heavenly realms, (Eph 1:19-20)
We believe that Jesus died and rose again and so we believe that God will bring with Jesus those who have fallen asleep in him. (1 Th 4:14)
Praise be to the God and Father of our Lord Jesus Christ! In his great mercy he has given us new birth into a living hope through the resurrection of Jesus Christ from the dead, (1 Pet 1:3)

2 **(1:4) Hope, Believer's—Inheritance, Spiritual**: there is the inheritance of the hope. The inheritance is the eternal life that God gives us, but the inheritance of eternal life involves the most wonderful gifts imaginable.

There Shall Be the Inheritance of a New Nature or State of Being
⇒ Being adopted (receiving the full rights) as a son of God (Gal.4:4-7; 1 Jn.3:1).
⇒ Being made blameless and pure (Ph.2:15).
⇒ Being given eternal life (Jn.3:16; 1 Tim.6:19).
⇒ Being given better and lasting possessions (Heb.10:34).
⇒ Being given a glorious body (Ph.3:11, 21; 1 Cor.15:42-44).
⇒ Being given eternal glory and honor and peace (Ro.2:10).
⇒ Being given eternal rest and peace (Heb.4:9; Rev.14:13).
⇒ Being given the blessings of the Lord (Pr.10:22).
⇒ Being given the knowledge of Christ Jesus (Ph.3:8).
⇒ Being given enduring wealth and prosperity (Pr.8:18).
⇒ Being made priests (Rev.20:6).

⇒ Being given a crown that will last forever (1 Cor.9:25).
⇒ Being given a crown of righteousness (2 Tim.4:8).
⇒ Being given a crown of life (Jas.1:12).
⇒ Being given a crown of glory (1 Pt.5:4).

There Shall Be the Inheritance of Work or Position and Rule
⇒ Being made exalted beings (Rev.7:9-12).
⇒ Being made ruler over or put in charge of many things (Mt.25:23).
⇒ Being given the Kingdom of God (Jas.2:5; Mt.25:34).
⇒ Being given a position of rule and authority (Lk.12:42-44; Lk.22:28-29; 1 Cor.6:2-3).
⇒ Being given eternal responsibility and happiness (Mt.25:21, 23).
⇒ Being given rule and authority over cities (Lk.19:17, 19).
⇒ Being given thrones and the privilege of reigning forever (Rev.20:4; 22:5).
⇒ Being given the privilege of surrounding the throne of God (Rev.7:9-13; 20:4).
⇒ Being made priests (Rev.20:6).
⇒ Being made kings (Rev.1:5; 5:10).

There Shall be the Inheritance of Wealth
⇒ Being made an heir of God (Ro.8:16-17; Tit.3:7).
⇒ Being given an inheritance that can never perish, spoil, nor fade away (1 Pt.1:3-4).
⇒ Being given the blessings of the Lord (Pr.10:22).
⇒ Being given enduring wealth and prosperity (Pr.8:18).
⇒ Being given unsearchable riches (Eph.3:8).
⇒ Being given treasures in heaven (Mt.19:21; Lk.12:33).

Note how our inheritance is described in verse four. It is most descriptive, an astounding picture of the new heavens and earth that are coming and of our life in God's new and eternal world.

And into an inheritance that can never perish, spoil or fade—kept in heaven for you, (v.4)

1. Our inheritance "can never perish; it is incorruptible" (aphtharton). The word means that it cannot perish; it does not age, deteriorate, or die; it does not have the seed of corruption within it.

Thought 1. Matthew Henry points out that everything on earth changes from better to worse, but not our inheritance. It is perfect and incorruptible. It never changes, and it shall never cease to be the most perfect inheritance and gift imaginable (*Matthew Henry's Commentary*, Vol.6. Old Tappan, NJ: Fleming H. Revell, p.1005.).

2. Our inheritance "can never spoil" (amianton). The word means that it cannot be polluted or defiled, dirtied or infected. It means that our inheritance will be without any flaw or defect; it will be perfectly free from sickness, disease, infections, accident, pollution, dirt—from any defilement whatsoever. There will never be any tears over

what happens to oneself or over the damage or loss of some possession.

3. Our inheritance *can never fade away* (amaranton). It will last forever and ever. The splendor and beauty of it all—of life and of all the positions and possessions which God shall give us—none of the splendor and beauty shall fade or diminish whatsoever. Nothing, not even our energy and bodies, shall wear out or waste away.

4. Our inheritance is in heaven; it is kept there for us. It is actually being held there by God for us. God is simply waiting for us to finish our task here on earth and to come to Him. Then He will give us our inheritance.

Note a critical point: the persons who are to receive the inheritance are those who have received the mercy of God, been born again, and are trusting the resurrection of Jesus Christ to cover their resurrection (v.3).

> **"Now I commit you to God and to the word of his grace, which can build you up and give you an inheritance among all those who are sanctified. (Acts 20:32)**
>
> **to open their eyes and turn them from darkness to light, and from the power of Satan to God, so that they may receive forgiveness of sins and a place among those who are sanctified by faith in me.' (Acts 26:18)**
>
> **The Spirit himself testifies with our spirit that we are God's children. Now if we are children, then we are heirs—heirs of God and co-heirs with Christ, if indeed we share in his sufferings in order that we may also share in his glory. (Rom 8:16-17)**
>
> **If you belong to Christ, then you are Abraham's seed, and heirs according to the promise. (Gal 3:29)**
>
> **[Christ] In him we were also chosen, having been predestined according to the plan of him who works out everything in conformity with the purpose of his will, (Eph 1:11)**
>
> **I pray also that the eyes of your heart may be enlightened in order that you may know the hope to which he has called you, the riches of his glorious inheritance in the saints, (Eph 1:18)**
>
> **Giving thanks to the Father, who has qualified you to share in the inheritance of the saints in the kingdom of light. (Col 1:12)**
>
> **Since you know that you will receive an inheritance from the Lord as a reward. It is the Lord Christ you are serving. (Col 3:24)**
>
> **So that, having been justified by his grace, we might become heirs having the hope of eternal life. (Titus 3:7)**
>
> **Are not all angels ministering spirits sent to serve those who will inherit salvation? (Heb 1:14)**
>
> **Because God wanted to make the unchanging nature of his purpose very clear to the heirs of what was promised, he confirmed it with an oath. (Heb 6:17)**
>
> **By faith Noah, when warned about things not yet seen, in holy fear built an ark to save his family. By his faith he condemned the world and became heir of the righteousness that comes by faith. (Heb 11:7)**
>
> **He regarded disgrace for the sake of Christ as of greater value than the treasures of Egypt, because he was looking ahead to his reward. (Heb 11:26)**
>
> **Listen, my dear brothers: Has not God chosen those who are poor in the eyes of the world to be rich in faith and to inherit the kingdom he promised those who love him? (James 2:5)**
>
> **And into an inheritance that can never perish, spoil or fade—kept in heaven for you, (1 Pet 1:4)**

3 (1:5) **Hope, Believer's**: there is the assurance of the hope. How do we know for sure that we will receive the inheritance? The temptations and trials of life are so forceful and threatening, how do we know that we will receive the living hope of eternal life and its glorious inheritance? How do we know that we will not fall and come short of the great day of redemption? There are two answers.

1. There is the assurance of God's power. God's power shields us. The word "shielded" (phrouroumenous) means to guard; to garrison; to protect. It is a military term; therefore it has the idea of might and strength. The might and strength of God's power protect us throughout our journey in life—through all the trials and temptations of life—and God will see to it that we shall reach the glorious end of life: salvation. God Himself, in His sovereign and omnipotent power, will see to it that we receive eternal life and the inheritance that is being kept for us.

> **I will remain in the world no longer, but they are still in the world, and I am coming to you. Holy Father, protect them by the power of your name—the name you gave me—so that they may be one as we are one. (John 17:11)**
>
> **Now to him who is able to establish you by my gospel and the proclamation of Jesus Christ, according to the revelation of the mystery hidden for long ages past, (Rom 16:25)**
>
> **But the Lord is faithful, and he will strengthen and protect you from the evil one. (2 Th 3:3)**
>
> **That is why I am suffering as I am. Yet I am not ashamed, because I know whom I have believed, and am convinced that he is able to guard what I have entrusted to him for that day. (2 Tim 1:12)**
>
> **And into an inheritance that can never perish, spoil or fade—kept in heaven for you, who through faith are shielded by God's power until the coming of the salvation that is ready to be revealed in the last time. (1 Pet 1:4-5)**
>
> **To him who is able to keep you from falling and to present you before his glorious presence without fault and with great joy— (Jude 1:24)**
>
> **Since you have kept my command to endure patiently, I will also keep you from the hour of trial that is going to come upon the whole world to test those who live on the earth. (Rev 3:10)**
>
> **I am with you and will watch over you wherever you go, and I will bring you back**

to this land. I will not leave you until I have done what I have promised you." (Gen 28:15)

For the LORD loves the just and will not forsake his faithful ones. They will be protected forever, but the offspring of the wicked will be cut off; (Psa 37:28)

Indeed, he who watches over Israel will neither slumber nor sleep. (Psa 121:4)

2. There is the assurance of faith. We are kept and shielded not only by God, but...

- by our faith in the Lord Jesus Christ.
- by our faith in God's power.

No person shall ever receive the hope of eternal life or of God's glorious inheritance unless he truly believes in God's Son, the Lord Jesus Christ. Belief in Christ is absolutely essential. But once we have truly trusted Christ as our Savior, we are saved; we shall receive eternal life and the great inheritance of God's promise.

But note: a true faith is a *continuing faith and trust* in God's power. And a *continuing faith* is diligent and vigilant. It is a faith that loves Christ with all its heart and life. It is a faith that seeks to follow Christ and to please Him in all that it does. Therefore, a continuing faith is a faith that lives a holy, righteous, and pure life and that serves the Lord Jesus Christ. Simply stated, the person who truly believes in Jesus Christ gives *all he is and has* to the Lord Jesus Christ: he gives *all that he is and has* to spread the love of Christ around the world. True faith is a real commitment that obeys and follows Christ and that trusts the power of God to deliver him through all the trials and temptations of life. This is the kind of faith that keeps a person. The person who has this kind of faith has the assurance that he will receive eternal life and the promise of the inheritance. God gives the true believer this kind of assurance.

That everyone who believes in him may have eternal life. (John 3:15)

"I tell you the truth, whoever hears my word and believes him who sent me has eternal life and will not be condemned; he has crossed over from death to life. (John 5:24)

Jesus said to her, "I am the resurrection and the life. He who believes in me will live, even though he dies; (John 11:25)

I have come into the world as a light, so that no one who believes in me should stay in darkness. (John 12:46)

But these are written that you may believe that Jesus is the Christ, the Son of God, and that by believing you may have life in his name. (John 20:31)

All the prophets testify about him that everyone who believes in him receives forgiveness of sins through his name." (Acts 10:43)

Through him everyone who believes is justified from everything you could not be justified from by the law of Moses. (Acts 13:39)

They replied, "Believe in the Lord Jesus, and you will be saved—you and your household." (Acts 16:31)

That if you confess with your mouth, "Jesus is Lord," and believe in your heart that God raised him from the dead, you will be saved. (Rom 10:9)

And how from infancy you have known the holy Scriptures, which are able to make you wise for salvation through faith in Christ Jesus. (2 Tim 3:15)

Everyone who believes that Jesus is the Christ is born of God, and everyone who loves the father loves his child as well. (1 John 5:1)

	C. Know the Truth About Trials & Temptations, 1:6-9	may be proved genuine and may result in praise, glory and honor when Jesus Christ is revealed.	b. To bring praise, glory, & honor to both Christ & us
1 Know the fact: Life is full of trials & temptations a. They are only for a season b. They bring heaviness **2 Know the purpose for trials & temptations** a. To test & prove our faith	6 In this you greatly rejoice, though now for a little while you may have had to suffer grief in all kinds of trials. 7 These have come so that your faith—of greater worth than gold, which perishes even though refined by fire—	8 Though you have not seen him, you love him; and even though you do not see him now, you believe in him and are filled with an inexpressible and glorious joy, 9 For you are receiving the goal of your faith, the salvation of your souls.	**3 Know how to conquer trials & temptations** a. By your love for Christ b. By your belief in Christ c. By your joy d. By your salvation

DIVISION I

HOW TO BE SECURE THROUGH SUFFERING: KNOW THAT YOU ARE SAVED, 1:1-12

C. Know the Truth About Trials and Temptations, 1:6-9

(1:6-9) **Introduction**: this passage is one of the great passages dealing with the trials and temptations of believers. The experience of trials obviously includes the experience of temptation. Some temptation always lies at the very core of any trial, no matter how light or severe the trial. There is always the temptation to buckle or to give up under the weight of a trial. Giving in and giving up is a constant threat to us all. Because of this, the subject of this passage is being expended to cover both the trials and temptations of life.

1. Know the fact: life is full of trials and temptations (v.6).
2. Know the purpose for trials and temptations (v.7).
3. Know how to conquer trials and temptations (v.8-9).

1 (1:6) **Trials—Temptations**: know the fact—life is full of trials and temptations. Any thinking person can look around and see that life is bombarded with all kinds of trials and temptations. There are all kinds of trials, such as…

- sickness
- disease
- suffering
- sorrows
- ridicule
- abuse
- loss
- disappointment
- criticism
- loneliness
- emptiness

There are also all kinds of trials and temptations such as…

- greed
- selfishness
- hoarding
- drunkenness
- deceit
- strife
- immorality
- sorcery
- indulgence
- backbiting
- whispering
- reveling
- drugs
- anger
- gluttony
- envy
- jealousy
- uncleanness

The list of trials and temptations in the world are as unlimited as acts of behavior. For every act there can be the sin of too much or the sin of too little, the sins of commission or the sins of omission. Life is fraught with trials and temptations.

This is especially true with genuine believers, for believers stand in opposition to the selfish, immoral, greedy, and unjust ways of the world. This goes against the grain of the world because the world is in opposition to God. Just note the world's cursing of God and its flaunting of sex even for advertising purposes. These are excellent examples of the world's opposition to God. Therefore, the world often persecutes believers who proclaim the need for man to turn to God. The world persecutes believers through ridicule, mockery, abuse, and silence; through bypassing them, holding them down, shutting them out, and ignoring them; through confiscating their property, destroying their reputation, and in some cases imprisoning and killing them. Every genuine believer who lives for Christ knows what it is to be shunned and withdrawn from and to be persecuted to some degree, no matter what society he lives in.

This was the case with the believers to whom Peter was writing. They were being severely persecuted because of their stand for Christ. They had been forced to flee for their lives and to leave everything behind: homes, property, estates, businesses, jobs, money, church, friends, and fellow believers. They were suffering trial after trial, experiencing what we see so often portrayed in the media: people flooding the roadways fleeing with whatever possessions they can carry by hand, fleeing the tyranny of the persecution of dictators and evil men. The difference with believers is that they often suffer at the hands of people because of their testimony for Christ. And this was, in fact, the case with the early believers who were receiving this letter from Peter.

As stated, the fact of trials and temptations is clear to any thinking person: we live in a world of trials and temptation. In addition, the believer has to bear the added trial of persecution because of his testimony for Christ. Now, note two things that are said.

1. Trials and temptations are only for a season; they are only for a little while, for a short time. The idea is that our salvation is at hand; we shall soon be delivered from the sufferings of this earth. Therefore, we can stand up under whatever suffering is attacking us.

2. Trials and temptations cause a heaviness within us. The words "suffer grief" (lupethentes) means to be grieving; to suffer sorrow, stress, and mental anguish. We all know what it is to feel heavy and weighed down with grief; to suffer stress and pressure; to be mentally in anguish, wondering, questioning, and suffering under the weight of trial or temptation.

Thought 1. This is a dark picture of the world and of life, a picture of all kinds of trials and temptations. But we must face reality; it is a fact. As we walk throughout life, we are bombarded with all kinds of

17

trials and temptations. Our human experience proves it. But why face it? Why think about it? Why not ignore the fact, think positively, and look at only the good and move on? There is one reason: facts cannot be handled unless they are dealt with. Ignoring and denying trials and temptations will not conquer them, not permanently and not eternally. The only way we can ever conquer anything—no matter the trial or temptation—is to squarely face it and fight against it. The way to conquer the trials and temptations of life is the subject of this great passage.

> **Strengthening the disciples and encouraging them to remain true to the faith. "We must go through many hardships to enter the kingdom of God," they said. (Acts 14:22)**
>
> **Through whom we have gained access by faith into this grace in which we now stand. And we rejoice in the hope of the glory of God. Not only so, but we also rejoice in our sufferings, because we know that suffering produces perseverance; (Rom 5:2-3)**
>
> **I do not understand what I do. For what I want to do I do not do, but what I hate I do. (Rom 7:15)**
>
> **No temptation has seized you except what is common to man. And God is faithful; he will not let you be tempted beyond what you can bear. But when you are tempted, he will also provide a way out so that you can stand up under it. (1 Cor 10:13)**
>
> **We are hard pressed on every side, but not crushed; perplexed, but not in despair; (2 Cor 4:8)**
>
> **In fact, when we were with you, we kept telling you that we would be persecuted. And it turned out that way, as you well know. (1 Th 3:4)**
>
> **I know your afflictions and your poverty—yet you are rich! I know the slander of those who say they are Jews and are not, but are a synagogue of Satan. Do not be afraid of what you are about to suffer. I tell you, the devil will put some of you in prison to test you, and you will suffer persecution for ten days. Be faithful, even to the point of death, and I will give you the crown of life. (Rev 2:9-10)**
>
> **"Man born of woman is of few days and full of trouble. (Job 14:1)**
>
> **Trouble and distress have come upon me, but your commands are my delight. (Psa 119:143)**

2 (1:7) **Trials—Temptations**: know the purpose for trials and temptations. When a believer is saved, why does God not just go ahead and give him a trouble-free, perfect life? Sometimes it would seem that God should do this. If God loves us and really cares for us then He should not let terrible things happen to us. Why does God let them happen? Why do the trials and temptations of life fall upon us, especially with such heaviness and sorrow? Scripture says there are two reasons why the believer is tried and tempted.

1. The believer's faith must be tried. The word "refined" (dokimion) means to prove; to test; to

strengthen; to show that your faith is genuine (A.T. Robertson. *Word Pictures In The New Testament*, Vol.6. Nashville, TN: Broadman Press, 1933, p.83).

It is just like gold. Gold has to be put to the fire in order to clean out all the impurities and dross and to make it pure and clean. Now note what this verse says: we are much more precious than gold. Gold perishes, but not believers. Believers are to live forever. Therefore, if gold has to be put to the fire to be made clean and pure, how much more do we?

The point is striking: God uses the fire of trials and temptations for a good purpose. He uses them to make us clean and pure and to make us trust Him more and more.

⇒ When we are faced with some trial or temptation, we draw nearer to God. We cry out to God more than when things go well. We even tend to clean up our lives in order to secure His help us as we go through the trial. We just live more pure, clean, and righteous lives. In fact, the greater the trial and temptation, the more we see that we need God. And the more we see our need for God, the closer we usually draw to Him; and the closer we draw to Him, the cleaner we live. The fire of trials causes us to live purer, cleaner lives, while learning to trust God more and more.

This is a most wonderful point: our trials and temptations are purposeful. God uses them to make us much more pure and to stir us to draw closer and closer to Him and to trust Him more and more. We become a stronger person through trials—much stronger, much more steadfast, persevering, and enduring.

There is another fact that should be noted as well. When our faith is tried and proven, when we walk strongly through the trials and temptations of life, the world sees it. They see the power of Christ in our lives and the rejoicing of our hearts in Him. Some are attracted and want to know Christ for themselves. Standing fast through the trials and temptations of life wins people to Christ. God uses the trials and sufferings of life to pour His strength into us and to attract the lost to want Him in their lives.

> **For you, O God, tested us; you refined us like silver. (Psa 66:10)**
>
> **See, I have refined you, though not as silver; I have tested you in the furnace of affliction. (Isa 48:10)**
>
> **In all their distress he too was distressed, and the angel of his presence saved them. In his love and mercy he redeemed them; he lifted them up and carried them all the days of old. (Isa 63:9)**
>
> **He is like a man building a house, who dug down deep and laid the foundation on rock. When a flood came, the torrent struck that house but could not shake it, because it was well built. (Luke 6:48)**
>
> **His work will be shown for what it is, because the Day will bring it to light. It will be revealed with fire, and the fire will test the quality of each man's work. (1 Cor 3:13)**
>
> **Though you probe my heart and examine me at night, though you test me, you will find nothing; I have resolved that my mouth will not sin. (Psa 17:3)**
>
> **Before I was afflicted I went astray, but now I obey your word. (Psa 119:67)**
>
> **This third I will bring into the fire; I**

will refine them like silver and test them like gold. They will call on my name and I will answer them; I will say, 'They are my people,' and they will say, 'The LORD is our God.'" (Zec 13:9)

He will sit as a refiner and purifier of silver; he will purify the Levites and refine them like gold and silver. Then the LORD will have men who will bring offerings in righteousness, (Mal 3:3)

But he knows the way that I take; when he has tested me, I will come forth as gold. (Job 23:10)

No discipline seems pleasant at the time, but painful. Later on, however, it produces a harvest of righteousness and peace for those who have been trained by it. (Heb 12:11)

These have come so that your faith—of greater worth than gold, which perishes even though refined by fire—may be proved genuine and may result in praise, glory and honor when Jesus Christ is revealed. (1 Pet 1:7)

Dear friends, do not be surprised at the painful trial you are suffering, as though something strange were happening to you. (1 Pet 4:12)

2. The believer's faith is refined in order to show forth the praise, glory, and honor of Jesus Christ and of the believer. When Jesus Christ appears—when He returns to earth—two things are going to be seen.

⇒ First, Jesus Christ is going to be seen exalted higher than the heavens themselves; He is going to be seen in all the honor and glory of the universe.

⇒ Second, believers are going to be seen exalted higher than anyone could ever ask or even think; they are going to be exalted in the very same honor and glory of Christ Himself. They are going to be seen as joint-heirs with Christ in receiving all the inheritance that God Himself possesses. Just imagine! All the honor and glory that the Lord Jesus Christ Himself possesses shall be poured out upon believers.

This is the reason God allows us to suffer trials and temptations on earth: not only to make us purer and stronger, but to better prepare us for the honor and glory of heaven. The more we suffer here on earth, the more we ache for heaven. There is also the idea of vindication, of proving that the claims of Christ and of our faith in His claims are true. In that glorious day when Christ returns, the world of unbelievers—all of them—will see once for all that Jesus Christ is truly the Son of God and that our faith in Him is real. Christ and His followers will be vindicated. Christ and all believers shall be exalted in the honor and glory of all the worlds and of all the dimensions of beings. And all unbelievers shall witness the glorious event.

"Blessed are you when people insult you, persecute you and falsely say all kinds of evil against you because of me. Rejoice and be glad, because great is your reward in heaven, for in the same way they persecuted the prophets who were before you. (Mat 5:11-12)

Then the righteous will shine like the sun in the kingdom of their Father. He who

has ears, let him hear. (Mat 13:43)

It will be good for those servants whose master finds them watching when he comes. I tell you the truth, he will dress himself to serve, will have them recline at the table and will come and wait on them. (Luke 12:37)

And if I go and prepare a place for you, I will come back and take you to be with me that you also may be where I am. (John 14:3)

Now if we are children, then we are heirs—heirs of God and co-heirs with Christ, if indeed we share in his sufferings in order that we may also share in his glory. (Rom 8:17)

For our light and momentary troubles are achieving for us an eternal glory that far outweighs them all. (2 Cor 4:17)

Who, by the power that enables him to bring everything under his control, will transform our lowly bodies so that they will be like his glorious body. (Phil 3:21)

When Christ, who is your life, appears, then you also will appear with him in glory. (Col 3:4)

And so that all will be condemned who have not believed the truth but have delighted in wickedness. (2 Th 2:12)

You sympathized with those in prison and joyfully accepted the confiscation of your property, because you knew that you yourselves had better and lasting possessions. (Heb 10:34)

He regarded disgrace for the sake of Christ as of greater value than the treasures of Egypt, because he was looking ahead to his reward. (Heb 11:26)

And when the Chief Shepherd appears, you will receive the crown of glory that will never fade away. (1 Pet 5:4)

Dear friends, now we are children of God, and what we will be has not yet been made known. But we know that when he appears, we shall be like him, for we shall see him as he is. (1 John 3:2)

3 (1:8-9) **Trials—Temptations**: know how to conquer trials and temptations. The trials and temptations of life are not to defeat or discourage us. On the contrary, we are to conquer them. We are to use them as stepping stones to become stronger and stronger in life. But how? How can we conquer trials and temptations when they are so devastating, destructive, powerful, damaging, and threatening?

Scripture gives four ways.

1. Trials and temptations are to be conquered by our love for Jesus Christ. We do not see Christ, but we love Him. Think about it: we have transgressed God's law. We have ignored, neglected, and disobeyed God; rejected and cursed God. We have even committed high treason and rebelled against God. Therefore, we are guilty and must bear the judgment and condemnation. We must bear the punishment for our rebellion against God. We are to die without God—to be exiled and cut off from God forever and ever. But note the glorious love of Jesus Christ. He has stepped forward and offered Himself as a substitute and sacrifice for us. Jesus Christ has taken our guilt upon Himself. He has died for us; He has borne our judgment, condemnation,

and punishment. No one could ever do any greater thing for us than what Jesus Christ has done. He has loved us supremely: He has died for us even when we have rejected and disbelieved Him. This is the great love of Jesus Christ for us. And this is the reason we love Him. We love Him because He has done so much for us—gone to the ultimate limit to save us by bearing the judgment for us.

Now, note what the verse says: we have not seen Him, but *we love Him*. We do not have to see Christ to stand up for Him and to please Him. Christ does not have to be standing over our shoulder for us to stand against trials and temptations. We love Christ; therefore, we...

- obey Him
- keep His commandments
- turn away from temptations
- walk through trials

It is our love for Christ that stirs us to stand up for Christ against all the trials and temptations of life, no matter how severe and ferocious they are. True love does all it can to keep from hurting the person loved. In fact, when we love someone, we do all we can to please that person, no matter what it may cost us—even if it costs us our life. So it is with our love for Christ. If we truly love Him, then we will never hurt Him—not by displeasing Him, not if we can help it. On the contrary, if we really love Christ, we do exactly what He says: we stand against all the destructive trials and temptations that devastate human life and doom it for eternity. We stand and bear all the sufferings in order to prove the power of Christ. We want some people to see the power of Christ and the great hope He gives—we want them to see so that they will turn to Him for salvation. How do we overcome trials and temptations? First, we conquer them by our love for Christ.

"If you love me, you will obey what I command. And I will ask the Father, and he will give you another Counselor to be with you forever— (John 14:15-16)

Jesus replied, "If anyone loves me, he will obey my teaching. My Father will love him, and we will come to him and make our home with him. (John 14:23)

If you obey my commands, you will remain in my love, just as I have obeyed my Father's commands and remain in his love...You are my friends if you do what I command. (John 15:10, 14)

Grace to all who love our Lord Jesus Christ with an undying love. (Eph 6:24)

I always thank my God as I remember you in my prayers, because I hear about your faith in the Lord Jesus and your love for all the saints. (Phile 1:4-5)

Though you have not seen him, you love him; and even though you do not see him now, you believe in him and are filled with an inexpressible and glorious joy, (1 Pet 1:8)

2. Trials and temptations are to be conquered by our belief in Jesus Christ. Again, note the verse: we do not see Jesus, but we do believe in Him. The word "believe" (pisteuontes) is in the present continuous tense. That is, it is continuous action, continuous belief—a belief that continues on and on in believing and trusting in Jesus Christ. The point is clear: if we are continuing to believe in Jesus Christ, then we are following Christ. We are doing what He says...

- rejecting and turning away from all temptations.
- standing firm and relying upon His presence and power to conquer and to carry us through all trials.

Then they asked him, "What must we do to do the works God requires?" Jesus answered, "The work of God is this: to believe in the one he has sent." (John 6:28-29)

In addition to all this, take up the shield of faith, with which you can extinguish all the flaming arrows of the evil one. (Eph 6:16)

And without faith it is impossible to please God, because anyone who comes to him must believe that he exists and that he rewards those who earnestly seek him. (Heb 11:6)

Consider it pure joy, my brothers, whenever you face trials of many kinds, because you know that the testing of your faith develops perseverance. Perseverance must finish its work so that you may be mature and complete, not lacking anything. If any of you lacks wisdom, he should ask God, who gives generously to all without finding fault, and it will be given to him. But when he asks, he must believe and not doubt, because he who doubts is like a wave of the sea, blown and tossed by the wind. (James 1:2-6)

In the same way, faith by itself, if it is not accompanied by action, is dead. (James 2:17)

And this is his command: to believe in the name of his Son, Jesus Christ, and to love one another as he commanded us. (1 John 3:23)

For everyone born of God overcomes the world. This is the victory that has overcome the world, even our faith. Who is it that overcomes the world? Only he who believes that Jesus is the Son of God. (1 John 5:4-5)

3. Trials and temptations are to be conquered by rejoicing and by an inexpressible joy that fills our hearts. The inexpressible joy of Christ is not always present, but it often is. We are creatures of emotion, creatures who do not experience any one feeling for more than a brief period. But every genuine believer experiences an inexpressible joy here and there. Words cannot describe it: it is just glorious, just as Scripture says in this verse. Matthew Henry states:

"This joy is inexpressible, it cannot be described by words; the best discovery is by an experimental taste of it; it is full of glory, full of heaven. There is much of heaven and the future glory in the present joys of...Christians" (*Matthew Henry's Commentary*, Vol.6, p.1007.)

The point is this: joying and rejoicing in the Lord and His presence will stir us to stand against temptations and trials. Joy and rejoicing will help us to focus upon Christ and His glorious power.

I have told you this so that my joy may be in you and that your joy may be complete. (John 15:11)

Until now you have not asked for anything in my name. Ask and you will receive, and your joy will be complete. (John 16:24)

The apostles left the Sanhedrin, rejoicing because they had been counted worthy of suffering disgrace for the Name. (Acts 5:41)

After they had been severely flogged, they were thrown into prison, and the jailer was commanded to guard them carefully. Upon receiving such orders, he put them in the inner cell and fastened their feet in the stocks. About midnight Paul and Silas were praying and singing hymns to God, and the other prisoners were listening to them. (Acts 16:23-25)

For the kingdom of God is not a matter of eating and drinking, but of righteousness, peace and joy in the Holy Spirit, (Rom 14:17)

Sorrowful, yet always rejoicing; poor, yet making many rich; having nothing, and yet possessing everything. (2 Cor 6:10)

Rejoice in the Lord always. I will say it again: Rejoice! (Phil 4:4)

And let us consider how we may spur one another on toward love and good deeds. (Heb 10:24)

Consider him who endured such opposition from sinful men, so that you will not grow weary and lose heart. (Heb 12:3)

Dear friends, do not be surprised at the painful trial you are suffering, as though something strange were happening to you. But rejoice that you participate in the sufferings of Christ, so that you may be overjoyed when his glory is revealed. (1 Pet 4:12-13)

Our mouths were filled with laughter, our tongues with songs of joy. Then it was said among the nations, "The LORD has done great things for them." (Psa 126:2)

I delight greatly in the LORD; my soul rejoices in my God. For he has clothed me with garments of salvation and arrayed me in a robe of righteousness, as a bridegroom adorns his head like a priest, and as a bride adorns herself with her jewels. (Isa 61:10)

4. Trials and temptations are to be conquered by keeping our eyes focused upon the salvation of our souls. This is the end, the very goal toward which we are moving, the salvation of our souls. As in any work or task, we must keep our eyes upon the goal. The more focused we are upon the goal, the stronger we become to stand against all obstacles. So it is with salvation. The more we focus upon the salvation of our souls, the stronger we become...

- to reject and turn away from temptation.
- to conquer the trials of life.

All men will hate you because of me, but he who stands firm to the end will be saved. (Mat 10:22)

Whoever believes in him is not condemned, but whoever does not believe stands condemned already because he has not believed in the name of God's one and only Son. (John 3:18)

"I tell you the truth, whoever hears my word and believes him who sent me has eternal life and will not be condemned; he has crossed over from death to life. (John 5:24)

Therefore, there is now no condemnation for those who are in Christ Jesus, (Rom 8:1)

Who is he that condemns? Christ Jesus, who died—more than that, who was raised to life—is at the right hand of God and is also interceding for us. (Rom 8:34)

That if you confess with your mouth, "Jesus is Lord," and believe in your heart that God raised him from the dead, you will be saved. For it is with your heart that you believe and are justified, and it is with your mouth that you confess and are saved. (Rom 10:9-10)

Therefore, get rid of all moral filth and the evil that is so prevalent and humbly accept the word planted in you, which can save you. (James 1:21)

Therefore, my brothers, be all the more eager to make your calling and election sure. For if you do these things, you will never fall, and you will receive a rich welcome into the eternal kingdom of our Lord and Savior Jesus Christ. (2 Pet 1:10-11)

"Blessed are those who wash their robes, that they may have the right to the tree of life and may go through the gates into the city. (Rev 22:14)

	D. Know the Wonder & Greatness of Salvation, 1:10-12
1 Salvation required special men, special prophets, to share the message	10 Concerning this salvation, the prophets, who spoke of the grace that was to come to you, searched intently and with the greatest care,
2 Salvation was to be the personal experience of God's grace	11 Trying to find out the time and circumstances to which the Spirit of Christ in them was pointing when he predicted the sufferings of Christ and the glories that would follow.
3 Salvation was a mystery	
4 Salvation was to be accomplished by the sufferings & glories of the Messiah	
5 Salvation was destined for future believers	12 It was revealed to them that they were not serving themselves but you, when they spoke of the things that have now been told you by those who have preached the gospel to you by the Holy Spirit sent from heaven. Even angels long to look into these things.
6 Salvation is now proclaimed in the gospel	
7 Salvation is so glorious that it arouses the angels to understand & look into it	

DIVISION I

HOW TO BE SECURE THROUGH SUFFERING: KNOW THAT YOU ARE SAVED, 1:1-12

D. Know the Wonder and Greatness of Salvation, 1:10-12

(1:10-12) **Introduction**: this is a great description of salvation. It describes the wonder and greatness of salvation, the glorious truth that God saves men from death and exalts them into the glories of heaven. Salvation is so glorious a work that even the angels are aroused to look into it and to understand what it means (v.12).

1. Salvation required special men, special prophets, to share the message (v.10).
2. Salvation was to be the personal experience of God's grace (v.10).
3. Salvation was a mystery (v.11).
4. Salvation was to be accomplished by the sufferings and glories of the Messiah (v.11).
5. Salvation was destined for future believers (v.12).
6. Salvation is now proclaimed in the gospel (v.12).
7. Salvation is so glorious that it arouses the angels to understand and look into it (v.12).

1 (1:10) **Salvation—Prophets**: salvation required special men, special prophets, to proclaim the message. The message of salvation was so important that a whole new order of men was required to proclaim it: that of prophets. The prophets were men who were called and chosen by God to do two things:

⇒ to *proclaim* God's salvation to man.
⇒ to *prophesy and predict* how God was going to save man.

Both functions were necessary. The prophet had to proclaim salvation to the people of his own generation and to predict how God was going to save the people of all generations. But note this: the predictions of the future salvation were not the prophet's own predictions. He had not been called to proclaim his own ideas and message; he had been called to proclaim the salvation of God Himself. He

was a man given a very special call, a call to the most important task in all the world: the task of proclaiming the glory and wonder of God's salvation. God was making it possible for man to be saved and to live eternally.

> **There came a man who was sent from God; his name was John. He came as a witness to testify concerning that light, so that through him all men might believe. (John 1:6-7)**

> **"The kingdom of heaven is like a king who prepared a wedding banquet for his son. He sent his servants to those who had been invited to the banquet to tell them to come, but they refused to come. (Mat 22:2-3)**

> **Then Moses said, "This is how you will know that the LORD has sent me to do all these things and that it was not my idea: (Num 16:28)**

> **Since then, no prophet has risen in Israel like Moses, whom the LORD knew face to face, (Deu 34:10)**

> **Then I heard the voice of the Lord saying, "Whom shall I send? And who will go for us?" And I said, "Here am I. Send me!" (Isa 6:8)**

> **"Come near me and listen to this: "From the first announcement I have not spoken in secret; at the time it happens, I am there." And now the Sovereign LORD has sent me, with his Spirit. (Isa 48:16)**

> **And though the LORD has sent all his servants the prophets to you again and again, you have not listened or paid any attention. (Jer 25:4)**

Again and again I sent all my servants the prophets to you. They said, "Each of you must turn from your wicked ways and reform your actions; do not follow other gods to serve them. Then you will live in the land I have given to you and your fathers." But you have not paid attention or listened to me. (Jer 35:15)

2 (1:10) **Salvation—Grace**: salvation was to be the personal experience of God's grace. Grace is the favor of God showered upon men—men who do not deserve His favor. Grace is the mercy and love that God gives to men who...

- ignore Him
- neglect Him
- rebel against Him
- curse Him
- reject Him
- disobey Him
- disbelieve Him
- transgress against Him
- sin against Him
- fail to love Him

This, of course, includes us all, for we have all *come short of God's glory*. We are all imperfect; we all have the perishable seed, the seed of corruption within our bodies that causes us to age, deteriorate, and move ever so rapidly toward the grave. But this is the grace of God: a way has been provided for us to be counted perfect—a way for the seed of corruption to be removed out of our body and to be replaced with an imperishable seed, a seed of incorruption—a way for us to be delivered from death and to live forever. How? By God's grace. The grace of God is the message of eternal salvation. We can now be saved from death and judgment—eternally saved—by experiencing God's grace.

No! We believe it is through the grace of our Lord Jesus that we are saved, just as they are." (Acts 15:11)

And are justified freely by his grace through the redemption that came by Christ Jesus. (Rom 3:24)

For the grace of God that brings salvation has appeared to all men. (Titus 2:11)

He saved us, not because of righteous things we had done, but because of his mercy. He saved us through the washing of rebirth and renewal by the Holy Spirit, whom he poured out on us generously through Jesus Christ our Savior, so that, having been justified by his grace, we might become heirs having the hope of eternal life. (Titus 3:5-7)

3 (1:11) **Salvation**: salvation was a mystery. The prophets did not understand all that God was telling them to proclaim. Note the verse: in particular, they did not know when the Messiah would be sent to earth. The Greek scholar A.T. Robertson states it well: "The prophets knew what they prophesied, but not at what time the Messianic prophecies would be fulfilled" (A.T. Robertson. *Word Pictures In The New Testament*, Vol.6, p.85).

The prophets prayed and asked God time and again, and they diligently sought to understand the age when the Messiah would be sent to save man. They wanted to know what the age would be like, the characteristics and signs of the time.

⇒ They wanted to know the very same thing that the Lord's disciples wanted to know when they asked about the Lord's return: "When will this happen, and what will be the sign of your coming and of the end of the age?" (Mt.24:3).

⇒ They wanted to know the very same thing that believers want to know today when they discuss the Lord's return: When is Christ going to return and what are the signs of His return?

The picture is this: they actually hungered and thirsted to understand all they could about God's promised Messiah and salvation. They prayed and diligently sought, sought just as diligently as miners who dig and dig down through the earth and then drill and drill through the rock until they reach the pure ore (Matthew Henry. *Matthew Henry's Commentary*, Vol.6, p.1008.).

Thought 1. What a challenge to us! If these great men of God had to search and search for the truth of God's Word and salvation, how much more do we? We are without excuse. We have the prophets as dynamic examples of men who hungered after God's salvation.

Jesus replied, "You do not realize now what I am doing, but later you will understand." (John 13:7)

"I have much more to say to you, more than you can now bear. (John 16:12)

Paul, a servant of Christ Jesus, called to be an apostle and set apart for the gospel of God— the gospel he promised beforehand through his prophets in the Holy Scriptures (Rom 1:1-2)

Now to him who is able to establish you by my gospel and the proclamation of Jesus Christ, according to the revelation of the mystery hidden for long ages past, (Rom 16:25)

Now we see but a poor reflection as in a mirror; then we shall see face to face. Now I know in part; then I shall know fully, even as I am fully known. (1 Cor 13:12)

Which was not made known to men in other generations as it has now been revealed by the Spirit to God's holy apostles and prophets. (Eph 3:5)

Do your best to present yourself to God as one approved, a workman who does not need to be ashamed and who correctly handles the word of truth. (2 Tim 2:15)

Like newborn babies, crave pure spiritual milk, so that by it you may grow up in your salvation, now that you have tasted that the Lord is good. (1 Pet 2:2-3)

Dear friends, now we are children of God, and what we will be has not yet been made known. But we know that when he appears, we shall be like him, for we shall see him as he is. (1 John 3:2)

4 (1:11) **Salvation—Jesus Christ, Death**: salvation was to be accomplished by the sufferings and glories of the Messiah. The Spirit of Christ, the Holy Spirit, told the prophets that God was going to save man by doing two things. (See note—Jn.1:45 for a complete list of the prophecies about Jesus Christ and their fulfillment.)

1. God would send the Messiah into the world to die for man's transgressions; the Messiah would take the guilt of

man's transgressions upon Himself and bear the judgment and punishment of man's guilt.

> Surely he took up our infirmities and carried our sorrows, yet we considered him stricken by God, smitten by him, and afflicted. But he was pierced for our transgressions, he was crushed for our iniquities; the punishment that brought us peace was upon him, and by his wounds we are healed. We all, like sheep, have gone astray, each of us has turned to his own way; and the LORD has laid on him the iniquity of us all. (Isa 53:4-6; cp. Ps.22; Is.52:13-15; 53:1-12).)

> But this is how God fulfilled what he had foretold through all the prophets, saying that his Christ would suffer. (Acts 3:18)

2. God would raise up the Messiah from the dead and exalt Him to the throne of God Himself.

> He will swallow up death forever. The Sovereign LORD will wipe away the tears from all faces; he will remove the disgrace of his people from all the earth. The LORD has spoken. (Isa 25:8. Fulfilled in 1 Cor.15:54)

> When the perishable has been clothed with the imperishable, and the mortal with immortality, then the saying that is written will come true: "Death has been swallowed up in victory." (1 Cor 15:54)

> For you will spread out to the right and to the left; your descendants will dispossess nations and settle in their desolate cities. (Isa 54:3. Fulfilled in Acts 13:34.)

> The fact that God raised him from the dead, never to decay, is stated in these words: "'I will give you the holy and sure blessings promised to David.' (Acts 13:34)

> Because you will not abandon me to the grave, nor will you let your Holy One see decay. (Psa 16:10. Fulfilled in Acts 2:25-28, 31.)

> David said about him: "'I saw the Lord always before me. Because he is at my right hand, I will not be shaken. Therefore my heart is glad and my tongue rejoices; my body also will live in hope, because you will not abandon me to the grave, nor will you let your Holy One see decay. You have made known to me the paths of life; you will fill me with joy in your presence.' Seeing what was ahead, he spoke of the resurrection of the Christ, that he was not abandoned to the grave, nor did his body see decay. (Acts 2:25-28, 31)

> But I have had God's help to this very day, and so I stand here and testify to small and great alike. I am saying nothing beyond what the prophets and Moses said would happen—that the Christ would suffer and, as the first to rise from the dead, would proclaim light to his own people and to the Gentiles." (Acts 26:22-23)

> He said to them, "How foolish you are, and how slow of heart to believe all that the prophets have spoken! Did not the Christ have to suffer these things and then enter his glory?" And beginning with Moses and all the Prophets, he explained to them what was said in all the Scriptures concerning himself. (Luke 24:25-27)

5 (1:12) **Salvation—Fullness of Time**: salvation was destined for future believers, for all who have lived since Christ came. The prophets proclaimed salvation through the coming Messiah. They even proclaimed that He was to suffer and die and be raised and exalted to God's right hand. But they never had the privilege to see Christ nor to know exactly how He would suffer and be raised from the dead and exalted. The fullness of time—zero B.C. and A.D.—had not yet happened. But now it has: the fullness of time has come and God has sent forth His Son, made of a woman, to redeem all mankind. Salvation and the full picture of how the Messiah would die for the sins of the world are now known. All men are, therefore, without excuse if they refuse the wonder and greatness of God's eternal salvation.

> But when the time had fully come, God sent his Son, born of a woman, born under law, to redeem those under law, that we might receive the full rights of sons. Because you are sons, God sent the Spirit of his Son into our hearts, the Spirit who calls out, "Abba, Father." (Gal 4:4-6)

> Be patient, then, brothers, until the Lord's coming. See how the farmer waits for the land to yield its valuable crop and how patient he is for the autumn and spring rains. (James 5:7)

> The Lord is not slow in keeping his promise, as some understand slowness. He is patient with you, not wanting anyone to perish, but everyone to come to repentance. (2 Pet 3:9)

> "I look for your deliverance, O LORD. (Gen 49:18)

> In that day they will say, "Surely this is our God; we trusted in him, and he saved us. This is the LORD, we trusted in him; let us rejoice and be glad in his salvation." (Isa 25:9)

> Yes, LORD, walking in the way of your laws, we wait for you; your name and renown are the desire of our hearts. (Isa 26:8)

> O LORD, be gracious to us; we long for you. Be our strength every morning, our salvation in time of distress. (Isa 33:2)

6 (1:12) **Salvation—Gospel**: salvation is now proclaimed in the gospel. The word *gospel* means good news and good tidings. It is the glorious message of God's salvation, of the death of Jesus Christ who died for our sins and was raised again for our justification. It is the glorious news that if we truly believe in Jesus Christ, then...

- God counts our faith as the righteousness of Jesus Christ. Therefore, we are able to stand before God as righteous, as acceptable to Him.
- God counts us as having already died in the death of Jesus Christ. Therefore, having died in Christ, we never have to die. We shall never taste or experience death. When we are ready to depart this world, in the blink of an eye God will transfer us into heaven and into His very presence.

This is the gospel, the good news of God's eternal salvation. The duty of man is clear: he must believe the gospel and commit his total being to Christ Jesus the Lord and begin to follow and live for Him. Note a significant fact: salvation is the good news of God. It is not the ideas, opinions, and thoughts of a man. Men may have their own ideas about how man can be saved, but their ideas are just that—ideas. Their thoughts are not the thoughts of God; their good news is not the good news of God. The end result of their ideas and opinions is the grave. No man can save men—not beyond the grave. At most, all man can do is delay and extend life a little while longer. No man can give life to any other man. The messages of men about life and the salvation of life are meaningless and empty. The only gospel that is true is God's gospel. His gospel and His gospel alone is the gospel of salvation. The *wonder and greatness of salvation* is just this: God has loved us and spoken to us. He has loved us so much that He has sent His Son into the world to die for us and to save us. God has saved us; He has spoken to us in His Son—spoken the glorious gospel of eternal salvation.

> That everyone who believes in him may have eternal life. "For God so loved the world that he gave his one and only Son, that whoever believes in him shall not perish but have eternal life. (John 3:15-16)
> "I tell you the truth, whoever hears my word and believes him who sent me has eternal life and will not be condemned; he has crossed over from death to life. (John 5:24)
> But these are written that you may believe that Jesus is the Christ, the Son of God, and that by believing you may have life in his name. (John 20:31)
> Therefore, since we have been justified through faith, we have peace with God through our Lord Jesus Christ, (Rom 5:1)
> That if you confess with your mouth, "Jesus is Lord," and believe in your heart that God raised him from the dead, you will be saved. For it is with your heart that you believe and are justified, and it is with your mouth that you confess and are saved. (Rom 10:9-10)
> Consider Abraham: "He believed God, and it was credited to him as righteousness." (Gal 3:6)
> And this gospel of the kingdom will be preached in the whole world as a testimony to all nations, and then the end will come. (Mat 24:14)
> He said to them, "Go into all the world and preach the good news to all creation. (Mark 16:15)
> Now, brothers, I want to remind you of the gospel I preached to you, which you received and on which you have taken your stand. By this gospel you are saved, if you hold firmly to the word I preached to you. Otherwise, you have believed in vain. For what I received I passed on to you as of first importance : that Christ died for our sins according to the Scriptures, that he

> was buried, that he was raised on the third day according to the Scriptures, (1 Cor 15:1-4)

7 (1:12) **Salvation—Angels**: salvation is so glorious that it arouses the angels to understand and look into it. The angels are not able to experience salvation, for they are of the spiritual world. But what God is doing in salvation is so astounding and glorious that they stand in stark amazement at God's workings (see note—Eph.3:10-12 for more discussion).

Thought 1. No believer, layman or minister, should ever treat the gospel of salvation lightly. It is so glorious and so astounding that it demands the utmost diligence and effort...
- in studying
- in witnessing
- in praying
- in living
- in teaching and preaching
- in ministering and serving

> Oh, the depth of the riches of the wisdom and knowledge of God! How unsearchable his judgments, and his paths beyond tracing out! (Rom 11:33)
> It is written: "'As surely as I live,' says the Lord, 'every knee will bow before me; every tongue will confess to God.'" (Rom 14:11)
> Therefore God exalted him to the highest place and gave him the name that is above every name, that at the name of Jesus every knee should bow, in heaven and on earth and under the earth, and every tongue confess that Jesus Christ is Lord, to the glory of God the Father. (Phil 2:9-11)
> And they sang a new song: "You are worthy to take the scroll and to open its seals, because you were slain, and with your blood you purchased men for God from every tribe and language and people and nation. You have made them to be a kingdom and priests to serve our God, and they will reign on the earth." Then I looked and heard the voice of many angels, numbering thousands upon thousands, and ten thousand times ten thousand. They encircled the throne and the living creatures and the elders. In a loud voice they sang: "Worthy is the Lamb, who was slain, to receive power and wealth and wisdom and strength and honor and glory and praise!" Then I heard every creature in heaven and on earth and under the earth and on the sea, and all that is in them, singing: "To him who sits on the throne and to the Lamb be praise and honor and glory and power, for ever and ever!" (Rev 5:9-13)

	II. HOW TO LIVE THROUGH SUFFERING: GIVE YOUR LIFE TO GOD, 1:13-3:12 **A. Get Your Mind Ready, 1:13-16**	fully on the grace to be given you when Jesus Christ is revealed. 14 As obedient children, do not conform to the evil desires you had when you lived in ignorance. 15 But just as he who called you is holy, so be holy in all you do; 16 For it is written: "Be holy, because I am holy."	b. Be self-controlled c. Hope to the end for God's salvation **2 Focus upon obedience** a. Do not be conformed b. Reason: No longer ignorant of God **3 Focus upon holiness**[DS1] a. God is holy b. God has called you c. Scripture demands holiness
1 Focus upon the coming grace & salvation of God a. Prepare your minds for action	13 Therefore, prepare your minds for action; be self-controlled; set your hope-		

DIVISION II

HOW TO LIVE THROUGH SUFFERING: GIVE YOUR LIFE TO GOD, 1:13-3:12

A. Get Your Mind Ready, 1:13-16

(1:13-16) Introduction: this passage begins the longest section of First Peter. Remember: the believers were suffering terrible persecution. They had lost their homes, property, money, possessions, and friends. They had been forced to flee for their lives, perhaps carrying only what they could by hand. They were being persecuted because of Christ. They were living for Christ and proclaiming the salvation and hope of eternal life in Him. People were willing to hear about salvation, hope, and eternal life in Christ; but they did not want to hear about repentance, that they had to repent in order to be saved and to receive eternal life. They were just like people of all ages: they did not want to hear about righteousness and godliness, about a Lord to whom they had to give *all they were and had.* Therefore, the people turned against the believers. The believers had fled into other countries trying to escape the fury of the persecution. They were naturally disappointed and experiencing the dread of fear. They needed to be encouraged and strengthened to continue on for Christ. But what was the best way for Peter to do this? What could be said to encourage a people who had lost everything and were having to flee for their lives?

There was only one message that could encourage and strengthen them: the glorious message of the gospel of salvation. They needed to keep their eyes upon the grace and salvation of God. This is what Peter had preached. Up until now he had proclaimed the wonder and greatness of salvation. Now something else was needed. When we are facing the trials and temptations of life, it is not enough to keep our eyes upon salvation. We must also act; we must do some things. When we undergo the trials of life, whether persecution and suffering or temptation and sin, we must act. We must dedicate our lives to God, and we must get our minds ready. We must concentrate upon some things. We must focus and zero in on three things in particular.

1. Focus upon the coming grace and salvation of God (v.13).
2. Focus upon obedience (v.14).
3. Focus upon holiness (v.15-16).

1 (1:13) **Grace—Mind—Sober—Hope**: focus upon the coming grace, the salvation of God. Remember: grace is the favor of God showered upon us. We do not deserve His favor, for we have not believed God, not perfectly. We have disobeyed, transgressed, cursed, neglected, ignored, and rebelled against God. Nevertheless God has favored us. He loves us; therefore He has provided a way for us to be saved. He has sent His Son into the world to take all of our transgressions upon Himself and to bear the judgment for us. This is what is meant when Scripture says that *Jesus Christ died for us.* He took the guilt of our transgressions against God upon Himself, and He bore the judgment and punishment for us. This is God's grace to us, the great favor and blessing which He has bestowed upon us, even our salvation. We can now be saved from sin and from death; we can now live with God eternally. But note a critical fact: we are not in heaven with God yet. We are not saved from the presence of sin and death yet. We are still living in this world and in the presence of evil and corruption. We shall be delivered some day; we shall be perfected and never know sin and death. But we are not there yet. However the day is coming, the day that is known as the glorious day of redemption or the glorious day of our salvation. The glorious day is coming, the day when Jesus Christ shall burst open the heavens above and return to earth to save and perfect us eternally. Therefore pursue that day; pursue the grace, the glorious salvation of God that is to be brought to us at the revelation of Jesus Christ. Go after God's grace—diligently go after it. Make sure, absolutely sure, that you do not miss God's grace. Pursue God's grace and salvation by doing three things.

1. Prepare your mind for action. This means to gather up all loose thoughts; to gird up your mind and thoughts; to concentrate and focus your attention upon your coming salvation. During Peter's day men wore robes, and they wore a belt around their waist. When they were set on some strenuous action, they gathered up their robe and tightened it under the belt so that the robe would not flop around and hinder their work. The believer is to gather up and prepare the thoughts of his mind, gather up all the loose thoughts and focus and concentrate upon the grace and salvation of God. He is to strain to control every thought, to focus upon...

- "whatever is *true*"
- "whatever is *honest*"
- "whatever is *just*"
- "whatever is *pure*"
- "whatever is *lovely*"
- "whatever is *of good report*"
- "if anything is excellent or praiseworthy—think about such things" (Ph.4:8).

Note how clearly and simply Scripture states this: we are not to allow our thoughts to roam about and harbor thoughts of lust and worldliness. We are to focus our thoughts upon things that are excellent or praiseworthy. We are not to allow thoughts that tear down our moral and godly fiber.

Scripture is even more clear and forceful in another passage:

> For though we live in the world, we do not wage war as the world does. The weapons we fight with are not the weapons of the world. On the contrary, they have divine power to demolish strongholds. We demolish arguments and every pretension that sets itself up against the knowledge of God, and we take captive every thought to make it obedient to Christ. (2 Cor 10:3-5)

The very warfare of the believer is spiritual and mental. Therefore, the believer must...
- demolish arguments or imaginations.
- demolish every pretension that sets itself up against the knowledge of God.
- take captive every thought to make it obedient to Christ.

Imagine—*every thought* is to be captivated for Christ. "Believers, prepare your minds for action. Gather up *all the thoughts* of your mind and focus upon the grace and salvation of God."

> Those who live according to the sinful nature have their minds set on what that nature desires; but those who live in accordance with the Spirit have their minds set on what the Spirit desires. The mind of sinful man is death, but the mind controlled by the Spirit is life and peace; (Rom 8:5-6)
> Therefore, I urge you, brothers, in view of God's mercy, to offer your bodies as living sacrifices, holy and pleasing to God—this is your spiritual act of worship. Do not conform any longer to the pattern of this world, but be transformed by the renewing of your mind. Then you will be able to test and approve what God's will is—his good, pleasing and perfect will. (Rom 12:1-2)
> "For who has known the mind of the Lord that he may instruct him?" But we have the mind of Christ. (1 Cor 2:16)
> For though we live in the world, we do not wage war as the world does. The weapons we fight with are not the weapons of the world. On the contrary, they have divine power to demolish strongholds. We demolish arguments and every pretension that sets itself up against the knowledge of God, and we take captive every thought to make it obedient to Christ. (2 Cor 10:3-5)
> To be made new in the attitude of your minds; and to put on the new self, created to be like God in true righteousness and holiness. (Eph 4:23-24)
> Your attitude should be the same as that of Christ Jesus: (Phil 2:5)
> Finally, brothers, whatever is true, whatever is noble, whatever is right, whatever is pure, whatever is lovely, whatever is admirable—if anything is excellent or praiseworthy—think about such things. (Phil 4:8)

> And have put on the new self, which is being renewed in knowledge in the image of its Creator. (Col 3:10)
> You will keep in perfect peace him whose mind is steadfast, because he trusts in you. (Isa 26:3)

2. Be "self-controlled" (nephontes). Self-controlled means two things:
⇒ Not to become intoxicated with drugs or alcohol of any kind.
⇒ To be self-controlled in mind and behavior; to be controlled in all things; not to be given over to indulgence, license, or extravagance. It is the opposite of indulgence, of indulging in anything such as eating, drinking, recreation, or whatever. It means to live a self-controlled and solid life.

The believer is to be self-controlled as he pursues the coming grace and salvation of God. He is not to indulge and gratify his flesh (sinful nature) in...

• drugs or alcohol	• position
• food	• recognition
• sleep	• authority
• recreation	• power
• sex	• pornography
• clothing	• vehicles
• possessions	• relaxation

The believer is to live a well-balanced life. He is to be self-controlled, solid, and steady. He is to keep all things in the proper place. He is to be self-controlled, focused and concentrated upon the grace and salvation of God.

> So then, let us not be like others, who are asleep, but let us be alert and self-controlled. For those who sleep, sleep at night, and those who get drunk, get drunk at night. But since we belong to the day, let us be self-controlled, putting on faith and love as a breastplate, and the hope of salvation as a helmet. (1 Th 5:6-8)
> In the same way, their wives are to be women worthy of respect, not malicious talkers but temperate and trustworthy in everything. (1 Tim 3:11)
> For the grace of God that brings salvation has appeared to all men. It teaches us to say "No" to ungodliness and worldly passions, and to live self-controlled, upright and godly lives in this present age, while we wait for the blessed hope—the glorious appearing of our great God and Savior, Jesus Christ, (Titus 2:11-13)
> Therefore, prepare your minds for action; be self-controlled; set your hope fully on the grace to be given you when Jesus Christ is revealed. (1 Pet 1:13)
> The end of all things is near. Therefore be clear minded and self-controlled so that you can pray. (1 Pet 4:7)

3. Set your hope fully on the grace and salvation of God. Our hope must be kept alive. There is a *dead hope* and a *lifeless hope*. A *dead hope* is the hope that so many people have, the hope that they will be acceptable to God when they die. But they seldom think about the fact; they just let their hope lie dormant in their mind. It is the hope, the feeling that most people have, the feeling that God

would never reject them, not in the final analysis. Whatever life there is that follows death—they are not sure what it will be like—they feel they will be okay and acceptable. They are not *perfect*, but they are not unacceptable to God. This is a *dead hope*, an occasional thought that they will be okay in whatever life follows death.

Note the exhortation of Scripture: hope to the end for the grace and salvation of God. Begin to hope now and keep on hoping to the very end. This is a living hope, the hope demanded by Scripture. Pursue, seek, and go after the grace and salvation of God. Hope for it and keep on hoping for it. Hope until the revelation of Jesus Christ. He is going to rent the clouds above and return to earth and save us from the sin and death and the evil and corruption of this world. Therefore, hope and keep on hoping, pursue and keep on pursuing, for the coming grace and salvation of God.

> **For in this hope we were saved. But hope that is seen is no hope at all. Who hopes for what he already has? (Rom 8:24)**
>
> **The faith and love that spring from the hope that is stored up for you in heaven and that you have already heard about in the word of truth, the gospel (Col 1:5)**
>
> **For the grace of God that brings salvation has appeared to all men. It teaches us to say "No" to ungodliness and worldly passions, and to live self-controlled, upright and godly lives in this present age, while we wait for the blessed hope—the glorious appearing of our great God and Savior, Jesus Christ, (Titus 2:11-13)**
>
> **God did this so that, by two unchangeable things in which it is impossible for God to lie, we who have fled to take hold of the hope offered to us may be greatly encouraged. We have this hope as an anchor for the soul, firm and secure. It enters the inner sanctuary behind the curtain, where Jesus, who went before us, has entered on our behalf. He has become a high priest forever, in the order of Melchizedek. (Heb 6:18-20)**
>
> **Praise be to the God and Father of our Lord Jesus Christ! In his great mercy he has given us new birth into a living hope through the resurrection of Jesus Christ from the dead, and into an inheritance that can never perish, spoil or fade—kept in heaven for you, (1 Pet 1:3-4)**
>
> **How great is the love the Father has lavished on us, that we should be called children of God! And that is what we are! The reason the world does not know us is that it did not know him. Dear friends, now we are children of God, and what we will be has not yet been made known. But we know that when he appears, we shall be like him, for we shall see him as he is. Everyone who has this hope in him purifies himself, just as he is pure. (1 John 3:1-3)**

2 (1:14) **Obedience**: focus upon obedience. There is a sharp contrast in this verse. Note exactly what it says.

> **As obedient children, do not conform to the evil desires you had when you lived in ignorance. (1 Pet 1:14)**

The phrase "obedient children" means *children of obedience*. That is, believers are to be so obedient to God that obedience becomes the basic trait of their lives. Obedience is to be so characteristic of our lives that we can be called *children of obedience*. However, in contrast to being *children of obedience* is the phrase "conform[ing] to the evil desires you had." As stated this is a sharp contrast. It pictures us as *children of evil desires*. That is, we used to be so given over to our own desires, to doing our own thing, that we could be called *children of evil desires*.

This is not a pretty picture, but it is exactly what a person without Christ is: a *child of desire*, a person who lives just like he wants to live. He does what he wants to do instead of what God says to do. He obeys himself, his own desires, not God and His Word. Therefore, he is a child of desires, *a child of evil desires*. What kind of lusts or desires are being talked about? All kinds. There are the lusts and desires for...

- money
- sex
- popularity
- authority
- possessions
- food

- recognition
- housing
- property
- position
- clothing

Man must have the necessities of life. God made him to desire these things. But when we begin to desire and lust and crave these things it becomes wrong. Our focus and concentration in life becomes the lust of these things, getting more and more of them and gratifying our flesh [sinful nature]. The lust of the flesh [sinful nature] and of the eyes will enslave and consume us. This is a fact of human nature that is too often ignored and neglected. Note why: because of man's ignorance.

Man is ignorant of God. Man does not know God, not personally, not in a close relationship that fellowships and communes with God day by day. When man thinks of God, he thinks of some misty Being or Force who is far away in outer space someplace, too far removed for us to relate to Him in a personal way. Therefore, man feels that he is free to do his own thing and to go his own way through life. And before man knows it, lust has gripped his life. Whatever it is that excites him or gives him purpose in this world, that thing enslaves man. The result is either obsession or emptiness. The person is either controlled and dominated by his lust or else left in despair and discouragement because his lust does not satisfy him.

The point is this: God is not far off and removed from man. God has revealed Himself in the Lord Jesus Christ. Therefore, man is to look at Jesus Christ and see God, and he is to follow the Lord Jesus Christ. Man is to obey God; he is to obey God so much that he will become a child of obedience. The world and its lusts or evil desires are no longer to control our lives. The Lord Jesus Christ is to dominate our lives. We are to focus and concentrate upon Him and the glorious grace and salvation that He is to bring at His revelation.

> **"Not everyone who says to me, 'Lord, Lord,' will enter the kingdom of heaven, but only he who does the will of my Father who is in heaven. (Mat 7:21)**
>
> **"Therefore everyone who hears these words of mine and puts them into practice**

is like a wise man who built his house on the rock. The rain came down, the streams rose, and the winds blew and beat against that house; yet it did not fall, because it had its foundation on the rock. But everyone who hears these words of mine and does not put them into practice is like a foolish man who built his house on sand. The rain came down, the streams rose, and the winds blew and beat against that house, and it fell with a great crash." (Mat 7:24-27)

For whoever does the will of my Father in heaven is my brother and sister and mother." (Mat 12:50)

Whoever has my commands and obeys them, he is the one who loves me. He who loves me will be loved by my Father, and I too will love him and show myself to him." (John 14:21)

Jesus replied, "If anyone loves me, he will obey my teaching. My Father will love him, and we will come to him and make our home with him. (John 14:23)

If you obey my commands, you will remain in my love, just as I have obeyed my Father's commands and remain in his love. You are my friends if you do what I command. (John 15:10, 14)

"Blessed are those who wash their robes, that they may have the right to the tree of life and may go through the gates into the city. (Rev 22:14)

The LORD your God commands you this day to follow these decrees and laws; carefully observe them with all your heart and with all your soul. (Deu 26:16)

Do not let this Book of the Law depart from your mouth; meditate on it day and night, so that you may be careful to do everything written in it. Then you will be prosperous and successful. (Josh 1:8)

3 (1:15-16) **Holiness**: focus upon holiness. Holy (hagios) means to be righteous, pure, sinless, and godly; to be perfect, complete, and fulfilled in every possible sense; to be separated and entirely different from all other beings and things. The believer is to be holy, that is…

- righteous, pure, sinless, and godly.
- perfect, complete, and fulfilled.
- separated, entirely different from all who live worldly.

There are three reasons why believers are to live holy lives.

1. God is holy. He is the very embodiment and perfection of absolute holiness (see DEEPER STUDY # 1, *Holy*— 1 Pt.1:15-16 for more discussion).

⇒ God is the embodiment of absolute righteousness, purity, sinlessness, and godliness.

⇒ God is the very embodiment of absolute perfection, completeness, and fulfillment.

⇒ God is the very embodiment of absolute separation—different and set apart and separated from all else.

2. God has called believers to be holy in all of life. God's very purpose in saving us is to have a people who

will be just like Him and who can live with Him eternally. God's purpose is for us…

- to be holy, righteous, pure, sinless, and godly.
- to be perfect, complete, and fulfilled.
- to be separated from the world and set apart unto Him.

God does not want us corruptible and dying with the world. God wants us holy; He wants us set apart to be just like Him. God wants us to live with Him eternally. But to live with Him eternally, we must be like Him: we must be holy. Therefore, we must pursue, seek, and go after holiness. We must live holy, pure, righteous, and godly lives. We must seek and go after God; we must seek to be like God while on this earth. If we do, then God gives us the most glorious of hopes: the hope of eternal salvation.

3. Scripture demands holiness. It is written in Scripture: "Be holy, because I am holy" (Lev.11:45; 19:2; 20:7, 26). We have no choice: this is the command of Scripture itself. If we wish to be God's, then we must live like God. We must live lives that are holy.

I am the LORD who brought you up out of Egypt to be your God; therefore be holy, because I am holy. (Lev 11:45)

To rescue us from the hand of our enemies, and to enable us to serve him without fear in holiness and righteousness before him all our days. (Luke 1:74-75)

Since we have these promises, dear friends, let us purify ourselves from everything that contaminates body and spirit, perfecting holiness out of reverence for God. (2 Cor 7:1)

Make every effort to live in peace with all men and to be holy; without holiness no one will see the Lord. (Heb 12:14)

For it is written: "Be holy, because I am holy." (1 Pet 1:16)

Since everything will be destroyed in this way, what kind of people ought you to be? You ought to live holy and godly lives (2 Pet 3:11)

Exalt the LORD our God and worship at his holy mountain, for the LORD our God is holy. (Psa 99:9)

And they were calling to one another: "Holy, holy, holy is the LORD Almighty; the whole earth is full of his glory." (Isa 6:3)

Who will not fear you, O Lord, and bring glory to your name? For you alone are holy. All nations will come and worship before you, for your righteous acts have been revealed." (Rev 15:4)

DEEPER STUDY # 1

(1:15-16) **Holy—Saint—Sanctification**: (hagios): all three of these words and their various forms (holiness, saints, and sanctification) are translated from one Greek word *hagios*. Its Hebrew equivalent is *kadosh*. It is difficult to translate into English although its meaning is easy to grasp. Its basic meaning is to be separated, set apart, and different. Morally, it means pure, sinless, righteous, holy. Something holy is set apart, separated, different from all other persons or things. It is something that God has set aside for Himself. Man cannot set it aside as holy. It has to be set aside by God Himself.

A study of the word *holy* shows the movement of God in history.

1. God is said to be preeminently and supremely holy (Lk.1:49; Jn.17:11; 1 Pt.1:15). He possesses an incomparable majesty, so supremely majestic that there are beings who do nothing but surround His throne day and night singing out the praises of His holiness (Is.6:1f; Rev.4:8).

2. Things that have a special connection to God are said to be holy. The ground upon which Moses stood when God confronted him was said to be holy (Ex.3:1-5; Acts 7:33). The temple was said to be holy (Mt.24:15), and the Most Holy Place in particular was holy (Heb.9:2-3). The mount where Christ was transfigured was called holy (2 Pt.1:18). The covenant that God made with Abraham was holy (Lk.1:35). The gospel and Scriptures are called holy (Mt.7:6; Ro.1:2). Anything that becomes associated with God is set apart unto God in a very special sense and becomes different from other things.

3. The Jews are called a *holy nation* (Ex.19:6). They were set apart in a very special way to God. The Old Testament deals primarily with the Jews and their special relationship to God: "You are to be holy to me because I, the LORD, am holy, and I have set you apart from the nations to be my own." (Lev.20:26; cp. Dan.7:18, 22).

⇒ The Jewish people were *holy* in that they were to be different from other nations, different in that they were to believe God and serve Him faithfully. God knew them in a very special way above all the nations of the earth (see DEEPER STUDY # 1—Jn.4:22; DEEPER STUDY # 1—Ro.4:1-25).

⇒ The Jewish priesthood was *holy*, different from other men (Lev.21:6). The people's tithe or tenth was *holy*, different from other money and goods and used for different purposes (Lev.27:30, 32). The temple was *holy*, different from other buildings (Ex.26:33).

But note this: the Jews refused to play the part in history that God wanted them to play. The Old Testament is a continuous record of their rejection of God's will. And when God sent His Son into the world, they committed the supreme and lasting rejection. They refused to acknowledge Him and put Him to death.

4. Jesus Christ is said to be holy in a very special way.
⇒ Before His birth, the angel said to Mary, "The holy One to be born will be called the Son of God" (Lk.1:35).

⇒ Mary worshipped Him in song and praise before His birth saying, "Holy is His name" (Lk.1:49f). He was the only begotten Son of God, *holy*, revered, and worthy of veneration and worship.
⇒ The people recognized that He was *sanctified* by God (Jn.10:36; cp. 6:69).
⇒ The mentally ill and demon-possessed recognized Him as the Holy One of God (Mk.1:24; Lk.4:34).
⇒ The church worshipped Him as "the Holy Child of God" (Acts 4:27, 30).

Note this: Jesus Christ Himself was the transition from God's dealing with the Jewish nation as holy to a new people as holy. When the Jews rejected God's Son, they showed their ultimate refusal to follow God, to be holy and separated unto Him. Therefore, God had no choice but to raise up another people to be separated unto Him. The new people are those of all nations and peoples who believe and follow Christ as the Lord of their lives.

5. The church is now said to be the holy people of God. The privileges and responsibilities of following God were taken from Israel and given to the church (Jn.17:14, 16; Ro.11:16f).
⇒ The church is called *a holy nation* and a *royal or holy priesthood*, a people made up of genuine believers from all nationalities and languages and races (1 Pt.2:5, 9).
⇒ The church is a people who set themselves apart unto God as holy and separated and different, who utterly trust Him and abandon themselves to follow Him.
⇒ The church is now the dwelling place for God's presence. Believers are being built "to become a dwelling in which God lives by His Spirit" (Eph.2:21-22). The church in some unique and spiritual sense, by an act of God, becomes the very body of Christ (Eph.1:22-23). The church, the body of believers when meeting together locally, now replaces the temple of the Old Testament (see note—1 Cor.3:16).

6. But there is something even more precious and hallowed to real believers. The body of the individual believer becomes holy, for the Spirit of God dwells within the believer's body (1 Cor.6:19-20). The body of the believer becomes the dwelling place for God's very presence, and the body replaces the holy of holies within the inner sanctuary of the temple. Thus, believers are called *saints or holy ones* (Acts 9:13, 32, 26:10; Ro.1:7. See note, *Saint*—Ph.1:1.)

	B. Live on Earth in the Fear & Reverence of God, 1:17-21	down to you from your forefathers,	redeemed by perishable, corruptible things
1 Bc. you call God "Father"	17 Since you call on a Father	19 But with the precious blood of Christ, a lamb without blemish or defect.	c. Redeemed by the blood of Christ
2 Bc. God will judge the world	who judges each man's work impartially, live your lives as	20 He was chosen before the creation of the world, but was	1) He was sinless
3 Bc. you are a stranger & alien on earth	strangers here in reverent fear.	revealed in these last times for your sake.	2) He was chosen
4 Bc. you have been redeemed	18 For you know that it was not with perishable things	21 Through him you believe in God, who raised him from	3) He has now come & been revealed
a. Redeemed from an empty life	such as silver or gold that you were redeemed from the	the dead and glorified him, and so your faith and hope	**5** Bc. you believe in the God who raised up & glorified Christ
b. Redeemed freely—not	empty way of life handed	are in God.	

DIVISION II

HOW TO LIVE THROUGH SUFFERING: GIVE YOUR LIFE TO GOD, 1:13-3:12

B. Live on Earth in the Fear and Reverence of God 1:17-21

(1:17-21) **Introduction**: How can we stand against the trials and temptations of life? When we are severely attacked to such a point that we cannot understand, how can we bear it? Is there anything anyplace that can help us to bear it? Yes! There is the fear of God. If a person fears God and fears Him enough, he will stand against temptation and he will endure the trials of life.

But note: most people do not like to talk about *fearing God*. To fear God is thought to be psychologically unsound and emotionally disturbing. It is said to drive people into all kinds of emotional problems. Because of these charges, many have shied away from preaching and teaching *the fear of God*. But note: Is this true? Is it true that preaching and teaching *the fear of God* causes problems for people? One thing is sure: this is not what Scripture proclaims. Scripture proclaims that man must fear God or else he will be doomed forever. Therefore, whatever is causing man's psychological and emotional problems, it is not the *fear of God*, not the *true fear of God*.

What does Scripture mean by the *fear of God*? It means two things.

⇒ To fear God means to hold Him in fear, dread, and terror.
⇒ To fear God means to hold Him in awe, to reverence the holiness, power, knowledge, wisdom, judgment and wrath of God.

What Scripture teaches is this: man must reverence God and hold God in the highest esteem and honor. Only if man reverences God will he worship and serve God. Therefore, the fear that God wants man to have is a fear of reverence and awe, a fear that will stir man to love God with the deepest of emotions, with a true honor and esteem. But if man fails to reverence and love God, then he must fear the judgment and wrath of God. Why? Because man will have to bear the judgment of God. Therefore, fear is man's only hope; it is one of the forces that can drive him to cry out for the mercy of God.

This is the subject of this passage. We are to live on earth in the fear of God.

1. Because you call God "Father" (v.17).
2. Because God will judge the world (v.17).
3. Because you are a stranger and alien (pilgrim) on earth (v.17).
4. Because you have been redeemed (v.18-20).
5. Because you believe in the God who raised up and glorified Christ (v.21).

1 (1:17) **God, Father**: believers are to reverence God because *they call God "Father"*. A father is to be reverenced: every child is to reverence his father. The word *reverence* means to hold one's father in the highest esteem and to honor and respect him. It means to hold one's father in such esteem that one fears lest he displease and hurt his father. This is especially true of God. God is our Father. He has adopted us as His children through the Lord Jesus Christ. Therefore, we are to reverence Him. We are...

• to honor and respect Him.
• to hold Him in the highest esteem.
• to fear lest we displease and dishonor Him and bring pain to His heart.

The point is this: if you call God "Father," then live like it. Stay true to Him. Stand against all the trials and persecutions, temptations and evils of this life. Call upon your Father; ask for His help and strength. But reverence Him; show honor and respect by living for Him.

> **"This, then, is how you should pray: "'Our Father in heaven, hallowed be your name, (Mat 6:9)**
> **If you, then, though you are evil, know how to give good gifts to your children, how much more will your Father in heaven give good gifts to those who ask him! (Mat 7:11)**
> **Yet to all who received him, to those who believed in his name, he gave the right to become children of God— (John 1:12)**
> **For you did not receive a spirit that makes you a slave again to fear, but you received the Spirit of sonship. And by him we cry, "Abba, Father." (Rom 8:15)**
> **"Therefore come out from them and be separate, says the Lord. Touch no unclean thing, and I will receive you." "I will be a Father to you, and you will be my sons and daughters, says the Lord Almighty." (2 Cor 6:17-18)**
> **But when the time had fully come, God sent his Son, born of a woman, born under law, to redeem those under law, that we might receive the full rights of sons. Because you are sons, God sent the Spirit of**

31

his Son into our hearts, the Spirit who calls out, "Abba, Father." (Gal 4:4-6)

Since you call on a Father who judges each man's work impartially, live your lives as strangers here in reverent fear. (1 Pet 1:17)

2 (1:17) **Judgment**: believers are to reverence God because *God will judge the world*. Note that the word "fear" (phoboi) is used. It means to hold God in reverence and awe. The judgment of God should strike fear, dread and terror within us, for it is to be the most fearful, dreaded and terrorizing experience imaginable. In fact, the human mind cannot even picture how awful and frightening it will be to be judged and cut off from God for eternity. Two things are said about the judgment of God.

1. Every person is going to be judged. No one shall escape. Every person will come to the day when he will stand all alone in a private interview with God. In that moment he shall stand face to face with God for one purpose and one purpose alone: to be judged.

2. It is the works of a person that are to be judged. No false profession will stand in that day. When God reveals the person's works, his works will show that he never really trusted in Christ. He only said that he believed Christ, but his life and works will prove differently. It will be seen that he lived a lie. His life and works will show that he lived for the world and its possessions and pleasure.

Thought 1. We must never forget: a person is saved by faith in Christ, by a faith that lives for Christ and continues to live for Christ. A person who believes in Christ lives for Him. The person believes; therefore he lives day by day doing exactly what he believes. There just is no such thing as faith without works to *back up the faith*. If a person truly believes, then he does what he believes. His works follow his belief. This is the reason it is our works that shall be judged: our works will reveal exactly what we believe.

3. God will judge without partiality. God has no favorites. It does not matter who the person is: high or low, rich or poor, sinner or saint, good or bad, righteous or evil—all shall be judged and favoritism will be shown to no one. Peter, Paul, Martin Luther, Pope Paul, Billy Graham, Caesar, George Washington, John Kennedy, Winston Churchill, Martin Luther King, Einstein, Hitler, Stalin, Genghis Khan, Bill, Henry, Jane, Elizabeth—every human being who has ever lived, both high and low, will be judged; and we shall all be judged on an equal basis. There will be no partiality and no favoritism shown to a single person.

For the Son of Man is going to come in his Father's glory with his angels, and then he will reward each person according to what he has done. (Mat 16:27)

"When the Son of Man comes in his glory, and all the angels with him, he will sit on his throne in heavenly glory. All the nations will be gathered before him, and he will separate the people one from another as a shepherd separates the sheep from the goats. (Mat 25:31-32)

For we must all appear before the judgment seat of Christ, that each one may receive what is due him for the things done while in the body, whether good or bad. (2 Cor 5:10)

Just as man is destined to die once, and after that to face judgment, (Heb 9:27)

Since you call on a Father who judges each man's work impartially, live your lives as strangers here in reverent fear. (1 Pet 1:17)

If this is so, then the Lord knows how to rescue godly men from trials and to hold the unrighteous for the day of judgment, while continuing their punishment. (2 Pet 2:9)

By the same word the present heavens and earth are reserved for fire, being kept for the day of judgment and destruction of ungodly men. (2 Pet 3:7)

In this way, love is made complete among us so that we will have confidence on the day of judgment, because in this world we are like him. (1 John 4:17)

Enoch, the seventh from Adam, prophesied about these men: "See, the Lord is coming with thousands upon thousands of his holy ones to judge everyone, and to convict all the ungodly of all the ungodly acts they have done in the ungodly way, and of all the harsh words ungodly sinners have spoken against him." (Jude 1:14-15)

And I saw the dead, great and small, standing before the throne, and books were opened. Another book was opened, which is the book of life. The dead were judged according to what they had done as recorded in the books. (Rev 20:12)

"Behold, I am coming soon! My reward is with me, and I will give to everyone according to what he has done. (Rev 22:12)

And that you, O Lord, are loving. Surely you will reward each person according to what he has done. (Psa 62:12)

"I the LORD search the heart and examine the mind, to reward a man according to his conduct, according to what his deeds deserve." (Jer 17:10)

3 (1:17) **Stranger—Alien (Pilgrim)—Worldliness**: believers are to reverence God because *they are strangers on earth*. The word "sojourning" (paroikais) means to dwell alongside; to be passing by. It is the picture of an alien or stranger who is in a foreign country and is only dwelling there or passing by for a brief time. This is the believer here on earth. He is not a permanent resident on earth. He is only passing through the earth to a better world. This means a most wonderful thing: when a person is a stranger or alien in a foreign land, his mind and heart are home. He lives in a consciousness of home. So it is with the believer: his thoughts are upon home. He lives and walks in the consciousness of being in heaven with God. This is his attitude and his thoughts as he walks through his pilgrimage upon earth. He travels through life with his mind and heart upon heaven, his permanent home.

All these people were still living by faith when they died. They did not receive the things promised; they only saw them and welcomed them from a distance. And they admitted that they were aliens and strangers on earth. People who say such things show that they are looking for a country of their own. If they had been thinking of the country they had left, they would have had opportunity to return. Instead, they were longing for a better country—a heavenly one. Therefore God is not ashamed to be called their God, for he has prepared a city for them. (Heb 11:13-16)

For here we do not have an enduring city, but we are looking for the city that is to come. (Heb 13:14)

Dear friends, I urge you, as aliens and strangers in the world, to abstain from sinful desires, which war against your soul. (1 Pet 2:11)

I also established my covenant with them to give them the land of Canaan, where they lived as aliens. (Exo 6:4)

We are aliens and strangers in your sight, as were all our forefathers. Our days on earth are like a shadow, without hope. (1 Chr 29:15)

"Hear my prayer, O LORD, listen to my cry for help; be not deaf to my weeping. For I dwell with you as an alien, a stranger, as all my fathers were. (Psa 39:12)

I am a stranger on earth; do not hide your commands from me. (Psa 119:19)

4 (1:18-20) **Redemption—Jesus Christ, Blood**: believers are to reverence God because *they have been redeemed*. The word "redeem" (lutron) means to set free or deliver by paying some ransom. Note three significant points.

1. We need to be redeemed, to be set free from the empty life that we have been taught to live by our forefathers. This is exactly what Scripture says:

For you...were redeemed from the empty way of life handed down to you from your forefathers, (v.18)

The life which most fathers teach is a vain and empty life. It focuses upon the world, its possessions and pleasures...

- jobs
- professions
- money
- housing
- property
- enjoyment
- ease
- investments
- retirement
- recreation
- position
- authority
- pleasure
- recognition
- fame
- popularity
- honor
- prestige
- comfort

Note carefully: these things do not satisfy the human heart. They are necessary to human life; we must have the basic necessities in order to sustain life. But physical and material things do not satisfy or fulfill the human heart. Only one thing can do that: God—the presence of God living in the heart and giving the person the perfect assurance of living forever with God. Therefore when a person focuses upon the world, its pleasures and possessions, he becomes vain. His heart becomes empty, void, unfulfilled, and incomplete. The worldly heart senses a lack of permanent purpose, meaning, and significance. Why?

⇒ Because the worldly person has little assurance that he is acceptable to God. Why? Because his life and thoughts are not focused upon God; they are focused upon the world.

⇒ Because the worldly person is not sure he will live forever. Why? Because his life is not focused upon heaven; it is focused upon this world, upon getting all the possessions and pleasures he can to live comfortably.

⇒ Because the worldly person transgresses the law of God. He neglects, ignores, rejects, rebels, and curses God. He is simply guilty of transgressing the law of God; therefore, he must bear the judgment and punishment for having violated God and His law. He must die, be exiled and cut off from God eternally. The worldly person has chosen to live without God; therefore, his desire will be granted. He will never have to live with God. He will continue on and on without God—exiled, cut off from God forever and ever.

The point is this: we need to be set free and delivered from the empty life that we have been taught to live. Our forefathers were wrong. A worldly life does not work. It only leaves us empty and void, incomplete and unfulfilled, and it dooms us to death, to an eternity apart from God.

He did evil in the eyes of the LORD, because he walked in the ways of his father and mother and in the ways of Jeroboam son of Nebat, who caused Israel to sin. (1 Ki 22:52)

He too walked in the ways of the house of Ahab, for his mother encouraged him in doing wrong. (2 Chr 22:3)

Instead, they have followed the stubbornness of their hearts; they have followed the Baals, as their fathers taught them." (Jer 9:14)

This is what the LORD says: "For three sins of Judah, even for four, I will not turn back my wrath. Because they have rejected the law of the LORD and have not kept his decrees, because they have been led astray by false gods, the gods their ancestors followed, (Amos 2:4)

Jesus replied, "And why do you break the command of God for the sake of your tradition [teaching]? (Mat 15:3)

In which you used to live when you followed the ways of this world and of the ruler of the kingdom of the air, the spirit who is now at work in those who are disobedient. All of us also lived among them at one time, gratifying the cravings of our sinful nature and following its desires and thoughts. Like the rest, we were by nature objects of wrath. (Eph 2:2-3)

See to it that no one takes you captive through hollow and deceptive philosophy, which depends on human tradition and the basic principles of this world rather than on Christ. (Col 2:8)

And will pay no attention to Jewish myths or to the commands of those who reject the truth. (Titus 1:14)

For you know that it was not with perishable things such as silver or gold that you were redeemed from the empty way of life handed down to you from your forefathers, (1 Pet 1:18)

For you have spent enough time in the past doing what pagans choose to do—living in debauchery, lust, drunkenness, orgies, carousing and detestable idolatry. (1 Pet 4:3)

2. We are freely redeemed: redemption does not cost us a penny. We are not redeemed by silver and gold. Note why. Because they are perishable, corruptible; that is, silver and gold perish. Money passes away. Therefore, if we were able to buy redemption with money, our redemption would last only as long as our money lasted. When it deteriorated and passed away, the payment for our ransom would no longer exist. Therefore, God's righteousness and justice would no longer be able to accept us. Once again, we would stand guilty before Him. Why? Because God is eternal; therefore, the ransom demanded by His justice is an eternal ransom. If we are going to be delivered from this perishable, corruptible world and given eternal life, then the ransom paid for our release has to be an eternal ransom—a ransom that will last as long as we are going to be living. This is the reason silver and gold are totally inadequate in redeeming us.

Thought 1. The most precious thing on earth to men is silver and gold. But even if a man had all the silver and gold in the world, he could not use them to buy his redemption. Yet, how many try to please God and to secure His approval by making gifts to the church and special projects to help the needy and the community?

3. We are redeemed by the precious blood of Christ. A.T. Robertson says, "The blood of anyone is 'precious' [costly] far above gold or silver, but that of Jesus immeasurably more so" (A.T. Robertson. *Word Pictures In The New Testament*, Vol.6, p.90). How is it that the blood of Christ redeems us?

a. First, Jesus Christ was just like the Passover lamb, "without blemish and without spot." When Jesus Christ came to earth, He never sinned; He never transgressed the law of God. He stood before God as the Perfect and Ideal Man. He was acceptable to God, perfectly acceptable. As the Ideal and Perfect Man, whatever Jesus Christ did, it would stand for and cover man. Therefore, when Jesus Christ died, He was able to take all of man's guilt and judgment upon Himself and die for man. He was able to bear the judgment and punishment of transgression for man. The death or blood of Jesus Christ is the eternal ransom for man. When we believe in Jesus Christ, really trust Him, God counts us as having died in Christ. Therefore, having died with Him, we shall never die. When it is time for us to depart this world, quicker than the blink of an eye, God shall transfer us into heaven, into His very own presence. Jesus Christ has redeemed us; He has paid the ransom and delivered and set us free from sin and its penalty of death.

And are justified freely by his grace through the redemption that came by Christ Jesus. (Rom 3:24)

Christ redeemed us from the curse of the law by becoming a curse for us, for it is written: "Cursed is everyone who is hung on a tree." (Gal 3:13)

In whom we have redemption, the forgiveness of sins. (Col 1:14)

Who [Christ] gave himself for us to redeem us from all wickedness and to purify

for himself a people that are his very own, eager to do what is good. (Titus 2:14)

He did not enter by means of the blood of goats and calves; but he entered the Most Holy Place once for all by his own blood, having obtained eternal redemption. (Heb 9:12)

For you know that it was not with perishable things such as silver or gold that you were redeemed from the empty way of life handed down to you from your forefathers, (1 Pet 1:18)

And they sang a new song: "You are worthy to take the scroll and to open its seals, because you were slain, and with your blood you purchased men for God from every tribe and language and people and nation. (Rev 5:9)

b. Second, God chose that Christ redeem us by His blood. He was chosen even before the creation of the world. The word "chosen" (proegnosmenou) means foreknown. The word is used three different ways in Scripture:
   ⇒ to know something beforehand, ahead of time.
   ⇒ to know something immediately by loving and accepting and approving it.
   ⇒ to elect, foreordain, and predetermine something.

Note that all three meanings are at work in this passage. Before the world was ever created, God knew, approved, and predestined Christ to redeem man by coming to earth and dying for man. (See DEEPER STUDY # 1, *Foreknowledge—* 1 Pt.1:2 for more discussion.)

That have been known for ages. (Acts 15:18)

For those God foreknew he also predestined to be conformed to the likeness of his Son, that he might be the firstborn among many brothers. (Rom 8:29)

God did not reject his people, whom he foreknew. Don't you know what the Scripture says in the passage about Elijah—how he appealed to God against Israel: (Rom 11:2)

For you know that it was not with perishable things such as silver or gold that you were redeemed from the empty way of life handed down to you from your forefathers, but with the precious blood of Christ, a lamb without blemish or defect. He was chosen before the creation of the world, but was revealed in these last times for your sake. (1 Pet 1:18-20)

Nevertheless, God's solid foundation stands firm, sealed with this inscription: "The Lord knows those who are his," and, "Everyone who confesses the name of the Lord must turn away from wickedness." (2 Tim 2:19)

Who have been chosen according to the foreknowledge of God the Father, through the sanctifying work of the Spirit, for obedience to Jesus Christ and sprinkling by his blood: Grace and peace be yours in abundance. (1 Pet 1:2)

c. Third, Christ has now come. God has now revealed and sent Him to redeem us. And note the statement: "in these last times." Time is short, very short. There is little time left for us to be redeemed. Century after century has already passed.

"The time has come," he said. "The kingdom of God is near. Repent and believe the good news!" (Mark 1:15)

But when the time had fully come, God sent his Son, born of a woman, born under law, to redeem those under law, that we might receive the full rights of sons. Because you are sons, God sent the Spirit of his Son into our hearts, the Spirit who calls out, "Abba, Father." (Gal 4:4-6)

This is good, and pleases God our Savior, who wants all men to be saved and to come to a knowledge of the truth. For there is one God and one mediator between God and men, the man Christ Jesus, who gave himself as a ransom for all men—the testimony given in its proper time. (1 Tim 2:3-6)

And at his appointed season he brought his word to light through the preaching entrusted to me by the command of God our Savior, (Titus 1:3)

Then Christ would have had to suffer many times since the creation of the world. But now he has appeared once for all at the end of the ages to do away with sin by the sacrifice of himself. (Heb 9:26)

5 (1:21) **Faith—Jesus Christ, Resurrection**: believers are to reverence God because they believe in God who raised up and glorified Christ. Who is the God whom believers trust and call upon? The God who raised up and glorified the Lord Jesus Christ. This means two most wonderful things: if God raised up Christ, He will also raise us up. If God glorified Christ, He will also glorify us. He knows how to raise us up and to glorify us and He has the power. He has proven it by raising up and glorifying Christ.

⇒ Jesus Christ pleased God, pleased Him perfectly. God accepted Jesus Christ, and He has proven it in the most supreme way possible: He has raised Christ up from the dead and glorified Him. Therefore, the person who believes in Jesus Christ—who really trusts the blood of Jesus Christ to cover his sins—who really honors God's Son enough to cast his whole life and eternity upon Christ—that person can rest assured that God will accept him. God will raise him up and glorify him with Christ.

⇒ God knows how to raise up and glorify the dead, and He has the power to do it. He has proven His omniscience (supreme knowledge) and omnipotence (supreme power) by raising up and glorifying Christ. Therefore, the person who believes in Jesus Christ can rest assured that God knows how to raise him up and to glorify him forever and ever.

Note one other fact: we believe in God "through Him," that is, through Christ. Christ is the Mediator between God and men, the only Person who is perfect and ideal. Therefore, He alone can make us acceptable to God. If we are going to approach God, we must come through Jesus Christ.

Then they asked him, "What must we do to do the works God requires?" Jesus answered, "The work of God is this: to believe in the one he has sent." (John 6:28-29)

For my Father's will is that everyone who looks to the Son and believes in him shall have eternal life, and I will raise him up at the last day." (John 6:40)

Jesus said to her, "I am the resurrection and the life. He who believes in me will live, even though he dies; (John 11:25)

Therefore, since we have been justified through faith, we have peace with God through our Lord Jesus Christ, (Rom 5:1)

That if you confess with your mouth, "Jesus is Lord," and believe in your heart that God raised him from the dead, you will be saved. For it is with your heart that you believe and are justified, and it is with your mouth that you confess and are saved. (Rom 10:9-10)

Now, brothers, I want to remind you of the gospel I preached to you, which you received and on which you have taken your stand. By this gospel you are saved, if you hold firmly to the word I preached to you. Otherwise, you have believed in vain. For what I received I passed on to you as of first importance : that Christ died for our sins according to the Scriptures, that he was buried, that he was raised on the third day according to the Scriptures, (1 Cor 15:1-4)

Because we know that the one who raised the Lord Jesus from the dead will also raise us with Jesus and present us with you in his presence. (2 Cor 4:14)

And his incomparably great power for us who believe. That power is like the working of his mighty strength, which he exerted in Christ when he raised him from the dead and seated him at his right hand in the heavenly realms, (Eph 1:19-20)

We believe that Jesus died and rose again and so we believe that God will bring with Jesus those who have fallen asleep in him. According to the Lord's own word, we tell you that we who are still alive, who are left till the coming of the Lord, will certainly not precede those who have fallen asleep. For the Lord himself will come down from heaven, with a loud command, with the voice of the archangel and with the trumpet call of God, and the dead in Christ will rise first. After that, we who are still alive and are left will be caught up together with them in the clouds to meet the Lord in the air. And so we will be with the Lord forever. Therefore encourage each other with these words. (1 Th 4:14-18)

Praise be to the God and Father of our Lord Jesus Christ! In his great mercy he has given us new birth into a living hope through the resurrection of Jesus Christ from the dead, (1 Pet 1:3)

And this is his command: to believe in the name of his Son, Jesus Christ, and to love one another as he commanded us. (1 John 3:23)

	C. Love One Another Fervently, 1:22-25	but of imperishable, through the living and enduring word of God.	a. The Word is imperishable, incorruptible
1 Reason 1: You have purified your souls	22 Now that you have puri-	24 For, "All men are like grass, and all their glory is	b. The Word lives forever
a. By obeying the truth	fied yourselves by obeying	like the flowers of the field;	**3 Reason 3: Your flesh withers & falls away**
b. By the Spirit's power	the truth so that you have sin-	the grass withers and the	a. Life is short, just like grass
	cere love for your brothers,	flowers fall,	
	love one another deeply, from	25 But the word of the Lord	
	the heart.	stands forever." And this is	b. The Word & the be-
2 Reason 2: You are born again through the Word of Godᴰˢ¹	23 For you have been born again, not of perishable seed,	the word that was preached to you.	liever endure forever

DIVISION II

HOW TO LIVE THROUGH SUFFERING: GIVE YOUR LIFE TO GOD, 1:13-3:12

C. Love One Another Fervently, 1:22-25

(1:22-25) **Introduction—Love**: there is no greater force than love. If two people truly love each other, they will do anything for the other. There is no greater bond on earth than true love. This is especially true of the love between believers. Why? Is there a difference between the love that believers have for one another and the love that neighbors have for one another? Scripture says yes, emphatically yes. Believers are to have a different kind of love than neighbors have for one another. The love that believers are to have for one another is what the Greek calls *philadelphia* love, a very special kind of love. The word is "scarcely found except in Christian writings" (B.C. Coffin. *First Peter*. "The Pulpit Commentary," Vol.22, ed. by HDM Spence and Joseph S. Exell. Grand Rapids, MI: Eerdmans, 1950, p.11.) *Philadelphia love* means *brotherly love*, the very special love that exists between the brothers and sisters within a loving family, brothers and sisters who truly cherish each other. It is the kind of love…

- that binds one another together as a family, as a brotherly clan.
- that binds one another in an unbreakable union.
- that holds one another ever so deeply within the heart.
- that knows deep affection for one another.
- that nourishes and nurtures one another.
- that shows concern and looks after the welfare of one another.

The importance of believers loving one another with a *philadelphia love* cannot be over-stressed. Note what verse 22 says:

⇒ We are to have *unfeigned love* for our Christian brothers. Unfeigned means genuine, sincere, without pretension, hypocrisy, or play-acting. We are not to pretend, play, and act like we love one another; we are to love one another genuinely and sincerely.

But note this: there can be no mistake about the importance of love, for verse 22 says more and it is forceful: "love one another deeply, from the heart." The word "deeply" (ektenos) "does not mean 'with warmth' but rather 'with full intensity'." It literally means to *stretch love fully out* or to love one another *in an all out manner* (Alan M. Stibbs. *The First Epistle General of Peter*. "The Tyndale New Testament Commentaries," ed. by RVG Tasker. Grand Rapids, MI: Eerdmans, 1959, p.94).

This is the love believers are to have for one another, a *philadelphia* kind of love. Now note: there are four reasons why we are to love one another fervently.

1. Reason 1: you have purified your souls (v.22).
2. Reason 2: you are born again through the Word of God (v.23).
3. Reason 3: your flesh withers and falls away (v.24-25).

1 (1:22) **Salvation—Obedience—Purity**: believers are to love one another because they have *purified their souls*. This means that the soul of a true believer is cleansed of sin. He is forgiven and purified from every sin he has ever committed. His soul is pure and clean, completely free from all guilt and moral dirt, pollution, and corruption. The true believer is no longer guilty of any misbehavior or sin, no matter what it is. He stands before God with a pure and clean soul, a soul that is perfect and acceptable to God.

But note a significant point—note what it is that cleanses the believer's soul: it is obedience to the truth. The believer obeys the truth and as he obeys the truth, the Spirit of God continually cleanses his soul from sin. This is critical to note: a person is cleansed only while he is walking in the truth, only while he is obeying the truth of God's light. When a person walks in the light of the truth, the Spirit cleanses his soul through the blood of Christ.

> **But if we walk in the light, as he is in the light, we have fellowship with one another, and the blood of Jesus, his Son, purifies us from all sin. (1 John 1:7)**

This is the reason we are to love our brothers. God has cleansed our souls from sin for the very purpose of loving others, and we are obedient when we love them. It is a circle: we are obedient when we love them and we love them when we are obedient. God has cleansed our souls so that we can love people with a clean and pure heart—with no restraints of guilt or shame or weakness whatsoever. Therefore, let us love one another in the freedom of a pure and clean soul.

> **"A new command I give you: Love one another. As I have loved you, so you must love one another. By this all men will know that you are my disciples, if you love one another." (John 13:34-35)**
> **Whoever has my commands and obeys them, he is the one who loves me. He who loves me will be loved by my Father, and I too will love him and show myself to him." (John 14:21)**

If you obey my commands, you will remain in my love, just as I have obeyed my Father's commands and remain in his love. I have told you this so that my joy may be in you and that your joy may be complete. My command is this: Love each other as I have loved you. (John 15:10-12)

Love must be sincere. Hate what is evil; cling to what is good. (Rom 12:9)

May the Lord make your love increase and overflow for each other and for everyone else, just as ours does for you. (1 Th 3:12)

The goal of this command is love, which comes from a pure heart and a good conscience and a sincere faith. (1 Tim 1:5)

Now that you have purified yourselves by obeying the truth so that you have sincere love for your brothers, love one another deeply, from the heart. (1 Pet 1:22)

And this is his command: to believe in the name of his Son, Jesus Christ, and to love one another as he commanded us. (1 John 3:23)

2 (1:23) **Born Again—New Birth—Word of God**: believers are to love one another because they have been born again through the Word of God. All believers have been spiritually born again and spiritually remade. They have been spiritually created into new men and new women, created anew by God to be brothers and sisters to one another and to love one another. Note two points.

1. First, believers are not born again by perishable, corruptible seed, that is, not by the seed of mere man who is perishable or corruptible. If we were born again by the work of some man, we would still be perishable. We would still be…

- abusive
- self-seeking
- hypocritical
- prideful
- angry
- selfish
- jealous
- withdrawn
- arrogant
- bitter
- deceptive
- envious
- snobbish
- neglectful
- hateful

This is the behavior of perishable, corruptible seed; it is the nature of human beings. It is the way man acts toward others. But this is not to be the nature of believers, for believers have been born again.

2. Second, believers are born again by the imperishable, incorruptible seed, through the Word of God itself. God spoke and convicted us and led us to repent of our sins and turn to Him. It may have happened when we were reading God's Word or thinking about God or when we were listening to some preacher proclaim God's Word. It does not matter when or how we were born again. What matters is that it has happened. When we turned from sin to God, God spoke the Word and made our spirits alive, making them alive to Him and His Word.

Note that God's Word is the *imperishable, incorruptible seed*; it is the seed that is planted within our hearts and lives. The word imperishable means that it does not perish. Imagine! The Word of God *recreates us*, and it is imperishable. This means a most wonderful thing: we are incorruptible; we will not age, perish, deteriorate, or decay. As this verse says, "the living and enduring Word of God." Therefore, we shall live and endure forever.

The point is this: as born again brothers and sisters, God has put His incorruptible Word into our hearts. And the very first Word or commandment to believers is to love one another. Therefore, we must love one another deeply, from the heart. We must obey God.

And this is his command: to believe in the name of his Son, Jesus Christ, and to love one another as he commanded us. (1 John 3:23)

In reply Jesus declared, "I tell you the truth, no one can see the kingdom of God unless he is born again." Jesus answered, "I tell you the truth, no one can enter the kingdom of God unless he is born of water and the Spirit. Flesh gives birth to flesh, but the Spirit gives birth to spirit. (John 3:3, 5-6)

Therefore, if anyone is in Christ, he is a new creation; the old has gone, the new has come! (2 Cor 5:17)

And to put on the new self, created to be like God in true righteousness and holiness. (Eph 4:24)

And have put on the new self, which is being renewed in knowledge in the image of its Creator. (Col 3:10)

He saved us, not because of righteous things we had done, but because of his mercy. He saved us through the washing of rebirth and renewal by the Holy Spirit, (Titus 3:5)

For you have been born again, not of perishable seed, but of imperishable, through the living and enduring word of God. (1 Pet 1:23)

Everyone who believes that Jesus is the Christ is born of God, and everyone who loves the father loves his child as well. (1 John 5:1)

DEEPER STUDY # 1

(1:23) **Born Again—New Birth**: a spiritual birth, a rebirth of one's spirit, a new life, a renewed soul, a regenerated spirit. It is the regeneration and renewal of one's spirit and behavior (2 Cor.5:17). It is the endowment of a new life, of a godly nature (2 Pt.1:4). The new birth is so radical a change in a person's life that it can be described only as being *born again*. Something so wonderful happens to the soul that it is just like a *new birth*. It is a spiritual birth, a birth beyond the grasp of man's hands and efforts. It is so radical, so life-changing, and so wonderful that it can be produced only by the love and power of God Himself.

The New Testament teaching on the new birth is rich and full.

1. The new birth is a necessity. A person will never see (Jn.3:3) nor ever enter (Jn.3:5) the Kingdom of God unless he is born again (Jn.3:7).

2. The new birth is a spiritual birth, the birth of a new power and spirit in life. It is not reformation of the old nature (Ro.6:6). It is the actual creation of a new birth within—spiritually (Jn.3:5-6; cp. Jn.1:12-13; 2 Cor.5:17; Eph.2:10; 4:24). (See notes—Eph.1:3; 4:17-19; DEEPER STUDY # 3—4:24.) A person is spiritually born again:

a. By water, even the Spirit (see DEEPER STUDY # 2—Jn.3:5).

b. By the will or choice of God (Jas.1:18).

c. By imperishable, incorruptible seed, even by the Word of God (1 Pt.1:23).

d. By God from above (1 Pt.1:3). The word new (ana) in the phrase "new birth" also means *above*. (Cp. Jn.1:12-13.)

e. By Christ, who gives both the *right* and *power* to be born again (Jn.1:12-13).

3. The new birth is a definite experience, a real experience. A person experiences the new birth:

a. By believing that Jesus is the Christ, the Son of God (1 Jn.5:1; cp. Jn.3:14-15).

b. By the gospel as it is shared by believers (1 Cor.4:15; Phile.10).

c. By the Word of God (1 Pt.1:23), or through the Word of Truth (Jas.1:18).

4. The new birth is a changed life, a totally new life. A person proves that he is born again:

a. By doing righteous acts (1 Jn.2:29; cp. Eph.2:10; 4:24).

b. By not practicing sin (1 Jn.3:9; 5:18).

c. By loving other believers (1 Jn.4:7).

d. By overcoming the world (1 Jn.5:4).

e. By not continuing to sin (1 Jn.5:18).

f. By possessing the divine seed or nature (1 Jn.3:9; 1 Pt.1:23; 2 Pt.1:14; cp. Col.1:27).

3 (1:24-25) **Death—Flesh—Body—Word of God**: believers are to love one another because their flesh (body) withers and falls away ever so quickly (cp. Is.6-8). Note two facts.

1. Life is ever so short. It lasts no longer than the grass that appears so quickly and then withers away or the flower that appears just as quickly and falls away.

Note the phrase "all their glory." People work and work to be glorious, to be...

- attractive
- acceptable
- honorable
- upstanding
- recognized
- charming
- appealing
- esteemed
- dignified
- beautiful

But no matter how much glory man achieves, he ages, wrinkles, deteriorates, and passes off the scene. His flesh is no more than the grass that withers, and the glory of his flesh is no more than the flower that falls away. But this is not true with the believer.

> You sweep men away in the sleep of death; they are like the new grass of the morning— though in the morning it springs up new, by evening it is dry and withered. May your deeds be shown to your servants, your splendor to their children. (Psa 90:5-6, 16)

> A voice says, "Cry out." And I said, "What shall I cry?" "All men are like grass, and all their glory is like the flowers of the field. The grass withers and the flowers fall, because the breath of the LORD blows on them. Surely the people are grass. (Isa 40:6-7)

> "I, even I, am he who comforts you. Who are you that you fear mortal men, the sons of men, who are but grass, (Isa 51:12)

> But the one who is rich should take pride in his low position, because he will pass away like a wild flower. (James 1:10)

> For, "All men are like grass, and all their glory is like the flowers of the field;

> the grass withers and the flowers fall, (1 Pet 1:24)

> You have made my days a mere handbreadth; the span of my years is as nothing before you. Each man's life is but a breath. Selah (Psa 39:5)

> But man, despite his riches, does not endure; he is like the beasts that perish. (Psa 49:12)

> For he will take nothing with him when he dies, his splendor will not descend with him. (Psa 49:17)

> He remembered that they were but flesh, a passing breeze that does not return. (Psa 78:39)

> For he knows how we are formed, he remembers that we are dust. (Psa 103:14)

> "My days are swifter than a weaver's shuttle, and they come to an end without hope. (Job 7:6)

> When a land falls into the hands of the wicked, he blindfolds its judges. If it is not he, then who is it? (Job 9:24)

> Stop trusting in man, who has but a breath in his nostrils. Of what account is he? (Isa 2:22)

> Therefore the grave enlarges its appetite and opens its mouth without limit; into it will descend their nobles and masses with all their brawlers and revelers. (Isa 5:14)

> Like a shepherd's tent my house has been pulled down and taken from me. Like a weaver I have rolled up my life, and he has cut me off from the loom; day and night you made an end of me. (Isa 38:12)

> Why, you do not even know what will happen tomorrow. What is your life? You are a mist that appears for a little while and then vanishes. (James 4:14)

2. The believer endures forever: "the Word of the Lord stands forever" (v.25). The Word of the Lord lives in the heart and life of the believer. Therefore, the believer lives forever (v.23). What is this word that stands forever? It is the Word of the gospel that is preached to you. If we receive the word of the gospel—really bring it into our lives—it will live within us forever and keep us living forever.

The point is this: believers have received the Word of the Lord into their lives. Therefore, they are going to be living together forever. We are the family of God. Therefore, we are to live and act like the family of God; we are to love one another deeply from the heart.

> Your word, O LORD, is eternal; it stands firm in the heavens. (Psa 119:89)

> The grass withers and the flowers fall, but the word of our God stands forever." (Isa 40:8)

> I tell you the truth, until heaven and earth disappear, not the smallest letter, not the least stroke of a pen, will by any means disappear from the Law until everything is accomplished. (Mat 5:18)

> Heaven and earth will pass away, but my words will never pass away. (Mat 24:35)

> But the word of the Lord stands forever." And this is the word that was

preached to you. (1 Pet 1:25)

"I tell you the truth, whoever hears my word and believes him who sent me has eternal life and will not be condemned; he has crossed over from death to life. (John 5:24)

For you did not receive a spirit that makes you a slave again to fear, but you received the Spirit of sonship. And by him we cry, "Abba, Father." The Spirit himself testifies with our spirit that we are God's children. Now if we are children, then we are heirs—heirs of God and co-heirs with Christ, if indeed we share in his sufferings in order that we may also share in his glory. (Rom 8:15-17)

Now, brothers, I want to remind you of the gospel I preached to you, which you re-ceived and on which you have taken your stand. By this gospel you are saved, if you hold firmly to the word I preached to you. Otherwise, you have believed in vain. For what I received I passed on to you as of first importance : that Christ died for our sins according to the Scriptures, that he was buried, that he was raised on the third day according to the Scriptures, (1 Cor 15:1-4)

But when the time had fully come, God sent his Son, born of a woman, born under law, to redeem those under law, that we might receive the full rights of sons. Because you are sons, God sent the Spirit of his Son into our hearts, the Spirit who calls out, "Abba, Father." (Gal 4:4-6)

	CHAPTER 2
	D. Strip Off Some Things & Crave the Word of God, 2:1-3
1 The things to strip off	Therefore, rid yourselves of all malice and all deceit, hypocrisy, envy, and slander of every kind.
a. Malice—deceit— hypocrisy	
b. Envy—all slander	
2 The one thing to crave: The Word	2 Like newborn babies, crave pure spiritual milk, so that by it you may grow up in your salvation,
a. The charge: Rave	
b. The purpose: To grow	
c. The result: You taste the Lord's goodness	3 Now that you have tasted that the Lord is good.

DIVISION II

HOW TO LIVE THROUGH SUFFERING: GIVE YOUR LIFE TO GOD, 1:13-3:12

D. Strip Off Some Things and Crave the Word of God, 2:1-3

(2:1-3) Introduction: this is a forceful passage of Scripture. It uses some descriptive, active words. The imperative "rid yourself" means *to strip off*, and the imperative "crave" means to *desire*. Believers are to strip off some things and crave the Word of God.

1. There are things that have to be stripped off (v.1).
2. There is one thing that has to be craved: the milk of God's Word (v.2-3).

1 (2:1) **Maturity—Growth, Spiritual**: the believer is to strip off some things. The Greek word for "rid yourself" (apothemenoi) means to put off one's clothing; to cleanse oneself of those things that defile. Both meanings are applicable in this verse (A.T. Robertson. *Word Pictures In The New Testament*, Vol.6, p.94). There are some things that defile the believer. He is to take these things and strip them off just as he would strip off his clothes; he is to cleanse himself from all that defiles him. Five things in particular are mentioned, and note: all five have to do with what has just been said in the former passage. We are to love one another deeply, from the heart. The very things that we are to strip off are the things that dirty and soil our love. They have to do with how we treat one another, with our behavior toward our Christian brothers and sisters.

1. Believers must strip off "malice" (kakian). The word means two things.
    a. In a general sense it means wickedness, all kinds and forms of evil. It is a word that strikes at all the vices of men.

> **They have become filled with every kind of wickedness, evil, greed and depravity. They are full of envy, murder, strife, deceit and malice. They are gossips, slanderers, God-haters, insolent, arrogant and boastful; they invent ways of doing evil; they disobey their parents; they are senseless, faithless, heartless, ruthless. Although they know God's righteous decree that those who do such things deserve death, they not only continue to do these very things but also approve of those who practice them. (Rom 1:29-32)**

    b. In a narrow sense it means malice, deep-seated feelings against a person; hatred that lasts on and on; intense and long-lasting bitterness against a person. It means ill will, actually wishing that something bad would happen to a person. It means to be vicious, spiteful, and to hold a grudge. It means that a person has turned his heart over to evil:
    ⇒ He no longer has any good feelings toward the other person—none whatsoever.
    ⇒ He could care less if something bad happened to the person.
    The charge is strong: believers are to strip off malice—all of their evil and wickedness and all of their ill feelings against others. Believers are to be pure and clean, and they are to live pure and clean lives before their brothers and sisters in the Lord.

> **Therefore let us keep the Festival, not with the old yeast, the yeast of malice and wickedness, but with bread without yeast, the bread of sincerity and truth. (1 Cor 5:8)**
> **Brothers, stop thinking like children. In regard to evil be infants, but in your thinking be adults. (1 Cor 14:20)**
> **Get rid of all bitterness, rage and anger, brawling and slander, along with every form of malice. (Eph 4:31)**
> **But now you must rid yourselves of all such things as these: anger, rage, malice, slander, and filthy language from your lips. (Col 3:8)**
> **At one time we too were foolish, disobedient, deceived and enslaved by all kinds of passions and pleasures. We lived in malice and envy, being hated and hating one another. (Titus 3:3)**
> **Therefore, rid yourselves of all malice and all deceit, hypocrisy, envy, and slander of every kind. (1 Pet 2:1)**

2. Believers must strip off "deceit" (dolon). The word means to deceive and mislead people; to set bait so as to catch them; to bait or deceive in order to achieve one's

own end. It means to be two-faced. Note that deceit or deception has to do primarily with words. When a person wants something, he tries to get it...

- by flattery
- by false promises
- by false tales
- by suggestive talk
- by off-colored suggestions
- by enticing words
- by outright lying

When a person wants something, he looks at the other person's weakness or ignorance, and he tries to appeal to it. He appeals to it by deceiving and beguiling the person. The exhortation is strong: believers must strip off deceit. We must not deceive and mislead people.

3. Believers must strip off "hypocrisy" (hupokriseis). The word means one who pretends, puts on a show, acts out something he is not. At first the word simply meant one who replied or answered another person. Then it came to mean acting, as actors play-acted the lines of a scene. Finally, the word was used in the worst sense: play-acting, pretending; one who wore a mask to hide his real self; one who acted one way, but who was really another way; one who put on an outward show.

All kinds of hypocrisies are meant. A person is a hypocrite...

- when he acts as though he loves and believes God, but he does not live like God tells him to live.
- when he pretends to be following God, but he is living like he wants to live.
- when he shows a concern for the things of God, but his real concern is for the things of the world.
- when he professes to believe God's Word, but he questions it and adds and takes away from it.
- when he acts as though he cares for people, but he is really full of selfishness, self-seeking, possessiveness, hoarding, envy, and pride.
- when he courts friends, but he is after something.
- when he acts friendly, but he could care less.
- when he promises, but he never intends to keep his promise.

Thought 1. Jesus warns hypocrites, severely warns them. Believers must, therefore, strip off any semblance of hypocrisy. Hypocrisy is one of the sins that God hates above all others.

⇒ Hypocrites shall receive the greater damnation (Mt.23:14).
⇒ Hypocrites are children of hell (Mt.23:15).
⇒ Hypocrites are fools and blind (Mt.23:17, 19).
⇒ Hypocrites are blind guides (Mt.23:24).
⇒ Hypocrites are full of extortion and excess (Mt.23:25).
⇒ Hypocrites are full of all uncleanness (Mt.23:27).
⇒ Hypocrites are serpents, a generation of vipers (Mt.23:33).
⇒ Hypocrites shall not escape the damnation of hell (Mt.23:33).

In the same way, on the outside you appear to people as righteous but on the inside you are full of hypocrisy and wickedness. (Mat 23:28)
Meanwhile, when a crowd of many thousands had gathered, so that they were trampling on one another, Jesus began to speak first to his disciples, saying: "Be on your guard against the yeast of the Pharisees, which is hypocrisy. (Luke 12:1)
The Spirit clearly says that in later times some will abandon the faith and follow deceiving spirits and things taught by demons. Such teachings come through hypocritical liars, whose consciences have been seared as with a hot iron. (1 Tim 4:1-2)
They claim to know God, but by their actions they deny him. They are detestable, disobedient and unfit for doing anything good. (Titus 1:16)
Therefore, rid yourselves of all malice and all deceit, hypocrisy, envy, and slander of every kind. (1 Pet 2:1)
For he is the kind of man who is always thinking about the cost. "Eat and drink," he says to you, but his heart is not with you. (Prov 23:7)
Though his speech is charming, do not believe him, for seven abominations fill his heart. (Prov 26:25)

4. Believers must strip off "envy" (phthonous): a person without God lives in envy (phthonoi). The word means that a person covets what someone else has, covets it so much that he wants it even if it has to be taken away from the other person. He may even wish that the other person did not have it or had not received it. We may look at people and envy their...

- money
- position
- looks
- possessions
- popularity
- clothes
- social status
- recognition
- authority

The word envy means all kinds of envies and jealousies; it means that we are not to look at a person and envy to be like them nor to have what they possess. The results of envy are terrible; envy takes a terrible toll upon the life and body of a person.

⇒ A person who envies *does not have peace or happiness*. He is dissatisfied with what he is and has and is always wanting more and more of what others have.
⇒ In addition to this, envy often drives a person into *crime and lawlessness* in order to get what he craves.
⇒ On top of this, envy often leads to *physical problems* such as migraine headaches, high blood pressure, ulcers, and other illnesses.
⇒ Envy also causes *emotional problems* ranging from mild neurosis or depression to psychotic behavior.

But thanks be to God our Savior. He saves and delivers us from envy. Through Christ He gives us real life, and He satisfies our hearts and lives with eternal pleasures (Ps.16:11). Therefore, we must strip off all envy. We must love one another and rejoice in the persons and possessions of others. We must love them, support and build them up, not envy and wish to see them torn down.

A heart at peace gives life to the body, but envy rots the bones. (Prov 14:30)

Do not let your heart envy sinners, but always be zealous for the fear of the LORD. (Prov 23:17)

Do not envy wicked men, do not desire their company; (Prov 24:1)

Let us behave decently, as in the daytime, not in orgies and drunkenness, not in sexual immorality and debauchery, not in dissension and jealousy. (Rom 13:13)

Love is patient, love is kind. It does not envy, it does not boast, it is not proud. (1 Cor 13:4)

Let us not become conceited, provoking and envying each other. (Gal 5:26)

5. Believers must strip off all "slander" (katalalias). This means to criticize, judge, backbite, gossip, censor, condemn, and grumble against another person. It means to talk about and to tear down another person; to spread tales about another person that cut and hurt him and that lower his image and reputation in the eyes of others. The word usually means to talk about a person behind his back when he is not present.

Note that the brother has sinned. He has broken the law of God. He has failed and his failure is known. It is public knowledge, and he is being judged and criticized for his failure. He is being talked about. What he has done is being buzzed and gossiped about, and it is hurting and cutting him and damaging him more and more in the eyes of the world. Now, if we are forbidden to slander a person who is really guilty of sin, how much more are we forbidden to speak against a person just because we dislike or disagree with him?

Note what the Scripture says: this is *slander*. Talking about a person is *evil*. It is just as much an evil as the failure of the other person. Therefore, the person who judges is as guilty as the sinner.

The exhortation is strong: Christian believers are not to judge and slander one another. The reason is clear: we are brothers, brothers of Christ and of one another. All of us are of the family of God. Therefore...

- we are to be loving, caring, and looking after each other, not destroying each other.
- we are to be supporting, encouraging, and building up one another, not tearing down one another.
- when one of us falls and gets into trouble, we are to be reaching out and helping him up, not pushing him farther down.

When we criticize a brother or sister in Christ, we are slandering one of God's own children. Just think: we are actually slandering a son or daughter of God. This alone should keep us from slandering of our brothers in Christ.

Think about something else as well: there is never a spirit of slander in the humble and loving person. There is only a loving compassion for others, especially for those who have come short and fallen. Therefore, when we speak evil of another person it means that we are neither humble nor loving, but the very opposite: prideful and hateful. We are slanderers.

Thought 1. There are several reasons why people tend to judge and criticize.

1) Criticism boosts our own self-image. Pointing out someone else's failure and tearing him down makes us seem a little bit better, at least in our own eyes. It adds to our own pride, ego, and self-image.

2) Criticism is simply enjoyed. There is a tendency in human nature to take pleasure in hearing and sharing bad news and shortcomings about others.

3) Criticism makes us feel that our own lives (morality and behavior) are better than the person who failed.

4) Criticism helps us justify the bad decisions we have made and the bad things we have done throughout our lives. We rationalize our decisions and acts by pointing out the failure of others.

5) Criticism points out to our friends how strong we are. Criticism gives good feelings because our *rigid beliefs* and *strong lives* are proven again. Proven how? By our brother's failure.

6) Criticism is an outlet for hurt and revenge. We feel *he deserves it*. Subconsciously, if not consciously, we think, "He hurt me so he deserves to hurt too." Therefore, we criticize the person who failed.

For I am afraid that when I come I may not find you as I want you to be, and you may not find me as you want me to be. I fear that there may be quarreling, jealousy, outbursts of anger, factions, slander, gossip, arrogance and disorder. (2 Cor 12:20)

Get rid of all bitterness, rage and anger, brawling and slander, along with every form of malice. (Eph 4:31)

Brothers, do not slander one another. Anyone who speaks against his brother or judges him speaks against the law and judges it. When you judge the law, you are not keeping it, but sitting in judgment on it. (James 4:11)

Therefore, rid yourselves of all malice and all deceit, hypocrisy, envy, and slander of every kind. (1 Pet 2:1)

Whoever slanders his neighbor in secret, him will I put to silence; whoever has haughty eyes and a proud heart, him will I not endure. (Psa 101:5)

2 (2:2-3) **Maturity—Growth, Spiritual**: the believer is to crave one thing—the milk of God's Word. Note three points.

1. The charge is an imperative, a command: "You desire, crave, and yearn for the pure spiritual milk [of the Word.] And the craving and yearning are to be constant."

a. The word "crave" (epipothesate) means to desire, yearn, and long for the Word of God. It is a strong word, very strong. It paints the picture of being an absolute essential, of hungering and thirsting after the Word. If a believer is to grow, it is absolutely essential that he hunger and thirst after the milk of the Word.

Thought 1. Too many believers crave the Word here and there, sporadically. Growth can come only as we live in the Word day by day.

b. The word "pure" (adolos) means unadulterated, unmixed with anything else. Men may seek the milk of other things; they may seek to be fed and satisfied by such things as...

- religion
- philosophy
- health
- science

- education
- possessions
- pleasure
- psychology
- counseling
- power
- fortune
- fame
- comfort

But none of these are pure. There are specks and dust and particles within every pursuit on earth—particles that make everything on earth weak and infirm and to some degree harmful. In addition and most tragic of all, every pursuit of man is doomed to pass away when man passes away. But there is one thing that is unadulterated; one thing that is completely and perfectly pure with no mixture whatsoever, and that is the Word of God. The Word of God lives and abides forever; therefore, we must crave and yearn for the Word of God. It is our only hope of enduring forever.

c. The word "milk" usually refers to the food needed by immature believers. That is, it is usually used to make a distinction between the milk and the meat or mature teachings of the Word. But this is not the case with the present passage. A distinction is not being made between believers. All believers are seen as needing to grow and to learn more about the Lord. All believers are to crave the pure spiritual milk (food) of the Word.

2. The purpose for craving and yearning after the Word is that we may grow. The most ancient Greek manuscripts have the words "in your salvation"—"that we may grow up in *salvation*." The idea is that we may grow up to full salvation, until we reach full maturity.

The Greek word that is translated "spiritual" (logikos) is translated by some commentators as *the word*. That is, the verse is made to read "desire the milk of the word" or "desire the reasonable and intelligent milk." This seems to be the correct translation: "crave the pure milk of the Word." This has clearly been the emphasis of Peter throughout this whole passage. His subject and thrust has been the Word of God (cp. 1 Pt.1:23-25). William Barclay states it as well as it can be stated:

"Logos is the Greek for word, and logikos means belonging to the word. This is the sense in which the Authorized Version takes the word, and we think that it is entirely correct. Peter has just been talking about the word of God which lives and abides for ever (1 Peter 1:23-25). It is the word of God which is in his mind; and we think that what Peter means here is that the Christian must desire with his whole heart the nourishment which comes from the word of God, for by that nourishment he can thrive and grow up until he reaches salvation itself. In face of all the evil of the heathen world the Christian must strengthen his soul and his life with the pure food of the word of God" (*The Letters of James and Peter*. "The Daily Study Bible." Philadelphia, PA: The Westminster Press, 1958, p.227).

3. The result of craving the Word of God is a most wonderful promise: we taste that the Lord is good. God feeds us, nourishes and nurtures us. He reveals and feeds our souls, teaching us all about His grace, His wonderful salvation and promises to us.

⇒ He teaches us how to live pure and clean lives; how to conquer the temptations of life; how to walk through the trials of life.
⇒ He teaches us all about the great salvation and promises He has made.
⇒ He teaches us all about Himself and the Lord Jesus Christ and the glorious hope we have of living with the Lord forever and ever.
⇒ He teaches us how to worship, praise, and honor Him as we walk in this corruptible world.

God just takes His Word and feeds us, nourishes and nurtures us in His marvelous goodness. As we crave and yearn for His Word, He grows us more and more into His image.

> **"Now I commit you to God and to the word of his grace, which can build you up and give you an inheritance among all those who are sanctified. (Acts 20:32)**
>
> **Let the word of Christ dwell in you richly as you teach and admonish one another with all wisdom, and as you sing psalms, hymns and spiritual songs with gratitude in your hearts to God. (Col 3:16)**
>
> **Do your best to present yourself to God as one approved, a workman who does not need to be ashamed and who correctly handles the word of truth. (2 Tim 2:15)**
>
> **All Scripture is God-breathed and is useful for teaching, rebuking, correcting and training in righteousness, (2 Tim 3:16)**
>
> **I have not departed from the commands of his lips; I have treasured the words of his mouth more than my daily bread. (Job 23:12)**
>
> **The precepts of the LORD are right, giving joy to the heart. The commands of the LORD are radiant, giving light to the eyes. (Psa 19:8)**
>
> **I have hidden your word in my heart that I might not sin against you. (Psa 119:11)**
>
> **How sweet are your words to my taste, sweeter than honey to my mouth! (Psa 119:103)**
>
> **Your word is a lamp to my feet and a light for my path. (Psa 119:105)**
>
> **The unfolding of your words gives light; it gives understanding to the simple. (Psa 119:130)**
>
> **When your words came, I ate them; they were my joy and my heart's delight, for I bear your name, O LORD God Almighty. (Jer 15:16)**
>
> **For you have been born again, not of perishable seed, but of imperishable, through the living and enduring word of God. (1 Pet 1:23)**
>
> **And we have the word of the prophets made more certain, and you will do well to pay attention to it, as to a light shining in a dark place, until the day dawns and the morning star rises in your hearts. (2 Pet 1:19)**
>
> **But grow in the grace and knowledge of our Lord and Savior Jesus Christ. To him be glory both now and forever! Amen. (2 Pet 3:18)**

	E. Come to Christ, the Living Stone, 2:4-8	chosen and precious cornerstone, and the one who trusts in him will never be put to shame."	
1 Picture 1: Christ is the Living Stone: He was rejected by men, but chosen by God	4 As you come to him, the living Stone—rejected by men but chosen by God and precious to him—	7 Now to you who believe, this stone is precious. But to those who do not believe, "The stone the builders rejected has become the capstone,"	**3 Picture 3: Unbelievers are disobedient builders** a. They disqualify the stone b. Christ is made the Head of the corner anyway
2 Picture 2: Believers are living stones a. Believers are being built into a spiritual house b. Believers are a holy priesthood c. Believers are a fulfillment of prophecy	5 You also, like living stones, are being built into a spiritual house to be a holy priesthood, offering spiritual sacrifices acceptable to God through Jesus Christ. 6 For in Scripture it says: "See, I lay a stone in Zion, a	8 And, "A stone that causes men to stumble and a rock that makes them fall." They stumble because they disobey the message—which is also what they were destined for.	c. They stumble & fall over the stone d. The reason: They disobey the message, the Word

DIVISION II

HOW TO LIVE THROUGH SUFFERING: GIVE YOUR LIFE TO GOD, 1:13-3:12

E. Come to Christ, the Living Stone, 2:4-8

(2:4-8) **Introduction**: this is a picture of the great house that God is building, the church of the Lord Jesus Christ. There are three pictures painted.

1. Picture 1: Christ is the Living Stone; He was rejected by men, but chosen by God (v.4).
2. Picture 2: believers are living stones (v.5-6).
3. Picture 3: unbelievers are disobedient builders (v.7-8).

1 (2:4) **Jesus Christ, Chief Cornerstone—Stone, The**: there is the first picture—Jesus Christ is the Living Stone. How can a stone be living? It cannot. This is simply a picture of how God looks at Christ and His followers: they are like a building that is being built by God Himself. The foundation of God's building is His Son, the Lord Jesus Christ. If a person wants to be a part of God's building, he has to place his life upon the foundation Stone, Christ Himself. But note what this verse says: the living stone was rejected by men. When men looked at the Stone (Christ)...

- it was not wanted.
- it did not fit in with their plans.
- it was useless and unsuitable for what they were building.
- it was not worth the price.

Men rejected Christ because they wanted to build their lives like they wanted. They wanted to do their own thing. Therefore, they cast the Stone of God aside. But note: the stone has been chosen of God. It is the very stone that God has chosen to be the foundation stone for life. It is the only stone that can support and bear the weight of life. And note: the stone chosen by God is a living stone. What does this mean? God is eternal; hence, the building of God will last forever and ever. Therefore, the cornerstone laid by God is bound to be eternal; it shall never deteriorate or waste away. The cornerstone is living and shall exist forever and ever.

The symbolism of the living cornerstone says three significant things.

1. The living cornerstone is the first stone laid. All other stones are placed after it. It is the *preeminent* stone in time. So it is with Christ; He is *the first* of God's new movement.

⇒ Christ is the author of salvation. All others are crew members who follow Him.

In bringing many sons to glory, it was fitting that God, for whom and through whom everything exists, should make the author of their salvation perfect through suffering. (Heb 2:10)

⇒ Christ is the source of eternal salvation, of our faith. All others are the readers of the story.

And, once made perfect, he became the source of eternal salvation for all who obey him (Heb 5:9)

Let us fix our eyes on Jesus, the author and perfecter of our faith, who for the joy set before him endured the cross, scorning its shame, and sat down at the right hand of the throne of God. (Heb 12:2)

⇒ Christ is the Alpha and the Omega, *beginning and the end*. All others come after Him and are under Him.

"I am the Alpha and the Omega," says the Lord God, "who is, and who was, and who is to come, the Almighty." (Rev 1:8; cp. 21:6; 22:13).

⇒ Christ is the forerunner, one who went before us into the very presence of God. All others enter God's presence after Him.

We have this hope as an anchor for the soul, firm and secure. It enters the inner sanctuary behind the curtain, where Jesus, who went before us, has entered on our behalf. He has become a high priest forever, in the order of Melchizedek. (Heb 6:19-20)

2. The cornerstone is the supportive stone. All other stones are placed upon it and held up by it. They all rest upon it. It is the preeminent stone in position and power. So it is with Christ; He is the support and power, the Foundation of God's new movement.

⇒ Christ is *the Head cornerstone*, the only true foundation upon which man can build. All crumble who are not laid upon Him.

> **For no one can lay any foundation other than the one already laid, which is Jesus Christ. (1 Cor 3:11)**

⇒ Christ is *the chief cornerstone* upon which all others are joined together. All who wish to be joined together have to be laid upon Him.

> **Built on the foundation of the apostles and prophets, with Christ Jesus himself as the chief cornerstone. In him the whole building is joined together and rises to become a holy temple in the Lord. And in him you too are being built together to become a dwelling in which God lives by his Spirit. (Eph 2:20-22)**

⇒ Christ is *the living Stone* upon which all others have to be built if they wish to live and be a part of God's spiritual house. All others have to be built upon Him if they wish to live and have their spiritual sacrifice accepted by God.

> **As you come to him, the living Stone— rejected by men but chosen by God and precious to him— you also, like living stones, are being built into a spiritual house to be a holy priesthood, offering spiritual sacrifices acceptable to God through Jesus Christ. (1 Pet 2:4-5)**

3. The living Stone is the stone to which men must come if they are to become a part of God's building. It is to Christ that we must come. No one can be a part of God's building unless he places himself upon the foundation stone laid by God. God accepts no one who refuses to become a part of His building. And God is just like all builders; He has a foundation upon which all workers must lay the stones of their lives.

> **"Therefore everyone who hears these words of mine and puts them into practice is like a wise man who built his house on the rock. The rain came down, the streams rose, and the winds blew and beat against that house; yet it did not fall, because it had its foundation on the rock. But everyone who hears these words of mine and does not put them into practice is like a foolish man who built his house on sand. The rain came down, the streams rose, and the winds blew and beat against that house, and it fell with a great crash." (Mat 7:24-27)**

> **For who among men knows the thoughts of a man except the man's spirit within him? In the same way no one knows the thoughts of God except the Spirit of God. (1 Cor 2:11)**

> **Nevertheless, God's solid foundation stands firm, sealed with this inscription: "The Lord knows those who are his," and, "Everyone who confesses the name of the Lord must turn away from wickedness." (2 Tim 2:19)**

2 (2:5-6) **Believers**: there is the second picture—believers are living stones. Remember: God is eternal which means that His building is eternal. The Foundation Stone laid by Him shall never decay nor waste away. Christ lives forever and ever. Therefore, when we place our lives upon the living stone of God, the living stone supports and holds us up eternally. We become living stones, stones that shall exist forever and ever. Note three significant facts.

1. Believers are being built into a spiritual house (v.5). This is a picture of the church that God is building all over the earth. It includes all believers of all generations. It is a picture of what is called the universal church or universal temple of God. Note that God's house is a *spiritual house*. What does this mean? It means that God's house is spiritual as opposed to physical. A physical house is not permanent; it ages, deteriorates, and wastes away. But not God's spiritual house. The spiritual world or dimension is the real world, the world that is permanent and eternal. Therefore, the spiritual house of God does not age, deteriorate or decay. This means two wonderful things.

   a. First, when we turn to God and lay our lives upon the foundation stone of Christ, we become a part of God's spiritual house. We shall never die or waste away, but we shall live permanently, forever and ever in God's spiritual and eternal house.

   b. Second, there are many stones who are going to live forever with us. It takes many stones to build a great building, and the same is true of God's spiritual house. We are only one of many who are being placed into God's great spiritual house. The point is this: there is no room for pride, arrogance, envy, jealousy, criticism, backbiting, anger, accusations, discrimination, prejudice, or wrath among God's building; no room for a stone to become puffed up over another stone.

   All living stones are needed in God's house. In fact, the house cannot be completed unless there are enough stones to build it. There is a place for all of us, and we are going to exist together forever. Therefore, we are to place ourselves and take our place in the house of God. We are to place ourselves right where we belong and do our part in holding up the building. We are not to seek the place or position or function of any other stone. We are not to weaken the building to any degree.

Thought 1. William Barclay tells a story from Sparta and then drives the point home with a striking application.

> "There is a famous story from Sparta. A Spartan king boasted to a visiting monarch about the walls of Sparta. The visiting monarch looked around and he could see no walls. He said to the Spartan king, 'Where are these walls about which you speak and boast so much?' The Spartan king pointed at his bodyguard of magnificent Spartan troops. 'These,' he said, 'are the walls of Sparta, and every man of them a brick.'

> "Now, the point is quite clear. So long as a brick lies by itself it is useless. It only becomes of use when it is built into a building. That is why it was made; and it is in being built into a building that it realizes its function and the reason for its existence. It is so with the individual Christian. To realize his destiny

45

he must not remain alone, but must be built into the fabric and edifice of the Church" (*The Letters of James and Peter*, p.231).

2. Believers are a holy priesthood (v.5). The chief function of the priest is to stand between God and men, to represent men before God and to present men to God. Man has just never felt worthy enough to approach God; he has usually felt that God was so far away that he could never reach God. Therefore, man has felt the need for priests to carry his case before God.

The point to note is man's thoughts about God, how far away he thinks God is—so far away that man needs a priest, some godly person to represent him before God. But note the Scripture: believers are being built up as an holy priesthood. Every single believer now stands before God as a priest. He can now approach God on his own. God is not far off and removed from man. Any person who turns to God and lays his life upon the foundation of Christ becomes a part of God's spiritual house. That person is in the very house of God itself. He can talk and share with God whenever he chooses. He can worship and praise God and cry out for God's help and deliverance any time he wishes. The believer himself is now a priest before God. (See DEEPER STUDY # 1, *Priest*—1 Pt.2:9 for more discussion.)

Thought 1. The priesthood of the believer is one of the great teachings of Scripture. Just imagine! We stand before God as a priest, as one who has access into God's presence any time of any day. There is no reason whatsoever why we should ever be overcome by any problem or trouble in this life. We are in the house of God. We can approach Him anytime and receive whatever we need to meet the demands of life: wisdom, provision, resource, or strength.

Now note why we are made priests before God: that we might offer spiritual sacrifices to God. In the past men have brought their sacrifices to priests and had the priests present their sacrifices to God. But now believers themselves are made priests for this very purpose: that they might offer up their own sacrifices to God. Men are now to bring their own offerings and sacrifices to God. They themselves are now the priests in the house of God. However, note a critical point: their sacrifices are made acceptable only by Jesus Christ. A person has to have his life lying upon the foundation of Christ. He must be trusting and believing in the support and power of Christ to make him a part of God's house. The only sacrifices that God accepts are the sacrifices made within His house. Scripture says that the believer is to make the following sacrifices.

⇒ He is to sacrifice his body as a living sacrifice to God. He is not to conform any longer to this world.

> Then he said to them all: "If anyone would come after me, he must deny himself and take up his cross daily and follow me. (Luke 9:23)
>
> And anyone who does not carry his cross and follow me cannot be my disciple. (Luke 14:27)
>
> For if you live according to the sinful nature, you will die; but if by the Spirit you put to death the misdeeds of the body, you will live, (Rom 8:13)
>
> Therefore, I urge you, brothers, in view of God's mercy, to offer your bodies

as living sacrifices, holy and pleasing to God—this is your spiritual act of worship. Do not conform any longer to the pattern of this world, but be transformed by the renewing of your mind. Then you will be able to test and approve what God's will is—his good, pleasing and perfect will. (Rom 12:1-2)

> Those who belong to Christ Jesus have crucified the sinful nature with its passions and desires. (Gal 5:24)
>
> But even if I am being poured out like a drink offering on the sacrifice and service coming from your faith, I am glad and rejoice with all of you. (Phil 2:17)
>
> For I am already being poured out like a drink offering, and the time has come for my departure. (2 Tim 4:6)

⇒ He is to sacrifice his life to God as he walks day by day. He is to follow God in love, even as Christ loved us and gave Himself as an offering and a sacrifice to God.

> Be imitators of God, therefore, as dearly loved children and live a life of love, just as Christ loved us and gave himself up for us as a fragrant offering and sacrifice to God. (Eph 5:1-2)
>
> This is how we know what love is: Jesus Christ laid down his life for us. And we ought to lay down our lives for our brothers. (1 John 3:16)

⇒ He is to offer the sacrifice of praise to God continually.

> Through Jesus, therefore, let us continually offer to God a sacrifice of praise—the fruit of lips that confess his name. (Heb 13:15)
>
> Let them sacrifice thank offerings and tell of his works with songs of joy. (Psa 107:22)
>
> I will sacrifice a thank offering to you and call on the name of the LORD. (Psa 116:17)
>
> The sounds of joy and gladness, the voices of bride and bridegroom, and the voices of those who bring thank offerings to the house of the LORD, saying, "Give thanks to the LORD Almighty, for the LORD is good; his love endures forever." For I will restore the fortunes of the land as they were before,' says the LORD. (Jer 33:11)
>
> But I, with a song of thanksgiving, will sacrifice to you. What I have vowed I will make good. Salvation comes from the LORD." (Jonah 2:9)

⇒ He is to offer the sacrifices of good works and gifts and money.

> And do not forget to do good and to share with others, for with such sacrifices God is pleased. (Heb 13:16)
>
> Sell your possessions and give to the poor. Provide purses for yourselves that will not wear out, a treasure in heaven that

will not be exhausted, where no thief comes near and no moth destroys. (Luke 12:33)

In everything I did, I showed you that by this kind of hard work we must help the weak, remembering the words the Lord Jesus himself said: 'It is more blessed to give than to receive.'" (Acts 20:35)

Share with God's people who are in need. Practice hospitality. (Rom 12:13)

Anyone who receives instruction in the word must share all good things with his instructor. Do not be deceived: God cannot be mocked. A man reaps what he sows. The one who sows to please his sinful nature, from that nature will reap destruction; the one who sows to please the Spirit, from the Spirit will reap eternal life. Let us not become weary in doing good, for at the proper time we will reap a harvest if we do not give up. Therefore, as we have opportunity, let us do good to all people, especially to those who belong to the family of believers. (Gal 6:6-10)

Command them to do good, to be rich in good deeds, and to be generous and willing to share. (1 Tim 6:18)

⇒ He is to offer spiritual sacrifices, that is, love, joy, peace, patience, kindness, goodness, faithfulness, gentleness, and self-control.

You also, like living stones, are being built into a spiritual house to be a holy priesthood, offering spiritual sacrifices acceptable to God through Jesus Christ. (1 Pet 2:5)

But the fruit of the Spirit is love, joy, peace, patience, kindness, goodness, faithfulness, gentleness and self-control. Against such things there is no law. (Gal 5:22-23)

Offer right sacrifices and trust in the LORD. (Psa 4:5)

⇒ He is to sacrifice his life in order to lead people to faith in Christ.

As you hold out the word of life—in order that I may boast on the day of Christ that I did not run or labor for nothing. But even if I am being poured out like a drink offering on the sacrifice and service coming from your faith, I am glad and rejoice with all of you. (Phil 2:16-17)

"Come, follow me," Jesus said, "and I will make you fishers of men." (Mat 4:19)

Do you not say, 'Four months more and then the harvest'? I tell you, open your eyes and look at the fields! They are ripe for harvest. (John 4:35)

Though I am free and belong to no man, I make myself a slave to everyone, to win as many as possible. To the Jews I became like a Jew, to win the Jews. To those under the law I became like one under the law, so as to win those under the law. To those not having the law I became like one not having the law, so as to win those not having the law. To the weak I became

weak, to win the weak. I have become all things to all men so that by all possible means I might save some. I do all this for the sake of the gospel, that I may share in its blessings. (1 Cor 9:19-23)

He who goes out weeping, carrying seed to sow, will return with songs of joy, carrying sheaves with him. (Psa 126:6)

2. Believers are a fulfillment of prophecy (v.6. Cp. Ps.118:22; Is.28:16.) The prediction that the Messiah would be the chief cornerstone of God's building was made centuries before Christ ever came into the world. Note the four great things predicted:

⇒ That God Himself would lay the cornerstone. God Himself would send the Messiah into the world and use Him as the foundation of God's eternal house.

⇒ That God would select or elect Him to be the cornerstone. There would be plenty of philosophies, religions, and ideas about how to best build a world and life for man. But God would choose only one foundation stone for the world and life: Jesus Christ.

⇒ That God would count His foundation stone precious. The stone selected by Him would be the most precious thing in all the universe: it would be His very own Son. He would choose His own Son to become the Foundation Stone for men's lives and for the eternal world God was planning. There is nothing in the world that is any more precious to God than His own dear Son. Therefore, God would count Him precious, the only thing precious enough to serve as the Foundation Stone for the eternal house of God.

⇒ That believers would not be put to shame (kataischunthei), that is, confounded, disappointed, and confused. Believing and trusting in Jesus Christ—leaning upon him and building upon Him—is the only way to keep from being eternally confused, shamed, and disappointed.

The point is this: believers—their salvation in Christ—are the fulfillment of this prophecy. God predicted that He would be building a spiritual and eternal house for believers. He laid the foundation when He sent Christ into the world, and believers have been laying the stones of their lives upon Christ ever since. How? By believing in Him, that is, by laying their lives upon Him or by building upon Him. The result has been phenomenal: those who have built upon Christ have experienced a most wonderful thing. All the confusion, shame, and disappointment in this life and the fear of judgment in the next life have disappeared. Believers are now flooded with life, a life that just overflows with love, joy, peace, victory, and triumph and with confidence and assurance that all things shall be well in the future.

Yet to all who received him, to those who believed in his name, he gave the right to become children of God— (John 1:12)

That everyone who believes in him may have eternal life. "For God so loved the world that he gave his one and only Son, that whoever believes in him shall not perish but have eternal life. (John 3:15-16)

I am not ashamed of the gospel, because it is the power of God for the salvation of everyone who believes: first for the Jew, then for the Gentile. (Rom 1:16)

3 (2:7-8) **Unbelievers—Lost, The—Unsaved, The**: the third picture—unbelievers are pictured as disobedient builders. Christ has done so much for man, He should be the most precious thing in a man's life. But the greatest tragedy in all of history is that He is not considered to be precious by some people. He is to believers, but they are a small minority of people. The vast, vast majority of people are unbelievers. They just do not believe that Jesus Christ is the foundation stone for their lives. The four points of the Scripture state it well.

1. Unbelievers disqualify and reject the stone. They look at the various foundation stones of life and...

- they do not want the Stone [Christ].
- they do not think that the Stone will fit in with their plans.
- they do not believe the Stone [Christ] will suit what they are building.
- they do not believe the Stone [Christ] is worth the price. They just do not think the Stone [Christ] is worth all they are and have.

The point is forceful: they reject and disqualify the stone. They do not want Christ enough to give all they are and have in order to get him.

2. Christ is made the Head of the corner anyway. Despite the rejection of men, Christ is made the cornerstone of the only permanent and lasting building. God selected and elected Him despite man. And if man is to become a part of an eternal house that lasts forever and that brings an abundance of life, he has to lay his life upon the foundation of Christ.

3. Unbelievers stumble over the stone of Christ. He is a rock that makes them fall. What does this mean? When people look at Jesus Christ, they stumble over Him; they do not understand...

- how He could be anything other than a man just like the rest of us.
- how He could be born of a virgin, God incarnate in human flesh.
- how He could live a sinless life, live without committing a single sin.
- how His death could be any more than the death of a martyr who died for a great cause.
- how His resurrection is anything but a tall tale made up by His followers to secure more and more followers.

Simply stated, many people do not understand nor believe that Jesus Christ is the Son of God, that He was sent into the world by God to save men; that He was able to live a sinless life because He was the God-Man who had come to earth for that very purpose; that He died and arose from the dead as the Perfect and Ideal Man so that His ideal death and resurrection could cover man.

People just stumble over the facts or else they fall because Christ lays the burden of total commitment upon man. After all, if Jesus Christ is truly who He claimed to be, we owe Him our lives—all that we *are and have*. Most men are not willing to give up the right to their lives and property. They fall at this demand of Christ. Therefore, they stumble over Him. But note:

⇒ to stumble means that we have tripped up and fallen, that we damage ourselves.
⇒ to fall means that we hurt ourselves.

Note another fact: what we are stumbling over. We are actually stumbling over the message, the very Word of God itself. What is so awful about this? The Word of God is the only incorruptible, imperishable seed on earth that lives and stands forever (cp. 1 Pt.1:23-25). If we reject the glorious gospel of God's Word, the glorious gospel that Jesus Christ is the Foundation Stone of God's building, then we are rejecting the only hope of living forever. We are appointing ourselves to a state of unbelief and disobedience to God. That is, we are steeping ourselves in more and more unbelief and becoming harder and harder to the gospel. We are living lives that are becoming more and more disobedient.

> "If you are the Christ, " they said, "tell us." Jesus answered, "If I tell you, you will not believe me, (Luke 22:67)
>
> I tell you the truth, we speak of what we know, and we testify to what we have seen, but still you people do not accept our testimony. (John 3:11)
>
> "For God so loved the world that he gave his one and only Son, that whoever believes in him shall not perish but have eternal life. For God did not send his Son into the world to condemn the world, but to save the world through him. Whoever believes in him is not condemned, but whoever does not believe stands condemned already because he has not believed in the name of God's one and only Son. (John 3:16-18)
>
> Whoever believes in the Son has eternal life, but whoever rejects the Son will not see life, for God's wrath remains on him." (John 3:36)
>
> I told you that you would die in your sins; if you do not believe that I am the one I claim to be, you will indeed die in your sins." (John 8:24)
>
> Even after Jesus had done all these miraculous signs in their presence, they still would not believe in him. (John 12:37)
>
> See to it, brothers, that none of you has a sinful, unbelieving heart that turns away from the living God. (Heb 3:12)
>
> Let us, therefore, make every effort to enter that rest, so that no one will fall by following their example of disobedience. (Heb 4:11)
>
> Are they ashamed of their loathsome conduct? No, they have no shame at all; they do not even know how to blush. So they will fall among the fallen; they will be brought down when I punish them," says the LORD. (Jer 6:15)

	F. Know Who You Are: The People of God, 2:9-10

1 Know what kind of people you are
  a. A chosen people
  b. A royal priesthood[DS1]
  c. A holy nation
  d. A people who belong to God
2 Know what your purpose is: To declare His praises
3 Know what has happened to you
  a. Have become the people of God
  b. Have now received mercy
	9 But you are a chosen people, a royal priesthood, a holy nation, a people belonging to God, that you may declare the praises of him who called you out of darkness into his wonderful light.
	10 Once you were not a people, but now you are the people of God; once you had not received mercy, but now you have received mercy.

DIVISION II

HOW TO LIVE THROUGH SUFFERING: GIVE YOUR LIFE TO GOD, 1:13-3:12

F. Know Who You Are: The People of God, 2:9-10

(2:9-10) **Introduction**: know who you are. You are not a people who stumble over Christ, a people who question His claims and deity and refuse to believe Him. You are a people who believe Christ, a people who are building your lives upon the Foundation Stone of God's Son. You have taken your lives and laid them upon Him; you have entrusted your whole being into the keeping of Christ. Therefore, know who you are: you are the people of God, the people He is building to live with Him forever and ever. (See outline and notes—1 Pt.2:4-8 for more discussion.)

1. Know what kind of people you are (v.9).
2. Know what your purpose is: to declare His praises (v.9).
3. Know what has happened to you (v.10).

1 (2:9) **Believers—Church**: know what kind of people you are. Once you believe in God's Son, the Lord Jesus Christ, you become very, very special to God. You become special because you trust His Son. God the Father has only one Son...

- only one Son who has God's perfect nature, who is holy, righteous, and pure, loving, kind and gentle just as God is.
- only one Son who came to earth to save men by dying for them by showing them how much God loves them.

God loves His Son so much that when a person trusts His Son—really believes and trusts Him—God will do anything for that person. The person becomes very, very special to God. God takes all believers and does four wonderful things for them.

1. Believers become a "chosen people" (genos eklekton). The Greek words actually mean a *chosen or elect race*. Peter takes the term from the Old Testament where God stated the same thing about Israel.

> **"My people, my chosen. The people I formed for myself" (Is.43:20-21).**

The idea is that of a new race of people, a new species that differs entirely from the other races upon earth. This is a shocking statement to some people; nevertheless it is exactly what the Word of God claims. God is actually creating a new race of people upon earth. How? How can it be that

believers from China, Russia, Asia, Africa, India, Europe, the Americas, the Islands, Canada, and all the other nations of the world form a new race of people? By the Spirit of God. The Spirit of God is changing people inwardly, not outwardly. He is not changing facial and skin features. These mean little; they are only superficial differences that change, age, perish, die, and decay ever so rapidly. God is changing people within their hearts and minds and lives, changing them where it really matters. God is implanting His divine nature within believers. When a person believes in Jesus Christ, God's divine nature is immediately implanted into his heart and life.

⇒ The person is *born again*.

> **In reply Jesus declared, "I tell you the truth, no one can see the kingdom of God unless he is born again." (John 3:3)**
>
> **Jesus answered, "I tell you the truth, no one can enter the kingdom of God unless he is born of water and the Spirit. Flesh gives birth to flesh, but the Spirit gives birth to spirit. (John 3:5-6)**
>
> **For you have been born again, not of perishable seed, but of imperishable, through the living and enduring word of God. (1 Pet 1:23)**
>
> **Everyone who believes that Jesus is the Christ is born of God, and everyone who loves the father loves his child as well. (1 John 5:1)**

⇒ The person receives a *renewed mind*.

> **Do not conform any longer to the pattern of this world, but be transformed by the renewing of your mind. Then you will be able to test and approve what God's will is—his good, pleasing and perfect will. (Rom 12:2)**
>
> **Those who live according to the sinful nature have their minds set on what that nature desires; but those who live in accordance with the Spirit have their minds set on what the Spirit desires. (Rom 8:5)**

⇒ The person becomes a *new creation*.

> **Therefore, if anyone is in Christ, he is a new creation; the old has gone, the new has come! (2 Cor 5:17)**
> **Neither circumcision nor uncircumcision means anything; what counts is a new creation. (Gal 6:15)**

⇒ The person becomes a *new person, a new self*.

> **And to put on the new self, created to be like God in true righteousness and holiness. (Eph 4:24)**
> **And have put on the new self, which is being renewed in knowledge in the image of its Creator. (Col 3:10)**

⇒ The person receives a *new spirit*.

> **I will give them an undivided heart and put a new spirit in them; I will remove from them their heart of stone and give them a heart of flesh. (Ezek 11:19)**
> **We were therefore buried with him through baptism into death in order that, just as Christ was raised from the dead through the glory of the Father, we too may live a new life. (Rom 6:4)**
> **But now, by dying to what once bound us, we have been released from the law so that we serve in the new way of the Spirit, and not in the old way of the written code. (Rom 7:6)**

(See note—Eph.4:17-19 for more discussion on the New Race of People God is creating.)

2. Believers become a *royal priesthood*. To a person who has never given his life to Jesus Christ, God seems far away and off in outer space someplace. God just does not seem that concerned with human life. There is no personal relationship and little, if any, fellowship and communion with God. A day by day relationship that praises and honors God and brings one's needs to God and knows that God will meet one's needs—all this is missing to the person who has never committed his life to Christ. God seems untouchable and unreachable and out of range of man's day to day affairs. Without Jesus Christ a person just has no access and no closeness to God. This is the reason men have always felt the need to have priests, a body of people who would dedicate their lives to God and who would carry the needs of men before God. Men have felt the need to have a representative before God, some godly priest who could present his needs to God.

This is the glorious message of the gospel: when we receive Jesus Christ as our Savior, God creates us into a royal priesthood. God makes a royal priest out of everyone of us. He gives us open access into His presence forever and ever. We can actually approach God anytime. In fact, God expects us to live in His presence—to fellowship, commune, and walk in His presence all day every day.

Note the word "*royal*," a royal priesthood. This simply means that we are priests of royalty, priests who belong to the Sovereign Majesty of the universe, the King of kings and Lord of lords. We are the priesthood of God Himself, the priests who rule and reign with Christ and who serve and worship God face to face, day by day, hour by hour and moment by moment. We are the priests who live and move and have our being in His presence, who walk and live in open communion with Him.

Thought 1. How many of us actually walk and live in the presence of God like this? How many know what it is to have an *unbroken communion* with God? How many know what it is to be praying always? May God convict our hearts and stir us to recommit our lives to prayer and communion—to praying always—to seeking an unbroken communion and fellowship with Him every moment of the twenty four hours of every day.

> **You also, like living stones, are being built into a spiritual house to be a holy priesthood, offering spiritual sacrifices acceptable to God through Jesus Christ. (1 Pet 2:5)**
> **And has made us to be a kingdom and priests to serve his God and Father—to him be glory and power for ever and ever! Amen. (Rev 1:6)**
> **Blessed and holy are those who have part in the first resurrection. The second death has no power over them, but they will be priests of God and of Christ and will reign with him for a thousand years. (Rev 20:6)**
> **You will be for me a kingdom of priests and a holy nation.' These are the words you are to speak to the Israelites." (Exo 19:6)**
> **If you remain in me and my words remain in you, ask whatever you wish, and it will be given you. (John 15:7)**
> **For though we live in the world, we do not wage war as the world does. The weapons we fight with are not the weapons of the world. On the contrary, they have divine power to demolish strongholds. We demolish arguments and every pretension that sets itself up against the knowledge of God, and we take captive every thought to make it obedient to Christ. (2 Cor 10:3-5)**
> **And pray in the Spirit on all occasions with all kinds of prayers and requests. With this in mind, be alert and always keep on praying for all the saints. (Eph 6:18)**
> **Do not be anxious about anything, but in everything, by prayer and petition, with thanksgiving, present your requests to God. And the peace of God, which transcends all understanding, will guard your hearts and your minds in Christ Jesus. Finally, brothers, whatever is true, whatever is noble, whatever is right, whatever is pure, whatever is lovely, whatever is admirable—if anything is excellent or praiseworthy—think about such things. (Phil 4:6-8)**
> **Pray continually; (1 Th 5:17)**
> **Let us draw near to God with a sincere heart in full assurance of faith, having our hearts sprinkled to cleanse us from a guilty conscience and having our bodies washed with pure water. (Heb 10:22)**
> **Come near to God and he will come near to you. Wash your hands, you sinners, and purify your hearts, you double-minded. (James 4:8)**

3. Believers become a *holy nation*. This is a very meaningful title for believers. Just think about it: God is building a *new nation* of people. He is drawing people

from all over the world, people from all the nations of the world, and creating a new nation. What is the nation? It is the *holy nation* of God. Remember: the word "holy" (hagios) means separated, set apart, and different. Any person who is willing to separate from the sin and evil of this world and set his life apart unto God, God will take that person and make him a citizen of His holy nation. This is what holy means: to be different from the world, from its sin, evil, and death. It means to be separated from the evil life of the world and set apart to the holy life of God. The person who turns to God becomes a citizen of God's holy nation:

⇒ He serves the Sovereign Head of God's nation, even God Himself.
⇒ He obeys the laws of God's nation.
⇒ He is dedicated to follow the customs and lifestyle of God's nation.
⇒ He speaks up for and defends the nation of God.

> **You will be for me a kingdom of priests and a holy nation.' These are the words you are to speak to the Israelites." (Exo 19:6)**

> **I am the LORD who brought you up out of Egypt to be your God; therefore be holy, because I am holy. (Lev 11:45)**

> **And a highway will be there; it will be called the Way of Holiness. The unclean will not journey on it; it will be for those who walk in that Way; wicked fools will not go about on it. (Isa 35:8)**

> **To rescue us from the hand of our enemies, and to enable us to serve him without fear in holiness and righteousness before him all our days. (Luke 1:74-75)**

> **Since we have these promises, dear friends, let us purify ourselves from everything that contaminates body and spirit, perfecting holiness out of reverence for God. (2 Cor 7:1)**

> **And to put on the new self, created to be like God in true righteousness and holiness. (Eph 4:24)**

> **May he strengthen your hearts so that you will be blameless and holy in the presence of our God and Father when our Lord Jesus comes with all his holy ones. (1 Th 3:13)**

> **For it is written: "Be holy, because I am holy." (1 Pet 1:16)**

> **But the day of the Lord will come like a thief. The heavens will disappear with a roar; the elements will be destroyed by fire, and the earth and everything in it will be laid bare. Since everything will be destroyed in this way, what kind of people ought you to be? You ought to live holy and godly lives as you look forward to the day of God and speed its coming. That day will bring about the destruction of the heavens by fire, and the elements will melt in the heat. (2 Pet 3:10-12)**

4. Believers become a "people who belong to God" (laos eis peripoiesin). The Greek means...
- "a people for God's own possession" (A.T. Robertson. *Word Pictures In The New Testament*, Vol.6, p.98).

- "the people to be His very own" (Charles B. Williams. *The New Testament in the Language of the People*. "The Four Translation New Testament." Printed for Decision Magazine by World Wide Publications of Minneapolis. New York, NY: Iversen Associates, 1966).
- "a people saved to be His own" (William F. Beck. *The New Testament in the Language of Today*. "The Four Translation New Testament." Printed for Decision Magazine by World Wide Publications of Minneapolis. New York, NY: Iversen Associates, 1966).

This is a most precious thought: that God makes us His very own people, a very special possession of His. Possession has the idea of value, of worth and preciousness. We are more precious to God than all the precious gems and treasures of the world. Possession also has the idea of provision, protection, and security. We are God's possession, His very special people; therefore, He will provide and protect us and make us secure in every sense of the word.

> **Now if you obey me fully and keep my covenant, then out of all nations you will be my treasured possession. Although the whole earth is mine, (Exo 19:5)**

> **For you are a people holy to the LORD your God. Out of all the peoples on the face of the earth, the LORD has chosen you to be his treasured possession. (Deu 14:2)**

> **But he brought his people out like a flock; he led them like sheep through the desert. (Psa 78:52)**

> **Know that the LORD is God. It is he who made us, and we are his ; we are his people, the sheep of his pasture. (Psa 100:3)**

> **And he will go on before the Lord, in the spirit and power of Elijah, to turn the hearts of the fathers to their children and the disobedient to the wisdom of the righteous—to make ready a people prepared for the Lord." (Luke 1:17)**

> **Simon has described to us how God at first showed his concern by taking from the Gentiles a people for himself. (Acts 15:14)**

> **And you also were included in Christ when you heard the word of truth, the gospel of your salvation. Having believed, you were marked in him with a seal, the promised Holy Spirit, who is a deposit guaranteeing our inheritance until the redemption of those who are God's possession—to the praise of his glory. (Eph 1:13-14)**

> **For the grace of God that brings salvation has appeared to all men. It teaches us to say "No" to ungodliness and worldly passions, and to live self-controlled, upright and godly lives in this present age, while we wait for the blessed hope—the glorious appearing of our great God and Savior, Jesus Christ, who gave himself for us to redeem us from all wickedness and to purify for himself a people that are his very own, eager to do what is good. (Titus 2:11-14)**

> **But you are a chosen people, a royal priesthood, a holy nation, a people belonging to God, that you may declare the**

praises of him who called you out of darkness into his wonderful light. (1 Pet 2:9)

And I heard a loud voice from the throne saying, "Now the dwelling of God is with men, and he will live with them. They will be his people, and God himself will be with them and be their God. (Rev 21:3)

DEEPER STUDY # 1

(2:9) **Priest—Priesthood—Mediator**: a priest is a person who has access into God's presence, who represents men before God and God before men. He is a mediator between God and men: he offers sacrifices and makes prayer to God for men. The priest was always looked upon as the one person who could carry a man's case before God and God would accept the man because of the priest's intercession.

1. Throughout Israel's history the high priest was the chief priest who essentially had four functions.
⇒ He supervised the other priests.
⇒ He made a sin offering (Lev.4).
⇒ He offered a sacrifice on the Day of Atonement (Lev.16).
⇒ He was shown the will of God (Num.27:21; Neh.7:65).

2. The development of the priesthood seems to have been as follows: at first, individuals were priests (Gen.4:3-4). Later on the head of a family, usually the father, began to serve as the priest (Gen.8:20; 12:7; 13:8; 26:25; 31:54). When God created the nation Israel and gave Israel the law at Mount Sinai, He said that the nation was to be unto God "a kingdom of priests" (Ex.19:6). But Israel failed to obey God's law. So God turned to one family of Israel, Aaron's family, and appointed them as the priests who were to minister to the nation (Ex.28:1; Lev.21:16-24).

3. In the New Testament Jesus Christ is said to be the perfect and eternal High Priest of God Himself (see outlines—Heb.7:1-8:5; 10:1-18). The sacrifice which He offered to God for men was the death of Himself. What this means is this: Jesus Christ has made the perfect and eternal sacrifice to God. He died for our sins, paid the penalty and judgment of death for us. No other sacrifice by death has to be made. God has accepted Christ's sacrifice of Himself—eternally.
Before Christ the presence of God was said to dwell in the Most Holy Place of the Tabernacle and Temple. Only the High Priest could enter the Most Holy Place and that only once a year. It was separated from men by a veil. But when Christ died, Scripture says that the veil was torn from top to bottom *by an act of God* (Mt.27:51). The torn veil is also said to be a symbol of Christ's body which was sacrificed or torn upon the cross (Heb.10:20). All believers now have access to God through the death of Christ—into the holiest of holies right along with Christ (Heb. 10:19-22).

4. Since Christ, the individual believer has become his own priest before God; that is, he has the right to approach God for himself. As priest, the believer has two functions: he is to offer intercession and he is to offer sacrifices to God. He makes the following sacrifices to God.
⇒ He sacrifices his own body (Ro.12:1; Ph.2:17; 2 Tim.4:6; Jas.1:27; 1 Jn.3:16).
⇒ He sacrifices praise to God continually (Heb.13:15; cp. Ex.25:22).
⇒ He sacrifices his substance (Ro.12:13; Gal.6:6, 10; Tit.3:14; Heb.13:2, 16; 3 Jn.5-8).
⇒ He sacrifices his service "to do good" (Heb.13:16).

---

2 (2:9) **Purpose, Believer's**: know what your purpose is. Why does God do so much for believers? There is one supreme reason:

That you may declare the praises of him who called you out of darkness into his wonderful light. (1 Pet 2:9 b)

The statement "that you may declare" (hopos exaggeilete) means to speak forth; to tell out; to publish abroad; to set forth. The word "praises" (aretas) means virtues, excellencies, and the supreme and eminent qualities of God (Alan Stibbs. *The First Epistle General of Peter*. "The Tyndale New Testament Commentaries," p.104). The very task of the believer is to witness for God, to share the glorious message of God. What is that message? Note the verse: "the praises of Him who called you out of darkness into His wonderful light." The message that we are to share is the glorious message of salvation. God will deliver man out of darkness into the light. This is what He has done for believers. Therefore, we are to proclaim the glorious truth that God has saved us through the Light of the world, through Jesus Christ Himself. He has saved us out of the darkness of sin and death and delivered us into the light of eternity. We shall live forever. We are to praise God, proclaim the glorious message of His wonderful light or salvation.

He said to them, "Go into all the world and preach the good news to all creation. (Mark 16:15)
It is written: "I believed; therefore I have spoken." With that same spirit of faith we also believe and therefore speak, (2 Cor 4:13)
We are therefore Christ's ambassadors, as though God were making his appeal through us. We implore you on Christ's behalf: Be reconciled to God. (2 Cor 5:20)
But you will receive power when the Holy Spirit comes on you; and you will be my witnesses in Jerusalem, and in all Judea and Samaria, and to the ends of the earth." (Acts 1:8)
For we cannot help speaking about what we have seen and heard." (Acts 4:20)
Come and listen, all you who fear God; let me tell you what he has done for me. (Psa 66:16)
I will tell of the kindnesses of the LORD, the deeds for which he is to be praised, according to all the LORD has done for us— yes, the many good things he has done for the house of Israel, according to his compassion and many kindnesses. (Isa 63:7)
Then those who feared the LORD talked with each other, and the LORD listened and heard. A scroll of remembrance was written in his presence concerning those who feared the LORD and honored his name. (Mal 3:16)

3 (2:10) **Believers**: know what has happened to you. Two great facts about believers are covered in this verse.

1. In the past believers were not a people, but now they have been made into the people of God. This is striking

language. What does it mean *not to be a people*? Are unbelievers not a people? It means to be without purpose and significance in life; to be missing the very point of life, the very reason for living. It means God created man and gave man life. If man does not live that life, then he is not living, not in the real sense of living. He exists, but he is missing out on life, on what life really is. He is missing the very purpose, meaning, and significance of life. He shall never fulfill, satisfy, or complete the purpose of life.

But when a person comes to God's Son, when a person enters the light of Christ, God saves him and gives him the light of life. He is given the light of life's purpose, meaning, and significance. He becomes a member of the people of God. He fulfills, satisfies, and completes life and all that life is meant to be.

> **Yet to all who received him, to those who believed in his name, he gave the right to become children of God— (John 1:12)**

> **For you did not receive a spirit that makes you a slave again to fear, but you received the Spirit of sonship. And by him we cry, "Abba, Father." (Rom 8:15)**

> **"Therefore come out from them and be separate, says the Lord. Touch no unclean thing, and I will receive you." "I will be a Father to you, and you will be my sons and daughters, says the Lord Almighty." (2 Cor 6:17-18)**

> **But when the time had fully come, God sent his Son, born of a woman, born under law, to redeem those under law, that we might receive the full rights of sons. Because you are sons, God sent the Spirit of his Son into our hearts, the Spirit who calls out, "Abba, Father." (Gal 4:4-6)**

> **For you are a people holy to the LORD your God. Out of all the peoples on the face of the earth, the LORD has chosen you to be his treasured possession. (Deu 14:2)**

> **"When Israel was a child, I loved him, and out of Egypt I called my son. (Hosea 11:1)**

2. In the past believers had not received mercy, but now they have received mercy. Before we were saved we were like everyone else: we ignored, neglected, cursed, rebelled against, and rejected God. We refused to change our lives and to cry out for the mercy of God; therefore, God could not have mercy upon us. But when we repented and turned to God, God had mercy upon us and saved us. He forgave our sin and neglect and brought us into His love and grace and gave us the glorious privilege of living with Him forever. God had mercy upon us and allowed us the glorious privilege of becoming a member of the people of God.

> **But because of his great love for us, God, who is rich in mercy, made us alive with Christ even when we were dead in transgressions—it is by grace you have been saved. And God raised us up with Christ and seated us with him in the heavenly realms in Christ Jesus, in order that in the coming ages he might show the incomparable riches of his grace, expressed in his kindness to us in Christ Jesus. For it is by grace you have been saved, through faith— and this not from yourselves, it is the gift of God— not by works, so that no one can boast. (Eph 2:4-9)**

> **He saved us, not because of righteous things we had done, but because of his mercy. He saved us through the washing of rebirth and renewal by the Holy Spirit, (Titus 3:5)**

> **But from everlasting to everlasting the Lord's love is with those who fear him, and his righteousness with their children's children— (Psa 103:17)**

> **Because of the Lord's great love we are not consumed, for his compassions never fail. They are new every morning; great is your faithfulness. (Lam 3:22-23)**

> **Rend your heart and not your garments. Return to the LORD your God, for he is gracious and compassionate, slow to anger and abounding in love, and he relents from sending calamity. (Joel 2:13)**

> **Who is a God like you, who pardons sin and forgives the transgression of the remnant of his inheritance? You do not stay angry forever but delight to show mercy. (Micah 7:18)**

	G. Abstain from Fleshly Lusts, 2:11-12

1 Reason 1: You are aliens & strangers on earth
2 Reason 2: Evil desires, lusts wars against your soul
3 Reason 3: Unbelievers are watching
  a. They speak against you
  b. They can experience the "day of visitation" through your testimony
    1) By your good works
    2) Will glorify God
	11 Dear friends, I urge you, as aliens and strangers in the world, to abstain from sinful desires, which war against your soul.
	12 Live such good lives among the pagans that, though they accuse you of doing wrong, they may see your good deeds and glorify God on the day he visits us.

DIVISION II

HOW TO LIVE THROUGH SUFFERING: GIVE YOUR LIFE TO GOD, 1:13-3:12

G. Abstain from Fleshly Lusts, 2:11-12

(2:11-12) **Introduction**: we live in a day when the flesh (sinful nature) is exalted and evil desires honored. A person's esteem and worth and image are often determined...

- by how much of the world he possesses
- by how much money he has
- by how much power he has
- by how much worldly recreation and pleasure he is able to enjoy
- by how famous he becomes
- by how many people he conquers in face to face confrontations or in bed sexually

The flesh (sinful nature) is exalted and evil desires honored. But this is not the way of God and His Word. Scripture is clear: abstain from evil, sinful desires.

1. Reason 1: you are aliens and strangers on earth (v.11).
2. Reason 2: evil desires, lusts war against your soul (v.11).
3. Reason 3: unbelievers are watching (v.12).

1 (2:11) **Aliens—Strangers**: abstain from evil desires because you are aliens and strangers on earth.

1. The word "alien" (parepidemos) has more of a temporary idea than *stranger* (paroikoi). Alien has the idea of a visitor or sojourner, of a foreigner who may be visiting and staying for a while but not long enough to lease a house.

The point is this: the believer is only passing through the earth on his way home to heaven. Heaven is his home, and his heart and mind are at home. He lives in a consciousness of home and his thoughts are upon home. He lives and walks in the consciousness of being in heaven with God. This is his attitude, his thoughts as he walks through his pilgrimage upon earth. He travels through life often moving from city to city, but his mind and heart are always upon heaven which is his permanent home.

Note what this means in so far as the world is concerned: the believer does not become entangled with the world and its affairs. His customs and lifestyle come from heaven, not from the earth. He does not practice the customs and lifestyle of the earth but of heaven.

> **By faith he made his home in the promised land like a stranger in a foreign country; he lived in tents, as did Isaac and Jacob, who were heirs with him of the same promise. For he was looking forward to the city with foundations, whose architect and builder is God. (Heb 11:9-10)**

> **All these people were still living by faith when they died. They did not receive the things promised; they only saw them and welcomed them from a distance. And they admitted that they were aliens and strangers on earth. People who say such things show that they are looking for a country of their own. If they had been thinking of the country they had left, they would have had opportunity to return. Instead, they were longing for a better country—a heavenly one. Therefore God is not ashamed to be called their God, for he has prepared a city for them. (Heb 11:13-16)**

> **For here we do not have an enduring city, but we are looking for the city that is to come. (Heb 13:14)**

2. The word "stranger" (paroikoi) means someone who dwells alongside or is exiled, but his home is elsewhere. It is the picture of a foreigner who is in a country for a while, long enough to rent or lease a house, but he is not a permanent resident. He has no legal rights or status. He is a stranger, an exile who dwells in a strange land (B.C. Coffin. *First Peter*. "The Pulpit Commentary," Vol.22, p.72). What Peter is saying is this: the believer is a stranger, a foreigner, an exile on earth. He is a resident, but he is not a citizen of this earth. He has no legal status in the world. He is not to follow the standards and the ways of the world. He belongs to God and to heaven; therefore, his legal status is in heaven. He is to follow the standards and the ways of God. The believer's laws are the laws of God, the highest and most moral and just laws in all the universe. The believer has no right to live by the standard and laws of the world, for they are far lower than the standards and laws of God. The believer is to live as a stranger on earth, as one whose heart and mind are upon a far greater home and world. The believer's heart is to be upon perfection of life and morality and justice, a home and world where perfection is the rule and standard.

Thought 1. This does not mean that the believer does not obey the legal laws of a land. He does; all foreigners are to obey the laws of a land when they visit that land. In fact, believers will go far beyond obeying human laws and do much more when they obey God's laws. God's laws and standards stress perfect behavior plus love, and there is no greater law than love. Therefore, the believer is to abstain from fleshly, sinful desires because such desires are of the world, and he has no right to partake of those fleshly, sinful desires. He is to obey the laws of God which forbid such sins and immoralities.

> **But our citizenship is in heaven. And we eagerly await a Savior from there, the Lord Jesus Christ, who, by the power that enables him to bring everything under his control, will transform our lowly bodies so that they will be like his glorious body. (Phil 3:20-21)**

> **Nothing impure will ever enter it, nor will anyone who does what is shameful or deceitful, but only those whose names are written in the Lamb's book of life. (Rev 21:27)**

> **We are aliens and strangers in your sight, as were all our forefathers. Our days on earth are like a shadow, without hope. (1 Chr 29:15)**

2 (2:11) **Sinful Desire—Flesh—Lust**: abstain from evil desires because they war against the soul. The term "sinful desires" (sarkikon epithumion) means the evil desires, urges, passions, lusts of the flesh, and cravings of the sinful nature. It means to have a yearning passion for the things of the flesh. Every person has experienced the flesh...

- yearning
- pulling
- desiring
- wanting
- craving
- hungering
- thirsting
- longing
- grasping
- grabbing
- taking

Every person knows what it is to have his flesh craving after something, to have it yearning and yearning to lay hold of something. The flesh is strong and difficult to control, and it never lets up its assault against the will.

1. What are the lusts of the flesh, the acts of the sinful nature? What kinds of sins are being referred to by Scripture? Scripture means far more than the sexual sins usually thought about when the lusts of the flesh are mentioned. They are listed in Galatians 5:19-21. When they are read they paint a picture of human nature that is seen or experienced by us all every day:

a. *Sexual immorality* (moicheia): a broad word including all forms of immoral and sexual acts. It is pre-marital sex and adultery; it is abnormal sex, all kinds of sexual vice, sexual unfaithfulness to husband or wife.

b. *Impurity* (akatharsia): moral impurity; doing things that dirty, pollute, and soil life.

c. *Debauchery* (aselgeia): filthiness, indecency, and shamefulness.

d. *Idolatry* (eidololatreia): the worship of idols, whether mental or material; the worship of some idea of what God is like, of an image of God within a person's mind; the giving of one's primary devotion (time and energy) to something other than God. (See note, *Idolatry*—1 Cor.6:9 for detailed discussion.)

e. *Witchcraft* (pharmakeia): sorcery; the use of drugs or of evil spirits to gain control over the lives of others or over one's own life. In the present context it would include all forms of seeking the control of one's fate including astrology, palm reading, seances, fortune telling, crystals, and other forms of witchcraft.

f. *Hatred* (echthrai): enmity, hostility, and animosity. It is the hatred that lingers and is held for a long time, a hatred that is deep within.

g. *Discord* (ereis): strife, contention, fighting, struggling, quarreling, dissension, and wrangling. It means that a man fights against another person in order to get something: position, promotion, property, honor, or recognition. He deceives, doing whatever has to be done to get what he is after.

h. *Jealousy* (zeloi): wanting and desiring to have what someone else has. It may be material things, recognition, honor, or position.

i. *Fits of rage* (thumoi): indignation; a violent, explosive temper; anger; quick and explosive reactions that arise from boiling emotions. But it is anger which fades away just as quickly as it arose. It is not anger that lasts.

j. *Selfish ambitions* (eritheia): self-seeking; craving position, power, fame for selfish ends; a strong desire for attainment or achievement to gain honor or recognition; pretension.

k. *Dissensions* (dichostasiai): division, rebellion, standing against others, and splitting off from others.

l. *Factions* (haireseis): sect, party, differences, heresies; some faction rejecting the fundamental beliefs of God, Christ, the Scriptures, and the church; believing and holding to some teaching other than the truth.

m. *Envy* (phthonoi): this word goes beyond jealousy. It is the spirit...

- that wants not only the things that another person has, but begrudges the fact that the person has them.
- that wants not only the things to be taken away from the person, but wants him to suffer through the loss of them.

n. *Drunkenness* (methai): taking drink or drugs to affect one's senses for lust or pleasure; becoming tipsy or intoxicated; partaking of drugs; seeking bodily or sexual pleasure through drink or drugs.

o. *Orgies* (komoi): carousing; uncontrolled license, indulgence, and pleasure; taking part in wild parties or in drinking parties; lying around indulging in feeding the lusts of the flesh.

2. Note that the flesh, sinful desires war against the soul. The flesh has within it base and unregulated urges and passions. A man senses the desire and urge to do what he likes, to lift the restraints and to follow his own desires and passions. He knows he should not do it, but the pull and desire tugs and struggles and wars against the soul.

a. The flesh or sinful nature keeps a person from doing what he would. Every person has experienced the power of the flesh; everyone has caved in to the flesh and done something that he did not want to do. He fought against doing it—knew it was harmful or hurtful—yet he could not resist the flesh. He gave in to the power of the flesh and did it. He...

- overate
- became angry
- began smoking
- got drunk
- did evil things
- lusted
- became prideful
- cursed
- acted selfishly
- committed immorality
- cheated, lied, or stole

Note another fact as well. All of us have been tempted, and we have known how to combat and overcome the temptation. However, the flesh was so strong we just did not struggle long enough to overcome it. The struggle we experienced involved that of...

- controlling
- reaching out
- loving
- sacrificing
- giving in

- being patient
- showing kindness
- giving
- helping
- showing kindness

The point is this: the flesh is so strong that it often keeps us from doing what we would. The only hope of ever controlling the flesh is to walk in the Spirit of God—in His presence and power.

I do not understand what I do. For what I want to do I do not do, but what I hate I do. And if I do what I do not want to do, I agree that the law is good. As it is, it is no longer I myself who do it, but it is sin living in me. I know that nothing good lives in me, that is, in my sinful nature. For I have the desire to do what is good, but I cannot carry it out. For what I do is not the good I want to do; no, the evil I do not want to do—this I keep on doing. Now if I do what I do not want to do, it is no longer I who do it, but it is sin living in me that does it. (Rom 7:15-20)

The weapons we fight with are not the weapons of the world. On the contrary, they have divine power to demolish strongholds. (2 Cor 10:4)

b. Now note a fact of critical importance: the flesh in itself is not sinful. The flesh or human body is God given; it is for God's use. In fact, when a person is converted to Christ, his body becomes a temple for God to dwell in through the Holy Spirit. The Christian is not told to cleanse himself from the flesh but from "the desires of the sinful nature" (Gal.5:16), from "everything that contaminates body and spirit" (2 Cor.7:1), and from "the acts of the sinful nature" (Ro.13:12; Gal.5:19). The acts of the sinful nature are the fruit of indwelling sin, and sin originates in the heart not in the flesh.

3. The exhortation is strong: "abstain from sinful desires, which war against the soul." We must abstain from them, for they do unbelievable harm and damage to the soul.

a. Sinful desires or fleshly lusts enslave and weaken the freedom of the soul. Sinful desire enslaves, no matter what the desires are:
⇒ Desire for drugs enslaves.
⇒ Desire for alcohol enslaves.
⇒ Desire for cigarettes enslaves.
⇒ Desire for sex enslaves.
⇒ Desire for pornography enslaves (films or magazines).
⇒ Desire for position and power enslaves.
⇒ Desire for money enslaves.

The more a man follows the desires of the sinful nature, the more freedom and liberty he loses. He becomes a slave to that which he sets his heart upon. If he sets his mind and thoughts upon the flesh and its desires, he will enslave himself to desires. He finds himself enslaved and in bondage to those desires and finds it very difficult to break away from them.

b. Desires disturb and often destroy the peace and security, assurance and confidence of the soul. When the believer came to Christ, one of the first things Christ did was give him peace and security of soul. If the believer turns back to the world and follows his desires, he breaks his peace with God and loses the security of God's presence and guidance and protection.

c. Desires hamper the growth of the soul. The soul living in the desires of the flesh [sinful nature] is destroying its fruit, not growing and proclaiming the fruit of the Spirit (Gal.5:22-23).

d. Fleshly desires doom the soul to defeat, sorrow, brokenness, and eventually to eternal separation from God.

Thought 1. The exhortation is strong: believers must abstain from fleshly lusts or desires, for they war against the soul.

If your right eye causes you to sin, gouge it out and throw it away. It is better for you to lose one part of your body than for your whole body to be thrown into hell. (Mat 5:29)

For we know that our old self was crucified with him so that the body of sin might be done away with, that we should no longer be slaves to sin— (Rom 6:6)

Rather, clothe yourselves with the Lord Jesus Christ, and do not think about how to gratify the desires of the sinful nature. (Rom 13:14)

So I say, live by the Spirit, and you will not gratify the desires of the sinful nature. (Gal 5:16)

Put to death, therefore, whatever belongs to your earthly nature: sexual immorality, impurity, lust, evil desires and greed, which is idolatry. (Col 3:5)

It is God's will that you should be sanctified: that you should avoid sexual immorality; (1 Th 4:3)

Avoid every kind of evil. (1 Th 5:22)

Dear friends, I urge you, as aliens and strangers in the world, to abstain from sinful desires, which war against your soul. (1 Pet 2:11)

As a result, he does not live the rest of his earthly life for evil human desires, but rather for the will of God. (1 Pet 4:2)

3 (2:12) **Witness—Witnessing:** abstain from evil, sinful desires because unbelievers are watching you. The world watches everything a genuine believer does. If a person really follows Christ—if he is genuine—then the world watches. This is the reason for this exhortation: we must live good lives before the world, always abstaining from evil desires.

The word "good" (kalos) means a good life, a life that is honorable, righteous, pure, lovely, decent, excellent, upright, and noble. It means a life that is without blame, that cannot be justly or accurately blamed with any sin or evil. The world watches a genuine believer to see if he really lives what he professes. Therefore, we must live good lives, lives that are just what we profess: holy, righteous, and pure. Note two reasons why:

1. Unbelievers accuse believers of doing wrong. Some will always accuse genuine believers. If a person really lives for Christ, his righteous and self-denying life convicts those who love the world and its pleasures and possessions. Therefore, they talk about, joke, mock, ridicule, abuse, and persecute the believer when they can.

The point is this: the believer must never add fuel to the fire. He must never give the world a chance to justly accuse and down him. The believer must abstain from evil, sinful desires: he must live a good life, do exactly what he proclaims and professes.

2. Unbelievers must have a chance to be saved. If we live bad and fleshly lives—go against all that we proclaim and stand for—then unbelievers will know we are hypocrites. They will not be attracted to Christ. We must, therefore, live for Christ and do good works. When unbelievers see our righteous lives and good deeds, they will experience the day of God's visitation and glorify God. The day God visits us means two things:

⇒ the day a man is visited by God to bring the man to repentance and salvation.
⇒ the day God will visit the earth for final judgment.

The day of visitation is the day of God's inspection and salvation, the day when He saves a man. It is also the day when He returns to earth as Savior and Lord. The idea is that unbelievers will be won to Christ by our good lives and glorify God in the great day when He shall visit the earth.

In the same way, let your light shine before men, that they may see your good deeds and praise your Father in heaven. (Mat 5:16)

The Lord's message rang out from you not only in Macedonia and Achaia—your faith in God has become known everywhere. Therefore we do not need to say anything about it, (1 Th 1:8)

Don't let anyone look down on you because you are young, but set an example for the believers in speech, in life, in love, in faith and in purity. (1 Tim 4:12)

In everything set them an example by doing what is good. In your teaching show integrity, seriousness (Titus 2:7)

But someone will say, "You have faith; I have deeds." Show me your faith without deeds, and I will show you my faith by what I do. (James 2:18)

Who is wise and understanding among you? Let him show it by his good life, by deeds done in the humility that comes from wisdom. (James 3:13)

Live such good lives among the pagans that, though they accuse you of doing wrong, they may see your good deeds and glorify God on the day he visits us. (1 Pet 2:12)

But the day of the Lord will come like a thief. The heavens will disappear with a roar; the elements will be destroyed by fire, and the earth and everything in it will be laid bare. Since everything will be destroyed in this way, what kind of people ought you to be? You ought to live holy and godly lives as you look forward to the day of God and speed its coming. That day will bring about the destruction of the heavens by fire, and the elements will melt in the heat. (2 Pet 3:10-12)

	H. Submit to the State, 2:13-17	15 For it is God's will that by doing good you should silence the ignorant talk of foolish men.	c. Because good behavior silences the critics of Christ
1 Submit to national & local officials[DS1] a. Because they are sent by God b. Because they execute justice for God	13 Submit yourselves for the Lord's sake to every authority instituted among men: whether to the king, as the supreme authority, 14 Or to governors, who are sent by him to punish those who do wrong and to commend those who do right.	16 Live as free men, but do not use your freedom as a cover-up for evil; live as servants of God. 17 Show proper respect to everyone: Love the brotherhood of believers, fear God, honor the king.	**2 Live as free citizens, yet as servants of God** a. Respect everyone, v.17 b. Love the brotherhood c. Reverence God d. Honor the king

DIVISION II

HOW TO LIVE THROUGH SUFFERING: GIVE YOUR LIFE TO GOD, 1:13-3:12

H. Submit to the State, 2:13-17

(2:13-17) **Introduction**: remember, the church and its believers were being severely persecuted by the government and the society of that day. The believers had even been forced to flee their homes. They had to leave everything behind: money, clothes, property, jobs, and professions. In light of such severe persecution, what was to be the attitude and behavior of the believers toward the government and its authorities? This is a critical question because of the periodic persecution of the church by society and government. History reveals that the genuine church is constantly suffering persecution of some sort.

1. Submit to national and local officials (v.13-15).
2. Live as free citizens, yet as servants of God (v.16-17).

1 (2:13-15) **Citizenship—Law, Civil—State**: first, submit to national and local officials. This is a hard pill to swallow when one is being persecuted and has lost so much because of the persecution. But note: the word *submit* is an imperative; it is a strong command. God expects believers to submit themselves to the laws of government, and note the word *every*: every authority or institution is to be obeyed. Every level of government, local as well as state and national government, is to be obeyed. Why is this so important? The reason is self-evident; it is perfectly clear: without law and the keeping of the law society would be in utter chaos.

⇒ Lawlessness would run wild.
⇒ No one would be safe to walk the streets.
⇒ People would have to live behind closed doors.
⇒ Abuse, attacks, murder, and war would be a constant threat.
⇒ No property would be safe.
⇒ There would be no public roads, transportation, water, sewage, or electrical systems, for there would be no law to collect taxes. And even if there was, no one would honor it.
⇒ There would be no military police or fire protection for the same reason.

Without law and the keeping of the law there can be no society and no community, no life together, no bond to tie people together. Law, rulers, and their authority are an utter necessity to keep people from becoming wild beasts in a jungle of unrestrained selfishness and lawlessness.

Chaos is not God's will for the world; law and order are God's will. God wills men to live in a world of love, joy, and peace—a world of perfect law and order. Therefore, the believer is to set the example: he is to obey the rulers and the laws of his community and nation. He is to show how *loving and joyful, peaceful and wonderful* life can be if people will obey God and obey the civil authorities of this world. (See notes—Ro.12:18; 13:1; 1 Pt.2:13-17 for the believer's duty when rulers and laws oppose God.) There are three reasons why believers are to obey civil rulers.

1. Civil rulers are sent by God; civil authority is ordained by God. That is, the existence, the authority, the position, the offices of government are ordained by God. It is God's will that government exist and that persons have the authority to rule within the state. There are three institutions ordained by God: the family, the church, and the government. All three exist because God set them up as the means by which men are to relate to each other and to Himself as God.

⇒ God has ordained that the family exist as the means by which family members share together, and that the office of parents rule within the family.
⇒ God has ordained that the church exist as the means by which people share with God, and that the office of church leaders exercise authority within the church.
⇒ God has ordained that the government exist as the means by which citizens relate to each other, and that the office of government officials exercise authority within the state.

The institutions and their authority are ordained by God, and men are responsible for how they carry out the functions of the institutions. Each of the three institutions have leaders who are faithful and do an excellent job, and each have leaders who are totally disobedient to God and do a terrible job. This includes the men who hold authority within various levels of government as well as men serving on various levels in the church and family. The fact to remember is that government is ordained by God, and rulers are answerable to Him: they shall give an account to God.

Everyone must submit himself to the governing authorities, for there is no authority except that which God has established. The authorities that exist have been established by God. (Rom 13:1)

Kings detest wrongdoing, for a throne is established through righteousness. (Prov 16:12)

58

In love a throne will be established; in faithfulness a man will sit on it— one from the house of David— one who in judging seeks justice and speeds the cause of righteousness. (Isa 16:5)

However, the *thrust* of this passage is not the rulers of government; the *thrust* is the believer and his duty to the state. Usually, the believer can do little about how the authorities in government conduct their affairs, but the believer can do a great deal about his behavior as a citizen within the state; and God is very, very clear about the believer's behavior. Keep in mind that the *infamous Nero* was ruling as the emperor when God led Peter to give these instructions. The believer is to obey all civil authority, no matter who it is.

2. Civil authorities execute justice for God. They rule to execute punishment for evil-doers and to reward those who do well and work good throughout the state. Rulers are not ordained by God to be a restraint upon good works, but upon evil. Civil authorities and laws exist to restrain evil; therefore, any believer who breaks the law can expect to be punished by the state. For this reason, the believer...

- should fear the state enough to obey its laws.
- should do that which is good and lawful.

By fearing and doing that which is good and lawful, the believer has the *commendation* of the state. The idea is that the believer contributes to the good and to the commendation of the state. He helps to build up righteousness and truth within the state, and thereby he is able to be the citizen of a good and commendable state. The believer has the *commendation* of the state; he is allowed to live in peace as a citizen of the state.

Thought 1. Note that civil government and law are a *restraint* upon evil. The power of evil and corruption is so strong that when men are without law, they go on a rampage of selfishness and sin, looting and stealing, assault and immorality, destruction and murder. History and the breakdown of law within communities, cities, societies, and even families provide ample evidence. When law does not exist or when law is not enforced, evil runs rampant. Society desperately needs to heed this fact.

We also know that law is made not for the righteous but for lawbreakers and rebels, the ungodly and sinful, the unholy and irreligious; for those who kill their fathers or mothers, for murderers, for adulterers and perverts, for slave traders and liars and perjurers—and for whatever else is contrary to the sound doctrine (1 Tim 1:9-10)

3. The believer's good behavior is to silence the critics of Christ. In the days of the early church, the church and its believers were under severe attack from the state and society. People wanted nothing to do with Christ and His demand for self-denial and holy living. They wanted to live like they wanted and to do their own thing. The very idea that a person had to give all he was and had to Christ and His cause of world-evangelization—that they had to sacrifice themselves to meet the desperate needs of a dying world—was the last thing upon their minds and the very last thing they were going to accept. Therefore, the government and society were set upon stamping out the church

and anyone who refused to turn away from Christ and His cause.

Note: the Scripture calls anyone who persecutes the church and believers "foolish men." Imagine rejecting a person just because he teaches...

- love and joy
- peace and health
- long-suffering and gentleness
- rule and authority
- morality and purity
- justice and righteousness
- discipline and control

Any person who opposes the great virtues of life and the teaching of the great virtues is doing a foolish thing, a very, very foolish thing. But note a significant fact: the believer who continues to live for Christ by doing good will eventually silence the critics. It may take some time, but eventually the righteous and godly behavior will overcome the lies and attacks of the vicious and evil of the earth. This is the third reason why we are to obey rulers—so that our lawful and righteous behavior will silence any question about Christ and His great cause. (Note: Is there ever a time when believers are not to obey the state? See DEEPER STUDY # 1—1 Pt.2:13-15 for more discussion.)

"Do not blaspheme God or curse the ruler of your people. (Exo 22:28)

Obey the king's command, I say, because you took an oath before God. (Eccl 8:2)

"Caesar's," they replied. Then he said to them, "Give to Caesar what is Caesar's, and to God what is God's." (Mat 22:21)

Paul replied, "Brothers, I did not realize that he was the high priest; for it is written: 'Do not speak evil about the ruler of your people.'" (Acts 23:5)

Everyone must submit himself to the governing authorities, for there is no authority except that which God has established. The authorities that exist have been established by God. (Rom 13:1)

Remind the people to be subject to rulers and authorities, to be obedient, to be ready to do whatever is good, (Titus 3:1)

Submit yourselves for the Lord's sake to every authority instituted among men: whether to the king, as the supreme authority, (1 Pet 2:13)

Show proper respect to everyone: Love the brotherhood of believers, fear God, honor the king. (1 Pet 2:17)

DEEPER STUDY # 1

(2:13-15) The State—Government: the Christian must give to Caesar the things of Caesar (Mt.22:21), but he must also give to God the things that are God's. He has a higher authority than the state—God Himself. Thus, when the state begins to fail in executing justice *under and for God*, the Christian must hearken to God and not to the state (cp. Acts 4:19; 5:29). There are times when the Christian serves the highest good of the state by refusing to obey the state and insisting on obedience to God. By such he bears a greater witness, and he works for greater justice by effecting change within the state. (See notes—Mk.12:16-17; Ro.13:1-7.)

---

2 (2:16-17) **Citizenship—Government**: live as free citizens, yet as servants of God. When a person receives Jesus Christ as his Savior, the person subjects himself to God above all other laws. If man's law stands against God's law, the believer obeys God rather than man. But note: there is a danger that the believer can use his liberty as a cover-up or veil to act maliciously against the state. He can disobey laws because he claims they are unjust when in fact they are not. It is just a matter that he does not like the law. William Barclay states it well:

> "Any great Christian doctrine can be perverted into an excuse for evil. The doctrine of grace can be perverted into an excuse for sinning to one's heart's content. The doctrine of the love of God can be sentimentalized into a defense for breaking the law of God. The doctrine of the life to come can be perverted into a reason for neglecting life in this world. And there is no doctrine so easy to pervert as the doctrine of Christian freedom and Christian liberty.
>
> "There are hints in the New Testament that it was frequently so perverted. Paul tells the Galatians that they have been called to liberty, but they must not use that liberty as an occasion for the flesh to do as it wills (Galatians 5:13). In 2 Peter we read of those who promise others liberty and who are themselves the servants of corruption (2 Peter 2:19)" (*The Letters of James and Peter*, p.245f).

The point is this: believers are the servants of God, not the servants of their own ideas and thoughts. They are to serve God and His call, not their own lusts and desires. They have no right to break the laws of government unless the laws are directly opposing God and His law. In dealing with government and living as citizens of the state, they have four clear duties. These duties are demanded of every servant of God. Note how pointed and brief they are.

1. Respect everyone. Respect and esteem all citizens as your fellow-citizens. Remember the early church and its believers: how they were surrounded by heathen worshippers of idols and by the most corrupt people who wallowed around in a cesspool of immoral, unjust, and drunken behavior. Yet, Scripture is here saying to show proper respect to *everyone*, these as well as the more controlled and disciplined. Note: this does not mean to respect them because of their sin, but to respect them...

- because they are God's creation.
- because their souls are of more value than all the wealth in the world.
- because of any virtue and good and order they have in their lives.
- because they contribute to the work, defense, and structure of the nation.

All persons are to be respected, honored, and esteemed. No person is to be mistreated, no matter who he may be: rich or poor, corrupt or clean, bad or good, evil or righteous, destructive or constructive. We must try to reach all persons on earth for Christ. They need to make their contribution to society. They need to be doing all the good they can for society. No person is to ever be counted beyond reach.

> But a Samaritan, as he traveled, came where the man was; and when he saw him, he took pity on him. He went to him and bandaged his wounds, pouring on oil and wine. Then he put the man on his own donkey, took him to an inn and took care of him. (Luke 10:33-34)
>
> The islanders showed us unusual kindness. They built a fire and welcomed us all because it was raining and cold. (Acts 28:2)
>
> Even as I try to please everybody in every way. For I am not seeking my own good but the good of many, so that they may be saved. (1 Cor 10:33)
>
> For you know the grace of our Lord Jesus Christ, that though he was rich, yet for your sakes he became poor, so that you through his poverty might become rich. (2 Cor 8:9)
>
> Do nothing out of selfish ambition or vain conceit, but in humility consider others better than yourselves. Each of you should look not only to your own interests, but also to the interests of others. (Phil 2:3-4)
>
> Show proper respect to everyone: Love the brotherhood of believers, fear God, honor the king. (1 Pet 2:17)

2. Love the brotherhood of believers. This means to love all believers whoever they may be, regardless of color, nationality, or beliefs. If a person is a *brother in Christ*, a true brother, we are to love him. Note: it is not enough to honor and respect a brother. Something far more is expected: love, a true brotherly love. And remember what love means: it means to care and look after one another...

- to teach one another
- to feed one another when needed
- to support one another
- to help one another
- to protect one another
- to share with one another
- to fellowship and commune with one another
- to pray and worship with one another

Love is the very opposite of criticizing, backbiting, grumbling, murmuring, and being divisive. We are to love the brotherhood of all believers everywhere.

> Jesus replied: "'Love the Lord your God with all your heart and with all your soul and with all your mind.' This is the first and greatest commandment. And the second is like it: 'Love your neighbor as yourself.' All the Law and the Prophets hang on these two commandments." (Mat 22:37-40)
>
> "A new command I give you: Love one another. As I have loved you, so you must love one another. By this all men will know that you are my disciples, if you love one another." (John 13:34-35)
>
> My command is this: Love each other as I have loved you. (John 15:12)
>
> Love must be sincere. Hate what is evil; cling to what is good. (Rom 12:9)
>
> May the Lord make your love increase and overflow for each other and for every-

one else, just as ours does for you. (1 Th 3:12)

Now that you have purified yourselves by obeying the truth so that you have sincere love for your brothers, love one another deeply, from the heart. (1 Pet 1:22)

3. Fear God. Do not fail in your duty to obey God as a citizen nor as a member of God's church. Fear God. His will and commandments are to be obeyed. Fear what will happen if you disobey God. The idea is that judgment is coming and disobedience will bring the judgment of God down upon you.

Do not be afraid of those who kill the body but cannot kill the soul. Rather, be afraid of the One who can destroy both soul and body in hell. (Mat 10:28)

Since you call on a Father who judges each man's work impartially, live your lives as strangers here in reverent fear. (1 Pet 1:17)

And now, O Israel, what does the LORD your God ask of you but to fear the LORD your God, to walk in all his ways, to love him, to serve the LORD your God with all your heart and with all your soul, (Deu 10:12)

The LORD Almighty is the one you are to regard as holy, he is the one you are to fear, he is the one you are to dread, (Isa 8:13)

4. Honor the king or supreme authority of the nation. Remember: the evil and infamous Nero was on the throne when this was being written and the believers were being persecuted by the authorities (Nero ruled A.D. 54-68). But note: believers are to be a people of order and discipline, of righteousness and justice. They are to set a dynamic example of love and peace so that some can be won to Christ and be saved for eternity.

Paul replied, "Brothers, I did not realize [know] that he was the high priest; for it is written: 'Do not speak evil about the ruler of your people.'" (Acts 23:5)

Everyone must submit himself to the governing authorities, for there is no authority except that which God has established. The authorities that exist have been established by God. (Rom 13:1)

"Do not blaspheme God or curse the ruler of your people. (Exo 22:28)

	I. Submit to Masters or Employers, 2:18-20
1 Submit with all respect	18 Slaves, submit yourselves to your masters with all respect, not only to those who are good and considerate, but also to those who are harsh.
2 Submit to both the good & the unfair master or employer	
3 Submit for conscience' sake, that is, being conscious of God	19 For it is commendable if a man bears up under the pain of unjust suffering because he is conscious of God.
4 Submit in order to secure God's commendation	20 But how is it to your credit if you receive a beating for doing wrong and endure it? But if you suffer for doing good and you endure it, this is commendable before God.

DIVISION II

HOW TO LIVE THROUGH SUFFERING: GIVE YOUR LIFE TO GOD, 1:13-3:12

I. Submit to Masters or Employers, 2:18-20

(2:18-20) **Introduction**: William Barclay points out that there were millions and millions of slaves in the Roman Empire during the days of Paul. He says that there were over sixty million (*The Letters of James and Peter*, p.249). The gospel was bound to reach many of these, and the churches all over the Empire were bound to be filled with slaves. For this reason the New Testament has much to say to slaves (1 Cor.7:21-22; Col.3:22; 4:1; 1 Tim.6:1-2; Tit.2:9-10; 1 Pt.2:18-25 and the whole book of Philemon is written to a slave). However, slavery is never directly attacked by the New Testament. If it had been, there would have probably been so much bloodshed the scene would have been unimaginable! The slave owners and government would have...

- attacked the church, its preachers and believers, seeking to destroy such a doctrine.
- imprisoned and executed any who refused to be silent about such a doctrine.
- reacted and killed all of the slaves who professed Christ.

The Expositors Greek Testament has an excellent statement on how Christianity went about destroying slavery:

"Here, as elsewhere in the NT, slavery is accepted as an existing institution, which is neither formally condemned nor formally approved. There is nothing to prompt revolutionary action, or to encourage repudiation of the position...the institution is left to be undermined and removed by the gradual operation of the great Christian principles of...
- the equality of men in the sight of God
- a common Christian brotherhood
- the spiritual freedom of the Christian man
- *the Lordship of Christ to which every other lordship is subordinate*" (Salmond, SDF. *The Epistle to the Ephesians.* "The Expositor's Greek Testament," Vol.3, ed. by W. Robertson Nicoll. Grand Rapids, MI: Eerdmans, 1970, p.377).

The instructions to slaves and masters in the New Testament are applicable to every generation of workmen. As Francis Foulkes says, "...the principles of the whole section apply to employees and employers in every age, whether in the home, in business, or in the state" (*The Epistle of Paul to the Ephesians.* "Tyndale New Testament Commentaries," ed. by RVG Tasker. Grand Rapids, MI: Eerdmans, p.167).

1. He is to submit with all respect (v.18).
2. He is to submit to both the good and the unfair master or employer (v.18).
3. He is to submit for conscience' sake, that is, being conscious of God (v.19).
4. He is to submit in order to secure God's commendation (v.20).

1 (2:18) **Slaves—Employees**: the Christian slave or workman is to submit himself to his master or employer with all respect. The word *submit* means to be submissive and to obey. He is to follow the instructions of the person over him. In the workplace there is no instruction that is not to be obeyed. This, of course, does not mean he is to obey when the orders are contrary to the teaching of Scripture and damaging to himself or to others. However, it does mean that the Christian workman is to do what he is told to do. Why? Because he has been given the privilege of a job, the privilege...

- to earn a livelihood and to provide for himself and his family.
- to serve humanity through providing some needed product or service.
- to earn enough to help meet the desperate needs of the world and to carry the gospel to the world.

The attitude of the Christian workman is that the energy and effort he puts into his job is important to the Lord. Note: the slave and employee is to submit "with all respect." He is to labor respecting the Lord. This is to be the very mark of the Christian workman. It is to be his respect and reverence for the Lord that stands out to those working around him. Every man is to be judged for what he does upon this earth, judged for the kinds of things he does and judged for how diligently he did the good things. The Christian workman knows…

- that God is watching his diligence.
- that God is going to reward him for his diligence.
- that the heavenly work that is to be awarded him is being determined by his faithfulness and diligence upon earth.

Therefore, the Christian workman labors ever so diligently in the respect and reverence of the Lord—labors arduously lest he become disqualified and miss out on the best that God has.

> **No, I beat my body and make it my slave so that after I have preached to others, I myself will not be disqualified for the prize. (1 Cor 9:27)**
>
> **Do not be afraid of those who kill the body but cannot kill the soul. Rather, be afraid of the One who can destroy both soul and body in hell. (Mat 10:28)**
>
> **His mercy extends to those who fear him, from generation to generation. (Luke 1:50)**
>
> **But accepts men from every nation who fear him and do what is right. (Acts 10:35)**
>
> **Since you call on a Father who judges each man's work impartially, live your lives as strangers here in reverent fear. (1 Pet 1:17)**
>
> **Who, then, is the man that fears the LORD? He will instruct him in the way chosen for him. (Psa 25:12)**
>
> **How great is your goodness, which you have stored up for those who fear you, which you bestow in the sight of men on those who take refuge in you. (Psa 31:19)**

2 (2:18) **Slaves—Employees—Masters—Employers**: the Christian slave or workman is to submit himself to both the good and the unfair master. Note two things.

1. It is a wonderful thing when a Christian workman can have a good and considerate master or employer. It is even more wonderful when the employer himself is a Christian. Under a good and considerate employer the workman can expect to be treated justly and fairly and in a brotherly spirit. However, the workman faces a serious danger, the danger of feeling that he should…

- be given special treatment.
- be allowed to slack off some.
- be treated with more leniency.
- be given more consideration.
- not be as readily corrected or rebuked for inefficiency or mistakes.

In the case of slaves in the Roman empire, or for that matter anywhere else, the slave would have faced the temptation to *despise or be disrespectful* of his master. He could have easily felt that a master, upon becoming a believer, should grant his freedom or at least show some favor. However, the fact that a master became a Christian did not mean that a believing slave was to appeal for better and easier treatment. On the contrary, the believing slave was to become the best worker he could because the master was now a Christian believer.

Once the believing slave became the best worker possible—once he began to work diligently as though he was working for Christ—then he could expect to reap some benefits from having a Christian master. He could expect to reap benefits such as fair and decent and brotherly treatment. Believing slaves were to treat believing masters as brothers, faithful and beloved, and there was to be a greater testimony because of greater production and efficiency and fruitfulness.

The point is this: the Christian workman is to give great service to a Christian employer because faithfulness bears fruit. Both the workman and employer doing the best they can will bear more fruit of the Spirit and a greater production of work. Thereby they will together bear a greater testimony for Christ.

> **Thought 1.** In reality, being a slave or a master has nothing to do with a person's commitment to life and work. The believing Christian, whether slave or master, is to do the very best he can at whatever he is doing. His state or condition or environment or circumstance is to have nothing to do with faithfulness to his work. He is to do his very best no matter who or where he is. (See note—1 Cor.7:20-23; 7:24. Cp.Eph.6:6-7; Col.3:23-25.)

2. There is the Christian workman's duty to the unfair and cruel masters or employers. The Christian workman is to subject even to the overbearing and crooked employers. Why? Why would Scripture demand such a thing? The Book of First Timothy tells us: "All who are under the yoke of slavery should consider their masters worthy of full respect, so that God's name and our teaching may not be slandered." (1 Tim.6:1).

God does not want His name blasphemed. He wants no believer failing in his duty to love and to witness to all men. God wants all men to be won to Christ, no matter who they are or how unfair and cruel they may be. This may be a bitter pill to swallow; nevertheless, it is what God says. What is often overlooked is this: if the workman does not give a full day's work for a full day's wage, he dishonors the name of Christ. If the workman is lazy, slothful, and beating time, or if he is disrespectful, the employer or supervisor knows something: the God of the new convert is a laugh, for He is inactive and dead. God has made no difference in the life of the workman. Therefore, the employer or supervisor slanders the name of God and the teachings of the gospel.

> **Slaves [workmen], obey your earthly masters with respect and fear, and with sincerity of heart, just as you would obey Christ. Obey them not only to win their favor when their eye is on you, but like slaves of Christ, doing the will of God from your heart. Serve wholeheartedly, as if you were serving the Lord, not men, because you know that the Lord will reward everyone for whatever good he does, whether he is slave or free. (Eph 6:5-8)**
>
> **Slaves, obey your earthly masters in everything; and do it, not only when their eye is on you and to win their favor, but with sincerity of heart and reverence for the Lord. Whatever you do, work at it with all your heart, as working for the Lord, not for men, since you know that you will receive an inheritance from the Lord as a reward. It is the Lord Christ you are serving.**

Anyone who does wrong will be repaid for his wrong, and there is no favoritism. (Col 3:22-25)

3 (2:19) **Slaves—Employees**: the Christian slave or workman is to submit for conscience' sake, that is, being conscious of God. As A.T. Robertson says: "Suffering is not a blessing in and of itself, but, if one's duty to God is involved (Acts 4:20), then one can meet it with gladness of heart" (*Word Pictures In The New Testament*, Vol.6, p.103).

Alan Stibbs says:

"[Conscience] is best understood in the sense of consciousness....The whole phrase, therefore, means prompted by a conscious awareness of God's presence and will. Such a man knows that God sees, and knows what God expects. His concern is to please Him" (*The First Epistle General of Peter*. "The Tyndale New Testament Commentaries," p.115).

Pulpit Commentary says:

"Conscience of God; that is, consciousness of God's presence, of His will, of our duties to Him" (B.C. Coffin. *First Peter*. "The Pulpit Commentary," Vol.22, p.75.)

The point is this: the Christian workman is to submit himself to his master or employer in order to please God. God loves all employers, no matter how unjust or unfair, and God wants every employer to be reached for Christ. The only hope of his ever being reached is for Christian believers to live pure, holy, and righteous lives before him and then sharing Christ with him as opportunity arises. If the Christian workman fails to live for Christ by shirking or failing in his duty at work, then he is failing to please God. His conscience is going to bug, convict, and cause problems for him. His fellowship with God is broken, and he is living a lie, walking contrary to God's standard.

So I strive always to keep my conscience clear before God and man. (Acts 24:16)
Therefore, it is necessary to submit to the authorities, not only because of possible punishment but also because of conscience. (Rom 13:5)
Now this is our boast: Our conscience testifies that we have conducted ourselves in the world, and especially in our relations with you, in the holiness and sincerity that are from God. We have done so not according to worldly wisdom but according to God's grace. (2 Cor 1:12)
The goal of this command is love, which comes from a pure heart and a good conscience and a sincere faith. (1 Tim 1:5)
Holding on to faith and a good conscience. Some have rejected these and so have shipwrecked their faith. (1 Tim 1:19)
How much more, then, will the blood of Christ, who through the eternal Spirit offered himself unblemished to God, cleanse our consciences from acts that lead to death, so that we may serve the living God! (Heb 9:14)

Keeping a clear conscience, so that those who speak maliciously against your good behavior in Christ may be ashamed of their slander. (1 Pet 3:16)

4 (2:20) **Slaves—Employees**: the Christian slave or workman is to submit in order to secure God's commendation. This verse is as direct and straightforward as it can be.

⇒ No person is going to be commendable to God if he does wrong; but if he does well, he shall be commendable to God. It is that simple; the fact that a person might suffer for doing good has nothing to do with it. God is good; therefore, for a person to be commendable to God, the person must do good.

Now, put the verse in context. It is talking about Christian slaves and workmen. It does no good and there is no glory to suffer for wrongdoing. But if you do good and people mistreat you for doing good, then you are going to be commendable to God. You are commendable not because you suffered, but because you did good. If a Christian workman is to be commendable to God, he must do good, work and labor just as Christ tells him to do.

The point is this: the Christian workman is to work at it with all his heart, as working for the Lord, not for men. This is exactly what Scripture declares.

Whatever you do, work at it with all your heart, as working for the Lord, not for men, since you know that you will receive an inheritance from the Lord as a reward. It is the Lord Christ you are serving. Anyone who does wrong will be repaid for his wrong, and there is no favoritism. (Col 3:23-25)

The phrase "all his heart" (ek pusches) means *out of the soul*. The Christian workman's labor is to arise out of his soul, from the innermost part of his being. He is not working for the men of this earth, but for the Lord. He is working for the deepest reason possible, for a reason that arises out of his very soul: the Lord Jesus Christ has told him to work and to work diligently. The Lord Jesus is his Lord; therefore, the Christian workman does what his Lord says. But note: there are two other critical reasons why he works diligently.

1. Diligent work will be rewarded by Christ. On earth the workman may be mistreated, used, misused, abused, cheated, by-passed, and taken advantage of; but the Lord knows, and He is going to abundantly reward the diligent workman. In fact, the reward of the inheritance simply explodes the human mind. It stretches far beyond and above all that we can ask or even think. It includes a new body that will be eternal, a new heavens and earth, and positions of enormous leadership, authority, and service for the Lord Jesus. (See notes—Lk.16:10-12; Ro.4:13; Deeper Study # 4—8:17 for more discussion.)

Now it is required that those who have been given a trust must prove faithful. (1 Cor 4:2)
Therefore, my dear brothers, stand firm. Let nothing move you. Always give yourselves fully to the work of the Lord, because you know that your labor in the Lord is not in vain. (1 Cor 15:58)

Each one should use whatever gift he has received to serve others, faithfully administering God's grace in its various forms. (1 Pet 4:10)

2. Slothful work and idleness will be judged by Christ. Many workmen do wrong on the job; they do wrong by...

- being slothful
- being lazy
- being irresponsible
- being unconcerned
- being unproductive
- being uncaring
- being prejudiced
- cheating
- stealing
- lying
- being careless
- being selfish
- being unfair

The list could go on and on. The point is this: every single person on earth is going to face God for the wrong he has done on the job. He will give an account for his labor and be judged exactly for what he has done. And note: there is no respect of persons. Everyone is going to stand before God—no matter who he is.

"His master replied, 'Well done, good and faithful servant! You have been faithful with a few things; I will put you in charge of many things. Come and share your master's happiness!' (Mat 25:23)

For we must all appear before the judgment seat of Christ, that each one may receive what is due him for the things done while in the body, whether good or bad. (2 Cor 5:10)

Anyone who does wrong will be repaid for his wrong, and there is no favoritism. (Col 3:25)

	J. Follow Christ's Great Suffering,DS1 2:21-25	taliate; when he suffered, he made no threats. Instead, he entrusted himself to him who judges justly.	
1 The great call of believers: To suffer for Christ even as He suffered for us	21 To this you were called, because Christ suffered for you, leaving you an example, that you should follow in his	24 He himself bore our sins in his body on the tree, so that we might die to sins and live for righteousness; by his	d. He suffered to the ultimate degree: Bore our sins in His body
2 The great suffering of Christ a. He suffered *for you*. b. He did not deserve to suffer: He had lived a sinless & perfect life	steps. 22 "He committed no sin, and no deceit was found in his mouth."	wounds you have been healed. 25 For you were like sheep going astray, but now you	e. He suffered that we might live for righteousness 3 The great need that believers haveDS2
c. He voluntarily & willingly suffered	23 When they hurled their insults at him, he did not re-	have returned to the Shepherd and Overseer of your souls.	a. We were going astray b. We have now returned

DIVISION II

HOW TO LIVE THROUGH SUFFERING: GIVE YOUR LIFE TO GOD, 1:13-3:12

J. Follow Christ's Great Suffering, 2:21-25

(2:21-25) **Introduction**: the one thing that God wants is a genuine life. He wants believers to live for Christ, to live exactly what they profess. He wants us to follow Christ ever so closely, and He wants us to bear whatever suffering has to be borne in following Him. This is the great discussion of this great passage: follow Christ in His suffering. In these words we have one of the clearest and most descriptive pictures of what the sufferings of Christ were.

1. The great call of believers: to suffer for Christ even as He suffered for us (v.21).
2. The great suffering of Christ (v.21-24).
3. The great need that believers have (v.25).

DEEPER STUDY # 1

(2:21-25) **Jesus Christ, Death**: there are at least four references to Isaiah 53 in this passage: v.22 (Is.53:9); v.23 (Is.53:7); v.24 (Is.53:5, 12); v.25 (Is.53:6).

It should be remembered that Peter was an eyewitness to Jesus' life and sufferings upon the cross. He says three things about the death of Christ (see note—Eph.5:2; cp. 2 Cor.5:21).

1. Christ "suffered for you" (v.21). That is, His death took the place of sinners.
2. Christ "committed no sin" (v.22). That is, He was sinless; He had lived a perfect and righteous life. Therefore the sins He bore in death were not His sins but the sins of men.
3. Christ "bore our sins in his body" (v.24). That is, the suffering Jesus bore was the penalty due sin.

In the Old Testament, the words "bore our sins" means to be answerable for sin; to endure its penalty; to die for sinners (Ex.28:43; Lev.24:15-16; Is.53:12). Thus, the death Jesus bore was substitution; He bore the sins due others. It is this act that shows the supreme love of God for man.

1 (2:21) **Suffering—Believers—Call**: there is the great call of believers—to suffer for Christ even as Christ suffered for us. Believers are called to suffer for Christ. What does this mean?

⇒ Any person who follows Christ—who lives a pure and righteous life—is going to be rejected by the world. The world wants little to do with purity and righteousness. People want to live like they want and to do their own thing. Therefore,

they ridicule, mock, ignore, abuse, bypass, ignore, and persecute anyone who lives a strict life of purity and righteousness.

⇒ Any person who lives a self-denying life—who sacrifices all he is and has to meet the needs of a lost and dying world—is going to be rejected by the world. People are not willing to live unselfish and sacrificial lives to meet the needs of the poor, starving, diseased, and lost masses of the world. People want more and more comfort and recognition, possessions and pleasure, money and property. Therefore, they want little to do with a person who sacrifices and proclaims a message of sacrifice.

But note: this is the very life to which Christ calls us. In fact, it is the only call Christ gives to men: the call to holy and sacrificial living—the call to love God and people, to love God so much that we live godly lives and to love people so much that we help them even to the point of sacrifice.

The point is this: Christ suffered for us. He gave everything He was and had to meet our need. Therefore, we are to follow His example. We are to live holy lives and sacrifice all we are and have to meet the needs of the world; and we are to suffer whatever ridicule, abuse, and persecution comes our way. Scripture is strong about this:

⇒ Note the word *example*. Christ has left us an "example" (hupogrammon). The word means the pattern of some picture or letter that a teacher gives to the pupil. The pattern is to be copied or reproduced. The idea is that an exact copy is to be made; every detail of the pattern is to be reproduced. The exhortation is that we are to be an exact copy of Christ; we are to follow the pattern of Christ in every detail.

⇒ The word "follow" (epakolouthesete) is the picture of a guide leading us along a most difficult and rocky path, so difficult that we must actually put our feet in his footprints (B.C. Coffin. *First Peter*. "The Pulpit Commentary," Vol.22, p.75.). We are to follow Christ step by step, moment by moment, and day by day.

Remember the point: Christ has given us a great call—to follow Him and to suffer for Him and His cause even as He suffered for us. What is His cause? To love God supremely by living a holy life and to love the lost and dying of the world by meeting their desperate needs.

2 (2:21-24) **Jesus Christ, Death**: there was the great suffering of Jesus Christ. Remember how close Peter was to Jesus. He was the big fisherman, the leader of the twelve apostles, one of the three closest persons to Christ when Christ was upon earth (James and John were the other two). If anyone knew Christ during the Lord's ministry, Peter knew Him. What we are about to read and study is exactly what Peter thought about Christ and His death. Therefore, what is being said needs to be closely observed and heeded. Peter says five things about the death of Christ.

1. Christ suffered "for you" (v.21). The word "for" (huper) is a simple word with profound meaning when used with the death of Christ. It proclaims the most wonderful truth known to man. Note this striking truth: it does *not mean* that Christ died only as an example for us, showing us how we should be willing to die for the truth or for some great cause. What it means is that Christ died *in our place, in our stead, in our room, as our substitute.* This meaning is unquestionably clear. (See notes—Eph.5:2; DEEPER STUDY # 1—1 Pt.2:21-25 for more discussion.)

   a. The idea of sacrifice to the Jewish and pagan mind of that day was the idea of a life given in another's place. It was *a substitutionary sacrifice.*

   b. The idea of sacrifice is often in the very context of the words, "Christ gave himself up *for us*" (Eph.5:2).

> **I am the living bread that came down from heaven. If anyone eats of this bread, he will live forever. This bread is my flesh, which I will give for the life of the world." (John 6:51)**
>
> **"I am the good shepherd. The good shepherd lays down his life for the sheep. (John 10:11)**
>
> **Just as the Father knows me and I know the Father—and I lay down my life for the sheep. (John 10:15)**
>
> **He did not say this on his own, but as high priest that year he prophesied that Jesus would die for the Jewish nation, (John 11:51)**
>
> **Greater love has no one than this, that he lay down his life for his friends. (John 15:13)**
>
> **For them I sanctify myself, that they too may be truly sanctified. (John 17:19) (Cp. Ro.8:32; Gal.1:4; 2:20; Eph.5:2; 1 Tim.2:6; Tit.2:14.)**

2. Christ did not deserve to suffer (v.22). He had lived a sinless and perfect life (v.22; cp. Is.53:9). Peter clearly says that Jesus Christ "committed no sin, and no deceit was found in his mouth." Jesus Christ never sinned and never deceived a person. Remember: Peter has already declared this amazing fact:

> **For you know that it was not with perishable things such as silver or gold that you were redeemed from the empty way of life handed down to you from your forefathers, but with the precious blood of Christ, a lamb without blemish or defect. (1 Pet 1:18-19)**

This means the most wonderful thing: Jesus Christ is the Perfect and Ideal Man. Since He never sinned, there is no unrighteousness in Him. He stands before God as the Perfect and Ideal Man, the very embodiment of righteousness. Therefore, His righteousness can cover and stand for man. Any person who truly believes in Jesus Christ is accepted in the righteousness of Jesus Christ. The person is covered by the perfect and ideal righteousness of Jesus Christ.

> **He was assigned a grave with the wicked, and with the rich in his death, though he had done no violence, nor was any deceit in his mouth. (Isa 53:9)**
>
> **Can any of you prove me guilty of sin? If I am telling the truth, why don't you believe me? (John 8:46)**
>
> **God made him who had no sin to be sin for us, so that in him we might become the righteousness of God. (2 Cor 5:21)**
>
> **For we do not have a high priest who is unable to sympathize with our weaknesses, but we have one who has been tempted in every way, just as we are—yet was without sin. (Heb 4:15)**
>
> **Such a high priest meets our need—one who is holy, blameless, pure, set apart from sinners, exalted above the heavens. (Heb 7:26)**
>
> **But with the precious blood of Christ, a lamb without blemish or defect. (1 Pet 1:19)**
>
> **"He committed no sin, and no deceit was found in his mouth." (1 Pet 2:22)**

3. Christ willingly and voluntarily suffered (v.23). This is seen in three facts.

   a. He was insulted, but He did not retaliate and hurl insults back at the attackers. The picture is that He was cursed, blasphemed, ridiculed, mocked, and insulted; but He bore it all willingly and voluntarily. He did not have to bear it. He was the Son of God, and He could have stopped everyone in their tracks. But He had come to save them, not to condemn them.

   b. He suffered, was abused, beaten, pushed around, and crowned with a crown of thorns; but He suffered it willingly. He did not even threaten the unbelievers and persecutors.

   c. He entrusted Himself to God knowing that God would vindicate Him. He knew that God judges righteously and fairly; therefore, He committed His life into the hands of God. The word "entrusted" (paredidou) means to hand over; to deliver into the hands of. Jesus Christ handed over His life to God; He delivered His life into the hands and keeping of God. Again, He did not have to suffer death, for He had the power to stop it all. But He had come to save men; therefore he willingly suffered, committing His death and cause into the hands of God. He knew that God would raise Him up and prove His claim to be the Son of God, the Savior of the world.

> **"I am the good shepherd. The good shepherd lays down his life for the sheep. (John 10:11)**
>
> **Just as the Father knows me and I know the Father—and I lay down my life for the sheep. (John 10:15)**

The reason my Father loves me is that I lay down my life—only to take it up again. No one takes it from me, but I lay it down of my own accord. I have authority to lay it down and authority to take it up again. This command I received from my Father." (John 10:17-18)

And live a life of love, just as Christ loved us and gave himself up for us as a fragrant offering and sacrifice to God. (Eph 5:2)

This is how we know what love is: Jesus Christ laid down his life for us. And we ought to lay down our lives for our brothers. (1 John 3:16)

4. Christ suffered to the ultimate degree: He bore our sins in His body (v.24). Nothing could be any clearer to the honest and open heart:

[Jesus Christ] himself bore our sins in his body on the tree (1 Pt.2:24).

Jesus Christ took our sins upon Himself—the guilt, judgment and punishment—and bore them for us. This is what is meant when we say that *Jesus Christ died for us*. He took all the sins of all men of all time upon Himself. He bore all the sin—all the guilt, judgment and punishment of sin and He died for it all. He bore the penalty for our sins.

How could Christ do this? How could one person bear the sins of all people? By having lived a sinless life. Jesus Christ was the Perfect and Ideal Man; therefore, whatever He did was acceptable to God. When Jesus Christ died, His death was the death of the Ideal and Perfect Man. Therefore, His death stands for and covers the death of all men.

But he was pierced for our transgressions, he was crushed for our iniquities; the punishment that brought us peace was upon him, and by his wounds we are healed. (Isa 53:5)

Christ redeemed us from the curse of the law by becoming a curse for us, for it is written: "Cursed is everyone who is hung on a tree." (Gal 3:13)

But we see Jesus, who was made a little lower than the angels, now crowned with glory and honor because he suffered death, so that by the grace of God he might taste death for everyone. (Heb 2:9)

For Christ died for sins once for all, the righteous for the unrighteous, to bring you to God. He was put to death in the body but made alive by the Spirit, (1 Pet 3:18)

5. Christ suffered for sins that we might die to sins and live for righteousness (v.24). What does this mean? How can a person die to sins? By believing in Jesus Christ and His death for our sins. There is no other way to die to sins. Every honest and thinking person knows this. We all sin and are ever so short of perfection and righteousness. Our only hope of ever being counted righteous and acceptable by God has to be through the righteousness of some ideal and perfect person. It has to be, for there is no righteous man. None of us have ever seen or ever will see a man who is perfect and sinless and righteous. But this is the glorious gospel: the righteousness and death of Jesus Christ

covers us. When we truly believe that Jesus Christ died for us, God takes our belief and counts it so.

⇒ He counts us as having died when Christ died.
⇒ He counts the death of Christ for our death.

Jesus Christ died for us; He bore the penalty, the judgment, and the punishment for our sin. Therefore, when we really believe and trust Jesus Christ as our Savior, we become free of sin. God actually accepts us in the righteousness of Jesus Christ. God no longer charges or counts sin against us. We are freed of sin and we stand before God as righteous and perfect—all because of Christ. We are healed of all our sins by the wounds which He suffered and bore. (See note, *Justified*—Ro.5:1 for more discussion.)

For all have sinned and fall short of the glory of God, and are justified freely by his grace through the redemption that came by Christ Jesus. (Rom 3:23-24)

Therefore, since we have been justified through faith, we have peace with God through our Lord Jesus Christ, (Rom 5:1)

Since we have now been justified by his blood, how much more shall we be saved from God's wrath through him! (Rom 5:9)

Because anyone who has died has been freed from sin. (Rom 6:7)

Who will bring any charge against those whom God has chosen? It is God who justifies. (Rom 8:33)

Consider Abraham: "He believed God, and it was credited to him as righteousness." (Gal 3:6)

Those who belong to Christ Jesus have crucified the sinful nature with its passions and desires. (Gal 5:24)

For you died, and your life is now hidden with Christ in God. (Col 3:3)

He himself bore our sins in his body on the tree, so that we might die to sins and live for righteousness; by his wounds you have been healed. (1 Pet 2:24)

3 (2:25) **Salvation—Jesus Christ, Names and Titles, Shepherd and Bishop:** there is the great need that believers have: to return to the Lord. Believers need to always remember what they were, and note: what is said about their past is true of all men.

1. Believers had been as sheep going astray. They had wandered away from God. They had been attracted by the greener grass of the world and had forsaken God for the world and its food and pleasures. They had wanted to live and wander about as they desired and to do their own thing. Therefore, they turned away from God and His pasture.

2. Believers had, however, returned to the Shepherd and Overseer of their souls. They had repented and turned back to God.

   a. They had returned to the Shepherd of their soul. The shepherd is a picture of Christ, a picture of the love, peace, joy, care, provision, protection, and security which He gives to those who turn to Him and follow Him day by day. (See DEEPER STUDY # 2—1 Pt.2:25 for more discussion.)

   b. They had returned to the Overseer of their souls. The word "overseer" (episkopon) means caretaker, guardian, protector, guide, and director (William Barclay. *The Letters of James and Peter,* p.258). It is the picture of Christ watching over our souls and looking after them with the greatest of care. Jesus Christ is our Overseer, Caretaker, Guardian, Protector, Guide, and Director. When we come to Him, He takes complete charge of our lives.

And saying, "Repent, for the kingdom of heaven is near." (Mat 3:2)

Blessed are those who mourn, for they will be comforted. (Mat 5:4)

Peter replied, "Repent and be baptized, every one of you, in the name of Jesus Christ for the forgiveness of your sins. And you will receive the gift of the Holy Spirit. (Acts 2:38)

Repent, then, and turn to God, so that your sins may be wiped out, that times of refreshing may come from the Lord, (Acts 3:19)

Repent of this wickedness and pray to the Lord. Perhaps he will forgive you for having such a thought in your heart. (Acts 8:22)

If my people, who are called by my name, will humble themselves and pray and seek my face and turn from their wicked ways, then will I hear from heaven and will forgive their sin and will heal their land. (2 Chr 7:14)

He who conceals his sins does not prosper, but whoever confesses and renounces them finds mercy. (Prov 28:13)

Let the wicked forsake his way and the evil man his thoughts. Let him turn to the LORD, and he will have mercy on him, and to our God, for he will freely pardon. (Isa 55:7)

Only acknowledge your guilt— you have rebelled against the LORD your God, you have scattered your favors to foreign gods under every spreading tree, and have not obeyed me,'" declares the LORD. (Jer 3:13)

"But if a wicked man turns away from all the sins he has committed and keeps all my decrees and does what is just and right, he will surely live; he will not die. (Ezek 18:21)

DEEPER STUDY # 2

(2:25) **Shepherd**: the Shepherd leads and shepherds the sheep. He loves them as His own; therefore He must lead them to the green pastures and still waters. He must see that they are nourished and protected and given the very best care possible. (See note—Mk.6:34 for more discussion, what happens to sheep without a Shepherd.)

1. He feeds the sheep even if He has to gather them in His arms and carry them to the feeding pasture.

**He tends his flock like a shepherd:
He gathers the lambs in his arms and**

carries them close to his heart; he gently leads those that have young. (Isa 40:11)

2. He guides the sheep to the pasture and away from the rough places and precipices.

A psalm of David. The LORD is my shepherd, I shall not be in want. He makes me lie down in green pastures, he leads me beside quiet waters, he restores my soul. He guides me in paths of righteousness for his name's sake. Even though I walk through the valley of the shadow of death, I will fear no evil, for you are with me; your rod and your staff, they comfort me. (Psa 23:1-4)

3. He seeks and saves the sheep who get lost.

"What do you think? If a man owns a hundred sheep, and one of them wanders away, will he not leave the ninety-nine on the hills and go to look for the one that wandered off? (Mat 18:12)

I will search for the lost and bring back the strays. I will bind up the injured and strengthen the weak, but the sleek and the strong I will destroy. I will shepherd the flock with justice. (Ezek 34:16)

4. He protects the sheep. He even sacrifices His life for the sheep.

"I am the good shepherd. The good shepherd lays down his life for the sheep. (John 10:11)

May the God of peace, who through the blood of the eternal covenant brought back from the dead our Lord Jesus, that great Shepherd of the sheep, (Heb 13:20)

5. He restores the sheep who go astray and return.

For you were like sheep going astray, but now you have returned to the Shepherd and Overseer of your souls. (1 Pet 2:25)

6. He rewards the sheep for obedience and faithfulness.

And when the Chief Shepherd appears, you will receive the crown of glory that will never fade away. (1 Pet 5:4)

7. He shall keep the sheep separate from the goats.

All the nations will be gathered before him, and he will separate the people one from another as a shepherd separates the sheep from the goats. He will put the sheep on his right and the goats on his left. (Mat 25:32-33)

	CHAPTER 3	elry and fine clothes.	
		4 Instead, it should be that of your inner self, the unfading beauty of a gentle and quiet spirit, which is of great worth in God's sight.	**5 Adorn or dress your heart with a gentle & quiet spirit**
	K. Submit to One's Own Husband, 3:1-6		a. The great example of the holy women of old
1 Live in submission to your own husband	**W**ives, in the same way be submissive to your husbands so that, if any of them do not believe the word, they may be won over without words by the behavior of their wives,	5 For this is the way the holy women of the past who put their hope in God used to make themselves beautiful. They were submissive to their own husbands,	b. The great example of Sarah, the spiritual mother of believers
2 Live a pure life	2 When they see the purity and reverence of your lives.	their own husbands,	
3 Live a reverent life before God	3 Your beauty should not come from outward adornment, such as braided hair and the wearing of gold jew-	6 Like Sarah, who obeyed Abraham and called him her master. You are her daughters if you do what is right and do not give way to fear.	
4 Do not dress to attract attention			

DIVISION II

HOW TO LIVE THROUGH SUFFERING: GIVE YOUR LIFE TO GOD, 1:13-3:12

K. Submit to One's Own Husband, 3:1-6

(3:1-6) **Introduction**: What is the duty of the Christian wife to her husband and of the Christian husband to his wife? This is the discussion of this passage and of the next passage. Remember: the major subject of chapters 1:13-3:12 is *giving your life to God*. If a woman wants to give her life to God, then she has to give herself, that is, submit herself, to her *own* husband. Scripture says that she has to do five specific things.

1. Live in submission to your own husband (v.1).
2. Live a pure life (v.2).
3. Live a reverent life before God (v.2).
4. Do not dress to attract attention (v.3).
5. Adorn or dress your heart with a gentle and quiet spirit (v.4-6).

1 (3:1) **Wife—Family—Marriage**: the wife's duty is to submit herself to her husband even if he does not believe God's Word. Scripture is clear and pointed about this. The word "submissive" (hupotassomenai) means just what it says—to be in submission; to submit oneself. The Greek scholar Marvin Vincent says that it is used of the *submission of servants* (*Word Studies In The New Testament*, Vol.1. Grand Rapids, MI: Eerdmans, 1946, p.65). (Cp. 1 Pt.2:18.) The word means that a Christian wife is to place herself under the authority and control of her husband; that she is to submit herself to her own husband's authority, control, and leadership. There is no question but that this is what the word means.

⇒ Vine says that it is primarily a military term meaning to *rank under* (*Expository Dictionary of New Testament Words*. Old Tappan, NJ: Fleming H. Revell, 1966). .

⇒ Robertson says that the word has a military air and that the word is the same kind of obedience that a citizen is to give to the government. (See his comments on Col.3:18, *Word Pictures In The New Testament*, Vol.6.)

In modern society this is strong; in fact, it is too strong for many. Many reject the idea of woman's submission as archaic, outdated, and old-fashioned. Some even react in anger and hostility against the Word of God and those who preach the duty of wives.

Are they right? Has Scripture gone too far in declaring that wives should be submissive to their husbands? Has God made a mistake within the order of the family? To the Christian, the answer is *no*. The problem is not in what God has said, but in our *understanding of what He has said* or in our rebellion against what He wills. Any wife who reacts to God's command is reacting either because she does not understand what God is saying or is just *unwilling to give her life to God and follow Him as He says*. What does God mean by submission? God does not mean *dictatorial submission*...

• that a wife is to submit herself to a tyrant.
• that a wife is to submit herself to the demands of a husband who acts like a beast.
• that a wife is to be a slave or footstool for the husband.
• that a wife is to serve her husband without restraint.
• that a wife is to be treated as inferior to her husband.

What God means by submission is order, cooperation, relationship, and partnership—that a husband and wife are to walk *together*, *hand in hand*, throughout life. Every body of people—even when the body is only two persons—must have a leader who takes the lead in plowing through the wilderness of the world and its trials and temptations and difficulties. Between the two, wife and husband, one of them has to be the primary leader. God's order for the two is that the husband take the lead. The Christian wife, in obedience to her Lord, submits herself to her husband's leadership, authority, and control.

Note one other factor that points out just how seriously God takes the wife's submission to her husband. Even if the husband does not believe God's Word, the wife is to submit herself to him. Imagine what is being said to the wife, how strong this exhortation is:

⇒ Some husbands are unbelievers; they just refuse to heed God's Word.
⇒ Some husbands not only fail to believe in God, they rebel against and curse God. And they make life difficult for their wives because their wives do trust God.

70

⇒ Some husbands show their unbelief in God's Word by living unholy and sinful lives, and they neglect and ignore their wives.

⇒ Some husbands are believers in Christ, but they do not obey God's Word. They, too, mistreat their wives.

What does God expect of the wife? This passage of Scripture is clear: the wife is to submit herself to her own husband. But note why: that the husband may be won to Christ by the godly behavior of the wife. By living a life of purity and reverence, and by demonstrating a quiet and gentle spirit, the wife stands a good chance of winning her husband to the Lord.

Just what Scripture means by submission is clearly stated. Four things are meant. These are covered in the next four notes.

2 (3:2) **Wife—Marriage**: the wife is to submit herself by living a pure life. The word "pure" (hagnen) means to be pure from all fault; to be clean and holy and free from all defilement; to act and behave in the most pure and modest way possible. When a woman marries a man, she sets herself apart for him and him alone. She keeps herself clean and pure for him and for him alone. Note that the verse says, "Wives, be submissive to your [own] *husbands*." She does not submit or give herself to some other husband or man. She is her husband's and his alone.

Thought 1. A dirty wife or husband is never to be named among Christian believers. Nothing destroys the testimony of believers any more than sexual impurity. And nothing affects the love and the trust that couples can put in one another any more than sexual impurity. For this reason, the Christian wife is to submit herself to her husband by living a pure life.

> **Blessed are the pure in heart, for they will see God. (Mat 5:8)**
>
> **But I tell you that anyone who looks at a woman lustfully has already committed adultery with her in his heart. (Mat 5:28)**
>
> **It is God's will that you should be sanctified: that you should avoid sexual immorality; (1 Th 4:3)**
>
> **The goal of this command is love, which comes from a pure heart and a good conscience and a sincere faith. (1 Tim 1:5)**
>
> **Then they can train the younger women to love their husbands and children, to be self-controlled and pure, to be busy at home, to be kind, and to be subject to their husbands, so that no one will malign the word of God. (Titus 2:4-5)**
>
> **These are those who did not defile themselves with women, for they kept themselves pure. They follow the Lamb wherever he goes. They were purchased from among men and offered as firstfruits to God and the Lamb. (Rev 14:4)**

3 (3:2) **Wife**: the wife is to submit herself out of her reverence for God. To reverence God means that the wife stands in awe and fear of all that God is—in fear and awe of the magnificence of God's being. She stands in awe and fear of His love, care, power, justice, and judgment. It is this that stirs her to live for God and to do what God says.

She knows that God will strengthen her to live as she should: to submit herself to her husband no matter how much he fails to believe God's Word. She fears lest she herself fall under the condemnation of God.

It is this reverence that makes her submit herself to her husband. It is this fear and reverence for God that attracts her husband and wins him to the Lord.

> **Do not be afraid of those who kill the body but cannot kill the soul. Rather, be afraid of the One who can destroy both soul and body in hell. (Mat 10:28)**
>
> **Since you call on a Father who judges each man's work impartially, live your lives as strangers here in reverent fear. (1 Pet 1:17)**
>
> **Show proper respect to everyone: Love the brotherhood of believers, fear God, honor the king. (1 Pet 2:17)**
>
> **Ascribe to the LORD the glory due his name; worship the LORD in the splendor of his holiness. (Psa 29:2)**
>
> **Let all the earth fear the LORD; let all the people of the world revere him. (Psa 33:8)**
>
> **Glorify the LORD with me; let us exalt his name together. (Psa 34:3)**
>
> **O LORD, you are my God; I will exalt you and praise your name, for in perfect faithfulness you have done marvelous things, things planned long ago. (Isa 25:1)**

4 (3:3) **Wife—Dress**: the wife is to submit herself by not dressing to attract attention. The word "adornment" is really an accurate translation of what Scripture means. The word means the dress, ornaments, and arrangement of clothing upon the body; but the word also refers to behavior and demeanor, that is, the way a woman carries herself, walks, moves, and behaves in public. Remember: this passage is being written to genuine Christian women—women who truly believe in the Lord and wish to honor the Lord and to have a strong testimony for Him. The Christian woman wants to guard her clothing and to dress modestly; she wants to watch the way she dresses, walks, moves, and behaves in public. She wants to bring honor to the Lord and to build a strong testimony—a testimony that she does love the Lord and has committed her life…

• to help people, not to seduce them.
• to serve people, not to destroy them.
• to point people to Jesus, not to attract them to herself.
• to teach people righteous behavior, not fleshly and worldly behavior.

The point is that the wife does not dress, walk, move, speak, or behave to attract attention to her body. She is not to adorn herself…

• with braided: elaborate hairstyles; hairstyles that are so different that they break away from acceptable custom and attract attention to herself.
• with gold or expensive clothing: elaborate jewelry and clothing that is extravagant, ostentatious, flamboyant, and that attracts attention to herself.

How a woman dresses shows whether she lives in the fear and reverence of God or has desires for the world and the gaping and lustful attention of men. The Christian wife is not to adorn herself in a sensual or excessive manner.

⇒ She is not to adorn herself with unusual hairstyles.

⇒ She is not to adorn herself with extremely expensive clothes and jewelry.

⇒ She is not to adorn herself in any manner that will be immodest or impure and unclean.

⇒ She must not dress or behave *in any manner that would not be modest enough to appear before and to be seen by God*—in any manner that does not show fear and reverence for God.

⇒ She must not adorn herself in any manner that would cause her to be proud or puffed up.

⇒ She must not adorn herself with any dress or behavior that would attract and cause sensual or tempting thoughts to a man. (This shows anything but fear and reverence for God.)

> **Do not offer the parts of your body to sin, as instruments of wickedness, but rather offer yourselves to God, as those who have been brought from death to life; and offer the parts of your body to him as instruments of righteousness. (Rom 6:13)**

> **I also want women to dress modestly, with decency and propriety, not with braided hair or gold or pearls or expensive clothes, but with good deeds, appropriate for women who profess to worship God. (1 Tim 2:9-10)**

> **Your beauty should not come from outward adornment, such as braided hair and the wearing of gold jewelry and fine clothes. Instead, it should be that of your inner self, the unfading beauty of a gentle and quiet spirit, which is of great worth in God's sight. For this is the way the holy women of the past who put their hope in God used to make themselves beautiful. They were submissive to their own husbands, (1 Pet 3:3-5)**

Thought 1. A wife who dresses, walks, moves, speaks, and behaves to attract attention to herself (her body) is a great disappointment to her husband. Such behavior cuts and hurts her husband deeply. He may not admit it, out of pride. But such behavior mars his respect and love for his wife, usually forever.

5 (3:4-6) **Wife—Dress**: the wife is to submit herself by adorning or dressing her heart and spirit, by focusing upon the inner self. The inner self means the inner life, the inward person, the new creation that Christ has made her. Jesus Christ has given her a new heart, a new life, a new character. He has made her a new person, a totally new person. He has recreated her heart and spirit. Therefore, the Christian woman, the woman who has truly believed and surrendered her heart to Jesus Christ, focuses upon adorning her heart and spirit, but...

• not with perishable *things* such as clothes which pass out of style, become moth-eaten, wear out, age, and deteriorate.

• not with perishable *things* such as gold and jewelry that can be stolen and that are useless when we lie sick and that are left behind when we die and that always deteriorate and waste away.

• not with perishable *things* such as hairstyles that soon pass out of style.

All earthly things are perishable and soon fall to the ground just as our hair does. These are not the things that a Christian wife focuses upon. She does not adorn herself with corruptible things. What then does she adorn herself with?

• *With a gentle and quiet spirit.*

The Christian woman focuses upon her heart, upon the things that are hidden and that cannot be seen by the naked eye, upon developing a gentle and quiet spirit.

⇒ A *gentle spirit* means a spirit that is gentle, tender, humble, mild, and considerate. It is a spirit that is disciplined and under control at all times. It does not flare up, talk back, act defensively, cut in, rant, rave, or go on and on, talking and talking. Neither does a gentle spirit whine or whimper or act persecuted or take on a martyr complex because the husband does not obey God's Word. A gentle spirit is as stated: gentle, tender, meek, considerate, disciplined, and controlled.

> **But the fruit of the Spirit is love, joy, peace, patience, kindness, goodness, faithfulness, gentleness and self-control. Against such things there is no law. (Gal 5:22-23)**

> **Therefore, get rid of all moral filth and the evil that is so prevalent and humbly accept the word planted in you, which can save you. (James 1:21)**

> **Instead, it should be that of your inner self, the unfading beauty of a gentle and quiet spirit, which is of great worth in God's sight. (1 Pet 3:4)**

⇒ A *quiet spirit* means a quiet and peaceful spirit, a spirit that is at peace with God and with itself and that builds peace with its husband. A quiet spirit spreads peace all throughout its home and around to everyone who enters its home.

Note that the gentle and quiet spirit is of great value to God. God has His eyes upon the Christian woman who has a gentle and quiet spirit: "which is of great worth in God's sight."

> **In your anger do not sin; when you are on your beds, search your hearts and be silent. Selah (Psa 4:4)**

> **"Be still, and know that I am God; I will be exalted among the nations, I will be exalted in the earth." (Psa 46:10)**

> **An evil man is bent only on rebellion; a merciless official will be sent against him. (Prov 17:11)**

> **Better one handful with tranquillity than two handfuls with toil and chasing after the wind. (Eccl 4:6)**

> **Make it your ambition to lead a quiet life, to mind your own business and to work with your hands, just as we told you, (1 Th 4:11)**

> **Instead, it should be that of your inner self, the unfading beauty of a gentle and quiet spirit, which is of great worth in God's sight. (1 Pet 3:4)**

There is a strong reason why Christian women should focus upon adorning their hearts with a gentle and quiet spirit. It was exactly what the holy women of history did, including Sarah who is the spiritual mother of every Christian woman. Note these facts.

⇒ This is not a new commandment. Holy women have always submitted themselves to their own husbands. Women who have loved and trusted God have submitted themselves to God and to their own husbands (v.5).

⇒ Holy women *trusted in God*, not in fashionable hairstyles, clothes, and jewelry (v.5).

⇒ Holy women, by trusting in God, sought inward beauty, not outward beauty. They adorned themselves with a gentle and quiet spirit, not with the worldly concerns and cares of this life (v.5).

⇒ Holy women, including Sarah, the spiritual mother of all believers, obeyed their own husbands and acknowledged their leadership in the family (v.6).

⇒ Christian women, the holy women of today, are not to live in fear and terror of their husbands, even if they do not believe God's Word. They are to trust God and His care and strength and to do well; that is, they are to adorn their hearts with a gentle and quiet spirit.

⇒ Christian women who truly trust God and who do well are the true daughters of Sarah. What is the significance of this? Sarah is the first great woman of belief. She stands as the spiritual mother of all women who believe. Every Christian woman who truly believes and adorns her heart with a quiet and gentle spirit is a daughter of Sarah, a true daughter of God.

Thought 1. The point is made as strongly as it can be made: the Christian wife must win her husband to the Lord by submitting herself to him. What is meant by submission? It means...

- that she lives a pure life.
- that she lives in the reverence of God.
- that she does not dress and behave to attract attention.
- that she adorns her heart with a gentle and quiet spirit.

To the married I give this command (not I, but the Lord): A wife must not separate from her husband. (1 Cor 7:10)

Wives, submit to your husbands, as is fitting in the Lord. (Col 3:18)

A woman should learn in quietness and full submission. I do not permit a woman to teach or to have authority over a man; she must be silent. For Adam was formed first, then Eve. (1 Tim 2:11-13)

In the same way, their wives are to be women worthy of respect, not malicious talkers but temperate and trustworthy in everything. (1 Tim 3:11)

Then they can train the younger women to love their husbands and children, (Titus 2:4)

Wives, in the same way be submissive to your husbands so that, if any of them do not believe the word, they may be won over without words by the behavior of their wives, (1 Pet 3:1)

She watches over the affairs of her household and does not eat the bread of idleness. (Prov 31:27)

To the woman he said, "I will greatly increase your pains in childbearing; with pain you will give birth to children. Your desire will be for your husband, and he will rule over you." (Gen 3:16)

	L. Understand One's Wife, 3:7
1 **Live with your wife** 2 **Live with your wife in understanding** 3 **Honor your wife** a. As the weaker partner b. As a joint heir c. The reason: Failure hinders your prayers	7 Husbands, in the same way be considerate as you live with your wives, and treat them with respect as the weaker partner and as heirs with you of the gracious gift of life, so that nothing will hinder your prayers.

DIVISION II

HOW TO LIVE THROUGH SUFFERING: GIVE YOUR LIFE TO GOD, 1:13-3:12

L. Understand One's Wife, 3:7

(3:7) **Introduction**: What is the duty of the Christian husband? Scripture pulls no punches with the husband. He is to live with his wife, not with some other woman, and he is to understand and honor her with the highest esteem.

1. Live with your wife (v.7).
2. Live with your wife in understanding (v.7).
3. Honor your wife (v.7).

1 (3:7) **Husbands—Family—Marriage**: husbands are to live with their wives. The Greek word "live with" (sunoikein) means to live with; to remain with; to reside with; to dwell together. Alan Stibbs points out that it is a word that is often used in the Greek for sexual intercourse. It is similar to the Hebrew verb *to know* which means that a man and woman *know* each other sexually (cp. Gen.4:1; Mt.1:25). (*The First Epistle General of Peter.* "The Tyndale New Testament Commentaries," p.127).

The point is this: the husband is to *live with his wife* and with no one else. He is not to *know* anyone else; he is not to have sexual intercourse with any other woman. The husband has a wife and he is to live with her in purity, righteousness, and holiness, and not as an adulterer.

Note one other fact as well: to live with his wife means that he is not to be gone all of the time. He stays at home and lives with her: he is a close and supportive companion. He is not out and away from the home all of the time pursuing his own interests and hobbies. A good husband lives at home; he is close to his wife and he is supportive of her in all of life. In fact, the term *live with* actually means to live together. The husband and wife are a team; they are as one body, one body that lives and moves together. This is not to do away with individuality. But individuality never has been and never will be the problem within a marriage of normal people. The problem with normal people will always be denying self and sacrificially giving oneself to one's spouse. *Husbands* must always remember this: they are to live with—to live and move and have their being with—their wives.

> 'For this reason a man will leave his father and mother and be united to his wife, and the two will become one flesh.' So they are no longer two, but one. Therefore what God has joined together, let man not separate." (Mark 10:7-9)
> The man said, "This is now bone of my bones and flesh of my flesh; she shall be called 'woman,' for she was taken out of man." For this reason a man will leave his father and mother and be united to his

wife, and they will become one flesh. (Gen 2:23-24)
> Enjoy life with your wife, whom you love, all the days of this meaningless life that God has given you under the sun— all your meaningless days. For this is your lot in life and in your toilsome labor under the sun. (Eccl 9:9)

2 (3:7) **Husbands—Family—Marriage**: husbands are to live with their wives in understanding. This is an eye-opener, a fact that is too often ignored and neglected. But the Scripture is clear: a husband is not to be ignorant in living with his wife. He is to be considerate. He is to know and understand...

- the marriage relationship: what marriage is and what it is to be.
- his wife: her nature and emotional makeup; what she needs and wants emotionally and spiritually, her strengths and weaknesses.
- the Word of God: what God says about the husband and his duties.

A husband is to be a knowledgeable and understanding person. He is to live with his wife, not as a thoughtless and ignorant fool, not as a blind and close-minded beast, not as a detached and inconsiderate observer. The husband is not to be a fool, beast, or observer. He is to be a man of understanding, a husband who knows and understands his wife and marriage and understands God and his own duty as a husband.

Thought 1. Matthew Henry states it in a simple and pointed way:

> "[Husbands are to live] with the wife according to knowledge; not according to lust, as brutes; nor according to passion, as devils; but according to knowledge, as wise and sober men, who know the word of God and their own duty" (*Matthew Henry's Commentary*, Vol.6, p.1023.)

3 (3:7) **Husband—Marriage**: husbands are to honor their wives. The word "respect" (timen) means to honor; to value; to esteem; to prize; to count as precious. A husband is to count his wife as a precious gem, as a prize of extreme value. He is to highly esteem her, set her up on a pedestal before his very eyes. Note three points.

1. The husband is to respect his wife as the weaker partner. By nature, the wife is just more delicate and frail. This means that the husband is...

- to protect her.
- to be the primary provider.
- to take the lead.
- to oversee the family and its welfare.
- to be the driving force.
- to plow the way.
- to be the initiator.

Husbands are to respect their wives by loving and tenderly taking care of them. They are to look after and care for them with warmth and tenderness, treating them in the most precious of spirits and esteeming them ever so highly.

> **Husbands, love your wives, just as Christ loved the church and gave himself up for her (Eph 5:25)**
> **May your fountain be blessed, and may you rejoice in the wife of your youth. (Prov 5:18)**

2. The husband is to respect his wife as a *joint heir* of the gracious gift of life. Note this point: in God's eyes men and women are joint or equal heirs. The husband is not above the wife nor the wife above the husband. God has no favorites. Spiritual gifts and rights are given equally to wives and husbands. Women receive the spiritual gifts of God just as readily as men do.

The point is well made: husbands are to respect their wives as being equal in life. Life is a gracious gift; it is an undeserved gift of God. Therefore in life, the husband is to treat the wife as an equal. He is not to be a tyrant, not to dominate and enslave her to serve and to meet his needs and wants. He is to be understanding, loving, gentle, and considerate. He is to respect her as a fellow heir of life, of the gracious gift of life that God has given us all.

> **For you did not receive a spirit that makes you a slave again to fear, but you received the Spirit of sonship. And by him we cry, "Abba, Father." The Spirit himself testifies with our spirit that we are God's children. Now if we are children, then we are heirs—heirs of God and co-heirs with Christ, if indeed we share in his sufferings in order that we may also share in his glory. (Rom 8:15-17)**
> **For all of you who were baptized into Christ have clothed yourselves with Christ. There is neither Jew nor Greek, slave nor free, male nor female, for you are all one in Christ Jesus. If you belong to Christ, then you are Abraham's seed, and heirs according to the promise. (Gal 3:27-29)**
> **So that, having been justified by his grace, we might become heirs having the hope of eternal life. (Titus 3:7)**

3. Failure to respect the wife hinders the prayers of the husband. God will not answer the prayers of any husband who does not respect his wife, no matter who he is or how much he professes Christ. What God hears is the sigh of the wife, not the prayers of a mean and domineering husband. The husband can cry out to God all he wants, but God's back is turned away from him and toward the sigh of the wife. God is going to hear the broken and contrite heart, not the prayers of the arrogant and dominating spirit. Both husband and wife must love one another and live as God says to live, both fulfilling their duty to one another, if they wish God to answer their prayers.

> **If I had cherished sin in my heart, the Lord would not have listened; (Psa 66:18)**
> **But your iniquities have separated you from your God; your sins have hidden his face from you, so that he will not hear. (Isa 59:2)**

	M. Live at Peace with Others, 3:8-9

1 **Live in harmony**
2 **Be sympathetic**
3 **Have brotherly love**
4 **Be compassionate**
5 **Be humble**
6 **Do not retaliate, but bless**
those who do evil against you
  a. Do not react
  b. Bless, that is, forgive
  c. You shall be rewarded
	8 Finally, all of you, live in harmony with one another; be sympathetic, love as brothers, be compassionate and humble.
	
	9 Do not repay evil with evil or insult with insult, but with blessing, because to this you were called so that you may inherit a blessing.

DIVISION II

HOW TO LIVE THROUGH SUFFERING: GIVE YOUR LIFE TO GOD, 1:13-3:12

M. Live at Peace with Others, 3:8-9

(3:8-9) **Believers—Peace**: this is a great passage for believers. It deals with peace. We are to live at peace with other Christian believers. When the world looks at believers, they are to see a most unusual unity, a spirit of oneness that is not found any place else on earth. They are to see believers who are so unified and so closely knit together that they are as brothers and sisters—brothers and sisters who stand together, who love and support each through all the trials and temptations of life. The world is not to see believers…

- arguing
- bickering
- biting
- brawling
- grumbling
- griping
- enticing
- complaining
- in division

The world is to see believers unified, standing together through thick and thin regardless of circumstances. How can believers live in unity? How can people with such diverse personalities and backgrounds be closer than earthly brothers and sisters? In the clearest of terms this verse spells out how in six points.

1. Live in harmony (v.8).
2. Be sympathetic (v.8).
3. Have brotherly love (v.8).
4. Be compassionate (v.8).
5. Be humble(v.8).
6. Do not retaliate, but bless those who do evil against you (v.9).

1 (3:8) **Unity—Brotherhood—Mind**: believers must live in harmony (homophrones). The word means to be like-minded; to be of the same mind. Believers must keep their minds on the same things. They must focus their minds upon Jesus Christ and His mission.

1. Believers must keep their minds upon becoming just like Jesus, upon being conformed to the image of Christ.

> For those God foreknew he also predestined to be conformed to the likeness of his Son, that he might be the firstborn among many brothers. (Rom 8:29)
> And we, who with unveiled faces all reflect the Lord's glory, are being transformed into his likeness with ever-increasing glory, which comes from the Lord, who is the Spirit. (2 Cor 3:18)

> I want to know Christ and the power of his resurrection and the fellowship of sharing in his sufferings, becoming like him in his death, (Phil 3:10)
> And have put on the new self, which is being renewed in knowledge in the image of its Creator. (Col 3:10)

2. Believers must keep their minds upon living holy, righteous, and pure lives.

> Therefore, I urge you, brothers, in view of God's mercy, to offer your bodies as living sacrifices, holy and pleasing to God—this is your spiritual act of worship. Do not conform any longer to the pattern of this world, but be transformed by the renewing of your mind. Then you will be able to test and approve what God's will is—his good, pleasing and perfect will. (Rom 12:1-2)
> Since we have these promises, dear friends, let us purify ourselves from everything that contaminates body and spirit, perfecting holiness out of reverence for God. (2 Cor 7:1)
> Make every effort to live in peace with all men and to be holy; without holiness no one will see the Lord. (Heb 12:14)
> But just as he who called you is holy, so be holy in all you do; for it is written: "Be holy, because I am holy." (1 Pet 1:15-16)
> Since everything will be destroyed in this way, what kind of people ought you to be? You ought to live holy and godly lives as you look forward to the day of God and speed its coming. That day will bring about the destruction of the heavens by fire, and the elements will melt in the heat. (2 Pet 3:11-12)

3. Believers must keep their minds upon developing spiritual character and fruit.

> But the fruit of the Spirit is love, joy, peace, patience, kindness, goodness, faithfulness, gentleness and self-control. Against such things there is no law. (Gal 5:22-23)

4. Believers must keep their minds upon carrying out the ministry and mission of Christ.

> Just as the Son of Man did not come to be served, but to serve, and to give his life as a ransom for many." (Mat 20:28)
> For the Son of Man came to seek and to save what was lost." (Luke 19:10)
> Again Jesus said, "Peace be with you! As the Father has sent me, I am sending you." (John 20:21)
> But you will receive power when the Holy Spirit comes on you; and you will be my witnesses in Jerusalem, and in all Judea and Samaria, and to the ends of the earth." (Acts 1:8)
> We are therefore Christ's ambassadors, as though God were making his appeal through us. We implore you on Christ's behalf: Be reconciled to God. (2 Cor 5:20)
> And the things you have heard me say in the presence of many witnesses entrust to reliable men who will also be qualified to teach others. (2 Tim 2:2)

2 (3:8) **Sympathy**: believers must have sympathy for one another. The word sympathetic (sumpatheis) means compassion; to actually feel with others. It means to feel for others so much that…

- one suffers with those who suffer.
- one weeps with those who weep.
- one rejoices when others are honored.
- one understands the pressure that a leader is under when he has to lead.
- one hurts with those who are criticized and attacked.
- one grieves with the sorrows of others.

Unity cannot exist unless believers feel sympathy for one another. Believers cannot be selfish and aloof; they cannot be seeking attention and seeking to get their own way if they are to be unified. Unity demands sympathy; unity demands that believers feel for one another—that they feel deeply, so deeply that they actually experience what other believers experience: pain, hurt, abuse, suffering, joy, and rejoicing.

> Rejoice with those who rejoice; mourn with those who mourn. (Rom 12:15)
> We who are strong ought to bear with the failings of the weak and not to please ourselves. (Rom 15:1)
> Carry each other's burdens, and in this way you will fulfill the law of Christ. (Gal 6:2)

3 (3:8) **Love, Brotherly**: believers must have brotherly love for one another. "Brotherly love" (philadelphoi) has already been discussed by Peter (see note, *Love—* 1 Pt.1:22-25 for discussion).

4 (3:8) **Compassion—Tenderhearted**: believers must have compassion for one another. The word "compassionate" (eusplagcnoi) means to be tenderhearted; to be sensitive and affectionate toward the needs of others;

to be moved with tender feelings over the pain and sufferings of others. We live in a world that desperately needs compassion, a world of extreme suffering. So many suffer and continue to suffer without ever having their needs met. The means and resources to meet their needs exist, but so many within the world have become hardened to the sufferings of others. They bank, hoard, and build up asset after asset instead of sacrificing and reaching out to meet the needs of the world. But this is not to be true of the believer. Believers are to have compassion upon the sufferings of others. Believers are to feel compassion to the point that they are moved to act, moved to sacrifice and to reach out and meet the needs of the suffering.

Again, note how compassion leaves no room for selfishness. Compassion demands that a person deny himself and help others in their desperate needs and sufferings. Note also how compassion draws people together. Helping and ministering to one another binds and knits people together. Having compassion—feeling for one another and sacrificing and reaching out to help one another—unites people together. A great bond is created between the believer and those to whom he ministers.

> In everything I did, I showed you that by this kind of hard work we must help the weak, remembering the words the Lord Jesus himself said: 'It is more blessed to give than to receive.'" (Acts 20:35)
> Remember those in prison as if you were their fellow prisoners, and those who are mistreated as if you yourselves were suffering. (Heb 13:3)
> Religion that God our Father accepts as pure and faultless is this: to look after orphans and widows in their distress and to keep oneself from being polluted by the world. (James 1:27)

5 (3:8) **Humility**: believers must be "humble" (tapeinophrones). The word means to be humble-minded; to be lowly in mind. It means to offer oneself as lowly and submissive; to walk in a spirit of lowliness; *to present* oneself as lowly; to be of low degree and low rank; not to be highminded, proud, haughty, arrogant, or assertive.

Note: a humble person may have a high position, power, wealth, fame, and much more; but he carries himself in a spirit of lowliness and submission. He denies himself for the sake of Christ and in order to help others.

Men have always looked upon humility as a vice. A lowly man is often looked upon as a coward, a cringing, despicable, slavish type of person. Men fear humility. They feel humility is a sign of weakness and will make them the object of contempt and abuse and cause them to be shunned and overlooked.

Because of all this, men ignore and shun the teaching of Christ on humility. This is tragic:

⇒ for a humble spirit is necessary for salvation (Mt.18:3-4).
⇒ for God's idea of humility is not weakness and cowardice.

God makes people strong, the strongest they can possibly be. By humility God does not mean what men mean. God infuses a new and strong spirit within a person and causes that person to conquer all throughout life. He just does not want the person walking around in pride. He wants the person to do what the definition says: *to offer* himself in a spirit of submissiveness and lowliness; not to act highminded, proud, haughty, arrogant, or assertive.

Humility is to be developed. Scripture tells us how:

> Take my yoke upon you and learn from me, for I am gentle and humble in heart, and you will find rest for your souls. (Mat 11:29)
>
> And he said: "I tell you the truth, unless you change and become like little children, you will never enter the kingdom of heaven. Therefore, whoever humbles himself like this child is the greatest in the kingdom of heaven. (Mat 18:3-4)
>
> For whoever exalts himself will be humbled, and whoever humbles himself will be exalted. (Mat 23:12)
>
> Live in harmony with one another. Do not be proud, but be willing to associate with people of low position. Do not be conceited. (Rom 12:16)
>
> As a prisoner for the Lord, then, I urge you to live a life worthy of the calling you have received. Be completely humble and gentle; be patient, bearing with one another in love. (Eph 4:1-2)
>
> Do nothing out of selfish ambition or vain conceit, but in humility consider others better than yourselves. Each of you should look not only to your own interests, but also to the interests of others. (Phil 2:3-4)
>
> Therefore, as God's chosen people, holy and dearly loved, clothe yourselves with compassion, kindness, humility, gentleness and patience. Bear with each other and forgive whatever grievances you may have against one another. Forgive as the Lord forgave you. (Col 3:12-13)
>
> Humble yourselves, therefore, under God's mighty hand, that he may lift you up in due time. (1 Pet 5:6)

6 (3:9) **Believers, Life and Walk**: do not retaliate, but bless those who do evil against you. This point refers to both believers and unbelievers. As tragic as it is, some believers do repay evil with evil and insult with insult against other believers. Nevertheless, no matter the source of the evil and insulting, true believers are not to retaliate. What are they to do when someone does evil against them?

1. The believer is not to react; he is not to return evil with evil to anyone. In the world and in the course of behavior between men, everyone is mistreated and reacted against at one time or another. Therefore, the believer suffers evil and mistreatment just as everyone else does—just in the course of behavior as a man. However, the genuine believer suffers additional evil: he suffers evil and mistreatment because he is a follower of Jesus Christ. As a follower of Christ...

- the believer is living a life of righteousness and purity, honesty and truthfulness; and such behavior is often opposed by the world. Therefore, the worldly person often opposes and abuses the believer.
- the believer is bearing testimony to the corruption of the world and to God's salvation; to man's need to escape the corruption by turning to Jesus Christ and His righteousness. Again, the

worldly person often opposes the message of Jesus Christ and His righteousness.

The point is this: the believer is not to react against a person who mistreats and does evil against him. There are at least two reasons why he is not to react.

a. Reaction will most likely lose the friendship of the person and lose all hope of ever reaching the person for Jesus Christ. The evil doer will be able to say, "A Christian did that to me." The believer will have made Christ an *unappealing* Savior. On the other hand, if the believer returns good for evil, he opens the door for eventual friendship and bears testimony to the love of God for all men, even for those who do evil.

b. Reaction is not the way of God or of Christ.

> But I tell you, Do not resist an evil person. If someone strikes you on the right cheek, turn to him the other also...that you may be sons of your Father in heaven. He causes his sun to rise on the evil and the good, and sends rain on the righteous and the unrighteous. (Mat 5:39,45)
>
> Do not repay evil with evil or insult with insult, but with blessing, because to this you were called so that you may inherit a blessing. (1 Pet 3:9)
>
> Make sure that nobody pays back wrong for wrong, but always try to be kind to each other and to everyone else. (1 Th 5:15)
>
> "'Do not seek revenge or bear a grudge against one of your people, but love your neighbor as yourself. I am the LORD. (Lev 19:18)
>
> Do not say, "I'll pay you back for this wrong!" Wait for the LORD, and he will deliver you. (Prov 20:22)
>
> Do not say, "I'll do to him as he has done to me; I'll pay that man back for what he did." (Prov 24:29)

2. The believer is to bless those who do evil against him. The word "bless" (eulogountes) means to speak well of.

a. It means to *speak well to our persecutors*. We do not react against them by cursing, speaking harshly, or striking out at them. We do not try to hurt them either verbally or physically. On the contrary, we seek to find something that is commendable about them and we commend them for it.

> Do not repay evil with evil or insult with insult, but with blessing, because to this you were called so that you may inherit a blessing. (1 Pet 3:9)
>
> Get rid of all bitterness, rage and anger, brawling and slander, along with every form of malice. Be kind and compassionate to one another, forgiving each other, just as in Christ God forgave you. (Eph 4:31-32)

b. It means to *speak well about our persecutors*. When speaking to others, we do not down the persecutor, but we mention some commendable trait. We praise some good thing about the person; we do not tear him down.

c. It means to pray *for our persecutors*. We must do as Jesus said and did.

But I tell you: Love your enemies and pray for those who persecute you, (Mat 5:44)

Jesus said, "Father, forgive them, for they do not know what they are doing." And they divided up his clothes by casting lots. (Luke 23:34)

Thought 1. Think of the impact upon persecutors when an attitude of love and blessing is demonstrated toward them. Every persecutor would not be won to Christ, but every persecutor would have a strong witness that could be used by the Holy Spirit in the persecutor's quiet, thoughtful moments; and some persecutors would be won to Christ. This is what God is after.

"For God so loved the world that he gave his one and only Son, that whoever believes in him shall not perish but have eternal life. (John 3:16)

d. It means to do good to our persecutors.

"But I tell you who hear me: Love your enemies, do good to those who hate you, (Luke 6:27)

But love your enemies, do good to them, and lend to them without expecting to get anything back. Then your reward will be great, and you will be sons of the Most High, because he is kind to the ungrateful and wicked. (Luke 6:35)

On the contrary: "If your enemy is hungry, feed him; if he is thirsty, give him something to drink. In doing this, you will heap burning coals on his head." (Rom 12:20)

Make sure that nobody pays back wrong for wrong, but always try to be kind to each other and to everyone else. (1 Th 5:15)

If you see the donkey of someone who hates you fallen down under its load, do not

leave it there; be sure you help him with it. (Exo 23:5)

If your enemy is hungry, give him food to eat; if he is thirsty, give him water to drink. (Prov 25:21)

3. The believer who blesses those who do evil against him will be greatly rewarded. Note: the believer is actually called to receive a blessing. The Amplified New Testament states it well:

Do not repay evil with evil or insult with insult, but with blessing, because to this you were called so that you may inherit a blessing. (v.9)

The idea is that believers shall inherit eternal life. If they forgive others, God will forgive them. God will forgive them and give them the inheritance of heaven, of eternal life itself.

But I tell you: Love your enemies and pray for those who persecute you, that you may be sons of your Father in heaven. He causes his sun to rise on the evil and the good, and sends rain on the righteous and the unrighteous. (Mat 5:44-45)

For if you forgive men when they sin against you, your heavenly Father will also forgive you. But if you do not forgive men their sins, your Father will not forgive your sins. (Mat 6:14-15)

And when you stand praying, if you hold anything against anyone, forgive him, so that your Father in heaven may forgive you your sins." (Mark 11:25)

Be kind and compassionate to one another, forgiving each other, just as in Christ God forgave you. (Eph 4:32)

Bear with each other and forgive whatever grievances you may have against one another. Forgive as the Lord forgave you. (Col 3:13)

	N. Love & Enjoy Life, 3:10-12
1 Step 1: Stop your tongue a. From speaking evil b. From speaking deceitfully **2 Step 2: Turn away from evil & do good** **3 Step 3: Seek peace & pursue it** **4 Step 4: Remember the source of life, the Lord Himself** a. He sees & hears the righteous b. He is against evildoers	10 For, "Whoever would love life and see good days must keep his tongue from evil and his lips from deceitful speech. 11 He must turn from evil and do good; he must seek peace and pursue it. 12 For the eyes of the Lord are on the righteous and his ears are attentive to their prayer, but the face of the Lord is against those who do evil."

DIVISION II

HOW TO LIVE THROUGH SUFFERING: GIVE YOUR LIFE TO GOD, 1:13-3:12

N. Love and Enjoy Life, 3:10-12

(3:10-12) **Introduction**: we live in a world that is full of sickness and desperate needs. Many are hungry, homeless, dressed in rags, diseased, and physically and emotionally ill. And to top it off, millions are lonely, empty, and unfulfilled. They feel they have no significant purpose in life. They do not love or enjoy life: life is more routine and drudgery than enjoyment. This is the subject of this great passage: how to love and enjoy life. There are four steps to loving and enjoying life. (Note that these verses are a quotation of Ps.34:12-16.)

1. Step 1: stop your tongue (v.10).
2. Step 2: turn away from evil and do good (v.11).
3. Step 3: seek peace and pursue it (v.11).
4. Step 4: remember the source of life, the Lord Himself (v.12).

1 (3:10) **Tongue**: first, stop your tongue. If you wish to love and enjoy life, the very first thing you must do is stop your tongue. Few tongues are disciplined and controlled. By far most tongues run, wag, and blaze ever so loosely.

The tongue is easily stirred to run loose. It is easily ignited and just as easily set ablaze. The tongues of so many people are ever so ready…

- to react
- to attack
- to defend
- to rail
- to poison
- to cut
- to hurt

A tongue that runs loose and is not controlled and disciplined knows little love and little enjoyment of life. What can be done? How can a person control and discipline his tongue? By doing two things:

1. A person must stop his tongue from speaking evil. Note: the honest and thinking person knows that no person can control and discipline his tongue perfectly. But Scripture is clear: God does not excuse us, and He expects us to stop our tongue from speaking evil. What we must remember—every couple and every believer—is that there is a vast difference between the *occasional offender* and the *constant offender*. An evil tongue is a tongue that constantly…

- cuts in and takes the floor
- reacts
- refuses instructions
- curses
- backbites
- argues
- interrupts and disrupts others
- defends oneself
- retaliates
- gossips
- criticizes

The list could go on and on until every act of behavior is covered. It is very difficult to live with a constant offender of the tongue. A person whose tongue constantly does evil is destroying his or her life. And we must always remember that an evil tongue is a tongue that is constantly doing evil, evil that ranges all the way from constantly interrupting and disrupting others over to cursing and blaspheming the name of God. An evil tongue shows disrespect for others regardless of what a person claims. It shows disrespect and displeasure.

Note what the antidote is: "[he] must keep his tongue from evil." This is an imperative, a command. The believer is personally responsible. He is to stop his tongue—hush, be quiet, quit allowing his tongue to do evil.

2. A person is to keep his lips from speaking deceitfully (dolon). A deceitful tongue is…

- a false tongue
- a cheating tongue
- a treacherous tongue
- a deceptive tongue
- a lying tongue
- a mistreating tongue
- a beguiling tongue
- a flattering tongue

We deceive and smooth talk others in order to get what we are after or to protect ourselves. But note what Scripture says: the very first step to loving and enjoying life is to keep our tongues from deceiving others. Deception leads to sin and sin destroys. Just think about the deceptive tongues that have…

- destroyed marriages
- damaged friendships
- caused wars
- caused injuries
- prevented promotions
- disturbed children
- ruined reputations
- aroused fights
- maimed bodies

If we wish to love and enjoy life, we must stop our tongues from doing evil and from deceiving others. We must control and discipline our tongues.

Thought 1. This is the duty of the believer. It is not something that God is going to do for the believer. Of course, God will help us and give us strength. Our tongues are controlled by us; they are under our power. We either do good or evil with our tongues.

> **Get rid of all bitterness, rage and anger, brawling and slander, along with every form of malice. (Eph 4:31)**
> **Remind the people to be subject to rulers and authorities, to be obedient, to be ready to do whatever is good, to slander no one, to be peaceable and considerate, and to show true humility toward all men. (Titus 3:1-2)**
> **The tongue also is a fire, a world of evil among the parts of the body. It corrupts the whole person, sets the whole course of his life on fire, and is itself set on fire by hell. (James 3:6)**
> **Brothers, do not slander one another. Anyone who speaks against his brother or judges him speaks against the law and judges it. When you judge the law, you are not keeping it, but sitting in judgment on it. (James 4:11)**
> **Therefore, rid yourselves of all malice and all deceit, hypocrisy, envy, and slander of every kind. (1 Pet 2:1)**
> **For I hear the slander of many; there is terror on every side; they conspire against me and plot to take my life. (Psa 31:13)**
> **Whoever slanders his neighbor in secret, him will I put to silence; whoever has haughty eyes and a proud heart, him will I not endure. (Psa 101:5)**
> **He who conceals his hatred has lying lips, and whoever spreads slander is a fool. (Prov 10:18)**
> **With his mouth the godless destroys his neighbor, but through knowledge the righteous escape. (Prov 11:9)**
> **"Beware of your friends; do not trust your brothers. For every brother is a deceiver, and every friend a slanderer. (Jer 9:4)**
> **For your hands are stained with blood, your fingers with guilt. Your lips have spoken lies, and your tongue mutters wicked things. (Isa 59:3)**
> **Make every effort to live in peace with all men and to be holy; without holiness no one will see the Lord. See to it that no one misses the grace of God and that no bitter root grows up to cause trouble and defile many. (Heb 12:14-15)**

2 (3:11) **Evil—Good Works:** second, turn away from evil and do good.

1. A person is to turn from evil. By turn from is meant to avoid and shun evil; to turn aside and away from evil. What evil is being talked about? Scripture clearly tells us what it is that we are to turn away from and flee. There are some things that we are to stop doing, some things that we are to turn away from and flee.

⇒ We must flee sexual immorality.

> **Flee from sexual immorality. All other sins a man commits are outside his body, but he who sins sexually sins against his own body. (1 Cor 6:18)**

⇒ We must flee idolatry.

> **Therefore, my dear friends, flee from idolatry. (1 Cor 10:14; cp. Acts 14:15)**

⇒ We are to flee foolish and harmful desires and the love of money.

> **People who want to get rich fall into temptation and a trap and into many foolish and harmful desires that plunge men into ruin and destruction. For the love of money is a root of all kinds of evil. Some people, eager for money, have wandered from the faith and pierced themselves with many griefs. But you, man of God, flee from all this, and pursue righteousness, godliness, faith, love, endurance and gentleness. (1 Tim 6:9-11)**

⇒ We are to flee the evil desires of youth.

> **Flee the evil desires of youth, and pursue righteousness, faith, love and peace, along with those who call on the Lord out of a pure heart. (2 Tim 2:22)**

⇒ We are to turn away from all forms of evil.

> **But mark this: There will be terrible times in the last days. People will be lovers of themselves, lovers of money, boastful, proud, abusive, disobedient to their parents, ungrateful, unholy, without love, unforgiving, slanderous, without self-control, brutal, not lovers of the good, treacherous, rash, conceited, lovers of pleasure rather than lovers of God— having a form of godliness but denying its power. Have nothing to do with them. (2 Tim 3:1-5)**

⇒ We are to stop and turn our tongue and lips away from evil.

> **For, "Whoever would love life and see good days must keep his tongue from evil and his lips from deceitful speech. (1 Pet 3:10)**

The charge is direct and forceful: we are to stop doing evil. The idea is that we are to stop dead in our tracks, snatch our hands back, snap our eyes away, shut our ears from the evil. We are to turn away and flee evil lest it consume and destroy us.

Note a crucial fact: evil is being pictured as a deliberate choice. We choose to do evil. The command of God is to turn away and flee evil. Turning away and fleeing is also a deliberate choice. Turning away and fleeing evil is up to us. We are the ones who have to repent; we are the ones who have to turn away from wrongdoing and turn to God. This is the second step to loving and enjoying life.

2. A person must do good. Note: it is not enough to turn away from evil. When a person turns away from evil, he is like a vacuum. All the things that had been filling his life are set aside and his life is left with empty spaces. Whereas he had been spending time in the pleasures of the world, he now has blocks of time that must be filled. What is it that is to fill these blocks of time? What is it that is to fill the life of the person who turns away from evil and turns to God? Good works. A person who truly turns to God is a person who gives all he is and has to God. He commits his life…

- to live a holy and righteous life.
- to make Christ known throughout his community and all over the world.
- to minister and meet the needs of the desperate in the world.

> **Turn from evil and do good; seek peace and pursue it. (Psa 34:14)**
>
> **But love your enemies, do good to them, and lend to them without expecting to get anything back. Then your reward will be great, and you will be sons of the Most High, because he is kind to the ungrateful and wicked. (Luke 6:35)**
>
> **And do not forget to do good and to share with others, for with such sacrifices God is pleased. (Heb 13:16)**
>
> **Anyone, then, who knows the good he ought to do and doesn't do it, sins. (James 4:17)**

3 (3:11) **Peace**: third, seek peace and pursue it. Believers are not only to desire peace, but they are to actively pursue and go after it. The word "pursue" (dioxato) means to run after, chase after, press after, and to pursue. It has the idea of swiftness and endurance—of hotly pursuing and staying after peace. We live in a world that is full of corruptible and evil people who could care less about peace and holiness just so they get what they are after. However, the believer must not give up, for peace is the very reason he is on earth.

The believer is to follow after peace (eirenen) with all men. The fact that he has to follow after peace means that peace is not always possible.

⇒ Some persons within the church are troublemakers: grumblers, complainers, gossipers, criticizers; some are self-centered leaders full of pride; some people within the church are just selfish and self-centered and care more about pushing themselves forward and getting their own way than they do about peace. Self is put before Christ and the church and its mission.

⇒ Some persons within the world are troublemakers and they cause great trouble for the believer. They oppose the believer: ridicule, mock, poke fun at, curse, abuse, persecute, ignore, and isolate him.

⇒ Some persons within the world are troublemakers for the world at large: dissenters, dividers, fighters, egotists, power-builders, and warmongers. Some people have no interest in peace whatever unless they can have their own way.

The point is this: the believer is to follow after peace with *all men*—no matter who they are. The very purpose for the believer being on earth is to bring peace between men and God and between men and all other men. Therefore, the believer is to do all he can to live at peace with everyone and to lead others to live in peace.

The believer is to live at peace with all men. The believer is to work for as much peace as possible. Some level of harmony and concord can be achieved at least some of the time. The believer is never to give up, not as long as there is hope for some degree of peace. He is to achieve as much peace as possible. However remember, peace is not always possible—not with everyone.

4 (3:12) **Life**: fourth, remember the source of life, the Lord Himself. No person has life apart from God, and God sees exactly who it is that is to receive life.

1. God sees the righteous, the very person who has been described in the first three points of the outline.

⇒ God sees the person who controls his tongue, who does not speak evil nor deceive people.

⇒ God sees the person who turns away and flees from evil.

⇒ God sees the person who seeks peace and pursues it.

This is the righteous person, the person to whom God gives life and good days. Note also that it is the righteous person whose prayers are answered. God's ears are open to their prayers. The idea is that He hears their cries in times of need and He meets their need. God cares and looks after the righteous day by day, never letting them suffer more than they can bear. This is a most wonderful thing: it means that the inner cry for life is met. God gives life, both abundant and eternal life, to the righteous, and He looks after them by answering their prayers while they journey throughout life.

> **If you remain in me and my words remain in you, ask whatever you wish, and it will be given you. (John 15:7)**
>
> **Let us then approach the throne of grace with confidence, so that we may receive mercy and find grace to help us in our time of need. (Heb 4:16)**
>
> **This is the confidence we have in approaching God: that if we ask anything according to his will, he hears us. And if we know that he hears us—whatever we ask—we know that we have what we asked of him. (1 John 5:14-15)**
>
> **The eyes of the LORD are on the righteous and his ears are attentive to their cry; (Psa 34:15)**
>
> **He will call upon me, and I will answer him; I will be with him in trouble, I will deliver him and honor him. (Psa 91:15)**
>
> **Before they call I will answer; while they are still speaking I will hear. (Isa 65:24)**

2. God sees those who do evil. Who are the evil? Being very specific, they are those who do not do what is covered in the first three points.

⇒ The evil are people who do not control their tongues and who speak evil and who deceive others with enticing and smooth talking words.

⇒ The evil are people who do not turn away from evil, who do not turn away from sexual immorality, idolatry, foolish and harmful desires, the love of money, the evil desires of youth, and all forms of evil.

⇒ The evil are people who do not seek and pursue peace, who are divisive, who grumble, complain, criticize, backbite, plot, fight, and war.

Note that the very face of God stands against those who do evil. The picture is that God does not only see the evil person, God stands *face to face against him.* He stands face to face to judge them.

Then I will tell them plainly, 'I never knew you. Away from me, you evildoers!' (Mat 7:23)

"Then the king told the attendants, 'Tie him hand and foot, and throw him outside, into the darkness, where there will be weeping and gnashing of teeth.' (Mat 22:13)

"Then he will say to those on his left, 'Depart from me, you who are cursed, into the eternal fire prepared for the devil and his angels. (Mat 25:41)

"Then they will go away to eternal punishment, but the righteous to eternal life." (Mat 25:46)

Whoever believes in the Son has eternal life, but whoever rejects the Son will not see life, for God's wrath remains on him." (John 3:36)

If this is so, then the Lord knows how to rescue godly men from trials and to hold the unrighteous for the day of judgment, while continuing their punishment. (2 Pet 2:9)

	III. HOW TO HANDLE OR CONQUER SUFFERING: LIVE FOR RIGHTEOUSNESS & NOT FOR EVIL, 3:13-4:19	frightened." 15 But in your hearts set apart Christ as Lord. Always be prepared to give an answer to everyone who asks you to give the reason for the hope that you have. But do this with gentleness and respect, 16 Keeping a clear conscience, so that those who speak maliciously against your good behavior in Christ may be ashamed of their slander. 17 It is better, if it is God's will, to suffer for doing good than for doing evil.	of persecution
	A. Stand Up For Christ: Suffer for Righteousness' Sake, 3:13-17		2 Second, set your heart on Christ & the great hope He gives 3 Third, readily answer & defend the hope of salvation 4 Fourth, keep a clear conscience
1 First, do what is right & good a. Will most likely not be persecuted b. Will be blessed c. Do not fear the terror		13 Who is going to harm you if you are eager to do good? 14 But even if you should suffer for what is right, you are blessed. "Do not fear what they fear ; do not be	a. Will put one's persecutors to shame b. Suffer for doing good & not for evil

DIVISION III

HOW TO HANDLE AND CONQUER SUFFERING: LIVE FOR RIGHTEOUSNESS AND NOT FOR EVIL, 3:13-4:19

A. Stand Up For Christ: Suffer for Righteousness' Sake, 3:13-17

(3:13-17) **Introduction**: this passage begins a new section dealing with persecution. Genuine believers suffer all kinds of persecution: being ridiculed and mocked, ignored and bypassed, isolated and cut off, abused and beaten, imprisoned and murdered. All genuine believers face some persecution at one time or another, all to varying degrees. The question is this: How can we bear up under the persecution? How can we be assured that we will stand up under the persecution and be counted faithful by God? How can we be assured that we will endure and inherit the hope of eternal life, of living with Christ forever and ever? There is only one way: we must stand up for Christ no matter the suffering or its ferociousness.

1. First, do what is right and good (v.13-14).
2. Second, set your heart on Christ and the great hope He gives (v.15).
3. Third, readily answer and defend the hope of salvation (v.15).
4. Fourth, keep a clear conscience (v.16-17).

1 (3:13-14) **Persecution—Zeal—Good Works**: the first answer to persecution is to do what is right and good. Note the verse: it actually says to become "eager to do good." The word "eager" (zelotai) means zealot. The believer is to be so zealous for what is right that he is actually known as a zealot for good. Imagine being gripped with so much passion and zeal for good that one becomes known as a zealot! This is the challenge of this passage. Several attitudes toward doing good permeate society.

⇒ Some persons have a *care less attitude* toward goodness. Doing what is right and good matters little. What is right and good is rebelled against, ignored, cursed, and rejected. The person has little conscience about right and wrong. His values are ever so weak. He could care less if he does what is right and good.

⇒ Some persons have a *selfish attitude* toward goodness. If doing what is right and good benefits them, then they do it. If it helps them, meets their need and enlarges their holdings, then they do what is right. But if it costs them, demands discipline and control, and takes away from their pleasure and holdings, then they reject the good and refuse to do what is right.

⇒ Some persons have a *surface or sentimental attitude* to what is good and right. They readily profess to believe in what is good and right and want to be known as moral and upright. But behind the scenes they go ahead and live like they want and do their own thing.

Some persons, of course, have a zealous attitude toward what is right and good. They have committed their lives to seeking and doing what they should. This is exactly what Scripture is saying: "Be a zealot—be a fanatic—be a passionate follower—after that which is good and right." Note three points.

1. The believer who does good will be less likely to suffer persecution (v.13). Most people will appreciate the good that we do, including our neighbors and civil authorities. Doing good will keep us from getting into trouble with the law and from offending our neighbors, fellow workers, and community. Therefore, the chance of our being persecuted becomes less likely.

Keep your lives free from the love of money and be content with what you have, because God has said, "Never will I leave you; never will I forsake you." So we say with confidence, "The Lord is my helper; I will not be afraid. What can man do to me?" (Heb 13:5-6)

Who is going to harm you if you are eager to do good? (1 Pet 3:13)

You will be secure, because there is hope; you will look about you and take your rest in safety. (Job 11:18)

You will not fear the terror of night, nor the arrow that flies by day, (Psa 91:5)

He will have no fear of bad news; his heart is steadfast, trusting in the LORD. (Psa 112:7)

When you lie down, you will not be afraid; when you lie down, your sleep will be sweet. (Prov 3:24)

2. The believer who suffers persecution will be blessed by God. How can a person who is suffering persecution be blessed? When a person focuses his mind and life upon the things of this world, they can be snatched from him overnight. The person can be stricken with a disease, suffer a heart attack, have an accident, go through bankruptcy, lose everything he has through an economic slump or stock market crash. A black Monday can happen anytime and anywhere in this world. A person of the world can suffer such a crushing blow that he is destroyed and left hopeless and helpless in life, but not a true believer. The mind and life of the true believer are focused upon Jesus Christ; therefore, no matter what he suffers, he still has his most cherished possession—Jesus Christ, the very Son of God. He knows that Jesus Christ is going to look after him and take care of him: that Christ is going to work everything out for good.

The very same thing happens when the believer is persecuted for righteousness' sake. His mind and life are focused upon Christ; therefore, he possesses Christ and all the promises of Christ. He possesses such promises as these:

⇒ God will work all things out for good for him.

> **And we know that in all things God works for the good of those who love him, who have been called according to his purpose. (Rom 8:28)**

⇒ God will provide all the necessities of life for him.

> **But seek first his kingdom and his righteousness, and all these things will be given to you as well. (Mat 6:33)**

⇒ God will give him a very special Spirit of glory to rest upon him.

> **If you are insulted because of the name of Christ, you are blessed, for the Spirit of glory and of God rests on you. (1 Pet 4:14)**

⇒ The life of Christ will be revealed in his body.

> **For we who are alive are always being given over to death for Jesus' sake, so that his life may be revealed in our mortal body. (2 Cor 4:11)**

⇒ God will give him a great reward in heaven.

> **"Blessed are you when people insult you, persecute you and falsely say all kinds of evil against you because of me. Rejoice and be glad, because great is your reward in heaven, for in the same way they persecuted the prophets who were before you. (Mat 5:11-12)**
> **If we endure, we will also reign with him. If we disown him, he will also disown us; (2 Tim 2:12)**
> **If we deliberately keep on sinning after we have received the knowledge of the truth, no sacrifice for sins is left, (Heb 10:26)**

⇒ The Lord will take him on to heaven and preserve him through all of eternity when the time comes for him to leave this earth.

> **The Lord will rescue me from every evil attack and will bring me safely to his heavenly kingdom. To him be glory for ever and ever. Amen. (2 Tim 4:18)**

Note how wonderful and glorious these promises are. There are so many more promises, so many in fact that, as John the Apostle says, the world itself could not contain enough shelves to hold the books if all the promises of God were written out (cp. Jn.21:25).

3. The believer is not to fear nor be troubled by the terror of persecution. No matter what the suffering is—ridicule, mockery, abuse, assault, rejection, being bypassed, imprisoned, or martyred—if the believer is persecuted because he stands up for Christ, he is not to fear. God will meet his need. God has great things in store for the believer; therefore, God shall never forsake him.

⇒ God will strengthen him to bear the persecution.
⇒ God will use his suffering as a strong testimony for Christ and touch the hearts of some of the persecutors.
⇒ God will use his suffering to make him a far stronger believer, to make him more and more secure in Christ.

> **The LORD will fight for you; you need only to be still." (Exo 14:14)**
> **Be strong and courageous. Do not be afraid or terrified because of them, for the LORD your God goes with you; he will never leave you nor forsake you." (Deu 31:6)**
> **For the eyes of the LORD range throughout the earth to strengthen those whose hearts are fully committed to him. You have done a foolish thing, and from now on you will be at war." (2 Chr 16:9)**
> **The angel of the LORD encamps around those who fear him, and he delivers them. (Psa 34:7)**
> **He will cover you with his feathers, and under his wings you will find refuge; his faithfulness will be your shield and rampart. (Psa 91:4)**
> **So do not fear, for I am with you; do not be dismayed, for I am your God. I will strengthen you and help you; I will uphold you with my righteous right hand. (Isa 41:10)**
> **For I am the LORD, your God, who takes hold of your right hand and says to you, Do not fear; I will help you. (Isa 41:13)**
> **But now, this is what the LORD says— he who created you, O Jacob, he who formed you, O Israel: "Fear not, for I have redeemed you; I have summoned you by name; you are mine. When you pass through the waters, I will be with you; and when you pass through the rivers, they will not sweep over you. When you walk through the fire, you will not be burned; the flames will not set you ablaze. (Isa 43:1-2)**
> **And even the very hairs of your head are all numbered. So don't be afraid; you are worth more than many sparrows. (Mat 10:30-31)**
> **Whatever happens, conduct yourselves in a manner worthy of the gospel of Christ.**

Then, whether I come and see you or only hear about you in my absence, I will know that you stand firm in one spirit, contending as one man for the faith of the gospel without being frightened in any way by those who oppose you. This is a sign to them that they will be destroyed, but that you will be saved—and that by God. For it has been granted to you on behalf of Christ not only to believe on him, but also to suffer for him, (Phil 1:27-29)

When I saw him, I fell at his feet as though dead. Then he placed his right hand on me and said: "Do not be afraid. I am the First and the Last. I am the Living One; I was dead, and behold I am alive for ever and ever! And I hold the keys of death and Hades. (Rev 1:17-18)

2 (3:15) **Persecution—Dedication**: the second answer to persecution is to set your heart upon Christ and the great hope He gives to believers. The believer is to receive Christ into his heart. Christ alone is to fill the heart of the believer. The believer's heart is to be sanctified, that is, filled with Christ and focused upon Christ. Why? Because Christ is his only hope of salvation. Jesus Christ promises to save all who receive Him into their hearts. Therefore, if a person wishes to be saved, he must have Jesus Christ in his heart.

The point is this: if Jesus Christ is in the heart of the believer, then the believer has the greatest of hopes, the hope of salvation and of living forever. It is this hope that stirs the believer to bear persecution. Christ, who lives within the believer, strengthens the believer. How? Christ stirs the hope of salvation within the heart of the believer and arouses him to endure the suffering no matter how fierce and threatening. Christ arouses great assurance within the believer, the assurance that the hope of salvation is true and that it is right around the corner. The person who has truly sanctified Christ within his heart loves Christ and wants to please Christ. He knows that Christ has died for him and is going to conform him into the very image of the Son of God Himself. Therefore, the true believer wants to please Christ. The believer would never think of displeasing Christ nor of hurting and causing Christ pain, especially by buckling under to persecution and denying Him. But remember: only the person who has sanctified Christ within his heart can stand fast against persecution. Our hearts must be filled with Christ and focused upon Christ to bear suffering for righteousness' sake.

I in them and you in me. May they be brought to complete unity to let the world know that you sent me and have loved them even as you have loved me. (John 17:23)

I have been crucified with Christ and I no longer live, but Christ lives in me. The life I live in the body, I live by faith in the Son of God, who loved me and gave himself for me. (Gal 2:20)

Blessed is the man who perseveres under trial, because when he has stood the test, he will receive the crown of life that God has promised to those who love him. (James 1:12)

If this is so, then the Lord knows how to rescue godly men from trials and to hold the unrighteous for the day of judgment, while continuing their punishment. (2 Pet 2:9)

Those who obey his commands live in him, and he in them. And this is how we know that he lives in us: We know it by the Spirit he gave us. (1 John 3:24)

Here I am! I stand at the door and knock. If anyone hears my voice and opens the door, I will come in and eat with him, and he with me. (Rev 3:20)

3 (3:15) **Persecution—Witnessing**: the third answer to persecution is to readily answer and defend the hope of salvation to every man, but to do so with meekness and fear. The word "answer" or "defend" (apologian) means just that, to answer back or to give a defense of the believer's hope (A.T. Robertson. *Word Pictures In The New Testament*, Vol.6, p.114).

1. The believer is to answer *every man* who asks him about his hope of salvation and of living forever. He is to answer every…

- neighbor
- foe
- employer
- classmate
- stranger
- friend
- civil authority
- employee
- legal authority
- fellow worker

The believer is to miss no opportunity to witness for Christ. He is not to shirk his duty in witnessing, and he is not to neglect or ignore anyone. Day by day as he crosses the path of others, he is to give an answer and defend the hope of salvation to all who ask and will listen.

2. The believer is *to be ready* to answer and defend the hope of salvation. This means preparation; it means study, meditation, and prayer. The believer must study the Scripture, study all about God and Christ, all about the salvation and promises of God. The believer must know the Scripture and live in prayer in order to be ready to witness.

Thought 1. The great tragedy is that most professing believers do not know what they believe. They know little about Christ, what it is that makes Him so unique and superior. Few can witness and lead anyone else to a saving knowledge of Jesus Christ. Few are willing to take the time or exert the effort to study God's Word and to learn the truth. Most are just not willing to pay the price to learn about God and Christ and to prepare themselves to be dynamic witnesses for Christ.

3. The believer is to be very careful about how he answers and defends the hope of salvation. He is to answer people with a spirit of gentleness and of respect before God.

⇒ By gentleness is meant a spirit of tenderness and softness, of care and love, of humility and brokenness. But note: gentleness also means a spirit of strength and courage. Gentleness does not put up with sin and shame, license and indulgence. It does all it can to relieve and correct evil and mistreatment. Too often witnessing is done in a spirit of superiority and arrogance, argument and controversy, criticism and divisiveness.

⇒ By respect is meant fearing God lest one misrepresent or twist the truth of God's salvation. It means to hold God in such reverence and awe that one bears witness only in a spirit of constant prayer and dependence upon God. One knows and acknowledges that God is the Source of salvation; He alone can save a person. Therefore, one is ever so careful to present only the truth of God's Word and of salvation.

Thought 1. Too often witnessing is done in a spirit of pride and bitterness, of pushing oneself forward instead of God. The spirit of fearing God is all but forgotten; God is not reverenced: the truth of His salvation is twisted to make oneself more acceptable and recognized.

The point is this: the answer to persecution is to bear a clear and strong witness for Christ, but to do so with meekness and in the fear of God. By bearing a strong but gentle witness, those who oppose us will understand more about why we hold to such a glorious hope. In some cases, some of them will even be saved.

Thought 2. Alan Stibbs has an excellent statement on this point that is well worth our noting:

"We have here some practical guidance concerning Christian witness. It is wrong to be always preaching at people. The Christian wife has been encouraged by Peter to seek to win her unbelieving husband without speaking to him on the subject (3:1). But the whole situation is changed if the other person asks for an explanation. Also, if Christians are on the alert, they may often rightly discern an implied question in some passing comment. Then is the time to speak; but one can do so only if one is seeking to be ready.

"The Christian is then to engage, not in an aggressive attack on the other person's will or prejudice, but in a logical account...or reasoned explanation of the hope that is [in him]" (*The First Epistle General of Peter.* "The Tyndale New Testament Commentaries," p.136).

Therefore go and make disciples of all nations, baptizing them in the name of the Father and of the Son and of the Holy Spirit, and teaching them to obey everything I have commanded you. And surely I am with you always, to the very end of the age." (Mat 28:19-20)

He said to them, "Go into all the world and preach the good news to all creation. (Mark 16:15)

For the Son of Man came to seek and to save what was lost." (Luke 19:10)

Again Jesus said, "Peace be with you! As the Father has sent me, I am sending you." (John 20:21)

But you will receive power when the Holy Spirit comes on you; and you will be my witnesses in Jerusalem, and in all Judea and Samaria, and to the ends of the earth." (Acts 1:8)

For we cannot help speaking about what we have seen and heard." (Acts 4:20)

It is written: "I believed; therefore I have spoken." With that same spirit of faith we also believe and therefore speak, (2 Cor 4:13)

So do not be ashamed to testify about our Lord, or ashamed of me his prisoner. But join with me in suffering for the gospel, by the power of God, (2 Tim 1:8)

And the things you have heard me say in the presence of many witnesses entrust to reliable men who will also be qualified to teach others. (2 Tim 2:2)

These, then, are the things you should teach. Encourage and rebuke with all authority. Do not let anyone despise you. (Titus 2:15)

But in your hearts set apart Christ as Lord. Always be prepared to give an answer to everyone who asks you to give the reason for the hope that you have. But do this with gentleness and respect, (1 Pet 3:15)

4 (3:16-17) **Persecution—Conscience**: the fourth answer to persecution is to keep a good conscience. Note the reference...

- to a good or clear conscience.
- to a good behavior, that is, good conduct.

The only way a person can have a clear conscience is to have good conduct. If the believer is to stand against persecution, he must have a clear conscience, and to have a clear conscience he must have good conduct and behavior. The believer must be living a good life; his conduct and behavior must be holy, righteous, pure, decent, upright, and above reproach. He must have a conscience and a behavior that are without blame, that cannot be justly blamed with any sin or evil. Note two points.

1. Those who oppose and persecute believers will be put to shame by the believer's good behavior and clear conscience. Some people will always oppose and persecute believers. If a person really lives for Jesus Christ, his righteousness and self-denial convicts those who love this world and its pleasures and possessions. Therefore, they often persecute the believer, ridicule, mock, isolate, abuse, imprison, or kill him. The worldly do all they can to stop the witness of the believer. But note: eventually those who oppose and persecute the believer will be put to shame. The good and righteous behavior of the believer will vindicate the believer either in this world or in the next world. The persecutor will stand ashamed of his attacks against the believer; the idea is that he will be eternally shamed.

2. It is better for believers to suffer for doing good than for doing evil. This is only common sense: a person can bear suffering much easier if he is suffering for a good and just cause. It is very difficult to stand up under suffering when it is an unjust and evil cause. Note also that it is the will of God for believers to suffer, that is to bear up under persecution, but not for doing evil. God wants believers living righteous and pure lives and He wants them witnessing for Him even if they do face persecution for it. This is the will of God; therefore, believers are to keep a good conscience before God.

In the same way, let your light shine before men, that they may see your good deeds and praise your Father in heaven. (Mat 5:16)

The Lord's message rang out from you not only in Macedonia and Achaia—your faith in God has become known everywhere. Therefore we do not need to say anything about it, (1 Th 1:8)

Don't let anyone look down on you because you are young, but set an example for the believers in speech, in life, in love, in faith and in purity. (1 Tim 4:12)

In everything set them an example by doing what is good. In your teaching show integrity, seriousness (Titus 2:7)

But someone will say, "You have faith; I have deeds." Show me your faith without deeds, and I will show you my faith by what I do. (James 2:18)

Who is wise and understanding among you? Let him show it by his good life, by deeds done in the humility that comes from wisdom. (James 3:13)

Live such good lives among the pagans that, though they accuse you of doing wrong, they may see your good deeds and glorify God on the day he visits us. (1 Pet 2:12)

But the day of the Lord will come like a thief. The heavens will disappear with a roar; the elements will be destroyed by fire, and the earth and everything in it will be laid bare. Since everything will be destroyed in this way, what kind of people ought you to be? You ought to live holy and godly lives as you look forward to the day of God and speed its coming. That day will bring about the destruction of the heavens by fire, and the elements will melt in the heat. (2 Pet 3:10-12)

	B. Understand the Death & Triumph of Christ, 3:18-22	in the days of Noah while the ark was being built. In it only a few people, eight in all, were saved through water, 21 And this water symbolizes baptism that now saves you also—not the removal of dirt from the body but the pledge of a good conscience toward God. It saves you by the resurrection of Jesus Christ,	2) To the disobedient of Noah's day
1 The death of Christ a. He died once for sins b. He died for the unjust c. He died to bring us to God **2 The triumph of Christ** a. He was made alive— raised from the dead b. He victoriously proclaimed His triumph 1) To the spirits in prison[DS1]	18 For Christ died for sins once for all, the righteous for the unrighteous, to bring you to God. He was put to death in the body but made alive by the Spirit, 19 Through whom also he went and preached to the spirits in prison 20 Who disobeyed long ago when God waited patiently		c. He saves the believer through baptism: Not baptism by water, but the baptism of a good conscience—brought about by the power of the resurrection of Jesus Christ d. He entered into heaven 1) Is at God's right hand 2) Is Lord over all

(continued, row spanning verse 22)

22 Who has gone into heaven and is at God's right hand—with angels, authorities and powers in submission to him.

DIVISION III

HOW TO HANDLE AND CONQUER SUFFERING: LIVE FOR RIGHTEOUSNESS AND NOT FOR EVIL, 3:13-4:19

B. Understand the Death and Triumph of Christ, 3:18-22

(3:18-22) **Introduction**: this is a great passage on the salvation wrought by the death of Jesus Christ. It is also an interesting passage in that it gives us some glimpse into what Jesus Christ was doing while he was dead, that is, between His crucifixion and resurrection. Two significant points are discussed.

1. The death of Christ (v.18).
2. The triumph of Christ (v.18-22).

1 (3:18) **Jesus Christ, Death**: there is the death of Christ. This is a verse that explains exactly what Christ did when He died. In the clearest of terms it tells us why Christ died and what the death of Christ does for man. In fact, this verse explains the death of Christ so clearly that it leaves the hearer without excuse if he fails to understand why Christ died. Because of its clarity every believer should study the verse in all of its depth and memorize it.

1. Christ died once for sins. It was for the sins of man that He died. Man is sinful; he is guilty before God, guilty...

- of disbelieving God. Just think how often people do not believe God, how often they do not take God and His Word seriously.
- of disobeying God. Just think how often people transgress and break the law of God.
- of cursing God. Just think how often people curse and blaspheme the name of God.
- of rebelling against God. Just think how often people choose to go their own way and do their own thing instead of doing what God says.
- of rejecting God. Just think how many people reject God.

This is sin—all of this and so much more. Man has transgressed the law of God, and when the law has been broken, the penalty has to be paid. Man has to be judged; he has to bear the punishment for his sins. What is the judgment and punishment? Death. Man has to die and he has to be separated from God forever. Why? Because God is perfect and only perfect beings can live in God's presence. This is the reason man's sin dooms him to death and eternal separation from God. But this is the glorious gospel; this is the declaration of this great verse: Jesus Christ died for our sins. He took the sin and guilt of man upon Himself and bore the judgment and punishment for man.

Note the words "for sins" (peri hamartion). These words are the very words used in the Old Testament for the sin offering (Lev.5:7; 6:30; cp. Ro.8:3; Heb.10:6, 8). The point is clear: Jesus Christ offered Himself *for sin*; He was the fulfillment of the sin-offering itself. This means a most wonderful thing: we can now become acceptable to God. We no longer have to stand before God guilty of sin, for Jesus Christ has died for our sin. If we trust His death to cover us, then sin and its guilt have been removed from us. *In Christ* we stand acceptable to God.

Note one other fact: Christ died *once* for our sins. His death never has to be repeated; His death upon the cross satisfies God completely and covers the sins and death of men forever. How? This is the discussion of the next point.

> **For what I received I passed on to you as of first importance : that Christ died for our sins according to the Scriptures, (1 Cor 15:3)**
>
> **Who gave himself for our sins to rescue us from the present evil age, according to the will of our God and Father, (Gal 1:4)**
>
> **And from Jesus Christ, who is the faithful witness, the firstborn from the dead, and the ruler of the kings of the earth. To him who loves us and has freed us from our sins by his blood, (Rev 1:5)**

2. Christ died vicariously; He was the just One dying for the unjust. What does this mean? It means two things.

a. Jesus Christ was *perfectly just* or righteous. He was sinless: as Man He lived a sinless life. Therefore, He stood before God as the Perfect and Ideal Man. He was the ideal pattern of what every man should be. His righteousness was the ideal righteousness. This means a most wonderful thing:

⇒ It means that whatever Jesus Christ did could stand for and cover all men.
⇒ It means that His righteousness could stand as the ideal and perfect righteousness. His ideal righteousness could cover every person and make him acceptable to God.
⇒ It means that His death could stand as the ideal and perfect death. His ideal death could

cover the death of every person and make him acceptable to God.

⇒ It means that Jesus Christ could become the ideal and perfect sin-offering for man. His ideal sin-offering could cover every man's sin-offering and make him acceptable to God.

> **Can any of you prove me guilty of sin? If I am telling the truth, why don't you believe me? (John 8:46)**
>
> **God made him who had no sin to be sin for us, so that in him we might become the righteousness of God. (2 Cor 5:21)**
>
> **For we do not have a high priest who is unable to sympathize with our weaknesses, but we have one who has been tempted in every way, just as we are—yet was without sin. (Heb 4:15)**
>
> **Such a high priest meets our need—one who is holy, blameless, pure, set apart from sinners, exalted above the heavens. (Heb 7:26)**
>
> **But with the precious blood of Christ, a lamb without blemish or defect. (1 Pet 1:19)**

b. Jesus Christ loves man; therefore, He gave His life for man. Man deserves to die and to be separated from God, for he is unjust and sinful. But Christ loves us; therefore He has become our substitute: borne our sin and judgment, condemnation and punishment. Therefore, we never have to die or be separated from God. If we surrender our lives to Christ—if we give ourselves over to Him—His righteousness covers us and His death covers us. *In Christ* we become acceptable to God. But we must always remember why. It is because *Christ died for us: the righteous One died for the unrighteous*. He sacrificed and substituted His life for us.

Note: this is the reason the death of Christ never has to be repeated. Christ never has to die again because He is the Perfect and Ideal Man. As the Ideal Man He has made the perfect sacrifice that satisfied the righteousness and justice of God. He has made the perfect sacrifice once-for-all (see notes—Heb.7:27; pt.3—Heb.9:11-14; 10:5-10 for more discussion).

> **And he died for all, that those who live should no longer live for themselves but for him who died for them and was raised again. (2 Cor 5:15)**
>
> **Christ redeemed us from the curse of the law by becoming a curse for us, for it is written: "Cursed is everyone who is hung on a tree." (Gal 3:13)**
>
> **But we see Jesus, who was made a little lower than the angels, now crowned with glory and honor because he suffered death, so that by the grace of God he might taste death for everyone. (Heb 2:9)**
>
> **For Christ died for sins once for all, the righteous for the unrighteous, to bring you to God. He was put to death in the body but made alive by the Spirit, (1 Pet 3:18)**

> **This is how we know what love is: Jesus Christ laid down his life for us. And we ought to lay down our lives for our brothers. (1 John 3:16)**
>
> **But he was pierced for our transgressions, he was crushed for our iniquities; the punishment that brought us peace was upon him, and by his wounds we are healed. (Isa 53:5)**

3. Christ died to bring us to God. How? It is our sin that separates and alienates us from God. It is sin that makes us imperfect and unacceptable to God. But note the most wonderful truth:

⇒ When Jesus Christ took our sin upon Himself, sin was removed from us. Therefore, we stand before God in the righteousness and sinlessness of Christ. *In Christ* we become acceptable to God.

⇒ When Jesus Christ took the guilt of our sin and died for us, our death penalty was paid. *In Christ* we no longer have to die or be separated from God.

However, note the critical point: we are acceptable to God only *in Christ*. That is, we must cast ourselves—all that we are and have, our mind, body, and soul, our past, present, and future—upon Christ. We must believe with our whole heart that Jesus Christ has died for our sins. When we genuinely believe, God accepts us *in Christ*, covering us in His righteousness and death.

> **Thought 1.** Note a terrible and tragic fact. Not everyone is *in Christ*. Not everyone *believes in Christ*. In fact, most people curse and reject Christ either by word or act. Few obey God and His Word; few trust Christ; few have given their lives to follow Christ fully and completely. Therefore, few people are covered by the death of Christ; few sins have been forgiven. Most people continue to bear their sins and the guilt of them.

> **Therefore, since we have been justified through faith, we have peace with God through our Lord Jesus Christ, (Rom 5:1)**
>
> **All this is from God, who reconciled us to himself through Christ and gave us the ministry of reconciliation: that God was reconciling the world to himself in Christ, not counting men's sins against them. And he has committed to us the message of reconciliation. (2 Cor 5:18-19)**
>
> **But now in Christ Jesus you who once were far away have been brought near through the blood of Christ. (Eph 2:13)**
>
> **And in this one body to reconcile both of them to God through the cross, by which he put to death their hostility. (Eph 2:16)**
>
> **And through him to reconcile to himself all things, whether things on earth or things in heaven, by making peace through his blood, shed on the cross. (Col 1:20)**
>
> **For this reason he had to be made like his brothers in every way, in order that he might become a merciful and faithful high priest in service to God, and that he might make atonement for the sins of the people. (Heb 2:17)**

2 (3:18-22) **Jesus Christ, Victory; Triumph; Resurrection**: there is the triumph of Christ. The triumph is seen in four glorious facts.

1. Jesus Christ was made alive. Jesus Christ was raised from the dead. Most translators say that the words *"the spirit"* refer to Jesus' spirit and not to the Holy Spirit. Jesus Christ was put to death in the flesh, but He was quickened, made alive in the spirit. In either case the meaning is pretty much the same: right after Jesus Christ died in the flesh, His spirit passed into a new life, a life that could not be tempted to sin nor undergo trials and sufferings. Jesus Christ was transferred into heaven, into the spiritual and perfect world or dimension where He lives, in the glory and majesty of God forever.

Thought 1. The same giving of life is experienced by every believer. The spirit of every true believer is quickened and made alive in Christ, made alive by God. And in that glorious day when it is time for the believer to depart this world and go on to live with God, God shall transfer the believer's spirit into heaven. Immediately—quicker than the eye can blink—the believer's spirit will be transferred into heaven, into the perfect and eternal world and dimension of being. The believer's spirit shall be perfected forever; it shall never again be subject to the trials and temptations of this corruptible world. The believer's spirit shall be perfected to live in the glory and majesty of God forever.

> **And who through the Spirit of holiness was declared with power to be the Son of God by his resurrection from the dead: Jesus Christ our Lord. (Rom 1:4)**
>
> **He was delivered over to death for our sins and was raised to life for our justification. (Rom 4:25)**
>
> **We were therefore buried with him through baptism into death in order that, just as Christ was raised from the dead through the glory of the Father, we too may live a new life. If we have been united with him like this in his death, we will certainly also be united with him in his resurrection. (Rom 6:4-5)**
>
> **And if the Spirit of him who raised Jesus from the dead is living in you, he who raised Christ from the dead will also give life to your mortal bodies through his Spirit, who lives in you. (Rom 8:11)**
>
> **For we who are alive are always being given over to death for Jesus' sake, so that his life may be revealed in our mortal body. (2 Cor 4:11)**
>
> **As for you, you were dead in your transgressions and sins, And God raised us up with Christ and seated us with him in the heavenly realms in Christ Jesus, (Eph 2:1, 6)**
>
> **Since, then, you have been raised with Christ, set your hearts on things above, where Christ is seated at the right hand of God. (Col 3:1)**
>
> **For you died, and your life is now hidden with Christ in God. When Christ, who is your life, appears, then you also will appear with him in glory. (Col 3:3-4)**

2. Jesus Christ victoriously proclaimed His triumph (v.19-20). He proclaimed the victory of His death and resurrection to the *spirits in prison* and to the *disobedient of Noah's day*. What does this mean? It means that right after Christ died, between the cross and His resurrection, He went before the *spirits in prison* and proclaimed that God's promise of salvation was fulfilled in Him, the Savior of the world. But who are the *spirits* to whom He preached? Scripture says that they were...

- the disobedient who were living upon earth while Noah was preparing the Ark.
- the disobedient toward whom God was long-suffering.
- the disobedient who were not saved during the flood.

This passage definitely says that Christ preached to the spirits of the unbelievers who had lived in Noah's day and were in *prison*, that is, the *prison of hell*. Does this mean that Christ gave them a second chance to be saved? No! It means that Jesus Christ went before them and *proclaimed His triumph*; that is, He went to *vindicate the way of faith*—to proclaim that the faith of Noah was victorious. Noah's life and his proclamation of faith in God were never vindicated in his day. Therefore, Christ Himself went before the spirits of unbelievers and personally proclaimed the victory.

Does this mean that Christ proclaimed His triumph only to the disobedient spirits of Noah's day? Not likely, for none of the Old Testament believers had ever had their faith vindicated and proven. They had only confessed that they believed in God and His promise to send the Messiah and Savior to the world. They never knew...

- who He would be
- how God would send Him
- how God would use Him to save the world
- when God would send Him

They knew little about the Savior, but they believed and trusted in Him before a mocking and unbelieving world. Therefore, it is most likely that Christ preached and vindicated the gospel before all the spirits who had disobeyed and rebelled against God. If this is so, then why did Peter focus only upon the disobedient spirits of Noah's day instead of mentioning all the spirits of the disobedient? Verse 21 tells us. Peter's very purpose is to stress how the triumph of Christ saves the believer, and he wants to stress the part that baptism (that is, the cleansing of the conscience) has in salvation. Therefore, Peter uses the saving of Noah and his family through the flooding waters as an illustration of his point.

Whatever the case, the point is this: Christ went before the spirits of the disobedient in the prison of hell and He proclaimed that God's salvation had been completed. He Himself was the Savior and Messiah of the world, the fulfillment of God's promise of salvation. Noah's faith (and the faith of all believers) was now fulfilled. Noah and the other seven members of His family were truly saved. (See DEEPER STUDY # 1—1 Pt.3:19-20 for more discussion.)

> **All men will hate you because of me, but he who stands firm to the end will be saved. (Mat 10:22)**
>
> **And all mankind will see God's salvation.'" (Luke 3:6)**
>
> **"For God so loved the world that he gave his one and only Son, that whoever believes in him shall not perish but have eternal life. (John 3:16)**

For the wages of sin is death, but the gift of God is eternal life in Christ Jesus our Lord. (Rom 6:23)

For it is by grace you have been saved, through faith—and this not from yourselves, it is the gift of God— not by works, so that no one can boast. (Eph 2:8-9)

For the grace of God that brings salvation has appeared to all men. It teaches us to say "No" to ungodliness and worldly passions, and to live self-controlled, upright and godly lives in this present age, (Titus 2:11-12)

Therefore, get rid of all moral filth and the evil that is so prevalent and humbly accept the word planted in you, which can save you. (James 1:21)

The Lord is not slow in keeping his promise, as some understand slowness. He is patient with you, not wanting anyone to perish, but everyone to come to repentance. (2 Pet 3:9)

3. Jesus Christ saves the believer through baptism: not the baptism by water, but the baptism of a good conscience—wrought by the power of the resurrection of Jesus Christ (v.21).

   a. The water which saved Noah and his family is a type of the cleansing that saves us. The water...
   - bore up the ark and saved them through the judgment of God.
   - delivered them from the ridicule and mockery of evil men.
   - delivered them from the corruption of the world and led them to a new life.
   - put to death the old world and gave them the hope of a new world.
   - put to death their old life and gave them a new beginning.
   - saved the race of man and created a new people of God.
   - delivered them from the old world right into the new world.

   What is Peter saying? Note the word "symbolizes" (antitupon). The symbol or picture of baptism is just like the water that saved Noah and his family.
   ⇒ The *flooding waters* of Noah's day picture the judgment of God upon sin. The flooding waters picture how man was saved from a corruptible world and carried into a new world.
   ⇒ The *baptismal water* pictures the judgment of God upon Christ, a judgment of death that was due sinners. It pictures how man is saved from a corruptible life and world and carried into a new life and world by the resurrection of Christ.

   b. Note: Peter says that baptism now saves us, but he *hastens* to explain what he means. He is not saying that the water or act of baptism saves us. Peter is clear about this, as clear as it can be stated.
   ⇒ It is not the cleansing of the flesh, not the outward form and ceremony that cleanses and saves. We may cleanse the outside with the most scrupulous care, but much more is needed in order to be saved.
   ⇒ It is the cleansing of a good conscience wrought by the power of the resurrection that

saves a person. The great Greek scholar A.T. Robertson says:

> "Baptism...does not wash away the filth of the flesh either in a literal sense, as a bath for the body, or in a metaphorical sense of the filth of the soul. No ceremonies really affect the conscience (Heb.9:13f)....[A person is saved] having repented and turned to God and now making this public proclamation...by means of baptism." (*Word Pictures In The New Testament*, Vol.6, p.119). (Underlining is done by us.)

Alan Stibbs says:

> "Peter deliberately adds two statements in parenthesis in order to make unmistakably plain that it is not...the outward form of baptism that saves. It is only Christ who can save through His death and resurrection, not the baptismal water and its administration. Those who would share in this salvation must enter into Christ crucified and risen" (*The First Epistle General of Peter*. "The Tyndale New Testament Commentaries," p.144).

The *Pulpit Commentary* states the significance of baptism well:

> "The outward and visible sign doth not save if separated from the inward and spiritual grace. The first [baptism] is necessary, for it is an outward sign appointed by Christ; but it will not save without the second; those who draw near to God must have their bodies washed with pure water, but also their hearts sprinkled from an evil conscience (Heb.10:22). The inner cleansing of the soul results in a good conscience, a consciousness of sincerity, of good intentions and desires, which will instinctively seek after God" (B.C. Coffin. *First Peter*. "The Pulpit Commentary," Vol.22, p.137.)

   c. Note that our consciences are cleansed by the resurrection of Christ. How does the resurrection cleanse our consciences?
   If God raised up Christ from the dead then it means that Christ is who He claimed to be: the Savior of the world. Therefore, He is able to save us from our sins. He is able to cleanse us from all sin and to free our consciences. He is able to give us a clear and pure conscience. (See note, pt.3— 1 Pt.1:3 for more discussion.)

   He was delivered over to death for our sins and was raised to life for our justification. (Rom 4:25)
   That if you confess with your mouth, "Jesus is Lord," and believe in your heart

that God raised him from the dead, you will be saved. For it is with your heart that you believe and are justified, and it is with your mouth that you confess and are saved. (Rom 10:9-10)

Now, brothers, I want to remind you of the gospel I preached to you, which you received and on which you have taken your stand. By this gospel you are saved, if you hold firmly to the word I preached to you. Otherwise, you have believed in vain. For what I received I passed on to you as of first importance : that Christ died for our sins according to the Scriptures, that he was buried, that he was raised on the third day according to the Scriptures, (1 Cor 15:1-4)

Now this is our boast: Our conscience testifies that we have conducted ourselves in the world, and especially in our relations with you, in the holiness and sincerity that are from God. We have done so not according to worldly wisdom but according to God's grace. (2 Cor 1:12)

How much more, then, will the blood of Christ, who through the eternal Spirit offered himself unblemished to God, cleanse our consciences from acts that lead to death, so that we may serve the living God! (Heb 9:14)

Holding on to faith and a good conscience. Some have rejected these and so have shipwrecked their faith. (1 Tim 1:19)

Praise be to the God and Father of our Lord Jesus Christ! In his great mercy he has given us new birth into a living hope through the resurrection of Jesus Christ from the dead, (1 Pet 1:3)

4. Jesus Christ saves the believer from all angels, authorities, and powers (v.22). All beings of all dimensions and worlds are submission to Him. He has gone into heaven and is on the right hand of God. He rules and reigns over all, submitting all to His sovereign will and power.

Thought 1. This means a most wonderful thing. Believers need never fear anyone or anything. Christ Jesus the Lord is looking after them. He will provide, protect, and deliver through all the trials and temptations of life no matter how terrible and severe.

And his incomparably great power for us who believe. That power is like the working of his mighty strength, which he exerted in Christ when he raised him from the dead and seated him at his right hand in the heavenly realms, far above all rule and authority, power and dominion, and every title that can be given, not only in the present age but also in the one to come. And God placed all things under his feet and appointed him to be head over everything for the church, (Eph 1:19-22)

Therefore God exalted him to the highest place and gave him the name that is above every name, (Phil 2:9)

Therefore, since we have a great high priest who has gone through the heavens,

Jesus the Son of God, let us hold firmly to the faith we profess. For we do not have a high priest who is unable to sympathize with our weaknesses, but we have one who has been tempted in every way, just as we are—yet was without sin. Let us then approach the throne of grace with confidence, so that we may receive mercy and find grace to help us in our time of need. (Heb 4:14-16)

For Christ did not enter a man-made sanctuary that was only a copy of the true one; he entered heaven itself, now to appear for us in God's presence. (Heb 9:24)

For to us a child is born, to us a son is given, and the government will be on his shoulders. And he will be called Wonderful Counselor, Mighty God, Everlasting Father, Prince of Peace. (Isa 9:6)

DEEPER STUDY # 1

(3:19-20) **Hell—Jesus Christ, Triumph**: this passage clearly says that Jesus Christ "went and preached to the spirits in prison." It says in particular that He preached to the souls of those who had lived in the days of Noah but had rejected God's salvation and long-suffering. What does all this mean? In order to determine the meaning, we must note four points.

1. First, note where the spirits of unbelievers go when they leave this world. Scripture says that the place where unbelievers go is a *prison* (1 Pt.3:19), and the picture in the Greek is actually that of a prison. Just as men put rebellious people into prison, so God shall imprison those who rebel against Him. Scripture even pictures God having Satan bound with a chain and cast into the prison of the bottomless pit. It also pictures God having the angels who rebelled with Satan bound with the chains of darkness and cast into the prison of hell. The point is that hell, the place where unbelievers go after leaving this world, is pictured as a prison. Scripture uses four words or terms to describe the prison. Note how each word or term describes a different section or cell block or compartment to the prison of hell.

a. There is the cell block or compartment which is called *Hell* or what the Greeks called *Hades* and the Hebrews called *Sheol*. This is the place where unbelievers go when they die and enter into the next world. Hell is the torment section for the human race, the place where all unbelievers are placed and punished until the end of the world. At the end of the world, they are all taken out of hell and cast into the lake of fire (cp. Lk.16:19-31. See DEEPER STUDY # 2—Mt.5:22 for more discussion.)

Do not be afraid of those who kill the body but cannot kill the soul. Rather, be afraid of the One who can destroy both soul and body in hell. (Mat 10:28)

"You snakes! You brood of vipers! How will you escape being condemned to hell? (Mat 23:33)

b. There is the cell block or compartment of *Tartarus*. This is the place where fallen angels are kept until the end of the world. At the end of the world they too shall be cast into the lake of fire. Note the description of Tartarus. It is a place…

- of imprisonment where fallen angels are chained in gloomy dungeons (2 Pt.2:4; Jude 6).

- of darkness (Jude 6).
- of punishment (Jude 7).
- of eternal fire (Jude 7).

Note: some commentators interpret the "sons of God" of Genesis 6:1-4 as angels and say that they are the only angels imprisoned in Tartarus. In this view Tartarus is thought to be the worst of all *hells* because the sin of Gen.6:1-4 is thought to be the worst imaginable sin. In this view some of the other angels are said to be imprisoned in the bottomless pit and still others are thought to be roaming throughout the universe working for Satan and oppressing men.

For if God did not spare angels when they sinned, but sent them to hell, putting them into gloomy dungeons to be held for judgment; (2 Pet 2:4)
And the angels who did not keep their positions of authority but abandoned their own home—these he has kept in darkness, bound with everlasting chains for judgment on the great Day. In a similar way, Sodom and Gomorrah and the surrounding towns gave themselves up to sexual immorality and perversion. They serve as an example of those who suffer the punishment of eternal fire. (Jude 1:6-7)

c. There is the cell block or compartment called the *Abyss* or the *Bottomless Pit*. This is the place where demons and evil spirits are kept until the end of the world. As pointed out in the previous point, some commentators think that some angels are also imprisoned in the *Abyss*.

And they [evil spirits] begged him repeatedly not to order them to go into the Abyss. (Luke 8:31)
The fifth angel sounded his trumpet, and I saw a star that had fallen from the sky to the earth. The star was given the key to the shaft of the Abyss. When he opened the Abyss, smoke rose from it like the smoke from a gigantic furnace. The sun and sky were darkened by the smoke from the Abyss. And out of the smoke locusts came down upon the earth and were given power like that of scorpions of the earth. They had as king over them the angel of the Abyss, whose name in Hebrew is Abaddon, and in Greek, Apollyon. (Rev 9:1-3, 11)
Now when they have finished their testimony, the beast that comes up from the Abyss will attack them, and overpower and kill them. (Rev 11:7)
The beast [antichrist] , which you saw, once was, now is not, and will come up out of the Abyss and go to his destruction. The inhabitants of the earth whose names have not been written in the book of life from the creation of the world will be astonished when they see the beast, because he once was, now is not, and yet will come. (Rev 17:8)
And I saw an angel coming down out of heaven, having the key to the Abyss and holding in his hand a great chain. He seized

the dragon, that ancient serpent, who is the devil, or Satan, and bound him for a thousand years. (Rev 20:1-2)

d. There is the cell block or compartment called *Gehenna* or the *Lake of Fire*. This is the place where all those who have rebelled against God are to be cast at the end of the world—all unbelieving men, fallen angels, demons, and the devil. At the final judgment of unbelievers, the lake of fire is the *final hell* to which all the wicked shall be judged and condemned, and the judgment of Gehenna is said to be eternal.

The Son of Man will send out his angels, and they will weed out of his kingdom everything that causes sin and all who do evil. They will throw them into the fiery furnace, where there will be weeping and gnashing of teeth. (Mat 13:41-42)
If your hand or your foot causes you to sin cut it off and throw it away. It is better for you to enter life maimed or crippled than to have two hands or two feet and be thrown into eternal fire. (Mat 18:8)
And the devil, who deceived them, was thrown into the lake of burning sulfur, where the beast and the false prophet had been thrown. They will be tormented day and night for ever and ever. (Rev 20:10)
"Then he will say to those on his left, 'Depart from me, you who are cursed, into the eternal fire prepared for the devil and his angels. "Then they will go away to eternal punishment, but the righteous to eternal life." (Mat 25:41, 46)
Then I saw a great white throne and him who was seated on it. Earth and sky fled from his presence, and there was no place for them. And I saw the dead, great and small, standing before the throne, and books were opened. Another book was opened, which is the book of life. The dead were judged according to what they had done as recorded in the books. The sea gave up the dead that were in it, and death and Hades gave up the dead that were in them, and each person was judged according to what he had done. Then death and Hades were thrown into the lake of fire. The lake of fire is the second death. If anyone's name was not found written in the book of life, he was thrown into the lake of fire. (Rev 20:11-15)
But the cowardly, the unbelieving, the vile, the murderers, the sexually immoral, those who practice magic arts, the idolaters and all liars—their place will be in the fiery lake of burning sulfur. This is the second death." (Rev 21:8)

2. Second, note where believers go when they leave this world. Scripture says that the place where believers go is paradise or heaven, and after the end of the world they shall become the citizens of the new heavens and earth.

a. There is paradise or heaven, the place of perfection and glory where God is perfectly glorified, worshipped, and served. It should be noted that some scholars say that paradise is one compartment or place in God's presence and that heaven is another compartment or place. They say that paradise was the place where all believers went before Christ, but now, since Christ, believers are much more honored and glorified. Believers are now taken to the compartment and place of heaven. (See DEEPER STUDY # 3, *Paradise*—Lk.16:23.) However, note this: the word *paradise* is found only three times in the New Testament.

> **Jesus answered him, "I tell you the truth, today you will be with me in paradise." (Luke 23:43)**
> **I know a man in Christ who fourteen years ago was caught up to the third heaven. Whether it was in the body or out of the body I do not know—God knows. And I know that this man—whether in the body or apart from the body I do not know, but God knows— was caught up to paradise. He heard inexpressible things, things that man is not permitted to tell. (2 Cor 12:2-4. Note that Paul says that the third heaven is the same as paradise, v.2, 4)**
> **He who has an ear, let him hear what the Spirit says to the churches. To him who overcomes, I will give the right to eat from the tree of life, which is in the paradise of God. (Rev 2:7)**

Scripture is clear about where believers go since the death and resurrection of Christ: they go immediately to be with Christ. Genuine believers never taste or experience death. They are transferred into heaven, transferred quicker than the eye can blink.

> **We are confident, I say, and would prefer to be away from the body and at home with the Lord. (2 Cor 5:8)**
> **I am torn between the two: I desire to depart and be with Christ, which is better by far; (Phil 1:23)**
> **After that, we who are still alive and are left will be caught up together with them in the clouds to meet the Lord in the air. And so we will be with the Lord forever. (1 Th 4:17)**

b. There is the *new heavens and earth*. The present heavens and earth are to be destroyed by fire and recreated. They are to be remade and created perfect without any seed of corruption whatsoever. The new heavens and earth are to be the eternal dwelling place for both Christ and believers.

> **But the day of the Lord will come like a thief. The heavens will disappear with a roar; the elements will be destroyed by fire, and the earth and everything in it will be laid bare. Since everything will be destroyed in this way, what kind of people ought you to be? You ought to live holy and godly lives as you look forward to the day of God and speed its coming. That day will bring about the destruction of the heavens by fire, and the elements will melt in the heat. But in keeping with his promise we are looking forward to a new heaven and a**

> **new earth, the home of righteousness. (2 Pet 3:10-13)**
> **Then I saw a new heaven and a new earth, for the first heaven and the first earth had passed away, and there was no longer any sea. I saw the Holy City, the new Jerusalem, coming down out of heaven from God, prepared as a bride beautifully dressed for her husband. And I heard a loud voice from the throne saying, "Now the dwelling of God is with men, and he will live with them. They will be his people, and God himself will be with them and be their God. He will wipe every tear from their eyes. There will be no more death or mourning or crying or pain, for the old order of things has passed away." He who was seated on the throne said, "I am making everything new!" Then he said, "Write this down, for these words are trustworthy and true." (Rev 21:1-5)**
> **"Behold, I will create new heavens and a new earth. The former things will not be remembered, nor will they come to mind. (Isa 65:17)**
> **"As the new heavens and the new earth that I make will endure before me," declares the LORD, "so will your name and descendants endure. (Isa 66:22)**

3. Third, note exactly what this verse says: "He [Christ] went and preached to the spirits in prison." What spirits? Who were the spirits to whom Christ went and preached? Note that the unbelievers of Noah's day are mentioned. But did Christ proclaim His triumph only to them? Not likely. He probably proclaimed His triumph to all those who had rebelled against God from the beginning of time.

a. He probably proclaimed His triumph to all the unbelievers in *hell*. He vindicated *the way of faith*, proclaimed that the faith of Noah and of all other believers was victorious. Remember that Noah's faith and life were never vindicated during his lifetime. He was mocked, abused, and rejected by the people of his day. Therefore, Christ Himself proclaimed the victory personally. The same shall be true in the end time. Scripture says that Christ shall vindicate the faith of His followers before all the enemies of God's people. The way of faith will triumph and Christ Himself will once again go before all men and proclaim the triumph of the way of faith. He shall be exalted as Lord, to the glory of God the Father (Ph.2:9-11). (See note, pt.2—Eph.4:8-10 for more discussion.)

b. He probably proclaimed His triumph to the fallen angels in *Tartarus*. All through history the fallen angels have rebelled against God and fought to keep the promised seed of the Savior from coming to earth. They have done all they can to lead men to reject God. Jesus Christ was able to stand before them and proclaim that He was the promised seed, the Savior of the world, and that the way of salvation was now provided for man.

If the angels in Tartarus are the "sons of God" mentioned in Gen.6:1-4, then they were trying to destroy the human race and to prevent the promised seed, the Savior, from ever coming. Christ would then be appearing before them to proclaim that their plan did not work and to vindicate the love and power of God to carry out His will. Christ was able to declare, "Here I am. God's plan has triumphed; He has now fulfilled His promise of salvation through my death and resurrection."

c. He probably proclaimed His triumph to the demons and evil spirits in the *abyss*. He probably vindicated the faith of all believers who had been oppressed by the evil spirits down through the centuries.

d. If paradise is a separate place or compartment from heaven, then Christ probably showed Himself to the Old Testament saints in paradise, proclaiming the fulfillment of their salvation. It should also be noted that some interpreters hold that He opened the door to paradise and took the Old Testament saints to heaven with Him when He arose from the dead. Remember: some of the Old Testament believers were raised and appeared to many in Jerusalem when Christ arose (Mt. 27:52-53). This would have been to confirm and strengthen the faith of the early believers—to make them stronger witnesses for the Lord. By seeing their loved ones raised from the dead, they would know beyond any question that Jesus is who He claimed: the Son of God, the Savior of the world.

4. Fourth, note a significant question: if the fallen angels and demons are in the prison of hell, how then can they attack and oppress man? There are at least two possible answers.

a. All fallen angels and demons are not in the prison of hell and its various compartments. Some are still able to roam about the universe and have access to oppress and influence men. However, if this is true, why are some imprisoned by God and some are not? Since they are all guilty of rebellion against God, it seems unlikely that God would imprison some and not others.

b. The prison of hell is another dimension of being, a spiritual world or dimension of corruption and suffering. It is a world of so much corruption and punishment that it can be called the prison of hell. An example would be the prison of corruption and suffering that man experiences. All men, including believers even after they are saved, are imprisoned and enslaved to corruption and suffering. Perhaps angels and evil spirits live in a sphere, dimension, compartment, or section of the spiritual world that is totally corrupt and involves the torment of judgment and punishment. If hell is another dimension of being, a spiritual world of corruption and suffering, then this would explain the influence of angels and demons on this world. The spiritual world definitely has access to the physical world. Therefore, fallen angels and demons, who are spiritual beings, are able to influence and oppress men so long as men are in the physical world. The spiritual world is a spiritual dimension of being just as the physical world is a material dimension of being. The spiritual world or dimension is much greater in power; therefore, it has access to the physical dimension or world.

Another way to say the same thing is this. Within the spiritual world there are good spirits and bad spirits. Therefore, the spiritual world has a good section or compartment called heaven and a bad section or compartment called hell. Hell, which can be called a prison, has several sections or compartments. As just stated above, the spiritual world or dimension has greater power and has access to the physical world. This would explain why Satan and the fallen angels and the demons of the other world have access to influence and oppress men. This would also fit what we scientifically know today about the possibility of other dimensions of being.

	CHAPTER 4 **C. Arm Yourself with the Mind of Christ, 4:1-6**	in debauchery, lust, drunkenness, orgies, carousing and detestable idolatry.	
1 It is dying to self—denying oneself—giving up sin	Therefore, since Christ suffered in his body, arm yourselves also with the same attitude, because he who has suffered in his body is done with sin.	4 They think it strange that you do not plunge with them into the same flood of dissipation, and they heap abuse on you. 5 But they will have to give account to him who is ready to judge the living and the dead.	**4 It is bearing the strange look by the world** a. They think believers are strange b. They slander believers c. They shall be judged
2 It is doing God's will for the rest of one's days	2 As a result, he does not live the rest of his earthly life for evil human desires, but rather for the will of God.	6 For this is the reason the gospel was preached even to those who are now dead, so that they might be judged according to men in regard to	**5 It is following the example of those gone before** a. The gospel was preached to them
3 It is being fed up with sin, knowing that one has sinned enough	3 For you have spent enough time in the past doing what pagans choose to do—living	the body, but live according to God in regard to the spirit.	b. They responded & escaped judgment (cp.v.5)

DIVISION III

HOW TO HANDLE AND CONQUER SUFFERING: LIVE FOR RIGHTEOUSNESS AND NOT FOR EVIL, 3:13-4:19

C. Arm Yourself with the Mind of Christ, 4:1-6

(4:1-6) Introduction: living for Jesus Christ is not easy. When we live for Christ, really live righteous and godly lives, the unbelievers of the world reject us. They want little to do with pure righteousness and pure godliness. A godly life convicts them and demands that they live like God or else face His judgment. Therefore, the world often ridicules, mocks, abuses, and sometimes kills the genuine believer. How can the believer handle and conquer such persecution when he is so unjustly treated? There is one way: he should arm himself with the attitude of Jesus Christ. Jesus Christ suffered persecution and He suffered persecution to the ultimate degree. He has shown us how to handle and conquer persecution. Therefore, arm yourself with the mind of Christ.

1. It is dying to self, denying oneself, giving up sin (v.1).
2. It is doing God's will for the rest of one's days (v.2).
3. It is being fed up with sin, knowing that one has sinned enough (v.3).
4. It is bearing the strange look by the world (v.4-5).
5. It is following the example of those gone before (v.6).

1 (4:1) **Self-Denial—Suffering**: arm yourself with the attitude of Christ. What does this mean? First, it means to die to self; to deny oneself. Jesus Christ denied Himself to the ultimate degree: He suffered for us in His body. Jesus Christ lived a pure and righteous life and men persecuted Him for it. But He bore the humiliation, ridicule, mockery, beatings, and even death in order to please God and to save men. In His body He did not want to suffer. He had a body just like ours, the body of humanity; therefore, His body wanted and desired to escape the abuse of men (cp. Heb.2:14-15). But Jesus Christ denied Himself and went ahead and did the will of God. The exhortation is strong:

"Now, you do the same thing. Arm yourself with the attitude of Christ. You are in a warfare with the desires and lusts of the flesh; the acts of the sinful nature and they are going to destroy you unless you conquer them. Therefore, you must arm yourself; you must put on the armor that will protect you. What is that armor?

⇒ The attitudes of Christ. The very same attitudes that delivered and saved Christ. Christ kept His attitudes and thoughts upon righteousness and salvation. Therefore, Christ gave Himself up—denied Himself—and suffered for us. We must do the same: we must keep our attitudes upon righteousness and salvation. We must die to self and suffer for Christ. We must become identified with Christ in His self-denial and suffering of death. We must identify with Him by denying ourselves and suffering for His name. Jesus Christ denied the desires of the flesh in order to please God and to save us. We are to do the same; we are to deny the desires of the flesh in order to please God and save men. We do this by keeping our thoughts upon the suffering and self-denial of Christ. We can conquer the flesh (sinful nature) and its desires by arming ourselves with the attitude of Christ. Therefore, our attitudes and thoughts are to be armed, that is, clothed, with the very armor of Christ's attitude.

Note one other significant fact: the person who suffers in the body has *given up sin, is done with sin once for all."* What does this mean? When the world persecutes us, we do not want to suffer and bear the judgment of ridicule, mockery, and abuse of men. Now if we give in to the fleshly desires and go along with the world, we sin and doom ourselves. But if we arm ourselves with the attitude of Christ, deny our fleshly desires and suffer for Christ and for the salvation of men, then we deny sin. We do just what Christ did: we deny sin and live righteously. Our suffering for Christ has delivered us from sin and it has caused us to give up sin, to be done with sin once for all. We have done the right thing, and in doing the right thing, we are delivered from sin. We are living righteously—all for Christ and His cause.

Another way to say the same thing is this: the person who suffers for Christ has chosen to identify himself with Christ. He has chosen to deny himself and his fleshly desires and to identify himself with Christ and His sufferings of death. Therefore, in suffering for Christ, the person is not sinning; he is living righteously. He is doing the right thing; he has done away with sin. Note this: the more a person suffers for Christ, the closer he becomes to Christ; and the closer he becomes to Christ, the more the desires and lusts of the flesh (sin) lose their appeal and power over the person.

> **By no means! We died to sin; how can we live in it any longer? Or don't you know that all of us who were baptized into Christ Jesus were baptized into his death? We were therefore buried with him through baptism into death in order that, just as Christ was raised from the dead through the glory of the Father, we too may live a new life. (Rom 6:2-4)**

> For we know that our old self was crucified with him so that the body of sin might be done away with, that we should no longer be slaves to sin— because anyone who has died has been freed from sin. Now if we died with Christ, we believe that we will also live with him. For we know that since Christ was raised from the dead, he cannot die again; death no longer has mastery over him. The death he died, he died to sin once for all; but the life he lives, he lives to God. In the same way, count yourselves dead to sin but alive to God in Christ Jesus. Therefore do not let sin reign in your mortal body so that you obey its evil desires. Do not offer the parts of your body to sin, as instruments of wickedness, but rather offer yourselves to God, as those who have been brought from death to life; and offer the parts of your body to him as instruments of righteousness. (Rom 6:6-13)

> I have been crucified with Christ and I no longer live, but Christ lives in me. The life I live in the body, I live by faith in the Son of God, who loved me and gave himself for me. (Gal 2:20)

> Those who belong to Christ Jesus have crucified the sinful nature with its passions and desires. (Gal 5:24)

> For you died, and your life is now hidden with Christ in God. (Col 3:3)

> He himself bore our sins in his body on the tree, so that we might die to sins and live for righteousness; by his wounds you have been healed. (1 Pet 2:24)

2 (4:2) **God, Will—Believer, Life and Walk**: arm yourself with the attitude of Christ. What does this mean? Second, it means to do the will of God—do it for the rest of your days. Note that the phrase "evil human desires" is plural. It is the picture of the believer being pulled every which way by different persons or groups. The believer is being pulled to live like the world lives, fulfilling the desires and lusts of the flesh. Men lust after the pleasures and possessions of the world...

- houses
- lands
- wealth
- position
- power
- recognition

- drink
- sex
- stimulation
- partying
- recreation
- excitement

Lusting after these things is not the will of God. God's will is for believers to live pure and righteous lives and to focus upon proclaiming the gospel of eternal life to a lost and dying world. Genuine believers do this. They do not make the lusts and desires of men the rule of their lives. The rule of their lives is God. And note the Scripture: they have committed the *rest of their days* to the will of God. This is what the mind of Christ means: just as Christ was totally committed to the will of God, so we are totally committed to the will of God. Just as His thoughts were consumed with God's will, so our thoughts are consumed with God's will. We arm ourselves with the very attitude of Christ: we become consumed in attitude and thought with the will of God, not with the lusts of men. We focus and concentrate upon living righteous lives and upon carrying the gospel to every person in the world (cp. v.6).

> **For whoever does the will of my Father in heaven is my brother and sister and mother." (Mat 12:50)**

> For we know that our old self was crucified with him so that the body of sin might be done away with, that we should no longer be slaves to sin— (Rom 6:6)

> In the same way, count yourselves dead to sin but alive to God in Christ Jesus. (Rom 6:11)

> Rather, clothe yourselves with the Lord Jesus Christ, and do not think about how to gratify the desires of the sinful nature. (Rom 13:14)

> If we live, we live to the Lord; and if we die, we die to the Lord. So, whether we live or die, we belong to the Lord. (Rom 14:8)

> And he died for all, that those who live should no longer live for themselves but for him who died for them and was raised again. (2 Cor 5:15)

> And do not forget to do good and to share with others, for with such sacrifices God is pleased. (Heb 13:16)

> I desire to do your will, O my God; your law is within my heart." (Psa 40:8)

> Teach me to do your will, for you are my God; may your good Spirit lead me on level ground. (Psa 143:10)

3 (4:3) **Sin**: arm yourself with the attitude of Christ. What does this mean? Third, it means being fed up with sin, knowing that one has sinned enough. The believer's life is divided into two parts: *his old life and his new life*. Note the force of this verse: in his *old life*, he sinned enough. He has already followed the desires and lusts of the ungodly (Gentiles) enough. He has already worked the will of the ungodly. He has walked after them, walked just as they walk, and enough is enough. The believer is no longer to fulfill the desires of the flesh (sinful nature). Note that six sins in particular are mentioned.

1. *Debauchery* (aselgeiai): filthiness, indecency, shamelessness, license, without restraint. A chief characteristic of the behavior is open and shameless indecency. It means unrestrained evil thoughts and behavior. It is giving in to brutish and lustful desires, a readiness for any pleasure. It is a man who knows no restraint, a man who has sinned so much that he no longer cares what people say or think. It is something far more distasteful than just doing wrong. The man who misbehaves usually tries to hide his wrong, but a lascivious man does not care who knows about his exploits or shame. He wants; therefore he seeks to take and gratify.

Decency and opinion do not matter. Initially when he began to sin, he did as all men do: he misbehaved in secret. But eventually, the sin got the best of him—to the point that he no longer cared who saw or knew. He became the subject of a master—the master of habit, of the thing itself. Men become the slaves of such things as unbridled lust, wantonness, licentiousness, outrageousness, shamelessness, insolence (Mk.7:22); lewd manners, filthy words, indecent body movements, immoral handling of males and females (Ro.13:13); public display of affection, carnality, gluttony, sexual immorality (1 Pt.4:3; 2 Pt.2:2, 18). (Cp. 2 Cor. 12:21; Gal.5:19; Eph.4:19; 2 Pt.2:7.)

> In the same way the men also abandoned natural relations with women and were inflamed with lust for one another. Men committed indecent acts with other men [homosexuality], and received in themselves the due penalty for their perversion. (Rom 1:27)

> Having lost all sensitivity, they have given themselves over to sensuality so as to indulge in every kind of impurity, with a continual lust for more. (Eph 4:19)

> For certain men whose condemnation was written about long ago have secretly slipped in among you. They are godless men, who change the grace of our God into a license for immorality and deny Jesus Christ our only Sovereign and Lord. In a similar way, Sodom and Gomorrah and the surrounding towns gave themselves up to sexual immorality and perversion. They serve as an example of those who suffer the punishment of eternal fire. (Jude 1:4, 7)

> For you have spent enough time in the past doing what pagans choose to do—living in debauchery, lust, drunkenness, orgies, carousing and detestable idolatry. (1 Pet 4:3)

2. *Lust* (epithumias): the word means strong desire or craving and passion; it means that the pull of sin is sometimes very, very strong. All men know what it is to lust after things, after more and more, and never to be satisfied even after the things are secured. (See note—1 Pt.1:14; 2:11 for more discussion.)

> Rather, clothe yourselves with the Lord Jesus Christ, and do not think about how to gratify the desires of the sinful nature. (Rom 13:14)

> Dear friends, I urge you, as aliens and strangers in the world, to abstain from sinful desires, which war against your soul. (1 Pet 2:11)

> As a result, he does not live the rest of his earthly life for evil human desires, but rather for the will of God. (1 Pet 4:2)

3. *Drunkenness* (oinophlugiai): excess amounts of wine, drunkenness, winebibbing. It would include taking drink or drugs to affect one's senses for lust or pleasure; becoming tipsy or intoxicated; partaking of drugs; seeking to loosen moral restraint for bodily pleasure.

> "Be careful, or your hearts will be weighed down with dissipation, drunken ness and the anxieties of life, and that day will close on you unexpectedly like a trap. (Luke 21:34)

> Let us behave decently, as in the daytime, not in orgies and drunkenness, not in sexual immorality and debauchery, not in dissension and jealousy. (Rom 13:13)

> Nor thieves nor the greedy nor drunkards nor slanderers nor swindlers will inherit the kingdom of God. (1 Cor 6:10)

> Do not get drunk on wine, which leads to debauchery. Instead, be filled with the Spirit. (Eph 5:18)

> For those who sleep, sleep at night, and those who get drunk, get drunk at night. (1 Th 5:7)

> Wine is a mocker and beer a brawler; whoever is led astray by them is not wise. (Prov 20:1)

> Who has woe? Who has sorrow? Who has strife? Who has complaints? Who has needless bruises? Who has bloodshot eyes? Those who linger over wine, who go to sample bowls of mixed wine. (Prov 23:29-30)

> Woe to those who rise early in the morning to run after their drinks, who stay up late at night till they are inflamed with wine. (Isa 5:11)

> They will be entangled among thorns and drunk from their wine; they will be consumed like dry stubble. (Nahum 1:10)

4. *Orgies* (komois): carousing; uncontrolled license, indulgence, and pleasure; taking part in wild parties or in drinking parties or in orgies; lying around indulging in feeding the lusts of the flesh (sinful nature).

> For you have spent enough time in the past doing what pagans choose to do—living in debauchery, lust, drunkenness, orgies, carousing and detestable idolatry. (1 Pet 4:3)

> They will be paid back with harm for the harm they have done. Their idea of pleasure is to carouse in broad daylight. They are blots and blemishes, reveling in their pleasures while they feast with you. With eyes full of adultery, they never stop sinning; they seduce the unstable; they are experts in greed—an accursed brood! (2 Pet 2:13-14)

> And envy; drunkenness, orgies, and the like. I warn you, as I did before, that those who live like this will not inherit the kingdom of God. (Gal 5:21)

> So the next day the people rose early and sacrificed burnt offerings and presented fellowship offerings. Afterward they sat down to eat and drink and got up to indulge in revelry. (Exo 32:6; cp. Judges 9:27; 1 Sam.30:16)

5. *Carousing* (potoi): drinking parties; partying and getting drunk.

> Let us behave decently, as in the daytime, not in orgies and drunkenness, not in sexual immorality and debauchery, not in dissension and jealousy. (Rom 13:13)

For you have spent enough time in the past doing what pagans choose to do—living in debauchery, lust, drunkenness, orgies, carousing and detestable idolatry. (1 Pet 4:3)

For those who sleep, sleep at night, and those who get drunk, get drunk at night. (1 Th 5:7)

6. *Detestable idolatry* (athemitois eidoloatriais): the worship of idols, whether mental or made by man's hands; the worship of some idea of what God is like, of an image of God within a person's mind; the giving of one's primary devotion (time and energy) to something other than God. (See note, *Idolatry*—1 Cor.6:9 for detailed discussion.)

Therefore, my dear friends, flee from idolatry. (1 Cor 10:14)

The acts of the sinful nature are obvious: sexual immorality, impurity and debauchery; idolatry and witchcraft; hatred, discord, jealousy, fits of rage, selfish ambition, dissensions, factions and envy; drunkenness, orgies, and the like. I warn you, as I did before, that those who live like this will not inherit the kingdom of God. (Gal 5:19-21)

For of this you can be sure: No immoral, impure or greedy person—such a man is an idolater—has any inheritance in the kingdom of Christ and of God. (Eph 5:5)

Put to death, therefore, whatever belongs to your earthly nature: sexual immorality, impurity, lust, evil desires and greed, which is idolatry. Because of these, the wrath of God is coming. (Col 3:5-6)

But the cowardly, the unbelieving, the vile, the murderers, the sexually immoral, those who practice magic arts, the idolaters and all liars—their place will be in the fiery lake of burning sulfur. This is the second death." (Rev 21:8)

Outside are the dogs, those who practice magic arts, the sexually immoral, the murderers, the idolaters and everyone who loves and practices falsehood. (Rev 22:15)

4 (4:4-5) **Persecution—Judgment**: arm yourself with the attitude of Christ. What does this mean? Fourth, it means to bear the strange look of the world. This fact is easily understood and it is often experienced by believers. The worldly just cannot understand...

- why a genuine believer separates himself from the world and does not participate in its pleasures and in getting all of the possessions he can.
- why a genuine believer gives all he is and has to spreading the gospel around the world and meeting the desperate needs of the world.

This is particularly true if the believer participated in the pleasures and ways of the world before his conversion. Once he has been converted and begins to separate himself from his old life, his former associates begin to look at him as a strange creature, and they often begin to slander and heap abuse upon him. They ridicule, mock, and withdraw from him because he no longer shares with them in the drinking parties or in the crooked and covetous ways of the world.

Note: the worldly and ungodly shall be judged. They shall give an account to Christ for all their ridicule, abuse, and persecution of believers. And Scripture is clear: Christ is *ready to judge* both the living and the dead.

All the nations will be gathered before him, and he will separate the people one from another as a shepherd separates the sheep from the goats. (Mat 25:32)

Moreover, the Father judges no one, but has entrusted all judgment to the Son, (John 5:22)

For he has set a day when he will judge the world with justice by the man he has appointed. He has given proof of this to all men by raising him from the dead." (Acts 17:31)

This will take place on the day when God will judge men's secrets through Jesus Christ, as my gospel declares. (Rom 2:16)

You, then, why do you judge your brother? Or why do you look down on your brother? For we will all stand before God's judgment seat. (Rom 14:10)

In the presence of God and of Christ Jesus, who will judge the living and the dead, and in view of his appearing and his kingdom, I give you this charge: (2 Tim 4:1)

And I saw the dead, great and small, standing before the throne, and books were opened. Another book was opened, which is the book of life. The dead were judged according to what they had done as recorded in the books. (Rev 20:12)

"Behold, I am coming soon! My reward is with me, and I will give to everyone according to what he has done. (Rev 22:12)

"I the LORD search the heart and examine the mind, to reward a man according to his conduct, according to what his deeds deserve." (Jer 17:10)

5 (4:6) **Gospel—Preaching**: arm yourself with the attitude of Christ. What does this mean? Fifth, it means to follow the example of believers who have gone before. God is going to judge the world. This is the reason He has seen to it that the gospel be preached. And note: the gospel was preached to believers who have already died.

⇒ The gospel was preached in order to judge them while they were still men in regard to the body: preached to condemn them for living after the sinful ways of men; preached to convict them of sin, and righteousness, and judgment.
⇒ The gospel was preached in order to give them life, a spiritual life, a life that is just like God's life; a life that has the power to live in the spirit forever and ever, to live just like God; a life that is eternal; a life that is eternal just like God's life.

The point is this: believers who have gone on heard the gospel. They heard the judgment and condemnation of the gospel while they were living on earth, and they accepted the gospel. Therefore, they shall escape the judgment to come (v.5). They now live with God, possessing the very life of God Himself which is eternal life. They shall live forever and ever with God. It is this that we are to keep our attitudes upon. We are to arm ourselves with the example of those who have gone on before. We must let the gospel judge and convict us of sin, and we must repent. We must turn away from sin and turn to God. When we so respond to the gospel, we receive the very life of God Himself. We shall live with God forever and ever just like those who have gone on and now live in His presence.

"I tell you the truth, whoever hears my word and believes him who sent me has eternal life and will not be condemned; he has crossed over from death to life. (John 5:24)

For the wages of sin is death, but the gift of God is eternal life in Christ Jesus our Lord. (Rom 6:23)

For we who are alive are always being given over to death for Jesus' sake, so that his life may be revealed in our mortal body. (2 Cor 4:11)

For to me, to live is Christ and to die is gain. (Phil 1:21)

We know that we have passed from death to life, because we love our brothers. Anyone who does not love remains in death. (1 John 3:14)

	D. Live Under the Shadow of History's Climax, 4:7-11	10 Each one should use whatever gift he has received to serve others, faithfully administering God's grace in its various forms.	5 Live using your gift a. Serve—ministering to one another b. Serve—faithfully
1 Live being clear-minded and self-controlled	7 The end of all things is near. Therefore be clear minded and self-controlled so that you can pray.	11 If anyone speaks, he should do it as one speaking the very words of God. If anyone serves, he should do it with the strength God provides, so that in all things God may be praised through Jesus Christ. To him be the glory and the power for ever and ever. Amen.	c. Serve—speaking the Word of God d. Serve—ministering in the strength of God e. Serve—that God may be glorified in all things.
2 Live watching & praying			
3 Live with fervent love a. Among brothers b. Because love covers a multitude of sins	8 Above all, love each other deeply, because love covers over a multitude of sins.		
4 Live showing hospitality & do it cheerfully	9 Offer hospitality to one another without grumbling.		

DIVISION III

HOW TO HANDLE AND CONQUER SUFFERING: LIVE FOR RIGHTEOUSNESS AND NOT FOR EVIL, 3:13-4:19

D. Live Under the Shadow of History's Climax, 4:7-11

(4:7-11) **Introduction—History, Climax—End Time**: believers often suffer. They suffer ridicule and abuse on the job and in their community. They suffer all forms of persecution at the hands of their neighbors, fellow workers, employers, competitors, school mates, society, and civil authorities. How can the believer handle and conquer suffering? By living under the shadow of history's climax. Note verse seven: "the end of all things is near." All things are soon to be consummated; the climax of history is at hand. Jesus Christ is returning and He is returning soon. Our suffering is to end; we are going to be freed from all the sufferings and trials of this corruptible and evil world. And not only this: the consummation of our faith is to soon take place. We are going to see Jesus face to face and be given the glorious privilege of living with Him and serving Him forever and ever (cp. Ro.13:12; Ph.4:5; Jas.5:8; 1 Jn.2:18; Rev.1:3; 22:20).

How can we handle and conquer all the trials and sufferings of this life? By living under the climax of history. How do we live under the climax of history? By doing five things.

1. Live being clear-minded and self-controlled (v.7).
2. Live watching and praying (v.7).
3. Live with fervent love (v.8).
4. Live showing hospitality and do it cheerfully (v.9).
5. Live using your gift (v.10-11).

1 (4:7) **Sober—Believers, Life and Walk**: How do we live under the climax of history? We live lives that are "clear-minded and self-controlled" (sophronein). This means to be serious and to have a sound mind; to be in control of oneself and to be self-restrained; to be calm and sensible. The believer lives under the climax of history; he keeps his mind upon the return of Christ by doing three things.

1. He keeps a serious and sound mind about everything. He is not a jolly, back-slapping, frivolous type of person. He takes life seriously, knowing that man has a purpose for being on earth, that life is the most meaningful and significant possession that man has. Therefore, he measures the importance of things. He measures all things in light of eternity as well as time. He considers the future as well as the present. He knows that his life could be snatched from him overnight by some accident or by the news of some disease. The believer who keeps his mind upon the climax

of history, upon the return of the Lord Jesus Christ, is a sober person; he is a serious and sound minded person.

2. He controls and restrains his desires and lusts and appetites. He never gives in to excess—to the lust for more and more. He controls sex and uses it for marriage. He controls desire for food and uses it for health. He controls the desire for material possessions and uses it to meet the needs of his family and the desperate needs of the world.

3. He is calm and sensible about all things. He is not overly shaken by trouble, problems, or circumstances that arise within his family, employment, society, or world. Family problems and world events just do not shake him. He is concerned but not shaken. He does not get overly excited with recreation, sports, or any other happening of life. He enjoys the happenings and experiences of life, but he keeps a sensible perspective of all things and gives each thing its proper place.

> **For by the grace given me I say to every one of you: Do not think of yourself more highly than you ought, but rather think of yourself with sober judgment, in accordance with the measure of faith God has given you. (Rom 12:3)**
>
> **So then, let us not be like others, who are asleep, but let us be alert and self-controlled. For those who sleep, sleep at night, and those who get drunk, get drunk at night. But since we belong to the day, let us be self-controlled, putting on faith and love as a breastplate, and the hope of salvation as a helmet. For God did not appoint us to suffer wrath but to receive salvation through our Lord Jesus Christ. (1 Th 5:6-9)**
>
> **For the grace of God that brings salvation has appeared to all men. It teaches us to say "No" to ungodliness and worldly passions, and to live self-controlled, upright and godly lives in this present age, (Titus 2:11-12)**
>
> **Therefore, prepare your minds for action; be self-controlled; set your hope fully on the grace to be given you when Jesus Christ is revealed. (1 Pet 1:13)**

> Be self-controlled and alert. Your enemy the devil prowls around like a roaring lion looking for someone to devour. (1 Pet 5:8)

2 (4:7) **Prayer—Watch**: How do we live under the climax of history? We watch and pray. The word "self-controlled" (nephate) means to stay sober and alert and awake at all times. This says two things.

1. The believer is to keep his mind sober, always watching. He is not to drink intoxicating beverages or take drugs or do anything else that dulls and numbs his mind. He is to keep his mind sober and alert at all times. He is not to be escaping reality; he is to be grasping reality. He is to be praying always for all things, and he cannot be praying if his mind is dull and numb because of drink and drugs.

2. The believer is to keep his mind alert, keep it from being sleepy-eyed and lazy and wandering about. The mind is always thinking; it is always upon something; it is never without thought. Therefore, the believer is to keep his mind alert and active. He is to control his thoughts even to the point of captivating every thought. Every moment that his thoughts are not engaged with the necessary activities of life, he is to focus his thoughts upon prayer. Even while carrying on the activities of life, he needs to flicker his thoughts to prayer here and there. He needs to acknowledge God in all His ways. This is what it means to watch and pray. The believer is to stay sober and alert to every opportunity to pray.

> **Thought 1.** Imagine how much better the world would be if believers prayed all the time! How much better the world would be if God were really sought this much! If His people never left the throne of God seeking His love and power for the earth!

> **"Ask and it will be given to you; seek and you will find; knock and the door will be opened to you. (Mat 7:7)**
> **It will be good for those servants whose master finds them watching when he comes. I tell you the truth, he will dress himself to serve, will have them recline at the table and will come and wait on them. (Luke 12:37)**
> **Devote yourselves to prayer, being watchful and thankful. (Col 4:2)**
> **You are all sons of the light and sons of the day. We do not belong to the night or to the darkness. So then, let us not be like others, who are asleep, but let us be alert and self-controlled. (1 Th 5:5-6)**
> **Submit yourselves, then, to God. Resist the devil, and he will flee from you. Come near to God and he will come near to you. Wash your hands, you sinners, and purify your hearts, you double-minded. (James 4:7-8)**
> **Be self-controlled and alert. Your enemy the devil prowls around like a roaring lion looking for someone to devour. (1 Pet 5:8)**

3 (4:8) **Love**: How do we live under the climax of history? We live with fervent love for one another. The word "deeply" (ektenes) is an athletic word. It means to be fer-

vent; to stretch and reach out; to strain and exert to the utmost degree just like an athlete in a race. It has the idea of burning and boiling and of being passionate about loving one's brother in Christ. Note how a fervent love is far more than the human love of warm feelings and attraction. It is far more than sentimental and caring feelings for a person.

The believer is to love with the ultimate love, the love of fervency. And note: fervent love is to be put before all else. It is the most important duty of the believer. We are to strain every ounce of energy in our minds and hearts to love. This means that we love others even when they...

- hurt us
- persecute us
- oppose us
- ridicule us
- abuse us
- speak evil against us
- injure us
- mock us

The most wonderful thing happens when we love each other with a fervent love: a multitude of sins is covered. What does this mean?

⇒ It means that when we love, we are not hating and reacting and sinning.

⇒ It means that when we love, we are living with a forgiving spirit and we are forgiving others, not living with a sinful and unforgiving spirit.

⇒ It means that when we love, we are more likely to reach those who do evil toward us and thereby to win them to Christ and to a life of love and ministry upon the earth.

> **"A new command I give you: Love one another. As I have loved you, so you must love one another. By this all men will know that you are my disciples, if you love one another." (John 13:34-35)**
> **My command is this: Love each other as I have loved you. (John 15:12)**
> **Love must be sincere. Hate what is evil; cling to what is good. (Rom 12:9)**
> **And now these three remain: faith, hope and love. But the greatest of these is love. (1 Cor 13:13)**
> **And over all these virtues put on love, which binds them all together in perfect unity. (Col 3:14)**
> **May the Lord make your love increase and overflow for each other and for everyone else, just as ours does for you. (1 Th 3:12)**
> **Now that you have purified yourselves by obeying the truth so that you have sincere love for your brothers, love one another deeply, from the heart. (1 Pet 1:22)**

4 (4:9) **Hospitality**: How do we live under the climax of history? We show hospitality and we do it cheerfully. The early believers had to open their homes to one another or else the church would have had difficulty surviving. The reasons are clear:

⇒ When believers were persecuted and forced to flee to other cities, they had no place to live.

⇒ When missionaries and evangelists traveled about, they needed a place to stay, and many of them were poor. The inns were just too dirty and immoral; therefore, room and board had to be provided for them.

⇒ When the jobs of Christians required them to travel, they needed homes to stay in because of the unsuitability of the inns.

⇒ In addition to this, we must always remember what William Barclay points out: there were no church buildings until about two hundred years after Christ. Therefore, the early believers had to meet for worship in the homes of willing believers. (*The Letters of James and Peter*, p.302.)

Hospitality was an absolute essential for the early church, and it is an absolute essential within the church today. Why? For love and care and ministry and close fellowship. It is almost impossible to maintain a loving and caring church and a dynamic ministry unless believers are fellowshipping together in their homes. In fact, Christ taught that we are to use our homes as centers of Christian love, fellowship, and outreach. This is a fact that is often unknown or ignored (see DEEPER STUDY # 1—Lk.9:4; note—10:5-6).

Note that we are to open our homes without grumbling, that is, without murmuring or complaining. We are to willingly and cordially open our homes, open them joyfully expecting great things of God.

> **Thought 1.** What would happen if we began to set up a home within every community for Christ, a home that was a center for love, fellowship, worship, and outreach. May God touch the hearts of many ministers and churches to adopt the very method laid down by Christ Himself (see outline and DEEPER STUDY #1—Lk.9:4; 10:5-6).

⇒ The overseer or minister must be given to hospitality.

> **Now the overseer must be above reproach, the husband of but one wife, temperate, self-controlled, respectable, hospitable, able to teach, (1 Tim 3:2)**
>
> **Rather he must be hospitable, one who loves what is good, who is self-controlled, upright, holy and disciplined. (Titus 1:8)**

⇒ All believers must open their door—even to strangers in need.

> **Do not forget to entertain strangers, for by so doing some people have entertained angels without knowing it. (Heb 13:2)**

⇒ All believers must use hospitality as a means to minister and use it without grumbling.

> **Practice hospitality. (Rom 12:13)**
> **Offer hospitality to one another without grumbling. (1 Pet 4:9)**

⇒ Widows in particular are to use hospitality as a means to minister.

> **And is well known for her good deeds, such as bringing up children, showing hospitality, washing the feet of the saints, helping those in trouble and devoting herself to all kinds of good deeds. (1 Tim 5:10)**

5 (4:10-11) **Spiritual Gifts:** How do we live under the climax of history? We use our gifts ministering as good stewards of God. The word "gift" (charisma) means the very special ability given to the believer by God. Note that the gift is from God; it is not a natural talent. The believer could not have attained nor secured the ability himself. It is a spiritual gift; that is, it is given by the Spirit of God for spiritual purposes. It is given to the believer so that he can fulfill his task on earth.

1. Note: believers are to *use their gifts serving and ministering to one another*. Every believer's task is to use his gift to build up believers in the church and in witnessing and ministering to the world. What are the spiritual gifts that God gives to believers? The great tragedy is that most believers just do not know anything about spiritual gifts, yet God covers them in His Word. They should be diligently studied (see outline and notes—Ro.12:6-8; 1 Cor.12:8-11; Eph.4:11 for discussion).

> **And if anyone gives even a cup of cold water to one of these little ones because he is my disciple, I tell you the truth, he will certainly not lose his reward." (Mat 10:42)**
>
> **We have different gifts, according to the grace given us. If a man's gift is prophesying, let him use it in proportion to his faith. If it is serving, let him serve; if it is teaching, let him teach; if it is encouraging, let him encourage; if it is contributing to the needs of others, let him give generously; if it is leadership, let him govern diligently; if it is showing mercy, let him do it cheerfully. Love must be sincere. Hate what is evil; cling to what is good. Be devoted to one another in brotherly love. Honor one another above yourselves. Never be lacking in zeal, but keep your spiritual fervor, serving the Lord. Be joyful in hope, patient in affliction, faithful in prayer. Share with God's people who are in need. Practice hospitality. Bless those who persecute you; bless and do not curse. Rejoice with those who rejoice; mourn with those who mourn. (Rom 12:6-15)**
>
> **There are different kinds of gifts, but the same Spirit. There are different kinds of service, but the same Lord. There are different kinds of working, but the same God works all of them in all men. Now to each one the manifestation of the Spirit is given for the common good. To one there is given through the Spirit the message of wisdom, to another the message of knowledge by means of the same Spirit, to another faith by the same Spirit, to another gifts of healing by that one Spirit, to another miraculous powers, to another prophecy, to another distinguishing between spirits, to another speaking in different kinds of tongues, and to still another the interpretation of tongues. All these are the work of one and the same Spirit, and he gives them to each one, just as he determines. (1 Cor 12:4-11)**
>
> **Therefore, as we have opportunity, let us do good to all people, especially to those who belong to the family of believers. (Gal 6:10)**
>
> **It was he who gave some to be apostles, some to be prophets, some to be evangelists, and some to be pastors and teachers, to prepare God's people for works of serv-**

ice, so that the body of Christ may be built up (Eph 4:11-12)

2. Note: the believer is to *serve by faithfully administering God's grace*. Scripture says he is a steward of God's grace. The steward was a slave who was given the responsibility of the master's estate, both his home and property. He was in full charge of all the affairs of the master. The believer is the steward of God; he is in full charge of the grace and gift which God has given him. No one else can look after or use the gift he has. If it is to be used, the believer has to use it. Think about this: the awesome responsibility has been placed into our hands. No one can exercise the gift of the believer except the believer himself. The only energy and effort that can arouse and use the gift is the believer's own energy and effort. If he fails to exercise and use his gift, then the gift lies dormant and is never used. He fails in his task. His mission upon earth is unfulfilled. And he has to face God as a failure in life. He failed to use the gift God had given him, failed to complete his task and mission upon earth. But note: this is not to be the case with believers. Believers are to use their gifts, and they are to be as faithful as enslaved stewards in carrying out their tasks upon earth. Two gifts in particular are mentioned. They are covered in the next two points.

"Again, it will be like a man going on a journey, who called his servants and entrusted his property to them. To one he gave five talents of money, to another two talents, and to another one talent, each according to his ability. Then he went on his journey. (Mat 25:14-15)

So he called ten of his servants and gave them ten minas. 'Put this money to work,' he said, 'until I come back.' (Luke 19:13)

Now it is required that those who have been given a trust must prove faithful. (1 Cor 4:2)

You were bought at a price. Therefore honor God with your body. (1 Cor 6:20)

Timothy, guard what has been entrusted to your care. Turn away from godless chatter and the opposing ideas of what is falsely called knowledge, (1 Tim 6:20)

Each one should use whatever gift he has received to serve others, faithfully administering God's grace in its various forms. (1 Pet 4:10)

3. Believers are to *serve by speaking the Word of God*. This would include such gifts as teaching, preaching, exhortation, prophesy, and the other gifts that involve proclaiming the Word of God. Note: we are to speak as one speaking the very words *of God*. This means two things. We are to speak for the Word of God and the Word of God alone, and we are to let God speak through us. We are to depend upon God to do the speaking, totally depend upon Him.

And teaching them to obey everything I have commanded you. And surely I am with you always, to the very end of the age." (Mat 28:20)

But everyone who prophesies speaks to men for their strengthening, encouragement and comfort. (1 Cor 14:3)

It was he who gave some to be apostles, some to be prophets, some to be evangelists, and some to be pastors and teachers, (Eph 4:11)

Preach the Word; be prepared in season and out of season; correct, rebuke and encourage—with great patience and careful instruction. (2 Tim 4:2)

He must hold firmly to the trustworthy message as it has been taught, so that he can encourage others by sound doctrine and refute those who oppose it. (Titus 1:9)

For the grace of God that brings salvation has appeared to all men. It teaches us to say "No" to ungodliness and worldly passions, and to live self-controlled, upright and godly lives in this present age, while we wait for the blessed hope—the glorious appearing of our great God and Savior, Jesus Christ, who gave himself for us to redeem us from all wickedness and to purify for himself a people that are his very own, eager to do what is good. These, then, are the things you should teach. Encourage and rebuke with all authority. Do not let anyone despise you. (Titus 2:11-15)

4. Believers are to *serve by ministering with the strength of God*. This would include such gifts as hospitality, visiting, mercy, giving, and the other gifts of ministering to people. Note: the believer who ministers is to do it in the ability and strength of the Lord. This also means that we minister acknowledging that our strength and ability come from God and from Him alone.

The point is this: How can we handle and conquer suffering in this life? By living under the climax of history. By being so occupied and set upon our ministry and task upon earth that nothing deters or sidetracks us. We are to be obsessed with God's gift and call, with the mission and task He has given us. We are to be so obsessed that absolutely nothing, not even suffering and persecution, can keep us from using God's gifts and from completing our task and mission.

And if anyone gives even a cup of cold water to one of these little ones because he is my disciple, I tell you the truth, he will certainly not lose his reward." (Mat 10:42)

Therefore, as we have opportunity, let us do good to all people, especially to those who belong to the family of believers. (Gal 6:10)

On the first day of every week, each one of you should set aside a sum of money in keeping with his income, saving it up, so that when I come no collections will have to be made. (1 Cor 16:2)

Each man should give what he has decided in his heart to give, not reluctantly or under compulsion, for God loves a cheerful giver. (2 Cor 9:7)

Religion that God our Father accepts as pure and faultless is this: to look after orphans and widows in their distress and to keep oneself from being polluted by the world. (James 1:27)

5. Believers are to *serve so that God may be glorified in all things through Jesus Christ*. This is the sole aim of the believer. He does not preach or teach to draw attention and gain a name for himself. He proclaims God's Word in order to glorify God through Jesus Christ. He does not minister, visit, and give to secure recognition, honor, or praise. He ministers to stir praise and thanksgiving to God in the name of Jesus Christ. God and Christ alone deserve all the praise and dominion throughout the universe. No man deserves this; God alone is sovereign.

In the same way, let your light shine before men, that they may see your good deeds and praise your Father in heaven. (Mat 5:16)

This is to my Father's glory, that you bear much fruit, showing yourselves to be my disciples. (John 15:8)

So that with one heart and mouth you may glorify the God and Father of our Lord Jesus Christ. (Rom 15:6)

You were bought at a price. Therefore honor God with your body. (1 Cor 6:20)

Through Jesus, therefore, let us continually offer to God a sacrifice of praise—the fruit of lips that confess his name. (Heb 13:15)

But you are a chosen people, a royal priesthood, a holy nation, a people belonging to God, that you may declare the praises of him who called you out of darkness into his wonderful light. (1 Pet 2:9)

Sing praises to the LORD, enthroned in Zion; proclaim among the nations what he has done. (Psa 9:11)

May the peoples praise you, O God; may all the peoples praise you. (Psa 67:3)

1 First, do not be surprised that you suffer persecution[DS1]	E. Stand Up Under the Fiery Trial of Persecution, 4:12-19	any other kind of criminal, or even as a meddler.	suffering & persecution upon yourself
a. Persecution can be fiery		16 However, if you suffer as a Christian, do not be ashamed, but praise God that you bear that name.	5 Fifth, do not be ashamed to suffer for being a Christian
b. Persecution is a test	12 Dear friends, do not be surprised at the painful trial you are suffering, as though something strange were happening to you.		
2 Second, rejoice in persecution		17 For it is time for judgment to begin with the family of God; and if it begins with us, what will the outcome be for those who do not obey the gospel of God?	6 Sixth, accept persecution as the purifying judgment of God
a. Because you share in Christ's sufferings	13 But rejoice that you participate in the sufferings of Christ, so that you may be overjoyed when his glory is revealed.		a. Because believers are scarcely saved
b. Because you shall be rewarded		18 And, "If it is hard for the righteous to be saved, what will become of the ungodly and the sinner?"	b. Because unbelievers have a terrible end
3 Third, know God's Spirit, that a glow of God's glory rests upon you	14 If you are insulted because of the name of Christ, you are blessed, for the Spirit of glory and of God rests on you.	19 So then, those who suffer according to God's will should commit themselves to their faithful Creator and continue to do good.	7 Seventh, keep on doing good and commit your self to God
4 Fourth, do not bring	15 If you suffer, it should not be as a murderer or thief or		

DIVISION III

HOW TO HANDLE AND CONQUER SUFFERING: LIVE FOR RIGHTEOUSNESS AND NOT FOR EVIL, 3:13-4:19

E. Stand Up Under the Fiery Trial of Persecution, 4:12-19

(4:12-19) **Introduction**: persecution is a strange thing. Why would God ever allow a person who believes in God, who really loves and follows God, to suffer persecution? This is the point of this passage, to discuss the question of persecution, of the fiery trial that the believer sometimes has to suffer. The believer is to stand up under the fiery trials of persecution.

1. First, do not be surprised that you suffer persecution (v.12).
2. Second, rejoice in persecution (v.13).
3. Third, know God's Spirit, that a glow of God's glory rests upon you (v.14).
4. Fourth, do not bring suffering and persecution upon yourself (v.15).
5. Fifth, do not be ashamed to suffer for being a Christian (v.16).
6. Sixth, accept persecution as the purifying judgment of God (v.17-18).
7. Seventh, keep on doing good and commit yourself to God (v.19).

1 (4:12) **Persecution—Suffering**: first, do not be surprised that you are persecuted and have to suffer. (See note—
1 Pt.1:12 for more discussion.) Believers often do not understand why they have to suffer. When they suffer, they are surprised and astonished, and they wonder why God does not protect them from suffering and from persecution. This is especially true when persecution is fiery and painful, and so long as the believer is upon earth, he is going to be called upon to face painful trials. Being a genuine believer in a corrupt world is difficult. People often oppose the believer's stand for Christ. The world just cannot understand the demands of Christ for self-denial and discipline, for purity and righteousness, and in particular His insistence that they give all they are and have to His cause. Therefore, when a person really begins to live for Christ, the world often wants little to do with him. It may be next

door, in the office, in school, in the government, or a hundred other places, but the genuine Christian is often...

• avoided	• cursed
• ridiculed	• questioned
• mocked	• abused
• isolated	• mistreated
• ignored	• slandered
• neglected	• persecuted
• overlooked	• imprisoned
• by-passed	• martyred

Why does God allow the believer to suffer persecution? This verse says that God allows it for one very basic reason: to test and try and prove us. This means at least four things.

⇒ Persecution measures how strong our faith is. Any person's faith can be measured by how much he is willing to sacrifice and bear for it. Suffering persecution for Christ shows how strong or weak our faith really is.

⇒ Persecution proves our trust in God and teaches us to depend upon God more and more. The more we suffer for Christ, the more we draw near God and plead for His help and strength. This, of course, teaches us to trust and depend upon Him more and more.

⇒ Persecution proves and strengthens our patience and endurance. The more we are tried and persecuted, the more we endure; and the more we endure, the more we are taught to endure. Persecution strengthens our patience, endurance, perseverance, and steadfastness in Christ.

⇒ Persecution proves our faith and attracts others to Christ. When we suffer and are persecuted, others can see the strength of Christ in us. They see that our faith in Christ is a living reality and they are drawn to Christ, to His salvation and love and care and strength. When others see us suffer for the hope of salvation and eternal life, the Holy Spirit uses our suffering to speak to the hearts of the persecutors and observers. He convicts them, and some eventually turn to Christ. Our faith is proven to be true, and it bears fruit.

> If you belonged to the world, it would love you as its own. As it is, you do not belong to the world, but I have chosen you out of the world. That is why the world hates you. (John 15:19)
>
> "If the world hates you, keep in mind that it hated me first. If I had not come and spoken to them, they would not be guilty of sin. Now, however, they have no excuse for their sin. (John 15:18, 22)
>
> For it has been granted to you on behalf of Christ not only to believe on him, but also to suffer for him, (Phil 1:29)
>
> In fact, everyone who wants to live a godly life in Christ Jesus will be persecuted, (2 Tim 3:12)
>
> Do not be surprised, my brothers, if the world hates you. (1 John 3:13)

DEEPER STUDY # 1

(4:12) **Persecution—Suffering**: the sufferings of the early Christians were just what Peter says, "painful." Most of us have seen pictures of believers being fed to wild lions and burned at the stake. But these were mild deaths compared to what some believers suffered. Some had boiling lead poured over their scorching bodies; others had fiery red branding irons put to the private parts of their bodies; others were wrapped in the bloody skins of wild game and chased in a hunt by man and dogs; others were soaked with flammable oil and set aflame; others had their limbs torn apart from their bodies one by one, both by machine and animals; others were subjected to the most devilish imaginations in torture chambers; and so the list goes on and on. (See *Foxes Book of Martyrs* for a complete discussion of the persecution of believers down through the centuries.)

William Barclay points out that there were essentially five slanders made against the church in the early days of its history (*The Gospel of Matthew*, Mt.5:10, p.108-109. Cp. his commentary on Revelation 2:8-11, Vol.1, p.98.)

1. Christian believers were thought to be cannibals. There were two reasons for this slander. (1) The teaching that one had to eat the flesh of Christ and drink His blood in order to have life (Jn.6:51f). (2) The practice of the Lord's Supper and its words, "This is my body and this is my blood" (Mt.26:26; Mk.14:22; Lk.22:19; 1 Cor.11:24).

2. The church was also charged with breaking up homes and tampering with family relationships. This was because some members of families became believers and others did not (Mt.10:34-39).

3. The church was charged with heresy.

⇒ Judaism, the religion of the Jews, charged the Christians with heresy because the believers refused to put tradition before God and people, and they refused to obey the rules and regulations as prescribed by the traditional beliefs.

⇒ Other people charged believers with heresy because they refused to pay homage to Caesar and to worship the gods and goddesses of society.

4. The church was charged with lust and immorality. This was because they practiced the Agape or The Love Feast. This was simply a fellowship meal in which Christian brotherhood was shared and experienced. But because it was called "The Love Feast" and such a close bond was seen between Christians, their behavior was twisted to be immoral.

5. The church and its believers were charged with being revolutionary and with insurrection. They were thought to be traitors for three primary reasons.

a. Christians preached Jesus Christ the Lord who is to return and establish His kingdom right here upon earth.

b. Christians also preached the destruction of the world by fire.

c. Christians refused to worship Caesar, the symbol of Roman government. This was the major reason for the official persecution of Christians by the government.

Rome had conquered the world with its vast number of peoples and their different cultures, politics, beliefs, philosophies, and languages. How could one government pull and hold all the diverse people of the world together as one nation and one people?

Rome needed a symbol, an object, something that could be held up before the people that would naturally demand their loyalty. As Rome began to conquer the world, the leaders began to notice something. The conquered people eventually became settled and thankful for the peace, prosperity, and civilization that Rome brought to the world. They were glad for a one-world government. And in the eyes of the people that government was centered in the emperor. The emperor was therefore set up as the one unifying principle around which the vast empire was built and held together. A law was passed which demanded that every citizen go once a year and burn a dab of incense to the idol of Caesar and say, "Caesar is Lord." The worshipper was then given a certificate showing that he was loyal to the empire. He was free to worship as he wished for the rest of the year.

Christians were just unable to bow and worship and say "Caesar is Lord." Therefore, in the eyes of the government they were lawbreakers and disloyal to Rome. They were hunted down and charged with being revolutionaries and insurrectionists. The result was, of course, just what Peter says, "painful persecution."

2 (4:13) **Persecution**: second, rejoice in persecution. This is difficult to do, for no person likes to suffer abuse or pain of any sort, but especially when it is inflicted by neighbors, friends, or co-workers. No person likes to be isolated, ridiculed, bypassed, scorned, imprisoned, or called upon to face death. Therefore, it is difficult to rejoice in persecution. Nevertheless this is the exhortation of Scripture. But note: there is a way to rejoice in persecution. How? By keeping our eyes and minds upon two things.

1. When we suffer, we are sharing in Christ's sufferings. Christ was rejected by men because He lived and proclaimed the righteousness and salvation of God. Therefore, when we suffer for following Christ—for living and proclaiming the righteousness and salvation of God—we are suffering for the very same reason that Christ suffered. We are sharing in the very sufferings of Christ Himself. We are denying ourselves and suffering for God and His righteousness just as Christ did. We become identified with Christ, associated with Him in the deepest devotion possible, the very sacrifice of ourselves for the cause of God and His glorious salvation. No greater privilege could be given to a person than to become so devoted to God that he would join Christ in the sacrifice of himself to God. To be so identified with Christ, who is the very Son of God Him

self, is the height of privileges, a great reason for joy and rejoicing.

> The apostles left the Sanhedrin, rejoicing because they had been counted worthy of suffering disgrace for the Name. (Acts 5:41)
>
> After they had been severely flogged, they were thrown into prison, and the jailer was commanded to guard them carefully. Upon receiving such orders, he put them in the inner cell and fastened their feet in the stocks. About midnight Paul and Silas were praying and singing hymns to God, and the other prisoners were listening to them. (Acts 16:23-25)
>
> Sorrowful, yet always rejoicing; poor, yet making many rich; having nothing, and yet possessing everything. (2 Cor 6:10)
>
> You sympathized with those in prison and joyfully accepted the confiscation of your property, because you knew that you yourselves had better and lasting possessions. (Heb 10:34)
>
> If anyone speaks, he should do it as one speaking the very words of God. If anyone serves, he should do it with the strength God provides, so that in all things God may be praised through Jesus Christ. To him be the glory and the power for ever and ever. Amen. Dear friends, do not be surprised at the painful trial you are suffering, as though something strange were happening to you. (1 Pet 4:11-12)

2. When we suffer, we shall be greatly rewarded when Christ returns in glory. This is exactly what Scripture declares time and again. (See note, *Reward*—1 Pt.1:4 for discussion.)

> "Blessed are you when people insult you, persecute you and falsely say all kinds of evil against you because of me. Rejoice and be glad, because great is your reward in heaven, for in the same way they persecuted the prophets who were before you. (Mat 5:11-12)
>
> The Spirit himself testifies with our spirit that we are God's children. Now if we are children, then we are heirs—heirs of God and co-heirs with Christ, if indeed we share in his sufferings in order that we may also share in his glory. (Rom 8:16-17)
>
> For our light and momentary troubles are achieving for us an eternal glory that far outweighs them all. (2 Cor 4:17)
>
> Therefore I endure everything for the sake of the elect, that they too may obtain the salvation that is in Christ Jesus, with eternal glory. (2 Tim 2:10)
>
> Persecutions, sufferings—what kinds of things happened to me in Antioch, Iconium and Lystra, the persecutions I endured. Yet the Lord rescued me from all of them. (2 Tim 3:11)
>
> He regarded disgrace for the sake of Christ as of greater value than the treasures of Egypt, because he was looking ahead to his reward. (Heb 11:26)

3 (4:14) **Persecution:** third, know God's Spirit, that a glow of God's glory rests upon you. The words "insulted because of...Christ" mean suffering for righteousness; being persecuted or abused or ridiculed for Christ. When a believer suffers for Christ, "the Spirit of glory and of God rests on [him]." He is given a very special closeness, a oneness with Christ that is beyond imagination and unexplainable (Acts 7:54-60). The Holy Spirit infuses him with a deep, intense consciousness of the Lord's presence. The Holy Spirit actually causes a glow of God's glory to shine in and through the believer's body. This is apparently the Shekinah glory of God's presence. It is the same glory that shone upon Stephen's face when he was martyred. It is an anointing, a consciousness so deep that it cannot be experienced apart from some severe experience of suffering.

In suffering for Christ the believer also experiences a very special identification with Christ, an identification that stirs a sense of happiness and joy within him. The Lord suffered on behalf of the believer, so now the believer suffers on behalf of the Lord. There is a sense in which the believer's sufferings *fill up the sufferings of Christ* and complete the sufferings of Christ for the church (see note—Col.1:24).

These two experiences—gaining a deeper consciousness of the Lord's presence and being used to complete the sufferings for the church—are gained only through suffering. They make suffering a privilege and a joy for the believer, for the believer suffers even as his Lord suffered. Note: Christ is glorified by the believer's sufferings. The believer honors Christ and proves that Christ is the Savior of the world by standing up for Him.

4 (4:15) **Persecution:** fourth, do not bring suffering and persecution upon yourself by breaking some law or doing some evil thing. If a person violates the laws of the land and harms others, then he deserves to suffer. This is not suffering for Christ's name. Suffering for Christ means that a person is persecuted because he is living for and proclaiming Christ. Therefore, a believer is not to bring suffering upon himself. If he is ever to suffer or be persecuted, it is to be because he is living for Christ and not because he is a lawbreaker.

⇒ The believer is not to suffer as a murderer: he is not to take the life of another person. In fact, he is never to become unjustly angry or to demean another person.

⇒ The believer is not to suffer as a thief: he is not to steal, no matter how small the item is nor how much he may need or desire it.

⇒ The believer is not to suffer as an evil doer, as any kind of lawbreaker or evil person.

⇒ The believer is not to suffer as a busybody or meddler or troublemaker in other people's affairs. No believer is to interfere in the life or affairs of anyone else—never in matters that do not concern him.

> We also know that law is made not for the righteous but for lawbreakers and rebels, the ungodly and sinful, the unholy and irreligious; for those who kill their fathers or mothers, for murderers, for adulterers and perverts, for slave traders and liars and perjurers—and for whatever else is contrary to the sound doctrine (1 Tim 1:9-10)
>
> Let no one deceive you with empty words, for because of such things God's

wrath comes on those who are disobedient. (Eph 5:6)

For if the message spoken by angels was binding, and every violation and disobedience received its just punishment, how shall we escape if we ignore such a great salvation? This salvation, which was first announced by the Lord, was confirmed to us by those who heard him. (Heb 2:2-3)

5 (4:16) **Persecution**: fifth, do not be ashamed to suffer for being a Christian. The name Christian was given to the early believers by unbelievers. It was a name of derision and ridicule and mockery. Early believers called themselves *brothers, believers, disciples,* and *saints.* Apparently they did not call themselves Christians until much later. It is used only three times in the New Testament:

⇒ in Acts 11:26 where the world called the believers at Antioch *Christians.*
⇒ in Acts 26:28 where King Agrippa uses the name in scorn.
⇒ here in 1 Peter 4:16.

The point is this: if a believer is being ridiculed, mocked, cursed, abused, or persecuted because he is a Christian, he is not to be ashamed. No believer should ever be ashamed of the fact that he is a Christian. He is to take a stand for Christ and stand firm. He is to glorify God by standing up for and honoring the name of Christ.

Thought 1. The world will usually ridicule and mock or withdraw from and isolate us if we do not join them in their worldly parties and ways. But Scripture is clear:

I am not ashamed of the gospel, because it is the power of God for the salvation of everyone who believes: first for the Jew, then for the Gentile. (Rom 1:16)

I eagerly expect and hope that I will in no way be ashamed, but will have sufficient courage so that now as always Christ will be exalted in my body, whether by life or by death. (Phil 1:20)

However, if you suffer as a Christian, do not be ashamed, but praise God that you bear that name. (1 Pet 4:16)

And now, dear children, continue in him, so that when he appears we may be confident and unashamed before him at his coming. (1 John 2:28)

Ascribe to the LORD the glory due his name; worship the LORD in the splendor of his holiness. (Psa 29:2)

Glorify the LORD with me; let us exalt his name together. (Psa 34:3)

Be exalted, O God, above the heavens; let your glory be over all the earth. (Psa 57:5)

Let them exalt him in the assembly of the people and praise him in the council of the elders. (Psa 107:32)

O LORD, you are my God; I will exalt you and praise your name, for in perfect faithfulness you have done marvelous things, things planned long ago. (Isa 25:1)

6 (4:17-18) **Persecution—Judgment**: sixth, accept persecution as the purifying judgment of God. Note: Scripture clearly says that persecution is used by God as a judgment upon believers. Judgment, in fact, must begin at the house or church of God. What does this mean? When things are going well for the believer, he tends to feel more and more secure in himself and tends to partake of the world more and more. Perhaps he partakes of only little tidbits of the pleasure and possessions of the world, but nevertheless, he is still partaking of some worldliness. The result is that the believer does not concentrate and focus upon Christ like he should. When things are going well, he does not pray and worship nor fellowship and commune with God like he should. He becomes somewhat contaminated and polluted with a sense of self-sufficiency and worldliness. When this happens, God has to do something to awaken the believer. One thing that He often does is use persecution to arouse the believer. God can use persecution as a means of judgment, as a means to stir the believer to clean up his life and to draw closer to God. Think about it: When a believer is persecuted, to whom can he turn? There is only one sure deliverer and that is God. Therefore, persecution causes the believer to flee to God for deliverance and protection; it causes the believer to turn his attention from self and the world and to focus and concentrate upon God. Two things happen:

⇒ The believer forgets self and self-sufficiency and he acknowledges that he is totally dependent upon God.
⇒ The believer cleans up his life. He turns away from the tidbits of worldliness and focuses upon God, fellowshipping and communing with Him as God wills.

The point is this: persecution is used by God as a purifying judgment, as a means of chastening and cleaning up the life of the believer. Therefore, the believer is to stand fast against persecution knowing that God wants to use it to draw him closer and closer to Christ.

Note one other significant truth: if believers have to suffer the judgment of God while on earth—if the righteous are scarcely saved—where shall the ungodly and sinner appear? What shall be the end of the person who lives an impure and unrighteous life? Who disobeys God and rebels and rejects Him and curses His name? What kind of judgment shall they bear? The point is this: they will never be allowed to appear in God's presence; they will never be acceptable to God. Their judgment shall be terrible; they shall be eternally doomed from the presence of the Lord—forever and ever separated from Him.

"Then they will go away to eternal punishment, but the righteous to eternal life." (Mat 25:46)

But whoever blasphemes against the Holy Spirit will never be forgiven; he is guilty of an eternal sin." (Mark 3:29)

His winnowing fork is in his hand to clear his threshing floor and to gather the wheat into his barn, but he will burn up the chaff with unquenchable fire." (Luke 3:17)

But for those who are self-seeking and who reject the truth and follow evil, there will be wrath and anger. (Rom 2:8)

What benefit did you reap at that time from the things you are now ashamed of? Those things result in death! (Rom 6:21)

For, as I have often told you before and now say again even with tears, many live as enemies of the cross of Christ. Their destiny is destruction, their god is their stomach, and their glory is in their shame. Their mind is on earthly things. (Phil 3:18-19)

They will be punished with everlasting destruction and shut out from the presence of the Lord and from the majesty of his power (2 Th 1:9)

But land that produces thorns and thistles is worthless and is in danger of being cursed. In the end it will be burned. (Heb 6:8)

How much more severely do you think a man deserves to be punished who has trampled the Son of God under foot, who has treated as an unholy thing the blood of the covenant that sanctified him, and who has insulted the Spirit of grace? (Heb 10:29)

And, "If it is hard for the righteous to be saved, what will become of the ungodly and the sinner?" (1 Pet 4:18)

If this is so, then the Lord knows how to rescue godly men from trials and to hold the unrighteous for the day of judgment, while continuing their punishment. (2 Pet 2:9)

If anyone's name was not found written in the book of life, he was thrown into the lake of fire. (Rev 20:15)

But the cowardly, the unbelieving, the vile, the murderers, the sexually immoral, those who practice magic arts, the idolaters and all liars—their place will be in the fiery lake of burning sulfur. This is the second death." (Rev 21:8)

7 (4:19) **Persecution**: seventh, keep on doing good and commit yourself to God. Note that the believer's suffering is in *the will of God*. God is either glorifying the name of Christ or purifying the life of the believer by the suffering. Therefore, the believer must do two things:

⇒ He must keep on doing good.
⇒ He must *commit* himself to God.

The word "commit" (paratithesthosan) means to deposit; to entrust into the hands of a trusted banker or friend. God can be trusted; He will not fail the believer. He will either deliver the believer through the suffering or else bring him on home to be with Christ forever. God will save the believer's soul. The believer can trust God, trust Him far more than any friend on earth, for God never fails. God is a faithful Creator. He has created us to be with Him eternally, and His plan will not be defeated. If we commit our souls to Him, no matter what men may do to us, God will save us. He will fulfill His plan and purpose in our lives.

I will remain in the world no longer, but they are still in the world, and I am coming to you. Holy Father, protect them by the power of your name—the name you gave me—so that they may be one as we are one. (John 17:11)

That is why I am suffering as I am. Yet I am not ashamed, because I know whom I have believed, and am convinced that he is able to guard what I have entrusted to him for that day. (2 Tim 1:12)

The Lord will rescue me from every evil attack and will bring me safely to his heavenly kingdom. To him be glory for ever and ever. Amen. (2 Tim 4:18)

I am with you and will watch over you wherever you go, and I will bring you back to this land. I will not leave you until I have done what I have promised you." (Gen 28:15)

The LORD commanded us to obey all these decrees and to fear the LORD our God, so that we might always prosper and be kept alive, as is the case today. (Deu 6:24)

Love the LORD, all his saints! The LORD preserves the faithful, but the proud he pays back in full. (Psa 31:23)

For the LORD loves the just and will not forsake his faithful ones. They will be protected forever, but the offspring of the wicked will be cut off; (Psa 37:28)

Indeed, he who watches over Israel will neither slumber nor sleep. (Psa 121:4)

For he guards the course of the just and protects the way of his faithful ones. (Prov 2:8)

So do not fear, for I am with you; do not be dismayed, for I am your God. I will strengthen you and help you; I will uphold you with my righteous right hand. (Isa 41:10)

		vealed:	Jesus' glory
	CHAPTER 5	2 Be shepherds of God's flock that is under your care, serving as overseers—not because you must, but because you are willing, as God wants you to be; not greedy for money, but eager to serve;	**2 The charge: Shepherd, care for the flock of God** a. Willingly, not by force b. Readily, not for gain
	IV. HOW THE CHURCH IS TO FUNCTION UNDER SUFFERING: BE FAITHFUL, 5:1-11		
	A. The Duties of the Elder or Minister, 5:1-4	3 Not lording it over those entrusted to you, but being examples to the flock.	c. As an example, not dominating
1 Peter stresses his right to be heard a. He was an elder b. He was a witness of Jesus' death c. He was to be a partaker of	To the elders among you, I appeal as a of fellow elder, a witness Christ's sufferings and one who also will share in the glory to be re-	4 And when the Chief Shepherd appears, you will receive the crown of glory that will never fade away.	**3 The result: A crown of glory** a. From the Chief Shepherd b. At His appearance

DIVISION IV

HOW THE CHURCH IS TO FUNCTION UNDER SUFFERING: BE FAITHFUL, 5:1-11

A. The Duties of the Elder or Minister, 5:1-4

(5:1-4) **Introduction**: this is a critical passage. It is a personal message from Peter to the elders and ministers of the church. Never is the church in need of leadership any more than when it is being attacked and persecuted. At such times, the ministers must stand forth and be more vigilant than ever.

1. Peter stresses his right to be heard (v.1).
2. The charge: Shepherd, care for the flock of God (v.2-3).
3. The result: A crown of glory (v.4).

1 (5:1) **Peter**: Peter stresses his right to be heard and the importance of listening to him. Peter was deeply concerned for the believers of God's church. They were being persecuted and savagely attacked by the wolves of this world. They were just like sheep under attack, sheep who needed the pastoral care of the shepherd. This is the reason Peter writes this exhortation to the leaders of the church. The top leader was the elder or minister; he was the person most responsible for the church. He was the person who needed to take the lead in facing the persecution. He was the one who needed to feed the flock of God and to lead them to stand fast for Christ. But how? How could Peter stir the elders to take the lead and do their duty? How could he arouse them to stand in the forefront against such savage persecution? By stressing his right to be heard and the importance of listening to him. Note that Peter stresses three things that should arouse all ministers to heed his exhortation.

1. Peter himself was an elder, a man called by God to be a minister to the flock of God. Therefore, Peter held the very same calling and office as all other elders. He was one with them; he could identify with them. He knew what they felt and experienced, for he faced and went through the same experiences they did. He was the elder sharing with the elders. He was one who had been where they now were and who wanted to help them. Therefore, they needed to listen and hear what he had to say. (See Deeper Study # 1, *Elder*—Titus 1:5-9 for more discussion.)

Thought 1. Think about this fact for a moment: we hold the very same calling and office that Peter the great apostle did, the calling of being an elder, a minister of God's flock. Just think: these words are a special message to us—all elders and ministers—from Peter himself.

2. Peter was an eye-witness to the sufferings of Christ. He actually saw…
- the ridicule, mockery, and cursing of Christ.
- the questioning and doubting of Christ.
- the unbelief and rejection of Christ.
- the denial and rebellion against the claims of Christ.
- the accusation and charges against Christ.
- the sufferings of Christ in the Garden of Gethsemane.
- the beatings and abuse Christ bore in His trials.
- the mockery and death of Christ upon the cross.

Peter knew that the sufferings of Christ were real: that Jesus Christ actually did suffer for man. He knew that man could now be saved by the sufferings of the cross if man would only believe and endure to the end. Therefore, the elders—all ministers of the gospel—need to listen and hear the exhortation of Peter.

3. Peter was to be a partaker of Jesus' glory. Remember: Peter had witnessed the transfiguration of Christ. He had seen and experienced a little taste of the glory that is to come. While writing this his heart must have beat a little faster, for he was recalling the promise of the Lord to return. And the Lord gave the promise often, always sharing that His followers would share in the glory of the resurrection and of life eternal with Him (cp. Mt.5:11-12; 13:43; 19:28-29; 25:23; Lk.6:35; 13:29; Jn.5:24-26; 5:28-29; 6:40; 8:51; 11:25-26; 12:26; 14:2-3; 17:24).

This was the reason Peter was willing to serve Christ as a minister: he had witnessed and tasted a little of the glory of heaven. He knew what lay ahead. He knew that Christ was truly the Savior of the world and that His promise of eternal glory was true. Therefore, Peter was willing to serve and bear anything, no matter how severe the suffering. He knew that the glory of heaven was worth bearing anything, no matter how terrible.

Thought 1. These three reasons state clearly why all elders—all ministers of the Lord—must listen and heed Peter's exhortation.
⇒ Peter was an elder himself, one who could identify with us, one who experienced just what we experience.
⇒ Peter was an eyewitness of the Lord's sufferings. He actually saw Christ die; therefore, he

knows that the claims of Christ are true. Jesus Christ is the true Messiah, the Savior who died for our salvation.

⇒ Peter was a partaker of the glory that we are all to share. In the transfiguration of Christ he actually witnessed and tasted a little of the glory that is to be revealed and brought to us when Christ returns. He knew that heaven and the glory of life eternal are real.

2 (5:2-3) **Minister, Duty—Church**: the exhortation to ministers is direct and forceful, but as clear as it can be. "Be shepherds of God's flock." The word "shepherd" (poimanate) is an all inclusive word that covers all the duties of the minister. It means not only to preach and teach the Word of God, but to tend and shepherd the flock. It means to act like a shepherd, to carry out the duties of a shepherd. The duties of the shepherd are several fold (see DEEPER STUDY # 2—1 Pt.2:25 for more discussion):

⇒ to feed the sheep even if he has to gather them in his arms and carry them to the pasture.
⇒ to guide the sheep to the pasture and away from the rough places and precipices.
⇒ to seek and save the sheep who get lost.
⇒ to protect the sheep. He is even willing to sacrifice his life for the sheep.
⇒ to restore the sheep who go astray and return.
⇒ to reward the sheep for obedience and faithfulness.
⇒ to keep the sheep separate from the goats.

But note this: in all the duties of tending and looking after God's flock, we must never forget what the great Greek scholar W.E. Vine stresses:

"In the spiritual care of God's children, the feeding of the flock from the Word of God is the constant and regular necessity; it is to have the foremost place. The tending (which includes this) consists of other acts, of discipline, authority, restoration, material assistance of individuals, but they are incidental in comparison with the feeding" (*Expository Dictionary of New Testament Words*).

Note another significant fact: the flock is *God's flock*; it is not the flock of the minister. Ministers are only undershepherds to God. But they are to be undershepherds: they are to tend God's flock, to look after and care for the flock. The fact that God is the Chief Shepherd does not mean that the minister can leave the care of the flock up to God as though He was going to automatically care for the flock. God looks after the flock through the undershepherds whom He chooses. This is the way He shepherds. Therefore, every minister is important; every minister is to feed and tend and shepherd God's flock. And Scripture pulls no punches about the fact: Scripture lays down exactly how the minister is to go about caring for the flock.

1. The elder or minister is to take the oversight of the flock willingly, not by force. This does not mean that a person is not to feel the constraint of God and His love in the ministry. He is. All ministers are to sense the constraint of God. Paul forcefully declared the fact:

For I am compelled to preach. Woe to me if I do not preach the gospel! (1 Cor 9:16)

For Christ's love compels us (2 Cor 5:14)

The person should not have to be forced and coerced to minister. He should willingly shepherd God's flock. The minister must willingly do the will of God. He should never have to be compelled or coerced to minister to God's people.

Thought 1. The great tragedy is this: many have been called by God into the ministry, called to shepherd His flock, but they refused. Why?
⇒ Some felt unworthy and inadequate.
⇒ Some felt it would cost them too much.
⇒ Some felt it required too much sacrifice.
⇒ Some did not want to bear the reproach of the ministry.
⇒ Some felt the demands and duties and expectations were too much to bear.

On and on the list could go, but Scripture is clear. If we have been called into the ministry by God, we must not reject His call. We must not have to be compelled and coerced to do God's will. We must willingly minister and shepherd God's flock.

"Not everyone who says to me, 'Lord, Lord,' will enter the kingdom of heaven, but only he who does the will of my Father who is in heaven. (Mat 7:21)

For whoever does the will of my Father in heaven is my brother and sister and mother." (Mat 12:50)

"The man with the two talents also came. 'Master,' he said, 'you entrusted me with two talents; see, I have gained two more.' "His master replied, 'Well done, good and faithful servant! You have been faithful with a few things; I will put you in charge of many things. Come and share your master's happiness!' (Mat 25:22-23)

"My food," said Jesus, "is to do the will of him who sent me and to finish his work. (John 4:34)

You did not choose me, but I chose you and appointed you to go and bear fruit—fruit that will last. Then the Father will give you whatever you ask in my name. (John 15:16)

However, I consider my life worth nothing to me, if only I may finish the race and complete the task the Lord Jesus has given me—the task of testifying to the gospel of God's grace. (Acts 20:24)

We loved you so much that we were delighted to share with you not only the gospel of God but our lives as well, because you had become so dear to us. (1 Th 2:8)

I have fought the good fight, I have finished the race, I have kept the faith. Now there is in store for me the crown of righteousness, which the Lord, the righteous Judge, will award to me on that day—and not only to me, but also to all who have longed for his appearing. (2 Tim 4:7-8)

"Blessed are those who wash their robes, that they may have the right to the tree of life and may go through the gates into the city. (Rev 22:14)

2. The elder or minister must take the oversight of the flock not for personal profit and gain, but of a ready mind. The Greek says that no person is to enter the ministry "greedy for money" (mede aischrokerdos), that is, for base gain, or for some soiled and dirty advantage. No person should ever enter the ministry...

- as a profession.
- as a means of livelihood.
- as a means to serve mankind.
- because people say he has the gifts for it.
- because people say he would make a good minister.
- because family and friends encourage him to enter the ministry.

All of these reasons usually surround a person's entrance into the ministry. But they must never be *the reasons* why a person enters the ministry and cares for God's people. The ministry is a *call from God*, and no person dare enter the ministry without a personal call to the ministry. But note: when the call comes, the person is to have a ready mind. He is to minister to God's people; he is to shepherd God's flock.

> **Jesus answered, "If you want to be perfect, go, sell your possessions and give to the poor, and you will have treasure in heaven. Then come, follow me." (Mat 19:21)**
>
> **Peter said to him, "We have left everything to follow you!" (Mark 10:28)**
>
> **Then he said to them all: "If anyone would come after me, he must deny himself and take up his cross daily and follow me. (Luke 9:23)**
>
> **"If anyone comes to me and does not hate his father and mother, his wife and children, his brothers and sisters—yes, even his own life—he cannot be my disciple. And anyone who does not carry his cross and follow me cannot be my disciple. (Luke 14:26-27)**
>
> **In the same way, any of you who does not give up everything he has cannot be my disciple. (Luke 14:33)**
>
> **"I tell you the truth," Jesus said to them, "no one who has left home or wife or brothers or parents or children for the sake of the kingdom of God will fail to receive many times as much in this age and, in the age to come, eternal life." (Luke 18:29-30)**
>
> **I have not coveted anyone's silver or gold or clothing. (Acts 20:33)**
>
> **For if you live according to the sinful nature, you will die; but if by the Spirit you put to death the misdeeds of the body, you will live, (Rom 8:13)**
>
> **We who are strong ought to bear with the failings of the weak and not to please ourselves. (Rom 15:1)**
>
> **Nobody should seek his own good, but the good of others. (1 Cor 10:24)**
>
> **Those who belong to Christ Jesus have crucified the sinful nature with its passions and desires. (Gal 5:24)**
>
> **Each of you should look not only to your own interests, but also to the interests of others. (Phil 2:4)**
>
> **What is more, I consider everything a loss compared to the surpassing greatness of knowing Christ Jesus my Lord, for whose sake I have lost all things. I consider them rubbish, that I may gain Christ (Phil 3:8)**

3. The elder or minister is to take the oversight of the flock not as a lord, but by being an example. Note, some manuscripts add the phrase "God's heritage," stating that ministers are not to be "lords over God's heritage." The flock of God is called God's heritage (kleron). This is the word that was used of Israel in the Old Testament. It means that the Jews were the people who were set apart and allotted and assigned to God. They were His very special allotment and assignment, the people charged to His care and oversight. This is the picture painted of the elder or minister and the flock of God. God has given the minister a very special heritage or allotment and assignment: the minister has been assigned to feed the heritage of God, the very flock that belongs to God Himself.

Now note how the minister is to lead God's flock. He is not to lord it over them, but he is to lead by example. The minister...

- is not to be a dictator but an example.
- is not to preach one thing and do something else.

The minister is to lead people by living for Christ. He is to preach and teach Christ, but he is to first of all live a pure and righteous life just like Christ lived. The minister is to live exactly what he preaches. He is to be a pattern and model for Christ, a pattern and model of just what God wants His people to be.

> **"You are the salt of the earth. But if the salt loses its saltiness, how can it be made salty again? It is no longer good for anything, except to be thrown out and trampled by men. (Mat 5:13)**
>
> **Jesus called them together and said, "You know that those who are regarded as rulers of the Gentiles lord it over them, and their high officials exercise authority over them. Not so with you. Instead, whoever wants to become great among you must be your servant, and whoever wants to be first must be slave of all. (Mark 10:42-44)**
>
> **I have set you an example that you should do as I have done for you. (John 13:15)**
>
> **Don't let anyone look down on you because you are young, but set an example for the believers in speech, in life, in love, in faith and in purity. (1 Tim 4:12)**
>
> **In everything set them an example by doing what is good. In your teaching show integrity, seriousness (Titus 2:7)**
>
> **Brothers, as an example of patience in the face of suffering, take the prophets who spoke in the name of the Lord. (James 5:10)**
>
> **To this you were called, because Christ suffered for you, leaving you an example, that you should follow in his steps. (1 Pet 2:21)**

3 (5:4) **Minister—Reward**: the reward for elders or ministers is glorious. It is a crown of glory that never fades away. Note two things.

1. Jesus Christ is the Chief Shepherd and He is going to appear, that is, return, to earth. The idea is that nothing

will stop His return; He is going to appear and reward His ministers.

Note the title of Christ, the Chief Shepherd (archipoimenos). Alan Stibbs says that it is the "Archshepherd" or "Archbishop" who is over all and to whom we shall all give an account (*The First Epistle General of Peter*. "The Tyndale New Testament Commentaries," p.168).

The work of Jesus as the Shepherd is fourfold.

a. Jesus Christ is the *Good Shepherd*. He is called *good* because He risks and sacrifices His life for the sheep (Jn.10:11, 15; cp. Ps.22).

b. Jesus Christ is the *Great Shepherd*. He is called *great* because He arose from the dead and He perfects the sheep (Heb.13:20-21).

c. Jesus Christ is the *Shepherd and Overseer* of our souls. He is called the *shepherd and overseer* because He welcomes those who wandered off and went astray (1 Pt.2:25).

d. Jesus Christ is the *Chief Shepherd*. He is called *chief* because He is to appear and return to earth with great glory and reward the faithful (1 Pt.5:4).

2. The reward for elders is glorious: it is to be a crown of glory. What does this mean? It means that the faithful minister shall share in the glory of heaven and be crowned with a very special portion of glory. By crown is meant rule and reign, the assignment of heavenly service for Christ. (See note—1 Pt.1:4 for a list of all rewards.)

> **And if anyone gives even a cup of cold water to one of these little ones because he is my disciple, I tell you the truth, he will certainly not lose his reward." (Mat 10:42)**

> **"His master replied, 'Well done, good and faithful servant! You have been faithful with a few things; I will put you in charge of many things. Come and share your master's happiness!' (Mat 25:23)**

> **In my Father's house are many rooms; if it were not so, I would have told you. I am going there to prepare a place for you. (John 14:2)**

> **Because you know that the Lord will reward everyone for whatever good he does, whether he is slave or free. (Eph 6:8)**

> **And when the Chief Shepherd appears, you will receive the crown of glory that will never fade away. (1 Pet 5:4)**

> **I am coming soon. Hold on to what you have, so that no one will take your crown. (Rev 3:11)**

	B. The Duties of the Believer (Part I): Humility & Submission, 5:5-7
1 Submit to the elders **2 Submit to one another &** **be clothed with humility**	5 Young men, in the same way be submissive to those who are older. All of you, clothe yourselves with humility toward one another, because, "God opposes the proud but gives grace to the humble."

3 Humble yourself under
the mighty hand of God
a. Bc. God is to be feared
b. Bc. the day of exaltation
   is coming
c. Bc. God cares for us,
   cares about all anxiety
	6 Humble yourselves, therefore, under God's mighty hand, that he may lift you up in due time.
	7 Cast all your anxiety on him because he cares for you.

DIVISION IV

HOW THE CHURCH IS TO FUNCTION UNDER SUFFERING: BE FAITHFUL, 5:1-11

B. The Duties of the Believer (Part I): Humility and Submission, 5:5-7

(5:5-7) **Introduction**: this is a great passage on humility. Humility is one of the very first duties of the believer. Some people shrink back when they hear the word humility mentioned. When they think of humility, they picture a shy, weak, unimpressive type of person. But this is not what God means by humility. The humility demanded by God strengthens a person and makes him one of the most striking and impressive persons around.

1. Submit to the elders (v.5).
2. Submit to one another and be clothed with humility (v.5).
3. Humble yourself under the mighty hand of God (v.6-7).

1 (5:5) **Humility**: first, submit to the elders or ministers of the church. The word submissive (hopotagete) means to submit and to place oneself under the authority and leadership of the elder or minister. The minister is the leader of the church. God has chosen and ordained the minister to be the leader among the flock of God. Therefore, his leadership is to be...

- esteemed
- recognized
- acknowledged
- honored
- followed
- obeyed
- subjected to

But remember: the minister is not to be a lord over God's heritage, but an example to the flock (v.3). He is to lead and exercise his authority by being an example, not by using authoritarian methods and bypassing people. It is this that gives balance to the minister's authority. But at the same time, the flock of God is to submit to the authority of the minister.

Note: the word *young* is used to describe the laity or believers of a church. The idea being conveyed is that believers are to be as youth who sit at the feet of the parent to be fed and to learn and grow. The very term conveys the idea of submission. This shows how important this charge is to God—so important that he terms believers the *young*. However, it should be noted that some commentators say that this refers to the young people of the church. They are to submit themselves to the older believers. But this does not seem to fit the context in light of two facts:

⇒ The preceding verses discuss the elder or minister of the church.
⇒ The rest of verse 5 exhorts all believers to be submissive toward one another.

The thrust seems to be that *young* refers to believers. Simply put, believers are to submissive toward themselves to the minister as the parent of the church, the parent who shepherds and feeds them the Word of God and who willingly takes the oversight of their welfare (cp. v.2-3).

> **To submit to such as these and to everyone who joins in the work, and labors at it. (1 Cor 16:16)**
>
> **Now we ask you, brothers, to respect those who work hard among you, who are over you in the Lord and who admonish you. Hold them in the highest regard in love because of their work. Live in peace with each other. (1 Th 5:12-13)**
>
> **The elders who direct the affairs of the church well are worthy of double honor, especially those whose work is preaching and teaching. (1 Tim 5:17)**
>
> **Obey your leaders and submit to their authority. They keep watch over you as men who must give an account. Obey them so that their work will be a joy, not a burden, for that would be of no advantage to you. (Heb 13:17)**

2 (5:5) **Humility**: second, submit to one another and be clothed with humility. Not only are we to submit to our ministers, but we are to submit ourselves to one another. Note several things.

1. The word *all* means every one of us, all ages, sexes, and classes (A.T. Robertson. *Word Pictures In The New Testament*, Vol.6, p.132). No person is exempt. All of us are to submit ourselves to all believers no matter who we may be: male or female, poor or rich, young or old.

Thought 1. Submission takes concentration and effort. It takes a deliberate decision to submit to someone else. But this is just what Scripture is demanding. Every believer is unique to God and has a very special gift and contribution to make to the world and to the church. All believers are to submit themselves to one another, to each one's uniqueness and gift. All believers are to acknowledge, respect, and honor one another, all because of who each one is and because of the gift God has given each one of us.

2. Note: to be submissive toward one another is not enough, not for God. Scripture says that we must also "clothe [ourselves] with humility." The word "clothe" (egkombosasthe) means to gird oneself with an apron. It is the picture of what Jesus did in the upper room when He girded Himself with an apron and assumed the role of a servant and washed the feet of the disciples. Jesus, the Son of God and Sovereign Majesty of the universe, actually clothed Himself with the apron of humility and served the disciples. And, when he finished, He said:

> **"You call me 'Teacher' and 'Lord,' and rightly so, for that is what I am. Now that I, your Lord and Teacher, have washed your feet, you also should wash one another's feet. I have set you an example that you should do as I have done for you. (John 13:13-15)**

Alan Stibbs states it well: "The exhortation here is not to feel humble, nor to pray for humility, but to act it" (*The First Epistle General of Peter.* "The Tyndale New Testament Commentaries," p.169). The word "humility" (tapeinophrosunen) means to offer oneself as lowly and submissive; to walk in a spirit of lowliness; to present oneself as lowly; to act of low degree and low rank. It is the opposite of being high-minded, above and better than others, prideful, arrogant, superior, haughty, and self-assertive. The believer may have a high position, power, wealth, fame, and much more; but he is to carry himself in a spirit of lowliness and submission. He is to deny himself for the sake of Christ and in order to help others. (See note, *Humility*—1 Pt.3:8. See DEEPER STUDY # 1—Ph.2:3 for full discussion.)

3. Note why we are to be submissive toward to one another and to clothe ourselves with humility: because God opposes the proud but gives grace to the humble (cp. Pr.3:34).

a. God resists the proud. He stands against all...
- who look down upon others.
- who feel superior to others.
- who discriminate against others.
- who are prejudiced.
- who are boastful.
- who are haughty.

God opposes the proud—all who oppress others—no matter who they are. The word "opposes" (antitassetai) is a strong word. It is the picture of an army being set and arrayed against the enemy. Marvin Vincent says that "pride calls out God's armies. No wonder, therefore, that it 'goeth before destruction' " (*Word Studies In The New Testament*, Vol.1, p.668). Those who walk upon this earth exalting themselves above others shall be destroyed by God Himself.

b. God gives grace to the humble. Grace means the favor and blessings of God. The person who walks humbly before God, recognizing and acknowledging the value of others, shall receive the favor and blessings of God. He shall be highly favored and blessed—rewarded beyond all imagination. The humble person shall bear the fruit of God's spirit in this life...
- love
- joy
- peace
- patience
- kindness
- goodness
- faithfulness
- gentleness
- self-control

In addition, the humble person has the full assurance of being cared for and looked after by God, that God will work all things out for his good while he is on earth. And then in the future, when Christ returns, the humble person will be abundantly rewarded with the glorious privilege of living and reigning with Christ forever and ever. (See note—1 Pt.1:4 for a full list of the rewards.)

> **Take my yoke upon you and learn from me, for I am gentle and humble in heart, and you will find rest for your souls. (Mat 11:29)**
> **And he said: "I tell you the truth, unless you change and become like little children, you will never enter the kingdom of heaven. Therefore, whoever humbles himself like this child is the greatest in the kingdom of heaven. (Mat 18:3-4)**
> **For whoever exalts himself will be humbled, and whoever humbles himself will be exalted. (Mat 23:12)**
> **Live in harmony with one another. Do not be proud, but be willing to associate with people of low position. Do not be conceited. (Rom 12:16)**
> **As a prisoner for the Lord, then, I urge you to live a life worthy of the calling you have received. Be completely humble and gentle; be patient, bearing with one another in love. (Eph 4:1-2)**
> **Do nothing out of selfish ambition or vain conceit, but in humility consider others better than yourselves. Each of you should look not only to your own interests, but also to the interests of others. (Phil 2:3-4)**
> **Therefore, as God's chosen people, holy and dearly loved, clothe yourselves with compassion, kindness, humility, gentleness and patience. Bear with each other and forgive whatever grievances you may have against one another. Forgive as the Lord forgave you. (Col 3:12-13)**
> **Humble yourselves, therefore, under God's mighty hand, that he may lift you up in due time. (1 Pet 5:6)**

3 (5:6-7) **Humility—God, Hand of**: third, humble yourselves under the mighty hand of God. There are three reasons for this.

1. God is to be feared, for He stands opposed to the proud. The very thing we do not want to be is prideful. The only way to escape the judgment of God's hand is to humble ourselves under His mighty hand. If we stand up to His hand, we shall be stricken down, but if we humble ourselves under His hand, we shall be protected and lifted up,

exalted forever and ever. The picture of God's mighty hand is a different picture for the proud and the humble:

To the humble, God's mighty hand means…
- strength and power
- sovereignty and control
- salvation and security
- care and protection
- assurance and confidence

To the proud, God's mighty hand means…
- strength and power
- sovereignty and control
- warning and fear
- anger and wrath
- judgment and condemnation

Note: God's mighty hand provides two entirely different things for the humble and the proud. Right now the hand of God stands over the world in all of its strength and power and its sovereignty and control. God's hand stands to save everyone, even the proud if he will only humble himself. But if he refuses to humble himself, then the hand of God stands for something entirely different than salvation. The mighty hand of God stands…
- as a warning and a threat
- in anger and wrath
- in judgment and condemnation

This is the reason we must humble ourselves under the mighty hand of God—to escape the terrifying judgment of God.

My Father, who has given them to me, is greater than all ; no one can snatch them out of my Father's hand. (John 10:29)

Now to him who is able to establish you by my gospel and the proclamation of Jesus Christ, according to the revelation of the mystery hidden for long ages past, (Rom 16:25)

Humble yourselves, therefore, under God's mighty hand, that he may lift you up in due time. (1 Pet 5:6)

He did this so that all the peoples of the earth might know that the hand of the LORD is powerful and so that you might always fear the LORD your God." (Josh 4:24)

Your arm is endued with power; your hand is strong, your right hand exalted. (Psa 89:13)

A psalm. Sing to the LORD a new song, for he has done marvelous things; his right hand and his holy arm have worked salvation for him. (Psa 98:1)

Shouts of joy and victory resound in the tents of the righteous: "The Lord's right hand has done mighty things! The Lord's right hand is lifted high; the Lord's right hand has done mighty things!" I will not die but live, and will proclaim what the LORD has done. (Psa 118:15-17)

Surely the arm of the LORD is not too short to save, nor his ear too dull to hear. (Isa 59:1)

2. We should humble ourselves under God's mighty hand because He is going to exalt the humble. Note that the humble are not yet lifted up. But *in due time* they will be. The day is coming when they shall be lifted up, exalted in all the glory and majesty of Christ. They shall be exalted to live with Christ and to rule and reign with Him and to serve Him throughout the universe. They shall be with Christ, worshipping and serving Him forever and ever—all to His glory and praise, honor, and grace. (See note— 1 Pt.1:4 for more discussion.)

3. We should humble ourselves under the mighty hand of God because God cares for us; He cares about all our anxiety. Remember: the believers of Peter's day were suffering terrible persecution. They had been forced to flee for their lives, leaving everything behind: homes, jobs, and possessions. They had only what they could carry by hand, and they fled to whatever places they felt were safe. They were, so to speak, an underground people, having to live, work, and worship in secret and to find housing and food wherever they could. They never knew when they would be discovered and forced to flee again.

The point is this: imagine the anxiety, the pressure, tension, and stress being experienced by the believers. Yet there was great help: God was available to help them. Note that the exhortation is not only clearly stated; it is a command: "cast all your anxiety (merimna) on Him, because He cares for you." God's mighty hand will…
- save and deliver you
- look after and care for you
- strengthen and secure you
- provide and protect you
- give you assurance and confidence

So we say with confidence, "The Lord is my helper; I will not be afraid. What can man do to me?" (Heb 13:6)

Yet I am poor and needy; may the Lord think of me. You are my help and my deliverer; O my God, do not delay. (Psa 40:17)

But you, O God, will bring down the wicked into the pit of corruption; bloodthirsty and deceitful men will not live out half their days. But as for me, I trust in you. (Psa 55:23)

So do not fear, for I am with you; do not be dismayed, for I am your God. I will strengthen you and help you; I will uphold you with my righteous right hand. (Isa 41:10)

"Therefore I tell you, do not worry about your life, what you will eat or drink; or about your body, what you will wear. Is not life more important than food, and the body more important than clothes? But seek first his kingdom and his righteousness, and all these things will be given to you as well. (Mat 6:25, 33)

Indeed, the very hairs of your head are all numbered. Don't be afraid; you are worth more than many sparrows. (Luke 12:7)

"Be careful, or your hearts will be weighed down with dissipation, drunkenness and the anxieties of life, and that day will close on you unexpectedly like a trap. (Luke 21:34)

And we know that in all things God works for the good of those who love him, who have been called according to his purpose. (Rom 8:28)

Who shall separate us from the love of Christ? Shall trouble or hardship or perse-

cution or famine or nakedness or danger or sword? As it is written: "For your sake we face death all day long; we are considered as sheep to be slaughtered." No, in all these things we are more than conquerors through him who loved us. For I am convinced that neither death nor life, neither angels nor demons, neither the present nor the future, nor any powers, neither height nor depth, nor anything else in all creation, will be able to separate us from the love of God that is in Christ Jesus our Lord. (Rom 8:35-39)

Do not be anxious about anything, but in everything, by prayer and petition, with thanksgiving, present your requests to God. (Phil 4:6)

Cast all your anxiety on him because he cares for you. (1 Pet 5:7)

	C. The Duties of the Believer (Part II): Vigilance & Resistance Against the Devil, 5:8-9
1 **The way: Be self-controlled, be alert**	8 Be self-controlled and alert. Your enemy the devil prowls around like a roaring lion looking for someone to devour.
2 **The reason: The devil is your adversary, a roaring lion seeking to devour all whom he can**	9 Resist him, standing firm in the faith, because you know that your brothers throughout the world are undergoing the same kind of sufferings.
3 **The duty** a. To resist standing firm b. To know that other believers are suffering & conquering the attacks of Satan	

DIVISION IV

HOW THE CHURCH IS TO FUNCTION UNDER SUFFERING: BE FAITHFUL, 5:1-11

C. The Duties of the Believer (Part II): Vigilance and Resistance Against the Devil, 5:8-9

(5:8-9) **Introduction**: this is one of the most important duties of the believer. The believer must be vigilant in this duty or his life and testimony for Christ will be devoured and destroyed. What is the duty? Vigilance and resistance against the devil. The believer must constantly watch for and resist the devil.

1. The way: self-controlled and alert (v.8).
2. The reason: the devil is your adversary, a roaring lion seeking to devour all whom he can (v.8).
3. The duty (v.9).

1 (5:8) **Satan—Believer, Duty**: how can we stand against the attacks and temptations of the devil? There is only one way: we must be self-controlled and alert.

1. First, be self-controlled (nephate). The word means...

- not to become intoxicated with drugs or alcohol of any kind.
- to be self-controlled in mind and behavior; to be controlled in all things; not given over to indulgence, license, or extravagance. It is the opposite of indulgence in anything such as eating, drinking, and recreation. it means to live a sober, solid, controlled, and strong life.

The believer has to be sober as he watches for the attacks of the devil. If he is not sober, he will not be alert enough to conquer the attacks and the temptations of the devil. The believer will be overcome and led into sin and destruction. And no believer can be alert enough to stand up against the devil if he indulges and gratifies his flesh in...

- sex
- food
- sleep
- relaxation
- pornography
- position
- clothing
- possessions
- alcohol and drugs
- recognition
- power

The believer is to live a sober and controlled life. He is to stay alert to the devil and his temptations at all times. He must be alert enough to see the temptations and attacks coming and have a mind and spirit strong enough to stand against the temptations and attacks.

So then, let us not be like others, who are asleep, but let us be alert and self-controlled. For those who sleep, sleep at night, and those who get drunk, get drunk at night. But since we belong to the day, let us be self-controlled, putting on faith and love as a breastplate, and the hope of salvation as a helmet. (1 Th 5:6-8)

In the same way, their wives are to be women worthy of respect, not malicious talkers but temperate and trustworthy in everything. (1 Tim 3:11)

For the grace of God that brings salvation has appeared to all men. It teaches us to say "No" to ungodliness and worldly passions, and to live self-controlled, upright and godly lives in this present age, while we wait for the blessed hope—the glorious appearing of our great God and Savior, Jesus Christ, (Titus 2:11-13)

Therefore, prepare your minds for action; be self-controlled; set your hope fully on the grace to be given you when Jesus Christ is revealed. (1 Pet 1:13)

The end of all things is near. Therefore be clear minded and self-controlled so that you can pray. (1 Pet 4:7)

2. How do we stand against the devil? Second, be "alert" (gregoresate). The word means to be watchful and awake. It has the idea of being constantly aroused and on the lookout; to always be aroused, awake, and watching for the devil and his attacks. Again, if a person's mind and body are dull, flabby, and weak from drink, drugs, overeating, slothfulness, and indulgence in sleep, recreation, pleasure, or in anything else—that person cannot be watching and waiting; he cannot be constantly aroused to look for the devil's temptations and attacks.

The believer must be sober and serious about the devil; he must be alert in looking for the devil's temptations and attacks. It is the only conceivable way the believer can conquer and overcome in this life; it is the only way he can keep his life and testimony from being destroyed by the devil.

"Watch and pray so that you will not fall into temptation. The spirit is willing, but the body is weak." (Mat 26:41)

It will be good for those servants whose master finds them watching when he comes. I tell you the truth, he will dress himself to serve, will have them recline at the table and will come and wait on them. (Luke 12:37)

So, if you think you are standing firm, be careful that you don't fall! (1 Cor 10:12)

Be on your guard; stand firm in the faith; be men of courage; be strong. (1 Cor 16:13)

Devote yourselves to prayer, being watchful and thankful. (Col 4:2)

You are all sons of the light and sons of the day. We do not belong to the night or to the darkness. So then, let us not be like others, who are asleep, but let us be alert and self-controlled. (1 Th 5:5-6)

Be self-controlled and alert. Your enemy the devil prowls around like a roaring lion looking for someone to devour. (1 Pet 5:8)

"Behold, I come like a thief! Blessed is he who stays awake and keeps his clothes with him, so that he may not go naked and be shamefully exposed." (Rev 16:15)

2 (5:8) **Satan**: Why should we stand against the attacks and temptations of the devil? There is one strong reason: he is our adversary, a roaring lion who seeks all whom he can devour. Note three points.

1. The devil is our "enemy" (antidikos). The Greek word means a legal opponent such as an opponent in a lawsuit. It also means a common day-to-day opponent like a neighbor who opposes and stands as an enemy against us. The picture is that of the devil opposing us in every conceivable way.

⇒ It is the picture of Satan standing in a law court, standing as an adversary in the court of God and accusing us before God.
⇒ It is the picture of Satan standing here on earth, standing against us and doing all he can to trip us up and to defeat and destroy us.

2. The word "devil" (diabolos) itself means slanderer or false accuser. The devil is a malicious enemy who accuses us before God and makes false charges against us. Scripture teaches that Satan is constantly bringing up our sins and transgressions before God, that he is constantly reminding God of our disobedience. But note: the accusations against us are false. The charges are not true. How can they not be true when we are sinners, for no true believer denies his sin? By Christ. We believe Christ and we have cast ourselves upon Christ, upon the glorious fact that He died for our sins. We have trusted Christ for forgiveness of sin, and when He forgives us, our sins are removed from us. We are no longer guilty of sin. Therefore, the accusations and charges of Satan against us are false. Why then would he accuse and charge us before God? Why would he remind God time and again of our sins? To hurt God, to cut the heart of God. He is the devil, the one who stands opposed to God and to all that God stands for. Eons ago, sometime before the world was ever created, he was apparently the highest angel in all of creation. God had created him as the highest spiritual being in the universe. At that time his name was Lucifer. But he did what so many men do—rebelled against God—and he led other angelic beings to rebel with him. Therefore, God judged him and cast him from his exalted position in heaven. From what we can glean from Scripture this is what happened to Satan, how he became the devil, the terrible opponent to God. (See DEEPER STUDY # 1—Rev.12:9 for more discussion. Cp. Is.14:12-17; Ezk.28:11-19. Also see note—2 Cor.4:4.)

The point is this: the devil does all he can to cut and hurt the heart of God. Therefore, he constantly reminds God of our sins. This, of course, means that he does all he can to tempt and lead us into sin, for the more we sin the more he can hurt God.

Thought 1. Think what this means: how deeply God's heart must be cut and hurt when we sin. We are believers, persons for whom God gave His Son to die. When God paid such a price—actually cast His wrath against His own Son because of sin—think about how much He must hurt when we sin, especially when we profess to love Him. The devil is a slanderer; he will constantly slander us before God. He will use our sin to hurt God as much as possible. This is the reason we must stand against the devil: we must protect the heart of God. We must not bring hurt and pain to our Father's heart.

The great dragon was hurled down—that ancient serpent called the devil, or Satan, who leads the whole world astray. He was hurled to the earth, and his angels with him. Then I heard a loud voice in heaven say: "Now have come the salvation and the power and the kingdom of our God, and the authority of his Christ. For the accuser of our brothers, who accuses them before our God day and night, has been hurled down. (Rev 12:9-10)

One day the angels came to present themselves before the LORD, and Satan also came with them. The LORD said to Satan, "Where have you come from?" Satan answered the LORD, "From roaming through the earth and going back and forth in it." Then the LORD said to Satan, "Have you considered my servant Job? There is no one on earth like him; he is blameless and upright, a man who fears God and shuns evil." "Does Job fear God for nothing?" Satan replied. "Have you not put a hedge around him and his household and everything he has? You have blessed the work of his hands, so that his flocks and herds are spread throughout the land. But stretch out your hand and strike everything he has, and he will surely curse you to your face." The LORD said to Satan, "Very well, then, everything he has is in your hands, but on the man himself do not lay a finger." Then Satan went out from the presence of the LORD. (Job 1:6-12)

Then he showed me Joshua the high priest standing before the angel of the LORD, and Satan standing at his right side to accuse him. (Zec 3:1)

3. He is like a roaring lion seeking to devour all whom he can. The *roaring lion* is a picture of anger, strength, fierceness, and cruelty. Satan is being pictured as angry (against God and all believers), strong, fierce, and cruel.

Note: Scripture says he roams about roaring in anger and cruelty and in the roaring ferociousness of his strength, seeking someone to attack and devour. How can Satan devour a person? Jesus tells us in one of the most shocking statements ever made about man. He said that a person who does not trust and follow God as his Father is actually following the devil as his father. In other words, Jesus says that all unbelievers have the devil as their father.

You belong to your father, the devil, and you want to carry out your father's desire. He was a murderer from the beginning, not holding to the truth, for there is no truth in him. When he lies, he speaks his native language, for he is a liar and the father of lies. (John 8:44)

Note that Jesus is telling us how the devil devours man. He consumes man by leading him to do four things.

a. The devil leads us to lust, crave. He tempts us to give in to the lust of the flesh, and the lust of our eyes, and the pride of life (boasting in what we have and do).

Do not love the world or anything in the world. If anyone loves the world, the love of the Father is not in him. For everything in the world—the cravings of sinful man, the lust of his eyes and the boasting of what he has and does—comes not from the Father but from the world. (1 John 2:15-16)

b. The devil leads us to murder. The devil is behind the murder of human life and behind the loss of man experiencing real life here on earth. The devil destroys life and all abundant living when he can: all love, joy, peace, patience, kindness, goodness, faithfulness, gentleness, self-control.

When anyone hears the message about the kingdom and does not understand it, the evil one comes and snatches away what was sown in his heart. This is the seed sown along the path. (Mat 13:19)
Be self-controlled and alert. Your enemy the devil prowls around like a roaring lion looking for someone to devour. (1 Pet 5:8)
"Does Job fear God for nothing?" Satan replied. "Have you not put a hedge around him and his household and everything he has? You have blessed the work of his hands, so that his flocks and herds are spread throughout the land. But stretch out your hand and strike everything he has, and he will surely curse you to your face." (Job 1:9-11)

Jesus was saying that one thing is certain: God is not the father of murder—the devil is. They who commit murder are children of the devil. But note the real meaning of murder revealed by Jesus (see note—Mt.5:22 for discussion). Murder is…
- anger
- bitterness
- enmity
- an uncontrolled spirit
- desiring a person's ruin
- striking out at a person

- slandering, maligning, speaking ill about a person, and destroying a person's image (who is created in God's image)
- envying & killing a person's happiness

c. The devil leads men to reject the truth.

You belong to your father, the devil, and you want to carry out your father's desire. He was a murderer from the beginning, not holding to the truth, for there is no truth in him. When he lies, he speaks his native language, for he is a liar and the father of lies. (John 8:44)
He who does what is sinful is of the devil, because the devil has been sinning from the beginning. The reason the Son of God appeared was to destroy the devil's work. (1 John 3:8)

d. The devil leads men to lie and deceive.

And even if our gospel is veiled, it is veiled to those who are perishing. The god of this age has blinded the minds of unbelievers, so that they cannot see the light of the gospel of the glory of Christ, who is the image of God. (2 Cor 4:3-4)
For such men are false apostles, deceitful workmen, masquerading as apostles of Christ. And no wonder, for Satan himself masquerades as an angel of light. It is not surprising, then, if his servants masquerade as servants of righteousness. Their end will be what their actions deserve. (2 Cor 11:13-15)

3 (5:9) **Satan—Believer, Duty**: What is our duty in standing against the attacks and temptations of Satan? Our duty is twofold.
1. We must resist the devil; we must resist him standing firm in the faith. The word "resist" (antistete) means to withstand the devil; to stand firm against him; to strive and struggle against him. Note that we must stand firm in our resistance. We must not…
- let our guard down
- slip one step
- look one time
- touch at all
- taste a single bite
- listen to one word
- think a single thought
- give way to any desire
- loosen the restraint

It might look good, taste good, and feel good, but we must resist the desire and lust and be steadfast in our resistance. We must not give in at all. Giving in one step leads to a second step, and before we know it, we have caved in and are engaged in the sin. Satan has devoured us.

Our duty is to resist the devil and to stand firm in our resistance. Note what it is that Satan is after: the believer's faith. He wants the believer to deny his faith, to turn away from Christ. The devil's crowd may say…
- "Oh come on! It won't hurt you."
- "Do your own thing."
- "You're a fool if you don't get all you can."
- "Live, drink, and be merry."

A person's desires and lusts may want more and more of the possessions and pleasures of this world. The temptation will always be there to turn away from Christ and His righteousness, to turn away from one's faith and to return to the world and its ways. Our duty is to resist the devil by standing firm in the faith, trusting God for the necessary strength to conquer the temptation.

2. The believer is to keep in mind the fact that other believers are suffering the same kind of sufferings and they are conquering them. When a believer refuses to go along with the world and its ways, he is misunderstood, withdrawn from, ridiculed, mocked, abused, and persecuted by unbelievers. In addition he is attacked and tempted by the devil. The believers of Peter's day were suffering terrible attacks from Satan, attacks that had broken out in severe persecution. How do believers stand against so much? By keeping in mind that other believers are also being attacked, and many are faithfully resisting the devil. They are standing firm in their faith. Therefore, their example encourages us. We are not alone in the world. There are others suffering the very same kind of sufferings of the devil as we are, and they are resisting ever so faithfully. They are standing firm for Christ. Therefore, we must let their example stir us to firmly resist the devil. We must use their example to arouse us to stand firm for Christ.

> **Do not offer the parts of your body to sin, as instruments of wickedness, but rather offer yourselves to God, as those who have been brought from death to life; and offer the parts of your body to him as instruments of righteousness. (Rom 6:13)**

> **No temptation has seized you except what is common to man. And God is faithful; he will not let you be tempted beyond what you can bear. But when you are tempted, he will also provide a way out so that you can stand up under it. (1 Cor 10:13)**

> **"In your anger do not sin:" Do not let the sun go down while you are still angry, and do not give the devil a foothold. (Eph 4:26-27)**

> **Therefore put on the full armor of God, so that when the day of evil comes, you may be able to stand your ground, and after you have done everything, to stand. (Eph 6:13)**

> **Submit yourselves, then, to God. Resist the devil, and he will flee from you. (James 4:7)**

> **Be self-controlled and alert. Your enemy the devil prowls around like a roaring lion looking for someone to devour. Resist him, standing firm in the faith, because you know that your brothers throughout the world are undergoing the same kind of sufferings. (1 Pet 5:8-9)**

> **By the same word the present heavens and earth are reserved for fire, being kept for the day of judgment and destruction of ungodly men. (2 Pet 3:7)**

> **My son, if sinners entice you, do not give in to them. (Prov 1:10)**

> **Do not set foot on the path of the wicked or walk in the way of evil men. (Prov 4:14)**

	D. The Suffering of the Believer and God, 5:10-14	12 With the help of Silas, whom I regard as a faithful brother, I have written to you briefly, encouraging you and testifying that this is the true grace of God. Stand fast in it.	4 The final greeting
1 God's great resource	10 And the God of all grace, who called you to his eternal glory in Christ, after you have suffered a little while, will himself restore you and make you strong, firm and steadfast.		a. From a faithful brother: Silas
2 God's great provision			b. From a faithful minister: Peter, who had written to share the true grace of God
a. He restores			
b. He makes us strong		13 She who is in Babylon, chosen together with you, sends you her greetings, and so does my son Mark.	c. From the church at Babylon (Rome)
c. He makes us firm			d. From Mark
d. He makes us steadfast		14 Greet one another with a kiss of love. Peace to all of you who are in Christ.	5 The conclusion: The kiss of love & peace
3 God's great power	11 To him be the power for ever and ever. Amen.		

DIVISION IV

HOW THE CHURCH IS TO FUNCTION UNDER SUFFERING: BE FAITHFUL, 5:1-11

D. The Suffering of the Believer and God, 5:10-14

(5:10-14) **Introduction**: this passage concludes Peter's letter to the believers. But before he makes his concluding remarks, he has one more important subject to discuss: the suffering of the believer and God. The believer suffers greatly in this world. The believer not only bears the natural sufferings of this world that all men suffer, but he is attacked because of his faith in Christ. He is attacked by both the devil and unbelievers because he lives a righteous and godly life and proclaims the hope of salvation for all men. Most people want nothing to do with pure godliness and holiness: they want to live in the comfort and enjoyment of their desires and in the pleasures and possessions of this world. Therefore, they reject and oppose anyone who stresses pure godliness and holiness.

But the genuine believer has a great promise: God will take care of him through all the sufferings of this life. God will keep and preserve the believer and eventually take him on home to heaven. This is the great study of this passage.

1. God's great resource (v.10).
2. God's great provision (v.10).
3. God's great power (v.11).
4. The final greeting (v.12-13).
5. The conclusion: the kiss of love and peace (v.14).

1 (5:10) **God—Grace—Glory**: there is God's great resource. Two great resources are mentioned: His grace and His call to eternal glory. Everything that God does for the believer is because of His grace. Note that He is even called the *God of all grace*. Grace means favor, the favor of God. God favors us; therefore, He blesses us. Every blessing we ever receive comes from the favor of God, even life itself. All good things come from God and from His grace.

But note another fact as well: God has called us to eternal glory. He wants us in heaven with Him, free from all the sin, dirt, filth, evil, corruption, disease, and death of this world. God wants us perfected and glorified, made just like His Son, the Lord Jesus Christ. God wants us living with Him forever and ever, worshipping and serving Him. He has called the believer to eternal glory. Therefore, God will do anything—do what is necessary—to save and keep the believer for glory. God has called the believer to glory; therefore, He is committed to keep and preserve the believer for glory.

This is the glorious truth: God's grace and God's call to eternal glory will keep us through all the sufferings of this life. No matter how much Satan attacks us, no matter how severe the suffering, God will keep us. He will keep us…

- because He is gracious to us; He has favored us.
- because He has called us to His eternal glory.

The Spirit himself testifies with our spirit that we are God's children. Now if we are children, then we are heirs—heirs of God and co-heirs with Christ, if indeed we share in his sufferings in order that we may also share in his glory. (Rom 8:16-17)

But because of his great love for us, God, who is rich in mercy, made us alive with Christ even when we were dead in transgressions—it is by grace you have been saved. And God raised us up with Christ and seated us with him in the heavenly realms in Christ Jesus, in order that in the coming ages he might show the incomparable riches of his grace, expressed in his kindness to us in Christ Jesus. For it is by grace you have been saved, through faith—and this not from yourselves, it is the gift of God— (Eph 2:4-8)

But our citizenship is in heaven. And we eagerly await a Savior from there, the Lord Jesus Christ, who, by the power that enables him to bring everything under his control, will transform our lowly bodies so that they will be like his glorious body. (Phil 3:20-21)

And my God will meet all your needs according to his glorious riches in Christ Jesus. (Phil 4:19)

When Christ, who is your life, appears, then you also will appear with him in glory. (Col 3:4)

For the grace of God that brings salvation has appeared to all men. It teaches us to say "No" to ungodliness and worldly passions, and to live self-controlled, upright and godly lives in this present age, while we wait for the blessed hope—the glorious appearing of our great God and Savior, Jesus Christ, (Titus 2:11-13)

So that, having been justified by his grace, we might become heirs having the hope of eternal life. (Titus 3:7)

2 (5:10) **God**: there is God's great provision. How does God keep and preserve the believer? The temptations and trials of life are severe and fierce. How does God make sure the believer makes it to heaven and its eternal glory? God does four wonderful things for the believer. Note: in the Greek the emphasis is upon God Himself doing these things. God Himself becomes actively involved in taking care of the believer, in keeping and preserving and taking the believer to heaven and its glory.

1. God Himself uses the believer's suffering to perfect the believer. The word "restore" (katartisei) means to make fit or join together; to restore. The Greek authority Marvin Vincent says:

"The radical notion of the verb is...*adjustment*—the putting of all the parts into right relation and connection. We find it used...
- "of mending the nets (Mt.4:21)
- "of restoring an erring brother (Gal.6:1)
- "of framing the body and the worlds (Heb.10:5; 11:3)
- "of the union of members in the church (1 Cor.1:10; 2 Cor.13:11)

"Out of this comes the general sense of *perfecting* (Mt.21:16; Lk.6:40; 1 Th.3:10)." (*Word Studies In The New Testament*, Vol.1, p.671.) (Note: the paragraph has been outlined for simplicity.)

God takes all of the displaced joints and broken limbs of life and uses them to adjust our character. He uses all the trials and temptations, difficulties and persecutions—all the sufferings of life—and makes us more and more like Christ. If we are truly called of God and if we truly love God, then God will take all that ever happens to us and work it out for good. He will restore us, fit all the parts of life together and lead us to glory. This is the glorious grace and call of God to eternal glory.

> **Be perfect, therefore, as your heavenly Father is perfect. (Mat 5:48)**
>
> **To prepare God's people for works of service, so that the body of Christ may be built up until we all reach unity in the faith and in the knowledge of the Son of God and become mature, attaining to the whole measure of the fullness of Christ. (Eph 4:12-13)**
>
> **Because you know that the testing of your faith develops perseverance. Perseverance must finish its work so that you may be mature and complete, not lacking anything. (James 1:3-4)**
>
> **But if anyone obeys his word, God's love is truly made complete in him. This is how we know we are in him: (1 John 2:5)**

2. God Himself uses the believer's sufferings to make the believer strong. The word "strong" (sterixei) means to make steadfast, firm, and solid. It means to be firmly set, as firmly as if one was set in reinforced concrete. It means to be immovable. God is able to attach us to Himself to such a degree that we will be immovable, no matter how severe the attack of temptation or suffering. But remember our duty: we must resist the devil and resist him firmly (v.8). The promise is clear: if we resist the devil and draw near God, He will draw near us (Jas.4:7-8).

> **Submit yourselves, then, to God. Resist the devil, and he will flee from you. Come near to God and he will come near to you. Wash your hands, you sinners, and purify**

> **your hearts, you double-minded. (James 4:7-8)**
>
> **May he strengthen your hearts so that you will be blameless and holy in the presence of our God and Father when our Lord Jesus comes with all his holy ones. (1 Th 3:13)**
>
> **In their effort to keep us from speaking to the Gentiles so that they may be saved. In this way they always heap up their sins to the limit. The wrath of God has come upon them at last. But, brothers, when we were torn away from you for a short time (in person, not in thought), out of our intense longing we made every effort to see you. (1 Th 2:16-17)**
>
> **You too, be patient and stand firm, because the Lord's coming is near. (James 5:8)**

3. God Himself will make us "firm" (sthenosei). This is the only time this word is used in the New Testament. Most translators say that it means strength. It would, therefore, mean to be filled with all strength, with all the strength necessary to overcome all the trials and temptations and sufferings of life. Again, remember that it is only God Himself who can give us such enormous strength. And He will, if we will only draw near Him.

> **I pray that out of his glorious riches he may strengthen you with power through his Spirit in your inner being, (Eph 3:16)**
>
> **I can do everything through him who gives me strength. (Phil 4:13)**
>
> **Being strengthened with all power according to his glorious might so that you may have great endurance and patience, and joyfully (Col 1:11)**
>
> **But the Lord stood at my side and gave me strength, so that through me the message might be fully proclaimed and all the Gentiles might hear it. And I was delivered from the lion's mouth. (2 Tim 4:17)**

4. God Himself will *make us steadfast*. The word "steadfast" (themeliosei) means to secure as in a foundation; to ground with security. God is able to make us secure through all the sufferings of life, no matter what they are. He is able to settle and secure our nerves, thoughts, and fears—all the uneasy and unnerving emotions that disturb us. God can make us steadfast if we will only do one thing: resist the devil and draw near to Him.

> **So that Christ may dwell in your hearts through faith. And I pray that you, being rooted and established in love, (Eph 3:17)**
>
> **"Therefore everyone who hears these words of mine and puts them into practice is like a wise man who built his house on the rock. The rain came down, the streams rose, and the winds blew and beat against that house; yet it did not fall, because it had its foundation on the rock. (Mat 7:24-25)**
>
> **Do not be anxious about anything, but in everything, by prayer and petition, with thanksgiving, present your requests to God. And the peace of God, which transcends all understanding, will guard your hearts and your minds in Christ Jesus. (Phil 4:6-7)**

3 (5:11) **God—Power**: there is God's power. This is a doxology, an exclamation of praise. In thinking about all that God does for us, Peter just breaks forth with praise. God assures our salvation—despite all our sins, failures, shortcomings, weaknesses, and frailties—God calls us to eternal glory and secures us forever and ever. He restores us and makes us strong, firm, and steadfast through all the temptations and trials and sufferings of life. He is God who possesses all power—power which no person or thing can defeat. He is God, the glorious and Sovereign Majesty of the universe; therefore, He is able to secure us. "To Him be the power for ever and ever."

4 (5:12-13) **Believer's, Hall of Fame**: this is the final greeting of the letter of First Peter. Peter has completed his exhortation and is about to close his letter. It is now time to send greetings from those with him.

1. There was Silas. This was most likely the same Silas who served so much with Paul. He became one of the great missionaries of the early church (cp. Acts 15:40). He was an outstanding believer, a disciple and a close companion of Paul. He was apparently a Roman citizen (Acts 16:37). Silas...

• was a leader in the Jerusalem church (Acts 15:27).
• was sent to Antioch to share the great decree of salvation (Acts 15:27, 32-33).
• was a prophet (Acts 15:32).
• was a disciple of Paul, joining Paul on his second missionary journey (Acts 15:40).
• was imprisoned with Paul (Acts 16:19-40).
• remained in Berea with Timothy to minister to the believers (Acts 17:14).
• was with Paul in Corinth (Acts 18:5; 2 Cor.1:19).
• ministered with Peter, apparently after Paul's death (1 Pt.5:12).
• is mentioned in the following New Testament books: 1 Th.1:1; 2 Th.1:1; 2 Cor.1:19; 1 Pt.5:12.

2. There was Peter himself (see Introduction, Author). Note: Peter says that he had written for the purpose of declaring the truth of the grace of God.

   a. He declared the grace of God that has given us the incorruptible inheritance, an inheritance that can never perish.

   > **Praise be to the God and Father of our Lord Jesus Christ! In his great mercy he has given us new birth into a living hope through the resurrection of Jesus Christ from the dead, and into an inheritance that can never perish, spoil or fade—kept in heaven for you, who through faith are shielded by God's power until the coming of the salvation that is ready to be revealed in the last time. (1 Pet 1:3-5)**

   b. He declared the grace of God that has saved our souls, the salvation that had been prophesied by the prophets of the Old Testament.

   > **For you are receiving the goal of your faith, the salvation of your souls. Concerning this salvation, the prophets, who spoke of the grace that was to come to you, searched intently and with the greatest care, (1 Pet 1:9-10)**

   c. He declared the grace of God that has redeemed us.

   > **For you know that it was not with perishable things such as silver or gold that you were redeemed from the empty way of life handed down to you from your forefathers, but with the precious blood of Christ, a lamb without blemish or defect. (1 Pet 1:18-19)**

   d. He declared the grace of God that stirs us to be born again.

   > **For you have been born again, not of perishable seed, but of imperishable, through the living and enduring word of God. (1 Pet 1:23)**

   e. He declared the grace of God that makes us the very special people of God.

   > **But you are a chosen people, a royal priesthood, a holy nation, a people belonging to God, that you may declare the praises of him who called you out of darkness into his wonderful light. (1 Pet 2:9)**

   f. He declared the grace of God that led Christ to bear our sins in His own body on the tree.

   > **He himself bore our sins in his body on the tree, so that we might die to sins and live for righteousness; by his wounds you have been healed. (1 Pet 2:24)**

   g. He declared the grace of God that led Christ to suffer for sins, to die as the righteous for the unrighteous.

   > **For Christ died for sins once for all, the righteous for the unrighteous, to bring you to God. He was put to death in the body but made alive by the Spirit, (1 Pet 3:18)**

   h. He declared the grace of God that has exalted Christ over all the powers and enemies of men.

   > **Who has gone into heaven and is at God's right hand—with angels, authorities and powers in submission to him. (1 Pet 3:22)**

   i. He declared the grace of God that gives us the great privilege of suffering and living for Christ.

   > **Therefore, since Christ suffered in his body, arm yourselves also with the same attitude, because he who has suffered in his body is done with sin. As a result, he does not live the rest of his earthly life for evil human desires, but rather for the will of God. (1 Pet 4:1-2)**

   j. He declared the grace of God that shall lift us in due time.
   > **And when the Chief Shepherd appears, you will receive the crown of glory that will**

never fade away. Humble yourselves, therefore, under God's mighty hand, that he may lift you up in due time. (1 Pet 5:4, 6)

k. He declared the grace of God that shall keep and preserve us for eternal glory.

And the God of all grace, who called you to his eternal glory in Christ, after you have suffered a little while, will himself restore you and make you strong, firm and steadfast. (1 Pet 5:10)

3. There was the church at Babylon, that is, Rome. Remember: the believers were being severely persecuted throughout Rome during these days. Therefore when secrecy was necessary, believers referred to Rome as Babylon. Peter was apparently in Rome while he was writing this letter. Therefore, he uses the symbolic name Babylon.

4. There was Mark. Note that Peter calls Mark his son. His first name was John. John Mark had a godly mother (Acts 12:12). Her home seemed to be the center of the Christian church (Acts 12:12). In fact, her home may have been the upper room which Jesus used for the Last Supper (Lk.22:10f) and for Pentecost (Acts 1:13). John Mark was related to Barnabas (Col.4:10) and was a disciple of Paul and Barnabas (Acts 12:25). As a young man and disciple something happened that caused his faith to weaken, and he forsook Paul and Barnabas on their first missionary journey (Acts 13:13; 15:38). However, he later recommitted his life to missionary service and became so staunch in his commitment that he was willing to let Paul and Barnabas argue over his seriousness and divide their team efforts over him (Acts 15:36-40). Scripture is silent about what happened after this. Mark is seen only as a man who had redeemed himself in the eyes of Paul (Col.4:10; Phile.1:24; 2 Tim.4:11). And Peter said Mark was serving with him (1 Pt.5:13). When writing to the churches of Asia Minor, Peter sent his special greetings from Mark. This points toward the churches knowing Mark personally. Mark apparently joined Peter on his missionary journeys. This is significant, for it means that much of what is in Mark's gospel probably comes from what Peter had told him. The Gospel of Mark, which Mark wrote, was probably the preaching material of Peter. (See note—Acts 13:13.) John Mark also may have been the man carrying the pitcher of water as a sign for the disciples to approach him in order to secure a room for the Passover (Lk.22:10f). He was probably the young man who fled the scene of Jesus' arrest (Mk.14:51-52).

5 (5:14) **Conclusion**: the conclusion stresses two significant points.

1. Peter encourages the believers to greet one another with a kiss of love. This was an act of unity and brotherhood. Believers must stand together as one in facing the trials and sufferings of the world. Therefore, by doing this one simple act, believers would be reminded that they did not stand alone, and they would be encouraged by the expression of oneness and brotherly love.

2. Peter gives them the benediction of peace (see note— 1 Pt.1:2 for discussion).

THE
OUTLINE & SUBJECT INDEX

REMEMBER: When you look up a subject and turn to the Scripture reference, you have not only the Scripture, you have *an outline and a discussion* (commentary) of the Scripture and subject.

This is one of the *GREAT VALUES* of the **Preacher's Outline & Sermon Bible**®. Once you have all the volumes, you will have not only what all other Bible indexes give you, that is, a list of all the subjects and their Scripture references, *BUT* you will also have…

- An outline of *every* Scripture and subject in the Bible.
- A discussion (commentary) on every Scripture and subject.
- Every subject supported by other Scriptures or cross references.

DISCOVER THE GREAT VALUE for yourself. Quickly glance below to the very first subject of the Index of First Peter. It is:

ACCEPTANCE - ACCEPTABLE
Who - what is **a**.
    Spiritual sacrifices. 2:5
    Suffering for good. 2:20

Turn to the reference. Glance at the Scripture and outline of the Scripture, then read the commentary. You will immediately see the GREAT VALUE of the INDEX of The **Preacher's Outline & Sermon Bible**®.

OUTLINE AND SUBJECT INDEX

ABIDE - ABIDING (See **ENDURE**)

ACCEPTANCE - ACCEPTABLE
Who - what is **a**.
    Spiritual sacrifices. 2:5
    Suffering for good. 2:20

ACCOUNTABLE - ACCOUNTABILITY
Who is **a**.
    The living and the dead. 4:5-6
    The worldly. 4:3

ADMINISTRATION
Discussed. By the elder. 5:1-5
How to **a**.
    The church. 5:1-4
    The overseership. 5:1-4

ADVERSARY
Is Satan. 5:8

ALERT
Meaning. 5:8-9

ALIENS
Described as. Believers. 1:1; 2:11
Discussed. 1:1; 2:11
Meaning. 1:17; 2:11

ANGELS
Fact.
    Aroused to understand and to look into salvation. 1:12
    Stand in stark amazement at the glories of salvation. 1:12
Function toward Christ. To be subservient to. 3:22

ANXIETY
Duty. To cast all your **a**. on God. 5:5-7

ASHAMED
Things not to be **a** of. Being a Christian. 4:16

ASSURANCE (See **CARE - CARING; CHURCH; SECURITY**)
Comes by.
    God's keeping power. 1:5
    Receiving the Word as God's Word. 1:23; 1:24-25; 2:1-3
    Stirring hope. 1:3-5; 1:6-9

Discussed. 1:3-5; 1:3-6
Needed in.
    Salvation. 1:1-12
    Trials and persecution. 1:6-9; 5:10

ATTITUDE (See **MIND**)
Duty.
    To be armed with the **m**. of Christ. 4:1-6
    To prepare your **m** for action. 1:13
Essential. Is the major weapon for warfare. 4:1
Of Christ. Meaning. 4:1-6

AUTHORITY
Civil **a**.
    Discussed. 2:13-17
    Instituted. 2:13-14
Duty. To respect **a**. 2:16-17
Exercised by.
    Citizens. 2:13-17
    Rulers. 2:13-14

BABYLON
Symbol. Of Rome. 5:13

BANQUETINGS (See **CAROUSING**)

BAPTISM
Meaning. Illustrated by Noah and the flood. 3:18-22

BELIEVERS
Described as. Stranger or an alien on earth. 1:17
Duty.
    How to walk before unbelievers. 2:11-12
    To abstain from fleshly lusts, sinful desires. 2:11-12
    To be vigilant and to resist the devil. 5:8-9
    To bear the glory, glow of God. 4:14
    To enjoy life. 3:10-12
    To live at peace with others. 3:8-9
    To other believers. Sixfold. 3:8-9
    To pass one's time in reverence. 1:17-21
    To submit to ministers. 5:5-7
    To suffer for Christ even as Christ suffered for us. 2:21
Fact. Are watched by unbelievers. 2:11-12

Life - Walk.
    How to enjoy and love life. 3:10-12
    How to live under the shadow of history's climax. 4:7
    Vigilance against the devil. 5:8-9
Life of. Divided into two parts: the old life and new life. 4:3
Names - Titles.
    A spiritual people. 2:9
    Brotherhood of believers, The. 2:16-17
    Chosen people. 2:9
    Chosen of God. 1:1-2
    God's flock. 5:2
    God's very own possession. 2:9
    Holy nation. 2:9
    Holy priesthood. 2:5
    Living stones. 2:5
    New race of people. 2:9
    People of God. 2:9
    People who belong to God. 2:9
    Royal priesthood. 2:9
    Spiritual house. 2:5
    Strangers and aliens. 1:1
Position. What the believer becomes. 2:5-6; 2:9
Purpose of.
    To declare the praises of God. 2:9
    To obey God and share in Christ's blood. 1:2

BORN AGAIN
Discussed. 1:23
Results.
    A living hope. 1:3-5
    An inheritance that can never perish. 1:3-5
Source.
    Imperishable Seed. 1:23-25
    Word of God. 1:23

BROTHERHOOD
Duty. To live in harmony. 3:8
Of believers. Duty. To love. 2:16-17

CALL
Of believers. To suffer for Christ even as Christ suffered for us. 2:21

CARE
Duty.

INDEX

HOLY - HOLINESS
Comes through. Obedience. 1:14
Discussed. 1:15-16
Duty. To seek and pursue holiness. 1:13-16;
1:15-17

HOLY SPIRIT
Work of. Sanctifies. 1:2

HONEST (See **GOOD**)

HONOR (See **RESPECT**)
HOPE
Described. As a living hope. 1:3-5
Discussed. 1:3-5
Duty. To hope to the end of life. 1:13
Source. Threefold. 1:3
What the believer's hope is. Eternal life.
1:3

HOSPITALITY
Discussed. 4:9

HUMBLE-HUMILITY
Discussed. 3:8

HUMILITY
Discussed. 5:5-7
Duty. Threefold. 5:5-7
Meaning. 5:5

HYPOCRISIES (See **HYPOCRISY**)

HYPOCRISY
Meaning. 2:1

IDOLATRY
Meaning. 4:3

IDOLS - IDOLATERS
Described as. Detestable. 4:3
Results of. Judgment. 4:3-5

IMPERISHABLE
Vs. perishable. 1:4; 1:23

INCORRUPTION (See **IMPERISH-ABLE**)

INHERITANCE
Discussed. 1:4
Nature. Imperishable, undefiled, can
never fade away. 1:4
Surety of. Discussed. 1:3-5
What the **i.** is.
Listed. 1:4
Reward (See **REWARD**) 1:3-4
The new birth - the imperishable seed.
1:23

JESUS CHRIST
Blood. (See **JESUS CHRIST**, Death)
Discussed. 1:2
Redeems man. 1:18-20
Death. (See **JESUS CHRIST**, Blood of)
Did not want to die, but denied Him-
self and gave Himself up. 4:1
Died for man. 2:21-24
Died once-for-all. 3:18
Discussed. 2:21-25; 3:18
Purpose.
To bear sins. 2:24; 3:18
To bring us to God. 3:18
To preach to the spirits in prison.
3:18-22

Substitutionary. Discussed. 2:21-24;
3:18
Voluntary. Discussed. 2:21-24
Deity. Sinless. 1:19
Descent into hell. Discussed. 3:19-20;
3:19-22
Exalted - Exaltation.
Discussed. 3:22
Entered heaven. 3:22
Mind of.
Discussed. 4:1
Meaning. 4:1
Names - Titles.
Chief Cornerstone, capstone. 2:5-8
Chief Shepherd. 5:4
Foundation Stone. 2:5-8
Living Stone. 2:5-8
Overseer. 2:25
Shepherd. 2:25
Origin and nature. (See **JESUS
CHRIST**, Deity; Humanity; Incarna-
tion)
Without blemish or defect. 1:19
Prophecies fulfilled by. His sacrifice.
1:11-12
Resurrection.
Proves. Three things. 1:3
Purpose. To be raised to a new life.
3:18-22
Results. Gives great hope to man. 1:3
Source. God raised up Christ. 1:21
Sinless. Discussed. 2:21-24
Triumph - Victory of. Discussed. 3:18-22
Work of.
Discussed. 1:18-20
To be the ideal and perfect Man and
Sacrifice. 1:2
To redeem us. 1:18-20
To secure the ideal and perfect right-
eousness for man. 1:2
To vindicate salvation before the spir-
its in the prison of hell. 3:19-20;
3:19-22

JUDGMENT
Described.
A terrible end. 4:17-18
The Day God Visits us. 2:12
Fact. God sees all men. Stands against the
evil. 3:12
How God judges. Allows life to perish
and corrupt. 1:23
Of believers.
A terrible end. 4:17-18
Is for righteousness sake. 3:13-17
Of God. Three facts. 1:17
Of the church. Discussed. 2:9-10; 4:17-18
Of whom. The lost - the unbeliever. 2:9-10;
3:12

JUSTIFICATION
Discussed. 1:2

KISS
Of love. Meaning. 5:14

LABOR
Discussed. 2:18-20

LABORERS (See **WORK**)
Discussed. 2:18-20

LASCIVIOUSNESS (See **DEBAUCHERY**)

LAYING ASIDE (See **RID YOURSELF**)

LEADERS - LEADERSHIP (See **DEA-
CONS; MINISTERS** and Related Sub-
jects)
How to lead. Discussed. 5:1-4

LIBERTY (See **FREEDOM; LICENSE;
SANCTIFICATION; SEPARATION**)

LIBERTY, CHRISTIAN (See **FREE-
DOM, CHRISTIAN**)

LICENSE
Vs. freedom. 2:16-17

LIFE
Duty. To enjoy **l.** 3:10-12
Steps to **l.** Fourfold. 3:10-12

LIVE
Meaning. 3:7

LOVE
Discussed. 4:8
Duty.
To **l.** as brothers. 3:8
To **l.** one another deeply. 1:22-25
To **l.** the brotherhood, the church.
2:16-17
Kinds.
Brotherly **l.** Discussed. 3:8
Deep. 4:8
Meaning. Of *philadelphia* love. 1:22-25
Results.
Covers a multitude of sins. 4:8
Purifies souls. 1:22
Why **l.** Discussed. 1:22-25; 4:8

LUST (See **CRAVE**)

MALICE
Meaning. 2:1

MAN
Depravity.
Has not obtained mercy. 2:10
Is not of God. 2:10
Described. As sheep gone astray. 2:25
Duty toward. To honor all men. 2:16-27
Names - Titles. Builders. 2:7
State of - Present. Accuses believer. 2:12

MARK, JOHN
Discussed. 5:13
Is like a son to Peter. 5:13

MARRIAGE
Duty.
Of husband. Threefold. 3:7
Of wife. To submit to own husband.
3:1-6
To witness to one's spouse. 3:1-6

MASTERS
Duty toward. To submit to. 2:18-20

MEDIATOR (See **JESUS CHRIST**, Me-
diator)
Discussed. 2:9
Fact. Is no longer needed. 2:9

MERCY
Duty. To receive the **m.** of God. 2:10
Fact. Unbelievers have not obtained
mercy. 2:9-10

INDEX

MIND (See **ATTITUDE**)
Duty.
 To be armed with the **m**. of Christ.
  4:1-6
 To prepare your **m** for action. 1:13
Essential. Is the major weapon for warfare. 4:1
Of Christ. Meaning. 4:1-6

MINISTER
Authority of. Believers to submit to
 authority of **m**. 5:5
Call.
 Discussed. 5:2-3
 Not to enter the ministry as a profession. 5:2-3
 To willingly accept call. Not to hesitate. 5:2-3
Described. As a shepherd. 5:2-3
Duty.
 Discussed. 5:1-4
 To shepherd God's flock. 5:2-3
Names - Titles.
 Elder. 5:1
 Shepherd of the flock. 5:1-4
Reward. Discussed. 5:1; 5:4

NATION, NEW
Fact. Believers are being formed into a
 new and holy **n**. 2:9

NEW BIRTH
Discussed. 1:23
Nature. Imperishable. 1:23
Source. Word of God. 1:23

NOAH
Fact. Saved through the flood. 3:19-22
Type. Of salvation. 3:19-22

OBEDIENCE
Duty.
 To obey Christ. 1:2
 To seek and pursue **o**. 1:14
Importance of.
 Purifies the believer. 1:22
 The very purpose of election. 1:1-2
Results. Purifies the believer. 1:22

ORGIES
Meaning. 4:3

PARTYING (See **ORGIES**)

PEACE
Discussed. 3:8-9
Duty. To seek peace and pursue it. 3:11

PERFECT (See **RESTORE**)

PERISH
Cause of. Natural heritage - bearing perishable seed. 1:23
Deliverance - Escape.
 By being born again. 1:23
 By being redeemed. 1:18-20
 Not by perishable things. 1:18-20
Vs. imperishable. 1:23

PERSECUTION
By whom. The government or civil
 authorities. 2:13-17
Deliverance - How to stand against. 4:1-6
 By arming oneself with the attitude of
 Christ. 3:13-17; 4:1-6

How to be secure through **p**. 1:1-12
How to handle or conquer **p**. 3:13-4:19
Duty.
 Discussed. 4:12-19
 Not to be ashamed to suffer for being a
 Christian. 4:16
 To keep conscience clear in **p**. 3:16-17
 To stand up under the painful trial of
 p. 4:12-19
Fact. God gives a glow of His glory to
 persecuted believers. 4:14
Of early believers.
 Discussed. 1:1-2; 1:13-16
 Recipients of the letter of I Peter. 1:1;
 1:13-16
Why believers are persecuted.
 Are considered evil doers. 2:12; 3:16
 Are thought to be strange. 4:4-5
 For bearing the believer's hope. 3:15
 For bearing the name of Christ. 4:14
 For evil works. 3:13-14
 For misbehavior. 4:15
 For righteousness sake. 3:13-17

PETER, THE APOSTLE
Was a close companion of Christ. 5:1
Was an elder, a minister of the church.
 5:1

PILGRIMS (See **ALIENS**)

PITY (See **COMPASSION**)

POWER
Of God. Keeps, protects, assures, and secures the believer. 1:5

PRAISE - PRAISES
Meaning. 2:9
Purpose. **P**. is the very reason believers
 are saved. 2:9

PRAYER
Duty. To watch, stay alert, and pray. 4:7
Hindrances to.
 Failure of husband to respect wives.
 3:7
 Family problems. 3:7
When. As history's climax nears. 4:7
Who. Open to the righteous. 3:10-12

PREACHING (See **GOSPEL; MINISTER**)
Call. Enabled by the Spirit. 1:12

PREDESTINATED - PREDESTINATION
Purpose for **p**. 1:2
Who.
 Discussed. 1:18-20
 The chosen people of God. 1:2
 Unbelievers. Appointed to unbelief. 2:7-8

PRIDE
Overcome by. Submitting to others. 5:5-7

PRIEST
Discussed. 2:9

PRIESTHOOD
Discussed. 2:9
Need for. Felt by men throughout history.
 2:9
Of believers. Discussed. 2:9

PROMISES
Of God. To the persecuted believer. 3:13-14

PROPHETS
Call of. Purpose. To proclaim and predict
 God's great salvation. 1:10
Inspiration of. Discussed. 1:10-12
Predictions of.
 Sought to understand. 1:10-12
 Sufferings and glories of Christ. 1:10-12

PURE
Meaning. 2:2-3

PURITY
Duty. Of wives. 3:2

PURPOSE
Of all things. God's glory. 4:11

REDEEM - REDEMPTION
Discussed. 1:18-20
Meaning. 1:18-20
Source. Blood of Christ. 1:18-20

REJECT - REJECTION
Of Jesus Christ. By unbelievers. 2:7-8

RELIGION - RITUAL
Need. To be redeemed from empty **r**.
 1:18-20
True **r**. Redeemed from empty **r**. 1:18-20

RESIST
Meaning. 5:9

RESPECT
Duty.
 To **r**. all men. 2:17
 To **r**. the king. 2:16-27

RESTORE
Meaning. 5:10

RETALIATION
Discussed. 3:9

REVEALED - REVELATION (See **JESUS CHRIST**, Revealed as)
Is given. To prophets. 1:10-12

REVELLINGS (See **ORGIES**)

REVERENCE
Duty. To **r**. God. 1:17-21; 1:17
Of God. Discussed. 1:17-21; 1:17

REWARDS
Crowns. Of glory. 5:4
Described - Identified as.
 An inheritance. 1:3-5
 Crowns. 5:4
 Exaltation. If one humbles himself.
 5:5-7
How to secure. Enduring trials & temptation. 1:6-9
List of. 1:4

RID YOURSELF
Meaning. 2:1-3

ROME
Symbolic name of. Babylon. 5:13

INDEX

SAINT
Discussed. 1:15-16

SALVATION - SAVED
Assurance. Through persecution. 1:1-12
Deliverance - Purpose.
Through persecution. 1:1-12
Wonder of. 1:10-12
Discussed. 1:10-12
Fact. Scarcely s. 4:17-18
Source - How one is saved.
By coming to Christ, the living stone. 2:4-8
By following Christ's great suffering. 2:21-25
Must be covered by the blood of Christ. 1:2
Not with perishable things. 1:18-20
Through election. 1:1-2

SANCTIFY - SANCTIFICATION
Discussed. 1:15-16
Meaning. 1:2
Source. Holy Spirit. 1:2

SARAH
Wife of Abraham. Example of. A godly wife. 3:4-6

SATAN
Described.
As an enemy. 5:8
Like a roaring lion. 5:8
Discussed. 5:8-9
How to combat and overcome. Resist - do not give place to. 5:8-9
Names - Titles. Slanderer, accuser. 5:8
Work of. To devour. Discussed. 5:8

SCRIPTURES
Inspiration of.
Discussed. 1:10-12
Prophets searched to understand. 1:10-12

SECURITY
Source. God. Power of God. 1:5

SELF-CONTROLLED
Discussed. 1:13
Meaning. 1:13; 4:7; 5:8-9

SELF-DENIAL
Duty. To deny self even as Christ did. 4:1

SEPARATED - SEPARATION
Fact. Not understood by the world. 4:4-5

SETTLE (See **STEADFAST**)

SHEPHERD
Described. By Isaiah 40:1. 2:25
Discussed. 2:25; 5:2-3
Meaning. 5:2-3
Title. Of elder or minister. 5:1-4

SHOW FORTH (See **DECLARE**)

SILAS
Discussed. 5:12

SIN
Deliverance. To be fed up with. 4:1-6
Denying. 4:4-5
Lists of. 2:11; 4:3

SINCERE (See **PURE**)

SINFUL DESIRES
Described. List of acts of the sinful nature. 2:11
Discussed. 2:11
Meaning. 2:11
Works of. Wars against the soul. 2:11

SLANDER
Meaning. 2:1

SLAVES
Discussed. 2:18-20
Duty. To submit to masters. 2:18-20

SOBER (See **SELF-CONTROLLED**)

SOJOURNER (See **STRANGERS**)

SOUL
Discussed. Struggled against by the flesh, sinful nature. 2:11
Duty. To be cleansed and purified. 1:22

SPEAKING, EVIL (See **SLANDER**)

SPIRITUAL GIFTS
Discussed. 4:10

STABLISH (See **STRONG**)

STATE, CIVIL
Duty.
To respect civil authorities. 2:16-17
To submit to s. Reasons. 2:13-17
When disobedience is permitted. 2:13-14

STEADFAST
Meaning. 5:10

STONE, THE
Described.
Jesus Christ, the chief cornerstone. 2:4-8
Jesus Christ, the living stone. 2:4-8
Discussed. 2:4-8

STRANGERS
Described as. Believers. 1:1; 2:11
Discussed. 2:11
Meaning. 1:17

STRENGTH - STRENGTHEN
Meaning. 5:10

STRIP OFF (See **RID YOURSELF**)

SUBJECTION (See **SUBMIT-SUBMISSION**)

SUBMIT-SUBMISSION
Of believers. To elders & to one one another. Discussed. 5:5-7
Of employees. To employers. Discussed. 2:18-20
Of wife. To husband. Discussed. 3:1

SUFFER GRIEF
Meaning. 1:6

SUFFERING (See **PERSECUTION**)
Deliverance from.
Being armed with the attitude of Christ. 4:1-6
Following Christ's great s. 2:21-25
How to handle s. 3:3-4:19
Provision for. 5:10-11
Discussed. 5:10-11
How the church is to stand up under s. 5:1-11
Duty.
To participate in Christ's s. 4:12-19

To put on the mind of Christ. 4:1-6
To stand up under the painful trial of s. 4:12-19
To suffer before violating one's conscience. 2:18-20
Example. Christ. 3:18
Fact.
Are sharing in the s. of Christ. 4:12
God gives a glow of His glory to s. believer. 4:14
God and suffering. God's provision for s. 5:10-11
Of early church. Discussed. 4:12
Why God allows s. Discussed. 4:12

SYMPATHY
Duty. To be sympathetic. 3:8

TEMPTATIONS
Described. List of temptations. 1:6
Discussed. 1:6-9
How to conquer. Four ways. 1:8-9
Purpose. Discussed. 1:7

TENDERHEARTED
Discussed. 3:8

TEST - TESTING
By God. Discussed. 4:12

TESTIMONY
Discussed. 2:11-12
Fact.
Believers are seen as strange. 4:4-5
Silences critics. 2:15
Unbeliever watches believers. 2:11-12

TIME
Facts about. End of time is at hand. 4:7

TONGUE
Discussed. Evil and deception of. 3:10
Duty. To stop your tongue. 3:10
Sins of. Slander. 2:1

TRIALS - TRIBULATION
Deliverance through. How to act in t. 4:12-19
Described.
Believers' painful t. 4:12-19
List of trials. 1:6
Discussed. 1:6-9
How to conquer.
Discussed. 5:10-11
Four things. 1:8-9
Purpose. Discussed. 1:7

UNBELIEVERS
Facts.
Are not a people. Never complete or fulfill their purpose. 2:10
Watch and scrutinize lives of believers. 2:12
Fate. Are not the people of God. 2:10
Meaning.
Those offended by Christ, the rock. 2:7-8
Those who reject Jesus Christ. 2:7-8
Those who stumble at the Word. 2:7-8
Those who stumble over Christ, the stone. 2:7-8

UNITY
Duty. To live in harmony. 3:8

VIGILANCE (See **ALERT**)

INDEX

SECOND

PETER

2 PETER

INTRODUCTION

AUTHOR: Simon Peter, the Apostle (2 Pt.1:1). However, note several facts. (Much of the following is taken from Michael Green. He makes an excellent and scholarly case for Peter's authorship.) (*The Second Epistle of Peter and The Epistle of Jude.* "The Tyndale New Testament Commentaries," ed. by RVG Tasker. Grand Rapids, MI: Eerdmans, 1968, p.13f).

1. The author is questioned by many commentators. The questioning centers primarily around external evidence such as the following two facts.
   ⇒ There are no direct references to the book by the earliest Christian writers.
   ⇒ The first person to mention Second Peter by name was Origen who lived around the middle of the third century.

When all of the evidence is considered, however, it points to Peter being the author.
   a. The earliest church fathers do have statements that are similar to parts of II Peter: I Clement (A.D. 950), II Clement (A.D. 150), Aristides (A.D. 130), Valentinus (A.D. 130), and Hippolytus (A.D. 180).
   b. The discovery of Papyrus 72, dated in the third century, shows that II Peter was well known in Egypt long before. Eusebius also states that Clement of Alexandria had II Peter in his Bible and wrote a commentary on it.

2. II Peter was not fully accepted into the canon of Scripture until the middle or latter part of the fourth century. Why did it take the church so long to accept II Peter as part of the canon of Scripture? This can be explained by two facts.
   a. Some letters were sent to obscure destinations and were small in content (II Peter, Jude, I, II, and III John). This kept these particular letters from becoming well-known. When they were finally circulated, the church would naturally delay in accepting them as Scripture until they could be proven to be the Word of God.
   b. Peter's name was often used to try to secure acceptance of various letters circulating at that time. The church was bound to hesitate in accepting a writing which claimed to be Peter's until proof could be secured.

3. Despite the questioning of the external evidence, the internal evidence favors Peter rather convincingly.
   a. The epistle says that it was written by Peter (2 Pt.1:1).
   b. The author wrote a previous epistle to the same recipients (2 Pt.3:1).
   c. The author was familiar with Paul's writings that had been sent to the same recipients (2 Pt.3:15-16). He also knew Paul rather intimately. He calls him "our beloved Paul" (2 Pt.3:15; cp. Gal.2:18f).

4. The author was an eyewitness of the transfiguration (2 Pt.1:16-18).

5. The author was aware of his pending death (2 Pt.1:13), and Peter's death was predicted by Christ (2 Pt.1:14; cp. Jn.21:18-19).

6. The epistle possesses no teaching that is inconsistent with the rest of Scripture. It is entirely free of personal feats to build up the author, and it is free of imaginative fables which characterized the false writings of later centuries (apocryphal books). Its content fit in much better with the early church period.

Note: the persecution that so heavily concerns First Peter had apparently now passed.

DATE: Uncertain. A.D. 61-68.

TO WHOM WRITTEN: "To those who...have received a faith as precious as ours" (2 Pt.1:1). "Dear friends, this is now my second letter to you" (2 Pt.3:1).

The epistle was apparently sent to the same believers who had received I Peter. Remember: they were scattered all throughout Asia. It was also probably written from the same place, Rome. (See Introductory Notes, To Whom Written—I Peter.)

PURPOSE: To combat and warn the church against false teachers and false doctrine.

SPECIAL FEATURES:
1. II Peter is "A General Epistle." That is, it is not written to a specific church or individual, but rather, it is written to all Christian believers.

2. II Peter is "An Epistle Written to Combat False Teaching." From its earliest days, the church had been born in controversy.
   ⇒ At first, it was the judaizing or legalistic problem which arose at Antioch (see Acts 15:1f).
   ⇒ Then there was the denial of the literal resurrection of the body by some in the Corinthian church (1 Cor.15:1f).
   ⇒ There was also arising the corruptible beginnings of antinomianism and gnosticism. These false doctrines were appearing all throughout the Roman empire. They were using God's grace as an excuse for sinning (see Colossians, Introductory Notes, Purpose, and Master Subject Index). The epistles of II Peter, I, II, and III John, and Jude were written to combat such errors as these.

3. II Peter is "An Epistle Stressing the Importance of Knowledge." The words *know, knowing* and *knowledge* are used ten times. Knowing the truth is the answer to false teaching.

4. II Peter is "An Epistle Verifying the Inspiration of the Scripture." Peter says "Above all, you must understand that no prophecy of Scripture came about by the prophet's own interpretation. For prophecy never had its origin in the will of man, but men spoke from God as they were carried along by the Holy Spirit." (2 Pt.1:20-21). Peter's statement that Paul's writings were *Scripture* shows that the canon was already being formed by the early church even while the early apostles were still alive (2 Pt.3:16; cp. 2 Tim.2:15; 3:16). The word *canon* simply means a collection of the writings considered to be inspired and breathed forth by God.

5. II Peter is "An Epistle of the Missionary Apostle to the Jews." Peter was given the primary responsibility of reaching the Jews throughout the world. He was the apostle to the Jews (Gal.2:7-8, 11-21). (See Author, point 10.)

OUTLINE OF 2 PETER

THE PREACHER'S OUTLINE & SERMON BIBLE® is *unique*. It differs from all other Study Bibles & Sermon Resource Materials in that every Passage and Subject is outlined right beside the Scripture. When you choose any *Subject* below and turn to the reference, you have not only the Scripture, but you discover the Scripture and Subject *already outlined for you—verse by verse.*

For a quick example, choose one of the subjects below and turn over to the Scripture, and you will find this marvelous help for faster, easier, and more accurate use.

In addition, every point of the Scripture and Subject is *fully developed in a Commentary with supporting Scripture* at the bottom of the page. Again, this arrangement makes sermon preparation much easier and faster.

Note something else: The Subjects of SECOND PETER have titles that are both Biblical and *practical*. The practical titles sometimes have more appeal to people. This *benefit* is clearly seen for use on billboards, bulletins, church newsletters, etc.

A suggestion: For the quickest overview of SECOND PETER, first read *all the major titles* (I, II, III, etc.), then come back and read the subtitles.

OUTLINE OF 2 PETER

I. **THE GREAT SALVATION OF GOD, 1:1-21**

    A. The Great Gift of Christ the Messiah: Salvation, 1:1-4
    B. The Great Things of the Believer's Life, 1:5-15
    C. The Great Proof of Salvation, 1:16-21

II. **THE WARNING AGAINST FALSE TEACHERS, 2:1-22**

    A. The Description and Judgment of False Teachers, 2:1-9
    B. The Character and Conduct of False Teachers, 2:10-22

III. **THE COMING AGAIN OF JESUS CHRIST AND THE END OF THE WORLD, 3:1-18**

    A. The First Thing to Know: Scoffers Shall Come, 3:1-7
    B. The One Thing Not to Be Ignorant About: Why Christ Has Not Yet Returned, 3:8-10
    C. The Things Believers Must Do Since Jesus Christ is Coming Again (Part I), 3:11-14
    D. The Things Believers Must Do Since Jesus Christ is Coming Again (Part II), 3:15-18

CHAPTER 1

I. THE GREAT SALVA-TION OF GOD, 1:1-21

A. The Great Gift of Christ the Messiah: Salvation, 1:1-4

1 He is the Messiah worthy of total devotion
2 He is the Messiah of faith
  a. A most precious faith
  b. Is, received, not earned
  c. Thru the righteousness of God & Christ

Simon Peter, a servant and apostle of Jesus Christ, To those who through the righteousness of our God and Savior Jesus Christ have received a faith as precious as ours:

2 Grace and peace be yours in abundance through the knowledge of God and of Jesus our Lord.
3 His divine power has given us everything we need for life and godliness through our knowledge of him who called us by his own glory and goodness.
4 Through these he has given us his very great and precious promises, so that through them you may participate in the divine nature and escape the corruption in the world caused by evil desires.

3 He is the Messiah of grace & peace
  a. An abundance of both
  b. Thru knowledge of Him
4 He is the Messiah of life & godliness
  a. An abundance: Everything
  b. By His divine power
  c. Thru knowledge of Him

5 He is the Messiah of the divine nature
  a. By His promises

  b. Purpose: To escape corruption[DS1]

DIVISION I

THE GREAT SALVATION OF GOD, 1:1-21

A. The Great Gift of Christ the Messiah: Salvation, 1:1-4

(1:1-4) **Introduction**: this is a great passage of Scripture. In the mind of the author it is one of the greatest in all of Scripture. It is a passage that takes Jesus Christ and lifts Him up as the great Messiah, the Savior of the world who can meet the desperate needs of man. Here is Christ and here is the great gift of Christ the Messiah, the great gift of salvation.

1. He is the Messiah worthy of total devotion (v.1).
2. He is the Messiah of faith (v.1).
3. He is the Messiah of grace and peace (v.2).
4. He is the Messiah of life and godliness (v.3).
5. He is the Messiah of the divine nature (v.4).

1 (1:1) **Servant—Apostle**: Jesus Christ is the Messiah worthy of total devotion. This is seen in the two claims made by Peter.

1. Peter calls himself the servant of Christ. The word servant (doulos) means far more than just a servant. It means a slave totally possessed by the master. It is a *bond-servant* bound by law to a master.

A look at the slave market of Peter's day shows more clearly what Peter meant when he said he was a "slave of Jesus Christ."

  a. The slave was owned by his master; he was totally possessed by his master. This is what Peter meant. Peter was purchased and possessed by Christ. Christ had looked upon him and had seen his degraded and needful condition. And when Christ looked, the most wonderful thing happened: Christ *loved him and bought him*; therefore, he was now the possession of Christ.
  b. The slave existed for his master and he had no other reason for existence. He had no personal rights whatsoever. The same was true with Peter: he existed only for Christ. His rights were the rights of Christ only.
  c. The slave served his master and he existed only for the purpose of service. He was at the master's disposal any hour of the day. So it was with Peter: he lived only to serve Christ—hour by hour and day by day.

  d. The slave's will belonged to his master. He was allowed no will and no ambition other than the will and ambition of the master. He was completely subservient to the Master and owed total obedience to the will of the master. Peter belonged to Christ.
  e. There is a fifth and most precious thing that Peter meant by "a slave of Jesus Christ." He meant that he had the highest and most honored and kingly profession in all the world. Men of God, the greatest men of history, have always been called *the servants of God*. It was the highest title of honor. The believer's slavery to Jesus Christ is no cringing, cowardly, shameful subjection. It is the position of honor—the honor that bestows upon a man the privileges and responsibilities of serving the King of kings and Lord of lords.

  ⇒ Moses was the slave of God (Dt.34:5; Ps.105:26; Mal.4:4).
  ⇒ Joshua was the slave of God (Josh.24:9).
  ⇒ David was the slave of God (2 Sam.3:18; Ps.78:70).
  ⇒ Peter was the slave of Jesus Christ (Ro.1:1; Ph.1:1; Tit.1:1; 2 Pt.1:1).
  ⇒ James was the slave of God (Jas.1:1).
  ⇒ Jude was the slave of God (Jude 1).
  ⇒ The prophets were the slaves of God (Amos 3:7; Jer.7:25).
  ⇒ Christian believers are said to be the slaves of Jesus Christ (Acts 2:18; 1 Cor.7:22; Eph.6:6; Col.4:12; 2 Tim.2:24).

Whoever serves me must follow me; and where I am, my servant also will be. My Father will honor the one who serves me. (John 12:26; cp. Ro.12:1; 1 Cor.15:58)

Obey them not only to win their favor when their eye is on you, but like slaves of Christ, doing the will of God from your heart. Serve wholeheartedly, as if you were serving the Lord, not men, (Eph 6:6-7)

Whatever you do, work at it with all your heart, as working for the Lord, not for men, since you know that you will receive an inheritance from the Lord as a reward. It is the Lord Christ you are serving. (Col 3:23-24)

Therefore, since we are receiving a kingdom that cannot be shaken, let us be thankful, and so worship God acceptably with reverence and awe, (Heb 12:28)

Worship the LORD your God, and his blessing will be on your food and water. I will take away sickness from among you, (Exo 23:25)

And now, O Israel, what does the LORD your God ask of you but to fear the LORD your God, to walk in all his ways, to love him, to serve the LORD your God with all your heart and with all your soul, (Deu 10:12)

Serve the LORD with fear and rejoice with trembling. (Psa 2:11)

Worship the LORD with gladness; come before him with joyful songs. (Psa 100:2)

2. Peter calls himself an apostle of Jesus Christ. The word apostle (apostolos) means either a person who is sent out or a person who is sent forth. An apostle is a representative, an ambassador, a person who is sent out into one country to represent another country. Three things are true of the apostle: (1) he belongs to the One who has sent him out; (2) he is commissioned to be sent out; and (3) he possesses all the authority and power of the One who has sent him out.

Note three forceful lessons.

a. Peter said that he was *called* to be an apostle. He was not in the ministry because he...
- chose to be.
- had the ability.
- had been encouraged by others to choose the *ministerial profession.*
- enjoyed working with people.

He was an apostle, a minister of the gospel for one reason only: God had called him.

'Now get up and stand on your feet. I [the Lord] have appeared to you to appoint you as a servant and as a witness of what you have seen of me and what I will show you. (Acts 26:16)

I thank Christ Jesus our Lord, who has given me strength, that he considered me faithful, appointing me to his service. (1 Tim 1:12)

The LORD had said to Abram, "Leave your country, your people and your father's household and go to the land I will show you. (Gen 12:1)

So now, go. I am sending you [Moses] to Pharaoh to bring my people the Israelites out of Egypt." (Exo 3:10)

The LORD turned to him [Gideon] and said, "Go in the strength you have and save Israel out of Midian's hand. Am I not sending you?" (Judg 6:14)

Then I heard the voice of the Lord saying, "Whom shall I send? And who will go for us?" And I said, "Here am I. Send me!" (Isa 6:8)

b. Peter had heard and answered God's call. God did not override Peter's will—He wanted Peter in the ministry, so He called Peter. But note: it was up to Peter to hear and respond.

c. Peter was called to be an apostle, that is, to be a minister. He was not called to occupy a position of authority or to be honored by men.

Thought 1. These two points stress one thing: Peter thought that Jesus Christ was worthy of total devotion. Peter made a decision to deliberately and wholly give himself to Jesus Christ. He centered his whole life around Jesus Christ. Jesus Christ was the Messiah, the Savior of the world who had been promised by God from the beginning of time, the Messiah who was worthy of total devotion.

Peter said to him, "We have left everything to follow you!" (Mark 10:28)

And anyone who does not carry his cross and follow me cannot be my disciple. "Suppose one of you wants to build a tower. Will he not first sit down and estimate the cost to see if he has enough money to complete it? (Luke 14:27-28)

Then he said to them all: "If anyone would come after me, he must deny himself and take up his cross daily and follow me. (Luke 9:23)

"If anyone comes to me and does not hate his father and mother, his wife and children, his brothers and sisters—yes, even his own life—he cannot be my disciple. And anyone who does not carry his cross and follow me cannot be my disciple. (Luke 14:26-27)

In the same way, any of you who does not give up everything he has cannot be my disciple. (Luke 14:33)

"I tell you the truth," Jesus said to them, "no one who has left home or wife or brothers or parents or children for the sake of the kingdom of God will fail to receive many times as much in this age and, in the age to come, eternal life." (Luke 18:29-30)

Those who belong to Christ Jesus have crucified the sinful nature with its passions and desires. (Gal 5:24)

What is more, I consider everything a loss compared to the surpassing greatness of knowing Christ Jesus my Lord, for whose sake I have lost all things. I consider them rubbish, that I may gain Christ (Phil 3:8)

2 (1:1) **Faith—Righteousness**: Jesus Christ is the Messiah of *faith*; that is, He is the Messiah who has made us acceptable to God by faith.

1. The faith of Christ is a most *precious faith*. The word "precious" (time) means of great honor and price; of great value and privilege. The faith of Jesus Christ is precious because it makes us acceptable to God. It ushers us into the very presence of God Himself.

Note this: the faith of Jesus Christ is the *same precious faith* that is given to all believers. The Greek word that Peter uses for "precious" (isotimos) is an unusual word. This is the only time it is used in the New Testament. It is really a double word. The *isos* means *equal*, and *time* means *honor* (A.T. Robertson. *Word Pictures In The New Testament*, Vol.6, p.147). Therefore, by *precious faith* is meant *like faith*, a faith that is like everyone else's faith. This is a most wonderful thing. It means that we are all given the very same faith; we are all equal in value and honor and privilege before God. God does not discriminate; He does not have favorites. God loves us all equally and He values and honors us all as much as He did Peter and James and John and Paul.

Thought 1. This means that the faith of Jesus Christ eliminates prejudice and discrimination. We all stand on an equal footing before God...

- the rich and the poor
- the upper class and the lower class
- the well fed and the hungry
- the free person and the prisoner
- the religionists and the heathen
- the male and the female

If a person has obtained the precious faith of Jesus Christ, then he is acceptable to God no matter who he is. He receives the highest and most valued privilege in the whole universe: to live in the presence of God forever and ever.

2. The faith of Jesus Christ is received not earned. The word "received" (lachousin) means to secure by lot; to receive by allotment; to be given a share or a portion. No person deserves the precious faith of Jesus Christ. No person can work and earn it. It is a gift of God, a free gift that is given to every person who believes in Jesus Christ.

3. The faith of Jesus Christ comes through the righteousness of Christ. What is the righteousness of Christ? It is two things.

a. The righteousness of Christ means that He is the righteous Man, the Perfect and Ideal Man who can stand for and cover all men. Man is not perfect, but imperfect and unrighteous. Therefore, man by his very nature cannot live in God's presence, for God is perfect and the very embodiment of righteousness. How then can man ever become acceptable to God and be allowed to live in God's presence? Jesus Christ is the answer, for He is the righteousness of God. That is, God sent Jesus Christ to earth to live the *perfect, ideal*, and *sinless* life. Jesus Christ never sinned, not even once. Therefore, He stood before God and before the world as the Ideal Man, the Perfect Man, the Representative Man, the Perfect Righteousness that could stand for the righteousness of every man.

When a man believes in Jesus Christ—really believes—God takes that man's faith and counts it (his faith) as righteousness. The man is not righteous; he and everyone else knows it. But God counts his faith and belief as righteousness. Why would God do such an incredible thing? Because God loves His Son that much and God loves man that much. God loves so much that He will take any man who honors His Son by believing in Him and count that man's faith as though it were the real thing: righteousness. Very simply stated: Jesus Christ is the righteousness of God. He is the only way a man can become righteous and acceptable to God.

God made him who had no sin to be sin for us, so that in him we might become the righteousness of God. (2 Cor 5:21)

For we do not have a high priest who is unable to sympathize with our weaknesses, but we have one who has been tempted in every way, just as we are—yet was without sin. (Heb 4:15)

Therefore he is able to save completely those who come to God through him, because he always lives to intercede for them. Such a high priest meets our need—one who is holy, blameless, pure, set apart from sinners, exalted above the heavens. (Heb 7:25-26)

He himself bore our sins in his body on the tree, so that we might die to sins and live for righteousness; by his wounds you have been healed. (1 Pet 2:24)

For Christ died for sins once for all, the righteous for the unrighteous, to bring you to God. He was put to death in the body but made alive by the Spirit, (1 Pet 3:18)

b. The righteousness of Christ means that He bore the sins of men and died for them. It is not enough for the ideal and perfect righteousness to exist, for we are already sinners. We have already transgressed God's law; we have already rebelled against God and gone our own way in life, living just like we want instead of following God. Therefore, the penalty for rebellion and treason—for sinning against God—has to be paid. We have to die or else someone else has to die for us. That someone has to be the ideal and perfect Man, for only perfection is acceptable to God. This is just what Jesus Christ did; He died for our sins. He bore the penalty and punishment for our sins. And it was acceptable to God because He was the Ideal and Perfect Man. His death stands for and covers our sins and death. Therefore, we are completely and totally free of sin. We stand before God as righteous. Now we are not righteous; we of all people know that. But God counts us righteous by the death of Christ. He credits the death of Christ to our sins. He counts us free of sin—credits us as being righteous by the death of Christ.

When does God do this? When we believe in Jesus Christ. When we really believe, God counts the death of Jesus Christ *for our sins*; therefore, He is able to count us *free from sin*, as righteous before Him. This is the righteousness of Jesus Christ; this is the way we become acceptable to God.

You see, at just the right time, when we were still powerless, Christ died for the ungodly. (Rom 5:6)

But God demonstrates his own love for us in this: While we were still sinners, Christ died for us. Since we have now been justified by his blood, how much more shall we be saved from God's wrath through him! (Rom 5:8-9)

Get rid of the old yeast that you may be a new batch without yeast—as you really are. For Christ, our Passover lamb, has been sacrificed. (1 Cor 5:7)

God made him who had no sin to be sin for us, so that in him we might become the righteousness of God. (2 Cor 5:21)

Such a high priest meets our need—one who is holy, blameless, pure, set apart from sinners, exalted above the heavens. Unlike the other high priests, he does not need to offer sacrifices day after day, first for his own sins, and then for the sins of the people. He sacrificed for their sins once for all when he offered himself. (Heb 7:26-27)

The blood of goats and bulls and the ashes of a heifer sprinkled on those who are ceremonially unclean sanctify them so that they are outwardly clean. How much more, then, will the blood of Christ, who through the eternal Spirit offered himself unblemished to God, cleanse our consciences from acts that lead to death, so that we may serve the living God! (Heb 9:13-14)

Nor did he enter heaven to offer himself again and again, the way the high priest enters the Most Holy Place every year with blood that is not his own. Then Christ would have had to suffer many times since the creation of the world. But now he has appeared once for all at the end of the ages to do away with sin by the sacrifice of himself. (Heb 9:25-26)

So Christ was sacrificed once to take away the sins of many people; and he will appear a second time, not to bear sin, but to bring salvation to those who are waiting for him. (Heb 9:28)

But when this priest had offered for all time one sacrifice for sins, he sat down at the right hand of God. because by one sacrifice he has made perfect forever those who are being made holy. (Heb 10:12, 14)

He himself bore our sins in his body on the tree, so that we might die to sins and live for righteousness; by his wounds you have been healed. (1 Pet 2:24)

For Christ died for sins once for all, the righteous for the unrighteous, to bring you to God. He was put to death in the body but made alive by the Spirit, (1 Pet 3:18)

Surely he took up our infirmities and carried our sorrows, yet we considered him stricken by God, smitten by him, and afflicted. But he was pierced for our transgressions, he was crushed for our iniquities; the punishment that brought us peace was upon him, and by his wounds we are healed. We all, like sheep, have gone astray, each of us has turned to his own way; and the LORD has laid on him the iniquity of us all. (Isa 53:4-6)

3 (1:2) **Grace—Peace—Knowledge:** Jesus Christ is the Messiah of *grace and peace*. No greater gifts exist than grace and peace. Note three things.

1. Grace (charis) means the *undeserved favor and blessings* of God. (See notes—Ro.4:16; DEEPER STUDY # 1— 1 Cor.1:4; DEEPER STUDY # 1—Tit.2:11-15.) The word *undeserved* is the key to understanding grace. Man does not deserve God's favor; he cannot earn God's approval and blessings. God is too high and man is too low for man to

deserve anything from God. Man is imperfect and God is perfect; therefore, man cannot expect anything from God. (See DEEPER STUDY # 1, *Justification*—Gal.2:15-16 for more discussion.) Man has reacted against God too much. Man has...

- rejected God
- rebelled against God
- ignored God
- neglected God
- cursed God
- sinned against God
- disobeyed God
- denied God
- questioned God

Man deserves nothing from God except judgment, condemnation, and punishment. But God is love—perfect and absolute love. Therefore, God makes it possible for man to experience His grace, in particular the favor and blessing of salvation which is in His Son, Jesus Christ. (See DEEPER STUDY # 1 *Grace*—1 Cor.1:4 for more discussion.)

And are justified freely by his grace through the redemption that came by Christ Jesus. (Rom 3:24)

For you know the grace of our Lord Jesus Christ, that though he was rich, yet for your sakes he became poor, so that you through his poverty might become rich. (2 Cor 8:9)

In him we have redemption through his blood, the forgiveness of sins, in accordance with the riches of God's grace (Eph 1:7)

In order that in the coming ages he might show the incomparable riches of his grace, expressed in his kindness to us in Christ Jesus. (Eph 2:7)

And my God will meet all your needs according to his glorious riches in Christ Jesus. (Phil 4:19)

The grace of our Lord was poured out on me abundantly, along with the faith and love that are in Christ Jesus. (1 Tim 1:14)

2. Peace (eirene) means to be bound, joined, and woven together. It also means to be bound, joined, and woven together with others and with God. It means to be assured, confident, and secure in the love and care of God. It means to have a sense, a consciousness, a knowledge that God will...

- provide
- guide
- strengthen
- sustain
- deliver
- encourage
- save
- give real life both now and forever

A person can experience true peace only as he comes to know Jesus Christ. Only Christ can bring peace to the human heart, the kind of peace that brings deliverance and assurance to the human soul.

Peace I leave with you; my peace I give you. I do not give to you as the world gives. Do not let your hearts be troubled and do not be afraid. (John 14:27)

"I have told you these things, so that in me you may have peace. In this world you will have trouble. But take heart! I have overcome the world." (John 16:33)

Therefore, since we have been justified through faith, we have peace with God through our Lord Jesus Christ, (Rom 5:1)

The mind of sinful man is death, but the mind controlled by the Spirit is life and peace; (Rom 8:6)

> But the fruit of the Spirit is love, joy, peace, patience, kindness, goodness, faithfulness, gentleness and self-control. Against such things there is no law. (Gal 5:22-23)
>
> Finally, brothers, whatever is true, whatever is noble, whatever is right, whatever is pure, whatever is lovely, whatever is admirable—if anything is excellent or praiseworthy—think about such things. (Phil 4:8)

3. Note that Jesus Christ gives an abundance of grace and peace; He multiplies grace and peace; He causes grace and peace to overflow in the life of the genuine believer. There is never to be a lack of grace and peace in the life of any true believer. Every believer is to always be overflowing with joy, with the favor and blessings of God and with peace within his own spirit and with God and others.

How can a person always be overflowing with the grace and peace of God? Through the knowledge of God and of Jesus our Lord. We have to know God in order to receive the grace and peace of God. What does it mean to know God? The word "knowledge" (epignosei) means "full, personal, precise, and correct" knowledge (The Amplified New Testament).

⇒ It means to know Christ personally; to know Him by experience. It means to know Christ just like we know any person: by walking and talking with Him.

⇒ It means to know Christ fully; to know Him in all of His person, exactly who He is. It means to be precise and correct in what we know about Him.

The point is this: if a person knows Christ fully and personally, precisely and correctly, then he knows Christ as Savior and Lord. He knows Christ as the Son of God who was sent to earth by the Father to save the world. The person does not look upon Christ as a mere man, as a great religious leader who founded the religion of Christianity. The person looks upon Jesus Christ as the Savior and Lord of men, and he knows Christ personally. He experiences Christ: he comes to Christ and asks Christ to save him and to be the Lord of his life. He gives all that he is and has to Christ, surrendering totally to Christ as his Lord. It is the person who so surrenders to Christ that comes to know Christ, and day by day, the person experiences the overflow of the Lord's grace and peace.

> Jesus answered, "My teaching is not my own. It comes from him who sent me. If anyone chooses to do God's will, he will find out whether my teaching comes from God or whether I speak on my own. (John 7:16-17)
>
> Now this is eternal life: that they may know you, the only true God, and Jesus Christ, whom you have sent. (John 17:3)
>
> What is more, I consider everything a loss compared to the surpassing greatness of knowing Christ Jesus my Lord, for whose sake I have lost all things. I consider them rubbish, that I may gain Christ (Phil 3:8)
>
> I want to know Christ and the power of his resurrection and the fellowship of sharing in his sufferings, becoming like him in his death, (Phil 3:10)
>
> "You are my witnesses," declares the LORD, "and my servant whom I have chosen, so that you may know and believe me and understand that I am he. Before me no god was formed, nor will there be one after me. (Isa 43:10)

4 (1:3) **Life—Godliness**: Jesus Christ is the Messiah of *life and godliness*. What is meant by life and godliness? It means *everything* that is necessary for life.

First, life is the energy, the force, and the power of being. The life which Jesus Christ gives is a life of energy, force, and power.

⇒ The life given by Christ is the very opposite of perishing. It is deliverance from condemnation and death. It is the stopping or cessation of aging, deterioration, decay, and corruption. It is a life that is eternal, that lasts forever and ever. It is the very life of God Himself (Jn.17:3).

⇒ The life given by Christ is an abundant life, a life of the very highest quality, a life that overflows with all the good things of life: love, joy, peace, goodness, satisfaction, and security.

Whatever is necessary for life is given by Christ. He longs for man to live, to have an abundance of life; therefore He gives all things that will make a person overflow with life. (See DEEPER STUDY # 2, *Life*—Jn.1:4, DEEPER STUDY # 1—10:10; DEEPER STUDY # 1—17:2-3 for more discussion.)

Second, godliness is living like God and being a godly person. It is living life like it should be lived. God gave man life; therefore, God knows what life should be, and above all things life should be godly just like God. The word "godliness" (eusebeian) actually means to live in the reverence and awe of God; to be *so conscious* of God's presence that one lives just as God would live if He were walking upon earth. It means to live seeking to be like God; to seek to possess the very character, nature, and behavior of God. The man of God follows and runs after godliness. He seeks to gain a consciousness of God's presence—a consciousness so intense that he actually lives as God would live if He were on earth.

Note: godliness means to be *Christlike*. Godliness is *Christlikeness*: it is living upon earth just as Christ lived.

> And we, who with unveiled faces all reflect the Lord's glory, are being transformed into his likeness with ever-increasing glory, which comes from the Lord, who is the Spirit. (2 Cor 3:18)
>
> It teaches us to say "No" to ungodliness and worldly passions, and to live self-controlled, upright and godly lives in this present age, while we wait for the blessed hope—the glorious appearing of our great God and Savior, Jesus Christ, (Titus 2:12-13)
>
> Since everything will be destroyed in this way, what kind of people ought you to be? You ought to live holy and godly lives (2 Pet 3:11)

Now note the verse. Two significant points are made, points that are absolutely essential for us to heed if we wish to have real life.

1. Note where life comes from. It does not come from man himself; life is not in and of man himself. Man dies. He is a dying creature, always in the process of dying, always moving onward toward the grave. Man is as good as dead. And in the process of dying, he experiences all kinds of trials and sufferings such as sickness, disease, accident, emptiness, loneliness, corruption, evil, shortcomings, failures, lies, thefts, killings, wars, and death after death of friends and loved ones.

Man has anything but life; at best he only exists for a few years that are ever so short and frail. Where then can man find life? Who has the power to stop the process of death and to deliver us from death? No man has such power. But note this verse: there is "divine power," the very power of Christ Himself that can stop death and give us life—life abundant, life now and life eternally. Jesus Christ is the Son of God who came to earth...

- to secure the perfect and ideal life for us.
- to die for our sins in order to free us from sin so that we could stand sinless before God, perfectly righteous in the eyes of God.

This is the power of Christ, the power to save us from death and to give us life and godliness.

2. Note how we receive life and godliness: by the knowledge of Christ. We must know Christ personally. We must know Him as our Savior and Lord, surrendering all that we are and have to him. We must be willing to walk and share with Him all day every day, serving Him as the Lord of our lives. We must be willing to know Him by living a godly life, by actually experiencing the life of God as we walk day by day.

Note: Christ has called us to glory and virtue. This is the very life to which He has called us: a life of glory and moral excellence both here on this earth and in heaven. We are to live pure and righteous lives, glorious lives; and when we do, He promises to give us a place in the glory and perfection of heaven. Note that this may read in the Greek: "Christ has called us by His own glory and goodness." That is, it is His own glory and goodness (moral excellence) that attracts man and pulls man to seek life and godliness in Him.

> "I tell you the truth, whoever hears my word and believes him who sent me has eternal life and will not be condemned; he has crossed over from death to life. (John 5:24)
> For we who are alive are always being given over to death for Jesus' sake, so that his life may be revealed in our mortal body. (2 Cor 4:11)
> For to me, to live is Christ and to die is gain. (Phil 1:21)
> Those who obey his commands live in him, and he in them. And this is how we know that he lives in us: We know it by the Spirit he gave us. (1 John 3:24)

5 (1:4) **Divine Nature—New Self—New Person—New Creation—Corruption**: Jesus Christ is the Messiah of the *divine nature or new person, the new self*. Note: exceeding great and precious promises have been given to us. The promises are those that have to do with the *divine nature* of God, the divine nature that is planted within the heart of a person who believes in Jesus Christ. When a person believes in Jesus Christ, God sends His Spirit, the Holy Spirit, to indwell the heart of the believer. God places within the heart of the believer His own divine nature and makes him a new creature and a new man. The believer is actually *born again* spiritually. He actually participates in the divine nature of God through the presence of God's Holy Spirit.

And note what happens: the believer escapes the corruption that is in the world. He lives eternally, for the divine nature of God can never die. When it is time for the believer to depart this life, quicker than the blink of an eye, his spirit is transferred into heaven, into the very presence of God Himself. Why? Because of the divine presence of God: the believer is a new creation, a new self, a new man, a new person in whom the very Spirit of God Himself dwells; and the Spirit of God cannot die. The person thereby escapes the corruption of this world. (See DEEPER STUDY # 1, *Corruption*—2 Pt.1:4 for more discussion.)

⇒ The believer is born again.

> In reply Jesus declared, "I tell you the truth, no one can see the kingdom of God unless he is born again." "How can a man be born when he is old?" Nicodemus asked. "Surely he cannot enter a second time into his mother's womb to be born!" Jesus answered, "I tell you the truth, no one can enter the kingdom of God unless he is born of water and the Spirit. Flesh gives birth to flesh, but the Spirit gives birth to spirit. (John 3:3-6)
> Everyone who believes that Jesus is the Christ is born of God, and everyone who loves the father loves his child as well. (1 John 5:1)

⇒ The believer is made into a new creation.

> Therefore, if anyone is in Christ, he is a new creation; the old has gone, the new has come! (2 Cor 5:17)

⇒ The believer is made into a new self, a new person.

> And to put on the new self, created to be like God in true righteousness and holiness. (Eph 4:24)
> And have put on the new self, which is being renewed in knowledge in the image of its Creator. (Col 3:10)

⇒ The believer is given the divine nature of God.

> Through these he has given us his very great and precious promises, so that through them you may participate in the divine nature and escape the corruption in the world caused by evil desires. (2 Pet 1:4)

DEEPER STUDY # 1

(1:4) **Sin—Death—Corruption**: the body of man has within it the principle or the seed of corruption, and the world in which man lives has within it the principle or the seed of corruption. Therefore, man deteriorates and decays—he dies and returns to dust.

This seed of corruption is caused by sin. Sin is selfishness or lust. Sin is acting against God, against others, and even against oneself.

When a man offends—when he acts selfishly, does what he wants instead of what he should do—when he acts *against* instead of *for*—he energizes and sets in motion the process of corruption. Man's selfishness corrupts himself and the world in which he lives—including the ground and the air and the water of the earth (Ro.8:21). His selfishness corrupts the relationship between himself and God and between himself and other persons and even the relationship between other persons. His selfishness and sin corrupt his own body (1 Cor.15:42). It may be nothing more than eating too much or failing to stay physically fit, but his selfishness and sin set in motion the process of corruption. And the process of corruption just continues and continues to eat and eat away at life. Sin, that is, selfishness, has caused and is causing death, both physically and spiritually. (See notes—Mt.6:19-20; DEEPER STUDY # 2—8:17; DEEPER STUDY # 1,2—Ro.5:12; notes—1 Cor.15:50; 2 Cor.5:1-4; DEEPER STUDY # 1—Heb.9:27.)

	B. The Great Things of the Believer's Life, 1:5-15	10 Therefore, my brothers, be all the more eager to make your calling and election sure. For if you do these things, you will never fall,	d. These things keep you from falling
1 The charge to add "these things" to one's life a. Add goodness b. Add knowledge c. Add self-control d. Add perseverance e. Add godliness f. Add brotherly kindness g. Add love	5 For this very reason, make every effort to add to your faith goodness; and to goodness, knowledge; 6 And to knowledge, self-control; and to self-control, perseverance; and to perseverance, godliness; 7 And to godliness, brotherly kindness; and to brotherly kindness, love.	11 And you will receive a rich welcome into the eternal kingdom of our Lord and Savior Jesus Christ. 12 So I will always remind you of these things, even though you know them and are firmly established in the truth you now have.	e. These things give you eternal life & more **3 The great importance of "these things"** a. To always preach these things 1) Not to neglect them 2) To preach them although believers are grounded therein
2 The great power of "these things" a. These things keep you from being barren or unfruitful b. These things keep you from being spiritually blind c. These things keep you from forgetting that you have been cleansed from your sins	8 For if you possess these qualities in increasing measure, they will keep you from being ineffective and unproductive in your knowledge of our Lord Jesus Christ. 9 But if anyone does not have them, he is nearsighted and blind, and has forgotten that he has been cleansed from his past sins.	13 I think it is right to refresh your memory as long as I live in the tent of this body, 14 Because I know that I will soon put it aside, as our Lord Jesus Christ has made clear to me. 15 And I will make every effort to see that after my departure you will always be able to remember these things.	b. To always stir believers about these things, as long as you are alive c. To see that believers are stirred over these things even after your death 1) To die soon 2) To have a lasting ministry is essential

DIVISION I

THE GREAT SALVATION OF GOD, 1:1-21

B. The Great Things of the Believer's Life, 1:5-15

(1:5-15) **Introduction**: this is one of the most important passages in all of Scripture for the believer, a passage that must be studied and heeded time and again. It covers the great things (qualities and virtues) which are to be in the life of the believer. The great importance of these things is seen in three facts that are forcefully stressed by Peter.

First, a person is to give *make every effort*, to add "these things" to his faith and life. As Scripture says, the believer "is to work out his salvation" (Ph.2:12).

Second, the *great power* of "these things" stresses their importance. *These things* work within the life of the believer to meet five desperate needs of man, five things for which the soul of the believer aches and longs. Glancing at the five points of verses 8-11 in the outline of the Scripture will again show the great importance of these things in the believer's life.

Third, Peter's heavy stress upon the importance of "these things" is phenomenal.

⇒ Note v.12: Peter says that he is going to always preach *these things* despite the fact that the believer already knows them. But this is not all.

⇒ Note v.13: Peter says that as long as he is living, he is going to stir up the believers by reminding them of *these things*. But this is not all.

⇒ Note v.14-15: Peter says that *these things* are so important that he is going to see to it that the believers are reminded of them *even after his death*.

What more could Peter say?

Another way to look at this passage is this: verses 1-4 are God's part in salvation. God's part includes...
- faith and righteousness (v.1).
- grace and peace (v.2).
- life and godliness everything we need for life and godliness (v.3).
- the divine nature or new self (v.4).

Note that *God's part* in salvation involves *seven things*. Now note that *man's part* in salvation involves *seven things* (v.5-7). The *things* of the believer's life are of critical importance.
1. The charge to add *these things* (v.5-7).
2. The great power of *these things* (v.8-11).
3. The great importance of *these things* (v.12-15).

1 (1:5-7) **Believer, Duty of**: there is the charge to add *these things* to one's life. The word "add" (epichoregein) means in addition to God's great salvation—right along side of what God has done—add *these things*. And make every effort to add them. Hasten, jump, act now to add them; don't wait. Be energetic and earnest, strenuously work to add *these things* to your faith and salvation.

1. Add "goodness" (areten): moral excellence and goodness of character; moral strength and moral courage. It means manliness; being an excellent person in life, a real man or a real woman in life; living life just like one should, in the most excellent way. It means always choosing the excellent way.

> **Finally, brothers, we instructed you how to live in order to please God, as in fact you are living. Now we ask you and urge you in the Lord Jesus to do this more and more. For you know what instructions we gave you by the authority of the Lord Jesus. It is God's will that you should be sanctified: that you should avoid sexual immorality; that each of you should learn to control his own body in a way that is holy and honorable, not in passionate lust like the heathen, who do not know God; and that in this matter no one should**

wrong his brother or take advantage of him. The Lord will punish men for all such sins, as we have already told you and warned you. For God did not call us to be impure, but to live a holy life. (1 Th 4:1-7)

Make it your ambition to lead a quiet life, to mind your own business and to work with your hands, just as we told you, so that your daily life may win the respect of outsiders and so that you will not be dependent on anybody. (1 Th 4:11-12)

2. Add "knowledge" (gnosin): practical intelligence, practical wisdom, practical insight. It means knowing what to do in every situation and doing it; it is practical, day to day knowledge that sees situations and knows how to handle them. It is seeing the trials and temptations of life and knowing what to do with them and doing it.

Remember the charge: we must add knowledge to our faith. We must give diligent attention to the situations of life and figure out how to conquer them.

To the Jews who had believed him, Jesus said, "If you hold to my teaching, you are really my disciples. (John 8:31)

I myself am convinced, my brothers, that you yourselves are full of goodness, complete in knowledge and competent to instruct one another. (Rom 15:14)

For in him you have been enriched in every way—in all your speaking and in all your knowledge— (1 Cor 1:5)

In whom are hidden all the treasures of wisdom and knowledge. (Col 2:3)

Who is wise and understanding among you? Let him show it by his good life, by deeds done in the humility that comes from wisdom. (James 3:13)

And if you call out for insight and cry aloud for understanding, and if you look for it as for silver and search for it as for hidden treasure, then you will understand the fear of the LORD and find the knowledge of God. (Prov 2:3-5)

The discerning heart seeks knowledge, but the mouth of a fool feeds on folly. (Prov 15:14)

Buy the truth and do not sell it; get wisdom, discipline and understanding. (Prov 23:23)

Let us acknowledge the LORD; let us press on to acknowledge him. As surely as the sun rises, he will appear; he will come to us like the winter rains, like the spring rains that water the earth." (Hosea 6:3)

3. Add "self-control" (egkrateian): to master and control the body or the flesh with all of its evil desires. It means self-control, the master of desire, appetite and passion, especially sensual urges and cravings. It means to be strong and controlled and restrained. It means to stand against the lust of the flesh, (sinful nature) and the lust of the eye and the pride of life, the boasting of what a person has and does (1 Jn.2:15-16).

⇒ The believer is to know that self-control is of God, a fruit of the Holy Spirit.

But the fruit of the Spirit is love, joy, peace, patience, kindness, goodness, faithfulness, gentleness and self-control. Against such things there is no law. (Gal 5:22-23)

⇒ The believer is to proclaim self-control to the lost.

As Paul discoursed on righteousness, self-control and the judgment to come, Felix was afraid and said, "That's enough for now! You may leave. When I find it convenient, I will send for you." (Acts 24:25)

⇒ The believer is to control his sexual desires.

But if they cannot control themselves, they should marry, for it is better to marry than to burn with passion. (1 Cor 7:9)

⇒ The believer is to strenuously exercise self-control, just as an athlete controls himself.

Everyone who competes in the games goes into strict training. They do it to get a crown that will not last; but we do it to get a crown that will last forever. (1 Cor 9:25)

⇒ The believer is to grow in self-control.

And to knowledge, self-control; and to self-control, perseverance; and to perseverance, godliness; (2 Pet 1:6)

⇒ The avenged believer is especially to be on guard to control himself.

Teach the older men to be temperate, worthy of respect, self-controlled, and sound in faith, in love and in endurance. (Titus 2:2)

4. Add "perseverance" (hupomonein): endurance, fortitude, steadfastness, constancy. The word is not passive; it is active. It is not the spirit that just sits back and puts up with the trials of life, taking whatever may come. Rather it is the spirit that stands up and faces life's trials, that actively goes about conquering and overcoming them. When trials confront a man who is truly justified, he is stirred to arise and face the trials head on. He immediately sets out to conquer and overcome them. He knows that God is allowing the trials in order to teach him more and more to persevere.

By standing firm you will gain life. (Luke 21:19)

Be joyful in hope, patient in affliction, faithful in prayer. (Rom 12:12)

You need to persevere so that when you have done the will of God, you will receive what he has promised. (Heb 10:36)

Consider it pure joy, my brothers, whenever you face trials of many kinds, because you know that the testing of your faith develops perseverance. Perseverance must finish its work so that you may be mature and complete, not lacking anything. (James 1:2-4)

Be patient, then, brothers, until the Lord's coming. See how the farmer waits for the land to yield its valuable crop and how patient he is for the autumn and spring rains. (James 5:7)

5. Add "godliness" (eusebeian): see note, *Godliness—2 Pt.1:3* for discussion.

6. Add "brotherly kindness" (philadelphian): the very special love that exists between brothers and sisters within a loving family, brothers and sisters who truly cherish one another. It is the kind of love...

- that binds each other together as a family, as a brotherly clan.
- that binds each other in an unbreakable union.
- that holds each other ever so dearly within the heart.
- that knows deep affection for each other.
- that nourishes and nurtures each other.
- that shows concern and looks after the welfare of each other.

a. that joins hands with each other in a common purpose *under one father* (Leon Morris. *The Epistles of Paul to the Thessalonians.* "Tyndale New Testament Commentary," ed. by RVG Tasker. Grand Rapids, MI: Eerdmans, 1956, p.80).

How can people possibly love one another like this when they are not true blood brothers and sisters? Here is how. The Greek word "brother" (adelphos) means *from the same womb.* The word used for love is phileo which means deep-seated affection and care, deep and warm feelings within the heart. It is the kind of love that holds a person near and dear to one's heart. Now note: the two Greek words are combined together by the writer to convey what he means by *brotherly love.*

⇒ People who have *brotherly love* have come from the same womb, that is, from the same source. They have been *born again* by the Spirit of God through faith in the Lord Jesus Christ. When they receive this new birth, God gives them a new spirit—a spirit that melts and binds their hearts and lives in love for all the family of God.

Believers may not even know each other. They may even be from different parts of the world, but there is a *brotherly love* between them because they have been given a new birth and a new spirit of love by God. They are brothers and sisters in the family of God—the family of those who truly believe in God's Son, the Lord Jesus Christ—the family who has received a new spirit that binds them together in brotherly love. This new spirit, of course, comes from the Holy Spirit of God Himself. (See Deeper Study # 3, *Fellowship—Acts 2:42* for more discussion.)

> "A new command I give you: Love one another. As I have loved you, so you must love one another. By this all men will know that you are my disciples, if you love one another." (John 13:34-35)
>
> My command is this: Love each other as I have loved you. (John 15:12)
>
> This is my command: Love each other. (John 15:17)
>
> And hope does not disappoint us, because God has poured out his love into our hearts by the Holy Spirit, whom he has given us. (Rom 5:5)
>
> Be devoted to one another in brotherly love. Honor one another above yourselves. (Rom 12:10)
>
> But the fruit of the Spirit is love, joy, peace, patience, kindness, goodness, faithfulness, (Gal 5:22)
>
> Keep on loving each other as brothers. (Heb 13:1)
>
> Now that you have purified yourselves by obeying the truth so that you have sincere love for your brothers, love one another deeply, from the heart. (1 Pet 1:22)
>
> Finally, all of you, live in harmony with one another; be sympathetic, love as brothers, be compassionate and humble. (1 Pet 3:8)
>
> We know that we have passed from death to life, because we love our brothers. Anyone who does not love remains in death. (1 John 3:14)
>
> Dear children, let us not love with words or tongue but with actions and in truth. This then is how we know that we belong to the truth, and how we set our hearts at rest in his presence (1 John 3:18-19)
>
> Everyone who believes that Jesus is the Christ is born of God, and everyone who loves the father loves his child as well. (1 John 5:1)

7. Add "love" (agapen): the love of the mind, of the reason, of the will. It is the *agape love* of God, the love that goes so far...

- that it loves regardless of feelings—whether a person feels like loving or not.
- that it loves a person even if the person does not deserve to be loved.
- that it actually loves the person who is utterly unworthy of being loved.

Note four significant points about *agape love.*

a. Selfless or agape love is the love of God, the very love possessed by God Himself. It is the love demonstrated in the cross of Christ.

⇒ It is the love of God for the *ungodly.*

> You see, at just the right time, when we were still powerless, Christ died for the ungodly. (Rom 5:6)

⇒ It is the love of God for *unworthy sinners.*

> But God demonstrates his own love for us in this: While we were still sinners, Christ died for us. (Rom 5:8)

⇒ It is the love of God for *undeserving enemies.*

> For if, when we were God's enemies, we were reconciled to him through the death of his Son, how much more, having been reconciled, shall we be saved through his life! (Rom 5:10)

b. Selfless or agape love is a gift of God. It can be experienced only if a person knows God *personally*—only if a person has received the love of God, that is, Christ Jesus, into his heart and life. *Agape love* has to be shed abroad poured out, (flooded, spread about) by the Spirit of God within the heart of a person.

> And hope does not disappoint us, because God has poured out his love into our hearts by the Holy Spirit, whom he has given us. (Rom 5:5)

c. Selfless or agape love is the greatest thing in all of life according to the Lord Jesus Christ.

"The most important one," answered Jesus, "is this: 'Hear, O Israel, the Lord our God, the Lord is one. Love the Lord your God with all your heart and with all your soul and with all your mind and with all your strength.' The second is this: 'Love your neighbor as yourself.' There is no commandment greater than these." (Mark 12:29-31)

d. Selfless or agape love is the greatest possession and gift in human life according to the Scripture (1 Cor.13:1-13).

And now these three remain: faith, hope and love. But the greatest of these is love. (1 Cor 13:13)

2 (1:8-11) **Believer, Life and Walk—Salvation, Power of—Faith, Power of**: there is the great power of *these things*. Note how the great needs of man's heart and life are covered in these verses:

⇒ Man is *ineffective and* unproductive in life (v.8).
⇒ Man is blind, cannot see the purpose, meaning, and significance of life and cannot see how to be absolutely sure of tomorrow, much less the distant future (v.9).
⇒ Man forgets, does not know how to deal with sin. Or if he knows how—knows the gospel—he is unwilling to give up his sin (v.9).
⇒ Man does not know how to keep from falling in life, from failing and coming short. He does not know how to meet his full potential; how to control the problems of life; to bring love, peace, and joy to himself and his loved ones and the world (v.10).
⇒ Man does not know how to gain and be perfectly assured of eternal life; he does not know how to receive an abundant entrance into the everlasting kingdom of Christ (v.11).

But note: all these needs can be met perfectly. They are met if *these things* of verses 7-8 are added to our lives in abundance. The term "increasing measure" (pleonazonta) means to increase and grow; to overflow and be filled with more and more, ever learning how to increase these things in our lives. In other words, do not be satisfied...

• with your life as it is.
• with present growth.
• with staying where you are spiritually.
• with just knowing Jesus.
• with doing no more than what you are.

To have the needs of our hearts and lives met, we have to continue on in *these things*. We have to grow and grow in them; give them utmost attention; go after them ever so diligently, never slackening. If we abound in them, then the needs of our hearts and lives will be met to the fullest.

1. We will not be *ineffective and unproductive*.
⇒ The word "ineffective" (argous) means idle and slothful; being empty and useless. It is the very opposite of being fruitful and productive in life. Therefore if we do *these things*, if we really work at our salvation, we will not live a barren, dry life. We will not be unfruitful nor live a life that is empty and useless, idle and slothful. On the contrary, we will live a life that flows with nourishment and that bears the ripest of fruit: love, joy, and peace (cp. Gal.5:22-23).

But note the source of such a life: the source is our Lord Jesus Christ. We must know Him and grow in the knowledge of Him. The knowledge of Him must be our aim and purpose in life. Only as we know Him can we overcome being ineffective and unproductive. He and He alone can give us real life. Therefore, we must do *these things*—really work at our salvation—really seek fellowship and communion with Christ moment by moment and day by day—in order not to be ineffective and unproductive in the knowledge of Him. We must learn to pray all day long and to take *set times* for prayer every day, set times for concentrated prayer. We must learn to *keep our minds* on Christ.

But the one who received the seed that fell on good soil is the man who hears the word and understands it. He produces a crop, yielding a hundred, sixty or thirty times what was sown." (Mat 13:23)
"I am the vine; you are the branches. If a man remains in me and I in him, he will bear much fruit; apart from me you can do nothing. If anyone does not remain in me, he is like a branch that is thrown away and withers; such branches are picked up, thrown into the fire and burned. (John 15:5-6)
But the fruit of the Spirit is love, joy, peace, patience, kindness, goodness, faithfulness, gentleness and self-control. Against such things there is no law. (Gal 5:22-23)
Blessed is the man who does not walk in the counsel of the wicked or stand in the way of sinners or sit in the seat of mockers. But his delight is in the law of the LORD, and on his law he meditates day and night. He is like a tree planted by streams of water, which yields its fruit in season and whose leaf does not wither. Whatever he does prospers. (Psa 1:1-3)

2. We will not be near-sighted and blind. Without Christ men are blind. They do not see...
• the purpose, meaning, or significance to life.
• the importance of morality and goodness, love, joy, peace, and the goodness of God and Christ.
• the way to conquer sin and evil, trials and suffering, life and death.

Men are pictured as being unable to see afar off, as being near-sighted. They are pictured as keeping their eyes only on the earth and its pleasures and possessions, only upon enjoying life now, only upon living as they want and doing their own thing. They give little if any thought to the *eternal consequences* of their behavior and actions. The result is devastating: they are blind and shortsighted. They lack real and permanent purpose, meaning, and significance in life. They experience ever so much emptiness and loneliness, often wondering...
• what is life all about?
• what is its purpose and end?
• what is there after death?
• is there meaning to this life at all?

But note: if we do *these things*, if we work at our salvation, we will not be blind or unable to see ahead. We will not lack purpose, meaning, or significance in life. *These things*, the things of salvation, will not only give us purpose in this life, they will give us eternal purpose. We will understand life, what life is all about. We will know the purpose, meaning, and significance of life. We will never be empty or lonely, or without purpose in life.

But if your eyes are bad, your whole body will be full of darkness. If then the light within you is darkness, how great is that darkness! (Mat 6:23)

In him was life, and that life was the light of men. (John 1:4)

When Jesus spoke again to the people, he said, "I am the light of the world. Whoever follows me will never walk in darkness, but will have the light of life." (John 8:12)

Then Jesus told them, "You are going to have the light just a little while longer. Walk while you have the light, before darkness overtakes you. The man who walks in the dark does not know where he is going. (John 12:35)

The god of this age has blinded the minds of unbelievers, so that they cannot see the light of the gospel of the glory of Christ, who is the image of God. (2 Cor 4:4)

For God, who said, "Let light shine out of darkness," made his light shine in our hearts to give us the light of the knowledge of the glory of God in the face of Christ. (2 Cor 4:6)

They are darkened in their understanding and separated from the life of God because of the ignorance that is in them due to the hardening of their hearts. (Eph 4:18)

For you were once darkness, but now you are light in the Lord. Live as children of light (Eph 5:8)

For it is light that makes everything visible. This is why it is said: "Wake up, O sleeper, rise from the dead, and Christ will shine on you." (Eph 5:14)

So that you may become blameless and pure, children of God without fault in a crooked and depraved generation, in which you shine like stars in the universe (Phil 2:15)

The people walking in darkness have seen a great light; on those living in the land of the shadow of death a light has dawned. (Isa 9:2)

3. We will not forget that we have been cleansed from our sins. Very frankly, the person who fails to do *these things*, who fails to work out his own salvation, soon forgets the death of Christ. He forgets the great price that Christ paid to forgive his sins. The person becomes a backslider. How can we say this? Because a person is either moving ahead in Christ or else sliding back from Christ. And the person sliding back thinks little about sin and the consequences of sin. His thoughts and actions are in the world, and he is focusing upon the world and its pleasures and possessions. He has just forgotten that Christ purged him from his sins. He has slipped away from Christ and slipped back into the world.

The point is this: we must do *these things*, work out our salvation, or else we will backslide. We will forget Christ and His death and the glorious fact that He has forgiven our sins. *These things*, the wonderful things of salvation, have the power to keep us near Christ and to keep us from ever backsliding.

But now that you know God—or rather are known by God—how is it that you are turning back to those weak and miserable principles? Do you wish to be enslaved by them all over again? (Gal 4:9)

Be diligent in these matters; give yourself wholly to them, so that everyone may see your progress. (1 Tim 4:15)

Do your best to present yourself to God as one approved, a workman who does not need to be ashamed and who correctly handles the word of truth. (2 Tim 2:15)

Therefore let us leave the elementary teachings about Christ and go on to maturity, not laying again the foundation of repentance from acts that lead to death, and of faith in God, (Heb 6:1)

But my righteous one will live by faith. And if he shrinks back, I will not be pleased with him." (Heb 10:38)

Like newborn babies, crave pure spiritual milk, so that by it you may grow up in your salvation, now that you have tasted that the Lord is good. (1 Pet 2:2-3)

But grow in the grace and knowledge of our Lord and Savior Jesus Christ. To him be glory both now and forever! Amen. (2 Pet 3:18)

4. We will never fall. How often we come short, stumble, and fall. We just do not do what we should. If there is any single trait that runs through human life, it is stumbling, coming short, and falling. People stumble and come short and fall...

- in marriage
- in family duties
- in relationships
- in work
- in school
- in responsibilities
- in life
- in promises
- in planning
- in behavior
- in resolutions
- in the Christian life
- in devotions
- in witnessing
- in serving Christ
- in worship

How can we keep from stumbling and falling? God has called and elected us to live a rich and fruitful life and to be rich and fruitful for all of eternity. How can we live such a rich, fruitful life? Note the verse:

Be all the more eager to make your calling and election sure. For if you do these things, you will never fall, (v.10)

We must be diligent in doing *these things*. We must give ourselves totally to the things of salvation. We must work and work at them. If we do, then we shall never stumble and fall, not in a tragic, devastating or destructive sense. On the contrary, we will live the most abundant and fruitful life imaginable.

Therefore, my dear brothers, stand firm. Let nothing move you. Always give yourselves fully to the work of the Lord, because you know that your labor in the Lord is not in vain. (1 Cor 15:58)

We want each of you to show this same diligence to the very end, in order to make your hope sure. (Heb 6:11)

Therefore, my brothers, be all the more eager to make your calling and election sure. For if you do these things, you will never fall, (2 Pet 1:10)

But in keeping with his promise we are looking forward to a new heaven and a new earth, the home of righteousness. So then, dear friends, since you are looking forward to this, make every effort to be found spotless, blameless and at peace with him. (2 Pet 3:13-14)

5. We will be given eternal life and more. We will receive a rich welcome into the kingdom of our Lord and Savior Jesus Christ. We will be richly and gloriously welcomed into heaven. The idea is that there will be different degrees of reward, of richness and wealth in heaven. Some of us will not inherit the kingdom, wealth, and service that others will inherit. How can we be sure of receiving the richest entrance into heaven? By being diligent in doing *these things*, in working out our salvation. (See note, *Reward*—1 Pt.1:4 for a list of the rewards of the believer.)

"Then the King will say to those on his right, 'Come, you who are blessed by my Father; take your inheritance, the kingdom prepared for you since the creation of the world. For I was hungry and you gave me something to eat, I was thirsty and you gave me something to drink, I was a stranger and you invited me in, I needed clothes and you clothed me, I was sick and you looked after me, I was in prison and you came to visit me.' (Mat 25:34-36)

For our light and momentary troubles are achieving for us an eternal glory that far outweighs them all. (2 Cor 4:17)

Praise be to the God and Father of our Lord Jesus Christ! In his great mercy he has given us new birth into a living hope through the resurrection of Jesus Christ from the dead, and into an inheritance that can never perish, spoil or fade—kept in heaven for you, (1 Pet 1:3-4)

And you will receive a rich welcome into the eternal kingdom of our Lord and Savior Jesus Christ. (2 Pet 1:11)

3 (1:12-15) **Salvation—Peter**: the great importance of *these things*. What Peter now does is most interesting. He tells us how important he considers these things.

1. They are so important that he is always going to preach and teach these things. He is going to remind and remind believers of them. Genuine believers know them and are even established in *these things*. But Peter says he is going to repeat and repeat them. He will not neglect them.

One thing is sure: Peter thought that *these things*, the things of salvation, were essential. How much more should we stress them! But note the next point. Peter has even more to say about *these things*.

2. They are so important that he is going to stir believers to do them as long as he is alive. He is going to remind and remind them of these things as long as he is in "this tabernacle," the tent of his body. Peter has to repeat and repeat these things. Why? Because it is right (dikaion), the only right thing to do. Believers must do *these things* in or-

der to experience the rich and fruitful life Christ gives. Therefore, he must stress them and drive them home to the hearts of his dear people. But note: this is not all that Peter has to say about *these things*.

3. They are so important that Peter is going to see that believers are stirred to do *these things* even after his death. Peter apparently knew that he was soon to be taken on home to heaven. But *these things* were so important that he was going to make arrangements with those left behind to teach *these things*.

Thought 1. How important are *these things*? How important is it that we preach *these things*? Few Scriptures are stressed and emphasized as much as these. Peter says he is going to see to it these things are taught to believers; he says this three times. This alone should stir us to preach and teach them—always—ever so diligently and faithfully.

Therefore go and make disciples of all nations, baptizing them in the name of the Father and of the Son and of the Holy Spirit, and teaching them to obey everything I have commanded you. And surely I am with you always, to the very end of the age." (Mat 28:19-20)

He said to them, "Go into all the world and preach the good news to all creation. (Mark 16:15)

Again Jesus said, "Peace be with you! As the Father has sent me, I am sending you." (John 20:21)

Again Jesus said, "Simon son of John, do you truly love me?" He answered, "Yes, Lord, you know that I love you." Jesus said, "Take care of my sheep." (John 21:16)

But you will receive power when the Holy Spirit comes on you; and you will be my witnesses in Jerusalem, and in all Judea and Samaria, and to the ends of the earth." (Acts 1:8)

For we cannot help speaking about what we have seen and heard." (Acts 4:20)

It is written: "I believed; therefore I have spoken." With that same spirit of faith we also believe and therefore speak, (2 Cor 4:13)

For you know what instructions we gave you by the authority of the Lord Jesus. (1 Th 4:2)

If you point these things out to the brothers, you will be a good minister of Christ Jesus, brought up in the truths of the faith and of the good teaching that you have followed. (1 Tim 4:6)

Be shepherds of God's flock that is under your care, serving as overseers—not because you must, but because you are willing, as God wants you to be; not greedy for money, but eager to serve; (1 Pet 5:2)

"You are my witnesses," declares the LORD, "and my servant whom I have chosen, so that you may know and believe me and understand that I am he. Before me no god was formed, nor will there be one after me. (Isa 43:10)

	C. The Great Proof of Salvation, 1:16-21	when we were with him on the sacred mountain. 19 And we have the word of the prophets made more certain, and you will do well to pay attention to it, as to a light shining in a dark place, until the day dawns and the morning star rises in your hearts.	3 The second proof of salvation: Scripture—the more certain account of prophecy or Scripture*DS1,2* a. Scripture is more sure than an eyewitness account b. Scripture is to be heeded
1 The great truth: Salvation is not a fable; it is the power and coming of Christ 2 The first proof of salvation: The great eyewitness account of Christ's majesty & transfiguration a. The honor & glory of God b. The voice from heaven c. The testimony: "We heard"	16 We did not follow cleverly invented stories when we told you about the power and coming of our Lord Jesus Christ, but we were eyewitnesses of his majesty. 17 For he received honor and glory from God the Father when the voice came to him from the Majestic Glory, saying, "This is my Son, whom I love; with him I am well pleased." 18 We ourselves heard this voice that came from heaven	20 Above all, you must understand that no prophecy of Scripture came about by the prophet's own interpretation. 21 For prophecy never had its origin in the will of man, but men spoke from God as they were carried along by the Holy Spirit.	c. Scripture is not of one's own interpretation 1) Because it is not given by man's will 2) Because it is given by the Spirit

DIVISION I

THE GREAT SALVATION OF GOD, 1:1-21

C. The Great Proof of Salvation, 1:16-21

(1:16-21) **Introduction**: How do we know that we can really be saved? That the glorious gospel of salvation is true? How do we know that Jesus Christ is really the Son of God, the Messiah and Savior of the world? This is the subject of this great passage—*the great proof of salvation.*

1. The great truth: salvation is not a fable; it is the power and coming of Christ (v.16).
2. The first proof of salvation: the great eyewitness account of Christ's majesty and transfiguration (v.16-18).
3. The second proof of salvation: Scripture—the more sure account of prophecy or Scripture (v.19-21).

1 (1:16) **Salvation, Proof of**: there is the great truth—salvation is not a fable; it is the power and coming of our Lord Jesus Christ.

1. The word *stories* is called *a cleverly invented story.* The gospel of salvation is not a story, not a fable, not some fictitious creation of man's mind. It is not an invention of man's imagination. It has not been thought up in order to give man more…

- peace
- security
- love
- joy
- morality

- goodness
- righteousness
- justice
- life

Man has created great value systems, religions, and laws to meet his need for peace, security, hope, and life. Some persons even declare that science and technology, education and social services are the answer to meeting man's needs. They think through the problems of life, and with great creative imagination they work out how technology and education can meet these needs. They then put their thoughts in writing and declare to the world that the salvation of man is found in technology and education. They declare that the needs of man for peace, security, and life are found in the works of man's own hands…

- in human religion and value systems
- in human laws and good behavior
- in science and technology
- in education and social services

But note: there is one terrible flaw in all this. Nothing on this earth is permanent; nothing lasts, not beyond this life. The cry of man's heart is for life, for fullness of life, for completeness, fulfillment, and satisfaction. Man longs for life, for more and more life, for security, hope, assurance, and peace. Man cries out for an abundance of life both now and in the future, life in this world and in the next world. In addition to the cry for life, man has a spiritual sense of God and of living forever, the need to worship God and to live with Him forever. But man dies and leaves this world. If he depends upon his own man-made efforts to meet his needs, then his efforts die when he dies. Why? Because no man can give him life beyond the grave. He depended upon his own mind and hands to make him secure in the future and in the hereafter, but when his mind and hands died, they were dead. His mind and hands could not deliver him; they were lifeless and powerless.

This means something: all the man-made efforts to save man, all the creations of man's mind and hands that claim to be the salvation of man—they are all fabrications of the human mind. They are the real *cleverly invented stories.* They may be helpful to man; they may meet some needs to some degree. In fact, all great thoughts and acts of men do help to some degree. But no thought of man and no act of man can meet the needs of man, *not perfectly and not eternally.* For all men die. In just a few short years there will not be a single person alive who is living upon the earth today—not a single person. We shall all be gone forever, never to return. No matter how great a thought we think and no matter how great a human salvation we make with our hands, we shall be gone forever. If we are going to meet our needs for life, if we are going to live abundantly both now and in the other world (heaven), then God Himself has to show us how to live and how to get into the other world. God Himself has to show us how to please Him so that He will take us there.

Note: if there is a God in another world, in a spiritual dimension, who has made us and the world, then He is interested in our getting to where He is. He is interested in our living with Him. There is too much good and love within the world and too much longing for Him and for life eternal within us for God not to love us. And this is the glorious gospel: God does love us. He has not left us in the dark to grope and grasp after Him. He has revealed Himself and shown us how to reach and please Him. He has shown us how to be acceptable to Him and to receive eternal life. The gospel of salvation is not a fable; it is not a cleverly invented story of man's imagination that deceives people. It is the truth that God loves us and has provided a way for us to be saved, a way for us to have peace and life now while on this earth and eternally when we enter the next world.

> "Watch out for false prophets. They come to you in sheep's clothing, but inwardly they are ferocious wolves. (Mat 7:15)
>
> For such men are false apostles, deceitful workmen, masquerading as apostles of Christ. And no wonder, for Satan himself masquerades as an angel of light. It is not surprising, then, if his servants masquerade as servants of righteousness. Their end will be what their actions deserve. (2 Cor 11:13-15)
>
> I am astonished that you are so quickly deserting the one who called you by the grace of Christ and are turning to a different gospel— which is really no gospel at all. Evidently some people are throwing you into confusion and are trying to pervert the gospel of Christ. But even if we or an angel from heaven should preach a gospel other than the one we preached to you, let him be eternally condemned! As we have already said, so now I say again: If anybody is preaching to you a gospel other than what you accepted, let him be eternally condemned! Am I now trying to win the approval of men, or of God? Or am I trying to please men? If I were still trying to please men, I would not be a servant of Christ. (Gal 1:6-10)
>
> For, as I have often told you before and now say again even with tears, many live as enemies of the cross of Christ. Their destiny is destruction, their god is their stomach, and their glory is in their shame. Their mind is on earthly things. (Phil 3:18-19)
>
> Nor to devote themselves to myths and endless genealogies. These promote controversies rather than God's work—which is by faith. (1 Tim 1:4)
>
> The Spirit clearly says that in later times some will abandon the faith and follow deceiving spirits and things taught by demons. (1 Tim 4:1)
>
> Have nothing to do with godless myths and old wives' tales; rather, train yourself to be godly. (1 Tim 4:7)
>
> And will pay no attention to Jewish myths or to the commands of those who reject the truth. (Titus 1:14)
>
> We did not follow cleverly invented stories when we told you about the power and coming of our Lord Jesus Christ, but we were eyewitnesses of his majesty. (2 Pet 1:16)
>
> But there were also false prophets among the people, just as there will be false teachers among you. They will secretly introduce destructive heresies, even denying the sovereign Lord who bought them— bringing swift destruction on themselves. Many will follow their shameful ways and will bring the way of truth into disrepute. In their greed these teachers will exploit you with stories they have made up. Their condemnation has long been hanging over them, and their destruction has not been sleeping. (2 Pet 2:1-3)
>
> Dear friends, do not believe every spirit, but test the spirits to see whether they are from God, because many false prophets have gone out into the world. This is how you can recognize the Spirit of God: Every spirit that acknowledges that Jesus Christ has come in the flesh is from God, but every spirit that does not acknowledge Jesus is not from God. This is the spirit of the antichrist, which you have heard is coming and even now is already in the world. (1 John 4:1-3)

2. Salvation is the power and coming of our Lord Jesus Christ. What does this mean?

a. First, it means the first coming of Jesus Christ. God has not left man in the dark to seek and search for peace and life—to see if there is such a thing as absolute peace of heart and such a thing as real life both now and hereafter. Only a *God of hate* would leave man in the dark to grasp and grasp after the truth within a corruptible world. But this is not God, not the true and living God. God is love and He cares deeply for man. How do we know this? By Jesus Christ. By the power and coming of Jesus Christ into this world. God loves man so much that He has sent His own Son into the world to save man. And note this:

⇒ The fact that God sent Christ into the world to save us means that God loves us, and God has the power to save us. God loves us enough and has enough power to give us peace and life both now and eternally. The power and coming of Jesus Christ into the world proves this.

> "For God so loved the world that he gave his one and only Son, that whoever believes in him shall not perish but have eternal life. For God did not send his Son into the world to condemn the world, but to save the world through him. (John 3:16-17)
>
> "I tell you the truth, whoever hears my word and believes him who sent me has eternal life and will not be condemned; he has crossed over from death to life. (John 5:24)
>
> The thief comes only to steal and kill and destroy; I have come that they may have life, and have it to the full. (John 10:10)
>
> For what the law was powerless to do in that it was weakened by the sinful nature, God did by sending his own Son in the likeness of sinful man to be a sin offering. And so he condemned sin in sinful man, (Rom 8:3)
>
> But when the time had fully come, God sent his Son, born of a woman,

born under law, to redeem those under law, that we might receive the full rights of sons. Because you are sons, God sent the Spirit of his Son into our hearts, the Spirit who calls out, "Abba, Father." So you are no longer a slave, but a son; and since you are a son, God has made you also an heir. (Gal 4:4-7)

Beyond all question, the mystery of godliness is great: He appeared in a body, was vindicated by the Spirit, was seen by angels, was preached among the nations, was believed on in the world, was taken up in glory. (1 Tim 3:16)

Since the children have flesh and blood, he too shared in their humanity so that by his death he might destroy him who holds the power of death—that is, the devil— and free those who all their lives were held in slavery by their fear of death. (Heb 2:14-15)

This is how you can recognize the Spirit of God: Every spirit that acknowledges that Jesus Christ has come in the flesh is from God, but every spirit that does not acknowledge Jesus is not from God. This is the spirit of the antichrist, which you have heard is coming and even now is already in the world. (1 John 4:2-3)

b. Second, it means the second coming of Christ. God is going to reveal His love and power again; God is going to prove His power to give us peace and life by sending Christ back to earth. Jesus Christ is going to come again just as He came before. Note the verse: this is not a "cleverly invented story...the power and coming of our Lord Jesus Christ." God has the power to bring peace to this earth, and He is going to personally come to earth to bring peace to it. He is coming again in the person of His Son Jesus Christ.

For as lightning that comes from the east is visible even in the west, so will be the coming of the Son of Man. (Mat 24:27)

In my Father's house are many rooms; if it were not so, I would have told you. I am going there to prepare a place for you. And if I go and prepare a place for you, I will come back and take you to be with me that you also may be where I am. (John 14:2-3)

For the Lord himself will come down from heaven, with a loud command, with the voice of the archangel and with the trumpet call of God, and the dead in Christ will rise first. After that, we who are still alive and are left will be caught up together with them in the clouds to meet the Lord in the air. And so we will be with the Lord forever. Therefore encourage each other with these words. (1 Th 4:16-18)

It teaches us to say "No" to ungodliness and worldly passions, and to live self-controlled, upright and godly lives in this present age, while we wait for the blessed hope—the glorious appearing of our great God and Savior, Jesus Christ, (Titus 2:12-13)

So Christ was sacrificed once to take away the sins of many people; and he will appear a second time, not to bear sin, but to bring salvation to those who are waiting for him. (Heb 9:28)

You too, be patient and stand firm, because the Lord's coming is near. (James 5:8)

2 (1:16-18) **Salvation, Proof—Jesus Christ, Deity:** there is the first proof of salvation, the great eyewitness account of Christ's majesty. The word "majesty" (megaleiotes) means the majesty of God, the *divine nature* of God (Michael Green. *The Second Epistle of Peter and The Epistle of Jude.* "The Tyndale New Testament Commentaries," p.83). It means that the *majesty and glory* of God filled and surrounded Christ when He walked upon earth. The early disciples and believers knew that Jesus Christ was the Savior of men because they saw the majesty and glory of God in His life and works. Jesus Christ went to great pains to reveal the majesty and glory of God; He proved time and again that He was the Son of God.

Now note verses 17-18: there was one event where the majesty and glory of God was allowed to shine out of Christ's very being; one event where the light of God's glory was so clearly seen that it proves beyond question that Jesus Christ is the Savior of the world, the very Son of God Himself. What was that event? It was the transfiguration of Christ. In the transfiguration of Christ, the very glory of God was *seen to be in Christ.* Scripture actually says that He was "transformed" (metamorphothe). The word means a change into another form; to undergo a transformation, a change of countenance; a complete change. Luke said, "the appearance of his face changed" (Lk.9:29). Note how the gospel writers described what happened.

There he was transfigured before them. His face shone like the sun, and his clothes became as white as the light. (Mat 17:2)

His clothes became dazzling white, whiter than anyone in the world could bleach them. (Mark 9:3)

As he was praying, the appearance of his face changed, and his clothes became as bright as a flash of lightning. (Luke 9:29)

Apparently *the glory* of His Godly nature was allowed to shine through His body to some degree. "The glory [He] had with God before the world" shone through His body, shone right through His clothes (Jn.17:5). Peter said, "We were eyewitnesses of His majesty." In John's vision of Christ in *The Revelation*, he described the glory of Christ as the sun which shines in all its brilliance (Rev.1:16).

The scripture says:

God is light (1 John 1:5)
[God]...who lives in unapproachable light, whom no one has seen or can see. (1 Tim 6:16)
He [God] wraps himself in light as with a garment (Psa 104:2)

Peter, James, and John witnessed the event; they had the wonderful privilege of tasting a little of heaven's glory. They experienced the very presence of God Himself and tasted some of heaven's peace, joy, security, fulfillment, and perfection. Note that...

- they saw the honor and glory of Christ.
- they heard God call Jesus His Son; they actually heard God say, "This is my Son, whom I love; with him I am well pleased" (Matt.17:5).

Note also the exact words concerning the voice. The fact is repeated in both verse 17 and verse 18.

The voice came to him [Christ] (2 Pet 1:17)

This voice that came from heaven (2 Pet 1:18)

Peter emphatically stresses that they heard the voice from heaven. It was not a dream nor a vision nor a figment of their imagination. A voice from heaven actually called Jesus Christ His Son.

Thought 1. Peter unequivocally claims that he, the other apostles, and all the early believers witnessed the power and coming of the Lord Jesus Christ. He claims that they were eyewitnesses of God's great love, that God loves the world and has sent His Son into the world to save men. We either believe or do not believe their eyewitness account. It is that simple: we believe or do not believe their testimony.

The Word became flesh and made his dwelling among us. We have seen his glory, the glory of the One and Only, who came from the Father, full of grace and truth. (John 1:14)

Many have undertaken to draw up an account of the things that have been fulfilled among us, just as they were handed down to us by those who from the first were eyewitnesses and servants of the word. Therefore, since I myself have carefully investigated everything from the beginning, it seemed good also to me to write an orderly account for you, most excellent Theophilus, so that you may know the certainty of the things you have been taught. (Luke 1:1-4)

We are witnesses of these things, and so is the Holy Spirit, whom God has given to those who obey him." (Acts 5:32)

"We are witnesses of everything he did in the country of the Jews and in Jerusalem. They killed him by hanging him on a tree, (Acts 10:39)

And for many days he was seen by those who had traveled with him from Galilee to Jerusalem. They are now his witnesses to our people. (Acts 13:31)

Now, brothers, I want to remind you of the gospel I preached to you, which you received and on which you have taken your stand. By this gospel you are saved, if you hold firmly to the word I preached to you. Otherwise, you have believed in vain. For what I received I passed on to you as of first importance : that Christ died for our sins according to the Scriptures, that he

was buried, that he was raised on the third day according to the Scriptures, and that he appeared to Peter, and then to the Twelve. After that, he appeared to more than five hundred of the brothers at the same time, most of whom are still living, though some have fallen asleep. Then he appeared to James, then to all the apostles, and last of all he appeared to me also, as to one abnormally born. (1 Cor 15:1-8)

To the elders among you, I appeal as a fellow elder, a witness of Christ's sufferings and one who also will share in the glory to be revealed: (1 Pet 5:1)

We did not follow cleverly invented stories when we told you about the power and coming of our Lord Jesus Christ, but we were eyewitnesses of his majesty. (2 Pet 1:16)

3 (1:19-21) **Salvation, Proof of—The Word of God**: the second proof of salvation is the more certain account of prophecy or Scripture. Note three significant points.

1. Scripture is more sure than an eyewitness account. The phrase *word of the prophets* is better translated the prophetic Word (A.T. Robertson. *Word Pictures In The New Testament*, Vol.6, p.157). There are an enormous number of prophecies in the Scripture about the coming Messiah and Savior of the world. When they are studied, it is clearly seen that Jesus Christ is the promised Savior. He fulfills all the prophecies perfectly. Therefore, the prophetic Word is a much *more certain account* of salvation. Just by the sheer number of prophecies and their fulfillment in Christ, the Scriptures prove themselves to be a far greater witness to Jesus Christ. (See DEEPER STUDY # 1, *Prophecy*—2 Pt.1:19-21 for a list of the Old Testament prophecies and their fulfillment in Christ.)

Thought 1. If the transfiguration of Christ had never taken place, the prophetic Scripture would still stand and prove that Jesus Christ is the Savior of the world. But if the prophetic Scriptures did not exist, the transfiguration by itself would be a much weaker proof that Christ is the Savior of the world. The transfiguration itself is greatly supported and substantiated by the prophetic Word. The prophetic Word helps tremendously to explain who Christ is and what was happening on the mount of transfiguration.

2. Scripture is to be heeded. This is descriptive language: we are to pay attention to the Word of God, for the Word of God is like "a light shining in a dark place, until the day dawns, and the morning star rises in your hearts" (v.19). What does this mean?

⇒ The Word of God is like a light that shines in dark places. It shows us how to walk in the dark forest of this world. It reveals the narrow path to follow and exposes the stumbling stones and dangerous pits and poisonous creatures along the path.

⇒ The Word of God will show us how to walk "until the day dawn." What day? The glorious day of Christ's return. In that day, "the morning star [Christ Himself shall] rises in our hearts" and perfect us. Our great salvation will be fulfilled and completed. We shall be transformed into His image, for we shall see Him as He is (1 Jn.3:2).

Michael Green has an excellent comment on the glorious day when the morning star (Christ) shall rise in our hearts:

"Our inner transformation, deepened continually by the Spirit as we study the Scriptures (2 Cor.3:18), will be completed on the great day when we shall see Him as He is, and be made like Him (1 Jn.3:2)" (The Second Epistle of Peter and The Epistle of Jude. "The Tyndale New Testament Commentaries," p.89).

Thought 1. The point is this: we are to study and heed, pay attention to the Scripture. We are to study the Old Testament and the New Testament, the prophecies of Christ and the fulfillment of the prophecies by Christ. The Scripture is the light that guides us through this dark and dangerous world.

3. Scripture is not of one's own interpretation (v.20-21). What does this mean? Verse 21 tells us. Men cannot interpret Scripture as they want. Scripture is to be interpreted by Scripture itself and by the Holy Spirit who dwells within the believer to teach him the truth. Note what verse 21 says.

a. First, Scripture did not come from the will of man. No prophecy of Scripture arose out of the prophet's own interpretation. God moved upon the prophet's heart and gave him a vision and then the prophet wrote down exactly what the Spirit of God spoke to him. The prophet did not seek to place his own interpretation upon God's Word. Scripture is not of the will or mind of man. It is of God. (See note, *Scripture*—2 Tim.3:16 for more discussion.)

b. Second, Scripture was given by the Holy Spirit. Men were carried along (borne along, moved, impelled) by the Holy Spirit to speak the Word *from God*. (*From God* is the Greek phrase, A.T. Robertson. *Word Pictures In The New Testament*, Vol.6, p.159).

I tell you the truth, until heaven and earth disappear, not the smallest letter, not the least stroke of a pen, will by any means disappear from the Law until everything is accomplished. (Mat 5:18)

For everything that was written in the past was written to teach us, so that through endurance and the encouragement of the Scriptures we might have hope. (Rom 15:4)

All Scripture is God-breathed and is useful for teaching, rebuking, correcting and training in righteousness, (2 Tim 3:16)

For prophecy never had its origin in the will of man, but men spoke from God as they were carried along by the Holy Spirit. (2 Pet 1:21)

I write these things to you who believe in the name of the Son of God so that you may know that you have eternal life. (1 John 5:13)

The point is this: Scripture can be trusted; it is the Word of God. Therefore, Jesus Christ is the Savior of the world. Man can be saved; his needs can be met. We can now have peace and life eternally. Salvation is now available through Jesus Christ our Lord. The proof is twofold: the eyewitnesses of the Lord and the prophetic Scriptures. Both prove beyond any question that Jesus Christ is the Son of God, the Savior and Lord of all men.

DEEPER STUDY # 1
(1:19-21) **Prophecy, Fulfilled—Scripture, Fulfilled**:

OLD TESTAMENT PROPHECIES OF JESUS AND THEIR FULFILLMENT IN THE NEW TESTAMENT

Prophecies		**Fulfillment**
Gen.3:15	The Promised Seed of a Woman	Gal.4:4; Lk.2:7; Rev.12:5
Gen.12:3; 18:18; 22:18	The Promised Seed of Abraham	Acts 3:25; Gal.3:8 (Mt.1:1; Lk.3:34)
Gen.17:19; 22:16-17	The Promised Seed of Isaac	Mt.1:2; Lk.1:55, 72-74
Gen.28:14 (Num.24:17)	The Promised Seed of Jacob	Lk.3:34 (Mt.1:2)
Gen.49:10[a]	Will Spring From The Royal Tribe of Judah	Lk.3:33; Heb.7:14
Dt.18:15, 18	Will Be a Prophet	John 6:14; Acts 3:22-23
2 Sam.7:13[b] (2 Sam.7:13; Is.9:1, 7; 11:1-5)	Will Be the Eternal Heir to David's Throne	Mt.1:1 (Mt.1:6; Lk.1:32-33)
2 Sam.7:14[a]	Will be God's Son	Mk.1:1
Is.35:6; 61:1-2 (cp.Ps.72:2; 146:8; Zech.11:11)	Will Meet the Desperate Needs of Men	Mt.11:4-6
Job 17:3	Will Ransom Men	Eph.1:7 (1 Jn.2:1-2)
Ps.2:1-2	Will Be Rejected By the Nations	Lk.23:36[a], 38
Ps.2:7	The Son of God	Acts 13:33; Heb.1:5; 5:5
Ps.8:2	Is to Be Praised	Mt.21:16
Ps.16:8-11	Will Be Resurrected	Acts 13:34-35; 2:25-28, 31 (Mt.28:1-2; Mk.16:6, 12, 14; Lk.24:1-53)

Ps.22:1	Will be Forsaken by God	Mt.27:46; Mk.15:34
Ps.22:7	People Will Shake Their Heads at the Cross	Mt.27:39
Ps.22:18	Clothes Gambled For	Mt.27:35; Mk.15:24; Lk.23:34; Jn.19:24
Ps.22:22	To Secure Many Brothers	Heb.2:12
Ps.31:5	Commends His Spirit to God	Lk.23:46
Ps.40:6-8	Fulfills God's Will	Heb.10:5-7
Ps.41:9	Is Betrayed by Judas	Jn.13:18; Acts 1:16
Ps.45:6, 7	Is Eternal & Preeminent	Heb.1:8, 9
Ps.68:18	Will Lead Captives in His Train	Eph.4:8-10
Ps.69:21	Offered Drugs on the Cross	Mt.27:48; Mk.15:36; Lk.23:36; Jn.19:28, 29
Ps.69:25; 109:8	Judas' Fate	Acts 1:20
Ps.89:26-27	Exaltation	Ph.2:9 (cp. Rev.11:15)
Ps.95:7-11	Hearts Hardened Against	Heb.3:7-11; 4:3, 5-7
Ps.102:25-27	Is Creator & Eternal	Heb.1:10-12
Ps.110:1	To Be Exalted	Mt.22:44; Mk.12:36; Lk.20:42; Acts 2:34, 35; Heb.1:13
Ps.110:4	The High Priest	Heb.5:6
Ps.118:22, 23	The Stone	Mt.21:42; Mk.12:10; Lk.20:17; Acts 4:11
Ps.118:25, 26	The Triumphal Entry	Mt.21:9; Mk.11:9; Jn.12:13
Ps.132:11, 17	The Son of David	Lk.1:69; Acts 2:30
Is.7:14	The Virgin Birth	Mt.1:23
Is.9:1, 2	A Light to Those in Darkness	Mt.4:15, 16
Is.11:2	The Spirit Rests Upon in a Special Way	Lk.4:18-21 (cp. Mt.12:18; Jn.3:34)
Is.11:10	To Save the Nations	Ro.15:12
Is.25:8	To Conquer Death	1 Cor.15:54
Is.28:16	The Stone	Ro.9:33; 1 Pt.2:6
Is.40:3-5	To Have a Forerunner	Mt.3:3; Mk.1:3; Lk.3:4-6
Is.42:1-4	To Minister to the Nations	Mt.12:17-21
Is.49:6	A Light for the Gentiles	Lk.2:32; Acts 13:47, 48; 26:23
Is.53:1	Would Not Be Believed	Jn.12:38; Ro.10:16
Is.53:3-6	To Die and Arise	Acts 26:22, 23
Is.53:4-6, 11	To Die for Man's Sins	1 Pt.2:24, 25
Is.53:4	To Heal & Bear Man's Sickness	Mt.8:17
Is.53:9	To Be Sinless	1 Pt.2:22
Is.53:12	To Be Counted a Sinner	Mk.15:28; Lk.22:37
Is.54:13	To Teach as God	Jn.6:45
Is.55:3	To Be Raised	Acts 13:34
Is.59:20, 21	To Save Israel	Ro.11:26, 27
Jer.31:31-34	To Make a New Covenant with Man	Heb.8:8-12; 10:16, 17
Hos.1:10-11	To Bring About the Restoration of Israel	Ro.11:1-36
Hos.1:10	The Conversion of the Gentiles	Ro.9:26
Hos.2:23	The Conversion of the Gentiles	Ro.9:25; 1 Pt.2:10
Joel 2:28-32	The Promise of the Spirit	Acts 2:16-21
Amos 9:11, 12	The Lord's Return & David's Kingdom Re-established	Acts 15:16, 17
Mic.5:2	The Birthplace of Messiah	Mt.2:5, 6; Jn.7:42
Hab.1:5	The Jews' Unbelief	Acts 13:40, 41
Hag.2:6	The Return of Christ	Heb.12:26
Zech.9:9	The Triumphal Entry	Mt.21:4, 5; Jn.12:14, 15
Zech.11:13	Judas' Betrayal	Mt.27:9, 10
Zech.12:10	The Spear Pierced in His Side	Jn.19:37
Zech.13:7	The Scattering of the Disciples at the Cross	Mt.26:31, 56; Mk.14:27, 50
Mal.3:1	The Forerunner, John the Baptist	Mt.11:10; Mk.1:2; Lk.7:27
Mal.4:5, 6	The Forerunner, John the Baptist	Mt.11:13, 14; 17:10-13; Mk.9:11-13; Lk.1:16, 17

DEEPER STUDY # 2

(1:19-21) **The Bible—Scripture**: "word of prophecy" is better translated *prophetic word*, referring to the whole prophetic message centered in Jesus Christ. The *prophetic word* did not begin or originate in the mind of man, but in the mind of God. However, God used men as instruments and authors to communicate His message to the world. Over a period of some 1500 years He chose kings, soldiers, peasants, farmers, scholars, priests, statesmen—approximately thirty-five authors from different nations, professions, and social strata. The original manuscripts were written in three different languages—Hebrew, Aramaic, and Greek.

1. The word *Bible* comes from the Greek word *biblos*, meaning *a book*. The Bible is also called "the Scriptures" (1 Cor.15:3-4) and "the Word of God" (Heb.4:12). The Bible is divided into two parts:
   ⇒ The first part, the *Old* Testament, was written before Christ.
   ⇒ The second part, the *New* Testament, was written after Christ came. The word *testament* means a *covenant or an agreement*. Therefore, the Bible is God's covenant, an agreement He has made with man. The Old Testament is His covenant with man before Christ came, and the New Testament is His covenant with man after Christ came.

2. The Old Testament has thirty-nine books which were designated as "the Law, the Prophets, and the Holy Writings or Psalms" (Lk.24:25-27). The books are sometimes divided as follows:
   ⇒ Five Law Books: Genesis, Exodus, Leviticus, Numbers and Deuteronomy. These five are known as the Pentateuch.
   ⇒ Twelve History Books: Joshua, Judges, Ruth, I and II Samuel, I and II Kings, I and II Chronicles, Ezra, Nehemiah, and Esther.
   ⇒ Five Poetic Books: Job, Psalms, Proverbs, Ecclesiastes, and the Song of Solomon.
   ⇒ Twelve Short or Minor Prophetic Books: Hosea, Joel, Amos, Obadiah, Jonah, Micah, Nahum, Habakkuk, Zephaniah, Haggai, Zechariah, and Malachi.
   ⇒ Five Long or Major Prophetic Books: Isaiah, Jeremiah, Lamentations, Ezekiel, and Daniel.

3. The New Testament has twenty-seven books which are sometimes divided as follows:
   ⇒ Four Gospels which cover the life of Christ: Matthew, Mark, Luke, and John.
   ⇒ One History Book which deals with the early believers and early church: Acts.
   ⇒ Fourteen Pauline Letters or Epistles written to specific churches or individual Christians: Romans, I and II Corinthians, Galatians, Ephesians, Philippians, Colossians, I and II Thessalonians, I and II Timothy, Titus, Philemon, and perhaps Hebrews.
   ⇒ Seven General Letters or Epistles written by other men to specific groups, each bearing the author's name: James, I and II Peter, I, II, and III John, Jude.
   ⇒ One Prophetic Book: Revelation.

4. The Bible has one central theme: Jesus Christ. He is the key to understanding what God reveals. He is the focal point of human history. In Him God reveals His purpose and program for the ages (Heb.1:1-2).

5. The unity of the Bible is a miracle of God. Think of the facts: thirty-five different authors from unbelievably diverse backgrounds wrote over a 1500 year period. Think of the number and diversity of subjects, yet look at the harmony of purpose and theme. There is only one explanation. God has spoken and has preserved an authoritative record of His message: "Men spoke from God as they were carried along by the Holy Spirit" (2 Pt.1:21).

6. The Bible claims to be the record of Jesus Christ (Jn.5:39), and it claims to be the written Word of God (2 Pt.1:21). As such it is inseparably linked with the living Word of God, Jesus Christ (Heb.4:12; 1 Pt.1:23). Jesus Christ is the *living Word of God* and the Bible is the *written Word of God*. The written Word testifies to the living Word even as the living Word [Christ Himself] testified to the written Word.

	CHAPTER 2	angels when they sinned, but sent them to hell, putting them into gloomy dungeons to be held for judgment;	angels who sinned
	II. THE WARNING AGAINST FALSE TEACHERS, 2:1-22	5 If he did not spare the ancient world when he brought the flood on its ungodly people, but protected Noah, a preacher of righteousness, and seven others;	b. God did not spare the ancient world, but He did deliver Noah
	A. The Description & Judgment of False Teachers, 2:1-9	6 If he condemned the cities of Sodom and Gomorrah by burning them to ashes, and	c. God destroyed Sodom & Gomorrah, but He did deliver Lot
1 False teachers have always existed	But there were also false prophets among the people, just as there will be false teachers among you. They will secretly introduce destructive heresies, even denying the sovereign Lord who bought them—bringing swift destruction on themselves.	made them an example of what is going to happen to the ungodly; 7 And if he rescued Lot, a righteous man, who was distressed by the filthy lives of lawless men	1) The cities turned to ashes 2) The cities were made an example 3) The reasons: Their immoral lives & the distress they caused for the souls of the righteous
2 False teachers teach destructive heresies			
a. The most tragic heresy: They deny the Lord			
b. The result: Swift destruction			
3 False teachers mislead people	2 Many will follow their shameful ways and will bring the way of truth into disrepute.	8 (For that righteous man, living among them day after day, was tormented in his righteous soul by the lawless deeds he saw and heard)—	
a. They lead them to live immoral lives			
b. They cause slander	3 In their greed these teachers will exploit you with stories they have made up. Their condemnation has long been hanging over them, and their destruction has not been sleeping.	9 If this is so, then the Lord knows how to rescue godly men from trials and to hold the unrighteous for the day of judgment, while continuing their punishment.	d. God knows how to deliver the righteous & to hold the unrighteous until judgment
4 False teachers exploit people			
5 False teachers shall be judged & destroyed			
a. God did not spare the	4 For if God did not spare		

DIVISION II

THE WARNING AGAINST FALSE TEACHERS, 2:1-22

A. The Description and Judgment of False Teachers, 2:1-9

(2:1-9) **Introduction**: if the world ever needed a warning, it needs to be warned against false teachers. Why? Because false teachers lead a person to doom himself quicker than any other single thing. Too many people are too quick to believe a lie. Why? So they can go ahead and live like they want. They want some excuse to get away from the restraints and demands that Jesus Christ puts upon them. Therefore, they grope after any teaching that lowers the Person of Christ. The more He is lowered, the less binding His demands are. But note: there is one major problem with false teaching. It is a lie; it is not the truth. A person dooms himself to an eternal hell if he follows false teaching. This is the critical message of this section of Second Peter: the warning against false teachers. This particular passage describes false teachers for us.

1. False teachers have always existed (v.1).
2. False teachers teach destructive heresies (v.1).
3. False teachers mislead people (v.2).
4. False teachers exploit people (v.3).
5. False teachers shall be judged and destroyed (v.3-9).

1 (2:1) **Teachers, False—Heresy**: false teachers and false prophets have always existed. They have always carried on their destructive work. Note the verse:

> There were also false prophets among the people, just as there will be false teachers among you. (v.1)

When did the false prophets do their destructive work in the world? When did the false prophets move among the people and introduce their destructive heresies? Note the previous verse along with this verse:

> For prophecy never had its origin in the will of man, but men spoke from God as they were carried along by the Holy Spirit. But there were also false prophets among the people, just as there will be false teachers among you. They will secretly introduce destructive heresies, even denying the sovereign Lord who bought them-- bringing swift destruction on themselves. (2 Pet 1:21-2:1)

The false prophets were at work while God was giving His Word to men. Imagine! Even while God was speaking and giving His Word to men there were some who were denying His Word and teaching destructive heresies and misleading people. There were false prophets all throughout the Old Testament period. They were the people who were denying God and His Word. But note: false teachers did not only exist throughout the Old Testament period. Scripture declares plainly: "there will be false teachers among you." The idea is this: there will always be false teachers; false teachers will fill every generation of man and they will continue to introduce their destructive heresies until the world ends.

Thought 1. This means there are false teachers among us. We must, therefore, be alert to what every man and woman teaches. This does not mean that we should be on a witch hunt; it means that we should test all preaching and teaching by the Word of God.

> **"Watch out for false prophets. They come to you in sheep's clothing, but inwardly they are ferocious wolves. (Mat 7:15)**
>
> **They worship me in vain; their teachings are but rules taught by men.'" (Mat 15:9)**
>
> **As I urged you when I went into Macedonia, stay there in Ephesus so that you may command certain men not to teach false doctrines any longer (1 Tim 1:3)**
>
> **The Spirit clearly says that in later times some will abandon the faith and follow deceiving spirits and things taught by demons. Such teachings come through hypocritical liars, whose consciences have been seared as with a hot iron. (1 Tim 4:1-2)**
>
> **For the time will come when men will not put up with sound doctrine. Instead, to suit their own desires, they will gather around them a great number of teachers to say what their itching ears want to hear. They will turn their ears away from the truth and turn aside to myths. (2 Tim 4:3-4)**
>
> **For there are many rebellious people, mere talkers and deceivers, especially those of the circumcision group. (Titus 1:10)**
>
> **Dear friends, do not believe every spirit, but test the spirits to see whether they are from God, because many false prophets have gone out into the world. (1 John 4:1)**

2 **(2:1) Teachers, False—Heresy—Destruction**: false teachers secretly teach destructive heresies. Note: Scripture says that false teachers secretly introduce or bring in destructive heresies. They teach destructive heresies, but they do not do it openly. They do it deceptively, quietly, secretly, slipping in false doctrine here and there.

Note where false teachers teach their destructive heresies. In the church, right among believers. The false teachers are not out in the world, but they are within the church. They have joined the church and they have been outstanding members long enough to become teachers and preachers within the church. They hold leadership positions from which they can teach their destructive heresies. Note that the word "heresies" (haireseis) is plural. What are the heresies being referred to? Any teaching that goes contrary to the Scripture, that is, the Word of God or Bible. This is clearly what is meant, for the exhortation has just been given: "Pay attention to the word of the prophets, to the Scripture" (cp. 2 Pt.1:19-21).

> **And we have the word of the prophets [scripture] made more certain, and you will do well to pay attention to it...For prophecy never had its origin in the will of man, but men spoke from God as they were carried along by the Holy Spirit. (2 Pet 1:19, 21)**

The point is this: any teaching that is contrary to God's Word is a destructive heresy. It destroys God's purpose for the church, and it destroys the lives of people within the church. Teachings that are contrary to God's Word are destructive and there is no escaping the fact. No matter how personable a person may be, no matter how much we may like him, if he is teaching a destructive heresy, he is destroying the church and the lives of people. William Barclay states it well:

> "A heretic [is]...a man who believes what he wishes to believe instead of accepting the truth of God which he must believe.
>
> "What was happening in the case of Peter's people was that certain men, who claimed to be prophets, were insidiously persuading men to believe the things they wished to be true rather than the things which God has revealed as true. They did not set themselves up as opponents of Christianity. Far from it. Rather they set themselves up as the finest fruits of Christian thinking. Insidiously, unconsciously, imperceptible, so gradually and so subtly that they did not even notice it, people were being lured away from God's truth to men's private opinions, for that is what heresy is" (*The Letters of James and Peter*, p.374).

1. The most tragic heresy is the heresy that denies the Lord who bought us. Jesus Christ has bought us, and He has paid the supreme price to buy us. He gave all that He is and all that He has—even His life—in order to buy us out of sin and death. We owe our lives to Him; we owe everything to Him. The picture is that of a servant: we owe Christ our minds and hearts, our duty and service. Therefore, to deny Him is to deny our Lord and Master. And we all know what happens to the servant who denies his Lord and Master: swift destruction. No matter who the servant is, no matter how high a position he holds or how influential he is, if he denies his Master, he brings swift destruction upon himself. What does it mean to deny Christ? It means...

- to deny that Jesus Christ is the Son of God: that He left heaven above and came to earth as Man (the God-Man) to reveal God's great love for man.
- to deny that Jesus Christ is the Savior of the world: that He lived a perfect and sinless life and secured the perfect righteousness for man.
- to deny that Jesus Christ died *for man*: that He took man's sin upon Himself and bore the judgment and condemnation and punishment for man.
- to deny that Jesus Christ arose from the dead and conquered death for man.
- to deny that Jesus Christ is seated at the right hand of God to receive all the worship and glory and honor and praise of the universe.

The list could go on and on to include all that the Scriptures teach about Christ. To deny any teaching of Scripture about Christ is to deny Christ. This is the very point that Peter is making: we must take heed to the Scriptures...

- for the Scriptures have been given by God Himself (2 Pt.1:21), and there are false teachers among us.

Thought 1. Remember: these men are in the church. They are the preachers and teachers who profess Christ and say that they are following Christ and building up His church. But what they are preaching and teaching is a complete denial of Him, and it is destroying the church.

"Not everyone who says to me, 'Lord, Lord,' will enter the kingdom of heaven, but only he who does the will of my Father who is in heaven. (Mat 7:21)

But whoever disowns me before men, I will disown him before my Father in heaven. (Mat 10:33)

If anyone is ashamed of me and my words in this adulterous and sinful generation, the Son of Man will be ashamed of him when he comes in his Father's glory with the holy angels." (Mark 8:38)

If we endure, we will also reign with him. If we disown him, he will also disown us; (2 Tim 2:12)

But there were also false prophets among the people, just as there will be false teachers among you. They will secretly introduce destructive heresies, even denying the sovereign Lord who bought them—bringing swift destruction on themselves. (2 Pet 2:1)

Who is the liar? It is the man who denies that Jesus is the Christ. Such a man is the antichrist—he denies the Father and the Son. (1 John 2:22)

Many deceivers, who do not acknowledge Jesus Christ as coming in the flesh, have gone out into the world. Any such person is the deceiver and the antichrist. (2 John 1:7)

2. False teachers shall be destroyed swiftly. Note that they bring destruction upon themselves. They are responsible for their own actions. They do not have to teach false doctrine; they make the choice to teach it. They could teach the truth [the Holy Scriptures], but they make a deliberate choice to teach contrary to what God has said. Therefore, they shall bring swift destruction upon themselves. The idea of swift is both certain and quick. When the judgment comes, there will be no discussion about the matter—no questioning, no leniency, no mercy, no love. There will be pure justice: swift, immediate judgment and destruction.

⇒ The word "destruction" (apoleian) means to lose one's well being; to be ruined; to be wasted; to perish; to be destroyed; to suffer perdition.

The Son of Man will send out his angels, and they will weed out of his kingdom everything that causes sin and all who do evil. They will throw them into the fiery furnace, where there will be weeping and gnashing of teeth. (Mat 13:41-42)

"You snakes! You brood of vipers! How will you escape being condemned to hell? (Mat 23:33)

He will cut him to pieces and assign him a place with the hypocrites, where there will be weeping and gnashing of teeth. (Mat 24:51)

"Then he will say to those on his left, 'Depart from me, you who are cursed, into the eternal fire prepared for the devil and his angels. (Mat 25:41)

If your hand causes you to sin, cut it off. It is better for you to enter life maimed than with two hands to go into hell, where the fire never goes out. And if your foot causes you to sin, cut it off. It is better for you to enter life crippled than to have two feet and be thrown into hell. And if your eye causes you to sin, pluck it out. It is better for you to enter the kingdom of God with one eye than to have two eyes and be thrown into hell, where "'their worm does not die, and the fire is not quenched.' (Mark 9:43-48)

Whoever believes in the Son has eternal life, but whoever rejects the Son will not see life, for God's wrath remains on him." (John 3:36)

If anyone destroys God's temple, God will destroy him; for God's temple is sacred, and you are that temple. (1 Cor 3:17)

For if the message spoken by angels was binding, and every violation and disobedience received its just punishment, how shall we escape if we ignore such a great salvation? This salvation, which was first announced by the Lord, was confirmed to us by those who heard him. (Heb 2:2-3)

How much more severely do you think a man deserves to be punished who has trampled the Son of God under foot, who has treated as an unholy thing the blood of the covenant that sanctified him, and who has insulted the Spirit of grace? (Heb 10:29)

They [False teachers] are wild waves of the sea, foaming up their shame; wandering stars, for whom blackest darkness has been reserved forever. (Jude 1:13)

3 (2:2) **Teachers, False—Grace, Abuse of—Love**: false teachers mislead many people. False teachers do two terrible things.

1. False teachers encourage people to live immoral and licentious lives. This is what is meant by *shameful ways*. *Shameful* means the ways of immorality and of the flesh (sinful nature). How do false teachers lead men to live worldly and fleshly lives?

a. False teachers say this: Christ is not the Son of God and the Bible is not the Word of God. But note this: if this is so, then there is no Lord over our lives and God has not told us how to live. There is no absolute authority over us, no absolute Word telling us how to live and how to get to God. The only authority that we have is the best thinking we as men can do. This teaching, of course, leads to worldly and fleshly living, for man cannot lead men above what he himself is. And man by nature is worldly and fleshly. If there is no absolute truth, no instructions telling us how to live, then we are free to live pretty much as we want just so we turn to some idea of God—some idea that we have of what He is like—just so we turn to Him every now and then. And if God has not instructed us how to live—clearly instructed us—then He cannot hold us accountable if we mess up here and there. As stated, this kind of teaching lends itself to worldly and fleshly living. And remember: any religion and any philosophy that stresses that man is his own authority can go no higher than man. And man is worldly and fleshly by nature.

b. False teachers take the love of God and twist it. They say that God is so loving that He would never condemn man to an eternity of hell. They say that a man must believe in Christ and follow Him, but if he fails, God still loves him and will forgive him and will never condemn and punish him—certainly not for long if at all.

Of course, the consequence of this teaching is devastating. For if a man is not to be judged and punished for his sin, he can go ahead and live like he wants. He will never be condemned or punished for his sin, not for long if at all.

c. False teachers take the grace of God and faith and pervert them. They say that a person must believe in Jesus Christ. This, of course, is true: we are saved by believing in Jesus Christ; we are saved by grace through faith. But false teachers add that once we believe, we are okay forever and ever even if we do return to the world and live in sin. False teachers say that God accepts us even if we live like the devil and live after the world and flesh—just so we believe in Jesus Christ. False teachers say that faith exists without ever producing fruit: that a person can believe in Jesus Christ...

- without repenting
- without changing his life
- without separating from the world
- without denying and controlling his flesh
- without following Christ

False teachers say that God's love and grace are so inexhaustible that a man is free to sin just so he believes in Jesus Christ. The result of this teaching, of course, is the indulgence and license to sin. A man never has to worry about being rejected by God. He can live like he wants and sin as much as he wants just so he believes in Jesus Christ, for God's grace will forgive him and still make him acceptable.

For such people are not serving our Lord Christ, but their own appetites. By smooth talk and flattery they deceive the minds of naive people. (Rom 16:18)

For such men are false apostles, deceitful workmen, masquerading as apostles of Christ. And no wonder, for Satan himself masquerades as an angel of light. It is not surprising, then, if his servants masquerade as servants of righteousness. Their end will be what their actions deserve. (2 Cor 11:13-15)

While evil men and impostors will go from bad to worse, deceiving and being deceived. (2 Tim 3:13)

Therefore, dear friends, since you already know this, be on your guard so that you may not be carried away by the error of lawless men and fall from your secure position. (2 Pet 3:17)

2. False teachers cause the name of Christ to be abused. They cause people to slander God, Christ, the church, believers, and the Scriptures. The very name of God is blasphemed because of hypocritical living and false profession. How often we hear comments such as "those hypocrites." Note that the blame lies at the feet of the false teachers. It is they who mislead people.

You who brag about the law, do you dishonor God by breaking the law? As it is written: "God's name is blasphemed among the Gentiles because of you." (Rom 2:23-24)

Likewise, teach the older women to be reverent in the way they live, not to be slanderers or addicted to much wine, but to teach what is good. Then they can train the younger women to love their husbands and children, to be self-controlled and pure, to be busy at home, to be kind, and to be subject to their husbands, so that no one will malign the word of God. (Titus 2:3-5)

But because by doing this you have made the enemies of the LORD show utter contempt, the son born to you will die." (2 Sam 12:14)

So I continued, "What you are doing is not right. Shouldn't you walk in the fear of our God to avoid the reproach of our Gentile enemies? (Neh 5:9)

4 (2:3) **Teachers, False**: false teachers exploit people. They use people just like they use merchandise, for their own ends. They are in the church ministering and teaching, but they are covetous, full of greed and lust. What is it that they are coveting?

⇒ popularity	⇒ attention
⇒ recognition	⇒ a following
⇒ a large church	⇒ success
⇒ livelihood	⇒ money
⇒ security	⇒ increased salaries
⇒ position	⇒ gifts
⇒ leadership	⇒ fame

A false teacher is often more interested in being popular and having the people accept him and his idea than he is in ministering to them. He is more concerned with a people following him, thinking he is a good teacher or preacher than he is in ministering to them. False ministers exploit people for their own ends.

Then he said to them, "Watch out! Be on your guard against all kinds of greed; a man's life does not consist in the abundance of his possessions." (Luke 12:15)

Even from your own number men will arise and distort the truth in order to draw away disciples after them. (Acts 20:30)

For such people are not serving our Lord Christ, but their own appetites. By smooth talk and flattery they deceive the minds of naive people. (Rom 16:18)

For there are many rebellious people, mere talkers and deceivers, especially those of the circumcision group. They must be silenced, because they are ruining whole households by teaching things they ought not to teach—and that for the sake of dishonest gain. (Titus 1:10-11)

Israel's watchmen are blind, they all lack knowledge; they are all mute dogs, they cannot bark; they lie around and dream, they love to sleep. They are dogs with mighty appetites; they never have enough. They are shepherds who lack understanding; they all turn to their own way, each seeks his own gain. (Isa 56:10-11)

"Son of man, prophesy against the shepherds of Israel; prophesy and say to them: 'This is what the Sovereign LORD says: Woe to the shepherds of Israel who only take care of themselves! Should not shepherds take care of the flock? You eat the curds, clothe yourselves with the wool and slaughter the choice animals, but you do not take care of the flock. (Ezek 34:2-3)

5 (2:3-9) **Judgment—Teachers, False**: false teachers shall be judged and destroyed. Verse 3 is descriptive language. Upon earth it may seem that false teaching goes on and on forever without ever being corrected or handled by God. But no matter how successful or prosperous a false teacher may seem to be, judgment does not linger; it is not idle. The damnation of false teachers has not fallen asleep. The day is coming when all false teachers will pay for teaching destructive heresies. They will be damned (apoleia), that is, destroyed, because they did not teach the truth of Christ and of God's Word. (See note, pt. 2, *Teachers, False*—2 Pt.2:1 for discussion.)

Now, how do we know that false teachers will be judged and destroyed? Because God is God, which means that He is not only love but He is also *just*. He has the power not only to love people with a perfect love, but He also has the power to judge people with a perfect justice. Note four clear facts.

1. God did not spare the angels who sinned (v.4). He sent them to hell (tartarus). (See DEEPER STUDY # 1, pt.1— 1 Pt.3:19-20 for discussion.) Eons ago in the distant past, Satan was apparently the highest created being ever created by God. At that time his name was Lucifer. But he did what so many people have done: he chose to go his own way; he rebelled against God. And he led a host of angels to rebel with him. Therefore, God judged him and sent him from his exalted position into hell. From what we can glean from Scripture, this is how Satan and the angels fell and became antagonists of God. (See note, *Satan*, pt.2— 1 Pt.5:8 for more discussion.)

The point is this: even angels were sent to hell and chained with darkness. And God is *holding them for eternal judgment*. If God judged such glorious beings as Lucifer and the angels, how much more will He judge men, especially if they teach false doctrine and mislead people? (See DEEPER STUDY # 1, pt.1, 3, 4—1 Pt.3:19-20; note— 1 Pt.5:8-9 for more discussion.)

Through whom also he went and preached to the spirits in prison who disobeyed long ago when God waited patiently in the days of Noah while the ark was being built. In it only a few people, eight in all, were saved through water, (1 Pet 3:19-20) For if God did not spare angels when they sinned, but sent them to hell, putting them into gloomy dungeons to be held for judgment; (2 Pet 2:4) And the angels who did not keep their positions of authority but abandoned their

own home—these he has kept in darkness, bound with everlasting chains for judgment on the great Day. (Jude 1:6)

The woman fled into the desert to a place prepared for her by God, where she might be taken care of for 1,260 days. And there was war in heaven. Michael and his angels fought against the dragon, and the dragon and his angels fought back. But he was not strong enough, and they lost their place in heaven. (Rev 12:6-8)

How you have fallen from heaven, O morning star, son of the dawn! You have been cast down to the earth, you who once laid low the nations! You said in your heart, "I will ascend to heaven; I will raise my throne above the stars of God; I will sit enthroned on the mount of assembly, on the utmost heights of the sacred mountain. I will ascend above the tops of the clouds; I will make myself like the Most High." But you are brought down to the grave, to the depths of the pit. (Isa 14:12-15)

The word of the LORD came to me: "Son of man, take up a lament concerning the king of Tyre and say to him: 'This is what the Sovereign LORD says: "'You were the model of perfection, full of wisdom and perfect in beauty. You were in Eden, the garden of God; every precious stone adorned you: ruby, topaz and emerald, chrysolite, onyx and jasper, sapphire, turquoise and beryl. Your settings and mountings were made of gold; on the day you were created they were prepared. You were anointed as a guardian cherub, for so I ordained you. You were on the holy mount of God; you walked among the fiery stones. You were blameless in your ways from the day you were created till wickedness was found in you. Through your widespread trade you were filled with violence, and you sinned. So I drove you in disgrace from the mount of God, and I expelled you, O guardian cherub, from among the fiery stones. Your heart became proud on account of your beauty, and you corrupted your wisdom because of your splendor. So I threw you to the earth; I made a spectacle of you before kings. By your many sins and dishonest trade you have desecrated your sanctuaries. So I made a fire come out from you, and it consumed you, and I reduced you to ashes on the ground in the sight of all who were watching. All the nations who knew you are appalled at you; you have come to a horrible end and will be no more.'" (Ezek 28:11-19)

2. God did not spare the ancient world (v.5; cp. Gen.6:5f). The world had become totally wicked; wickedness prevailed in every mind, heart, and life.

The LORD saw how great man's wickedness on the earth had become, and that every inclination of the thoughts of his heart was only evil all the time. (Gen 6:5)

He destroyed the whole world of the ungodly by a flood. God had no choice; His righteousness demanded that He judge the world of the ungodly. And this He did. God sent a flood of water to cover the world, and all the ungodly were destroyed. But note: there was one family saved—a preacher and his family. The preacher's name was Noah, and note what he preached: righteousness. He preached the righteousness of God. All the other preachers and priests of that day perished with all the other ungodly. But not Noah; he was saved, and the reason he was saved was because he was faithful to God and His righteousness. He lived and preached the truth of God and His Word.

The point is this: if God judged and destroyed the *whole world of the ungodly people*, He will certainly judge and destroy a false teacher.

3. God destroyed Sodom and Gomorrah (v.6-8; cp. Gen.19:1f). God caused an explosion, a combustion of fire, to fall upon Sodom and Gomorrah. Note the facts of the outline:

a. The cities were turned into ashes (v.6).
b. The cities were made an example to all who live ungodly lives (v.6).
c. The reason for the judgment and destruction was twofold:
⇒ The citizens were living filthy, immoral, and unjust lives.
⇒ The sin and shame of the citizens were disturbing the heart of Lot. There was so much sin and shame that Lot's heart was distressed and tortured to see the law of God violated so much.

Note what happened: everyone in the city was judged and destroyed except one man, Lot. And note why he was saved—because he was righteous. (A study of Lot's life shows a selfish and carnal man; nevertheless, Lot believed God and when the time came, he separated from the ungodly and the world. He obeyed God.)

The point is this: if God judged and destroyed two great cities and all the people in them, He will certainly judge and destroy a false teacher.

4. God knows how to deliver the godly and reserve the unjust until the day of judgment to be punished. This verse completes the sentence begun in verse 4. Note what it is that God delivers the godly from: temptations and trials (peirasmou); all the temptations and trials of life. There is no excuse for a false teacher preaching or teaching false doctrine—no excuse for him to fear other preachers or teachers or other men within his church nor to shy away from the truth—for God knows how to meet the needs of the man. God knows how to deliver the man from every obstacle and through every difficulty, no matter how great a trial or temptation. No matter who opposes the teacher, God knows how to deliver him. He delivered Noah and Lot both through the most trying opposition and ungodliness. But note this: God also knows how to keep the ungodly until the day of judgment and doom. All false teachers shall be judged and doomed to punishment.

> **Do not be afraid of those who kill the body but cannot kill the soul. Rather, be afraid of the One who can destroy both soul and body in hell. (Mat 10:28)**
> **The Son of Man will send out his angels, and they will weed out of his kingdom**
everything that causes sin and all who do evil. They will throw them into the fiery furnace, where there will be weeping and gnashing of teeth. (Mat 13:41-42)

> **But if anyone causes one of these little ones who believe in me to sin, it would be better for him to have a large millstone hung around his neck and to be drowned in the depths of the sea. If your hand or your foot causes you to sin cut it off and throw it away. It is better for you to enter life maimed or crippled than to have two hands or two feet and be thrown into eternal fire. And if your eye causes you to sin, gouge it out and throw it away. It is better for you to enter life with one eye than to have two eyes and be thrown into the fire of hell. (Mat 18:6, 8-9)**

> **"Then he will say to those on his left, 'Depart from me, you who are cursed, into the eternal fire prepared for the devil and his angels. (Mat 25:41)**

> **"Then they will go away to eternal punishment, but the righteous to eternal life." (Mat 25:46)**

> **If anyone is ashamed of me and my words in this adulterous and sinful generation, the Son of Man will be ashamed of him when he comes in his Father's glory with the holy angels." (Mark 8:38)**

> **This is the verdict: Light has come into the world, but men loved darkness instead of light because their deeds were evil. (John 3:19)**

> **And give relief to you who are troubled, and to us as well. This will happen when the Lord Jesus is revealed from heaven in blazing fire with his powerful angels. He will punish those who do not know God and do not obey the gospel of our Lord Jesus. (2 Th 1:7-8)**

> **How much more severely do you think a man deserves to be punished who has trampled the Son of God under foot, who has treated as an unholy thing the blood of the covenant that sanctified him, and who has insulted the Spirit of grace? (Heb 10:29)**

> **By the same word the present heavens and earth are reserved for fire, being kept for the day of judgment and destruction of ungodly men. (2 Pet 3:7)**

> **Enoch, the seventh from Adam, prophesied about these men: "See, the Lord is coming with thousands upon thousands of his holy ones to judge everyone, and to convict all the ungodly of all the ungodly acts they have done in the ungodly way, and of all the harsh words ungodly sinners have spoken against him." (Jude 1:14-15)**

> **If anyone's name was not found written in the book of life, he was thrown into the lake of fire. (Rev 20:15)**

	B. The Character & Conduct of False Teachers, 2:10-22	16 But he was rebuked for his wrongdoing by a donkey—a beast without speech—who spoke with a man's voice and restrained the prophet's madness.	
1 They indulge the flesh 2 They despise authority 3 They are bold and proud 4 They are arrogant 5 They slander spiritual beings	10 This is especially true of those who follow the corrupt desire of the sinful nature and despise authority. Bold and arrogant, these men are not afraid to slander celestial beings;	17 These men are springs without water and mists driven by a storm. Blackest darkness is reserved for them.	11 They are filled with emptiness & instability
	11 Yet even angels, although they are stronger and more powerful, do not bring slanderous accusations against such beings in the presence of the Lord.	18 For they mouth empty, boastful words and, by appealing to the lustful desires of sinful human nature, they entice people who are just escaping from those who live in error.	12 They speak empty, boastful words 13 They set traps baited with lustful desires
	12 But these men blaspheme in matters they do not understand. They are like brute beasts, creatures of instinct, born only to be caught and destroyed, and like beasts they too will perish.	19 They promise them freedom, while they themselves are slaves of depravity—for a man is a slave to whatever has mastered him.	14 They promise freedom, but they only enslave people
6 They carouse around in pleasure & they do it openly, that is, along with the unbelievers of the world	13 They will be paid back with harm for the harm they have done. Their idea of pleasure is to carouse in broad daylight. They are blots and blemishes, reveling in their pleasures while they feast with you.	20 If they have escaped the corruption of the world by knowing our Lord and Savior Jesus Christ and are again entangled in it and overcome, they are worse off at the end than they were at the beginning.	15 The conclusion: A warning to false teachers a. Against returning to the world & its entanglements 1) If one escapes the world's corruption 2) Then turns back 3) One is worse off at the end
7 They have eyes full of adultery 8 They entice unstable souls 9 They are greedy	14 With eyes full of adultery, they never stop sinning; they seduce the unstable; they are experts in greed—an accursed brood!	21 It would have been better for them not to have known the way of righteousness, than to have known it and then to turn their backs on the sacred command that was passed on to them.	b. Against turning from the sacred commandment
10 They have wandered off the right road	15 They have left the straight way and wandered off to follow the way of Balaam son of Beor, who loved the wages of wickedness.	22 Of them the proverbs are true: "A dog returns to its vomit," and, "A sow that is washed goes back to her wallowing in the mud."	c. Against becoming uncouth, repulsive to God

DIVISION II

THE WARNING AGAINST FALSE TEACHERS, 2:1-22

B. The Character and Conduct of False Teachers, 2:10-22

(2:10-22) **Introduction**: this is a graphic picture of false teachers. It shows how horrible God considers false teachers to be, and it serves as a severe warning to every person who would even dare to deny Christ and the teachings of God's Word. No matter who the teacher is—no matter how suave and charismatic, no matter how fluent and great an orator, no matter how creative and sharp a thinker, no matter how well liked and appreciated—if he teaches and denies Christ and God's Word, then he is a false teacher (cp. 2 Pt.2:1).

Here is one of the most horrible pictures painted in all the Bible. It is the picture of the character and conduct of false teachers.

1. They indulge the flesh (v.10).
2. They despise authority (v.10).
3. They are bold and proud (v.10).
4. They are arrogant (v.10).
5. They slander spiritual beings (v.10-12).
6. They carouse around in pleasure and they do it openly, that is, along with the unbelievers of the world (v.13).
7. They have eyes full of adultery (v.14).
8. They entice unstable souls (v.14).
9. They are greedy (v.14).
10. They have wandered off the right road (v.15-16).
11. They are filled with emptiness and instability (v.17).
12. They speak empty, boastful words (v.18).
13. They set traps baited with lustful desires (v.18).
14. They promise freedom, but they only enslave people (v.19).
15. The conclusion: a warning to false teachers (v.20-22).

1 (2:10) **False Teachers—Flesh, The**: false teachers *indulge the flesh*. The flesh itself is not evil. It is what man does with the flesh that is evil. Man is both flesh and spirit. The spirit desires God; and the flesh desires food, security, recognition, love, companionship, and all the other necessities of life. But note: these are normal and natural desires. If we did not have these desires, we could not survive in the world. Again, man is both flesh and spirit. But note what the false teachers do: they follow the corrupt desire of the sinful nature. They ignore the spirit and follow the passions of the flesh. They indulge and gratify the flesh. They teach their false doctrine for personal gain. They desire...

- to live like they want.
- to gain recognition and honor and a following.
- to gain a livelihood and security.
- to gain worldly freedom and do away with godly restraints and demands.

As stated, the flesh desires these things and there is nothing wrong with them: a person needs recognition to feel that he is meaningful and significant. He also needs freedom and a livelihood. But when a person seeks more and more of these, when he takes the desires of the flesh and begins to lust and lust after the desires, they become harmful and sinful.

⇒ One helping of food is good; two helpings are damaging to the body.

⇒ Some recognition is good; too much leads to pride and arrogance or indulgent selfishness.

⇒ Being free to secure the necessities of life is right, but trying to seek them without law leads to sinful transgression and lawlessness. As an example, we have all seen scenes of a community without law, all the looting and evil that runs rampant.

The point is this: false teachers follow the corrupt desire of the sinful nature, not the spirit. They are teaching in order to satisfy the flesh, to please people and to gain recognition, security, or livelihood. They teach a false doctrine in order to do away with the Lordship of Christ, for the Lordship of Christ demands the sacrifice of all one is and has. They want to live like they want, to do their own thing; therefore, they try to do away with the demands of God as much as they can. Again, false teachers follow the corrupt desire of the sinful nature, not the spirit.

> **For, as I have often told you before and now say again even with tears, many live as enemies of the cross of Christ. Their destiny is destruction, their god is their stomach, and their glory is in their shame. Their mind is on earthly things. (Phil 3:18-19)**
>
> **Dear friends, I urge you, as aliens and strangers in the world, to abstain from sinful desires, which war against your soul. (1 Pet 2:11)**
>
> **As a result, he does not live the rest of his earthly life for evil human desires, but rather for the will of God. (1 Pet 4:2)**
>
> **First of all, you must understand that in the last days scoffers will come, scoffing and following their own evil desires. (2 Pet 3:3)**
>
> **They said to you, "In the last times there will be scoffers who will follow their own ungodly desires." (Jude 1:18)**

2 (2:10) **False Teachers—Authority**: false teachers *despise authority*. They stress rights, freedom, and liberty. They stress the right to live like they want, to do their own thing. They want few if any restraints or control over them. What is wrong with this? There is nothing wrong with rights, freedom, and liberty. But law is necessary, especially the law of God. Without God's law to control us,

man becomes selfish and indulgent, and he gives license to his own personal desires. Without God's authority, man grabs for more and more; he takes more and more away from the earth and from the weaker people of the earth. This is a picture of the false teacher and his doctrine. He denies the Lord Jesus Christ. If Jesus Christ is not Lord, then His demand for self-denial and the sacrifice of all one is and has is not valid. The false teacher can pretty much live like he wants.

Thought 1. Despising authority within society is dangerous. What happens is that those in power create human laws that favor themselves, the rich and the powerful. Human law is not enough for man, for man cannot create a law higher than himself. Therefore, whoever is in power will always be influenced by some selfishness. He will seldom if ever give all he is and has to be perfectly just and equal to all. Therefore, God's law is necessary. Man must have a law that is above and beyond himself. Man must have a law that controls and governs all men. And more than this, man must have a living Lord who can give him the power and who can motivate him to live like he should. This is the reason the Lord Jesus Christ, who reveals and fulfills the law of God perfectly, must be proclaimed. He must be exalted and not denied. The only hope for man is to deny himself and give all he is and has to meet the desperate needs of *all the people and not of just a few*.

> **Take care that what the prophets have said does not happen to you: "'Look, you scoffers, wonder and perish, for I am going to do something in your days that you would never believe, even if someone told you.'" (Acts 13:40-41)**
>
> **Or do you show contempt for the riches of his kindness, tolerance and patience, not realizing that God's kindness leads you toward repentance? (Rom 2:4)**
>
> **Anyone who rejected the law of Moses died without mercy on the testimony of two or three witnesses. How much more severely do you think a man deserves to be punished who has trampled the Son of God under foot, who has treated as an unholy thing the blood of the covenant that sanctified him, and who has insulted the Spirit of grace? (Heb 10:28-29)**

3 (2:10) **False Teachers—Presumption**: false teachers *are bold and proud*, that is, arrogant, rash, or daring in a bad sense. A daring spirit can be good; it can be courageous and brave. A person can set out on a daring venture for a good cause that reaps great benefits. But a daring spirit can be bad, very bad. A person can dare to do something that is difficult, but if it is wrong, he should not do it. His daring is nothing more than arrogance.

False teachers are daring and presumptuous. They venture into the theory of some false teaching, feeling courageous because they have the gumption to question God's Word and Christ. But note: this kind of daring is wrong. It is presumptuous. It is arrogance against the truth and against God.

> **Live in harmony with one another. Do not be proud, but be willing to associate**

with people of low position. Do not be conceited. (Rom 12:16)

The man who thinks he knows something does not yet know as he ought to know. (1 Cor 8:2)

As it is, you boast and brag. All such boasting is evil. (James 4:16)

For everything in the world—the cravings of sinful man, the lust of his eyes and the boasting of what he has and does—comes not from the Father but from the world. (1 John 2:16)

Therefore pride is their necklace; they clothe themselves with violence. (Psa 73:6)

When pride comes, then comes disgrace, but with humility comes wisdom. (Prov 11:2)

Pride goes before destruction, a haughty spirit before a fall. (Prov 16:18)

A greedy man stirs up dissension, but he who trusts in the LORD will prosper. (Prov 28:25)

4 (2:10) **False Teachers—Stubborn**: false teachers are *arrogant* in the most stubborn sense possible. They are set on doing what they want, and nothing is going to stop them. They are going to claim the right of free thought and free speech, the right to teach what they want. They are going to get what they are after, and no one is going to change them. The false teacher is going to share his opinion and denial of Christ and the Word of God even if it does hurt and damage others. Note the hardness of heart and obstinacy and stubbornness in this spirit.

For this people's heart has become calloused; they hardly hear with their ears, and they have closed their eyes. Otherwise they might see with their eyes, hear with their ears, understand with their hearts and turn, and I would heal them.' (Acts 28:27)

They are darkened in their understanding and separated from the life of God because of the ignorance that is in them due to the hardening of their hearts. (Eph 4:18)

The Spirit clearly says that in later times some will abandon the faith and follow deceiving spirits and things taught by demons. Such teachings come through hypocritical liars, whose consciences have been seared as with a hot iron. (1 Tim 4:1-2)

But encourage one another daily, as long as it is called Today, so that none of you may be hardened by sin's deceitfulness. (Heb 3:13)

A man who remains stiff-necked after many rebukes will suddenly be destroyed—without remedy. (Prov 29:1)

5 (2:10-12) **False Teachers—Unbelief**: false teachers *slander spiritual beings*. This means speaking against God Himself and doubting and questioning spiritual beings such as angels and the cherubim and seraphim. They ridicule the ideas of Christ and angels and other spiritual beings living in a spiritual world. They question whether there are even beings in a spiritual world, beings who are living and functioning just as we are in this world.

⇒ The idea of another dimension of being, of a spiritual world that is as real and alive as the physical world is questioned.

⇒ The idea of levels of authority in a spiritual world or some other dimension, of principalities and powers and rulers in a spiritual world, is mocked.

⇒ The idea of Christ being exalted to the right hand of God, of believers someday ruling and serving and ministering for Christ in a new heavens and earth, is doubted and often ridiculed.

But note two things.

1. The angels themselves do not dare hurl insults and mock the principalities and powers of the spiritual world. This is a strong warning to the false teachers.

For our struggle is not against flesh and blood, but against the rulers, against the authorities, against the powers of this dark world and against the spiritual forces of evil in the heavenly realms. (Eph 6:12)

For by him all things were created: things in heaven and on earth, visible and invisible, whether thrones or powers or rulers or authorities; all things were created by him and for him. (Col 1:16)

And [Christ] having disarmed the powers and authorities, he made a public spectacle of them, triumphing over them by the cross. (Col 2:15)

2. False teachers are like brute beasts who have no understanding. They are speaking of things they do not understand. No person knows what the spiritual world is like, for no person has ever been there. There is only one Person who has ever been there, and that is the Person who came to earth from the other world, the Lord Jesus Christ. He alone knows what the other world is like. This is the very reason He came to earth: to bring the Word and promise of heaven to us. We either believe Him or not. It is that simple. But note this: the Word of God is the prophecy and record concerning the Lord Jesus Christ. If a person does not believe Christ, then he has no right to claim to be a follower and minister of Christ. He should not abuse the Word of God through hypocrisy. When he does he is as a brute beast, speaking of things he knows nothing about. And note what the Scripture says about him:

⇒ He is as a beast made to be taken and destroyed (v.12).

⇒ He shall utterly perish in his own corruption. That is, in trying to pollute the Word of God and Christ, he destroys lives; therefore, he shall be utterly destroyed. His own corruption shall destroy him.

But if your eyes are bad, your whole body will be full of darkness. If then the light within you is darkness, how great is that darkness! (Mat 6:23)

This is the verdict: Light has come into the world, but men loved darkness instead of light because their deeds were evil. (John 3:19)

For, "Everyone who calls on the name of the Lord will be saved." (Rom 10:13)

The god of this age has blinded the minds of unbelievers, so that they cannot see the light of the gospel of the glory of Christ, who is the image of God. (2 Cor 4:4)

They are darkened in their understanding and separated from the life of God because of the ignorance that is in them due to the hardening of their hearts. (Eph 4:18)

If we claim to have fellowship with him yet walk in the darkness, we lie and do not live by the truth. (1 John 1:6)

"My people are fools; they do not know me. They are senseless children; they have no understanding. They are skilled in doing evil; they know not how to do good." (Jer 4:22)

6 (2:13) **False Teachers—Carousing—Pleasure Seeking**: false teachers *carouse around in pleasure and they do it openly*; that is, they carouse around with the unbelievers of the world. They reject the Lordship of Jesus Christ and the strict demands of God's Word. Therefore, the demand for separation from the world and its pleasures and possessions are rejected. False teachers, therefore, participate and share in the world, in its parties, social affairs, drinking, eating, smoking, and in being merry. They join in with the worldly, indulging the flesh. The ideas of Christian separation and sanctification are rejected by them. They reject the Lordship of Christ and His demand for total separation and self-denial and the sacrifice of all one is and has.

Note: Scripture says that false teachers are deceived. They think that sharing and participating in the world is acceptable. But they are wrong and deceived. They are blots and blemishes on the name of Christ and on the church. They soil and dirty the name *Christian*. They profess to be believers and are even teachers of God's Word, but they are not pure. Their worldliness—their partying, drinking, indulgence, and pleasure—dirties and blemishes the name of Christ.

Therefore, I urge you, brothers, in view of God's mercy, to offer your bodies as living sacrifices, holy and pleasing to God—this is your spiritual act of worship. Do not conform any longer to the pattern of this world, but be transformed by the renewing of your mind. Then you will be able to test and approve what God's will is—his good, pleasing and perfect will. (Rom 12:1-2)

"Therefore come out from them and be separate, says the Lord. Touch no unclean thing, and I will receive you." "I will be a Father to you, and you will be my sons and daughters, says the Lord Almighty." (2 Cor 6:17-18)

Do not love the world or anything in the world. If anyone loves the world, the love of the Father is not in him. For everything in the world—the cravings of sinful man, the lust of his eyes and the boasting of what he has and does—comes not from the Father but from the world. (1 John 2:15-16)

7 (2:14) **False Teachers—Immorality**: false teachers *have eyes full of adultery, that never stop sinning*. The world has always worshipped at the shrine of sex. Even today, in a society that has learned so much about human behavior and health, sex is used to sell everything from cars to soap. The human body is exposed to attract attention and to stir action whether to buy or to boost one's image. The result is loose morals and adultery.

The point is this: false teachers have chosen to deny Christ and the supreme authority of God's Word. Therefore, they feel more free to share in the ways of the world. By sharing in the worldliness of the world, they are attracted to look and think about the opposite sex. Thereby they are more easily aroused and stirred to desire. The result is catastrophic. They fall into immorality, desiring and lusting...

- to read or look at pornographic material
- to look at attractive bodies
- to make suggestive remarks
- to have adulterous affairs

But note: Christ is clear about the lust of the flesh and immorality, the cravings of the sinful nature.

"You shall not commit adultery. (Exo 20:14)

But I tell you that anyone who looks at a woman lustfully has already committed adultery with her in his heart. If your right eye causes you to sin, gouge it out and throw it away. It is better for you to lose one part of your body than for your whole body to be thrown into hell. And if your right hand causes you to sin, cut it off and throw it away. It is better for you to lose one part of your body than for your whole body to go into hell. (Mat 5:28-30)

The acts of the sinful nature are obvious: sexual immorality, impurity and debauchery; and envy; drunkenness, orgies, and the like. I warn you, as I did before, that those who live like this will not inherit the kingdom of God. (Gal 5:19, 21)

It is God's will that you should be sanctified: that you should avoid sexual immorality; that each of you should learn to control his own body in a way that is holy and honorable, not in passionate lust like the heathen, who do not know God; and that in this matter no one should wrong his brother or take advantage of him. The Lord will punish men for all such sins, as we have already told you and warned you. For God did not call us to be impure, but to live a holy life. (1 Th 4:3-7)

8 (2:14) **False Teachers**: false teachers *seduce and entice and lure away unstable souls*. They trap people with their false teaching. They take people who are not grounded in the faith and lure them over to their opinion. They want the recognition or following...

- as a thinker or learned person
- as the creator of a new and creative idea
- as a great teacher or preacher
- as an influential leader

Whatever the reason, false teachers reach out with their opinions. They reach out to seduce the unstable souls to approve and accept their opinion.

> **"Woe to you, teachers of the law and Pharisees, you hypocrites! You shut the kingdom of heaven in men's faces. You yourselves do not enter, nor will you let those enter who are trying to. (Mat 23:13)**
>
> **"And if anyone causes one of these little ones who believe in me to sin, it would be better for him to be thrown into the sea with a large millstone tied around his neck. (Mark 9:42)**
>
> **For such people are not serving our Lord Christ, but their own appetites. By smooth talk and flattery they deceive the minds of naive people. (Rom 16:18)**
>
> **For such men are false apostles, deceitful workmen, masquerading as apostles of Christ. And no wonder, for Satan himself masquerades as an angel of light. It is not surprising, then, if his servants masquerade as servants of righteousness. Their end will be what their actions deserve. (2 Cor 11:13-15)**

9 (2:14) **False Teachers—Greed—Covetousness**: false teachers *are experts in greed*. They are worldly minded, desiring the pleasures and possessions of the world...

- popularity
- attention
- recognition
- a following
- large churches
- success
- money
- raises
- gifts
- livelihood
- security
- position
- leadership
- fame
- possessions

They have coveted and coveted until their hearts are set on their worldly ambitions. They have struggled and struggled against God, conscience, Scripture, and what they know is right. They have focused upon their ambition and it alone, focused so much that their hearts are now trained to focus only upon their ambition. The truth of Christ and of God's Word no longer matter at all. All that matters is whatever the false teacher is after. Therefore, he drives and drives to get across his false doctrine.

Note: false teachers are said to be doomed, "an accursed brood." They are living under the curse of God and shall be destroyed.

> **"You shall not covet your neighbor's house. You shall not covet your neighbor's wife, or his manservant or maidservant, his ox or donkey, or anything that belongs to your neighbor." (Exo 20:17)**
>
> **Then he said to them, "Watch out! Be on your guard against all kinds of greed; a man's life does not consist in the abundance of his possessions." (Luke 12:15)**
>
> **"From the least to the greatest, all are greedy for gain; prophets and priests alike, all practice deceit. (Jer 6:13)**
>
> **"Woe to him who builds his realm by unjust gain to set his nest on high, to escape the clutches of ruin! (Hab 2:9)**

10 (2:15-16) **False Teachers—Backsliding—Balaam**: false teachers *have wandered off the right road*. Jesus Christ is the way to God. He said, "I am the way, the truth, and the life" (Jn.14:6). Therefore, if a person denies Jesus Christ, he has...

- forsaken the way to God
- forsaken the truth of God
- forsaken the life of God

The false teacher has forsaken the right road and wandered off. He has forsaken the road that leads to life and has wandered off, following the road that leads to death. Note that Balaam is used as an example (cp. Num.22:1f). The king of Moab, Balak, began to fear the strength of Israel. Therefore, he sent messengers to a diviner named Balaam to come and put a curse upon Israel. At first Balaam refused to go and discuss the matter with the king. But the king continued to offer more and more position and wealth to Balaam. Finally the offer was so much that Balaam's heart coveted after the world. Therefore, he agreed to go and meet with the king. However, along the way, God gave the power of speech to the donkey that Balaam was riding and God rebuked Balaam through the donkey. Balaam was also the person who was later to turn Israel away from God and lead them into sin (Num.31:16; cp. Num.3:1f).

The point is this: Balaam is an example of a false teacher who became worldly and led God's people into sin and destruction. All false teachers who deny the Lord Jesus Christ...

- become worldly (seeking the possessions, acceptance, and security of the world) and wandered off the right road.
- lead people into sin and destruction.

> **"Enter through the narrow gate. For wide is the gate and broad is the road that leads to destruction, and many enter through it. (Mat 7:13)**
>
> **Join with others in following my example, brothers, and take note of those who live according to the pattern we gave you. For, as I have often told you before and now say again even with tears, many live as enemies of the cross of Christ. Their destiny is destruction, their god is their stomach, and their glory is in their shame. Their mind is on earthly things. (Phil 3:17-19)**
>
> **For you have spent enough time in the past doing what pagans choose to do—living in debauchery, lust, drunkenness, orgies, carousing and detestable idolatry. They think it strange that you do not plunge with them into the same flood of dissipation, and they heap abuse on you. But they will have to give account to him who is ready to judge the living and the dead. (1 Pet 4:3-5)**
>
> **First of all, you must understand that in the last days scoffers will come, scoffing and following their own evil desires. (2 Pet 3:3)**
>
> **They said to you, "In the last times there will be scoffers who will follow their own ungodly desires." (Jude 1:18)**

11 (2:17) **False Teachers—Emptiness—Instability**: false teachers are *filled with emptiness and instability*. Two illustrations are given that describe false teachers.

⇒ They are like springs that offer water to travelers who have been crossing a dry, barren desert. But when the travelers reach the springs, they are dry.

⇒ They are like mists that offer rain to the farmer. But when the mists arrive, they are driven away by the rushing wind of a storm.

The picture is that of the false teacher offering hope to people, but his hope is empty and unstable, just as empty and unstable as the desert of the world itself. The false teacher cannot quench the thirst of people nor water the seed of God's Word in people's hearts. His false teaching is nothing more than the idea of a man; therefore, it ends up where all the ideas of men end—in the grave. The opinion of the false teacher cannot give hope at the end of life's journey nor in facing the trials and temptations of life. In dealing with eternity and God and Christ and Scripture, the false teacher is a spring without water, as mists driven away by the winds of a storm.

Note: the mist or gloom of darkness is forever reserved for false teachers. They are going to remain in darkness forever, both in this life and hereafter, unless they surrender to the Lordship of Jesus Christ.

> **So I tell you this, and insist on it in the Lord, that you must no longer live as the Gentiles do, in the futility [emptiness] of their thinking. (Eph 4:17)**
>
> **In the morning you will say, "If only it were evening!" and in the evening, "If only it were morning!"—because of the terror that will fill your hearts and the sights that your eyes will see. (Deu 28:67)**
>
> **Yet when I surveyed all that my hands had done and what I had toiled to achieve, everything was meaningless, a chasing after the wind; nothing was gained under the sun. (Eccl 2:11)**
>
> **All his days his work is pain and grief; even at night his mind does not rest. This too is meaningless. (Eccl 2:23)**
>
> **Why spend money on what is not bread, and your labor on what does not satisfy? Listen, listen to me, and eat what is good, and your soul will delight in the richest of fare. (Isa 55:2)**
>
> **But the wicked are like the tossing sea, which cannot rest, whose waves cast up mire and mud. (Isa 57:20)**

12 (2:18) **False Teachers**: false teachers *speak empty boastful words*. They use lofty words, excellency of speech, flowery language, and descriptive phrases; but what they say is empty. It is not the truth. It is only their own idea and opinion. As stated above, their false teaching can offer no hope, not in dealing with the trials and temptations of life and not in dealing with death. Their teaching ends up empty and unstable. Their teaching dies with the grave. It cannot carry us across the portals of death into life everlasting. Only Jesus Christ can do that. Therefore, if the teacher's message denies Jesus Christ, there is no hope of heaven, not a true hope.

> **For such people are not serving our Lord Christ, but their own appetites. By smooth talk and flattery they deceive the minds of naive people. (Rom 16:18)**
>
> **What you heard from me, keep as the pattern of sound teaching, with faith and love in Christ Jesus. (2 Tim 1:13)**
>
> **While evil men and impostors will go from bad to worse, deceiving and being deceived. (2 Tim 3:13)**
>
> **For there are many rebellious people, mere talkers and deceivers, especially those of the circumcision group. They must be silenced, because they are ruining whole households by teaching things they ought not to teach—and that for the sake of dishonest gain. (Titus 1:10-11)**
>
> **Would he argue with useless words, with speeches that have no value? (Job 15:3)**
>
> **At the beginning his words are folly; at the end they are wicked madness— (Eccl 10:13)**

13 (2:18) **False Teachers**: false teachers lure people through the lusts of the flesh. They set traps baited with lustful desires. (see note, *False Teachers*—2 Pt.2:2 for discussion). Note who it is that the false teachers entice: the immature believer and the young believer, those who have barely escaped the world. This is a warning to those who are not rooted and grounded in the Lord and in God's Word. Believers must be consistent in studying God's Word and in following Christ. This is the believer's only hope to escape the doom that is to fall upon those who follow false teachers.

14 (2:19) **False Teachers—Sin, Enslaves**: false teachers *promise freedom, but they only enslave* people. Sin always enslaves. No matter what the false teaching is, it will enslave. The false teacher who denies Christ and God's Word removes the supreme authority over man's life. Therefore, man is pretty much free to live in selfishness and greed, desire and lust. He is pretty much left to seek as much pleasure and as many possessions as he desires upon earth. But in the end, man discovers something. The more he gets, the more he wants. It may be comfort, money, sex, position, or authority; it does not matter. Man's nature is such that he wants more and more. Man must be restrained by an authority above himself, that is, by God and by God's Word. If he is not, then he becomes enslaved to his passions and to the corruption of the world. This is one of the terrible fallacies of all false teachings. They all enslave man to this world: not a single false teaching can usher a man through the door of death into eternal life. Only Jesus Christ can do that. Note the clear truth: A man is a slave to whatever has mastered him, that very thing enslaves him.

⇒ If a false teacher overcomes a man, then the man is enslaved to that teaching.

⇒ If the world overcomes a man, then the man is enslaved by the world.

> **Jesus replied, "I tell you the truth, everyone who sins is a slave to sin. (John 8:34)**
>
> **Don't you know that when you offer yourselves to someone to obey him as slaves, you are slaves to the one whom you**

obey—whether you are slaves to sin, which leads to death, or to obedience, which leads to righteousness? (Rom 6:16)

But I see another law at work in the members of my body, waging war against the law of my mind and making me a prisoner of the law of sin at work within my members. (Rom 7:23)

And that they will come to their senses and escape from the trap of the devil, who has taken them captive to do his will. (2 Tim 2:26)

They promise them freedom, while they themselves are slaves of depravity—for a man is a slave to whatever has mastered him. (2 Pet 2:19)

The evil deeds of a wicked man ensnare him; the cords of his sin hold him fast. (Prov 5:22)

15

(2:20-22) **False Teachers—Warning**: this is a strong warning to false teachers, a threefold warning.

1. Warning one: against returning to the world and its entanglements. If a false teacher once knew Christ and has returned to the world, his fate is going to be worse than if he had never begun with Christ. Why? Because he has known the truth and he has chosen to deliberately reject it. And even more, he is teaching against it. He has corrupted the truth of Christ and is leading others into destruction, dooming their very souls.

Thought 1. Teaching is the most responsible profession on earth. Therefore, the greater accountability falls upon the teacher's shoulders. God will have no mercy upon a false teacher; the false teacher will be judged much more severely than a person who never knew the truth.

2. Warning two: against turning from the way of righteousness and from the sacred command.

⇒ The way of righteousness is Jesus Christ. He is the One who has made it possible for God to count us righteous and to accept us (see note, pt.3—2 Pt.1:1 for more discussion).

⇒ The sacred command is the Word of God, that is, all the commandments of God.

It is far better for a person not to have ever known Christ or God's Word than to have known them and to turn back. The judgment shall be far worse, much more severe upon such persons.

3. Warning three: against becoming uncouth, repulsive to God. The illustration given is clear. Imagine being compared to a dog that returns to its vomit and to a washed hog that returns to wallowing around in the foul, smelly mud. The judgment of God will be severe and terrible for all false teachers. (See note, *Destruction*—2 Pt.2:1 for more discussion.)

But I tell you, it will be more bearable for Tyre and Sidon on the day of judgment than for you. (Mat 11:22)

For the Son of Man is going to come in his Father's glory with his angels, and then he will reward each person according to what he has done. (Mat 16:27)

When his parents saw him, they were astonished. His mother said to him, "Son, why have you treated us like this? Your father and I have been anxiously searching for you." (Luke 2:48)

This is the verdict: Light has come into the world, but men loved darkness instead of light because their deeds were evil. (John 3:19)

For we must all appear before the judgment seat of Christ, that each one may receive what is due him for the things done while in the body, whether good or bad. (2 Cor 5:10)

Since you call on a Father who judges each man's work impartially, live your lives as strangers here in reverent fear. (1 Pet 1:17)

And I saw the dead, great and small, standing before the throne, and books were opened. Another book was opened, which is the book of life. The dead were judged according to what they had done as recorded in the books. (Rev 20:12)

"Behold, I am coming soon! My reward is with me, and I will give to everyone according to what he has done. (Rev 22:12)

	CHAPTER 3	derstand that in the last days scoffers will come, scoffing and following their own evil desires.	**in our day & time** 3 **They walk after passion**
	III. THE SECOND COMING OF CHRIST AND THE END OF THE WORLD, 3:1-18	4 They will say, "Where is this 'coming' he promised? Ever since our fathers died, everything goes on as it has since the beginning of creation."	4 **They scoff & ridicule the return of Christ**
	A. The First Thing to Know: Scoffers Shall Come, 3:1-7		
1 **Arouse your minds to be pure, wholesome thinking; so you can remember**	Dear friends, this is now my second letter to you. I have written both of them as reminders to stimulate you to wholesome thinking.	5 But they deliberately forget that long ago by God's word the heavens existed and the earth was formed out of water and by water.	5 **They deliberately forget** a. That God's Word created the world
a. Remember the words of the prophets b. Remember what has been preached	2 I want you to recall the words spoken in the past by the holy prophets and the command given by our Lord and Savior through your apostles.	6 By these waters also the world of that time was deluged and destroyed. 7 By the same word the present heavens and earth are reserved for fire, being kept for the day of judgment and destruction of ungodly men.	b. That God's Word destroyed the world c. That God's Word reserves the world for destruction by fire
2 **They come in the last days,**	3 First of all, you must un-		

DIVISION III

THE COMING AGAIN OF JESUS CHRIST AND THE END OF THE WORLD, 3:1-18

A. The First Thing to Know: Scoffers Shall Come, 3:1-7

(3:1-7) **Introduction**: the coming again of Jesus Christ and the end of the world—this is the subject of this final section of the book of Second Peter. This is a subject that literally fascinates tens of thousands of people. But note: fascination is not what God is after in discussing the return of His Son and the end of the world. What God is after is *preparation*—for man to prepare himself to receive God's Son. Man must be ready for the return of Christ or else he will be doomed. This first passage covers a critical subject: *the first thing to know—scoffers shall come.*

1. Arouse your minds to be pure, wholesome thinking; so you can remember (v.1-2).
2. They come in the last days, in our day and time (v.3).
3. They walk after passion (v.3).
4. They scoff and ridicule the return of Christ (v.4).
5. They deliberately forget (v.5-7).

1 (3:1-2) **Mind—Word of God—Preaching—Teaching**: arouse your pure mind; arouse it so that you can remember. If a person is to know and understand the return of the Lord, his mind has to be aroused. The mind cannot be lazy or wandering about. It has to be watchful, alert, focused, concentrated, and actively engaged upon two things.

First, the mind must remember the words spoken by the prophets. They had much to say about the return of Christ to earth.

Second, the mind must remember the commandments of the Lord that have been preached and taught by the apostles. Jesus Christ taught much about His return. The apostles in turn shared His teachings with their people.

The importance of the mind being aroused cannot be overstressed. Note how Peter drives the point home:

⇒ "Stimulate …wholesome thinking" (v.1)
⇒ "Recall" (v.2)
⇒ "First of all" (v.3)
⇒ "Do not forget this one thing" (v.8)

The phrase "wholesome thinking" (eilikrine dianoian) means to have a clear, pure, unmixed, uncontaminated, focused, and concentrating mind. It is the picture of thoughts being sifted just like wheat is sifted in order to be separated from the chaff. Thoughts are to be sifted in order to separate the true and pure from the untrue and impure. There is always so much false teaching about the end time that the mind must be pure, wholesome in order to sift the true teaching from the false. The picture of a pure, wholesome mind is this: the mind must be exposed to the light of the sun and be found flawless. The mind must be pure and clear from wandering and impure thoughts if it is to study the Word of God and learn its great teachings. The mind must be pure and clear if it is to grasp the great truth of the return of Jesus Christ to earth.

Note one other fact in these first two verses: the unity of Scripture. The prophets of the Old Testament and the words of Jesus Christ and the preaching and teaching of the apostles are all tied together and put on an equal footing—at least by the time the letter of Second Peter was written—They were all considered to be authoritative, to be the Word of God. Note that Paul's writings were also considered to be Scripture by Peter when he was writing this letter (v.15-16). Paul's writings were already considered to be the very Word of God to men.

Thought 1. The stress is upon the mind—a pure, wholesome mind that thinks, a mind that is focused and learning and remembering what it has been taught. But note this: before a person can remember something, he first has to study and learn the facts. This stresses the utter necessity for him to study the Scriptures, to learn all he can about the return of Christ to earth. There is no place in the Christian life for lazy, lethargic, unfocused, and wandering minds. Christ demands total dedication from a person, the total commitment of a person's mind and life to His teaching. This requires intense and diligent study of the Word of God.

This also speaks directly to preachers and teachers. The early apostles studied the prophets and the words of Jesus. They studied the Scripture; therefore they knew all about the return of Christ to earth. Consequently, they were able to offer great hope to their people, the great hope of the second coming of Christ to earth.

2 (3:3) **Last Days—Jesus Christ, Return—Scoffers—World, Judgment of**: know that in the last days scoffers will come." The first coming of Jesus Christ to earth was the pivotal point of human history.

⇒ Jesus Christ came when "the time had fully come" (Gal.4:4).

⇒ Jesus Christ came "in these last times for you" (1 Pt.1:20).

⇒ God has "in these last days he has spoken to us by his Son" (Heb.1:2).

⇒ John the Apostle says, "it is the last time" (1 Jn.2:18).

Since Jesus Christ first came to earth, history is in its last stage. Right now, the time between Christ's first coming and His second coming, is called the age of grace—the age when God's mercy and grace are flowing out to the world through His Son, the Lord Jesus Christ. The thing to remember is that this period of history is called...

• "these last times" (1 Pt.1:20).
• "the last days" (2 Pt.3:3; 2 Tim.3:1).
• "these last days" (Heb.1:2).
• "the last hour" (1 Jn.2:18).
• "the last times" (Jude 18).

Note John's term for the end time: "the last hour" (eschate hora). The Greek really means the last hour, the midnight hour when the world is to end. But note this: the end time does not mean annihilation; it does not mean that everything will cease to exist. As William Barclay describes so well:

> "In biblical thought the last time is the end of one age and the beginning of another. It is not only a time of ending; it is a time of new beginning. It is not only a time of destruction; it is a time of recreation. It is last in the sense that things as they are pass away; but leads not to world obliteration, but world recreation. In other words, the last hour and the last days lead not to extinction, but to consummation" (*The Letters of John and Jude.* "The Daily Study Bible." Philadelphia, PA: The Westminster Press, 1958, p.71).

The final chapter of human history is now being written. Soon Jesus Christ will return to earth and time will be no more. When? Jesus Christ said that no man knows nor can know. Only God knows. And we must always keep in mind what verse eight says, "that a thousand years is as one day" with the Lord. Therefore, we must not be projecting dates. What we must do is obey the Lord's exhortation to watch and be ready. We are to look for His return every day and be prepared for His return any moment. And when He returns, not only will the earth and the heavens be destroyed, but He is going to recreate the whole universe, both the heavens and the earth. The new universe will be the home of all those who have followed Jesus Christ.

Thought 1. This then is the message that we must heed: it is the *last days*. What are we going to do about it? Are we going to attach ourselves to the world and be destroyed with it or attach ourselves to Jesus Christ and enter into the glory of the new world that is soon coming? The choice is ours. We either follow the world that is doomed to destruction or else we follow Jesus Christ and enter the new world promised by Him. The end time, the destruction of the world that is coming, is not a message of gloom; it is the most glorious message of hope—the hope of a new world. There is a new world coming that will be gloriously perfected: no corruption, evil, sin, or death—only glory and splendor, health and life; and it will last forever and ever, world without end.

But note the point: there are scoffers in these last days, people who scoff at the idea of Christ returning to earth and recreating the universe. Three significant facts are said about the scoffers. The next three notes discuss these facts.

> **A group of Epicurean and Stoic philosophers began to dispute with him. Some of them asked, "What is this babbler trying to say?" Others remarked, "He seems to be advocating foreign gods." They said this because Paul was preaching the good news about Jesus and the resurrection. (Acts 17:18)**

> **First of all, you must understand that in the last days scoffers will come, scoffing and following their own evil desires. (2 Pet 3:3)**

> **They said to you, "In the last times there will be scoffers who will follow their own ungodly desires." These are the men who divide you, who follow mere natural instincts and do not have the Spirit. (Jude 1:18-19)**

> **They say, "How can God know? Does the Most High have knowledge?" (Psa 73:11)**

> **To those who say, "Let God hurry, let him hasten his work so we may see it. Let it approach, let the plan of the Holy One of Israel come, so we may know it." (Isa 5:19)**

> **They keep saying to me, "Where is the word of the LORD? Let it now be fulfilled!" (Jer 17:15)**

3 (3:3) **Jesus Christ, Return—Scoffers**: know that scoffers follow their own evil desires. They live like they want and do their own thing. They want the possessions and pleasures of this world.

⇒ They want the right to seek and keep as much as they can of money, houses, lands, furnishings, recognition, popularity, honor, position, authority, power, fame, recreation, comfort.

⇒ They want the right to enjoy all the pleasure they feel safe doing such as partying, drinking, eating, and engaging in suggestive immoralities and sexual relationships.

These are the mockers, people who follow their own evil desires. They have to mock and reject the second coming of Christ. If they accepted it, they would have to change their lives; they would have to repent and turn to Christ or else live under the terrible fear of eternal judgment. They are unwilling to change their lives; therefore, they reject Jesus Christ and His return to earth in judgment.

> **The acts of the sinful nature are obvious: sexual immorality, impurity and debauchery; idolatry and witchcraft; hatred, discord, jealousy, fits of rage, selfish ambition, dissensions, factions and envy; drunkenness, orgies, and the like. I warn you, as I did before, that those who live like this will not inherit the kingdom of God. (Gal 5:19-21)**
>
> **All of us also lived among them at one time, gratifying the cravings of our sinful nature and following its desires and thoughts. Like the rest, we were by nature objects of wrath. (Eph 2:3)**
>
> **Put to death, therefore, whatever belongs to your earthly nature: sexual immorality, impurity, lust, evil desires and greed, which is idolatry. Because of these, the wrath of God is coming. (Col 3:5-6)**
>
> **That each of you should learn to control his own body in a way that is holy and honorable, not in passionate lust like the heathen, who do not know God; (1 Th 4:4-5)**
>
> **What causes fights and quarrels among you? Don't they come from your desires that battle within you? You want something but don't get it. You kill and covet, but you cannot have what you want. You quarrel and fight. You do not have, because you do not ask God. (James 4:1-2)**
>
> **For everything in the world—the cravings of sinful man, the lust of his eyes and the boasting of what he has and does—comes not from the Father but from the world. (1 John 2:16)**

4 (3:4) **Jesus Christ, Return—Scoffers**: know that scoffers ridicule the return of Jesus Christ. They scoff for two reasons.

1. They scoff because it has been thousands of years since Jesus Christ came to earth the first time. They scoffingly ask:

> "Where is the promise of Christ's return? What has happened to His promise? It has been thousands of years since He first came, and Christians have always been proclaiming that He was coming soon. Even today you are declaring that He is coming soon, declaring that His coming is just around the corner, declaring that everyone must expect His return today. What has happened? Where is He? If He was coming back to earth, He would have surely returned by now."

Some mockers even argue this:

> "There is so much suffering and evil in the world, Christ would have certainly returned by now if He was going to. He would have returned and brought the peace and abundance of life that Christians proclaim."

Note: the first argument of the scoffers is based upon the teaching that the second coming is false. They feel that Christ would have returned long ago if the teaching were true. The fact that He has not yet returned proves that the teaching of the second coming is false. Christ is not return-

ing to earth. A person can, therefore, forget the doctrine and go ahead and live like he wishes.

> **For as lightning that comes from the east is visible even in the west, so will be the coming of the Son of Man. "No one knows about that day or hour, not even the angels in heaven, nor the Son, but only the Father. (Mat 24:27, 36)**
>
> **At that time they will see the Son of Man coming in a cloud with power and great glory. (Luke 21:27)**
>
> **"Men of Galilee," they said, "why do you stand here looking into the sky? This same Jesus, who has been taken from you into heaven, will come back in the same way you have seen him go into heaven." (Acts 1:11)**
>
> **So Christ was sacrificed once to take away the sins of many people; and he will appear a second time, not to bear sin, but to bring salvation to those who are waiting for him. (Heb 9:28)**

2. They scoff because the world continues on just as it always has. They argue:

> "There has never been a change in the way the world operates; there has not been a change since creation itself, not a convulsive event that would shake the world like the return of Jesus Christ to earth in a worldwide judgment."

Note: this second argument is based upon the stability of the universe and its laws, upon the fact that the laws of nature run the world and keep it stable and functioning. The laws of nature have kept the universe running on and on without any major convulsive event. Therefore they argue:

> "Why then should people get excited and become concerned about the world ending? The laws of nature run the universe, not an imaginary God. Nothing has ever changed the world; the world has been going on for millions of years. In fact, it has been continuing on for thousands of years since Christ came. Why then get concerned about a change now? The laws of nature will continue to run the universe and keep it stable."

> **And I'll say to myself, "You have plenty of good things laid up for many years. Take life easy; eat, drink and be merry."' (Luke 12:19)**
>
> **So, if you think you are standing firm, be careful that you don't fall! (1 Cor 10:12)**
>
> **"Now then, listen, you wanton creature, lounging in your security and saying to yourself, 'I am, and there is none besides me. I will never be a widow or suffer the loss of children.' (Isa 47:8)**
>
> **They have lied about the LORD; they said, "He will do nothing! No harm will come to us; we will never see sword or famine. (Jer 5:12)**
>
> **The pride of your heart has deceived you, you who live in the clefts of the rocks and make your home on the heights, you**

who say to yourself, 'Who can bring me down to the ground?' (Oba 1:3)

Like clouds and wind without rain is a man who boasts of gifts he does not give. (Prov 25:14)

Do you see a man wise in his own eyes? There is more hope for a fool than for him. (Prov 26:12)

Do not boast about tomorrow, for you do not know what a day may bring forth. (Prov 27:1)

5 (3:5-7) **Jesus Christ, Return**: the scoffers are ignorant of three facts, and note, Scripture says that they *deliberately forget*. They choose to ignore, to be unreasonable, and to reject the fact that God is the Creator and Sustainer of the world. Note these facts.

1. Scripture declares that the world is not self-creating and self-sufficient (v.5). It was not made by the laws of nature and it does not run and operate itself by the laws of nature. The heavens and earth were created by *the Word of God*. It was God, His speaking the world into existence, who created the universe and the laws of nature. The heavens and earth were created by God simply speaking and bringing them into being. God is God, the Supreme Intelligence and Power; therefore, God can simply will and speak, and His Word creates whatever He wills.

The point is this: mockers willingly choose to ignore and reject God, to deny God's absolute intelligence and power. Therefore, they deliberately forget that God created the world and that He sustains it by the mere power of His Word. The world and its laws are existing today only because God keeps them existing today. The only reason Jesus Christ has not yet returned to earth is because it is not yet God's time. God is not yet ready for Christ to return. When God's day arrives, God will simply speak the Word and Christ will return. The final chapter of human history will then be closed.

In the beginning God created the heavens and the earth. (Gen 1:1)

You alone are the LORD. You made the heavens, even the highest heavens, and all their starry host, the earth and all that is on it, the seas and all that is in them. You give life to everything, and the multitudes of heaven worship you. (Neh 9:6)

He spreads out the northern skies over empty space; he suspends the earth over nothing. (Job 26:7)

In the beginning you laid the foundations of the earth, and the heavens are the work of your hands. (Psa 102:25)

"Men, why are you doing this? We too are only men, human like you. We are bringing you good news, telling you to turn from these worthless things to the living God, who made heaven and earth and sea and everything in them. (Acts 14:15)

By faith we understand that the universe was formed at God's command, so that what is seen was not made out of what was visible. (Heb 11:3)

2. Scripture declares that the world has not always continued on as it presently does (v.6). The idea that world-wide convulsive events do not happen is totally false. The earth has perished before; God spoke the Word and judged

the world. His Word destroyed the world with a flood and all life was destroyed except Noah and his family and two of every creature. God did not let people go on and on in their sin forever. God judged and punished sinners. The world is a moral universe. God created it to be moral, and He expects man to live righteous and godly lives while here on earth. If they refuse, then He speaks His Word and judges the earth.

Again, note that the mockers deliberately forget the facts about a flood that destroyed all of life. The bones and the imprint of the bones of sea life can be found all over the dry land of the earth, yet men continue to reject the evidence of a cataclysmic flood that destroyed life upon earth. They ignore and reject that this is a moral universe that is answerable to a loving and just God. They reject Him because they want to control their own lives and live as they wish (v.3).

The point is this: the world was destroyed by God's Word once; it can therefore be destroyed by God's Word again. One cataclysmic destruction took place; therefore, another catastrophic destruction can occur. In fact, the only reason the world has not yet been destroyed is that it is not yet God's time. But Scripture is clear; God has spoken: Jesus Christ is going to return to the world and the world is going to be judged and destroyed again.

"No one knows about that day or hour, not even the angels in heaven, nor the Son, but only the Father. As it was in the days of Noah, so it will be at the coming of the Son of Man. For in the days before the flood, people were eating and drinking, marrying and giving in marriage, up to the day Noah entered the ark; and they knew nothing about what would happen until the flood came and took them all away. That is how it will be at the coming of the Son of Man. (Mat 24:36-39)

Who disobeyed long ago when God waited patiently in the days of Noah while the ark was being built. In it only a few people, eight in all, were saved through water, (1 Pet 3:20)

If he did not spare the ancient world when he brought the flood on its ungodly people, but protected Noah, a preacher of righteousness, and seven others; (2 Pet 2:5)

The LORD saw how great man's wickedness on the earth had become, and that every inclination of the thoughts of his heart was only evil all the time. The LORD was grieved that he had made man on the earth, and his heart was filled with pain. So the LORD said, "I will wipe mankind, whom I have created, from the face of the earth—men and animals, and creatures that move along the ground, and birds of the air—for I am grieved that I have made them." (Gen 6:5-7)

I am going to bring floodwaters on the earth to destroy all life under the heavens, every creature that has the breath of life in it. Everything on earth will perish. (Gen 6:17)

In the six hundredth year of Noah's life, on the seventeenth day of the second month—on that day all the springs of the great deep burst forth, and the floodgates of the heavens were opened. (Gen 7:11)

Will you keep to the old path that evil men have trod? They were carried off before their time, their foundations washed away by a flood. They said to God, 'Leave us alone! What can the Almighty do to us?' (Job 22:15-17)

"To me this is like the days of Noah, when I swore that the waters of Noah would never again cover the earth. So now I have sworn not to be angry with you, never to rebuke you again. (Isa 54:9)

3. Scripture declares that the heavens and earth are being kept, reserved, and stored up for destruction by fire (v.7). How? By God's Word. God is controlling the heavens and the earth. They have not yet been destroyed because God has not yet spoken the Word. But note: he is keeping, reserving, and storing up the world for destruction by fire. Why? Because of ungodly men. As stated, this is a moral universe and God expects men to live moral and pure lives. The day of judgment and destruction is coming because men have chosen to live ungodly lives. It is this that men and mockers have chosen to ignore and reject: they are accountable to a loving, holy, and just God. It is this that they refuse to study and know and submit to. Therefore, they continue on in their selfish and hoarding and unjust and immoral ways. And they continue to scoff at the coming again of the Lord Jesus Christ to judge the earth.

"When the Son of Man comes in his glory, and all the angels with him, he will sit on his throne in heavenly glory. All the nations will be gathered before him, and he will separate the people one from another as a shepherd separates the sheep from the goats. (Mat 25:31-32)

Just as man is destined to die once, and after that to face judgment, (Heb 9:27)

If this is so, then the Lord knows how to rescue godly men from trials and to hold the unrighteous for the day of judgment, while continuing their punishment. (2 Pet 2:9)

By the same word the present heavens and earth are reserved for fire, being kept for the day of judgment and destruction of ungodly men. (2 Pet 3:7)

Enoch, the seventh from Adam, prophesied about these men: "See, the Lord is coming with thousands upon thousands of his holy ones to judge everyone, and to convict all the ungodly of all the ungodly acts they have done in the ungodly way, and of all the harsh words ungodly sinners have spoken against him." (Jude 1:14-15)

For your hands are stained with blood, your fingers with guilt. Your lips have spoken lies, and your tongue mutters wicked things. (Isa 59:3)

Make every effort to live in peace with all men and to be holy; without holiness no one will see the Lord. See to it that no one misses the grace of God and that no bitter root grows up to cause trouble and defile many. (Heb 12:14-15)

177

	B. The One Thing Not to Forget: Why Christ Has Not Yet Returned, 3:8-10	understand slowness. He is patient with you, not wanting anyone to perish, but everyone to come to repentance.	earth, but patient, cp. v.15 a. He wants none to perish b. He wants all to repent[DS1]
1 The Lord does not measure time the same as man	8 But do not forget this one thing, dear friends: With the Lord a day is like a thousand years, and a thousand years are like a day.	10 But the day of the Lord will come like a thief. The heavens will disappear with a roar; the elements will be destroyed by fire, and the earth and everything in it will be laid	3 The Day of the Lord is coming, v.10 a. As a thief—unexpected b. The heavens will pass away with a roar c. The elements will melt with intense heat he earth will burn up
2 The Lord is not slow in sending Christ back to	9 The Lord is not slow in keeping his promise, as some	bare.	e. All things shall be dissolved

DIVISION III

THE COMING AGAIN OF JESUS CHRIST AND THE END OF THE WORLD, 3:1-18

B. The One Thing Not to Forget: Why Christ Has Not Yet Returned, 3:8-10

(3:8-10) **Introduction**: Jesus Christ is coming back to earth. This is the declaration of Scripture time and again.

> "Yes, it is as you say," Jesus replied. "But I say to all of you: In the future you will see the Son of Man sitting at the right hand of the Mighty One and coming on the clouds of heaven." (Mat 26:64)
>
> At that time they will see the Son of Man coming in a cloud with power and great glory. (Luke 21:27)
>
> "Men of Galilee," they said, "why do you stand here looking into the sky? This same Jesus, who has been taken from you into heaven, will come back in the same way you have seen him go into heaven." (Acts 1:11)
>
> So Christ was sacrificed once to take away the sins of many people; and he will appear a second time, not to bear sin, but to bring salvation to those who are waiting for him. (Heb 9:28)
>
> For the Son of Man is going to come in his Father's glory with his angels, and then he will reward each person according to what he has done. (Mat 16:27)
>
> "When the Son of Man comes in his glory, and all the angels with him, he will sit on his throne in heavenly glory. All the nations will be gathered before him, and he will separate the people one from another as a shepherd separates the sheep from the goats. (Mat 25:31-32)
>
> Therefore judge nothing before the appointed time; wait till the Lord comes. He will bring to light what is hidden in darkness and will expose the motives of men's hearts. At that time each will receive his praise from God. (1 Cor 4:5)
>
> In the presence of God and of Christ Jesus, who will judge the living and the dead, and in view of his appearing and his kingdom, I give you this charge: (2 Tim 4:1)
>
> Enoch, the seventh from Adam, prophesied about these men: "See, the Lord is coming with thousands upon thousands of his holy ones to judge everyone, and to convict all the ungodly of all the ungodly acts they have done in the ungodly way, and of all the harsh words ungodly sinners have spoken against him." (Jude 1:14-15)

Every generation of believers has proclaimed that Jesus Christ is *coming soon*. Even believers today proclaim that He is returning and that His return is just over the horizon. But it has been two thousand years since these promises were made. Does this mean then that the teaching of His return is false, that Jesus Christ is not going to return to earth? Have Christians been wrong in declaring that Jesus Christ was to return soon? How can thousands of years be said to be soon? There are those who ask questions like this and there are even those who use these questions to mock the return of Christ. The mockers of the second coming of Christ were the discussion of the former passage (see outline and notes—2 Pt.3:1-7 for discussion). But what are the answers to these questions? Why has Christ not yet returned? This is the one thing we must not be ignorant about: *why Christ has not yet returned to earth.*

1. The Lord does not measure time the same as man (v.8).
2. The Lord is not slow in sending Christ back to earth, but patient (v.9).
3. The Day of the Lord is coming (v.10).

1 (3:8) **Time—Jesus Christ, Return**: Why has Christ not yet returned to earth? First, because God does not measure time the same as man. There are two differences between the time of God and the time of man.

1. There is the *span of time*. To God, a thousand years are *like a day*. God is eternal. Think of thousands of years heaped upon thousands of years. Multiply ten thousand years times ten thousand and then multiply that by thousands of years again and keep on multiplying, never quitting. That is eternity. What then is one thousand years? Time is relative; it has no span to God. But this is not so to man. Man measures time by days and years, and he walks minute by minute throughout the day, all 365 days of the year. Therefore, time stretches on and on to him. But to God, who is eternal, it takes one thousand years to make a day. Therefore, to ask why Jesus Christ has not yet returned after two thousand years is ridiculous. To God it has only been about two days since Christ died and arose. Two thousand years may seem like a long time to man, but not to God. To God two days is only a drop in a bucket.

The point is this: believers must not be discouraged because Christ has not yet returned. God may want a lot more to take place on earth before He sends Christ back to earth. Our task is not to question when He is returning, but to watch and be ready in case He returns before we depart this life and go to Him.

2. There is the *intensity of time*. Note that one day with God is *like a thousand years*. Picture one day on the earth and consider...

- all the trials and temptations
- all the suffering and pain
- all the accidents and diseases
- all the sin and evil
- all the cursing and blasphemy against God
- all the selfishness and hoarding while millions are in desperate need
- all the people dying and being sent to hell

God feels every ounce of all the events. He loves us; therefore He feels it all. He suffers along with us, and the intensity of His feeling is absolute. God is absolute and perfect; therefore He feels in an absolute and perfect sense. He suffers with us with such intensity that we could never even imagine the experience. This is what is meant by the statement "with the Lord a day is like a thousand years." The feelings of one day are so intense that it feels like a thousand years. Whereas we bear only the sufferings of our own personal experience, God bears the sufferings of all the experiences of *all people*. Therefore, to God the experience during just one day of an evil earth is like a thousand years to Him.

This point is significant: it is a warning to man. God will not bear evil forever. He will not suffer the rejection and rebellion of men too long. He will speak the Word and send Christ back to judge the world. Scripture definitely teaches that we are living in the last days.

> **But mark this: There will be terrible times in the last days. People will be lovers of themselves, lovers of money, boastful, proud, abusive, disobedient to their parents, ungrateful, unholy, without love, unforgiving, slanderous, without self-control, brutal, not lovers of the good, treacherous, rash, conceited, lovers of pleasure rather than lovers of God— having a form of godliness but denying its power. Have nothing to do with them. (2 Tim 3:1-5)**
>
> **But in these last days he has spoken to us by his Son, whom he appointed heir of all things, and through whom he made the universe. (Heb 1:2)**
>
> **For you know that it was not with perishable things such as silver or gold that you were redeemed from the empty way of life handed down to you from your forefathers, but with the precious blood of Christ, a lamb without blemish or defect. He was chosen before the creation of the world, but was revealed in these last times for your sake. (1 Pet 1:18-20)**
>
> **First of all, you must understand that in the last days scoffers will come, scoffing and following their own evil desires. (2 Pet 3:3)**
>
> **Dear children, this is the last hour; and as you have heard that the antichrist is coming, even now many antichrists have come. This is how we know it is the last hour. (1 John 2:18)**
>
> **But, dear friends, remember what the apostles of our Lord Jesus Christ foretold.**

> **They said to you, "In the last times there will be scoffers who will follow their own ungodly desires." (Jude 1:17-18)**

2 (3:9) **Salvation—Longsuffering**: Why has Christ not yet returned to earth? Because God loves man; He does not want any person to perish, not a single person. God is not slack in fulfilling His promise nor is He powerless to return and judge the earth. He has not returned for one reason and one reason only. He wants more and more people to come to repentance. Note two significant points.

1. God is patient (makrothumei). The word means...

- that God is patient with us.
- that God bears and suffers a long time with us.
- that God perseveres and is constant in suffering with us.
- that God is steadfast and enduring in being patient with us.

Very simply, God is slow to give in and to judge and condemn us. God loves and cares for us despite our sin and rebellion, cursing and rejection. This is the very reason He sent Christ to save us. He loves and cares for us; therefore, He is suffering a long time with us.

> **In the past God overlooked such ignorance, but now he commands all people everywhere to repent. For he has set a day when he will judge the world with justice by the man he has appointed. He has given proof of this to all men by raising him from the dead." (Acts 17:30-31)**
>
> **Or do you show contempt for the riches of his kindness, tolerance and patience, not realizing that God's kindness leads you toward repentance? (Rom 2:4)**
>
> **God presented him as a sacrifice of atonement, through faith in his blood. He did this to demonstrate his justice, because in his forbearance he had left the sins committed beforehand unpunished— (Rom 3:25)**
>
> **But concerning Israel he says, "All day long I have held out my hands to a disobedient and obstinate people." (Rom 10:21)**

2. God wants no person to perish. To perish is a terrible thing. It means to be utterly lost and destroyed. It means to lose eternal life and to be cut off from life forever and ever. It means to be spiritually destitute, completely empty of all good. It means to suffer the judgment, condemnation, and punishment of separation from God forever and ever. It means to perish; to be in a state of suffering forever and ever apart from God.

The point is this: God does not want us perishing; He does not want us cut off and separated from Him. God wants us to spend eternity with Him not apart from Him.

> **"For God so loved the world that he gave his one and only Son, that whoever believes in him shall not perish but have eternal life. (John 3:16)**
>
> **But God demonstrates his own love for us in this: While we were still sinners, Christ died for us. (Rom 5:8)**
>
> **But because of his great love for us, God, who is rich in mercy, made us alive with Christ even when we were dead in transgressions—it is by grace you have been saved. (Eph 2:4-5)**

How great is the love the Father has lavished on us, that we should be called children of God! And that is what we are! The reason the world does not know us is that it did not know him. (1 John 3:1)

3. God wants everyone to come to repentance (see DEEPER STUDY # 1—2 Pt.3:9 for discussion).

DEEPER STUDY # 1

(3:9) **Repent—Repentance**: to change; to turn; to change one's mind; to turn one's life. It is a turning away from sin and turning to God. It is a change of mind, a forsaking of sin. It is putting sin out of one's thoughts and behavior. It is resolving never to think or do a thing again. (Cp. Mt.3:2; Lk.13:2-3; Acts 2:38; 3:19; 8:22; 26:20.) The change is turning away from lying, stealing, cheating, immorality, cursing, drunkenness, and the other so-called glaring *sins of the flesh (the sinful nature)*. But the change is also turning away from *the silent sins of the spirit* such as self-centeredness, selfishness, envy, bitterness, pride, greed, anger, evil thoughts, hopelessness, laziness, jealousy, and lust.

1. Repentance involves two turns. There is a negative turn away from sin and a positive turn toward God. It is a turning to God away from sin, whether sins of thought or action. (See note, *Repentance*—Lk.3:3. Cp. 1 Th.1:9; Acts 14:15.)

2. Repentance is more than sorrow. Sorrow may or may not be involved in repentance. A person may repent simply because he wills and acts to change; or a person may repent because he senses an agonizing sorrow within. But the sense or feeling of sorrow is not repentance. Repentance is both the change of mind and the actual turning of one's life away from sin and toward God. (See DEEPER STUDY # 1—2 Cor.7:10.)

And saying, "Repent, for the kingdom of heaven is near." (Mat 3:2)

I tell you, no! But unless you repent, you too will all perish. (Luke 13:3)

Peter replied, "Repent and be baptized, every one of you, in the name of Jesus Christ for the forgiveness of your sins. And you will receive the gift of the Holy Spirit. (Acts 2:38)

Repent, then, and turn to God, so that your sins may be wiped out, that times of refreshing may come from the Lord, (Acts 3:19)

Repent of this wickedness and pray to the Lord. Perhaps he will forgive you for having such a thought in your heart. (Acts 8:22)

In the past God overlooked such ignorance, but now he commands all people everywhere to repent. (Acts 17:30)

---

3 (3:10) **Day of the Lord—Jesus Christ, Return**: Why has Christ not yet returned to earth? The glorious fact is that He shall return. The Day of the Lord is coming. He is going to bring about the glorious day of redemption, giving all believers the wonderful privilege of living with Him forever and ever.

1. The day of the Lord will come like a thief. Note a significant fact: a man never knows when a thief is going to hit his house. No thief tells a man ahead of time that he is going to strike his house. If a man knew, he would watch and prepare. This is just the point: the Lord Jesus Christ has told us that He is coming back to earth. He has forewarned us, but He has not told us when. Why?

⇒ Not knowing when Jesus is returning keeps us focused upon Him and His return. It keeps us looking and longing for Him. It keeps us watching, and it stirs us to live pure and holy lives.

⇒ Not knowing when Jesus is returning serves as a warning to unbelievers. It warns them that they must repent now, today, for He could return today and catch them unprepared.

The day of the Lord is coming, but it is coming like a thief. His return is going to be totally unexpected by most people. The believer must...

• not be careless: get tired of waiting up, get sleepy, be caught off guard, begin to disbelieve. (All of this can happen to a house owner waiting on a burglar.)

• watch: sit up, stay awake, listen, look, take notice of all noises and sights (signs). (The burglar always comes in an unexpected hour.)

"Therefore keep watch because you do not know when the owner of the house will come back—whether in the evening, or at midnight, or when the rooster crows, or at dawn. (Mark 13:35)

For as lightning that comes from the east is visible even in the west, so will be the coming of the Son of Man. (Mat 24:27)

"No one knows about that day or hour, not even the angels in heaven, nor the Son, but only the Father. (Mat 24:36)

So you also must be ready, because the Son of Man will come at an hour when you do not expect him. (Mat 24:44)

"But while they were on their way to buy the oil, the bridegroom arrived. The virgins who were ready went in with him to the wedding banquet. And the door was shut. "Later the others also came. 'Sir! Sir!' they said. 'Open the door for us!' "But he replied, 'I tell you the truth, I don't know you.' "Therefore keep watch, because you do not know the day or the hour. (Mat 25:10-13, cp. v. 6-9)

For you know very well that the day of the Lord will come like a thief in the night. (1 Th 5:2)

Remember, therefore, what you have received and heard; obey it, and repent. But if you do not wake up, I will come like a thief, and you will not know at what time I will come to you. (Rev 3:3)

"Behold, I come like a thief! Blessed is he who stays awake and keeps his clothes with him, so that he may not go naked and be shamefully exposed." (Rev 16:15)

2. The heavens and universe shall pass away: all "the elements will be destroyed by fire, and the earth and everything in it." Based upon what we know about the universe today—the basic elements such as the atom—nothing really needs to be said about how the universe is going to be destroyed. It is rather a matter of belief in God, that God is God, the Supreme Intelligence and Force of the universe. If a person believes in God, then he knows that God can destroy the universe. How? By doing what He did when He created

the world and when He destroyed the earth the first time (cp. v.5-6), that is, by simply speaking the Word, by simply commanding a universal atomic explosion to take place.

Man himself has enough intelligence to burst the atom and to cause a chain reaction that would be so devastating that it would destroy the earth and melt the elements of the earth with fervent heat. Man himself can cause an atomic explosion so severe that every element of the earth would melt with fervent heat. Why then doubt God?

All God has to do is speak the Word and all the atoms throughout the universe will burn up in a chain reaction. There would be an atomic explosion that would destroy the whole universe.

The point is this: "the day of the Lord *will come.*" There is no question about it.

⇒ Just as God spoke the Word and created the world...

⇒ just as God spoke the Word and destroyed the earth in Noah's day...

⇒ so God is going to speak the Word and the day of the Lord will come.

> **"The heavens will disappear with a roar, the elements will be destroyed by fire, and the earth and everything in it will be laid bare" (v.10).**

Now note: Why is God going to destroy both heaven and earth? There is one glorious reason and verse thirteen tells us: so that He can create a new heavens and earth where righteousness dwells. God wants a perfect world in which there will be nothing but righteousness. Note: verse ten says that the earth and "everything in it will be laid bare." By "everything" is meant all the works of man's hands:

⇒ buildings	⇒ services
⇒ offices	⇒ evil works
⇒ houses	⇒ businesses
⇒ religion	⇒ murder
⇒ governments	⇒ wars

Everything that man has ever done, all of his corruptible works, shall be burned up and destroyed by the fire of God's judgment. The whole universe will be destroyed by fire; a fiery explosion will take place and the fire will be so hot that every element will melt from the fervent heat. But note: it is all so that God's eternal purpose for the universe can be fulfilled. God is going to create a new heavens and earth in which only righteousness will exist. The righteous, those who have trusted the Lord Jesus Christ for righteousness, shall be the citizens of the new heavens and earth. The new heavens and earth will be the home where God's people will live and serve Him for all of eternity.

Thought 1. What man must do is watch and prepare. He must repent, turn to God, and turn away from his sin and the coming destruction. Scripture is clear, and it is stated as clearly as it can be.

> I tell you the truth, until heaven and earth disappear, not the smallest letter, not the least stroke of a pen, will by any means disappear from the Law until everything is accomplished. (Mat 5:18)
>
> Heaven and earth will pass away, but my words will never pass away. (Mat 24:35)
>
> Now, brothers, about times and dates we do not need to write to you, for you know very well that the day of the Lord will come like a thief in the night. While people are saying, "Peace and safety," destruction will come on them suddenly, as labor pains on a pregnant woman, and they will not escape. (1 Th 5:1-3)
>
> But the day of the Lord will come like a thief. The heavens will disappear with a roar; the elements will be destroyed by fire, and the earth and everything in it will be laid bare. Since everything will be destroyed in this way, what kind of people ought you to be? You ought to live holy and godly lives as you look forward to the day of God and speed its coming. That day will bring about the destruction of the heavens by fire, and the elements will melt in the heat. But in keeping with his promise we are looking forward to a new heaven and a new earth, the home of righteousness. (2 Pet 3:10-13)
>
> And the angels who did not keep their positions of authority but abandoned their own home—these he has kept in darkness, bound with everlasting chains for judgment on the great Day. (Jude 1:6)
>
> Enoch, the seventh from Adam, prophesied about these men: "See, the Lord is coming with thousands upon thousands of his holy ones to judge everyone, and to convict all the ungodly of all the ungodly acts they have done in the ungodly way, and of all the harsh words ungodly sinners have spoken against him." (Jude 1:14-15)
>
> For the great day of their wrath has come, and who can stand?" (Rev 6:17)
>
> Then I saw a new heaven and a new earth, for the first heaven and the first earth had passed away, and there was no longer any sea. (Rev 21:1)
>
> "Behold, I will create new heavens and a new earth. The former things will not be remembered, nor will they come to mind. (Isa 65:17)
>
> "As the new heavens and the new earth that I make will endure before me," declares the LORD, "so will your name and descendants endure. (Isa 66:22)
>
> In the beginning you laid the foundations of the earth, and the heavens are the work of your hands. They will perish, but you remain; they will all wear out like a garment. Like clothing you will change them and they will be discarded. But you remain the same, and your years will never end. (Psa 102:25-27)
>
> All the stars of the heavens will be dissolved and the sky rolled up like a scroll; all the starry host will fall like withered leaves from the vine, like shriveled figs from the fig tree. (Isa 34:4)
>
> Lift up your eyes to the heavens, look at the earth beneath; the heavens will vanish like smoke, the earth will wear out like a garment and its inhabitants die like flies. But my salvation will last forever, my righteousness will never fail. (Isa 51:6)

		C. The Things Believers Must Do Since Jesus Christ is Coming Again (Part I), 3:11-14	about the destruction of the heavens by fire, and the elements will melt in the heat. 13 But in keeping with his promise we are looking forward to a new heaven and a new earth, the home of righteousness.	3	Believers must look for the new heavens & new earth
1	Believers must live holy & godly lives	11 Since everything will be destroyed in this way, what kind of people ought you to be? You ought to live holy and godly lives			
2	Believers must look for & speed up the Day of God	12 As you look forward to the day of God and speed its coming. That day will bring	14 So then, dear friends, since you are looking forward to this, make every effort to be found spotless, blameless and at peace with him.	4	Believers must be prepared for the coming of Christ a. Must be spotless b. Must be blameless c. Must be found in peace

DIVISION III

THE COMING AGAIN OF JESUS CHRIST AND THE END OF THE WORLD, 3:1-18

C. The Things Believers Must Do Since Jesus Christ is Coming Again (Part I), 3:11-14

(3:11-14) **Introduction**: Jesus Christ is coming to earth again. Therefore, there are some things that believers must do, and they are of critical importance.

1. Believers must live holy and godly lives (v.11).
2. Believers must look for and speed up the day of God (v.12).
3. Believers must look for the new heavens and new earth (v.13).
4. Believers must be prepared for the coming of Christ (v.14).

1 (3:11) **Jesus Christ, Return—Holiness—Godliness—World, Judgment of**: believers must live holy and godly lives. In fact, note the Scripture: *all of our behavior* must be holy and godly. There is to be no area of our lives—no part, no act—that is not holy and godly. Why? Why such a stress upon holiness and godliness? One strong reason is given.

The heavens and earth are to be dissolved because of the sin and evil of man. It is the sin and evil of man that has made the world so corrupt—corrupt beyond repair. God will be forced to destroy the world because of our sin and evil. The sin and evil of man has put the world under a curse of destruction. Sin and evil are therefore terrible things, abominable things! They should be hated and despised by every man, woman, and child. All sin and evil should be despised because of the terrible things they do and have done. They have caused a curse of corruption and utter destruction upon the earth. For this reason, we should hate sin and evil and love holiness and godliness. We should be holy and godly in all of our behavior.

1. *Holy* means that our behavior is sanctified, that is, set apart unto God; separated from the world and given over to God; given over to live pure and righteous lives (see DEEPER STUDY # 1, *Holy*—1 Pt.1:15-16).

> I am the LORD who brought you up out of Egypt to be your God; therefore be holy, because I am holy. (Lev 11:45)
> To rescue us from the hand of our enemies, and to enable us to serve him without fear in holiness and righteousness before him all our days. (Luke 1:74-75)
> Since we have these promises, dear friends, let us purify ourselves from everything that contaminates body and spirit,

perfecting holiness out of reverence for God. (2 Cor 7:1)
> Make every effort to live in peace with all men and to be holy; without holiness no one will see the Lord. (Heb 12:14)
> For it is written: "Be holy, because I am holy." (1 Pet 1:16)
> Since everything will be destroyed in this way, what kind of people ought you to be? You ought to live holy and godly lives (2 Pet 3:11)
> Exalt the LORD our God and worship at his holy mountain, for the LORD our God is holy. (Psa 99:9)
> And they were calling to one another: "Holy, holy, holy is the LORD Almighty; the whole earth is full of his glory." (Isa 6:3)
> Who will not fear you, O Lord, and bring glory to your name? For you alone are holy. All nations will come and worship before you, for your righteous acts have been revealed." (Rev 15:4)

2. *Godly* means that we live like God and seek to be a godly person; that we live and do all things in the reverence and awe of God; that we are so conscious of God's presence that we live like God would live if He were walking upon earth (see note, *Godliness*—2 Pt.1:3).

Thought 1. Note: godly means to be *Christlike*. Godliness is *Christlikeness*: it is living upon earth just as Christ lived.

> And we, who with unveiled faces all reflect the Lord's glory, are being transformed into his likeness with ever-increasing glory, which comes from the Lord, who is the Spirit. (2 Cor 3:18)
> It teaches us to say "No" to ungodliness and worldly passions, and to live self-controlled, upright and godly lives in this present age, while we wait for the blessed hope—the glorious appearing of our great God and Savior, Jesus Christ, (Titus 2:12-13)
> Since everything will be destroyed in this way, what kind of people ought you to be? You ought to live holy and godly lives (2 Pet 3:11)

2 (3:12) **Jesus Christ, Return—World, Judgment of; Destruction of**: believers must look for and seek to bring the day of God about. The day of God refers to the day when God shall dissolve and destroy the heavens and earth, the day when the universe shall be "set aflame by fire and the elements will melt in the heat" (v.12; see note— 2 Pt.3:10 for discussion). What is to be the attitude of the believer toward the *day of God*?

1. The believer is to "look forward" (prosdokontas) the day of God. The word means to wait; to wait patiently but expectantly; to eagerly anticipate and long for the day of God; to be in expectation (W.E. Vine. *Expository Dictionary of New Testament Words*).

2. The believer is to *speed the coming of* the day of God. The term "speed its coming" (speudontas) can mean two things.

a. *To speed its coming* can mean to hurry after; to earnestly desire; to rush toward. The believer is to live a holy and godly life looking for and hastening toward the day of God. Keeping his eyes upon that terrible day of judgment is to *arouse him* to live a holy and godly life. Every day that he lives upon earth is to be a day in which he hastens toward the judgment of God; he should never take his eyes off the terrible day of God that is coming. If he takes his eyes off that day, if he fails to direct his life toward the day of God, then he will most likely slip into unholiness and ungodliness. He must, therefore, stay focused upon the day of God, the day of the terrible judgment to come upon the heavens and earth.

b. *To speed its coming* can also mean to *speed up* the day of God; to rush the coming of Christ; to cause the day of God to come sooner. The believer has a part in bringing about the eternal kingdom of God; he has a part in bringing about the return of Christ and the great day of God. How? God is "patient...not wanting anyone to perish" (v.9). This is the reason He is delaying the return of Christ. Apparently, God has a certain number of believers that He has ordained to be brothers and sisters of His dear Son; apparently there are to be a certain number of believers to rule and manage the new heavens and earth for Christ. In His eternal knowledge God certainly knows the number who will be saved and serving His dear Son. Whatever the number and whatever the case, that number has to be reached before Christ can come and before the great day of God can destroy the universe and make a new heavens and earth. This much is known for sure:

⇒ God does have a certain number of believers in mind. Being God, He has purposed that His Son have many brothers who will reign with Him and who will worship and serve God through all eternity (cp. Ro.8:28-29 where God will allow nothing to stop Him from giving Christ "many brothers.")

⇒ This Scripture tells us that we are to *speed its coming*, to help bring about the day of God.

Thought 1. How can we help the day of God to come? How can we quicken the return of Christ and the end of the world? By living more holy and godly lives so that more people will more readily be attracted to Christ. The more they see *Christ in us*, His presence and power carrying us through the trials and temptations of life, the more they are going to want

Christ and His power in their lives. The more holy and godly we live the more people will see the things for which they long...

- strength to conquer the trials and temptations of life
- hope in the future
- assurance and confidence of living forever
- conviction, purpose, meaning, and significance in life
- love, joy, and peace

When people see these things, the things for which they long, they will be attracted to Christ much quicker. The result will be more souls for Christ. They will be won much quicker and the number that God has in mind will be reached much sooner. Therefore, the way we are to *speed up* the day of God is to live more dynamic lives for Christ. We must live more holy and godly lives for Christ, and we must witness more diligently than ever before. We must begin to tell everyone that the Messiah, the Savior of the world, has come—that He has come to save us from the sin and death of the world and to give us a life of love, joy, peace, and power—the power to live abundantly both now and forever.

> **And I have the same hope in God as these men, that there will be a resurrection of both the righteous and the wicked. (Acts 24:15)**
>
> **The faith and love that spring from the hope that is stored up for you in heaven and that you have already heard about in the word of truth, the gospel that has come to you. All over the world this gospel is bearing fruit and growing, just as it has been doing among you since the day you heard it and understood God's grace in all its truth. (Col 1:5-6)**
>
> **It teaches us to say "No" to ungodliness and worldly passions, and to live self-controlled, upright and godly lives in this present age, while we wait for the blessed hope—the glorious appearing of our great God and Savior, Jesus Christ, (Titus 2:12-13)**
>
> **Praise be to the God and Father of our Lord Jesus Christ! In his great mercy he has given us new birth into a living hope through the resurrection of Jesus Christ from the dead, (1 Pet 1:3)**
>
> **But in your hearts set apart Christ as Lord. Always be prepared to give an answer to everyone who asks you to give the reason for the hope that you have. But do this with gentleness and respect, (1 Pet 3:15)**
>
> **If this is so, then the Lord knows how to rescue godly men from trials and to hold the unrighteous for the day of judgment, while continuing their punishment. (2 Pet 2:9)**
>
> **How great is the love the Father has lavished on us, that we should be called children of God! And that is what we are! The reason the world does not know us is that it did not know him. Dear friends, now we are children of God, and what we will be has not yet been made known. But we know that when he appears, we shall be like him, for we shall see him as he is. Everyone who has this hope in him purifies himself, just as he is pure. (1 John 3:1-3)**

3 (3:13) **Jesus Christ, Return—New Heavens and Earth**: believers must look for a new heavens and earth. Scripture clearly says that God is going to create a new heavens and a new earth. No matter what men may think and say about the issue, God declares as simply and as clearly as human language can describe that He is going to make a *new heavens and a new earth*. Why? So that the world will be perfect and nothing but righteousness will exist therein. God has *ordained* a perfect world, a world in which only righteous people will live. God wants a world where there will be no more sin and evil, no more accidents, disease, suffering, murder, drunkenness, drugs, adultery, sexual perversion, war, or death. God wants a people who know only the fullness of love, joy, and peace, a people who worship and serve Him forever and ever. (See note, pt.2—2 Pt.3:10 for more discussion.) The old but great *Pulpit Commentary* says:

> "St. John, like St. Peter, speaks of a new earth, and tells us that that new earth will be the dwelling place of the blessed [believer]. He saw the holy city, new Jerusalem, coming down from God out of heaven; the throne of God and of the Lamb (he tells us shall be in it). 'The tabernacle of God is with men, and he will dwell with them.' The holy city, Jerusalem, which is above, is in heaven now....But heaven will come down to earth; the throne of God and of the Lamb shall be there [upon earth]; there his servants shall serve him" (*The Pulpit Commentary*, Vol.22, p.69f).

The great Biblical commentator Matthew Henry says:

> "In these new heavens and earth...only righteousness shall dwell; this is to be the habitation of such righteous persons as do righteousness, and are free from the power and pollution of sin...those only who are clothed with the righteousness of Christ, and sanctified by the Holy Ghost, shall be admitted to dwell in this holy place" (*Matthew Henry's Commentary*, Vol.6, p.1057.)

I consider that our present sufferings are not worth comparing with the glory that will be revealed in us. The creation waits in eager expectation for the sons of God to be revealed. For the creation was subjected to frustration, not by its own choice, but by the will of the one who subjected it, in hope that the creation itself will be liberated from its bondage to decay and brought into the glorious freedom of the children of God. We know that the whole creation has been groaning as in the pains of childbirth right up to the present time. (Rom 8:18-22)

For he was looking forward to the city with foundations, whose architect and builder is God. (Heb 11:10)

All these people were still living by faith when they died. They did not receive the things promised; they only saw them and welcomed them from a distance. And they admitted that they were aliens and strangers on earth. People who say such things show that they are looking for a country of their own. If they had been thinking of the country they had left, they would have had opportunity to return. Instead, they were longing for a better country—a heavenly one. Therefore God is not ashamed to be called their God, for he has prepared a city for them. (Heb 11:13-16)

But in keeping with his promise we are looking forward to a new heaven and a new earth, the home of righteousness. (2 Pet 3:13)

Then I saw a new heaven and a new earth, for the first heaven and the first earth had passed away, and there was no longer any sea. I saw the Holy City, the new Jerusalem, coming down out of heaven from God, prepared as a bride beautifully dressed for her husband. And I heard a loud voice from the throne saying, "Now the dwelling of God is with men, and he will live with them. They will be his people, and God himself will be with them and be their God. He will wipe every tear from their eyes. There will be no more death or mourning or crying or pain, for the old order of things has passed away." He who was seated on the throne said, "I am making everything new!" Then he said, "Write this down, for these words are trustworthy and true." (Rev 21:1-5)

"Behold, I will create new heavens and a new earth. The former things will not be remembered, nor will they come to mind. (Isa 65:17)

"As the new heavens and the new earth that I make will endure before me," declares the LORD, "so will your name and descendants endure. (Isa 66:22)

4 (3:14) **Jesus Christ, Return—Believer, Life and Walk—Blameless**: believers must make every effort and be prepared for the coming of Christ. The word "effort" (spoudasate) means to be eager; to strive earnestly; to be zealous in seeking after. The believer is to be diligent, that is, eager, earnest and zealous in preparing himself for the return of the Lord. Why? So that the Lord will find him prepared. Note that three preparations are necessary.

1. The believer must be *found spotless*. This means to be clean, pure, and unsoiled; to have no dirt, pollution, or contamination of sin whatsoever. The believer is to be confessing his sins always, all day long. He is to be walking in constant communion and fellowship with Christ, walking in open confession, confessing all the sin and contamination that he picks up from the world. Just being in the world means that some of the pollution of sin catches the eye and ears of the believer and causes unclean thoughts to cross his mind. The believer must walk in open confession, praying always for the power of Christ's blood to cleanse him and to keep him pure. This is the only way a believer can ever be found spotless by Christ when He returns.

If we confess our sins, he is faithful and just and will forgive us our sins and purify us from all unrighteousness. (1 John 1:9)

"Therefore, my brothers, I want you to know that through Jesus the forgiveness of sins is proclaimed to you. (Acts 13:38)

In him we have redemption through his blood, the forgiveness of sins, in accordance with the riches of God's grace (Eph 1:7)

Let the wicked forsake his way and the evil man his thoughts. Let him turn to the LORD, and he will have mercy on him, and to our God, for he will freely pardon. (Isa 55:7)

2. The believer must be found *"blameless"* (amometoi). The word means free from fault and censure; to be faultless; above reproach and rebuke. The believer is to live a blameless, faultless, and pure life, both in the church and in the world. No one is to be able to point to the Christian and accuse or blame him with anything. The Christian is to be clean, unpolluted, spotless, holy, righteous, and pure before man and God.

Everyone has heard about your obedience, so I am full of joy over you; but I want you to be wise about what is good, and innocent about what is evil. (Rom 16:19)

So that you may be able to discern what is best and may be pure and blameless until the day of Christ, (Phil 1:10)

So that you may become blameless and pure, children of God without fault in a crooked and depraved generation, in which you shine like stars in the universe (Phil 2:15)

The Lord will rescue me from every evil attack and will bring me safely to his heavenly kingdom. To him be glory for ever and ever. Amen. (2 Tim 4:18)

Such a high priest meets our need—one who is holy, blameless, pure, set apart from sinners, exalted above the heavens. (Heb 7:26)

So then, dear friends, since you are looking forward to this, make every effort to be found spotless, blameless and at peace with him. (2 Pet 3:14)

To him who is able to keep you from falling and to present you before his glorious presence without fault and with great joy— (Jude 1:24)

3. The believer must be found in *peace*. He must be at peace with *both God and man*. He must not be living in rebellion against God nor be divided against his brothers and sisters. He must not be…
- living like he wants instead of how God says
- doing his own thing
- disobeying God
- living in sin
- cheating, lying, or stealing

- being selfish and hateful
- gossiping and criticizing
- grumbling and backbiting
- stirring up trouble within the church
- neglecting and ignoring God

The believer must be at peace with God and with men. He must be living just like God says to live, and he must be living as one with his brothers and sisters. When Christ comes, no believer dare be found criticizing and being divided from a brother or sister. And no believer dare be found at odds with Christ and not living for Christ. Such sinful behavior will be severely judged.

Therefore, since we have been justified through faith, we have peace with God through our Lord Jesus Christ, (Rom 5:1)

I appeal to you, brothers, in the name of our Lord Jesus Christ, that all of you agree with one another so that there may be no divisions among you and that you may be perfectly united in mind and thought. (1 Cor 1:10)

Finally, brothers, good-by. Aim for perfection, listen to my appeal, be of one mind, live in peace. And the God of love and peace will be with you. (2 Cor 13:11)

For he himself is our peace, who has made the two one and has destroyed the barrier, the dividing wall of hostility, (Eph 2:14)

Make every effort to keep the unity of the Spirit through the bond of peace. (Eph 4:3)

Whatever happens, conduct yourselves in a manner worthy of the gospel of Christ. Then, whether I come and see you or only hear about you in my absence, I will know that you stand firm in one spirit, contending as one man for the faith of the gospel (Phil 1:27)

And through him to reconcile to himself all things, whether things on earth or things in heaven, by making peace through his blood, shed on the cross. (Col 1:20)

Let the peace of Christ rule in your hearts, since as members of one body you were called to peace. And be thankful. (Col 3:15)

Finally, all of you, live in harmony with one another; be sympathetic, love as brothers, be compassionate and humble. (1 Pet 3:8)

"Submit to God and be at peace with him; in this way prosperity will come to you. (Job 22:21)

Turn from evil and do good; seek peace and pursue it. (Psa 34:14)

	D. The Things Believers Must Do Since Jesus Christ is Coming Again (Part II), 3:15-18	which ignorant and unstable people distort, as they do the other Scriptures, to their own destruction.	
1 Believers must count the Lord's patience as salvation a. God is working to save more & more people b. Paul confirms the same point c. Some twist the Scriptures to their own destruction	15 Bear in mind that our Lord's patience means salvation, just as our dear brother Paul also wrote you with the wisdom that God gave him. 16 He writes the same way in all his letters, speaking in them of these matters. His letters contain some things that are hard to understand,	17 Therefore, dear friends, since you already know this, be on your guard so that you may not be carried away by the error of lawless men and fall from your secure position. 18 But grow in the grace and knowledge of our Lord and Savior Jesus Christ. To him be glory both now and forever! Amen.	**2 Believers must beware lest they be led into error** **3 Believers must grow in the grace & knowledge of our Lord**

DIVISION III

THE COMING AGAIN OF JESUS CHRIST AND THE END OF THE WORLD, 3:1-18

D. The Things Believers Must Do Since Jesus Christ is Coming Again (Part II), 3:15-18

(3:15-18) **Introduction**: this passage concludes the second letter of Peter. The emphasis of this concluding exhortation is striking. Jesus Christ is coming again, but His coming has been delayed. Believers are still on earth waiting for Him to come. What then are we to be doing? There are some critical things we should be doing. What are they? (Note: this is a continuation of the former passage and subject, 2 Pt.3:11-14.)

1. Believers must count the Lord's patience as salvation (v.15-16).
2. Believers must beware lest they be led into error (v.17).
3. Believers must grow in the grace and knowledge of our Lord (v.18).

1 (3:15-16) **God, Patience—Longsuffering—Salvation—Paul**: believers must count the patience, the longsuffering of the Lord as salvation.

1. Remember: scoffers ridicule the coming again of Jesus Christ. They say such is foolishness. They say that the world is operated and run by the natural laws of nature; they say that if God existed and cared about the world, He would have come long ago and saved the world from all the evil, corruption, murder, and war that rages on and on (v.3-4). Remember what Scripture says, why it is that Jesus Christ has not yet come: because God is patient, longsuffering and does not want any person to perish. He wants all to repent and to be saved (v.9). Now note: this is what the present verse is referring to. We are to count the patience, the longsuffering of God as salvation. The Lord Jesus has not yet returned to earth for one reason and one reason only: that more and more people might be saved, that more and more might be snatched out of the claws of death and judgment. This is the reason the Lord delays His return. His delay...

- is not because He has forgotten the earth.
- is not because He is angry with man because man has not paid more attention to His Word and teaching.
- is not because He does not care and love man enough to deliver him out of the evil, corruption, and suffering of the world.

The Lord cares and loves man so much that He wants all men to be saved. He longs for *all men* to repent and turn to Him. He shrinks from the thought of returning because He knows that when He returns every single unbeliever is doomed forever and ever. Therefore, He waits one more day; He waits longing for a few more to be saved; He waits because He knows that all unbelievers will be doomed to judgment and destruction.

The point is this: the believer must count the patience of the Lord as salvation, as His concern for souls. We must never look upon the Lord's delay as unconcern or lack of care for His people and for the world. God loves all people, every single person on earth; therefore, He is longsuffering with the sin and evil of men. He is suffering a long time with man and his cursing and rebellion and rejection. But the day will come when God cannot bear sin and evil any longer. When that day comes, He will return and all the unbelievers and ungodly of this world will fall into the hands of an angry God, a God who is just and holy and righteous—just as much so as He was loving and patient and caring.

2. Note a significant fact: Peter says that Paul wrote the same thing in his writings. That is, Paul taught that God delayed the coming of Christ so that more and more people could be saved.

> **Or do you show contempt for the riches of his kindness, tolerance and patience, not realizing that God's kindness leads you toward repentance? (Rom 2:4)**
>
> **And are justified freely by his grace through the redemption that came by Christ Jesus. God presented him as a sacrifice of atonement, through faith in his blood. He did this to demonstrate his justice, because in his forbearance he had left the sins committed beforehand unpunished— (Rom 3:24-25)**
>
> **What if God, choosing to show his wrath and make his power known, bore with great patience the objects of his wrath—prepared for destruction? What if**

he did this to make the riches of his glory known to the objects of his mercy, whom he prepared in advance for glory— (Rom 9:22-23)

For if God did not spare the natural branches, he will not spare you either. Consider therefore the kindness and sternness of God: sternness to those who fell, but kindness to you, provided that you continue in his kindness. Otherwise, you also will be cut off. (Rom 11:21-22)

3. Note that some people twist the Scripture to their viewpoint. The point is this: believers are not to take the delay of Christ and assume that it is going to be years and years before He ever comes and before we have to face judgment. We must keep our eyes on His return, watch, prepare, and be ready at all times. If we are not watching, then we are being lazy and complacent and are much more likely to fall into sin and worldliness. And if this happens, we will be caught unprepared and be spotted and dirtied with sin and stand blamable before Him (cp. v.14).

The Lord is not delaying His return so that we can enjoy this world and its pleasures and possessions more. This earth is to be dissolved, utterly destroyed, and melted down. The Lord is delaying His return because He is patient, wanting more and more people to be saved. Our task is to be more evangelistic; to live more spotless and blameless lives so that we can reach more and more people for Christ. The delay of Christ should not cause us to become lethargic and complacent and worldly; it should stir us to be more diligent in the mission of Christ. If we twist the Scripture, allowing the patience of God to stir the thought that we have a little more time to wait, then we are destroying ourselves.

Jesus replied, "You are in error because you do not know the Scriptures or the power of God. (Mat 22:29)

Unlike so many, we do not peddle the word of God for profit. On the contrary, in Christ we speak before God with sincerity, like men sent from God. (2 Cor 2:17)

Rather, we have renounced secret and shameful ways; we do not use deception, nor do we distort the word of God. On the contrary, by setting forth the truth plainly we commend ourselves to every man's conscience in the sight of God. (2 Cor 4:2)

On the contrary, we speak as men approved by God to be entrusted with the gospel. We are not trying to please men but God, who tests our hearts. You know we never used flattery, nor did we put on a mask to cover up greed—God is our witness. (1 Th 2:4-5)

And we also thank God continually because, when you received the word of God, which you heard from us, you accepted it not as the word of men, but as it actually is, the word of God, which is at work in you who believe. (1 Th 2:13)

He writes the same way in all his letters, speaking in them of these matters. His letters contain some things that are hard to understand, which ignorant and unstable people distort, as they do the other Scriptures, to their own destruction. (2 Pet 3:16)

Thought 1. Note two things.
1) Peter said that Paul wrote some things that were difficult to understand. He also says that some people twisted what Paul said just as they twisted the truth of God's patience. What were those things?
   ⇒ Paul's teaching on justification by faith. This teaching led some people to say that when a person believed in Christ, he was saved no matter how he lived. Even if a person lived like the devil himself, if he believed in Christ, he was saved. This, of course, leads to the abuse of grace (cp. Ro.3:5-8; 6:1f; Jas.2:14-26).
   ⇒ Paul's teaching on Christian liberty and freedom. This teaching led some people to say that Paul was removing the restrictions of God upon behavior and giving license to live and do as one likes (Ro.8:1-2; 7:4; 14:1-23; 1 Cor.6:12; Gal.3:10; 5:13).
2) Peter said that Paul's writings were accepted as Scripture by the early church (v.16). He says that they twisted Paul's writings even as they did "the other Scriptures." The great Greek scholar A.T. Robertson says:

"There is no doubt that the apostles claimed to speak by the help of the Holy Spirit (1 Th.5:27; Col.4:16) just as the prophets of old did (2 Pt.1:20f.). Peter thus puts Paul's Epistles on the same plane with the Old Testament, which was also misused (Mt.5:21-44; 15:3-6; 19:3-10)" (*Word Pictures In The New Testament*, Vol.6, p.179).

The commentator Michael Green says:

"Notice how Peter admires Paul's wisdom—not without reason! Yet his is a gift from God, as Paul was the first to admit (1 Cor.3:10; 2:6, 16). Polycarp writes in the same vein (c AD 115), 'Neither I nor anyone like me can attain to (lit. 'keep up with') the wisdom of the blessed and glorious Paul, who also, when he was absent from you, wrote you letters. It is interesting to see the difference here between the first and early second century references to Paul. To Peter he is a 'beloved brother': to Polycarp, though himself one of the most distinguished of subapostolic bishops and a sufferer for the faith, he had already become 'the blessed and glorious Paul'. If 2 Peter is a pseudepigraph, it is a very good one!" (*The Second Epistle of Peter and The Epistle of Jude*. "The Tyndale New Testament Commentaries," p.146).

Michael Green again says:

> "There can, in any case be no question that long before AD 60 Christian writings were being read in church alongside the Old Testament, and consequently were well on the way to being rated as equivalent in value to it....The point was this. The apostles were conscious that they spoke the word of the Lord (1 Th.2:13) as surely as did any of the prophets. There is nothing, therefore, unnatural about their placing each other alongside the Old Testament prophets. The same Holy Spirit who inspired the prophets was active in themselves. That is quite enough to explain how Peter could have put Paul alongside the Old Testament writers in this verse. Bigg [of the International Critical Commentaries] remarks that, so far from having an inferiority complex about Moses and the prophets, the apostles believed themselves to be even higher in the purposes of God. St. Paul sets apostles before prophets (Eph.4:11)...And it follows from 1 Pt.1:12 that the Christian evangelist was superior to the old prophets, as Christ Himself was greater than Moses'" (*The Second Epistle of Peter and The Epistle of Jude*. "The Tyndale New Testament Commentaries," p.148f).

2 (3:17) **Believer, Duty**: believers must beware lest they be led into error. Note that Peter addresses the believers of the churches as *dear friends*. He loves God's people, and it has been his love that has stirred him to warn them of the great day of God that is coming, the terrible judgment and destruction of the ungodly and of the heavens and earth. Now Peter gives the believers who are dear friends one more warning:

> **Therefore, dear friends, since you already know this, be on your guard so that you may not be carried away by the error of lawless men and fall from your secure position. (v.17)**

The believer has been warned; he now knows all about these things. He has read and studied the letter of Second Peter...

- the message of the great love and salvation of God and of the coming judgment of God upon man and his world.
- the message that warns against false teachers who pervert and twist the Scriptures. They deny the Lord (2 Pt.2:1f) and the Scripture (2 Pt.2:1f) and the return of Christ and the judgment to come (2 Pt.3:3f).

The believer has been warned; therefore, he must now beware, guard and stand against the error of false teachers. If he does not stay alert and guard against the teaching of false teachers, he will be led away by their error. The believer will fall and no longer be steadfast. He will lose the exciting hope of the Lord's return and no longer look forward to the glorious union with Christ nor to eternal life with God the Father.

> **"Watch and pray so that you will not fall into temptation. The spirit is willing, but the body is weak." (Mat 26:41)**

> **So be on your guard! Remember that for three years I never stopped warning each of you night and day with tears. (Acts 20:31)**

> **So, if you think you are standing firm, be careful that you don't fall! (1 Cor 10:12)**

> **Be on your guard; stand firm in the faith; be men of courage; be strong. (1 Cor 16:13)**

> **Be self-controlled and alert. Your enemy the devil prowls around like a roaring lion looking for someone to devour. (1 Pet 5:8)**

> **Jesus said to them: "Watch out that no one deceives you. (Mark 13:5)**

> **Be on guard! Be alert ! You do not know when that time will come. (Mark 13:33)**

> **The Spirit clearly says that in later times some will abandon the faith and follow deceiving spirits and things taught by demons. (1 Tim 4:1)**

> **For the time will come when men will not put up with sound doctrine. Instead, to suit their own desires, they will gather around them a great number of teachers to say what their itching ears want to hear. They will turn their ears away from the truth and turn aside to myths. (2 Tim 4:3-4)**

> **See to it, brothers, that none of you has a sinful, unbelieving heart that turns away from the living God. (Heb 3:12)**

> **Therefore, dear friends, since you already know this, be on your guard so that you may not be carried away by the error of lawless men and fall from your secure position. (2 Pet 3:17)**

> **Do not set foot on the path of the wicked or walk in the way of evil men. (Prov 4:14)**

3 (3:18) **Grace—Knowledge**: believers must grow in the grace and knowledge of our Lord and Savior Jesus Christ. (See note—2 Pt.1:2 for discussion.)

Note the close of Peter's letter, a glorious exaltation of praise: "To Him be glory both now and forever." All the glory that belongs to God, Peter says belongs to Jesus Christ. And if any one person should know, Peter should. Peter is the *big fisherman*, the man chosen by Christ to be one of His closest associates and to be the leader of His small apostolic band. No one knew Jesus Christ any better than Peter. And Peter says that the glory due God belongs to Jesus Christ. Jesus Christ is God incarnate in human flesh, God who came down to earth to reveal Himself and to save men.

> "What a telling final ejaculation! It reveals the mainspring of Peter's Christianity. Christ the Saviour; Christ the Lord; to Christ belongs glory for ever. In this incidental phrase we have the highest possible Christology. For glory belongs to God (Ro.11:36,

Jude 25). But Peter had learnt that 'all men should honour the Son even as they honour the Father' (Jn.5:23)" (Michael Green. *The Second Epistle of Peter and The Epistle of Jude*. "The Tyndale New Testament Commentaries," p.151).

Matthew Henry says:

"We must grow in the knowledge of our Lord Jesus Christ. Follow on to know the Lord. Labour to know him more clearly and more fully, to know more of Christ...so as to be more like him and to love him better. This is the knowledge of Christ the apostle Paul reached after and desired to attain, Ph.3:10. Such a knowledge of Christ as conforms us more to him and [will] preserve us from falling off in times of...apostasy; and those who experience...the knowledge of the Lord and Saviour Jesus Christ will...give thanks and praise to him, and join with our apostle in saying, To him be glory both now and for ever. Amen" (*Matthew Henry's Commentary*, Vol.6, p.1059).

THE

OUTLINE & SUBJECT INDEX

REMEMBER: When you look up a subject and turn to the Scripture reference, you have not only the Scripture, you have *an outline and a discussion* (commentary) of the Scripture and subject.

This is one of the *GREAT VALUES* of **The Preacher's Outline & Sermon Bible®**. Once you have all the volumes, you will have not only what all other Bible indexes give you, that is, a list of all the subjects and their Scripture references, *BUT* you will also have…

- An outline of *every* Scripture and subject in the Bible.
- A discussion (commentary) on every Scripture and subject.
- Every subject supported by other Scriptures or cross references.

DISCOVER THE GREAT VALUE for yourself. Quickly glance below to the very first subject of the Index of Second Peter. It is:

> **ADULTERY**
> Sin of. Trait of false teachers. 2:14

Turn to the reference. Glance at the Scripture and outline of the Scripture, then read the commentary. You will immediately see the GREAT VALUE of the INDEX of **The Preacher's Outline & Sermon Bible®**.

OUTLINE AND SUBJECT INDEX

ABOUND (See **INCREASING MEAS-URE**)

ADULTERY
Sin of. Trait of false teachers. 2:14

ANGELS
Power of. Greater than man's. 2:10-19

ANGELS, FALLEN
Fall of. Discussed. 2:4
Judgment of. Discussed. 2:4

APOSTASY
Danger - fate of.
Blackest darkness. 2:17; 2:10-22
Judgment. 2:1
Deliverance from. By going on to matur-ity. 1:10
Described as.
A time existing now. In the church now. 2:1-3; 2:10-22
A time in the future. The last times. 3:3
A time past.
At the flood. 2:5
When Sodom was destroyed. 2:6
When the angels sinned. 2:4
Discussed. 2:1-22
Marks of - Characteristics of.
Denying the Lord's return. 3:3-7
Greed-seeking followers. 2:3; 2:18-19
Returning to immorality. 2:14-16; 2:20
Source of.
False prophets and teachers. 2:1-22
Scoffers. 3:3-7
Servants of corruption. 2:18-19

APOSTLE
Discussed. 1:1

AUTHORITY
Despised by false teachers. 2:10

BALAAM
Example of. Leading others to sin. 2:15-16

BARREN (See **INEFFECTIVE**)

BELIEVERS
Duty.
Discussed. 1:5-7
How to live in light of the new heav-ens and earth. 3:11-14
Must do some things since Jesus Christ is coming again. 3:11-14; 3:15-18
Response to world's end. 3:15-18
To add certain things. 1:5-7
To be diligent in working out one's own salvation. 1:5-15
To beware lest they fall into error. 3:17
To look for a new heavens and earth. 3:12-15
To teach the things of salvation and to teach diligently. 1:12-15
To work out one's own salvation. 1:5-15
Life - Walk. Great things of salvation.
Discussed. 1:5-15
Need. To be stirred constantly. 1:12-15

BIBLE
Discussed. Books and contents of. 1:19-21

BLAMELESS
Meaning. 3:14

BLIND, SPIRITUALLY
Discussed. 1:8-11

CALL - CALLED (See **MINISTER**)
Duty of. To make one's c. sure. 1:10
Purpose of.
To be excellent, good. 1:5-7
To obtain glory. 1:3

CAROUSING
Sin of. 2:13

CASTAWAY (See **SENT**)

CHANCE, SECOND
Not given after death.
To fallen angels. 2:4
To those before the flood. 2:5-6

CHURCH
Need. To be stirred constantly. 1:12-15

CONVERSION
Warning. Can be ignored and forgotten. 1:9

CORRUPT - CORRUPTION
Cause of. Lust. 1:4
Deliverance from. By participating in God's nature. 1:4
Meaning. 1:4
Seed of **c**. Is within the world. 1:4
Who is **c**. False teachers. 2:19

COVET - COVETOUSNESS (See **GREED**)

CREATION
By God. By the Word of God. 3:5
Of new heavens and earth. 3:13-14

DAMNATION
Meaning. 2:1

DAY OF THE LORD
Discussed. 3:10

DAYS, THE LAST
Discussed. 3:3

DEAD - DEATH
Caused by. Sin and corruption. 1:4
Deliverance from.
By the power of Christ. 1:3
Through the divine nature. 1:4
Meaning. Corruption - perishing. 1:4; 2:19

DESTRUCTION
Meaning. 2:1

DILIGENT (See **EFFORT**)

DISCRIMINATION
How to overcome. By faith. 1:1

EARTH
Destruction of. Discussed. 3:10; 3:12
Fact. To be a new heavens and earth. 3:10; 3:13

EFFORT
Meaning. 3:14

EMPTINESS
Caused by. False teaching. 2:18

FIRST

JOHN

1 JOHN

INTRODUCTION

AUTHOR: John, the Apostle (see the Gospel of John, Introductory Notes, Author).

The author does not give his name nor give himself a title. But the author is easily identifiable. The style, vocabulary, and content point to the same author writing the Gospel of John and the Epistles of I, II, and III John.

John Stott points out that all three epistles are found in the earliest Greek manuscripts. There has never been any question about their being Scripture. The earliest reference to the three epistles was by Polycarp (about A.D. 155 in his letter to the Philippians, 7th chapter). But there are what seem to be quotations from the epistles made by earlier writers (Clement of Rome, the Didache, and the Epistle to Diogenetus). Eusebius verifies that John wrote at least the first two epistles. And Clement of Alexandria mentions "the greater epistle" of John which shows that he knew of more than one letter (John RW Stott. *The Epistles of John.* "Tyndale New Testament Commentary," ed. by RVG Tasker. Grand Rapids, MI: Eerdmans, 1964, p.14f).

It should be mentioned, however, that some say there were two Johns: John the Apostle and John the Elder, who is said to have been a member or minister of the church at Ephesus. But the weight of evidence points directly to John the Apostle as the author of all four books.

DATE: Uncertain. Probably A.D. 85-90 (see the Gospel of John, Introductory Notes, Date).

There is no mention of the persecution under the Emperor Domitian in A.D. 95, so the letter most likely was written before that date. It is thought that the three epistles were written about the same time. Some even feel that II and III John were written and sent at the same time as First John. If both Second and Third John are personal letters to individuals, they could have easily accompanied the letter of First John to the church.

TO WHOM WRITTEN: To the church at large. Note: there is no greeting, farewell, or personal references that would reveal the recipients. This means a most wonderful thing: each local church can look upon First John as though the letter has been personally written to it.

Tradition says that all three epistles were written from Ephesus where John pastored during the latter years of his life.

PURPOSE: "I write these things to you...so that you may know that you have eternal life" (5:13) (see Special Features, point 3). However, John also wrote to defend the faith and to strengthen the church against false teachers and heretical doctrine. John confronted the first stages of the same heretical teachings that Paul often confronted—the beginning stages of Gnosticism. Briefly stated, Gnosticism said that the human body was evil. This teaching resulted in two different attitudes toward the body and life.

⇒ Some said that the body needed to be disciplined, controlled, and taken care of as much as possible. By controlling its urges and appetites and keeping it fit, the corruption and evil of the body could be mastered more easily.

⇒ Others said that what was done with the body mattered little, for it was evil and doomed to death. Therefore, if a person took care of his spirit, he could eat, drink, and be merry and do whatever else he wanted with his body.

  a. The parallel with the false teaching of today is clearly seen.

⇒ Some concentrate upon the body and its health through recreation and discipline, seeking to overcome the evil, that is, the corruption, disease, aging, and dying of the body as much as possible.

⇒ Others live as they please, eating and drinking and partying as they wish, thinking that it matters little how they live. Just think how many people feel that they can do their own thing—what they want, when they want—just so they believe in God and worship occasionally and do a good deed here and there.

The point to see is this: each person gives attention to the spiritual only as he wishes, only as much as he feels is necessary to keep his spirit in touch with God. But his concentration is the body and its pleasure, whether the pleasure is the exhibition of discipline and control or the stimulating of the flesh.

There are teeming millions, and have been since Christ, who believe that they are safe and acceptable to God just so they have been baptized, belong to a church, practice the rituals of the church, and worship here and there. They think they can pretty much live like they want during the week: eat, drink, party, seek the pleasures and possessions of the world, bank, hoard, even curse and be immoral here and there. What they do with their bodies, just so it is not too serious in their minds, does not matter that much. What it is that makes them acceptable to God is what has just been stated: being baptized and belonging to the church.

  b. Note how the truth destroys this life-style and teaching. The human body is not evil; Jesus Christ, the image of God, came to earth in a human body. Therefore, the human body could not be evil, for God cannot be touched with evil. He is perfect. The conclusion is shocking and convulsive for the life of man. Since the body is honorable, it means that everything a man does with his body *is important to his spiritual welfare*. What he does with his body determines his relationship and destiny with God. It is totally impossible to keep one's spirit right with God and let one's body go its own way. A person is a person, both spirit and body. Therefore, he is to honor God with both his spirit and body, just as Jesus Christ did in the body given him by God. (See outline and notes—Ro.12:1-2; 1 Cor.6:12-20 for more discussion. See Colossians, Introductory Notes, Purpose. Also see note, pt.2—Col.1:15 for more detailed discussion.)

SPECIAL FEATURES:

1. I John is "A General Epistle." That is, it is not written to a specific church, but rather it is written to all Christian believers. It is "An Epistle Written From a Father to His Children." It is written from the heart of a pastor who feels the tenderness of a father for his children (1 Jn.2:1, 12, 18, 28; 3:1, 2, 7, 18, 21; 4:1, 4, 7, 11; 5:2, 21). See James, Introductory Notes, Special Features, point 1.)

2. I John is "An Epistle Combating False Teachers and Doctrinal Error." (See Purpose above.)

3. I John is "An Epistle of Christian Certainty or Assurance." The phrase "we know" is used seventeen times to give assurance to the believer. The epistle assures the believer time and again that God has sent His Son, the Lord Jesus Christ, into the world to save man (the incarnation). In addition, John assures the believer of eternal life. In contrast, the Gospel of John was written to stir faith "that you may believe that Jesus is the Christ, the Son of God...." (Jn.20:31).

4. I John is "The Epistle of Tests." It was written to give the believer test after test by which he could prove whether or not he knows God. The tests also strengthen the believer's faith and love for God. A quick glance at the outline will show this.

5. I John is "A Personal and a Spiritual Epistle." It is not written so much from a doctrinal point of view, although it is filled with doctrinal teaching. Its emphasis is personal righteousness, purity, love, and a knowledge and loyalty to Jesus Christ, the Son of God Himself.

6. I John is "An Epistle that Stresses Love" (1 Jn.2:7-11; 3:1-3; 3:11-17; 3:23; 4:7-21).

7. I John is "An Epistle that Stresses that Jesus Christ is the Son of God, the Messiah, the Anointed One of God" (1 Jn.1:7; 2:1, 22; 3:8; 4:9-10, 14-15; 5:1, 5, 9-13, 18, 20).

8. I John is "An Epistle that Stresses that Jesus Christ Did Come As a Man" (1 Jn.1:1-3, 5, 8; 4:2-3, 9-10, 14; 5:6, 8, 20).

9. I John is "An Epistle that Stresses that Jesus Christ is the Savior: He Did Die for Man's Sins" (1 Jn.1:7; 2:1-2; 3:5, 8, 16; 4:9-10, 14).

10. I John is "An Epistle that Stresses the Spirit Living Within the Believer" (1 Jn.2:20, 27; 3:24; 4:13, 15-16; 5:12).

11. I John is "An Epistle that Stresses the Need for Separation From the World" (1 Jn.2:15-17; 3:1, 3, 13; 4:3-5; 5:4; 5:19).

12. I John is "An Epistle that Stresses Righteousness and Obedience to God's Commandments" (1 Jn.2:3-8, 29; 3:3-15, 22-24; 4:20-21; 5:2-4, 17-19, 21).

OUTLINE OF 1 JOHN

THE PREACHER'S OUTLINE & SERMON BIBLE®
is *unique*. It differs from all other Study Bibles & Sermon
Resource Materials in that every Passage and Subject is
outlined right beside the Scripture. When you choose any
Subject below and turn to the reference, you have not only
the Scripture, but you discover the Scripture and Subject
already outlined for you—verse by verse.

For a quick example, choose one of the subjects below
and turn over to the Scripture, and you will find this
marvelous help for faster, easier, and more accurate use.

In addition, every point of the Scripture and Subject is
fully developed in a Commentary with supporting Scripture
at the bottom of the page. Again, this arrangement makes
sermon preparation much easier and faster.

Note something else: The Subjects of FIRST JOHN have
titles that are both Biblical and *practical*. The practical
titles sometimes have more appeal to people. This *benefit* is
clearly seen for use on billboards, bulletins, church
newsletters, etc.

A suggestion: For the quickest overview of FIRST
JOHN, first read *all the major titles* (I, II, III, etc.), then
come back and read the subtitles.

OUTLINE OF 1 JOHN

I. **THE GREAT TESTIMONY OF JOHN: THE SON OF GOD HAS COME TO EARTH, 1:1-5**

II. **THE THREE MISCONCEPTIONS OF MAN, 1:6-2:2**

   A. Misconception 1: Man Can Fellowship with God and Still Walk in Sin, 1:6-7

   B. Misconception 2: Man is Not Totally Sinful and Depraved, 1:8-9

   C. Misconception 3: Man Can Become Sinless and Righteous on His Own, 1:10-2:2

III. **THE PROOF THAT ONE REALLY KNOWS GOD: SEVEN TESTS, 2:3-29**

   A. Test 1: Obeying God's Commands, 2:3-6

   B. Test 2: Loving One's Neighbor, 2:7-11

   C. Test 3: Remembering Your Spiritual Growth, 2:12-14

   D. Test 4: Not Loving the World, 2:15-17

   E. Test 5: Guarding Against Antichrists or False Teachers, 2:18-23

   F. Test 6: Letting the Gospel Remain in You, 2:24-27

   G. Test 7: Continuing, Abiding in Christ, 2:28-29

IV. **THE PROOF THAT ONE REALLY LOVES GOD: SIX TESTS, 3:1-4:21**

   A. Test 1: Experiencing God's Incredible Love, 3:1-3

   B. Test 2: Turning Away from Sin and Its Enslavement, 3:4-9

   C. Test 3: Being Marked by Love, 3:10-17

   D. Test 4: Having a Clean Heart, 3:18-24

   E. Test 5: Testing the Spirits of False Teachers, 4:1-6

   F. Test 6: Loving One Another, 4:7-21

V. **THE PROOF THAT ONE REALLY BELIEVES IN GOD: FOUR TESTS, 5:1-21**

   A. Test 1: Being Born Again, 5:1-5

   B. Test 2: Believing the Witness About Christ: That He is the Son of God (Part I), 5:6-8

   C. Test 3: Believing the Witness About Christ: That He is the Son of God (Part II), 5:9-15

   D. Test 4: Living Free of Sin, 5:16-21

CHAPTER 1

I. THE GREAT TESTIMONY OF JOHN: THE SON OF GOD HAS COME TO EARTH, 1:1-5

1 **Jesus Christ has always existed**
2 **Jesus Christ has proven who He is**
3 **Jesus Christ has revealed who He is: The Word of Life**
  a. By appearing, revealing Himself
  b. By identifying with men

That which was from the beginning, which we have heard, which we have seen with our eyes, which we have looked at and our hands have touched—this we proclaim concerning the Word of life.
2 The life appeared; we have seen it and testify to it, and we proclaim to you the eternal life, which was with the Father and has appeared to us.
3 We proclaim to you what we have seen and heard, so that you also may have fellowship with us. And our fellowship is with the Father and with his Son, Jesus Christ.
4 We write this to make our joy complete.
5 This is the message we have heard from him and declare to you: God is light; in him there is no darkness at all.

4 **Jesus Christ came to earth for the most glorious purpose**
  a. That we might have fellowship with God & His Son Jesus Christ
  b. That our joy be complete[DS1]

5 **Jesus Christ preached the most wonderful message**
  a. That God is Light
  b. That there is no darkness in God at all[DS2]

DIVISION I

THE GREAT TESTIMONY OF JOHN: THE SON OF GOD HAS COME TO EARTH, 1:1-5

(1:1-5) **Introduction**: John jumps right into the great subject he wants to cover. There is no greeting and no salutation. What he has to say is of unparalleled importance; he must get right to the point: God's Son has come to earth. God is not living off in outer space someplace like so many people think and say; God has not forgotten the earth. God is not unconcerned and disinterested in the world. The very opposite is true. God loves and cares for us and He has proven it in the most supreme way possible: God has sent His Son into the world. This is the glorious testimony of John: God's Son has come into the world and His name is Jesus Christ. Jesus is the Messiah, the Savior of the world.

1. Jesus Christ has always existed (v.1).
2. Jesus Christ has proven who He is (v.1).
3. Jesus Christ has revealed who He is: the Word of Life (v.1-2).
4. Jesus Christ came to earth for the most glorious purpose (v.3-4).
5. Jesus Christ preached the most wonderful message (v.5).

(1:1-5) **Another Outline**: The Son of God Has Come to Earth.
1. The basic fact: He has always existed (v.1).
2. The clear proof: Man heard, saw, looked upon, and handled (v.1).
3. The most glorious revelation (v.1-2).
  a. He appeared, revealed Himself, revealed the life to us.
  b. He identified with man: Gave man the opportunity to see Him.
4. The most glorious purpose (v.3-4).
  a. That we might have fellowship together.
  b. That our joy be complete (v.4).
5. The most wonderful message (v.5).
  a. That God is light.
  b. That there is no darkness in God.

1 (1:1) **Jesus Christ, Son of God—Eternal—Pre-existent**: Jesus Christ has always existed. This is what is meant by the words "that which was from the beginning." Jesus Christ was existing before the world was ever created. He was living and had always been living. He possessed life—the energy, the force, the power of life. He was the very being and essence of life, the very embodiment of life. Life was wrapped up in Him, for He was the very energy and force of life itself.

Thought 1. The point is clear: from the beginning Jesus Christ was already there. He did not have a beginning; He was not created. He "was from the beginning with God." Our Lord and Savior knows what the other world is all about, for He has come from there. Therefore, all that He told us is true. We can trust His Word.

> **In the beginning was the Word, and the Word was with God, and the Word was God. (John 1:1)**
> **Before the mountains were born or you brought forth the earth and the world, from everlasting to everlasting you are God. (Psa 90:2)**
> **I was appointed from eternity, from the beginning, before the world began. (Prov 8:23)**
> **And now, Father, glorify me in your presence with the glory I had with you before the world began. (John 17:5)**
> **[Christ Jesus] Who, being in very nature God, did not consider equality with God something to be grasped, but made himself nothing, taking the very nature of a servant, being made in human likeness. And being found in appearance as a man, he humbled himself and became obedient to death— even death on a cross! (Phil 2:6-8; cp. 2 Cor. 8:9)**

2 (1:1) **Jesus Christ, Deity; Revelation, Proof of—John, Testimony of**: Jesus Christ proved who He is. How? By partaking of human flesh, by becoming a man and letting people hear, see, look upon, and handle him.

1. John and the early believers *heard the Son of God.* The Son of God actually partook of flesh and blood and became a man and *spoke to men* (cp. Heb.2:14-15). They heard Him teach and share the glorious news that God loves man, that man can be delivered from sin and death and live forever with God. The twelve apostles and thousands of others not only *heard about Him,* they actually *heard Him* proclaim the words of life. They heard Him deal with individuals and heard Him teach audiences of thousands. They themselves spoke to Him and heard Him speak to them. For three years John and the apostles and many others were in constant conversation with Him, listening and hanging on to every word He said.

Thought 1. One of the great needs of man is a Word from God—a Word that tells us the truth about God and about life—who we are, why we are here, and where we are going.

Jesus answered, "My teaching is not my own. It comes from him who sent me. If anyone chooses to do God's will, he will find out whether my teaching comes from God or whether I speak on my own. (John 7:16-17)
To the Jews who had believed him, Jesus said, "If you hold to my teaching, you are really my disciples. Then you will know the truth, and the truth will set you free." (John 8:31-32)

2. John and the early believers *saw the Son of God with their eyes.* The Son of God actually became a man. Men saw Him in the flesh just as they see all other men. Note: John says they saw Him *with their eyes.* He wants us to know that Jesus Christ was not a phantom, ghost, or spirit. He was real; He had actually partaken of flesh and blood and become a man. He and the others saw Him with their eyes. They were as Matthew Henry says, "Eyewitnesses as well as ear-witnesses" (*Matthew Henry's Commentary,* Vol.6, p.1061).

⇒ They were witnesses of His life upon earth for three years, from His baptism by John the Baptist to His resurrection from the dead. They saw all his wonderful works: the healings and miracles and good deeds that He ministered to people. They saw the most wonderful event of all, His resurrection and conquest of death for man.

Therefore it is necessary to choose one of the men who have been with us the whole time the Lord Jesus went in and out among us, beginning from John's baptism to the time when Jesus was taken up from us. For one of these must become a witness with us of his resurrection." (Acts 1:21-22)

⇒ They were eyewitnesses of His majesty and they declare the truth to us.

We did not follow cleverly invented stories when we told you about the power and coming of our Lord Jesus Christ, but we were eyewitnesses of his majesty. (2 Pet 1:16)

3. John and the early believers *looked at the Son of God.* This means more than just seeing Jesus Christ in a human body. The Greek word for "looked at" (etheasametha) means to gaze and look upon for a long time in order to study and understand and grasp. It means to look intensely and earnestly; it means to grasp the meaning and significance of a person. John is testifying that he and the other apostles and believers looked and gazed at Jesus Christ in order...
• to study and understand Him.
• to seek and grasp the meaning and significance of His person.

Thought 1. A person will never see and understand who Christ is by just glancing at Him. If a person wants to know Christ, he has to look intensely and seriously; he has to seek to understand if Christ really is who John and other believers claim He is.

But let him who boasts boast about this: that he understands and knows me, that I am the LORD, who exercises kindness, justice and righteousness on earth, for in these I delight," declares the LORD. (Jer 9:24)
Let us acknowledge the LORD; let us press on to acknowledge him. As surely as the sun rises, he will appear; he will come to us like the winter rains, like the spring rains that water the earth." (Hosea 6:3)
Jesus answered, "My teaching is not my own. It comes from him who sent me. If anyone chooses to do God's will, he will find out whether my teaching comes from God or whether I speak on my own. (John 7:16-17)
To the Jews who had believed him, Jesus said, "If you hold to my teaching, you are really my disciples. Then you will know the truth, and the truth will set you free." (John 8:31-32)

4. John and the early believers *touched* Jesus Christ, the Son of God. The word "touched" (epselaphesan) means more than just touching. It means to grope and grasp after in order to understand; to handle in order to examine closely (John RW Stott. *The Epistles of John.* "Tyndale New Testament Commentary," p.60). A.T. Robertson, the Greek scholar, says that it is a graphic word, the very same word that Jesus used to prove that He was not a spirit after His resurrection (*Word Pictures In The New Testament,* Vol.6, p.205).

Look at my hands and my feet. It is I myself! Touch me and see; a ghost does not have flesh and bones, as you see I have." (Luke 24:39)
Then he said to Thomas, "Put your finger here; see my hands. Reach out your hand and put it into my side. Stop doubting and believe." (John 20:27)

Thought 1. The Son of God came to earth; He partook of flesh and blood and became a Man just like all other men. He is called Jesus Christ or Jesus the Messiah, the Savior of the world. He was heard, seen, intensely looked at and touched by John and the other apostles and by many others who believed and followed Him. Jesus Christ did everything He could to show man that the Son of God had come to earth—that He had come to save man, to deliver man from this corruptible world of sin and death—that He had come to give man life eternal, the glorious privilege of living in heaven with God forever and ever.

> **The Son is the radiance of God's glory and the exact representation of his being, sustaining all things by his powerful word. After he had provided purification for sins, he sat down at the right hand of the Majesty in heaven. (Heb 1:3)**

> **Jesus answered: "Don't you know me, Philip, even after I have been among you such a long time? Anyone who has seen me has seen the Father. How can you say, 'Show us the Father'? (John 14:9)**

> **Theirs are the patriarchs, and from them is traced the human ancestry of Christ, who is God over all, forever praised! Amen. (Rom 9:5)**

> **He is the image of the invisible God, the firstborn over all creation. (Col 1:15)**

> **For in Christ all the fullness of the Deity lives in bodily form, (Col 2:9)**

> **Beyond all question, the mystery of godliness is great: He appeared in a body, was vindicated by the Spirit, was seen by angels, was preached among the nations, was believed on in the world, was taken up in glory. (1 Tim 3:16)**

> **Which God [Jesus Christ] will bring about in his own time—God, the blessed and only Ruler, the King of kings and Lord of lords, who alone is immortal and who lives in unapproachable light, whom no one has seen or can see. To him be honor and might forever. Amen. (1 Tim 6:15-16)**

> **On his robe and on his thigh he has this name written: KING OF KINGS AND LORD OF LORDS. (Rev 19:16)**

3 (1:1-2) **Jesus Christ, Person—Revelation—Word, The**: Jesus Christ revealed who He was, the *Word of Life*. This means two things:

⇒ First, Jesus Christ Himself is *the Word*. Remember what a word is: it is the expression of an idea, a thought, an image in the mind of a person. A word describes what is in the mind of a person. John is saying this: in the life of Jesus Christ, God was speaking to the world, speaking and demonstrating just what He wanted to say to man. This means the most wonderful thing. It means that God has given us much more than mere words in the Holy Scriptures. God has given us Jesus Christ, *The Word*. As *The Word*, Jesus Christ was the picture, the expression, the pattern, the very image of what God wished to say to man. The very image within God's mind of the *Ideal Man* was demonstrated in the life of Jesus Christ. Jesus Christ was the perfect expression of all that God wishes man to be. Jesus Christ was God's utterance, God's speech, *God's Word* to man. Jesus Christ was the *Word of life who came to earth to show us that the very energy, force, power, and essence of life is in God and in God alone. Therefore, if a person wants life, he must trust and depend upon God for life. For life in all of its energy and force and being exists only in God.*

> **In the beginning was the Word, and the Word was with God, and the Word was God. (John 1:1)**

⇒ Second, Jesus Christ Himself is *the Word of life*, the very message of life, the good news (gospel) of life. He is the very embodiment of life, the energy and force of life; therefore, when He came to earth, He brought the Word of life to man. Jesus Christ—His life, His acts, His teaching—tells men how to live. In Jesus Christ and in Jesus Christ alone is the Word of life, the Word that tells man how to conquer death and to live abundantly both now and eternally. Jesus Christ is the *Word of life*. This is the great thing that He revealed to man. But note: How did He reveal this great message to man? Verse two tells us in clear language. The verse is here given just as it reads in the Greek text:

> "(And the life was revealed, and we have seen and bear witness, and report to you the life, the eternal, which was with the Father, and was revealed to us)."

1. Jesus Christ *revealed* the life to us (v.2). That is, He came to earth, appeared to us and showed us the life that was in Him. He showed us what life is...

⇒ that it is the very energy and force of living forever just as God Himself lives. Life never dies and never ceases to be.

⇒ that it is the very energy and force of living abundantly, of experiencing love, joy, and peace just as God experiences. Life never lacks and never ceases to experience the fullness of life to the ultimate.

Thought 1. The point is this. Jesus Christ revealed who He was; He came to earth and showed us life—showed us that life is in God and in God alone. Therefore, if man wants to really live, he has to put his life into the hands of God, for life exists only in God. God alone can give man life.

2. But Jesus Christ did a second thing: He identified with man. He gave men the opportunity to see Him and the life which He was bringing to man. As covered in verse one, men heard, saw, looked at, and touched Christ. He made Himself available to men, allowed them to use all their physical senses in order to prove that He was indeed the Son of God, the very embodiment of life eternal. He allowed men to use all their physical senses so they could have perfect proof and never be able to question that the Son of God had come to earth, not if they were honest and willing to study and know the truth.

Note the testimony of John: "we have seen and testify to it, and we proclaim to you the eternal life, which was with the Father and appeared to us" (v.2). There is compulsion here: the witnesses to the Son of God must proclaim the truth. The Son of God, Jesus Christ, has come to earth. He came to bring the glorious message of the Word of life. Men do not have to live in sin and the dread of corruption and death; men can live in the abundance of love, joy, and peace with God, both now and eternally.

> **Just as Moses lifted up the snake in the desert, so the Son of Man must be lifted**

up, that everyone who believes in him may have eternal life. (John 3:14-15)

Whoever believes in the Son has eternal life, but whoever rejects the Son will not see life, for God's wrath remains on him." (John 3:36)

"I tell you the truth, whoever hears my word and believes him who sent me has eternal life and will not be condemned; he has crossed over from death to life. (John 5:24)

For my Father's will is that everyone who looks to the Son and believes in him shall have eternal life, and I will raise him up at the last day." (John 6:40)

Jesus said to her, "I am the resurrection and the life. He who believes in me will live, even though he dies; and whoever lives and believes in me will never die. Do you believe this?" "Yes, Lord," she told him, "I believe that you are the Christ, the Son of God, who was to come into the world." And after she had said this, she went back and called her sister Mary aside. "The Teacher is here," she said, "and is asking for you." (John 11:25-28)

The man who loves his life will lose it, while the man who hates his life in this world will keep it for eternal life. (John 12:25)

So that, just as sin reigned in death, so also grace might reign through righteousness to bring eternal life through Jesus Christ our Lord. (Rom 5:21)

The one who sows to please his sinful nature, from that nature will reap destruction; the one who sows to please the Spirit, from the Spirit will reap eternal life. (Gal 6:8)

But it has now been revealed through the appearing of our Savior, Christ Jesus, who has destroyed death and has brought life and immortality to light through the gospel. (2 Tim 1:10)

We know that we have passed from death to life, because we love our brothers. Anyone who does not love remains in death. (1 John 3:14)

And this is the testimony: God has given us eternal life, and this life is in his Son. He who has the Son has life; he who does not have the Son of God does not have life. (1 John 5:11-12)

4 (1:3-4) **Jesus Christ, Purpose—Fellowship**: Jesus Christ came to earth for the greatest of purposes.

1. Jesus Christ came that men might have fellowship with God and with His Son Jesus Christ and with one another. This is the most wonderful declaration, for it means that God is not far off in outer space someplace. God is not disinterested and uncaring about what happens to man. God has not left us to fend for ourselves upon earth with nothing but death and the grave to look forward to. The very opposite is true: God has revealed Himself in the Lord Jesus Christ and has shown us that He deeply loves and cares for us and that He wants to fellowship with us. Imagine! Jesus Christ, the Son of God, came to earth to show us that we can know God personally and fellowship with Him. We can actually fellowship with God...

- become acceptable to Him
- relate to Him and talk and share with Him
- have Him walk with us throughout the day, looking after and caring for us step by step
- cast our problems upon Him
- trust Him to help us in meeting our needs
- ask Him for strength to conquer the trials and temptations of life
- know that He will constantly give us a life of love, joy, and peace
- know that He will deliver us from sin and death and give us life eternal
- depend upon Him for righteousness so that we can be acceptable to Him

We can know both God and His Son, the Lord Jesus Christ, know them personally just like all the above describes. And we can experience fullness of life with all other believers who truly give their lives to follow Christ. We can all have fellowship together, the kind of fellowship that exists within the greatest of all families—the family of God Himself.

2. Jesus Christ came that our joy might be made complete (see DEEPER STUDY # 1, *Joy*—1 Jn.1:4 for discussion).

DEEPER STUDY # 1

(1:4) **Joy** (chara): an inner gladness; a deep seated pleasure. It is a depth of assurance and confidence that ignites a cheerful heart. It is a cheerful heart that leads to cheerful behavior.

Several things need to be said about the believer's joy.

1. Joy is divine. It is possessed and given only by God. Its roots are not in earthly or material things or cheap triumphs. It is the joy of the Holy Spirit, a joy based in the Lord. It is His very own joy (Jn.15:11; Acts 13:52; Ro.14:17; Gal.5:22; 1 Th.1:6).

2. Joy does not depend on circumstances or happiness. Happiness depends upon happenings, but the joy that God implants in the believer's heart overrides all, even the matters of life and death (Ps.5:11; 2 Cor.6:10; 7:4).

3. Joy springs from faith (Ro.15:13; Ph.1:25; 2 Tim.1:4; cp. Mt.2:10).

4. Joy of future reward makes and keeps one faithful (Mt.25:21, 23; Acts 20:24; Heb.12:2).

The source of the believer's joy is several fold.

1. The fellowship of the Father and His Son brings joy (1 Jn.1:3-4).

2. Victory over sin, death, and hell brings joy (Jn.14:28; 16:20-22).

3. Repentance brings joy (Lk.15:7, 10).

4. The hope of glory brings joy (Ro.14:17; Heb.12:2; 1 Pt.4:13).

5. The Lord's Word—the revelations, commandments, and promises which He made—brings joy (Jn.15:11).

6. The commandments of Christ and the will of God bring joy. Obeying and doing a good job stirs joy within the believer's heart (Jn.15:11, 32; 17:13; Acts 13:52).

7. Prayer brings joy (Jn.16:24).

8. The presence and fellowship of believers brings joy (1 Jn.1:3-4).

9. Converts bring joy (Lk.15:5; Ph.4:1; 1 Th.2:19-20).

10. Hearing that others walk in the truth brings joy (3 Jn.1:4).

11. Giving brings joy (2 Cor.8:2; Heb.10:34).

5 (1:5) **Jesus Christ, Message of—God, Nature—Light**: Jesus Christ preached the most wonderful message. It included two wonderful things.

1. *God is light*. What does this mean? It means several things.

a. God is light by nature and character. Light is what God is within Himself, within His being, essence, nature, and character. God dwells in the splendor, glory, and brilliance of light. Wherever He is, the splendor, glory, and brilliance of light shines out of His being. In fact, there is not even a need for the sun when God's glory is present. The glory of His presence just beams forth the most brilliant light imaginable, so brilliant and glorious that it would consume human flesh.

> **The city does not need the sun or the moon to shine on it, for the glory of God gives it light, and the Lamb is its lamp. (Rev 21:23)**
> **There will be no more night. They will not need the light of a lamp or the light of the sun, for the Lord God will give them light. And they will reign for ever and ever. (Rev 22:5)**

b. God is light in that He reveals the light of all things, the truth of all things.

⇒ Jesus, the Light, tells us that God is holy, righteous, and pure. Light is the symbol of purity and holiness. Light means the absence of darkness and blindness; it has no spots of darkness and blackness, of sin and shame.

⇒ Jesus, the Light, reveals. His light shows clearly the nature, the meaning, and the destiny of all things. His light beams in, spots, opens up, identifies, illuminates, and shows things as they really are. The light of Jesus Christ shows the truth about the world and man and God. The light of Christ reveals that God loves and cares for man and wants man to love and care for Him.

⇒ Jesus, the Light, guides. His light allows a man to walk out of darkness. Man no longer has to grope, grasp, and stumble about trying to find his way through life. The path of life can now be clearly seen.

⇒ Jesus, the Light, does away with darkness and with chaos. His light routs, wipes out, strips away and erases the darkness. The empty chaos of creation was routed by the light given by God (Gen.1:3). Jesus Christ is the Light that can save man from chaos (Jn.14:1, 17; 12:46; 16:33).

2. There is no darkness in God. What does this mean? (See DEEPER STUDY # 2, *Darkness*—1 Jn.1:5 for discussion. Observe that none of the descriptions of darkness are true of God.) (Also see DEEPER STUDY # 2, *Darkness*—Jn.8:12 for more discussion.)

DEEPER STUDY # 2

(1:5) **Darkness** (skotos, skotia): the word darkness describes both the state and works of a person. It symbolizes evil and sin, everything that life should not be and everything that a person should not do.

1. The darkness means that man is ignorant of God.

⇒ The darkness means that a person is foolish; he is futile in his thinking about God.

> **For although they knew God, they neither glorified him as God nor gave thanks to him, but their thinking became futile and their foolish hearts were darkened. (Rom 1:21)**

⇒ The darkness means that a person does not live and walk in the light of God and Christ.

> **When Jesus spoke again to the people, he said, "I am the light of the world. Whoever follows me will never walk in darkness, but will have the light of life." (John 8:12)**

⇒ The darkness means that a person is blind to the light of Christ and stumbles about through life.

> **Jesus answered, "Are there not twelve hours of daylight? A man who walks by day will not stumble, for he sees by this world's light. It is when he walks by night that he stumbles, for he has no light." (John 11:9-10)**

⇒ The darkness means that a person does not understand the light and is powerless to extinguish the light.

> **The light shines in the darkness, but the darkness has not understood it [or extinguished it]. (John 1:5)**

⇒ The darkness means that a person does not see the glory of God in the face of Jesus Christ.

> **For God, who said, "Let light shine out of darkness," made his light shine in our hearts to give us the light of the knowledge of the glory of God in the face of Christ. (2 Cor 4:6)**

2. The darkness means evil behavior and deeds.

⇒ The darkness means that a person's deeds are evil and that he hates the light.

> **This is the verdict: Light has come into the world, but men loved darkness instead of light because their deeds were evil. Everyone who does evil hates the light, and will not come into the light for fear that his deeds will be exposed. But whoever lives by the truth comes into the light, so that it may be seen plainly that what he has done has been done through God." (John 3:19-21)**

⇒ The darkness means that a person walks in the darkness of hate and antagonism against others.

> **Anyone who claims to be in the light but hates his brother is still in the darkness. Whoever loves his brother lives in the light, and there is nothing in him to make him stumble. But whoever hates his brother is in the darkness and walks around in the darkness; he does not know where he is**

going, because the darkness has blinded him. (1 John 2:9-11)

⇒ The darkness means that a person lives a secretive life, a life that is gripped by what is hidden in darkness, that cannot bear the light.

Therefore judge nothing before the appointed time; wait till the Lord comes. He will bring to light what is hidden in darkness and will expose the motives of men's hearts. At that time each will receive his praise from God. (1 Cor 4:5)

3. The darkness means man's nature, that his nature is darkness.

⇒ The darkness means that a person is the very embodiment of darkness, that his very nature and character are that of darkness.

For you were once darkness, but now you are light in the Lord. Live as children of light (Eph 5:8)

⇒ The darkness means that a person's eye is focused upon evil; therefore, his whole being is full of darkness or evil.

"The eye is the lamp of the body. If your eyes are good, your whole body will be full of light. But if your eyes are bad, your whole body will be full of darkness. If then the light within you is darkness, how great is that darkness! (Mat 6:22-23)

⇒ The darkness means that a person is an unbeliever and has fellowship with darkness.

Do not be yoked together with unbelievers. For what do righteousness and wickedness have in common? Or what fellowship can light have with darkness? (2 Cor 6:14)

4. The darkness means that man is fruitless in life.

Have nothing to do with the fruitless deeds of darkness, but rather expose them. (Eph 5:11)

5. The darkness means that man dwells in darkness.

⇒ The darkness means that a person dwells in darkness and is blind to the glorious day of salvation and of the Lord's return.

But you, brothers, are not in darkness so that this day should surprise you like a thief. You are all sons of the light and sons of the day. We do not belong to the night or to the darkness. (1 Th 5:4-5)

⇒ The darkness means that a person has rejected the call of God and still dwells in darkness.

If this is so, then the Lord knows how to rescue godly men from trials and to hold the unrighteous for the day of judgment, while continuing their punishment. This is especially true of those who follow the corrupt desire of the sinful nature and despise authority. Bold and arrogant, these men are not afraid to slander celestial beings; (2 Pet 2:9-10)

6. The darkness means the influence and power of Satan.

⇒ The darkness means that a person is under the power of Satan and is guilty of sin; that his sins are not forgiven.

To open their eyes and turn them from darkness to light, and from the power of Satan to God, so that they may receive forgiveness of sins and a place among those who are sanctified by faith in me.' (Acts 26:18)

7. The darkness means the place of punishment and hell, the pit of darkness.

⇒ The darkness means the place of punishment and hell where all the ungodly shall be cast in the final judgment.

For our struggle is not against flesh and blood, but against the rulers, against the authorities, against the powers of this dark world and against the spiritual forces of evil in the heavenly realms. (Eph 6:12)

If this is so, then the Lord knows how to rescue godly men from trials and to hold the unrighteous for the day of judgment, while continuing their punishment. (2 Pet 2:9)

They are wild waves of the sea, foaming up their shame; wandering stars, for whom blackest darkness has been reserved forever. (Jude 1:13)

	II. THE THREE MISCON-CEPTIONS OF MAN, 1:6-2:2 A. Misconception 1: Man Can Fellowship with God and Still Walk in Sin, 1:6-7
1 **We can fellowship with God & walk in darkness** a. This is a lie b. This is not the truth 2 **The truth: We must walk in the light** a. Then we have true fellowship b. Then we are cleansed from sin	6 If we claim to have fellowship with him yet walk in the darkness, we lie and do not live by the truth. 7 But if we walk in the light, as he is in the light, we have fellowship with one another, and the blood of Jesus, his Son, purifies us from all sin.

DIVISION II

THE THREE MISCONCEPTIONS OF MAN, 1:6-2:2

A. Misconception 1: Man Can Fellowship with God and Still Walk in Sin, 1:6-7

(1:6-7) **Introduction—Man, Unbelief**: the Son of God has come to earth. This is the great testimony of John the Apostle. He came to earth so that man can have *fellowship with God and with His Son Jesus Christ.*

"But wait," man shouts. "We already have fellowship with God. We already worship God and feel safe and acceptable in our religion. We do not need someone else to show us how to become acceptable to God. We can reach God on our own; we can secure His approval by ourselves. We don't need someone else telling us how to approach God and how we should worship God and secure His approval."

This is the great subject of this particular section (1 Jn.1:6-2:2). Man objects to the idea that Jesus Christ is the Son of God, that He is truly God's very own Son. Man objects to the idea...

- that the way he worships is wrong.
- that he has no merit with God.
- that he is unacceptable to God.

This is the reason many reject John's declaration: "the Son of God has come to earth." Jesus Christ came so that man can have *true* fellowship with God. But man objects to the idea that he needs help in reaching God. He feels sufficient within himself. He objects to the idea that he cannot reach God on his own. This passage strikes at these objections and exposes their fallacies. There are basically three misconceptions of man.

1. Misconception 1: man can fellowship with God and still walk in sin (1:6-7).
2. Misconception 2: man is not totally sinful and depraved (1:8-9).
3. Misconception 3: man can become righteous and sinless on his own (1:10-2:2).

The first misconception is the subject of the present passage. The other two misconceptions are discussed in the next two studies. Note that the first misconception strikes at the belief that is held by most people on earth. Most people believe that they can *fellowship with God even while they walk in darkness and sin.*

1. We can fellowship with God and walk in darkness (v.6).

a. This is a lie.
b. This is not the truth.
2. The truth: we must walk in the light (v.7).
a. Then we have fellowship.
b. Then we are cleansed from sin.

1 (1:6) **Fellowship—Darkness—Man—Salvation**: first, why does man object to the deity of Jesus Christ? To the Son of God coming to earth? That it was *necessary* for Him to come? Because they believe that man can fellowship with God and walk in darkness at the same time. What does it mean to walk in darkness?

⇒ It means that the world is in the dark about God. Man cannot see God nor talk face to face with God. Man cannot hear God nor touch God. How then can man know that God really exists? Man and his world are in the dark about God.

⇒ It means that man does not know exactly how God wants him to live: how moral and pure, how righteous and just. Man cannot talk with God; he has no way to communicate with God, for he cannot see God and he does not know where God is so that he can set up communication with Him. Therefore, man has no way to discover God nor to find out how God wants him to live.

Note four significant facts.

1. First, the world is in the dark about God. When it comes to God, man is in darkness, for he cannot see God nor talk with God. He cannot even be sure that God exists, not absolutely sure. Why? Because man's physical senses and flesh (sinful nature) can know only the things of the physical and material world. If there is a God, if there is a spiritual world, man has absolutely no way to penetrate it. Man can take all his technology and science, all his intellectual and creative reasoning, and he will never be able to penetrate the spiritual world, not with his physical and material nature. The physical and material world cannot and never will be able to penetrate and cross over into the spiritual world. Man and his world are completely in the dark about God. No matter what any person claims, no matter how religious or how much a spiritist the person may be, no person from the physical world can cross over

and enter into the spiritual world to find out if God exists, much less fellowship with God.

2. Second, how then can man ever know God and fellowship with God? There is only one way: God has to leave the spiritual world and dimension and enter the physical world and dimension. God has to come to earth and reveal Himself to us. This is the only conceivable way man could ever fellowship with God. This is the glorious gospel: this is exactly what John declares: that the Son of God has come to earth. He came to reveal God to us (see outline and notes—1 Jn.1:1-5 for discussion).

3. Third, note the foolishness of man: man rejects the Son of God and declares...

"We [can] have fellowship with God yet walk in darkness."

- Man declares that he can find God on his own, that he can relate to God and be good enough to fellowship with God and to secure God's approval by himself.
- Man believes that he can use his own mind and reasonings and find out enough about God to become acceptable to Him and to fellowship with Him.
- Man believes that he can use his own hands and energy and do enough to please God and to receive His approval.

Man thinks this: if he believes in God and does half-way right, then his belief and good deeds will put God in debt to him. God will never reject him; God will accept him. Therefore, man concludes that he can reject Jesus Christ as the Son of God. He concludes that he can fellowship and become acceptable to God by believing that God exists and by doing enough good to please God.

4. Fourth, note what the Scripture says to any of us who say this: we lie and do not live by the truth. No matter how great our minds and thoughts imagine God to be—no matter how many good works we do—we are not living by the truth. And note: a thinking and honest person knows this, for no person can cross over into the spiritual world. If we are ever to know God, God Himself has to come to us. It would not even be enough for some lesser spiritual being to come, for he would not be God. The only way we can ever hope to *know God* and to *know Him accurately* is for God Himself to come to earth. Therefore, to profess that "we can fellowship with God yet walk in darkness" is a lie. Whatever we do—all the approaches to God that men use—they are not the truth. By taking any approach to God other than by the Son of God, we do not take the true approach; we take a false approach.

> **Thought 1.** The Word of God is strong. It says this: if a person says that he is saved, and then lives in the darkness of this world, he lies. God is light; therefore, if a person walks in darkness, he does not know God. He is not fellowshipping with God. Light and darkness cannot dwell together. A person has to choose in which he wants to live: he has to choose to live in either the light of God or in the darkness of the world.

> **For as I walked around and looked carefully at your objects of worship, I even found an altar with this inscription: TO AN UNKNOWN GOD. Now what you worship as something unknown I am going to proclaim to you. (Acts 17:23)**

The light shines in the darkness, but the darkness has not understood it. (John 1:5)

He was in the world, and though the world was made through him, the world did not recognize him. (John 1:10)

This is the verdict: Light has come into the world, but men loved darkness instead of light because their deeds were evil. (John 3:19)

Jesus answered her, "If you knew the gift of God and who it is that asks you for a drink, you would have asked him and he would have given you living water." (John 4:10)

Then they asked him, "Where is your father?" "You do not know me or my Father," Jesus replied. "If you knew me, you would know my Father also." (John 8:19)

The man answered, "Now that is remarkable! You don't know where he comes from, yet he opened my eyes. (John 9:30)

Jesus answered: "Don't you know me, Philip, even after I have been among you such a long time? Anyone who has seen me has seen the Father. How can you say, 'Show us the Father'? (John 14:9)

If we claim to have fellowship with him yet walk in the darkness, we lie and do not live by the truth. (1 John 1:6)

"They know nothing, they understand nothing. They walk about in darkness; all the foundations of the earth are shaken. (Psa 82:5)

But the way of the wicked is like deep darkness; they do not know what makes them stumble. (Prov 4:19)

"My people are fools; they do not know me. They are senseless children; they have no understanding. They are skilled in doing evil; they know not how to do good." (Jer 4:22)

"Therefore their path will become slippery; they will be banished to darkness and there they will fall. I will bring disaster [judgment] on them in the year they are punished," declares the LORD. (Jer 23:12)

2 (1:7) **Light—Fellowship—Forgiveness of Sin**: man cannot fellowship with God and walk in darkness. The truth is that man must walk in the light if he is to fellowship with God. What is the light of God?

⇒ The light of God is the revelation of God Himself. The Lord Jesus Christ came to earth to reveal God. Jesus Christ has the very nature of God; therefore, He was able to show us exactly what God is like.

⇒ The light of God is the revelation of just how God wants us to live while upon earth. When the Son of God came to earth He told us and showed us exactly how to live, exactly what God expects of us.

Therefore, to walk in the light means to believe in the Son of God who came to earth and to follow Him. If we walk upon earth believing in Jesus Christ and doing exactly what He said to do, then we are in the light just "as he is in the light." Note: this is exactly what this verse says: we are to "walk in the light, as he is in the light." This means two most wonderful things.

1. If we walk in the light of Christ, then we have fellowship with Christ and with God and with all other believers. Jesus Christ is the Son of God; therefore, when He was upon earth, He was in constant fellowship with God. He is the One who shows us how to relate to and fellowship with God. Therefore, when we walk in the light of Christ, we do what Christ did. We approach God through Christ and fellowship with God just as Christ showed us. The result is glorious. It means that we have true fellowship—that we actually know God and fellowship with God, that we actually know and fellowship with His Son, the Lord Jesus Christ, and with all who believe and walk in His light.

> **Thought 1.** Note: God is light and in Him is no darkness at all. Few if any persons would deny this. But note this: it is impossible to walk in both light and darkness at the same time. Therefore, if we walk in darkness, we are not walking and fellowshipping with God. As stated, it is totally impossible.

> **Jesus answered, "I am the way and the truth and the life. No one comes to the Father except through me. (John 14:6)**
>
> **Now this is eternal life: that they may know you, the only true God, and Jesus Christ, whom you have sent. (John 17:3)**
>
> **We proclaim to you what we have seen and heard, so that you also may have fellowship with us. And our fellowship is with the Father and with his Son, Jesus Christ. (1 John 1:3)**
>
> **But if we walk in the light, as he is in the light, we have fellowship with one another, and the blood of Jesus, his Son, purifies us from all sin. (1 John 1:7)**
>
> **Here I am! I stand at the door and knock. If anyone hears my voice and opens the door, I will come in and eat with him, and he with me. (Rev 3:20)**
>
> **I am a friend to all who fear you, to all who follow your precepts. (Psa 119:63)**
>
> **Then those who feared the LORD talked with each other, and the LORD listened and heard. A scroll of remembrance was written in his presence concerning those who feared the LORD and honored his name. (Mal 3:16)**

2. If we walk in the light of Christ, then the blood of Jesus Christ, God's Son, cleanses us from all sin. This is a critical point to note. It was not enough for God's Son to come to earth and reveal God to man. Man is sinful; he has transgressed God's law. Man has chosen to live like he wants to live upon earth, to do his own thing. Man has…

- ignored God
- neglected God
- disbelieved God
- disobeyed God
- cursed God
- rebelled against God
- rejected God

Man is guilty of offending God and of transgressing God's law. Therefore, just as with any law, when the law is broken, the penalty has to be paid. The lawbreaker has to pay or else someone has to step forward to pay the penalty for him. This is just what Jesus Christ did. He not only came to reveal God to us, He came to take our sins and transgressions upon Himself—all the guilt of them. Jesus Christ died for our sins.

⇒ He faced the judgment for us.
⇒ He suffered the punishment for us.
⇒ He bore the condemnation for us.

The blood of Jesus Christ was shed upon the cross for us. Therefore, to walk in the light of Christ means that we walk believing that Christ died for us. It means that we believe His blood cleanses us; it "purifies us" from sin, that He actually paid the penalty for our sins, that we are thereby freed from the guilt of sin. When we walk in the light of Christ, God sees our sins covered by the blood of Christ. He accepts us in Christ. Our sins are forgiven by the blood of God's Son.

But note: the word "purifies" is in the present tense. This means…

- that the blood of Christ *continually purifies* us from sin.
- that if we are walking in the light of Jesus Christ, then His blood is *always purifying* us from our sins.
- that if we walk in fellowship with Jesus Christ we are *constantly confessing* our sins, we are living in *open confession* before Him.

The believer is to walk in fellowship with Christ *all day long every day*. He is to walk acknowledging God in *all His ways*, praying, praising, and confessing his shortcomings and sins *all day long*. The believer who walks in fellowship with Jesus Christ like this is being *constantly cleansed, constantly purified* by the blood of Jesus Christ.

> **Thought 1.** This is the point so often missed by man: he cannot erase the sins of his past. He has no way to pay the penalty and judgment of his sins, and they have already been committed. Therefore, the penalty has to be paid. And note: the payment has to be made by Someone who is perfect, for God is perfect. Only perfect sacrifices can be acceptable to God. And this is the terrible problem that man faces, for who is perfect other than God? No man is; only the Son of God is perfect. This is the reason the Son of God had to come to earth. He had to come to sacrifice Himself for man. He had to take man's sins upon Himself and become man's substitute in death. He had to die for man. It is His death, the sacrifice of the blood of God's Son, that covers our sins. No person is ever acceptable to God unless he is free of sin, unless his sins are purified and forgiven by the blood of Christ.

> **This is my blood of the covenant, which is poured out for many for the forgiveness of sins. (Mat 26:28)**
>
> **But God demonstrates his own love for us in this: While we were still sinners, Christ died for us. Since we have now been justified by his blood, how much more shall we be saved from God's wrath through him! (Rom 5:8-9)**
>
> **In him we have redemption through his blood, the forgiveness of sins, in accordance with the riches of God's grace (Eph 1:7)**
>
> **In whom we have redemption, the forgiveness of sins. (Col 1:14)**

How much more, then, will the blood of Christ, who through the eternal Spirit offered himself unblemished to God, cleanse our consciences from acts that lead to death, so that we may serve the living God! (Heb 9:14)

For you know that it was not with perishable things such as silver or gold that you were redeemed from the empty way of life handed down to you from your forefathers, but with the precious blood of Christ, a lamb without blemish or defect. (1 Pet 1:18-19)

But if we walk in the light, as he is in the light, we have fellowship with one another, and the blood of Jesus, his Son, purifies us from all sin. (1 John 1:7)

To him who loves us and has freed us from our sins by his blood, (Rev 1:5)

	B. Misconception 2: Man is Not Totally Sinful & Depraved, 1:8-9

1 We are not totally sinful & depraved
   a. This is a deception
   b. The truth is not in us
2 The truth: We must confess our sins
   a. Because God is faithful & just
   b. Because God forgives
	8 If we claim to be without sin, we deceive ourselves and the truth is not in us.
	9 If we confess our sins, he is faithful and just and will forgive us our sins and purify us from all unrighteousness.

DIVISION I

THE THREE MISCONCEPTIONS OF MAN, 1:6-2:2

B. Misconception 2: Man is Not Totally Sinful and Depraved, 1:8-9

(1:8-9) **Introduction**: the great testimony has been borne; the great proclamation has been made. John the apostle has declared: "the Son of God has come to earth. He has come to earth to reveal who God is and what God is like and how God wants us to live. In addition to this, He has come to die for us and to cleanse us from our sin."

But note: man objects to the idea that Jesus Christ *had to die* for our sins. Man shouts at the idea:

"We are not that sinful, so sinful that we cannot handle the problem of sin ourselves. We can change our behavior and act responsibly. Man has the capacity to reform himself, to discipline and control his own life. Man has the ability to live a responsible life: he can resolve to change and live a decent, moral, and responsible life. Man has the power to please God himself. Man can do good and be good enough to make himself acceptable to God. Man is not so terrible a sinner, not down deep within. Man can become a moral and righteous person on his own. All he needs is...

- to be educated to understand himself and his world.
- to have a set of moral values and religious worship to encourage him in his values.
- to use his technology and science for moral and just causes."

The point is this: man rejects the idea that he needs someone to die for his sins, that he cannot become acceptable to God on his own. Man objects to the idea that the perfect and sinless Son of God had to come to earth to die for his sins. Man objects because it means that man is...

- sinful and depraved.
- so sinful and depraved that he is totally unacceptable to God.
- so sinful and depraved that he cannot become acceptable to God by his own efforts.
- so sinful and depraved that no matter what he does, he cannot secure God's approval.
- so sinful and depraved that he can never fellowship with God, that all his prayers, worship, and thoughts about God are vain and empty.

This is the reason many persons object to Jesus Christ. This is the reason many accept Him as a great religious teacher, but reject His claim to be the Son of God and the Savior of the world. They are unwilling to accept the fact that man is depraved, totally sinful. This is the great subject of this passage, the second major misconception of man about the deity of Jesus Christ, about the Son of God coming to earth: *man is not totally sinful and depraved.*

1. We are not totally sinful and depraved (v.8).
   a. This is a deception.
   b. The truth is not in us.
2. The truth: we must confess our sins (v.9).
   a. Because God is faithful and just.
   b. Because God forgives.

1 (1:8) **Man—Sin—Depravity**: the misconception is forcefully stated—"we claim to be without sin." Note that the word *sin* is not plural but singular. The sin being talked about is *sin as a root within man*, as a part of man's nature, as a principle, a law, a force, an energy within man. Persons who say that they can approach God on their own are saying that they have no sin, no root of sin, no nature of sin, no principle of sin within them. They are saying...

- that they can handle sin themselves; that they can change their lives and stop sinning enough to please God and to become acceptable to Him.
- that they do not need the Son of God to come to earth and die for their sins.
- that they can control their lives enough to keep from sinning.

Note what Scripture says about this misconception: we deceive ourselves and the truth is not in us. No person can keep from sinning. If any person thinks that he can keep from sinning, the truth is not in him; he is utterly deceived. And note: if we cannot keep from sinning, this means that we have a nature, a root of sin within us. The force and energy of the root shoots out and we sin. As stated, we cannot keep from sinning: this fact alone proves that we have sin within our nature, a nature that is depraved. To say differently is to be deceived and to deny the truth of all human experience. Remember: sin is imperfection. Sin is falling short of God's glory and perfection, missing the mark of His glory and perfection. This is the reason no person can ever live with God. God is perfect; therefore, only perfection can live in His presence. Man is imperfect and short of God's glory; he is sinful. Therefore, man can never live in God's presence. This is what the objector needs to see. If he misses this, then he will miss the eternal salvation that is in Christ Jesus our Lord, the very Son of God who came to earth to die for our sins.

Thought 1. Note a significant fact. There are those who say that man is not responsible for his sin; therefore, he cannot be charged with sin. They say that man acts the way he does because of his upbringing, parents, society, environment, education or the lack of it, playmates and associates. They say that man is a product of his environment; therefore, God cannot charge man with guilt. Man just is not responsible for his behavior. For this reason, God nor society can hold man accountable for his actions. The reason man sins is because someone else made him do it.

The problem with this is that it is only partly true. Environment and upbringing do affect us and have some bearing on our actions. But this is not all that we are; we are not just robots responding to the trigger of environment. We are free moral creatures with a free will that chooses to sin or not to sin. And it is deception to deny the fact. The truth is just not in us if we deny that we have a great degree of freedom in all that we do. The problem is not our environment; we just cannot keep from sinning and acting irresponsibly. We sin because there is a root, a nature, a force of sin within us. To object to what is so clear and visible is to be deceived, to show that the truth is not in us.

Thought 2. The person who thinks that he can control sin enough to become acceptable to God has a low view of God and too high a view of himself. Think how weak man really is: how weak his flesh is. He is not only sinful by acts, but he walks short of God's glory every day. And he is so corruptible that he dies after just a few brief years on earth.

> "Not everyone who says to me, 'Lord, Lord,' will enter the kingdom of heaven, but only he who does the will of my Father who is in heaven. Many will say to me on that day, 'Lord, Lord, did we not prophesy in your name, and in your name drive out demons and perform many miracles?' Then I will tell them plainly, 'I never knew you. Away from me, you evildoers!' (Mat 7:21-23)

> For all have sinned and fall short of the glory of God, (Rom 3:23)

> Therefore, just as sin entered the world through one man, and death through sin, and in this way death came to all men, because all sinned— (Rom 5:12)

> If we claim to be without sin, we deceive ourselves and the truth is not in us. (1 John 1:8)

> We know that we are children of God, and that the whole world is under the control of the evil one. (1 John 5:19)

> So, because you are lukewarm—neither hot nor cold—I am about to spit you out of my mouth. You say, 'I am rich; I have acquired wealth and do not need a thing.' But you do not realize that you are wretched, pitiful, poor, blind and naked. I counsel you to buy from me gold refined in the fire, so you can become rich; and white clothes to wear, so you can cover your shameful nakedness; and salve to put on your eyes, so you can see. (Rev 3:16-18)

> The LORD saw how great man's wickedness on the earth had become, and that every inclination of the thoughts of his heart was only evil all the time. (Gen 6:5)

> Everyone has turned away, they have together become corrupt; there is no one who does good, not even one. (Psa 53:3)

> Who can say, "I have kept my heart pure; I am clean and without sin"? (Prov 20:9)

> All of us have become like one who is unclean, and all our righteous acts are like filthy rags; we all shrivel up like a leaf, and like the wind our sins sweep us away. (Isa 64:6)

2 (1:9) **Confession of Sins—Forgiveness of Sin**: the truth is this—we must confess our sins. Man is deceived if he denies that he has sinned, if he denies that he has a root and force of sin within him. He deceives himself if he says that he does not need the Son of God to deliver him from sin and its guilt. Remember: the Son of God came to die for our sins, and it is His blood that cleanses us from sin. Therefore, if we will confess our sins, God will forgive our sins. And He will do even more: He not only will forgive us for the sins we know about and confess, He will purify us from *all unrighteousness*.

⇒ *To forgive our sins* means that God forgives the *guilt of sin*. God justifies us: He counts the death of Christ as our punishment. Jesus Christ bore our guilt of sin. When we believe in Jesus Christ and confess our sins, God counts our belief and confession as the guilt which Christ bore. We stand before God, no longer guilty of sin.

⇒ *To purify us from all unrighteousness* means that God cleanses us from all the dirt, filth, pollution, and contamination of sin. Not a single stain or spot of sin remains on us. We stand before God sinless and perfect, but remember why: because we believe in Jesus Christ and confess that we are sinners who trust the blood of God's Son to purify our sins.

How do we know that God will forgive our sins and purify us? How do we know that God will count the death of Jesus Christ as the punishment for our sins? Because God is faithful and just or righteous.

⇒ God is perfectly just or righteous; therefore He must condemn and punish sin. But note: God is also perfect love and mercy; therefore, He must demonstrate His love and mercy and provide a way of forgiveness for man. This is exactly what He has done in Jesus Christ. God has demonstrated His love in the most perfect and supreme way possible: He has given His Son to die for the sins of man.

The point is this: having done this for man—having given His Son to die for man's sins—God will forgive man. He is faithful and righteous; therefore, He will keep His Word. He will do exactly what He says. He would be unfaithful and unrighteous if He did not forgive us. Therefore, God will forgive any repentant sinner who truly turns away from his sin and turns to God and confesses his sin. God is faithful and just to forgive us our sins.

> God exalted him to his own right hand as Prince and Savior that he might give repentance and forgiveness of sins to Israel. (Acts 5:31)

> "Therefore, my brothers, I want you to know that through Jesus the forgiveness of sins is proclaimed to you. (Acts 13:38)

In him we have redemption through his blood, the forgiveness of sins, in accordance with the riches of God's grace (Eph 1:7)

If we confess our sins, he is faithful and just and will forgive us our sins and purify us from all unrighteousness. (1 John 1:9)

Now make confession to the LORD, the God of your fathers, and do his will. Separate yourselves from the peoples around you and from your foreign wives." (Ezra 10:11)

He who conceals his sins does not prosper, but whoever confesses and renounces them finds mercy. (Prov 28:13)

"I, even I, am he who blots out your transgressions, for my own sake, and remembers your sins no more. (Isa 43:25)

I have swept away your offenses like a cloud, your sins like the morning mist. Return to me, for I have redeemed you." (Isa 44:22)

We all, like sheep, have gone astray, each of us has turned to his own way; and the LORD has laid on him the iniquity of us all. He was oppressed and afflicted, yet he did not open his mouth; he was led like a lamb to the slaughter, and as a sheep before her shearers is silent, so he did not open his mouth. (Isa 53:6-7)

Let the wicked forsake his way and the evil man his thoughts. Let him turn to the LORD, and he will have mercy on him, and to our God, for he will freely pardon. (Isa 55:7)

Only acknowledge your guilt— you have rebelled against the LORD your God, you have scattered your favors to foreign gods under every spreading tree, and have not obeyed me,'" declares the LORD. (Jer 3:13)

		C. Misconception 3: Man Can Become Sinless & Righteous on His Own, 1:10-2:2
1	We can become righteous & sinless on our own	10 If we claim we have not sinned, we make him out to be a liar and his word has no place in our lives.
		CHAPTER 2
2	The truth: We are sinful, but we should not sin	My dear children, I write this to you so that you will not sin. But if anybody does sin, we have one who speaks to the Father in our defense— Jesus Christ, the Righteous One.
3	The provision is made if we do sin	
	a. Jesus Christ, the Advocate, the one who pleads for us	
	b. Jesus Christ, the propitiation, the atoning sacrifice, for our sins^DS1	2 He is the atoning sacrifice for our sins, and not only for ours but also for the sins of the whole world.

DIVISION I

THE THREE MISCONCEPTIONS OF MAN, 1:6-2:2

C. Misconception 3: Man Can Become Sinless and Righteous on His Own, 1:10-2:2

(1:10-2:2) **Introduction**: sin is a terrible thing. We see it blazed across the headlines of news reports every day: murder, mayhem, assault, fraud, cheating, lying, deceit, adultery, divorce, fightings, wars. Sin is so corrupt and common that every conceivable sin is seen or heard about in one form or another practically every day. Sin is so much a part of human life that we hardly pay attention to it unless it is some major crime or else it involves our own lives and families. Sin is just everywhere. No matter where we turn we see people mistreating others—criticizing, backbiting, and gossiping about them. We see people verbally tearing other people down. We see husbands and wives living together but lacking true love. They are just together, living in coldness and being withdrawn from one another. We see all kinds of selfishness in children and fellow workers. We see lying, deception, stealing, cheating, and all sorts of sexual immorality. We see people dressing in tight clothes or else exposing parts of the human body in order to attract attention, and then we see all kinds of promiscuity and rapes, assaults and murders. The list of sins and shortcomings in life could fill a book.

But the point is this: some people say they have not sinned. Despite all the sin in the world—all the sin that swirls around and engulfs human lives and society—some persons say that they can become righteous on their own. They say they can become so righteous that God will approve their behavior—that God will accept them because of their own righteousness and sinlessness. They say they do not need a Savior; they are able to save themselves. They say that the Son of God does not need to die for the sins of man because man can become righteous and sinless enough on his own, righteous and sinless enough to become acceptable to God.

This is the subject of the present passage. There are those who object to the idea that Jesus Christ *had to die* for the sins of man. They object to the preaching of sin, the idea that they are sinners, to the idea that they need the blood of God's Son to cleanse their sins. They object and declare that *man can become righteous and sinless on His own*.

1. We can become righteous and sinless on our own (v.10).
2. The truth: we are sinful, but we should not sin (Ch.2:1).
3. The provision is made if we do sin (v.1-2).
   a. Jesus Christ, the Advocate.
   b. Jesus Christ, the propitiation, the atoning sacrifice, for our sins.

1 (1:10) **Sin—Self-righteousness—Self-Sufficient**: the misconception is forcefully stated—"we have not sinned." How could any person conceivably claim this? Who would claim such a thing in light of all the sin that swirls and engulfs man and society? Many people! There are many people who object to being called *sinners*, and they are insistent in their objection. They believe they are righteous and sinless enough that God would never reject them. They believe they can become good enough and sinless and righteous enough for God to accept them. They accept Jesus Christ as a great moral teacher and as the founder of Christianity, one of the great religions of the world. And they claim to be Christians; they follow the teachings of Jesus Christ. But they reject His deity, the fact that He is the Son of God who had to die for the sins of the world. They look upon the death of Jesus Christ as the death of a martyr, as a great man who was showing us how we should be willing to pay any price for what we believe—even death.

Who would make such a claim? Who would say "we have not sinned"? Who is it that objects to being called *a sinner*?

⇒ There is the *religious perfectionist*. This is a person who actually believes that he can achieve a state of sinlessness. Often he believes in Christ, but he believes that once he is saved, he can live so righteous and so pure a life that he can achieve a state of sinlessness and righteousness before God. He believes that the Holy Spirit will help him to *walk perfectly* before God.

⇒ There is the *social perfectionist*. This is a person who is a social Christian, who accepts Jesus Christ as a great teacher but rejects Him as the Savior from sin. He objects to being called *a sinner*; he objects to the fact that he is sinful enough that he can be termed *a sinner*. He believes that he is righteous and sinless enough for God to accept, that God would never reject them. He believes he is too good for God to reject. He cannot accept the fact that he is bad enough and sinful enough for God to condemn him.

Note what the problem is with these two objectors. They just do not have a clear view of what sin is. To them sin is the gross violation of law and morality, the thing that society looks upon as gross sins: murder, fraud, and abuse—the kinds of things that would grab a neighbor's attention and cause talk. They fail to see what sin is to God. God is perfect; therefore, to God:

⇒ Sin is any imperfection.
⇒ Sin is falling short of God's glory.
⇒ Sin is missing the mark of God's perfection.

This is the reason no person can ever live with God. God is perfect; therefore, only perfection can live in His presence. Man is imperfect and short of God's glory; he is sinful. Therefore, man can never live in God's presence. This is what the objector needs to see. To God man is *a sinner*, a person who is ever so short of God's glory, a person...

- who fails to use his mind to the fullest degree and who focuses it upon evil.
- who sometimes thinks impure and wrong thoughts and who commits impurity.
- who sometimes acts unlovely and mean to people.
- who sometimes acts impatiently and abuses others.
- who sometimes acts selfishly and steals.
- who sometimes owns too much and banks and hoards instead of living sacrificially to meet the desperate needs of the world.

All men are short in so much—short in worshipping God like they should, short in praying and fellowshipping and communing with God. No person obeys God perfectly all the time. All men come short of loving others like they should, short in witnessing and sharing Christ and in sacrificing and reaching out to help everywhere they should. No person is perfect; all are ever so short and sinful, so sinful that to God we are all sinners. We are sinners who need a Savior, the very Son of God Himself, to save us from our sins. Now, note what the verse says:

If we claim we have not sinned, we make him out to be a liar and his word has no place in our lives. (v.10)

God's Word plainly tells us that we are sinners, and it tells us often. If we, therefore, deny sin, we make God out to be a liar. In addition, we show that God's Word is not in us; that is, we are not acceptable to God. No matter what we may claim, we are not acceptable to God...

- if God's Word is not in us.
- if we call God a liar.

- if we say we do not need God's Son to save us from our sin.
- if we say we can become good enough and righteous enough and sinless enough to be acceptable to God.

For all have sinned and fall short of the glory of God, (Rom 3:23)

At one time we too were foolish, disobedient, deceived and enslaved by all kinds of passions and pleasures. We lived in malice and envy, being hated and hating one another. (Titus 3:3)

Anyone, then, who knows the good he ought to do and doesn't do it, sins. (James 4:17)

If we claim to be without sin, we deceive ourselves and the truth is not in us. (1 John 1:8)

We know that we are children of God, and that the whole world is under the control of the evil one. (1 John 5:19)

There is not a righteous man on earth who does what is right and never sins. (Eccl 7:20)

The LORD saw how great man's wickedness on the earth had become, and that every inclination of the thoughts of his heart was only evil all the time. (Gen 6:5)

Everyone has turned away, they have together become corrupt; there is no one who does good, not even one. (Psa 53:3)

Who can say, "I have kept my heart pure; I am clean and without sin"? (Prov 20:9)

We all, like sheep, have gone astray, each of us has turned to his own way; and the LORD has laid on him the iniquity of us all. (Isa 53:6)

All of us have become like one who is unclean, and all our righteous acts are like filthy rags; we all shrivel up like a leaf, and like the wind our sins sweep us away. (Isa 64:6)

2 (2:1) **Sin—Spiritual Struggle**: the truth is that we are sinful, but *we should not sin*. This is a tender exhortation: John addresses the believers "my dear children." They are very, very dear to him. He was their pastor, their spiritual father; and they were his spiritual children, the ones under his care. He loved them with the love of a strong and caring father. Therefore, he must exhort them. He must exhort them in the areas where they needed strength. Where was that? In sinning. Note exactly what John says:

My dear children, I write this to you so that you will not sin. (1 John 2:1)

"*I write this*" refer to the things John has just said, to the fact that all have sinned and all do sin. Because of man's nature, the very fact that he lives within a corruptible world, he *cannot keep from sinning*. But note the strong exhortation: "I write this to you so that you will not sin." The believer lives in a corruptible world, and he is housed in a body of flesh that is so easily aroused and attracted to eat more, take more, have more, be more, and receive more. But the believer is to struggle and fight against sin. He is not to give in to sin. He is to *cast down imaginations*, *demolish arguments* and struggle to captivate every thought for Christ (2 Cor.10:5). He is to do all he can to become more and more like Christ and to be a stronger and stronger witness for righteousness in the world. He will never achieve perfection; he will never be sinless so long as he is in the flesh and in this corruptible world. But he is to struggle to be as good as he can. He is to be as righteous as possible and he is to gain ground; he is to grow in righteousness. The believer is to become more and more like Christ as long as he is on earth.

Thought 1. Believers must prove they are sincere when they come to Christ for forgiveness of sins. Christ has no patience with hypocrisy and no place for half-hearted commitment. He can look at our lives and tell whether we love Him or not, whether we are sincere or not. He can watch our struggle against sin and tell if we really want to follow Him or not. The genuine believer struggles against sin; he fights, wrestles, and wars against sin with every ounce of energy he has. He does all he can to please God and to receive God's approval.

> **Wash and make yourselves clean. Take your evil deeds out of my sight! Stop doing wrong, (Isa 1:16)**
>
> **Later Jesus found him at the temple and said to him, "See, you are well again. Stop sinning or something worse may happen to you." (John 5:14)**
>
> **"No one, sir," she said. "Then neither do I condemn you," Jesus declared. "Go now and leave your life of sin." (John 8:11)**
>
> **Therefore do not let sin reign in your mortal body so that you obey its evil desires. (Rom 6:12)**
>
> **Come back to your senses as you ought, and stop sinning; for there are some who are ignorant of God—I say this to your shame. (1 Cor 15:34)**
>
> **If you put away the sin that is in your hand and allow no evil to dwell in your tent, (Job 11:14)**
>
> **Let the wicked forsake his way and the evil man his thoughts. Let him turn to the LORD, and he will have mercy on him, and to our God, for he will freely pardon. (Isa 55:7)**
>
> **You were taught, with regard to your former way of life, to put off your old self, which is being corrupted by its deceitful desires; (Eph 4:22)**
>
> **Therefore, since we are surrounded by such a great cloud of witnesses, let us throw off everything that hinders and the sin that so easily entangles, and let us run with perseverance the race marked out for us. (Heb 12:1)**
>
> **Dear friends, I urge you, as aliens and strangers in the world, to abstain from sinful desires, which war against your soul. (1 Pet 2:11)**
>
> **My dear children, I write this to you so that you will not sin. But if anybody does sin, we have one who speaks to the Father in our defense—Jesus Christ, the Righteous One. (1 John 2:1)**

3 (2:1-2) **Jesus Christ, Death**: there is the great provision. The believer is not to sin, but if he sins he has the most wonderful provision—that is Jesus Christ, the Son of God Himself. Two things are said about Jesus Christ that show the wonderful provision God has made for us.

1. Jesus Christ is our "Advocate," the one who speaks to the father in our defense (parakleton). The word *"advocate or defender"* means someone who is called in to stand by the side of another. The purpose is to help in any way possible. (This is the word [parakletos] used of the Holy Spirit. See DEEPER STUDY # 1—Jn.14:16 for discussion.)

⇒ There is the picture of a friend called in to help a person who is troubled or distressed or confused.

⇒ There is the picture of a commander called in to help a discouraged and dispirited army.

⇒ There is the picture of a lawyer, an advocate called in to help a defendant who needs his case pleaded.

There is no one word that can adequately translate *paracletos*. The word that probably comes closest is simply *helper*. Sin causes the believer to be distressed and confused, discouraged and dispirited. Sin separates the believer from God and makes him guilty of transgression and worthy of condemnation and punishment. But Jesus Christ is the believer's *Advocate*. Jesus Christ stands before God and pleads the case of the believer. Note two significant points.

a. What is it that gives Jesus Christ the right to plead the case of the believer? Note exactly what the verse says: Jesus Christ is *the righteous One*. He is the Son of God who came to earth and lived a sinless life as man. He is the One who secured the *perfect and ideal righteousness* for man. Therefore, Jesus Christ is the *only Person* who has the right to stand before God. Why? Because God is perfect, and only a perfect person can stand in God's presence. This is the reason man must approach God through Jesus Christ: He alone is perfect and righteous. He alone has the right to stand in the court of God as the Advocate or attorney to represent man. There is no other righteousness, no other goodness that is acceptable to God; only the perfect and ideal righteousness of Christ has been approved to stand as the advocate in the court of heaven.

This means a most wonderful thing. God will never turn down a person who has Jesus Christ as his advocate. The person who has Jesus Christ to approach God for him will never be turned down, for Jesus Christ has the right to stand as the advocate before God in the court of heaven.

b. What is it that Jesus Christ pleads?

⇒ He does not plead the reputation of the believer.

⇒ He does not plead the good works of the believer.

⇒ He does not plead *not guilty*, that the believer did not commit sin.

⇒ He does not plead the personal righteousness of the believer.

⇒ He does not plead that the believer has been as good as he can be.

What is it that Jesus Christ pleads? Again, note the verse:

We have one who speaks to the Father in our defense—Jesus Christ, the Righteous One. (1 John 2:1)

He pleads His own righteousness. How can He do this? This is the discussion of the next point.

Who is he that condemns? Christ Jesus, who died—more than that, who was raised to life—is at the right hand of God and is also interceding for us. (Rom 8:34)

For this reason he had to be made like his brothers in every way, in order that he might become a merciful and faithful high priest in service to God, and that he might make atonement for the sins of the people. (Heb 2:17)

Therefore, since we have a great high priest who has gone through the heavens, Jesus the Son of God, let us hold firmly to the faith we profess. For we do not have a high priest who is unable to sympathize with our weaknesses, but we have one who has been tempted in every way, just as we are—yet was without sin. (Heb 4:14-15)

Therefore he is able to save completely those who come to God through him, because he always lives to intercede for them. Such a high priest meets our need—one who is holy, blameless, pure, set apart from sinners, exalted above the heavens. (Heb 7:25-26)

The point of what we are saying is this: We do have such a high priest, who sat down at the right hand of the throne of the Majesty in heaven, (Heb 8:1)

For Christ did not enter a man-made sanctuary that was only a copy of the true one; he entered heaven itself, now to appear for us in God's presence. (Heb 9:24)

2. Jesus Christ is the *propitiation, the atoning sacrifice for our sins.* "Atoning sacrifice" (hilasmos) means to be a sacrifice, a covering, a satisfaction, a payment, an appeasement for sin. It means to turn away anger or to make reconciliation between God and man. Remember: God is holy and just. He is perfect love, but He is also perfect holiness and justice. Therefore He must execute justice against the sinner. He must judge and condemn sin. His justice must be perfectly satisfied. Now there is only one way God's justice can be perfectly satisfied: His justice has to be cast against the perfect sacrifice. If there was a Perfect and Ideal Man, then that Man could accept the guilt and punishment for sin. The Perfect Man could step forward and bear the punishment for sin and satisfy the justice of God.

This is the glorious gospel, the wonderful love and provision of God. Jesus Christ is the Ideal and Perfect Man. Therefore, He sacrificed His life for man and His sacrifice covered all men. As the Ideal Man, Jesus Christ accepted the guilt and punishment of sin for all men. He died for all men. When He died, He died as the perfect sacrifice for sins. Therefore, God accepts His death...

- as the *sacrifice* for our sins.
- as the *covering* for our sins.
- as the *satisfaction* for our sins.
- as the *payment* for the penalty of our sins.
- as the *appeasement* of His wrath against sin.

When Jesus Christ carries a man's case before God, He pleads His own righteousness and death, and God accepts His righteousness and death for man. It is by this, by the sacrifice of His death for our sins, that we become acceptable to God.

Note one other point: Jesus Christ is the propitiation, the atoning sacrifice for the sins of the *whole world*. He is the eternal Son of God, the Ideal and Perfect Man. Therefore, all that He ever did covers eternity. His sacrifice for sin covers the first man ever born and spans all of time over to the last man, and then continues right on throughout all of eternity. Jesus Christ paid the penalty of sin for all sinners of all generations. He died for the sins of all people, no matter who they are or what they have done.

But note a critical fact: a person has to come to Jesus Christ and trust Him to be his advocate before God. Jesus Christ is the only Person who has the right to stand as an advocate in the court of God's perfect justice. He is the only Person who can present man's case before God and have man declared righteous. Therefore, a person is not covered by the advocacy of Christ unless he comes to Christ and has Christ represent him before God.

For this reason he had to be made like his brothers in every way, in order that he might become a merciful and faithful high priest in service to God, and that he might make atonement for the sins of the people. (Heb 2:17)

My dear children, I write this to you so that you will not sin. But if anybody does sin, we have one who speaks to the Father in our defense—Jesus Christ, the Righteous One. He is the atoning sacrifice for our sins, and not only for ours but also for the sins of the whole world. (1 John 2:1-2)

This is love: not that we loved God, but that he loved us and sent his Son as an atoning sacrifice for our sins. (1 John 4:10)

"But the tax collector stood at a distance. He would not even look up to heaven, but beat his breast and said, 'God, have mercy on me, a sinner.' (Luke 18:13)

DEEPER STUDY # 1

(2:2) Atoning Sacrifice—Propitiation (hilasmos): to sacrifice in order to appease; to satisfy; to cover; to pay the penalty for. It is a sacrificial word. In the Old Testament when a man sinned or something went wrong, he brought a sacrifice to God. The idea was that the sacrifice would appease and pacify and satisfy God. He thought God would be gracious to him and place the punishment for his sin upon the animal. When things go wrong, man has always offered to fast and pray and serve with renewed vigor, or else he has offered to give up some meaningful pleasure or possession. There is a feeling that this kind of denial or renewed sacrifice appeases and satisfies God.

It is true that God told Israel to offer sacrifices. But He did it for a reason: to teach Israel, and through them the world, that the answer does not lie in human or animal sacrifice. A human sacrifice cannot bring about a right relationship with God. Man's problem is too deep for human sacrifice; his contamination too severe; his disease too terrible; his infection too deadly. The paraphernalia of earthly sacrifice can never put things right with God.

The reason is simply stated. Man's sin has cut him off from God, severed his relationship with God, put God out of *arm's reach*. Man instinctively senses this. Thus, when man fails to get satisfaction from his sacrifice, he often returns to his former behavior and practices.

What man needs is to be disinfected, to have his sins covered. He needs to know beyond a doubt that God does accept him and is satisfied with him. And then he needs a power to live for God.

This comes about through propitiation. Four things need to be said about propitiation.

1. God is the One who has to be appeased, satisfied, and propitiated. The Bible is not speaking of reconciliation. The Bible never says that God has to be reconciled to man. God is already the friend of man; He loves man. It is man who needs to be reconciled to God. Man is the one who holds enmity, who ignores, neglects, and rejects God. Thus, God is the One who has to be appeased or propitiated (cp. Lk.18:13).

There is another thought here as well. God is righteous and holy, and His righteousness and holiness have to be satisfied. He can only accept a person who is perfectly righteous and holy. It might be said that anything less than perfection would contaminate the very atmosphere around God. And the presence and dwelling place of God would no longer be the utopia which God has prepared for the believer and for which man dreams.

2. Jesus Christ is the propitiation, the atoning sacrifice, the satisfaction for sins. Christ was completely righteous and holy; therefore, He was the perfect and ideal Man. This means that His death was the perfect and ideal sacrifice. God was able to satisfy His justice against sins by casting it against Christ. The perfect sacrifice of Jesus Christ completely satisfied and appeased the righteousness of God (1 Jn.4:9-10).

3. Propitiation means *coverage*. Christ covers our sins so that God no longer can see them (Ro.3:25; Heb.2:17; 1 Jn.2:2).

4. Propitiation finds its type in the mercy seat, that is, in the lid of the ark (Heb.9:5). God had said that man was to approach Him through the sacrifice of an animal, through the shedding of blood. The lid or covering of the ark was sprinkled once a year with the blood of a perfect animal. This signified that the life of the people was being offered to God in the blood of the victim. God was thereby appeased and satisfied. (Cp. Lk.18:13; Ro.3:25; Heb.2:17; 1 Jn.2:2; 4:10.)

	III. THE PROOF THAT ONE REALLY KNOWS GOD: SEVEN TESTS, 2:3-29 A. Test 1: Obeying God's Commands, 2:3-6	4 The man who says, "I know him," but does not do what he commands is a liar, and the truth is not in him. 5 But if anyone obeys his word, God's love is truly made complete in him. This is how we know we are in him:	2 The professing man: Says he knows God but does not obey His commands 3 The obedient man: Obeys God's Word
1 The test: Do we obey God's commands?	3 We know that we have come to know him if we obey his commands.	6 Whoever claims to live in him must walk as Jesus did.	4 The responsible man: Lives up to his profession

DIVISION III

THE PROOF THAT ONE REALLY KNOWS GOD: SEVEN TESTS, 2:3-29

A. Test 1: Obeying God's Commands, 2:3-6

(2:3-6) **Introduction**: How do we know if we really know God? We live in a day when many people are not even interested in knowing God. They could care less about knowing God. They want to live like they want and get all the possessions and enjoy all the pleasures of the world they can. To know God is the furthest thing from their minds. But this is dangerous ground, for if God really exists then the rejecters of God are going to miss out:

⇒ They are going to miss out on the purpose, meaning, and significance of life; they are going to miss out on real love, joy, and peace and the abundance of a rich and full life both now and eternally. If God really exists and they fail to know Him, they are going to miss out on all of what life really is. Why? Because God created life and He knows what life should be. Therefore, if we do not know God, God who gave us life, then we miss out on everything that God meant life to be. But this is not all that the rejecters will face if they do not know God.

⇒ If God exists, then it means that all those who reject Him must face His holiness and justice. They must stand before Him having rejected Him and face His judgment.

The point is clear: we must know God. But how can we tell if we really know Him? There are seven tests that will show us. The first test is the discussion of this passage: Do we obey God's commands?

1. The test: do we obey God's commands (v.3)?
2. The professing man: says he knows God but does not obey His commands (v.4).
3. The obedient man: obeys God's Word (v.5).
4. The responsible man: lives up to his profession (v.6).

1 (2:3) **Commandments—Knowledge, of God—Believers**: How do we know if we really know God? There is a test that will show us. Do we obey God's commands? Man faces an enormous problem, a problem that any thinking and honest person can see. If God really exists, man can never know it—not by his own reasoning and energy or effort. No matter how much thought or creative thinking and *inner feelings* man may have, man can never know for sure if God exists—not in and of himself. There is a clear reason for this. Man lives in a physical and material world, and the physical and material world cannot penetrate or cross over into the other world, that is, into the spiritual world. If man is ever to *know* the spiritual world, if he is ever to know God, then God has to enter the physical and material world and reveal Himself to man. And note: this

is exactly what God has done. God has sent His Son Jesus Christ into the world to tell man the truth: the truth about God, about man himself, about the world in which man lives, and about the world to come. This is exactly what Jesus Christ and His followers said time and again. This is exactly what Jesus Christ and Scripture declare:

⇒ No man has ever crossed over into the spirit world and returned, no man but Jesus Christ.

No one has ever gone into heaven except the one who came from heaven—the Son of Man. (John 3:13)
For the bread of God is he who comes down from heaven and gives life to the world." For I have come down from heaven not to do my will but to do the will of him who sent me. (John 6:33, 38)
But here is the bread that comes down from heaven, which a man may eat and not die. I am the living bread that came down from heaven. If anyone eats of this bread, he will live forever. This bread is my flesh, which I will give for the life of the world." (John 6:50-51)
Jesus said to them, "If God were your Father, you would love me, for I came from God and now am here. I have not come on my own; but he sent me. (John 8:42)
Jesus knew that the Father had put all things under his power, and that he had come from God and was returning to God; (John 13:3)
And now, Father, glorify me in your presence with the glory I had with you before the world began. (John 17:5)

⇒ Jesus Christ came to save man from perishing and to give man a full, abundant life both now and eternally.

"For God so loved the world that he gave his one and only Son, that whoever believes in him shall not perish but have eternal life. (John 3:16)
Whoever believes in the Son has eternal life, but whoever rejects the Son will not see life, for God's wrath remains on him." (John 3:36)
"I tell you the truth, whoever hears my word and believes him who sent me has eter-

nal life and will not be condemned; he has crossed over from death to life. (John 5:24)

The thief comes only to steal and kill and destroy; I have come that they may have life, and have it to the full. (John 10:10)

⇒ Jesus Christ said that God had sent Him to make God known.

Nor does his word dwell in you, for you do not believe the one he sent. (John 5:38)

Jesus answered, "The work of God is this: to believe in the one he has sent." (John 6:29)

Then Jesus, still teaching in the temple courts, cried out, "Yes, you know me, and you know where I am from. I am not here on my own, but he who sent me is true. You do not know him, (John 7:28)

"I have much to say in judgment of you. But he who sent me is reliable, and what I have heard from him I tell the world." (John 8:26)

When he looks at me, he sees the one who sent me. (John 12:45)

If you really knew me, you would know my Father as well. From now on, you do know him and have seen him." (John 14:7)

All that belongs to the Father is mine. That is why I said the Spirit will take from what is mine and make it known to you. (John 16:15)

For in Christ all the fullness of the Deity lives in bodily form, (Col 2:9)

Beyond all question, the mystery of godliness is great: He appeared in a body, was vindicated by the Spirit, was seen by angels, was preached among the nations, was believed on in the world, was taken up in glory. (1 Tim 3:16)

The Son is the radiance of God's glory and the exact representation of his being, sustaining all things by his powerful word. After he had provided purification for sins, he sat down at the right hand of the Majesty in heaven. (Heb 1:3)

This means something very significant: if we are to know God, we must know Jesus Christ. God has revealed Himself and made Himself known through Jesus Christ and through Christ alone. Therefore, to know God we must know Jesus Christ whom He has sent. How do we know if we know God? If we know Jesus Christ, then we know God.

Now, note exactly what the verse says.

We know that we have come to know him if we obey his commands. (v.3)

This verse says explicitly that we know God if we obey God's commands. What are God's commands?

And this is his command: to believe in the name of his Son, Jesus Christ, and to love one another as he commanded us. (1 John 3:23)

God's chief command is this: that we believe in the name of His Son Jesus Christ and love one another. There are two things said here.

1. First, to know God we must believe on the name of His Son Jesus Christ. If we believe in Christ, then we come to know God, for Jesus Christ came to earth to reveal God. By believing in Jesus Christ we keep God's commandment.

2. Second, to know God we must love one another. Love covers all the commandments of God. If we love one another, we will not hurt or cause pain for one another; we will not offend or sin against one another. We will be obeying all the commands of God. This is exactly what Scripture declares.

Let no debt remain outstanding, except the continuing debt to love one another, for he who loves his fellowman has fulfilled the law. The commandments, "Do not commit adultery," "Do not murder," "Do not steal," "Do not covet," and whatever other commandment there may be, are summed up in this one rule: "Love your neighbor as yourself." Love does no harm to its neighbor. Therefore love is the fulfillment of the law. (Rom 13:8-10)

The point is this: How do we know if we know God? Take a test: Do we obey God's commands? If we obey God's commands, then we believe in Jesus Christ, that He is God's Son, and we love one another. We surrender all we are and have to Jesus Christ and to loving one another. Unless we are doing these two things, we do not know God. No matter what a person may say, he does not know God if he has never given his life to Jesus Christ. And he does not know God if he criticizes, grumbles, and backbites his brother and commits adultery, kills, steals, lies, covets, or does anything else against his brother. If a person really knows God, then he wants to please God. He wants to know more and more about God, and the only way he can know more and more about God is to follow God. He has to do the things that God does, to walk and love as God walks and loves. The more we walk and love as God does, the more we will come to know God. Therefore, if we obey His commands, we know Him. This is the way we can tell if we know Him, the only way.

Jesus answered, "My teaching is not my own. It comes from him who sent me. If anyone chooses to do God's will, he will find out whether my teaching comes from God or whether I speak on my own. (John 7:16-17)

To the Jews who had believed him, Jesus said, "If you hold to my teaching, you are really my disciples. (John 8:31)

I tell you the truth, if anyone keeps my word, he will never see death." (John 8:51)

We know that we have come to know him if we obey his commands. (1 John 2:3)

Let us acknowledge the LORD; let us press on to acknowledge him. As surely as the sun rises, he will appear; he will come to us like the winter rains, like the spring rains that water the earth." (Hosea 6:3)

Thought 1. Some people seek to know God. They seek after God, but they do it in the wrong way.

1) Some speculate about God. This is the route most people take in trying to know God. They imagine what God is like and hold that image in their mind and try to live by what they imagine. They have their own teachings and their own images of what God is like, and they govern their lives by that image.

220

2) Some try to seek and know God by mystical or emotional experiences. They seek to know the spiritual world and its focus through spiritists, astrology, seances, magic, and a host of other man-made mystical experiences.

2 (2:4) **Profession, False**: there is the man who makes a false profession. Scripture is direct and pulls no punches:

**The man who says, "I know him," but
does not do what he commands is a liar,
and the truth is not in him. (v.4)**

It is absolutely impossible to know God and not to obey His commands. Why? For one clear reason: if God really exists, then He created us. We came from God. He created us for some purpose; He put us on earth for some reason. Therefore, He is bound to tell us why He created us; He is bound to tell us what He wants us to do and exactly how to do it. He would defeat His purpose if He did not. Therefore, God would never leave us in the dark, groping and grasping and trying to find out the truth. He would be a God of hate if He left us in the dark, and He is the farthest thing from hate. Jesus Christ has shown us that God is love, that God loves us so much that He has given us the Holy Scriptures to tell us what to do. But more than this, God has shown us His love by giving His Son to live the truth out right before our eyes. God has not only given us His written Word that tells us how to live, He has given us the *Living Word* in the life of His Son. God has sent His very own Son to live the perfect and ideal life upon earth so that we might know how to live. Jesus Christ lived out the will of God; He lived just like God commands man to live. Therefore, He knew God perfectly. He had perfect communion and fellowship with God.

The point is this: if a person says that he knows God and does not keep God's commands, he is a liar. The only way a person can know God is to follow Jesus Christ, to walk in fellowship with God just like Jesus Christ did. A person has to follow the perfect and ideal life of Jesus Christ. The person has to walk and live as Jesus Christ walked and lived; he has to follow Jesus Christ and do exactly what Jesus Christ says in order to know God. This is what Jesus Christ did: He obeyed all the commands of God; therefore, He knew God perfectly. This is exactly what man must do. Man must follow Jesus Christ and do exactly what Christ did: obey the commands of God. When man obeys the commands of God, then he will come to know God.

But note: the converse is also true. If a man does not keep God's commandments, then he does not know God. This is exactly what this verse says. Note it again.

**The man who says, "I know him," but
does not do what he commands is a liar,
and the truth is not in him. (v.4)**

Note: this person makes a false profession. His knowledge of God—what he thinks God is like—is false. His image of God and the ideas within his mind of God are not true. They are false, counterfeit, not genuine. The person does not know God at all. How can we tell? Because he does not obey the commands of God. He has not truly believed in Jesus Christ, nor is he loving his brother like God commands. He is not walking like Jesus Christ walked, not obeying God nor doing what God says to do. The verse is clear; note it: the person is a liar and the truth is not in him. He is making a false profession.

"Not everyone who says to me, 'Lord, Lord,' will enter the kingdom of heaven, but only he who does the will of my Father who is in heaven. (Mat 7:21)

He replied, "Isaiah was right when he prophesied about you hypocrites; as it is written: "'These people honor me with their lips, but their hearts are far from me. (Mark 7:6)

By this all men will know that you are my disciples, if you love one another." (John 13:35)

They claim to know God, but by their actions they deny him. They are detestable, disobedient and unfit for doing anything good. (Titus 1:16)

Be imitators of God, therefore, as dearly loved children and live a life of love, just as Christ loved us and gave himself up for us as a fragrant offering and sacrifice to God. But among you there must not be even a hint of sexual immorality, or of any kind of impurity, or of greed, because these are improper for God's holy people. Nor should there be obscenity, foolish talk or coarse joking, which are out of place, but rather thanksgiving. For of this you can be sure: No immoral, impure or greedy person—such a man is an idolater—has any inheritance in the kingdom of Christ and of God. Let no one deceive you with empty words, for because of such things God's wrath comes on those who are disobedient. (Eph 5:1-6)

They remembered that God was their Rock, that God Most High was their Redeemer. But then they would flatter him with their mouths, lying to him with their tongues; (Psa 78:35-36)

My people come to you, as they usually do, and sit before you to listen to your words, but they do not put them into practice. With their mouths they express devotion, but their hearts are greedy for unjust gain. Indeed, to them you are nothing more than one who sings love songs with a beautiful voice and plays an instrument well, for they hear your words but do not put them into practice. (Ezek 33:31-32)

3 (2:5) **Profession, True—Obedience**: there is the obedient man. The obedient man obeys God's Word and knows God and loves God. Note how obedience is tied to knowing and loving God. All these things are involved in knowing anyone. The only way to know anyone is...

- to get near them.
- to study them, learn all about them—all about their will, desires, and wants, their nature and thoughts and behavior.

The same is true with God. The only way to know God is to get near Him and study Him, learning all we can about His will, desires, and wants; all about His nature and thoughts and behavior. But how can we do this when God is in the spiritual world, another whole dimension of being, a world that is far removed from this world? By Jesus Christ. Remember: Jesus Christ came to earth to reveal God and to show us how to draw near God. Therefore, to know God, we must draw near Jesus Christ and follow the example He left us. We must follow the Word of Christ; we must keep the Word of Christ, living exactly as He lived. This is the person who knows God.

Note a most wonderful result: the person who obeys God's Word has God's love made complete in his life. What does this mean? When we draw near God and begin to keep His Word, we begin to *establish a relationship* with God. It is just like a boy who meets a girl and begins to draw near her. He begins to know her and to develop affection for her, and the more he associates with her, the more he loves her. So it is with God. The more we draw near Him and obey His Word and please Him, the more we learn about Him and love Him. The word "obeys" (terei) is continuous action. It means to continue on and not to stop. It means day by day obedience. If we obey God's Word day by day, then we learn more and more about God; we learn to love Him more and more. His love becomes completed and fulfilled in us.

The obedient person is the person who knows God and loves God. He is the person who knows the love of God; he knows all the fullness of life that God's love brings. No matter what a person may profess—no matter how religious a person may be—if he does not obey God, he does not know God. Neither does he love God.

> The rain came down, the streams rose, and the winds blew and beat against that house; yet it did not fall, because it had its foundation on the rock. But everyone who hears these words of mine and does not put them into practice is like a foolish man who built his house on sand. The rain came down, the streams rose, and the winds blew and beat against that house, and it fell with a great crash." (Mat 7:25-27)
>
> For whoever does the will of my Father in heaven is my brother and sister and mother." (Mat 12:50)
>
> If anyone chooses to do God's will, he will find out whether my teaching comes from God or whether I speak on my own. (John 7:17)
>
> Jesus replied, "If anyone loves me, he will obey my teaching. My Father will love him, and we will come to him and make our home with him. (John 14:23)
>
> But the world must learn that I love the Father and that I do exactly what my Father has commanded me. "Come now; let us leave [that I may die]. (John 14:31)
>
> If you obey my commands, you will remain in my love, just as I have obeyed my Father's commands and remain in his love. (John 15:10)
>
> You are my friends if you do what I command. (John 15:14)
>
> "Blessed are those who wash their robes, that they may have the right to the tree of life and may go through the gates into the city. (Rev 22:14)
>
> Oh, that their hearts would be inclined to fear me and keep all my commands always, so that it might go well with them and their children forever! (Deu 5:29)

4 (2:6) **Believer, Duty—Walk, Spiritual**: there is the responsible man, the man who lives up to his profession. The word "walk" (peripatein) is continuous action. It means to keep on walking; to continuously walk. If a person says that he abides in Christ, he must be a responsible person. He ought to walk as Jesus Christ walked. In fact, the word *must* means debt, constraint, obligation. The person who professes Jesus Christ, who claims that he knows God, is obligated to walk as Jesus Christ walked. He is in debt to walk as Christ walked. How did Christ walk upon earth? He walked...

- believing and trusting God
- worshipping and praying to God
- fellowshipping and communing with God
- giving and sacrificing all He was and had to God
- seeking and following after God
- teaching and telling others about God
- loving and caring for others just as God said to do
- obeying all of God's commands

This is the responsible man, the man who lives what he professes. If he professes to know God, he walks even as the Lord Jesus Christ walked upon earth. He believes and trusts God; he worships and prays to God, and he does all the other things that Christ did. He walks in the footsteps of Christ, doing exactly what Christ did. This is the person who knows God.

> We were therefore buried with him through baptism into death in order that, just as Christ was raised from the dead through the glory of the Father, we too may live a new life. (Rom 6:4)
>
> We live by faith, not by sight. (2 Cor 5:7)
>
> So I say, live by the Spirit, and you will not gratify the desires of the sinful nature. (Gal 5:16)
>
> As a prisoner for the Lord, then, I urge you to live a life worthy of the calling you have received. (Eph 4:1)
>
> And live a life of love, just as Christ loved us and gave himself up for us as a fragrant offering and sacrifice to God. (Eph 5:2)
>
> Be very careful, then, how you live— not as unwise but as wise, (Eph 5:15)
>
> But if we walk in the light, as he is in the light, we have fellowship with one another, and the blood of Jesus, his Son, purifies us from all sin. (1 John 1:7)
>
> Whoever claims to live in him must walk as Jesus did. (1 John 2:6)
>
> Then Jesus said to his disciples, "If anyone would come after me, he must deny himself and take up his cross and follow me. (Mat 16:24)
>
> I have set you an example that you should do as I have done for you. (John 13:15)
>
> Your attitude should be the same as that of Christ Jesus: (Phil 2:5)
>
> Bear with each other and forgive whatever grievances you may have against one another. Forgive as the Lord forgave you. (Col 3:13)
>
> Therefore, holy brothers, who share in the heavenly calling, fix your thoughts on Jesus, the apostle and high priest whom we confess. He was faithful to the one who appointed him, just as Moses was faithful in all God's house. (Heb 3:1-2)
>
> To this you were called, because Christ suffered for you, leaving you an example, that you should follow in his steps. (1 Pet 2:21)

	B. Test 2: Loving One's Neighbor, 2:7-11	shining.	erases darkness
1 The test: The supreme command—love a. Is an old command: Already in the Scripture b. Is a new command that is in Christ & in His disciples c. Is now made known by the true light that shines &	7 Dear friends, I am not writing you a new command but an old one, which you have had since the beginning. This old command is the message you have heard. 8 Yet I am writing you a new command; its truth is seen in him and you, because the darkness is passing and the true light is already	9 Anyone who claims to be in the light but hates his brother is still in the darkness. 10 Whoever loves his brother lives in the light, and there is nothing in him to make him stumble. 11 But whoever hates his brother is in the darkness and walks around in the darkness; he does not know where he is going, because the darkness has blinded him.	**2 The professing man: Professes God but hates his brother** **3 The obedient man: Loves his brother** a. Lives, abides in the light b. Does not stumble **4 The bitter & hating man**^{DS1} a. Is in darkness & walks in darkness b. Has no direction & is blind

DIVISION III

THE PROOF THAT ONE REALLY KNOWS GOD: SEVEN TESTS, 2:3-29

B. Test 2: Loving One's Neighbor, 2:7-11

(2:7-11) **Introduction**: How do we know if we really know God? (See note—1 Jn.2:3-6 for introductory discussion.) There are seven tests that will show us. This passage covers the second test: it deals with love. Do we love our neighbors? If we criticize, grumble, gripe, backbite, ignore, neglect, curse, abuse, slander, hate, or mistreat our neighbors in any way, then we do not know God. No matter what we may claim nor how loudly we claim it, we do not know God if we do not love our neighbors. God is love; therefore any person who truly knows God is bound to love. Loving others is a strong test of our knowledge of God. We can tell whether or not we know God by testing our love for others.

1. The test: the supreme command—love (v.7-8).
2. The professing man: professes God but hates his brother (v.9).
3. The obedient man: loves his brother (v.10).
4. The bitter and hating man (v.11).
   a. Is in darkness and walks in darkness.
   b. Has no direction and is blind.

1 (2:7-8) **Command—Love**: How do we know if we know God? There is a test that shows us: Do we follow after the supreme command, the command to love our neighbors? Note three significant facts.

1. This is not a new command, but an old command. Observe: John does not come right out and say that he is talking about love, not immediately. He says that the command he is about to talk about…
   • is not a new command but an old command.
   • is the command that they had heard from the beginning of time.

One of the very first things that God ever said to man was this: man must love his neighbor (Lev.19:18). Why then would John not just go ahead and mention the command? Why take a backdoor approach to the subject of love? John had a very good reason: what John is about to say is new, so new that people would say that it was his own idea and not the truth. Therefore, John had to establish the fact that God had said the same thing from the beginning of time. But note a crucial question: If the command of love has been with man from the beginning of time, how can it be a new command? What is there about the command that might upset people and cause them to

turn away from John's exhortation? This is the second thing discussed by John.

2. The command is a new command (v.8). It is not only an old command but a new command. Again, what is so new about love? Jesus Christ! Jesus Christ gave love a new meaning. Jesus Christ…
   • loved not only friends, but enemies.
   • loved not only good people, but bad people.
   • loved not only the righteous, but the sinner.
   • loved not only the acceptable, but the rejected.
   • loved not only the clean, but the dirty.

Jesus Christ Himself stated the fact as clearly as it can be stated:

> **"You have heard that it was said, 'Love your neighbor and hate your enemy.' But I tell you: Love your enemies and pray for those who persecute you, that you may be sons of your Father in heaven. He causes his sun to rise on the evil and the good, and sends rain on the righteous and the unrighteous. (Mat 5:43-45)**

This was a totally new concept of love. Man has always felt free to mistreat others, especially those who had mistreated him. He has felt free to…

• hate	• criticize
• strike back	• be unkind
• hurt	• backbite
• ignore	• retaliate
• neglect	

But Jesus Christ has shown that we cannot mistreat people *no matter what they have done*, that we must love everyone no matter who they are. Note His words: "That you may be sons of your Father in heaven" (Mt.5:45). The only way we can become children of God is to love even as God loves. If we do not love, then we do not know God, for God is love. He is the love that loves all people no matter who they are. Note another statement of Jesus Christ:

> **"A new command I give you: Love one another. As I have loved you, so you must love one another. By this all men will know that you are my disciples, if you love one another." (John 13:34-35)**

Jesus Christ says an astounding thing: the only way people can tell that we are His disciples is by our love for one another. Our discipleship and our knowledge of God can be measured by whether or not we love our brothers and sisters in the Lord. This is exactly what John says in verse 8: "A new command; its truth is seen in him [Christ] and you [true believers]." The person who truly follows God has the love of God in him. The love of God dwells not only in Christ but in the believer also.

3. Note another fact about the new command of love. Love is now made known by the true light that shines and erases the darkness (v.8). "The darkness is passing and the true light is already shining" (v.8).

The darkness refers to man's old idea of love, that he could react against anyone who mistreated him. But Jesus Christ, who is the light of the world, has now shone forth the truth. Man is to love his neighbor no matter what the neighbor does. In fact, man is to love all men no matter who they are or what they have done. God is love; therefore man is to be as God: man is to love. It is by his love that man knows whether or not he knows God. No man knows God unless he loves as Christ loves, loves even his enemies.

> **When Jesus spoke again to the people, he said, "I am the light of the world. Whoever follows me will never walk in darkness, but will have the light of life." (John 8:12)**

> **Then Jesus told them, "You are going to have the light just a little while longer. Walk while you have the light, before darkness overtakes you. The man who walks in the dark does not know where he is going. (John 12:35)**

> **For God, who said, "Let light shine out of darkness," made his light shine in our hearts to give us the light of the knowledge of the glory of God in the face of Christ. (2 Cor 4:6)**

> **For it is shameful even to mention what the disobedient do in secret. (Eph 5:12)**

> **The people walking in darkness have seen a great light; on those living in the land of the shadow of death a light has dawned. (Isa 9:2)**

2 (2:9) **Hate—Profession, False:** there is the professing man, the man who professes that he knows God but who hates his brother. How many persons do just what this scene pictures? A person says that he is *in the light*, that is, that he is *in Christ*. He says that he…

- believes in Christ
- has been baptized in Christ
- belongs to the church of Christ
- has been confirmed in Christ
- takes the supper of Christ
- reads the Word of Christ
- prays to Christ
- lives for Christ
- teaches for Christ

But the person hates his brother. He says, "Oh, I don't hate my brother. I just don't like him. I don't know how to get along with him." Or, "He just turns me off: his appearance, his behavior." Or, "He did me wrong; he mistreated me." Whatever the reason, it is not love. Love is love; it is not mistreatment or hate. And Jesus Christ re-

vealed the light of love to us. We must love our neighbors, even those who are our enemies, if we are to become children of God and followers of Him. No man walks in the light of God, no man knows God, unless he loves his neighbor—even the neighbors who stand against him. If we hate our neighbors—neglect, dislike, disregard, criticize, backbite, and mistreat them—we are not living in the light, not living *in Christ*. We are making a false profession. We do not know God, not really, no matter what we claim. We are living in the darkness of this world—living like most people in the world live—hating some of our brothers.

> **But if your eyes are bad, your whole body will be full of darkness. If then the light within you is darkness, how great is that darkness! (Mat 6:23)**

> **"Not everyone who says to me, 'Lord, Lord,' will enter the kingdom of heaven, but only he who does the will of my Father who is in heaven. (Mat 7:21)**

> **This is the verdict: Light has come into the world, but men loved darkness instead of light because their deeds were evil. (John 3:19)**

> **Love is patient, love is kind. It does not envy, it does not boast, it is not proud. (1 Cor 13:4)**

> **Let us not become conceited, provoking and envying each other. (Gal 5:26)**

> **They claim to know God, but by their actions they deny him. They are detestable, disobedient and unfit for doing anything good. (Titus 1:16)**

> **If we claim to have fellowship with him yet walk in the darkness, we lie and do not live by the truth. (1 John 1:6)**

> **Anyone who claims to be in the light but hates his brother is still in the darkness. (1 John 2:9)**

> **Anyone who hates his brother is a murderer, and you know that no murderer has eternal life in him. (1 John 3:15)**

> **If anyone says, "I love God," yet hates his brother, he is a liar. For anyone who does not love his brother, whom he has seen, cannot love God, whom he has not seen. (1 John 4:20)**

> **"'Do not hate your brother in your heart. Rebuke your neighbor frankly so you will not share in his guilt. (Lev 19:17)**

> **Hatred stirs up dissension, but love covers over all wrongs. (Prov 10:12)**

> **Better a meal of vegetables where there is love than a fattened calf with hatred. (Prov 15:17)**

3 (2:10) **Love:** there is the obedient man, the man who loves his brother. Two wonderful things are said about the person who loves his brother.

1. He is a man who lives *in the light*, that is, *in Christ*. The obedient man lives and walks in Jesus Christ. He walks in love just as Jesus Christ walked in love. What does it mean to walk in love? Scripture spells out some very practical acts.

⇒ Love is patient.
⇒ Love is kind.
⇒ Love does not envy (is not jealous).
⇒ Love does not boast.

⇒ Love is not proud (is not arrogant, prideful).
⇒ Love is not rude (unbecoming, indecent, unmannerly).
⇒ Love is not self-seeking her own (is not selfish, insisting on one's rights and way).
⇒ Love is not easily angered (is not touchy, fretful, resentful).
⇒ Love keeps no record of wrongs (harbors no evil thought, takes no account of a wrong done it).
⇒ Love does not delight in evil (in wrong, sin, evil, injustice), but rejoices with the truth (in justice, in righteousness).
⇒ Love always protects.
⇒ Love always trusts (exercises faith in everything, under all circumstances).
⇒ Love always perseveres (never weakens; has the power to endure).

2. The man who loves his brother has nothing in him to make him stumble. There is nothing in him to make him stumble, nothing to trip him up in life, nothing to make him fall and hurt himself or destroy his life. How can this be? How can it be said of any man that he will not stumble? Because love is the great binding force of the universe.

⇒ God is love; therefore the more we love God, the closer and closer we draw to Him. And the closer we get to Him, the more we learn to trust His care, provision, protection, and power. When God is taking care of us, there is absolutely nothing that can touch us (cp. Ro.8:35-39).
⇒ The great need of man is love. Man needs to be loved, but not with the sentimental feelings and passions of the world that come and go as freely as the falling star that shoots across the sky. Man needs to be loved with the love of God, the kind of love just covered above, the kind of love that will help him to know that God loves him. Man needs to know that God cares for him and wants to deliver and strengthen him against all the trials of life. This kind of love will pull men together, not alienate them. The man who loves his neighbor like this will not fail to live the kind of life he should live.

And you are to love those who are aliens, for you yourselves were aliens in Egypt. (Deu 10:19)

And the second is like it: 'Love your neighbor as yourself.' (Mat 22:39)

By this all men will know that you are my disciples, if you love one another." (John 13:35)

My command is this: Love each other as I have loved you. (John 15:12)

Love must be sincere. Hate what is evil; cling to what is good. (Rom 12:9)

May the Lord make your love increase and overflow for each other and for everyone else, just as ours does for you. (1 Th 3:12)

Now that you have purified yourselves by obeying the truth so that you have sincere love for your brothers, love one another deeply, from the heart. (1 Pet 1:22)

DEEPER STUDY # 1

(2:11) **Hate—Darkness:** there is the bitter, hating man. This person differs from the professing person in that he does not profess to know God. He is a man who is totally lost in the darkness of this world. Several things are said about this man.

1. He is in darkness and walks in darkness. He is not in the light, not in Christ. Therefore, he does not know God. He does not even profess to know God. He is wrapped up and focused only upon the world. When it comes to God and Christ, he is totally in the dark and often could care less. He takes what he can and accumulates all that he can, no matter who it hurts. He cares little about other people except perhaps family and close friends. He lives mainly for the pleasures and passions of the world. Therefore, how he treats his neighbor matters little, just so he gets what he wants.

2. He has no direction and is blind. He does not look beyond this life and he is blind to it. He sees little if any meaning to life other than getting all he can of its comfort, pleasures, and possessions. Therefore, to hate his neighbor means nothing to him if his neighbor gets in the way.

Note: when a man hates or is bitter against another person, it blinds him even more. He often focuses upon getting back at the person and loses sight of what he should be doing. He just cannot see the truth.

Thought 1. How often a person has opposed a good project simply because he was upset with the leader. The great good of the project is often clearly visible, but hatred blinds the mind and more tragically the heart—so much so that a person makes a fool out of himself without even knowing it. But more tragically, he often causes damage and division among people, and his soul is doomed to be in darkness forever—forever separated from the light of God and of His Son, the Lord Jesus Christ.

The god of this age has blinded the minds of unbelievers, so that they cannot see the light of the gospel of the glory of Christ, who is the image of God. (2 Cor 4:4)

They are darkened in their understanding and separated from the life of God because of the ignorance that is in them due to the hardening of their hearts. (Eph 4:18)

But whoever hates his brother is in the darkness and walks around in the darkness; he does not know where he is going, because the darkness has blinded him. (1 John 2:11)

	C. Test 3: Remembering Your Spiritual Growth, 2:12-14	cause you have overcome the evil one. I write to you, dear children, because you have known the Father.	c. Young men: You have overcome—through God Himself (implied)
1 **Step 1: Remember your spiritual growth** a. Children: You are forgiven because of God's name's b. Fathers: You have known God Himself who is eternal	12 I write to you, dear children, because your sins have been forgiven on account of his name. 13 I write to you, fathers, because you have known him who is from the beginning. I write to you, young men, be-	14 I write to you, fathers, because you have known him who is from the beginning. I write to you, young men, because you are strong, and the word of God lives in you, and you have overcome the evil one.	2 **Step 2: Confirm who you are—your great relationship to God—over & over again**

DIVISION III

THE PROOF THAT ONE REALLY KNOWS GOD: SEVEN TESTS, 2:3-29

C. Test 3: Remembering Your Spiritual Growth, 2:12-14

(2:12-14) **Introduction**: note that three groups of people are addressed by John—*dear children, fathers, and young men*. Note also that each one is addressed twice. "I have written to you." Two questions immediately arise: Who are these people and why does John specifically address them?

1. First, who are the people John is addressing? Is he addressing the various age groups in the church: the children, the aged fathers, and the young men? Or is he talking about stages of spiritual growth? Now note a significant fact: there are within the church other adults other than fathers and young men. There are full grown men who are aged and there are women. It is doubtful that John would be referring to the various age groups within the church and addressing only the fathers and young men among the adults. This points rather strongly to John's classification being the stages of spiritual growth.

2. Second, why does John specifically address these people? For emphasis: John is driving home the point that believers must grow in Christ. They must confirm their growth in Christ, confirm their great relationship with God over and over again. To stress the point John says…

- "I am writing *this part of the letter* and what is to follow so that you will grow and grow in Christ."
- "I have written *the first part of the letter* so that you grow and grow in Christ."

The following chart will help us to grasp what John is doing. (Note: the idea of this chart was stirred by the chart of A. Plummer. *The Epistles of St. John.* "The Pulpit Commentary," Vol.22, ed. by HDM Spence and Joseph S. Exell. Grand Rapids, MI: Eerdmans, 1950, p.23.)

I *AM WRITING* this part of the letter…

- To the dear children among you, that is, the newborn Christians
- To spiritual fathers among you, that is, the spiritually mature with a deep and rich knowledge of God
- To the young men among you, that is, the mature believers

Reasons for writing

- Because your sins have been forgiven
- Because you have known God and have been from the beginning
- Because you have overcome the wicked one

I *HAVE WRITTEN* the first part of the letter…

- To dear children among you, that is, the newborn Christians
- To spiritual fathers among you, that is, the spiritually mature with a deep and rich knowledge of God
- To the young men among you, that is, the mature believers

Reasons for writing

- Because you have known the Father
- Because you have known God who is faithful from the beginning
- Because you are strong, have the Word of God abiding in you, and have overcome the evil one

Now, to the discussion of the passage. Remember the overall subject that John is discussing: How do we know if we really know God? (See note—1 Jn.2:3-6 for introductory discussion.) There are seven tests that will show us. This passage covers the third test, a test that shows us beyond any question whether or not we know God. It is the test of spiritual growth.

⇒ Do you remember your spiritual growth?

⇒ Do you remember how you have grown in Christ from the beginning of your conversion?
⇒ Do you remember how God has grown and matured and developed you in Christ?

If you really know Christ, then you have grown in Christ; you have developed and matured stage by stage. Have you grown in Christ since you professed Christ? If you have grown, then you know God. You are a child of God. If you have not grown in Christ, you do not know God. Once a person is truly converted he grows in Christ.

That is what *conversion* means: to convert over; to change over; to become a new person; to be born again; to exchange the old life without Christ for the new life with Christ. If a person is *truly born again* in Christ, then he begins to live and walk *in Christ*. If he is *truly converted* over to Christ, then he is a follower of Christ; he focuses upon Christ and grows in Christ.

The point is perfectly understandable to a clear and honest mind: a person who truly knows God follows God. He grows spiritually; he grows in the knowledge of God and of His Son, the Lord Jesus Christ. The person who truly knows God remembers his spiritual growth. He has a spiritual growth to remember.

1. Step 1: remember your spiritual growth (v.12-13).
2. Step 2: confirm who you are—your great relationship to God—over and over again (v.14).

1 (2:12-13) **Growth, Spiritual—Maturity—Stages, Spiritual**: first, remember your spiritual growth. In the church, in God's family, there are various stages of growth. Note: what John is writing applies to every stage of the believer's growth. No matter who the believer is, how weak or strong he is, this message applies to him. This is a message for the whole church.

1. There are *dear children*, people who have just received Jesus Christ and begun to follow Him. If you are a newborn Christian, remember this: your sins are forgiven. You are...

- no longer guilty of sin
- no longer to be judged for sin
- no longer to be condemned for sin
- no longer to be punished for sin

You have trusted Jesus Christ as the great Bearer of your sins. You believe that Jesus Christ took your sins upon Himself and bore the condemnation and punishment for them. You believe that Jesus Christ became your substitute in bearing the judgment for your sins. Therefore, you are cleansed of sin; your sins are forgiven.

But note why: "on account of his name." God forgives our sins *because of Christ*. He cleanses us for the sake of Christ far more than He does for us. God loves us perfectly, yes, but God loves His own Son with a very special love. God's Son, the Lord Jesus Christ, is God's Son by nature. In addition, Christ has obeyed and fulfilled the will of God perfectly. In obedience to God's will, He left the glory of heaven and came to this corrupt world to die for our sins. Jesus Christ did exactly what God willed and ordained; He obeyed God perfectly. Therefore, no person can ever take the place of Christ in the heart of God. For this reason God has destined that Jesus Christ have many *adopted brothers and sisters*, many believers who follow and attach themselves to Him. God has ordained that believers live forever with Christ, worshipping and serving Him throughout all eternity. This is what is meant by the words "because of Christ." Because of what Christ has done, for His sake, God has forgiven our sins. God loves His Son so much that He honors any person who honors His Son. Any person who believes in God's Son, who gives his life to Jesus Christ, God will take and do exactly what that person believes. He does it *for Christ's sake*—does it so that Jesus Christ will have another brother or sister to worship and serve Him throughout all eternity. Our sins are forgiven *for Christ's sake*.

The point is this: all believers must *remember* that their sins are forgiven. But young believers—you who are young children in the faith—you in particular must remember this. Because you are young in the faith, because you have just recently left the world and its pleasures and possessions, you are more likely to forget what Jesus Christ has done for you. You must focus and concentrate upon Jesus Christ, upon the glorious fact that He has forgiven your sins. You must guard against returning to the world and its enticements.

> **God exalted him to his own right hand as Prince and Savior that he might give repentance and forgiveness of sins to Israel. (Acts 5:31)**
>
> **"Therefore, my brothers, I want you to know that through Jesus the forgiveness of sins is proclaimed to you. (Acts 13:38)**
>
> **In him we have redemption through his blood, the forgiveness of sins, in accordance with the riches of God's grace (Eph 1:7)**
>
> **Be kind and compassionate to one another, forgiving each other, just as in Christ God forgave you. (Eph 4:32)**
>
> **If we confess our sins, he is faithful and just and will forgive us our sins and purify us from all unrighteousness. (1 John 1:9)**

2. There are *fathers*, spiritual fathers, believers who are spiritually mature with a deep and rich knowledge of God. What is the exhortation to these who have such a deep and rich knowledge of God? To these few who have walked so faithfully for so many years, the exhortation is this: remember, you have known God from the very beginning of your conversion, and you have faithfully and diligently served Him. Day by day you have...

- fed upon the Word of God.
- set aside time for prayer and learned to walk in prayer all day long.
- learned to fellowship and commune with God all day long, striving for an unbroken communion and fellowship with Him.
- witnessed to the saving power of Jesus Christ.
- been loyal to the church, its members, mission, and ministry.
- committed your life to minister to the needs surrounding you and reached out beyond to the world through your prayers and gifts.
- given all you are and have to Christ and His mission, meeting the desperate needs of the world.

The point is this: the spiritually mature who have a deep and rich knowledge of God must never forget where they have come from, never forget how they grew in Christ. They must remember how they grew and came to know the Father so well. They must remember how they gained such a deep and rich knowledge of God. Remembering and staying focused upon the Father is the only way a person can finish the Christian race faithfully and receive his reward. The spiritually mature, those with a deep and rich knowledge of God, must remember and continue to grow in the knowledge of God.

> **"Therefore everyone who hears these words of mine and puts them into practice is like a wise man who built his house on the rock. The rain came down, the streams rose, and the winds blew and beat against that house; yet it did not fall, because it had its foundation on the rock. But everyone who hears these words of mine and does not put them into practice is like a foolish man who built his house on sand.**

The rain came down, the streams rose, and the winds blew and beat against that house, and it fell with a great crash." (Mat 7:24-27)

To the Jews who had believed him, Jesus said, "If you hold to my teaching, you are really my disciples. Then you will know the truth, and the truth will set you free." (John 8:31-32)

Now this is eternal life: that they may know you, the only true God, and Jesus Christ, whom you have sent. (John 17:3)

But whatever was to my profit I now consider loss for the sake of Christ. What is more, I consider everything a loss compared to the surpassing greatness of knowing Christ Jesus my Lord, for whose sake I have lost all things. I consider them rubbish, that I may gain Christ and be found in him, not having a righteousness of my own that comes from the law, but that which is through faith in Christ—the righteousness that comes from God and is by faith. I want to know Christ and the power of his resurrection and the fellowship of sharing in his sufferings, becoming like him in his death, (Phil 3:7-10)

That is why I am suffering as I am. Yet I am not ashamed, because I know whom I have believed, and am convinced that he is able to guard what I have entrusted to him for that day. (2 Tim 1:12)

And how from infancy you have known the holy Scriptures, which are able to make you wise for salvation through faith in Christ Jesus. (2 Tim 3:15)

3. There are *young men*, mature believers in the church. These must remember how far they have come. They have come a long way: they have fought a long battle and they have now overcome the wicked one. The wicked one used to attack them right and left, at every turn. He attacked them with every temptation imaginable, but especially with the sins that were so common before their conversion, the sins of...

- evil and immoral thoughts
- illicit affairs
- immoral practices
- looking and lusting
- drunkenness
- shoplifting
- drugs
- stealing
- lying
- cheating
- pride
- arrogance
- covetousness
- hoarding
- gossiping
- backbiting
- hate
- anger
- loving money
- greed

The point is this: believers who have walked *faithfully with Christ* over a long period of time have overcome the temptations of the wicked one. The temptations do not strike as often nor with the force that they once did. It was a difficult struggle, a fierce battle all along the way, for it is never easy to die to self, never easy to deny self completely. It is never easy to give up all one is and has to Christ and His mission. In fact, after we have committed our lives and possessions to Christ, the wicked one attacks us more fiercely than ever before. Satan does not want to lose us and our loyalty to sin; he wants to cause God as much pain as possible. Therefore right after we accept Christ, he attacks us with far greater force than ever before. But the mature believer overcomes. However, he must remember how he overcame, for Satan stays after the believer as long as he is on earth. The attacks perhaps are not as often nor as fierce as when the believer was younger, but the believer must stay strong or else he will be caught off-guard and fall into sin. The mature believer must remember how he overcame the wicked one and continue to combat him in the Word.

Thought 1. How do believers overcome Satan?

⇒ They overcome by drawing near God, by praying and asking for wisdom.

If any of you lacks wisdom, he should ask God, who gives generously to all without finding fault, and it will be given to him. (James 1:5)

If this is so, then the Lord knows how to rescue godly men from trials and to hold the unrighteous for the day of judgment, while continuing their punishment. (2 Pet 2:9)

⇒ They overcome by using God's Word, quoting it over and over in their minds, to conquer the temptation.

Jesus answered, "It is written: 'Worship the Lord your God and serve him only.'" (Luke 4:8)

⇒ They overcome by learning and knowing that God allows temptation to teach endurance.

Consider it pure joy, my brothers, whenever you face trials of many kinds, because you know that the testing of your faith develops perseverance. (James 1:2-3)

⇒ They overcome by not offering their bodily parts to sin.

Do not offer the parts of your body to sin, as instruments of wickedness, but rather offer yourselves to God, as those who have been brought from death to life; and offer the parts of your body to him as instruments of righteousness. (Rom 6:13)

⇒ They overcome by clothing themselves with the armor of God.

Therefore put on the full armor of God, so that when the day of evil comes, you may be able to stand your ground, and after you have done everything, to stand. (Eph 6:13)

⇒ They overcome by being on guard and watching for the tempter's temptations.

Be self-controlled and alert. Your enemy the devil prowls around like a roaring lion looking for someone to devour. (1 Pet 5:8)

Therefore, dear friends, since you already know this, be on your guard so that you may not be carried away by the error of lawless men and fall from your secure position. (2 Pet 3:17)

⇒ They overcome by not giving in to anger nor giving a foot hold the devil.

"In your anger do not sin" : Do not let the sun go down while you are still angry, and do not give the devil a foothold. (Eph 4:26-27)

⇒ They overcome by submitting to God and resisting the devil.

Submit yourselves, then, to God. Resist the devil, and he will flee from you. (James 4:7)

⇒ They overcome by not giving in to the enticement of sinners.

My son, if sinners entice you, do not give in to them. (Prov 1:10)

⇒ They overcome by not setting foot on the path of the wicked.

Do not set foot on the path of the wicked or walk in the way of evil men. (Prov 4:14)

2 (2:14) **Growth, Spiritual—Maturity—Diligence—Faithfulness**: second, remember your great relationship to God over and over again. Note the emphasis in this second exhortation to each of the believers: the stress is upon the believer's relationship to God and His Word. What John has written has been written to stir up their relationship to the Father. Believers, no matter their stage of spiritual growth, must never forget who it is they know: God the Father. They have the greatest privilege in all the world, the privilege of knowing God Himself, of being adopted into the very family of God and of becoming a son or a daughter of God. The believer receives the great privilege of calling God "Father."

1. *Dear children*, young believers, must remember that they have known the Father. They have just been adopted into the family of God. God Himself, the Supreme Force of the universe, the Supreme Intelligence and Power of the universe, is not some abstract energy way off in outer space. God is a Person, the Supreme Person in all the universe, the only living and true God. And He desires the most wonderful thing in all the world: to relate to man. He wants to become a Father to people. He wants to adopt people as His children, to have people believe in Him and trust Him to look after them. Young believers know this; therefore they have come to God through Jesus Christ, and they have experienced the privilege of adoption. They now know God as their Father.

But note: young believers must remember this glorious truth. They must remember and focus upon God as their Father; they must not let the thought of God slip from their mind. They must come to God *day by day* as their Father. They must...

- bring their needs to Him
- trust Him to look after them
- ask and depend upon Him to teach them
- trust Him to discipline them when they need it
- study Him and His Word, and listen and do what He says

- fellowship and commune with Him
- love Him and receive His love
- do nothing that would shame Him
- share with others what a wonderful Father He is

"This, then, is how you should pray: "'Our Father in heaven, hallowed be your name, (Mat 6:9)
If you, then, though you are evil, know how to give good gifts to your children, how much more will your Father in heaven give good gifts to those who ask him! (Mat 7:11)
The Spirit himself testifies with our spirit that we are God's children. Now if we are children, then we are heirs—heirs of God and co-heirs with Christ, if indeed we share in his sufferings in order that we may also share in his glory. (Rom 8:16-17)
"Therefore come out from them and be separate, says the Lord. Touch no unclean thing, and I will receive you." "I will be a Father to you, and you will be my sons and daughters, says the Lord Almighty." (2 Cor 6:17-18)
But when the time had fully come, God sent his Son, born of a woman, born under law, to redeem those under law, that we might receive the full rights of sons. Because you are sons, God sent the Spirit of his Son into our hearts, the Spirit who calls out, "Abba, Father." (Gal 4:4-6)
Since you call on a Father who judges each man's work impartially, live your lives as strangers here in reverent fear. (1 Pet 1:17)

2. *Fathers*, the believers who have a deep and rich knowledge of God, must remember that they have known God who is from the beginning. They must remember everything that has been said to them in the above note (1 Jn.2:12-13). But in addition, they must never be lifted up with pride—no matter how long they have walked with God. Note the words: "him [God] who is from the beginning." God has been around from the beginning of time, much longer than the *fathers* of the faith. No matter how deep and rich the believer's knowledge of God is, there is so much more to know. God is eternal and He has an eternity of experience for us to learn about. Therefore, we must never be lifted up with pride as though we know God and have arrived. There is still an eternity of things to learn about God. Mature believers, those with a rich and full knowledge of God, must remember from where they have come and continue to seek to know God. They have known God from the beginning of their conversion and they must continue to grow and grow in their relationship with God.

When I was a child, I talked like a child, I thought like a child, I reasoned like a child. When I became a man, I put childish ways behind me. (1 Cor 13:11)
Brothers, stop thinking like children. In regard to evil be infants, but in your thinking be adults. (1 Cor 14:20)
Now he who supplies seed to the sower and bread for food will also supply and increase your store of seed and will enlarge

the harvest of your righteousness. (2 Cor 9:10)

To prepare God's people for works of service, so that the body of Christ may be built up until we all reach unity in the faith and in the knowledge of the Son of God and become mature, attaining to the whole measure of the fullness of Christ. (Eph 4:12-13)

But solid food is for the mature, who by constant use have trained themselves to distinguish good from evil. (Heb 5:14)

But grow in the grace and knowledge of our Lord and Savior Jesus Christ. To him be glory both now and forever! Amen. (2 Pet 3:18)

3. *Young men*, the mature believers, must remember three things.

a. Mature believers must remember that they are strong. They must know their strength and be assured and have confidence in the strength they have gained. But mature believers must remember where their strength comes from and how they became spiritually strong: all through Jesus Christ. Note: believers must never trust the power of the flesh (sinful nature) of mental determination. The flesh and the mind fail. Neither can be consistently strong in controlling the flesh. Both mind and body will eventually weaken and fail in spiritual warfare.

"I am the vine; you are the branches. If a man remains in me and I in him, he will bear much fruit; apart from me you can do nothing. (John 15:5)

But you will receive power when the Holy Spirit comes on you; and you will be my witnesses in Jerusalem, and in all Judea and Samaria, and to the ends of the earth." (Acts 1:8)

Now to him who is able to establish you by my gospel and the proclamation of Jesus Christ, according to the revelation of the mystery hidden for long ages past, but now revealed and made known through the prophetic writings by the command of the eternal God, so that all nations might believe and obey him— to the only wise God be glory forever through Jesus Christ! Amen. (Rom 16:25-27)

Not that we are competent in ourselves to claim anything for ourselves, but our competence comes from God. (2 Cor 3:5)

But he said to me, "My grace is sufficient for you, for my power is made perfect in weakness." Therefore I will boast all the more gladly about my weaknesses, so that Christ's power may rest on me. That is why, for Christ's sake, I delight in weaknesses, in insults, in hardships, in persecutions, in difficulties. For when I am weak, then I am strong. (2 Cor 12:9-10)

I pray that out of his glorious riches he may strengthen you with power through his Spirit in your inner being, (Eph 3:16)

Being strengthened with all power according to his glorious might so that you may have great endurance and patience, and joyfully (Col 1:11)

b. Mature believers must remember that the Word of God abides, lives in them. This is the key to spiritual growth and to pleasing and securing the approval of God. No matter what a person may think or say, there is no spiritual growth apart from God's Word. No person pleases or secures God's approval without studying and living in God's Word. Mature believers must never forget this, and they must continue to give their lives to studying and living in the Word of God.

"Then a famine struck all Egypt and Canaan, bringing great suffering, and our fathers could not find food. (Acts 7:11)

"Now I commit you to God and to the word of his grace, which can build you up and give you an inheritance among all those who are sanctified. (Acts 20:32)

Let the word of Christ dwell in you richly as you teach and admonish one another with all wisdom, and as you sing psalms, hymns and spiritual songs with gratitude in your hearts to God. (Col 3:16)

Do your best to present yourself to God as one approved, a workman who does not need to be ashamed and who correctly handles the word of truth. (2 Tim 2:15)

All Scripture is God-breathed and is useful for teaching, rebuking, correcting and training in righteousness, (2 Tim 3:16)

Like newborn babies, crave pure spiritual milk, so that by it you may grow up in your salvation, now that you have tasted that the Lord is good. (1 Pet 2:2-3)

c. Mature believers must remember that they have overcome the evil one (see note, pt.3—1 Jn.2:12-13 for discussion).

	D. Test 4: Not Loving the World, 2:15-17	man, the lust of his eyes and the boasting of what he has and does—comes not from the Father but from the world.	2) The lust of the eyes 3) The pride of life: boasting of what he has and does
1 The test: Do we love the world? **2 The professing man** a. He loves the world b. He follows after the world 1) The cravings of the flesh	15 Do not love the world or anything in the world. If anyone loves the world, the love of the Father is not in him. 16 For everything in the world—the cravings of sinful	17 The world and its desires pass away, but the man who does the will of God lives forever.	c. He is not of God **3 The obedient man: Is immortal**

DIVISION III

THE PROOF THAT ONE REALLY KNOWS GOD: SEVEN TESTS, 2:3-29

D. Test 4: Not Loving the World, 2:15-17

(2:15-17) **Introduction**: How do we know if we really know God? (See note—1 Jn.2:3-6 for introductory discussion.) This is the fourth test that proves whether or not we know God: Do we love the world? If a person loves the world, he does not know God. No matter what a person may feel or think, the Scripture is clear, and it is forceful in its statement: the person who loves the world does not know God.

1. The test: do we love the world (v.15)?
2. The professing man (v.15-16).
3. The obedient man: is immortal (v.17).

1 (2:15) **World—Worldliness**: the test is clearly stated—do we love the world? A believer can tell whether or not he knows God by taking this test. He can examine his life and see if he loves the world. What is meant by the world? Does this mean that we are not to appreciate the beauty, splendor, and resources of the earth and heavens? No! For we live of the earth, and God has given us the earth and the heavens in which to live, appreciate, and enjoy. What, then, does Scripture mean by *the world* and by the charge, *do not love the world*?

⇒ The world means the earth and the heavens that are passing away. The world is corruptible and deteriorating and will eventually be destroyed. Therefore, believers must not become attached to the world; they must be attached to God and to heaven. Believers are not to love the world so much that they desire to stay here more than they desire to be with God in heaven.

⇒ The world is a system of man-made governments and societies, some good and some bad, but none perfect. Therefore, believers must respect and be loyal to the good, but reject and stand against the bad. Believers must love none of them, not to the point that they are more attached to the systems of man's organizations than they are to God and heaven.

⇒ The world means a system of sin and lust and evil and pride and rebellion against God. The world is full of sinful people, people who are evil and full of lust and pride; it is full of people who are in rebellion against God. Therefore, believers must not love this sinful system of the world.

A person is not to love this world, the possessions and pleasures of this world; he is to love God. Of course, he is to appreciate and enjoy the beauty and the good things of both the earth and the heavens. But he is not to become more attached to this world than he is to God and heaven.

The believer's eyes are to be focused upon God, and he is to be attached to God, loving God before all else.

> **Do not conform any longer to the pattern of this world, but be transformed by the renewing of your mind. Then you will be able to test and approve what God's will is—his good, pleasing and perfect will. (Rom 12:2)**

> **Those who use the things of the world, as if not engrossed in them. For this world in its present form is passing away. (1 Cor 7:31)**

> **May I never boast except in the cross of our Lord Jesus Christ, through which the world has been crucified to me, and I to the world. (Gal 6:14)**

> **No one serving as a soldier gets involved in civilian affairs—he wants to please his commanding officer. (2 Tim 2:4)**

> **By faith Moses, when he had grown up, refused to be known as the son of Pharaoh's daughter. He chose to be mistreated along with the people of God rather than to enjoy the pleasures of sin for a short time. (Heb 11:24-25)**

> **Do not love the world or anything in the world. If anyone loves the world, the love of the Father is not in him. (1 John 2:15)**

> **If you belonged to the world, it would love you as its own. As it is, you do not belong to the world, but I have chosen you out of the world. That is why the world hates you. (John 15:19)**

> **Have nothing to do with the fruitless deeds of darkness, but rather expose them. (Eph 5:11)**

> **In the name of the Lord Jesus Christ, we command you, brothers, to keep away from every brother who is idle and does not live according to the teaching you received from us. (2 Th 3:6)**

> **Depart, depart, go out from there! Touch no unclean thing! Come out from it and be pure, you who carry the vessels of the LORD. (Isa 52:11)**

2 (2:15-16) **Lust—Flesh—Eyes—Pride**: there is the professing man. Note that a particular man is being talked about here, the man who *loves the world*. And note in verse 17 that another man is being talked about, the man who *does the will of God*. The first man is the professing man, the man who makes a false profession; the second man is the obedient man, the man who does exactly what God says. Four things are pointed out about the professing man.

1. The professing man loves the world. He loves and is attached more to this world than he is to God. The people to whom John is writing are church members. They have professed Christ, yet John is having to charge them not to love the world. Some in the church had returned or were apparently about to return to the world. Scripture pronounces the terrible truth: "the love of the father is not in [them]." Any person who loves the world does not love the Father.

Thought 1. Three things happen to believers that cause them to return to the world and to love the world.
1) Some begin to enjoy nature and the beauty of the earth so much that they no longer worship regularly. They forsake the worship of God and the study of His Word in order to be out in nature (cp. fishing, golfing, hiking, camping, and other forms of recreation out in nature).
2) Some become so involved in man's government and social organizations that they become more attached and faithful to them than they do to God and His church and its mission of salvation.
3) Some become so hungry for the world and its things that they begin to return to its pleasures and possessions.

2. The professing man follows after the world. There are three sins of worldliness.
   a. There is the lust of the flesh, cravings of sinful man. The *flesh or sinful man* has to do with feeling, touching, tasting, smelling, hearing, and seeing. It is the seat of desires and urges. Note that desires and urges are not wrong. A man has to have desires and urges in order to live a healthy and normal life. But the desires of the flesh, cravings of sinful man have to be controlled. If they are not controlled, then the flesh begins to desire and lust more and more. There are two times when the desires and urges of the flesh are wrong:
   ⇒ when the flesh desires something that is directly forbidden by God. (For example, sex is not wrong within marriage, but adultery and sexual immorality are wrong. One helping of food is not wrong, but several helpings is gluttony.)
   ⇒ when the flesh desires and desires and consumes and consumes, then it becomes indulgence and license. For example, we must desire food in order to maintain life. But if the flesh desires and desires food in order to consume and indulge, then food is wrong. Too much cake is wrong. The desire has become lust, consumption, indulgence, and license.

   What are the sins of the flesh, the acts of the sinful nature? They are far more than what people usually think, far more than just the immoral sins of society. The acts of the sinful nature are these (see outline and notes—Gal.5:19-21):
   ⇒ *Sexual immorality*: sexual unfaithfulness to husband or wife. It is also looking on a woman or a man to lust after her or him. Looking at and lusting after the opposite sex whether in person, magazines, books, on beaches or anywhere else is adultery. Imagining and lusting within the heart is the very same as committing the act including all forms of immoral and sexual acts. It is premarital sex and adultery; it is abnormal sex, all kinds of sexual vice.
   ⇒ *Impurity*: moral impurity; doing things that dirty, pollute, and soil life.
   ⇒ *Debauchery*: filthiness, indecency, shamelessness. A chief characteristic of the behavior is open and shameless indecency. It means unrestrained evil thoughts and behavior.
   ⇒ *Idolatry*: the worship of idols, whether mental or made by man's hands; the worship of some idea of what God is like, of an image of God within a person's mind; the giving of one's primary devotion (time and energy) to something other than God. (See note, *Idolatry*—1 Cor.6:9 for detailed discussion.)
   ⇒ *Witchcraft*: sorcery; the use of drugs or of evil spirits to gain control over the lives of others or over one's own life. In the present context it would include all forms of seeking the control of one's fate including astrology, palm reading, seances, fortune telling, crystals, and other forms of witchcraft.
   ⇒ *Hatred* (echthrai): enmity, hostility, animosity. It is the hatred that lingers and is held for a long time; a hatred that is deep within.
   ⇒ *Discord* (ereis): strife, discord, contention, fighting, struggling, quarreling, dissension, wrangling. It means that a man strives against another person in order to get something: position, promotion, property, honor, recognition. He deceives, doing whatever has to be done to get what he is after.
   ⇒ *Jealousy* (zeloi): wanting and desiring to have what someone else has. It may be material things, recognition, honor, or position.
   ⇒ *Fits of rage* (thumoi): indignation; a violent, explosive temper; anger; quick and explosive reactions that arise from stirred and boiling emotions. But it is anger which fades away just as quickly as it arose. It is not anger that lasts.
   ⇒ *Selfish ambition* (eritheiai): conflict, struggle, fight, contention, faction, dissension; a party spirit, a cliquish spirit.
   ⇒ *Dissensions* (dichostasiai): division, rebellion, standing against others, splitting off from others.
   ⇒ *Factions* (aireseis): rejecting the fundamental beliefs of God, Christ, the Scriptures, and the church; believing and holding to some teaching other than the truth.
   ⇒ *Envy* (phthonoi): this word goes beyond jealousy. It is the spirit...
   • that wants not only the things that another person has, but begrudges the fact that the person has them.
   • that wants a person to lose the things he has, and wants him to suffer through the loss of them.
   ⇒ *Drunkenness* (methai): taking drink or drugs to affect one's senses for lust or pleasure; becoming tipsy or intoxicated; partaking of

drugs; seeking to loosen moral restraint for bodily pleasure.

⇒ *Orgies* (komoi): carousing; uncontrolled license, indulgence, and pleasure; taking part in wild parties or in drinking parties; lying around indulging in feeding the lusts of the flesh, the cravings of sinful man.

b. There is the lust of the eyes. The eyes have to do with seeing and wanting to have what one sees. Again, there is nothing wrong with desiring what we see. Seeing and desiring is normal. It becomes wrong when two things happen:

⇒ When we see and desire what is directly forbidden by God.

⇒ When we see and desire in order to consume it upon our lusts and to indulge.

What are the sins of the eyes? Scripture says the following.

⇒ There is the lust of the eyes for sex.

> **But I tell you that anyone who looks at a woman lustfully has already committed adultery with her in his heart. (Mat 5:28)**
> **Because of this, God gave them over to shameful lusts. Even their women exchanged natural relations for unnatural ones. In the same way the men also abandoned natural relations with women and were inflamed with lust for one another. Men committed indecent acts with other men, and received in themselves the due penalty for their perversion. Furthermore, since they did not think it worthwhile to retain the knowledge of God, he gave them over to a depraved mind, to do what ought not to be done. (Rom 1:26-28)**
> **With eyes full of adultery, they never stop sinning; they seduce the unstable; they are experts in greed—an accursed brood! (2 Pet 2:14)**
> **"I made a covenant with my eyes not to look lustfully at a girl. (Job 31:1)**

⇒ There is the lust of the eyes that fills a person with darkness, great darkness.

> **But if your eyes are bad, your whole body will be full of darkness. If then the light within you is darkness, how great is that darkness! (Mat 6:23)**

⇒ There is the lust of the eyes after the things of other people.

> **He lies in wait near the villages; from ambush he murders the innocent, watching in secret for his victims. (Psa 10:8)**
> **Then he said to them, "Watch out! Be on your guard against all kinds of greed; a man's life does not consist in the abundance of his possessions." (Luke 12:15)**

⇒ There is the lust of the eyes after all the pleasures and possessions of the world.

> **I denied myself nothing my eyes desired; I refused my heart no pleasure. My heart took delight in all my work, and this was the reward for all my labor. (Eccl 2:10)**

⇒ There is the lust of the eyes after wine, drugs, and alcoholic drinks.

> **Who has woe? Who has sorrow? Who has strife? Who has complaints? Who has needless bruises? Who has bloodshot eyes? Those who linger over wine, who go to sample bowls of mixed wine. Do not gaze at wine when it is red, when it sparkles in the cup, when it goes down smoothly! (Prov 23:29-31)**

⇒ There is the lust of the eyes after other gods.

> **"'Do not make idols or set up an image or a sacred stone for yourselves, and do not place a carved stone in your land to bow down before it. I am the LORD your God. (Lev 26:1)**

c. There is the pride of life, boasting in what a person has and does. This is at least two things. First, boasting in what a person has and does means self-centeredness, a person who is focused upon himself and wants people to notice him. It is a person whose mind and thoughts are primarily upon himself, a person who...

- seeks attention through dress or looks
- seeks attention through rank or wealth
- seeks honor
- seeks recognition
- seeks fame
- seeks power
- seeks position
- seeks luxury
- seeks wealth for recognition and power
- seeks to outshine others
- seeks importance

Second, boasting in what a person has and does—pride of life means self-sufficiency, a person who is focused upon himself and feels completely capable of handling life himself. It is a person who feels that self-image, public image, ego and personal strength are the basis of life; a person who feels little if any need for God. He feels he can plow through life himself and conquer whatever problems and circumstances confront him. He feels that this world is an end within itself, that there is probably nothing beyond this life; therefore, he is to get all the comfort, pleasure, luxury, honor, and glory that he can while here. The pride of life—boasting in what a person has and does means self-sufficiency, a person who...

- is arrogant
- is conceited
- is boastful
- feels better than others because of rank or wealth

- feels superior to others in looks and ability

What are the sins of the boasting in what a person has and does? Scripture says the following:

⇒ There is the pride or boasting of self-sufficiency.

> You say, 'I am rich; I have acquired wealth and do not need a thing.' But you do not realize that you are wretched, pitiful, poor, blind and naked. (Rev 3:17)
> Do not boast about tomorrow, for you do not know what a day may bring forth. (Prov 27:1)

⇒ There is the pride or boasting of wealth.

> He boasts of the cravings of his heart; he blesses the greedy and reviles the LORD. (Psa 10:3)
> Man is a mere phantom as he goes to and fro: He bustles about, but only in vain; he heaps up wealth, not knowing who will get it. (Psa 39:6)
> Those who trust in their wealth and boast of their great riches? No man can redeem the life of another or give to God a ransom for him— (Psa 49:6-7)
> By your great skill in trading you have increased your wealth, and because of your wealth your heart has grown proud. (Ezek 28:5)

⇒ There is the pride or boasting of position.

> He must not be a recent convert [new believer], or he may become conceited and fall under the same judgment as the devil. (1 Tim 3:6)
> I wrote to the church, but Diotrephes[a church leader], who loves to be first, will have nothing to do with us. (3 John 1:9)
> "For God knows that when you eat of it your eyes will be opened, and you will be like God, knowing good and evil." (Gen 3:5)
> The word of the LORD came to me: "Son of man, take up a lament concerning the king of Tyre and say to him: 'This is what the Sovereign LORD says: "'You were the model of perfection, full of wisdom and perfect in beauty. You were in Eden, the garden of God; every precious stone adorned you: ruby, topaz and emerald, chrysolite, onyx and jasper, sapphire, turquoise and beryl. Your settings and mountings were made of gold; on the day you were created they were prepared. (Ezek 28:11-13)

⇒ There is the pride or boasting of power.

> I will break down your stubborn pride and make the sky above you like iron and the ground beneath you like bronze. (Lev 26:19)

⇒ There is the pride or boasting of intelligence and knowledge.

> The man who thinks he knows something does not yet know as he ought to know. (1 Cor 8:2)

⇒ There is the pride or boasting of being better and superior.

> If you are convinced that you are a guide for the blind, a light for those who are in the dark, (Rom 2:19)
> Like clouds and wind without rain is a man who boasts of gifts he does not give. (Prov 25:14)

⇒ There is the pride or boasting of conceit.

> Live in harmony with one another. Do not be proud, but be willing to associate with people of low position. Do not be conceited. (Rom 12:16)
> Do you see a man wise in his own eyes? There is more hope for a fool than for him. (Prov 26:12)

⇒ There is the pride or boasting of self-glory.

> For in his own eyes he flatters himself too much to detect or hate his sin. (Psa 36:2)

⇒ There is the pride or boasting of self-righteousness.

> The Pharisee stood up and prayed about himself: 'God, I thank you that I am not like other men—robbers, evildoers, adulterers—or even like this tax collector. (Luke 18:11)
> Since they did not know the righteousness that comes from God and sought to establish their own, they did not submit to God's righteousness. (Rom 10:3)
> 'I am pure and without sin; I am clean and free from guilt. (Job 33:9)

3. The professing man is not of God; he is of the world. To be of God means to be spiritually born of God. It means to be born again; to be made into a new creation; to be re-created into a new person, a new self; to have the divine seed and nature of God implanted into one's heart and life. But note: the professing man is of the world, not of God.

⇒ He has been born of the flesh, not of God (Jn.3:3, 5).
⇒ He is still the old creation of the earth, not the new creation of God (2 Cor.5:17).
⇒ He is still the old self of the earth, not the new self of God (Eph.4:24; Col.3:10).
⇒ He has only the perishable and dying nature of man, not the imperishable and eternal nature of God (1 Pt.1:23; 2 Pt.1:4).

3 (2:17) **Obedience**: there is the obedient man. The man who does the will of God lives forever. He knows something: the world and its lusts or desires will pass away. It is important to know this, for it means that the lusts of the world will pass away as well.

⇒ The world and its lusts pass away when he dies. Every man leaves behind the world and all he has secured. He loses all of the world he has accumulated and enjoyed. He will not be able to take a single pleasure or possession with him when he leaves the world. Imagine! He cannot take a single thing. The world will have passed away from him; time will be no more—not for him, not for his pleasures or possessions.

⇒ The world and its lusts will pass away at the end of the world. The world is to be destroyed by fire and a new heavens and earth will be created by God where only righteousness will dwell.

> But the day of the Lord will come like a thief. The heavens will disappear with a roar; the elements will be destroyed by fire, and the earth and everything in it will be laid bare. Since everything will be destroyed in this way, what kind of people ought you to be? You ought to live holy and godly lives as you look forward to the day of God and speed its coming. That day will bring about the destruction of the heavens by fire, and the elements will melt in the heat. But in keeping with his promise we are looking forward to a new heaven and a new earth, the home of righteousness. (2 Pet 3:10-13)

This is the reason the wise man turns away from the world and turns to God. He wants God and the life God offers, the life that is both abundant and eternal. Therefore, he seeks after the will of God, to do what God commands so that he may live with God forever.

> For whoever does the will of my Father in heaven is my brother and sister and mother." (Mat 12:50)
>
> "I tell you the truth, whoever hears my word and believes him who sent me has eternal life and will not be condemned; he has crossed over from death to life. (John 5:24)
>
> Jesus replied, "If anyone loves me, he will obey my teaching. My Father will love him, and we will come to him and make our home with him. (John 14:23)
>
> "Blessed are those who wash their robes, that they may have the right to the tree of life and may go through the gates into the city. (Rev 22:14)

	E. Test 5: Guarding Against Antichrists or False Teachers, 2:18-23	them belonged to us. 20 But you have an anointing from the Holy One, and all of you know the truth. 21 I do not write to you because you do not know the truth, but because you do know it and because no lie comes from the truth. 22 Who is the liar? It is the man who denies that Jesus is the Christ. Such a man is the antichrist—he denies the Father and the Son. 23 No one who denies the Son has the Father; whoever acknowledges the Son has the Father also.	3 The protection against antichrists a. The Savior's anointing^DS1 b. The truth—knowing it
1 The warning against antichrists a. It is the last hour b. It is time for antichrist c. Proof: There are many antichrists now 2 The origin of antichrists a. They were in the church b. They went out c. They did not continue d. Their going out proves they are not genuine	18 Dear children, this is the last hour; and as you have heard that the antichrist is coming, even now many antichrists have come. This is how we know it is the last hour. 19 They went out from us, but they did not really belong to us. For if they had belonged to us, they would have remained with us; but their going showed that none of		4 The false teaching of antichrists a. Denying Jesus is the Christ b. Denying identifies one as an antichrist c. Denying Jesus Christ denies God

DIVISION III

THE PROOF THAT ONE REALLY KNOWS GOD: SEVEN TESTS, 2:3-29

E. Test 5: Guarding Against Antichrists or False Teachers, 2:18-23

(2:18-23) **Introduction**: How do we know if we really know God? (See note—1 Jn.2:3-6 for introductory discussion.) This is the fifth test that proves whether or not we know God: Are we guarding against *antichrists*? Note that the word is plural, *antichrists*, not singular, antichrist. Scripture is speaking of false teachers. Are we guarding ourselves against false teachers? Or are we swallowing the false doctrine of false teachers? This is a test of our salvation, a test that will clearly show us whether or not we know God. We must guard against *antichrists*, against all false teachers.

1. The warning against antichrists (v.18).
2. The origin of antichrists (v.19).
3. The protection against antichrists (v.20-21).
4. The false teaching of antichrists (v.22-23).

1 (2:18) **Antichrist—Teachers, False—Last Hour**: there is the warning against antichrists. Note the tenderness with which John wants to issue this warning: he calls the believers "dear children." He is the aged minister, and the people are ever so dear to him. His heart beats ever so tenderly for their welfare. They are facing a critical period in their lives, the threat of false teaching, a teaching that can stir questions, doubts, unbelief, and denial of Jesus Christ. To him they are his dear children who must be warned against false teachers. The warning is for all believers. Note three facts.

1. Believers must know that it is the last hour, that the midnight hour is about to strike for the end of the world. Note the term "the last hour" (eschate hora). It really means *the last hour*, the midnight hour when the world is to end (see note, *Last Days*—2 Pt.3:3 for discussion).

2. Believers must know that it is time for the antichrist. We must be alert to the fact that the antichrist can appear upon the scene of world history anytime. Note this: the Bible definitely teaches that there will be a personal antichrist, a man to arise in the end time who will oppose and stand against Christ more fiercely than anyone else has ever done. Antichrist does not mean the spirit of evil that sweeps the world; it does not mean the spirit of false doctrine that is always presenting a problem for the church and

believers. The spirit of evil and of false doctrine do, of course, stand against Christ, and they do great harm. But this is not what is meant by the antichrist. The Bible is clear about this: the antichrist refers to a person, a man who is to arise upon the scene as a world leader—a world leader who is going to exalt the state and world government above all worship of God. Believers must know that the antichrist will come. Unless they know the teaching of the Bible, they will not be prepared. Believers must prepare and know that he is coming soon. They must sound forth the warning. (See DEEPER STUDY # 1, *Antichrist*—Mt.24:15; note—2 Th.2:3; 2:4-9; outline and notes—2 Th.2:10-12; Master Subject Index, *Antichrist* for discussion.)

> **And then the lawless one will be revealed, whom the Lord Jesus will overthrow with the breath of his mouth and destroy by the splendor of his coming. The coming of the lawless one will be in accordance with the work of Satan displayed in all kinds of counterfeit miracles, signs and wonders, (2 Th 2:8-9)**

3. How do we know that it is the last hour, that the world is about to end and Jesus Christ is about to return? Because there are many antichrists now, many who oppose and stand against Christ. The antichrist has his *forerunners* just as Jesus Christ had His prophets as forerunners. Many false prophets and teachers are on the world scene today. There are many persons—leaders, teachers, and even preachers—who are denying that Jesus Christ is the Son of God. How does this show us that it is the last time? Because this is exactly what Jesus Christ said. He said in the last days many would arise who would oppose and deny Him, and the emphasis is upon *many*. The world will be overflowing with false teachers, false preachers, and false leaders—all false prophets who proclaim a false message of hope to the world, a message that offers nothing beyond this life and the grave, nothing but judgment and hell. Note the forcefulness of John's declaration: "*We know* that it is the last time." We know because there are so many who are denying Jesus Christ.

⇒ They are *denying His deity*: that He is the Son of God who came *out of* (ek) heaven, out from the spiritual world and dimension into this world; who came through the womb of a virgin as the God-Man to save the world.

⇒ They are *denying that He is the sinless Son of God* who lived a perfect and righteous life and thereby secured the ideal and perfect righteousness for man.

⇒ They are *denying His death and resurrection*: that He died as the perfect sacrifice for man's sins and that He rose from the dead to conquer death for man.

⇒ They are *denying His Lordship*: that He is truly the Son of God who ascended into heaven and is now seated at the right hand of God as the Lord and God of the universe.

⇒ They are *denying His return to earth*: that He is coming again to execute judgment upon every person who has ever lived upon the earth.

But there is even more to show us that we are in the last days. Not only is the world full of false teachers, it is full of false messiahs. People all over the earth are proclaiming that they or some other person is the Messiah, the Savior of man. They are declaring that they have the answer to man's utopia, to man's hopes and dreams. The great tragedy is that millions of people are following these antichrists and false teachers of false hopes.

> **For when we were controlled by the sinful nature, the sinful passions aroused by the law were at work in our bodies, so that we bore fruit for death. (Rom 7:5)**

> **"Therefore everyone who hears these words of mine and puts them into practice is like a wise man who built his house on the rock. (Mat 7:24)**

> **For false Christs and false prophets will appear and perform signs and miracles to deceive the elect—if that were possible. (Mark 13:22)**

> **The Spirit clearly says that in later times some will abandon the faith and follow deceiving spirits and things taught by demons. Such teachings come through hypocritical liars, whose consciences have been seared as with a hot iron. (1 Tim 4:1-2)**

2 (2:19) **Teachers, False—Antichrists**: there is the origin of antichrists. From where do antichrists come from? Shockingly, they come from within the church. False teachers are teachers within the church; they hold positions of leadership within the church. Note exactly what John says: "They went out from us, but they did not really belong to us." They were within the church, but they were not true believers. They did not honestly believe that Jesus Christ is the Son of God, the Savior of the world. They professed Christ, were baptized, and joined the church. They even became teachers and ministers in the church, but they were not true believers.

Thought 1. How many ministers and teachers within the church do not truly believe that Jesus Christ is the Son of God, the Savior of the world? Only God knows. But all who claim to be ministers of Christ and of His church stand warned: Scripture calls them antichrists. If they were honest, they would admit that they do not belong in the church.

> **"Watch out for false prophets. They come to you in sheep's clothing, but inwardly they are ferocious wolves. By their fruit you will recognize them. Do people pick grapes from thornbushes, or figs from thistles? Likewise every good tree bears good fruit, but a bad tree bears bad fruit. A good tree cannot bear bad fruit, and a bad tree cannot bear good fruit. Every tree that does not bear good fruit is cut down and thrown into the fire. Thus, by their fruit you will recognize them. "Not everyone who says to me, 'Lord, Lord,' will enter the kingdom of heaven, but only he who does the will of my Father who is in heaven. Many will say to me on that day, 'Lord, Lord, did we not prophesy in your name, and in your name drive out demons and perform many miracles?' Then I will tell them plainly, 'I never knew you. Away from me, you evildoers!' (Mat 7:15-23)**

> **For such men are false apostles, deceitful workmen, masquerading as apostles of Christ. And no wonder, for Satan himself masquerades as an angel of light. It is not surprising, then, if his servants masquerade as servants of righteousness. Their end will be what their actions deserve. (2 Cor 11:13-15)**

> **They want to be teachers of the law, but they do not know what they are talking about or what they so confidently affirm. (1 Tim 1:7)**

> **The Spirit clearly says that in later times some will abandon the faith and follow deceiving spirits and things taught by demons. Such teachings come through hypocritical liars, whose consciences have been seared as with a hot iron. (1 Tim 4:1-2)**

> **If anyone teaches false doctrines and does not agree to the sound instruction of our Lord Jesus Christ and to godly teaching, he is conceited and understands nothing. He has an unhealthy interest in controversies and quarrels about words that result in envy, strife, malicious talk, evil suspicions and constant friction between men of corrupt mind, who have been robbed of the truth and who think that godliness is a means to financial gain. (1 Tim 6:3-5)**

> **For the time will come when men will not put up with sound doctrine. Instead, to suit their own desires, they will gather around them a great number of teachers to say what their itching ears want to hear. They will turn their ears away from the truth and turn aside to myths. (2 Tim 4:3-4)**

> **But there were also false prophets among the people, just as there will be false teachers among you. They will secretly introduce destructive heresies, even denying the sovereign Lord who bought them—bringing swift destruction on themselves. (2 Pet 2:1)**

> **"From the least to the greatest, all are greedy for gain; prophets and priests alike, all practice deceit. (Jer 6:13)**

"Both prophet and priest are godless; even in my temple I find their wickedness," declares the LORD. (Jer 23:11)

"My people have been lost sheep; their shepherds have led them astray and caused them to roam on the mountains. They wandered over mountain and hill and forgot their own resting place. (Jer 50:6)

But if the watchman sees the sword coming and does not blow the trumpet to warn the people and the sword comes and takes the life of one of them, that man will be taken away because of his sin, but I will hold the watchman accountable for his blood.' (Ezek 33:6)

3 (2:20-21) **Teachers, False:** there is the protection against antichrists. God gives the believer two protections.

1. God gives an anointing (chrisma) to the believer. Note who it is that anoints us: the Holy One, that is, God Himself. What is the anointing that He gives? The Holy Spirit. This is exactly what Scripture declares:

Now it is God who makes both us and you stand firm in Christ. He anointed us, set his seal of ownership on us, and put his Spirit in our hearts as a deposit, guaranteeing what is to come. (2 Cor 1:21-22)

Why does God give us the Holy Spirit? One of the major reasons is to teach us all things. This was the glorious promise of Jesus Christ.

But the Counselor, the Holy Spirit, whom the Father will send in my name, will teach you all things and will remind you of everything I have said to you. (John 14:26; cp. Jn.14:16-20; 16:7-11)

What is meant by *the truth*? Does it mean that the Holy Spirit teaches us all the skilled professions of the world such as science, history, and medicine? No, not in the technical sense. But note: the Holy Spirit does teach the believer to relate all professions to the truth. The believer knows that no profession stands as a *god* before men, as though it were the answer to man's basic problems. The Holy Spirit will also strengthen and help a sincere believer learn whatever field or profession he wishes to enter. But this is not the primary teaching that concerns the Holy Spirit. The primary concern of the Holy Spirit is the truth about Jesus Christ and about man and his world as they relate to Christ and to eternity. It means *the truth* that has to do with God and Christ and man's spiritual hunger; it means the truth that has to do with man and his world, their purpose and fate; it means the truth that has to do with Christianity and life, the purpose, meaning, and significance of life. This means a most wonderful thing: it means that any believer who has a question about some person's teaching can ask the Holy Spirit to teach him the truth. There is no excuse for any believer ever being misled by false teaching. God has given him the Holy Spirit to protect him.

2. God gives the truth to the believer. He gives us the truth in two ways.

　　a. God gives us the truth in Jesus Christ. Jesus Christ is the truth. He declared this emphatically:

Jesus answered, "I am the way and the truth and the life. No one comes to the Father except through me. (John 14:6)

Jesus Christ is the very embodiment of truth. He is the picture of truth. God not only talks to man about Himself in the Word of God, God shows man what He is like in the person of Jesus Christ. Man can look at Jesus Christ and see a perfect picture of the truth of God. Jesus Christ, the Son of God, shows us exactly what God is like.

I and the Father are one." (John 10:30)
Do not believe me unless I do what my Father does. But if I do it, even though you do not believe me, believe the miracles, that you may know and understand that the Father is in me, and I in the Father." (John 10:37-38)

Don't you believe that I am in the Father, and that the Father is in me? The words I say to you are not just my own. Rather, it is the Father, living in me, who is doing his work. (John 14:10)

I will remain in the world no longer, but they are still in the world, and I am coming to you. Holy Father, protect them by the power of your name—the name you gave me—so that they may be one as we are one. (John 17:11)

I have given them the glory that you gave me, that they may be one as we are one: (John 17:22)

As Jesus Christ says in Jn.14:6, "I am the way [to God], and the truth [of God] and the life [of God]." The truth is found in Jesus Christ. True believers know this. Therefore, there is never an excuse for believers to be led astray by false teachers or antichrists.

　　b. God gives us the truth in the Word of God, the Holy Scriptures or Holy Bible. Jesus Christ Himself and scripture declare:

To the Jews who had believed him, Jesus said, "If you hold to my teaching, you are really my disciples. Then you will know the truth, and the truth will set you free." (John 8:31-32)

Sanctify them by the truth; your word is truth. (John 17:17)

Do your best to present yourself to God as one approved, a workman who does not need to be ashamed and who correctly handles the word of truth. (2 Tim 2:15)

All Scripture is God-breathed and is useful for teaching, rebuking, correcting and training in righteousness, (2 Tim 3:16)

And we have the word of the prophets made more certain, and you will do well to pay attention to it, as to a light shining in a dark place, until the day dawns and the morning star rises in your hearts. Above all, you must understand that no prophecy of Scripture came about by the prophet's own interpretation. For prophecy never had its origin in the will of man, but men spoke from God as they were carried along by the Holy Spirit. (2 Pet 1:19-21)

The genuine believer knows the truth; he knows the Lord Jesus Christ is the Lord and Savior of men, the very Son of God Himself; and he has the Word of God itself. In addition to this, he has the Holy Spirit to teach him the truth and to help him remember the words of Christ. Therefore, there is no excuse for the believer ever being misled by antichrists or false teachers.

Note the words "no lie comes from the truth." No matter how attractive or appealing, no matter how much charisma a person may have, no matter how much we may like a person—if he teaches a doctrine that differs from the Word of God, it is a lie. It is not from the truth; it is a deception.

Thought 1. This lays an enormous obligation upon us, an obligation to study the Word of God and to depend upon the Holy Spirit to teach us. He will not teach a lethargic or lazy person. We must be diligent in studying the Word of God, in praying and seeking the leadership of the Spirit of God.

DEEPER STUDY # 1

(2:20) Anointed: this is the Holy Spirit. In the Old Testament only prophets, priests, and kings were anointed. They were anointed by pouring oil upon their heads. The oil symbolized the Spirit of God coming upon them for service. Such anointing was the privilege of only a few chosen people. But Jesus Christ changed this. He was anointed at His baptism—not with the *symbol* of the Spirit, that is, the oil, but rather with the Holy Spirit Himself (Lk.4:18; Acts 4:27; 10:38). What John is saying is this: the same anointing is no longer just the possession of only a chosen few. It is the possession of every believer (cp. Acts 8:17; 2 Cor.1:21-22; Col.1:28). The Holy Spirit is the believer's protective force against false teaching and seducing spirits, against antichrists.

---

4 (2:22-23) **Teachers, False—Unbelief—Apostasy**: there is the false teaching of antichrists or false teachers. The false teaching is stated as clearly as human language can state it:

> Who is the liar? It is the man who denies that Jesus is the Christ. Such a man is the antichrist—he denies the Father and the Son. (v.22)

The false teacher who is a forerunner of the antichrist is the person who denies that Jesus is the Messiah. He denies the very Son of God whom God had promised to send as the Savior of the world. Two terrible things are said about this person: first, he is a liar; and second, he denies the Father if he denies the Son, the Lord Jesus Christ. Why is this so? How is it that a person denies God if he denies Christ? The answer is twofold.

First, if a person denies that God sent His Son into the world, then his image of God differs entirely from the God who is the Father of Jesus Christ. God sent His Son into the world. Therefore, if we picture a *god* in our minds that did not send His Son, then our image of God differs entirely from the *true and living God*. The *true and living God* is love, perfect love. Therefore, He has loved man perfectly. God has done the greatest thing that can be done for man: He has sent His only Son into the world to save man by dying for man's sins. No greater love could ever be demonstrated for man. Therefore, if a man says that God did not send His Son into the world—that Jesus Christ is not the Son of God—then that man is thinking of some *god* other than the Father of the Lord Jesus Christ.

⇒ By denying Jesus Christ, the man denies the Father.

⇒ By denying the Son, the man does not have the Father. He is separated from the Father, standing against and opposed to both God and His Son, the Lord Jesus Christ. The man is doomed, for he has denied that God loves the world enough to send His Son to save the world.

Second, any person who denies Jesus Christ is denying the New Testament. Why? Because the New Testament says time and time again that Jesus Christ is the Son of God, the one Person who reveals God the Father to the world.

> "All things have been committed to me by my Father. No one knows the Son except the Father, and no one knows the Father except the Son and those to whom the Son chooses to reveal him. (Mat 11:27)
>
> Then Jesus cried out, "When a man believes in me, he does not believe in me only, but in the one who sent me. When he looks at me, he sees the one who sent me. (John 12:44-45)
>
> Jesus answered, "I am the way and the truth and the life. No one comes to the Father except through me. (John 14:6)
>
> Jesus answered: "Don't you know me, Philip, even after I have been among you such a long time? Anyone who has seen me has seen the Father. How can you say, 'Show us the Father'? Don't you believe that I am in the Father, and that the Father is in me? The words I say to you are not just my own. Rather, it is the Father, living in me, who is doing his work. Believe me when I say that I am in the Father and the Father is in me; or at least believe on the evidence of the miracles themselves. (John 14:9-11)

The point is clear: any person who denies Jesus Christ is denying God as well, the *only living and true God*. Any person who denies that Jesus Christ is the Son of God is a false teacher, a forerunner of the antichrist.

> But whoever disowns me before men, I will disown him before my Father in heaven. (Mat 10:33)
>
> If anyone is ashamed of me and my words in this adulterous and sinful generation, the Son of Man will be ashamed of him when he comes in his Father's glory with the holy angels." (Mark 8:38)
>
> That all may honor the Son just as they honor the Father. He who does not honor the Son does not honor the Father, who sent him. (John 5:23)
>
> I have come in my Father's name, and you do not accept me; but if someone else comes in his own name, you will accept him. (John 5:43)
>
> But there were also false prophets among the people, just as there will be false teachers among you. They will secretly introduce destructive heresies, even denying

the sovereign Lord who bought them—bringing swift destruction on themselves. (2 Pet 2:1)

Who is the liar? It is the man who denies that Jesus is the Christ. Such a man is the antichrist—he denies the Father and the Son. (1 John 2:22)

Many deceivers, who do not acknowledge Jesus Christ as coming in the flesh, have gone out into the world. Any such person is the deceiver and the antichrist.

Watch out that you do not lose what you have worked for, but that you may be rewarded fully. Anyone who runs ahead and does not continue in the teaching of Christ does not have God; whoever continues in the teaching has both the Father and the Son. If anyone comes to you and does not bring this teaching, do not take him into your house or welcome him. Anyone who welcomes him shares in his wicked work. (2 John 1:7-11)

		F. Test 6: Letting the Gospel Remain in You, 2:24-27	26 I am writing these things to you about those who are trying to lead you astray.	3 The warning: Some lead us astray from Christ

1 The test: Does the gospel remain in you?
  a. It is the old unchangeable message
  b. The evidence: You are continuing in the Son
2 The promise: Eternal life
		24 See that what you have heard from the beginning remains in you. If it does, you also will remain in the Son and in the Father.
		25 And this is what he promised us—even eternal life.
			27 As for you, the anointing you received from him remains in you, and you do not need anyone to teach you.
			28 But as his anointing teaches you about all things and as that anointing is real, not counterfeit—just as it has taught you, remain in him.
				4 The provision of God to protect us: The Holy Spirit
				  a. He is the anointing & He abides in us
				  b. He teaches us the truth
				  c. He seals us, assures us that we do abide in Christ

DIVISION III

THE PROOF THAT ONE REALLY KNOWS GOD: SEVEN TESTS, 2:3-29

F. Test 6: Letting the Gospel Remain in You, 2:24-27

(2:24-27) **Introduction**: How do we know if we really know God? (See note—1 Jn.2:3-6 for introductory discussion.) This is the sixth test that proves whether or not we know God: Does the gospel abide in us? How we live shows quicker than anything else whether or not we know God. If we have grasped the truth of God's Word, of His gospel, and are living it out in our lives, then we definitely know God. But the converse is also tragically true: if the gospel, God's Word, is not within us, if we are not living out the gospel, then we do not know God. Regardless of what we may feel or profess—regardless of what others may think—we do not know God. The gospel lives within the life of every genuine believer and the believer lives out the gospel.

1. The test: does the gospel remain in you (v.24)?
2. The promise: eternal life (v.25).
3. The warning: some lead us astray from Christ (v.26).
4. The provision of God to protect us: the Holy Spirit (v.27).

1 (2:24) **Gospel—Word of God—Truth**: the test is clearly stated—does the gospel remain in you? Note that the word gospel is not used in this passage. But note the exact words of the verse:

> See that what you have heard from the beginning remains in you. If it does, you also will remain in the Son and in the Father. (v.24)

What we heard from the beginning is the gospel. Glance back to verses 22-23 where the denial of Jesus Christ is discussed. False teachers were denying that Jesus Christ is the Son of God; they were denying the gospel. Therefore, "what you have heard from the beginning" is the message of the gospel...

• the gospel of Jesus Christ.
• the gospel of the truth, of the Word of God itself (v.21).
• the gospel of the apostolic message (cp. 1 Cor.15:1-4).
• the gospel of salvation (cp. Tit.2:11-14; 3:4-7).

Now note the evidence of salvation, of knowing God: if the gospel continues in you, "you also will remain in the Son and in the Father." The word "remain" (meneto) means to abide, dwell, remain. It means not to be carried away by false teaching or worldly pleasures and possessions. How do we know if we know God?

Does the gospel continue to live in our lives? Are we continuing to live in the Son and in the Father? Is the gospel being lived out in our lives? Are we confessing Jesus Christ to be the Son of God? Do we really believe that Jesus Christ is the Son of God? Are we letting Jesus Christ live His life out in us? This is the final proof that we know God.

> **"As the Father has loved me, so have I loved you. Now remain in my love. (John 15:9)**
>
> **I have been crucified with Christ and I no longer live, but Christ lives in me. The life I live in the body, I live by faith in the Son of God, who loved me and gave himself for me. (Gal 2:20)**
>
> **So then, just as you received Christ Jesus as Lord, continue to live in him, (Col 2:6)**
>
> **Therefore, prepare your minds for action; be self-controlled; set your hope fully on the grace to be given you when Jesus Christ is revealed. (1 Pet 1:13)**
>
> **Whoever claims to live in him must walk as Jesus did. (1 John 2:6)**
>
> **No one who lives in him keeps on sinning. No one who continues to sin has either seen him or known him. (1 John 3:6)**
>
> **Anyone who runs ahead and does not continue in the teaching of Christ does not have God; whoever continues in the teaching has both the Father and the Son. (2 John 1:9)**
>
> **I am coming soon. Hold on to what you have, so that no one will take your crown. (Rev 3:11)**
>
> **Here I am! I stand at the door and knock. If anyone hears my voice and opens the door, I will come in and eat with him, and he with me. (Rev 3:20)**

2 (2:25) **Eternal Life**: there is the promise of eternal life. This is the great promise of God to man. God has made many promises, but this is the one promise that supersedes all others. Eternal life is the supreme promise of God. But note the thrust of the verse: the gospel must remain in us if we are to receive eternal life (v.27). What is eternal life? It is life, real life. It is the very life of God Himself. It is the very energy, force, being, essence, principle, and power of life. It has to do with both quality and with what life really is, with duration. To live forever in the present world, with the world like it is, is not necessarily a good thing. The world and man's body need changing. That changed life is found only in eternal life. The only being who can be said to be eternal is God. Therefore, life—supreme life—is found only in God. To possess eternal life is to know God. Once a person knows God and Jesus Christ whom He has sent, that person has eternal life—he shall live forever. But more essential, the person has the supreme quality of life, the very life of God Himself. (See notes—Deeper Study # 2— Jn.1:4; Deeper Study # 1—10:10.)

Thought 1. Once a person believes in Jesus Christ, he has eternal life. That is, he immediately receives eternal life. It is not that he is going to receive eternal life; he has already received it. He begins to live eternally from that very moment onward. The day that he makes his decision for Christ is the first day of his eternal life. And every day of his life thereafter is another day in eternity for him. This is significant: it means that we should be very careful about how we live every day. For every day is another day lived in eternity. We shall never die. When God is ready to move us from this physical world into the spiritual world (heaven), He simply transfers us—all quicker than the blink of the eye.

Just as Moses lifted up the snake in the desert, so the Son of Man must be lifted up, that everyone who believes in him may have eternal life. (John 3:14-15)
Whoever believes in the Son has eternal life, but whoever rejects the Son will not see life, for God's wrath remains on him." (John 3:36)
"I tell you the truth, whoever hears my word and believes him who sent me has eternal life and will not be condemned; he has crossed over from death to life. (John 5:24)
For my Father's will is that everyone who looks to the Son and believes in him shall have eternal life, and I will raise him up at the last day." (John 6:40)
Jesus said to her, "I am the resurrection and the life. He who believes in me will live, even though he dies; and whoever lives and believes in me will never die. Do you believe this?" (John 11:25-26)
The man who loves his life will lose it, while the man who hates his life in this world will keep it for eternal life. (John 12:25)
So that, just as sin reigned in death, so also grace might reign through righteousness to bring eternal life through Jesus Christ our Lord. (Rom 5:21)
The one who sows to please his sinful nature, from that nature will reap destruction; the one who sows to please the Spirit, from the Spirit will reap eternal life. (Gal 6:8)
But it has now been revealed through the appearing of our Savior, Christ Jesus, who has destroyed death and has brought life and immortality to light through the gospel. (2 Tim 1:10)
We know that we have passed from death to life, because we love our brothers. Anyone who does not love remains in death. (1 John 3:14)
And this is the testimony: God has given us eternal life, and this life is in his Son. He who has the Son has life; he who

does not have the Son of God does not have life. (1 John 5:11-12)

3 (2:26) **Teachers, False—Seduction**: there is the warning—some do attempt to lead us astray. Why is John writing his letter to the believers? One of the major reasons is given here: there were false teachers who were trying to lead them astray. The word "astray" (planonton) means to deceive; to lead astray. A false teacher is one who attempts to lead us away from Jesus Christ, from the glorious truth that He is the Son of God who came to earth to die for our sins. The false teacher deceives people; that is, he teaches that man can become acceptable to God by some other way than Jesus Christ. He teaches that there are other ways to God, other approaches, other religions, other truths. He seduces and leads people astray; he deceives people into following some other teaching. Note this: the tense is continuous action in the Greek. That is, false teachers are continually teaching false doctrine. They are always teaching a false doctrine and always trying to lead people astray.

Thought 1. Believers must be on constant guard against false teaching. So much is at stake: the very promise of God. We will abandon the faith if we listen to the deception and go astray. We must continue to follow Christ; we must let the gospel abide and take up a permanent residence in our lives.

Thought 2. Note this: if God has really sent His Son into the world to save man, there is not a chance in eternity that He will allow a person to approach Him by any other way. His very purpose for sending His Son was to save man. If there was another way God would never have allowed His Son to leave the glory of heaven and be so humiliated as to come to such a corruptible world as ours.

4 (2:27) **Holy Spirit**: there is the provision of God to protect us—the Holy Spirit Himself.
1. The Holy Spirit is the anointing. It is He who abides and remains in us (see note, pt.1—1 Jn.2:20-21 for discussion).
2. The Holy Spirit is the One who teaches us the truth (see note, pt.2—1 Jn.2:20-21 for discussion).
3. The Holy Spirit seals us and guarantees and assures us that we do abide and remain in Christ.

The Spirit himself testifies with our spirit that we are God's children. Now if we are children, then we are heirs—heirs of God and co-heirs with Christ, if indeed we share in his sufferings in order that we may also share in his glory. (Rom 8:16-17)
Set his seal of ownership on us, and put his Spirit in our hearts as a deposit, guaranteeing what is to come. (2 Cor 1:22)
And you also were included in Christ when you heard the word of truth, the gospel of your salvation. Having believed, you were marked in him with a seal, the promised Holy Spirit, who is a deposit guaranteeing our inheritance until the redemption of those who are God's possession—to the praise of his glory. (Eph 1:13-14)
And do not grieve the Holy Spirit of God, with whom you were sealed for the day of redemption. (Eph 4:30)

	G. Test 7: Continuing, Continuing in Christ, 2:28-29
1 The test: Do we continue in Christ?	28 And now, dear children, continue in him, so that when he appears we may be confident and unashamed before him at his coming.
2 The purpose for continuing: That we may have confidence & not be ashamed at Christ's return	
3 The proof of continuing: Living a righteous life a. Knowing that He is righteous b. Being born again	29 If you know that he is righteous, you know that everyone who does what is right has been born of him.

DIVISION III

THE PROOF THAT ONE REALLY KNOWS GOD: SEVEN TESTS, 2:3-29

G. Test 7: Continuing in Christ, 2:28-29

(2:28-29) **Introduction**: How do we know if we really know God? (See note—1 Jn.2:3-6 for introductory discussion.) This is the seventh and final test that proves whether or not we know God: Do we continue in Christ? Remember: Christ is the only Person who ever came "*out of*" (ek) heaven, out of the spiritual world and dimension. He is the Son of God who came to earth to reveal who God is and to show us what life is all about. Jesus Christ is of the very nature of God. He is righteous just like God is righteous. He always did what was right; He was righteous in every detail of life just like God is righteous. Therefore, when we continue in Christ, we continue in the very nature of God. We live like God lives, and we live life like it should be lived. We live righteous lives; we try to do all things right just like God. Consequently, the person who continues and lives in Christ is the person who knows God, but the person who does not continue in Christ does not know God. The test of salvation, of whether or not we know God, is this: Do we continue in Christ?

1. The test: do we continue in Christ (v.28)?
2. The purpose for continuing: that we may have confidence and not be ashamed at Christ's return (v.28).
3. The proof of continuing: living a righteous life (v.29).

1 (2:28) **Continuing**: there is the test—do we continue in Christ? The word *continue* means to dwell, continue, stay, sojourn, rest in or upon. It is being set and fixed and remaining there; continuing on and on in a fixed state, condition, or being. It is being at home and being permanent and settled. Therefore, to continue in Christ means...

- to continue and stay in Christ
- to sojourn and rest in and upon Christ
- to be set and fixed in Christ and to remain in Him
- to continue on and on in Christ, in being fixed in Him
- to be at home in Christ; to find our permanent home in Him and to be settled in Him

The basic idea of *continuing in Christ* is that of dwelling. It is just like dwelling in a house. We are to dwell in Christ, in the kind of life He showed us how to live. He lived a righteous life, a life that was always right toward God and man. Therefore, we are to make our home in Christ, to dwell and move about in the righteous life of Christ. We are to be right with God and man just like He was.

Now, when a person continues in Christ, what kind of life does he live? Very practically, what kinds of things does he do? How does he behave toward God and man? Scripture says the following:

⇒ Continuing in Christ means that a person confesses that Jesus Christ is the Son of God. He believes the love that God has shown him in Christ, and he loves God because of what God has done for him.

If anyone acknowledges that Jesus is the Son of God, God lives in him and he in God. And so we know and rely on the love God has for us. God is love. Whoever lives in love lives in God, and God in him. (1 John 4:15-16)

⇒ Continuing in Christ means that a person walks and fellowships with Christ. He lives and moves and has his being in Christ. He communes and lives in a consciousness of the Lord's presence, and from the Lord's presence he learns of God, and he draws the strength and authority to live victoriously day by day.

Whoever claims to live in him must walk as Jesus did. (1 John 2:6)
As for you, the anointing you received from him remains in you, and you do not need anyone to teach you. But as his anointing teaches you about all things and as that anointing is real, not counterfeit— just as it has taught you, remain in him. (1 John 2:27; cp. Ps.16:11; Pr.3:5-6)

⇒ Continuing in Christ means that a person walks in open confession before God. He walks hour by hour all day long opening up his life to God; he constantly confesses that he is short of God's glory and any known sin that he slips into. He does not walk in sin, and he does not allow any sin to go unconfessed.

If we claim to have fellowship with him yet walk in the darkness, we lie and do not live by the truth. But if we walk in the light, as he is in the light, we have fellowship with one another, and the blood of Jesus, his Son, purifies us from all sin. If we claim to be without sin, we deceive our-

selves and the truth is not in us. If we confess our sins, he is faithful and just and will forgive us our sins and purify us from all unrighteousness. If we claim we have not sinned, we make him out to be a liar and his word has no place in our lives. (1 John 1:6-10)

⇒ Continuing in Christ means that a person continues in the Word of Christ and knows the truth.

To the Jews who had believed him, Jesus said, "If you hold to my teaching, you are really my disciples. Then you will know the truth, and the truth will set you free." (John 8:31-32)

⇒ Continuing in Christ means that a person lets the Word of God continue in his life.

I write to you, fathers, because you have known him who is from the beginning. I write to you, young men, because you are strong, and the word of God lives in you, and you have overcome the evil one. (1 John 2:14)
See that what you have heard from the beginning remains in you. If it does, you also will remain in the Son and in the Father. (1 John 2:24)

⇒ Continuing in Christ means that a person experiences the indwelling presence and witness of the Spirit.

No one has ever seen God; but if we love one another, God lives in us and his love is made complete in us. We know that we live in him and he in us, because he has given us of his Spirit. (1 John 4:12-13)

⇒ Continuing in Christ means that a person has power to live like he should.

If you remain in me and my words remain in you, ask whatever you wish, and it will be given you. (John 15:7)

⇒ Continuing in Christ means that a person dwells in love and in unity and fellowship with all other believers.

That all of them may be one, Father, just as you are in me and I am in you. May they also be in us so that the world may believe that you have sent me. I have given them the glory that you gave me, that they may be one as we are one: I in them and you in me. May they be brought to complete unity to let the world know that you sent me and have loved them even as you have loved me. (John 17:21-23)
And so we know and rely on the love God has for us. God is love. Whoever lives in love lives in God, and God in him. (1 John 4:16; cp. 1 Jn.4:20)

⇒ Continuing in Christ means that a person bears fruit and lives a very fruitful life.

"I am the vine; you are the branches. If a man remains in me and I in him, he will bear much fruit; apart from me you can do nothing. (John 15:5)
But the fruit of the Spirit is love, joy, peace, patience, kindness, goodness, faithfulness, gentleness and self-control. Against such things there is no law. (Gal 5:22-23)

⇒ Continuing in Christ means that a person loves others, that he lives and walks in love toward others.

No one has ever seen God; but if we love one another, God lives in us and his love is made complete in us. We know that we live in him and he in us, because he has given us of his Spirit. (1 John 4:12-13)

⇒ Continuing in Christ means that a person remains in the church; he has not gone out from the church.

They went out from us, but they did not really belong to us. For if they had belonged to us, they would have remained with us; but their going showed that none of them belonged to us. (1 John 2:19)
No one who lives in him keeps on sinning. No one who continues to sin has either seen him or known him. (1 John 3:6)

⇒ Continuing in Christ means that a person possesses confidence, an unashamedness in life that prepares him for eternity.

And now, dear children, continue in him, so that when he appears we may be confident and unashamed before him at his coming. (1 John 2:28)

⇒ Continuing in Christ means that a person actively surrenders himself to obey God's commandments.

Those who obey his commands live in him, and he in them. And this is how we know that he lives in us: We know it by the Spirit he gave us. (1 John 3:24)

⇒ Continuing in Christ means that a person loves his brother.

Whoever loves his brother lives in the light, and there is nothing in him to make him stumble. (1 John 2:10; cp. 1 Jn.3:14-15)

⇒ Continuing in Christ means that a person does the will of God.

The world and its desires pass away, but the man who does the will of God lives forever. (1 John 2:17)

⇒ Continuing in Christ means that a person experiences the continuous presence and anointing of the Holy Spirit.

As for you, the anointing you received from him remains in you, and you do not need anyone to teach you. But as his anointing teaches you about all things and as that anointing is real, not counterfeit—

just as it has taught you, remain in him. (1 John 2:27)

Those who obey his commands live in him, and he in them. And this is how we know that he lives in us: We know it by the Spirit he gave us. (1 John 3:24)

2 (2:28) **Continuing—Abiding—Jesus Christ, Return—Judgment—Unashamed**: there is the purpose for continuing—that we may have confidence and not be ashamed when Christ returns. Note two significant points.

1. Jesus Christ is coming again. Scripture emphatically declares that He is going to return to earth again. He is coming to consummate human history and to judge the earth—every man and woman who has ever lived. This is the constant declaration of Scripture.

For the Son of Man is going to come in his Father's glory with his angels, and then he will reward each person according to what he has done. (Mat 16:27)

"When the Son of Man comes in his glory, and all the angels with him, he will sit on his throne in heavenly glory. All the nations will be gathered before him, and he will separate the people one from another as a shepherd separates the sheep from the goats. (Mat 25:31-32)

Moreover, the Father judges no one, but has entrusted all judgment to the Son, "Do not be amazed at this, for a time is coming when all who are in their graves will hear his voice and come out—those who have done good will rise to live, and those who have done evil will rise to be condemned. (John 5:22, 28-29)

Therefore judge nothing before the appointed time; wait till the Lord comes. He will bring to light what is hidden in darkness and will expose the motives of men's hearts. At that time each will receive his praise from God. (1 Cor 4:5)

For we must all appear before the judgment seat of Christ, that each one may receive what is due him for the things done while in the body, whether good or bad. (2 Cor 5:10)

In the presence of God and of Christ Jesus, who will judge the living and the dead, and in view of his appearing and his kingdom, I give you this charge: (2 Tim 4:1)

Since you call on a Father who judges each man's work impartially, live your lives as strangers here in reverent fear. (1 Pet 1:17)

Enoch, the seventh from Adam, prophesied about these men: "See, the Lord is coming with thousands upon thousands of his holy ones to judge everyone, and to convict all the ungodly of all the ungodly acts they have done in the ungodly way, and of all the harsh words ungodly sinners have spoken against him." (Jude 1:14-15)

And I saw the dead, great and small, standing before the throne, and books were opened. Another book was opened, which is the book of life. The dead were judged according to what they had done as recorded in the books. (Rev 20:12)

"Behold, I am coming soon! My reward is with me, and I will give to everyone according to what he has done. (Rev 22:12)

2. The task of believers, yea of all people, is to be prepared for the return of Christ. How can we prepare ourselves? By doing just what is discussed above: *continuing in Christ*. If we *continue in Christ*, we will have confidence and not be ashamed before Him at His coming.

⇒ The word "confident" (parresian) means boldness, assurance. It has the idea of unshakable boldness and assurance. If we continue in Christ now, today, and every day hereafter, we can have unshakable confidence and assurance and even boldness when Jesus Christ returns to earth.

⇒ The word "unashamed" (me aischynomai) means not to shrink back; not to sense guilt and disgrace; not to feel embarrassment. If we do not continue in Christ, we shall be ashamed when Jesus Christ returns to earth.

Note a fact that is so often ignored by believers, a fact that is seldom if ever thought about. There shall be shame, disgrace, and embarrassment when Christ returns. Some believers will shrink back from Christ. The picture of nothing but joy and rejoicing when Christ returns is not a true picture. There is going to be judgment: the judgment of every man's works no matter what the works are, and there shall be the judgment of sinners no matter who they are, all unbelievers.

There will be joy and rejoicing for some believers, for those who have been continuing in Christ. But there will be shame, guilt, disgrace, and embarrassment—a shrinking back, for those who have been walking unfaithfully.

He commanded us to preach to the people and to testify that he is the one whom God appointed as judge of the living and the dead. (Acts 10:42)

For he has set a day when he will judge the world with justice by the man he has appointed. He has given proof of this to all men by raising him from the dead." (Acts 17:31)

This will take place on the day when God will judge men's secrets through Jesus Christ, as my gospel declares. (Rom 2:16)

You, then, why do you judge your brother? Or why do you look down on your brother? For we will all stand before God's judgment seat. (Rom 14:10)

If any man builds on this foundation using gold, silver, costly stones, wood, hay or straw, his work will be shown for what it is, because the Day will bring it to light. It will be revealed with fire, and the fire will test the quality of each man's work. If what he has built survives, he will receive his reward. If it is burned up, he will suffer loss; he himself will be saved, but only as one escaping through the flames. (1 Cor 3:12-15)

For we must all appear before the judgment seat of Christ, that each one may receive what is due him for the things done while in the body, whether good or bad. (2 Cor 5:10)

> In the presence of God and of Christ Jesus, who will judge the living and the dead, and in view of his appearing and his kingdom, I give you this charge: (2 Tim 4:1)

3 (2:29) **Righteousness—Jesus Christ, Sinless—New Birth**: there is the proof of continuing—living a righteous life. If a person continues in Jesus Christ, he lives a righteous life This is the supreme and final proof that a person knows God. We can always tell if a person knows God by the fruit and treasure of his life: Is he living a righteous life, a life just like Jesus Christ lived? This is exactly what Jesus Christ said.

> By their fruit you will recognize them. Do people pick grapes from thornbushes, or figs from thistles? Likewise every good tree bears good fruit, but a bad tree bears bad fruit. A good tree cannot bear bad fruit, and a bad tree cannot bear good fruit. (Mat 7:16-18)
>
> The good man brings good things out of the good stored up in him, and the evil man brings evil things out of the evil stored up in him. (Mat 12:35)

There is one reason why a person who knows Christ lives a righteous life. Note how significant this reason is: the person knows that Jesus Christ is righteous. The person knows that Jesus Christ is the sinless Son of God. Jesus Christ was sinless before He ever came to earth; He was the perfect and righteous Son of God throughout all of eternity. In addition to this, He was sinless when He lived on earth. He walked as a Man upon earth and He lived a perfect and righteous life as a Man. Therefore, He secured the perfect and ideal righteousness for man. This is the very reason Jesus Christ was able to bear the sins of man and die for them. As the Perfect and Ideal Man, God was able to accept His death as the perfect sacrifice for sin.

The point is this: everything that Jesus Christ did hinges upon His righteousness, upon the fact that He is the righteous and sinless Son of God. Therefore, the person who truly believes in Jesus Christ lives in the righteousness of Christ. He continues, dwells, lives, and moves in the righteousness of Jesus Christ. He trusts and casts himself upon the righteousness of Christ, and he continues day by day to trust and cast himself upon His precious Lord and His righteousness.

This is the way we can tell whether or not a person is born of God, whether or not God has given a new birth to a person. If a person honors God's Son by trusting and casting himself upon the righteousness of His Son, God takes that person and honors him. God gives him a new life, a spiritual birth. God makes a new creation out of him, a spiritual man. The true believer becomes a new creation, the new man of God. Now note the verse:

> If you know that he [Christ] is righteous, you know that everyone who does what is right has been born of him. (1 John 2:29)

Thought 1. The person who lives a righteous life is the person who knows God. God is righteous; His very nature is righteousness. Therefore, a person who lives a righteous life is the person who has the nature of God. He is the person who allows God's nature to be lived out and through his life. If a person does not have the nature of God, then he does not live out the life of God. He does not live a righteous life. We can tell whether or not a person knows God by the life he lives.

> In reply Jesus declared, "I tell you the truth, no one can see the kingdom of God unless he is born again." "How can a man be born when he is old?" Nicodemus asked. "Surely he cannot enter a second time into his mother's womb to be born!" Jesus answered, "I tell you the truth, no one can enter the kingdom of God unless he is born of water and the Spirit. (John 3:3-5)
>
> Therefore, if anyone is in Christ, he is a new creation; the old has gone, the new has come! (2 Cor 5:17)
>
> And to put on the new self, created to be like God in true righteousness and holiness. (Eph 4:24)
>
> And have put on the new self, which is being renewed in knowledge in the image of its Creator. (Col 3:10)
>
> For you have been born again, not of perishable seed, but of imperishable, through the living and enduring word of God. (1 Pet 1:23)
>
> Everyone who believes that Jesus is the Christ is born of God, and everyone who loves the father loves his child as well. (1 John 5:1)
>
> In reply Jesus declared, "I tell you the truth, no one can see the kingdom of God unless he is born again." "How can a man be born when he is old?" Nicodemus asked. "Surely he cannot enter a second time into his mother's womb to be born!" Jesus answered, "I tell you the truth, no one can enter the kingdom of God unless he is born of water and the Spirit. (John 3:3-5)
>
> Therefore, if anyone is in Christ, he is a new creation; the old has gone, the new has come! (2 Cor 5:17)
>
> And to put on the new self, created to be like God in true righteousness and holiness. (Eph 4:24)
>
> And have put on the new self, which is being renewed in knowledge in the image of its Creator. (Col 3:10)
>
> For you have been born again, not of perishable seed, but of imperishable, through the living and enduring word of God. (1 Pet 1:23)
>
> Everyone who believes that Jesus is the Christ is born of God, and everyone who loves the father loves his child as well. (1 John 5:1)

	CHAPTER 3 IV. THE PROOF THAT ONE REALLY LOVES GOD: SIX TESTS, 3:1-4:21 A. Test 1: Experiencing God's Incredible Love, 3:1-3	dren of God! And that is what we are! The reason the world does not know us is that it did not know him. 2 Dear friends, now we are children of God, and what we will be has not yet been made known. But we know that when he appears, we shall be like him, for we shall see him as he is.	a. Given by God b. The world does not know nor understand believers 2 **The great hope & mystery of God's love: Eternal transformation** a. What we shall be is unknown b. We shall be like Christ
1 **The privilege of God's love: We are called children of God**	How great is the love the Father has lavished on us, that we should be called chil-	3 Everyone who has this hope in him purifies himself, just as he is pure.	3 **The incentive of God's love: Purity**

DIVISION IV

THE PROOF THAT ONE REALLY LOVES GOD: SIX TESTS, 3:1-4:21

A. Test 1: Experiencing God's Incredible Love, 3:1-3

(3:1-3) **Introduction**: the love of God—there is no greater subject in all the world. Why? Because if God loves us, it means that He is not far off in outer space someplace. It means that God is not distant, unreachable, and unconcerned with the world. It means that God is not mean and vengeful, that He does not cause all the bad things that happen to us, things such as accidents, diseases, and death. It means that God is not hovering over us looking for every mistake we make so that He can punish us.

On the contrary, since God is love, it means that He is bound to show us His love and act for us. It means...

- that God cares and looks after us.
- that God will help us through all the trials and temptations of life.
- that God will save us from the sin, evil, corruption, and death of this world.
- that God will provide a way for us to be delivered from the coming judgment of His holy wrath against sin.

But note: if God loves us and has demonstrated His love to us, then He must expect us to respond. He must expect us to love Him. Love expects to be loved in return. In fact, if someone loves us and we do not receive his love, then his love never touches us. We never experience his love. To know love, we must receive love and share it. God loves us, but we have to receive His love in order to experience it. We have to enter a loving relationship with God in order to know the love of God. If we do not love God, then we can never know or experience God's love for us. His love will never touch us. It is absolutely essential that we love God if we wish to experience the love of God.

But note this: few people truly love God. Therefore, they have to walk through life without knowing God's love and care.

⇒ They have to face all the terrible trials and temptations of life alone. They have no help except what help man can give. They have rejected the love and help of God.

⇒ They have to face suffering and sorrow and the death of loved ones all alone. They do not have the supernatural power of God to help. They have rejected His love.

⇒ They have to confront death without really knowing if God is on the other side waiting to judge them.

⇒ They have no hope beyond this life, feeling that this life may be all, but not quite sure, wondering if perhaps there might be something after death.

We could go on and on listing the things that a person has to face if he does not love God. And note: he has to face them all alone. But thanks be to God, He loves the world. He loves all of us. Therefore, any of us who want to know God's love and care can do so. All we have to do is respond to His love—open up our lives and receive His love and love Him in return.

This is the discussion of this section of John's letter: the love of God and our love for Him. How can we really tell if we love God? How can we make sure that God is pleased with us, with what love we show Him? There are six tests that measure our love for God, six tests that will show if and how much we love God (1 Jn.3:1-4:21). The first test is the discussion of the present passage: Have we experienced God's incredible love?

1. The privilege of God's love: we are called children of God (v.1).
2. The great hope and mystery of God's love: eternal transformation (v.2).
3. The incentive of God's love: purity (v.3).

1 (3:1) **Believers, Children of God—Adoption—God, Love of**: there is the great privilege of God's love, the great privilege of being called the *children of God*. Think how astounding this is, to be called a child of the Supreme Majesty of the universe, of the Supreme Intelligence and Power that created all things. There is no greater privilege than to be called a child of God. Two significant points are made.

1. It is the love of God that has given us the privilege of adoption. No man is a child of God because of any merit or work of his own. Man has rebelled against God.

Man has chosen to go his own way in life and to do his own thing. He has wanted little if anything to do with God. He has not wanted the restraints of God upon his life; he has preferred to make his own way through life. Therefore, man has rebelled against God:

⇒ ignored God   ⇒ disbelieved God
⇒ neglected God   ⇒ rejected God
⇒ cursed God   ⇒ denied God
⇒ disobeyed God

It is this that makes the love of God so amazing. It was while we were rebelling and opposing God—while we were sinners and enemies of God—while we were standing against God—while we were in wrath and hostile with God—while we wanted little if anything to do with God—that God lavished His love upon us.

> **You see, at just the right time, when we were still powerless, Christ died for the ungodly. (Rom 5:6)**
> **But God demonstrates his own love for us in this: While we were still sinners, Christ died for us. (Rom 5:8)**
> **Since we have now been justified by his blood, how much more shall we be saved from God's wrath through him! For if, when we were God's enemies, we were reconciled to him through the death of his Son, how much more, having been reconciled, shall we be saved through his life! (Rom 5:9-10)**

Note that God's love is the giving of His Son to the world. God lavished His love upon us by giving His Son to die for our sins. We know that God loves us because He gave His Son to die for us. It is the death of Jesus Christ that makes it possible for us to become children of God. How?

⇒ When Jesus Christ took our sins upon Himself, our sins were removed from us.
⇒ When Jesus Christ died and paid the penalty for our sins, the penalty was removed from us.

Therefore, God is able to receive us as righteous men and women, as being free of sin. When Jesus Christ died for our sins, He removed all sin from us; He freed us of sin. Therefore, God is able to accept us into His family, the family of God. God is able to adopt us as children of God.

> **Yet to all who received him, to those who believed in his name, he gave the right to become children of God— (John 1:12)**
> **For you did not receive a spirit that makes you a slave again to fear, but you received the Spirit of sonship. And by him we cry, "Abba, Father." (Rom 8:15)**
> **"Therefore come out from them and be separate, says the Lord. Touch no unclean thing, and I will receive you." "I will be a Father to you, and you will be my sons and daughters, says the Lord Almighty." (2 Cor 6:17-18)**
> **But when the time had fully come, God sent his Son, born of a woman, born under law, to redeem those under law, that we might receive the full rights of sons. Because you are sons, God sent the Spirit of his Son into our hearts, the Spirit who calls out, "Abba, Father." (Gal 4:4-6)**

2. The world does not know nor understand believers. This explains why believers are ridiculed, mocked, ignored, opposed, abused, rejected, and persecuted by the world. The persecution may come at work, at school, in the neighborhood, or anywhere else; the world just does not understand why believers act and live the way they do. The world does not understand...

- why believers separate themselves from the pleasures and things of the world.
- why believers deny themselves and live sacrificially so that they can carry the message of Christ to the world and meet the needs of the desperate.
- why believers go to church so much and talk so much about Christ.

Note why the world does not understand believers: because the world did not know Jesus Christ. Think about it: God's very own Son came into the world, but the world did not know Him. They wanted nothing to do with Him; they rejected Him. Now if the world rejected Jesus Christ, God's very own Son, they are bound to reject God's adopted children. The world is just unwilling to recognize and acknowledge that God is righteous and pure and just. They want nothing to do with a lifestyle that demands all that a person *is and has*. They are just unwilling to give sacrificially to carry the gospel around the world and to meet the needs of the world. They do not understand the nature of believers—that they are the children of God; that they can live no other life than that of following God. Why? Because believers know God in all of His love and the majesty of His being. This the world cannot understand.

> **"Be on your guard against men; they will hand you over to the local councils and flog you in their synagogues. (Mat 10:17)**
> **"Then you will be handed over to be persecuted and put to death, and you will be hated by all nations because of me. (Mat 24:9)**
> **Remember the words I spoke to you: 'No servant is greater than his master.' If they persecuted me, they will persecute you also. If they obeyed my teaching, they will obey yours also. (John 15:20)**
> **For it has been granted to you on behalf of Christ not only to believe on him, but also to suffer for him, (Phil 1:29)**
> **So that no one would be unsettled by these trials. You know quite well that we were destined for them. (1 Th 3:3)**
> **In fact, everyone who wants to live a godly life in Christ Jesus will be persecuted, (2 Tim 3:12)**
> **Consider him who endured such opposition from sinful men, so that you will not grow weary and lose heart. (Heb 12:3)**
> **Dear friends, do not be surprised at the painful trial you are suffering, as though something strange were happening to you. But rejoice that you participate in the sufferings of Christ, so that you may be overjoyed when his glory is revealed. If you are insulted because of the name of Christ, you are blessed, for the Spirit of glory and of God rests on you. (1 Pet 4:12-14)**
> **However, if you suffer as a Christian, do not be ashamed, but praise God that you bear that name. (1 Pet 4:16)**
> **All your commands are trustworthy; help me, for men persecute me without cause. (Psa 119:86)**

2 (3:2) **Jesus, Return**: there is the great hope and mystery of God's love, the eternal transformation that believers shall undergo. Note the great declaration: "Dear friends, now we are children of God." It is not that we shall be God's children; we are already God's children. If we have trusted and given our lives to Jesus Christ, we are *now* the children of God. Now note the declaration again: "Dear friends, now we are children of God." We know what we are now, *but* "we know that when he [Christ] appears, we shall be like him, for we shall see him as he is." The contrast is emphatic: we know what we are now, the children of God, *but* we do not know what we shall be like when Christ returns. Oliver Greene has an excellent statement on this point:

> **While they were still talking about this, Jesus himself stood among them and said to them, "Peace be with you." They were startled and frightened, thinking they saw a ghost. He said to them, "Why are you troubled, and why do doubts rise in your minds? Look at my hands and my feet. It is I myself! Touch me and see; a ghost does not have flesh and bones, as you see I have." When he had said this, he showed them his hands and feet. And while they still did not believe it because of joy and amazement, he asked them, "Do you have anything here to eat?" They gave him a piece of broiled fish, and he took it and ate it in their presence. (Luke 24:36-43)**

> "We cannot understand a body, a personality, like that, we cannot comprehend such tremendous truth with these finite minds. Therefore God did not explain in detail what it will mean to be like Jesus. We will just wait and let Him show us in that glorious resurrection morning" (Oliver Greene. *The Epistles of John*. Greenville, SC: The Gospel Hour, 1966, p.112f).

Note the words: "When he appears we shall be like him, for we shall see him as he is." God is light; therefore, when we first see God face to face, His light will be transmitted to us and we shall become light even as He is light. *The Pulpit Commentary* has an excellent explanation of this fact:

> "'We shall be like him, because we shall see him.' God is light (ch.1:5), and light is seen. In this life we cannot see the light of the Divine nature 'as it is,' but only as it is reflected: and the reflected light cannot transmit to us the nature of the Divine original, though it prepares us to receive it. Hereafter the sight, 'face to face' (1 Cor.13:12), of the Light itself will illuminate us through and through, and we shall become like it" (A. Plummer. *The Pulpit Commentary*, Vol.22, p.71).

The believer is to be made just like Christ, conformed to His very image. This means that believers shall be like Christ in person and in character. Believers shall possess a perfect body and being (1 Cor.15:51-57).

> For he chose us in him before the creation of the world to be holy and blameless —eternally (Eph 1:4; 4:24)
> He predestined us to be adopted as his sons through Jesus Christ, —forever (Eph 1:5)
> And just as we have borne the likeness of the earthly man, so shall we bear the likeness of the man from heaven. (1 Cor 15:49; cp. Ph.3:21; 1 Jn.3:2)

This is a precious thought. It is more than just a general idea that believers are to be like Christ. It is a definite idea—the idea that what Christ is, believers shall be. The Scripture says in Ro.8:29, He is "a Son" (uios); so believers are *sons* (uioi). The Scripture also says in Ph.2:6, He was "in the very nature of God" (enmorphe theou); so believers shall be *very nature of God* (summorphoi). The believer is to have a *nature* (morphe) just like the *likeness* (eixon) of Christ—resemble Him in perfection as much as His very image is stamped with perfection. The whole precious idea is that Jesus Christ took the believer and purified and exalted him; therefore, the believer is to partake of the purity and holiness of Christ (see notes—Ro.8:29).

This much is known about the body that we shall receive: it will be a body just like the body that Jesus Christ has. This is made abundantly clear by the glorious promises of Scripture:

⇒ "Who, by the power that enables him to bring everything under his control, will transform our lowly bodies so that they will be like his glorious body." (Ph.3:21; cp. Mt.13:43; Ro.8:17; Col.3:4; Rev.22:5).

⇒ We shall be "conformed to the likeness of His Son" (Ro.8:29. Cp.1 Cor.15:49; 2 Cor.3:18.)

⇒ "We shall be like him, for we shall see him as he is" (1 Jn.3:2).

The body of the believer is to undergo a radical change just as the Lord's body was radically changed. Several changes are promised the believer.

1. The body will not be perishable but imperishable.

> **The body that is sown is perishable, it is raised imperishable; (1 Cor 15:42)**

Our earthly body is corruptible, perishable; our resurrected body will be incorruptible, imperishable. Corruptible, perishable means that our bodies age, deteriorate, die, decay, and decompose. But our heavenly bodies will differ radically. They shall be incorruptible, imperishable: never age, never deteriorate, never die, never decay, and never decompose. They will be transformed and never perish. They will be completely free from defilement and depravity, from death and decay.

2. The body will not be a body of dishonor but a resurrected body of glory.

> **It [the earthly body] is sown in dishonor, it is raised in glory; it is sown in weakness, it is raised in power; (1 Cor 15:43)**

Our earthly body is buried in dishonor; our resurrected body will be raised in glory. Our body is dishonorable, and nothing shows the body's dishonor any more than its death and burial. Every human body is ultimately shamed and disgraced, degraded and deprived of all it has. Every human body is doomed to become nothing more than a handful of dirt. Think about it. Nothing could be any more dis honorable than to take the wonderful mechanism and beauty of a man's body and see it become nothing more than dirt. Yet that is exactly what happens.

But not the resurrected body. The human body will be transformed into a body of glory. Glory means to possess and to be full of *perfect light*; to dwell in the perfect light, brilliance, splendor, brightness, luster, magnificence, dignity, majesty and grace of God Himself.

3. The body will not be a body of weakness but a body of power.

> It [the earthly body] is sown in dishonor, it is raised in glory; it is sown in weakness, it is raised in power; (1 Cor 15:43)

Our earthly body is buried in weakness; our resurrected body is raised in power. While on earth our body is ever so weak: subject to sickness, disease, and a host of other infirmities and limitations; and eventually it becomes so weak that it dies. In death the human body is utterly powerless: helpless, devoid of any strength and capability whatsoever. In death the human body is so powerless it is unable to lift a single finger. It can do nothing, absolutely nothing.

The resurrected body, however, is raised in power. It shall have a mind and body filled with strength, might, health, authority, and control. It will be a perfect body, never subject to disease, accident, or suffering. It will be a body so powerful that it will be able to control its acts and the circumstances around it—all for good.

3 (3:3) **Purity—Holiness**: there is the great motive of God's love—purity. God wants a people just like Himself, a people who are pure and holy and righteous just like Himself. God wants us living with Him in fellowship and communion; He wants us worshipping and serving Him forever and ever. This is the reason God has saved us in Jesus Christ and given us the great hope of being eternally transformed: all so that we can live with Him in glory. If we keep our eyes upon the great glory that lies ahead, it stirs us to live pure lives. God has done so much for us— He has loved us with such an incredible love—that we are stirred to live as Christ lived. We are aroused to please God, aroused to live a godly life. God is going to purify us, make us perfect in every sense of the word. In appreciation we must purify ourselves now, while on this earth. We must seek to be pure even as Christ Jesus is pure.

This is the test, the proof that we love God: Do we understand the incredible love of God? Are we stirred to live pure lives because of His incredible love for us?

Blessed are the pure in heart, for they will see God. (Mat 5:8)

And now what are you waiting for? Get up, be baptized and wash your sins away, calling on his name.' (Acts 22:16)

Since we have these promises, dear friends, let us purify ourselves from everything that contaminates body and spirit, perfecting holiness out of reverence for God. (2 Cor 7:1)

The goal of this command is love, which comes from a pure heart and a good conscience and a sincere faith. (1 Tim 1:5)

If a man cleanses himself from the latter, he will be an instrument for noble purposes, made holy, useful to the Master and prepared to do any good work. (2 Tim 2:21)

How much more, then, will the blood of Christ, who through the eternal Spirit offered himself unblemished to God, cleanse our consciences from acts that lead to death, so that we may serve the living God! (Heb 9:14)

Make every effort to live in peace with all men and to be holy; without holiness no one will see the Lord. (Heb 12:14)

Come near to God and he will come near to you. Wash your hands, you sinners, and purify your hearts, you double-minded. (James 4:8)

For it is written: "Be holy, because I am holy." (1 Pet 1:16)

Since everything will be destroyed in this way, what kind of people ought you to be? You ought to live holy and godly lives (2 Pet 3:11)

So then, dear friends, since you are looking forward to this, make every effort to be found spotless, blameless and at peace with him. (2 Pet 3:14)

Everyone who has this hope in him purifies himself, just as he is pure. (1 John 3:3)

Wash and make yourselves clean. Take your evil deeds out of my sight! Stop doing wrong, (Isa 1:16)

O Jerusalem, wash the evil from your heart and be saved. How long will you harbor wicked thoughts? (Jer 4:14)

	B. Test 2: Turning Away From Sin & Its Enslavement, 3:4-9	anyone lead you astray. He who does what is right is righteous, just as he is righteous.	c. We can be deceived about the matter of sin & righteousness
1 The need for deliverance: Man is sinful[DS1] a. He practices sin b. He breaks the law 2 The provision for deliverance: Christ took away our sins 3 The proof of deliverance a. If we abide, live in Christ, we do not sin b. If we sin, we do not know Christ	4 Everyone who sins breaks the law; in fact, sin is lawlessness. 5 But you know that he appeared so that he might take away our sins. And in him is no sin. 6 No one who lives in him keeps on sinning. No one who continues to sin has either seen him or known him. 7 Dear children, do not let	8 He who does what is sinful is of the devil, because the devil has been sinning from the beginning. The reason the Son of God appeared was to destroy the devil's work. 9 No one who is born of God will continue to sin, because God's seed remains in him; he cannot go on sinning, because he has been born of God.	4 The great conquest of Christ in deliverance a. The person who sins is of the devil b. The Son of God came to earth to destroy the devil's work 5 The result of deliverance: Being freed from living in sin

DIVISION IV

THE PROOF THAT ONE REALLY LOVES GOD: SIX TESTS, 3:1-4:21

B. Test 2: Turning Away from Sin and Its Enslavement, 3:4-9

(3:4-9) **Introduction**: Do we really love God? There are six tests that show us. This is the second test: Have we turned away from sin? Have we been born of God?

⇒ If we live in sin, if we are enslaved by the habits of sin, this is a clear sign we do not love God. But if we have turned away from sin, if the habits of sin have been broken by Christ and permanently conquered in our lives, this is a clear sign that we love God.

⇒ If we have been born of God, if we have participated in the divine nature of God, then we love God. If we have not been born of God, if we have not participated in the divine nature of God, then we do not love God.

When we love someone, we want to know and please him. We want his approval and acceptance; therefore, we do all we can to please him. So it is with God. If we love Him, we want to know Him and please Him. We want His approval and acceptance; therefore, we do all we can to please Him. God is righteous; He is pure and holy. There is no sin in Him at all. Therefore, the person who loves God lives a righteous life, a pure and holy life. He does not live in sin; he does not practice sin. He lives in righteousness and he practices righteousness. He does all he can to please Him whom he loves—the Lord God Himself.

This is the second test, the test that shows whether or not we love God. Have we turned away from sin? Have the habits of sin been broken and conquered in our lives? Have we been truly born again by the Spirit of God?

1. The need for deliverance: man is sinful (v.4).
2. The provision for deliverance: Christ took away our sins (v.5).
3. The proof of deliverance (v.6-7).
4. The great conquest of Christ in deliverance (v.8).
5. The result of deliverance: being freed from living in sin (v.9).

1 (3:4) **Sin—Transgression**: there is the need for deliverance. Man is sinful and he breaks the law. Few people like to be called a *sinner*. Some people even react to the statement that men are *sinners*. There is a reason for this. To most people sin is thought to be the gross sins of society, the crimes that make the headlines of our newspapers and telecasts. The sins committed by most people are not thought to be that serious. Most people think that what little wrong they do could never be interpreted as sin. Therefore, to them they only commit…

• a mistake
• a shortcoming
• a failure
• a psychological quirk
• a flaw of nature
• a bad decision
• an irrational act
• a social flaw

This is not what sin is, not to God and not to the Bible. Sin is the *lawlessness*. It is violating the law of God.

⇒ Sin is choosing to go one's own way in life, doing one's own thing instead of doing what God says.
⇒ Sin is living like one wants instead of living like God says.
⇒ Sin is disobeying God, not doing what God says to do and doing what God says not to do.
⇒ Sin is disbelieving God instead of believing what God says.
⇒ Sin is ignoring God and neglecting God instead of following and worshipping Him as He says.
⇒ Sin is rebelling against God instead of doing what God says.
⇒ Sin is rejecting God and denying God instead of confessing God and becoming a follower of God.

And note: God is perfect. Therefore, only perfection is acceptable to God. This is shocking; nevertheless it is true. If God lets anything less than perfection into heaven, then heaven would no longer be perfect. Therefore, God can never accept anything other than perfection. This is what sin is: imperfection—falling short of God's glory and of God's perfect nature. Consequently, man not only does things that come short of God's perfection; man himself is short of God's nature.

⇒ Man is a sinner. He himself is *short of God's glory, short of perfection*. Therefore, whatever he does is short of God; man's acts are imperfect. At the very root of things, this is what sin is: it is imperfection; it is being and coming short

251

of God's glory and nature. It is not only that we do things that are short of perfection, but we ourselves are short of God's glory, short by nature, short of what we should be.

⇒ Man is not only a sinner, he is sinful. The reason he is sinful is because he has *broken God's law.* If he had never broken the law of God, then he would have dwelt in the perfect nature of God. He would have always obeyed God; therefore, he would have lived in the glory of God and never come short of God's will and nature. It was lawlessness, going against God's law and nature, that caused the fall of man. Therefore, sin is lawlessness, disobeying God's law, falling short of what God says.

As it is written: "There is no one righteous, not even one; there is no one who understands, no one who seeks God. All have turned away, they have together become worthless; there is no one who does good, not even one." "Their throats are open graves; their tongues practice deceit." "The poison of vipers is on their lips." "Their mouths are full of cursing and bitterness." "Their feet are swift to shed blood; ruin and misery mark their ways, and the way of peace they do not know." "There is no fear of God before their eyes." Now we know that whatever the law says, it says to those who are under the law, so that every mouth may be silenced and the whole world held accountable to God. (Rom 3:10-19)

For all have sinned and fall short of the glory of God, (Rom 3:23)

But the Scripture declares that the whole world is a prisoner of sin, so that what was promised, being given through faith in Jesus Christ, might be given to those who believe. (Gal 3:22)

If we claim to be without sin, we deceive ourselves and the truth is not in us. (1 John 1:8)

For everyone born of God overcomes the world. This is the victory that has overcome the world, even our faith. (1 John 5:4)

All wrongdoing is sin, and there is sin that does not lead to death. (1 John 5:17)

The LORD saw how great man's wickedness on the earth had become, and that every inclination of the thoughts of his heart was only evil all the time. (Gen 6:5)

Everyone has turned away, they have together become corrupt; there is no one who does good, not even one. (Psa 53:3)

Who can say, "I have kept my heart pure; I am clean and without sin"? (Prov 20:9)

We all, like sheep, have gone astray, each of us has turned to his own way; and the LORD has laid on him the iniquity of us all. (Isa 53:6)

All of us have become like one who is unclean, and all our righteous acts are like filthy rags; we all shrivel up like a leaf, and like the wind our sins sweep us away. (Isa 64:6)

DEEPER STUDY # 1

(3:4) **Sin**: there are a number of Hebrew words and a number of Greek words for sin in the Bible. A literal translation of the major words will show the meaning of sin.

1. Sin is unbelief, the failure to believe God (Mt.13:58; 17:20; Ro.3:3; 4:20; 11:20, 23; 1 Tim.1:13; Heb.3:12, 19).

2. Sin is missing the mark, falling short of the glory of God (see note—Ro.3:23).

3. Sin is error, making a mistake; a wandering off of the right path (Ro.1:27; Jas.5:20; 2 Pt.2:18; 3:17; Jude 11).

4. Sin is ungodliness and unrighteousness (Ro.1:18; 11:26; 2 Tim.2:16; Tit.2:12; Jude 15, 18).

5. Sin is transgression, a stepping outside the law (Ro.3:23; 4:15; 5:13, 20; Heb.2:2; 9:15).

6. Sin is trespassing, intruding where one should not go (see note—Eph.2:1).

7. Sin is disobedience, a refusal to listen and hear and do (Eph.2:2; 5:6; Col.3:6).

8. Sin is lawlessness, rebellion, a rejection of God's will and law (1 Jn.3:4).

9. Sin is iniquity, doing evil, an inward contempt that leads to the continual practice of sin (Mt.7:23; Ro.6:19; 2 Th.2:3. Cp. Ro.1:21-23.)

All men have sinned (Ro.3:23). Sin first entered the world through Adam (Ro.5:12). Because of sin, all men are spiritually dead, forever, and are destined to die physically (Ro.6:23; cp. Gen.2:17; 3:19; Ezk.18:4, 20). But there is a deliverance from sin and from its penalty—the sacrificial death of Jesus Christ (Acts 4:12; Heb.9:26). (See DEEPER STUDY # 1—2 Pt.1:4.)

---

2 (3:5) **Sin, Deliverance—Jesus Christ, Death**: there is the provision for deliverance. Jesus Christ, the Son of God, came to earth to take away our sins. How is this possible? How is it possible for Christ to actually remove our sins and take them away so that God can accept us? By living a sinless life. Note the words of the verse: "in Him is no sin." When Jesus Christ came to earth as a Man, He lived a sinless life. He was perfectly righteous, the very embodiment of righteousness. He secured the perfect and ideal righteousness; He was the Perfect and Ideal Man. Therefore as the Ideal Man, whatever Jesus Christ did could stand for and cover man. What does this mean? Simply this: when Jesus Christ died, His death was the perfect sacrifice for sins. He was the Perfect Man so He was able to die as the perfect sacrifice. God was able to accept His death as the perfect sacrifice for sins.

What happens is this. When we really believe in Jesus Christ, God counts the sacrifice of Jesus Christ for us. God no longer sees our sins, for Jesus Christ took them and died for them. They are thereby removed from us, and we are counted free of sin. They are gone forever because Jesus Christ took them upon Himself and died for them. Consequently, being free of sin, we become acceptable to God.

Thought 1. This is the great love of God for man, the giving of His Son to die for the sins of man. If a person truly loves God, then that person bows in humble adoration before God's Son. The person loves God because God sacrificed His own Son in order to save man. This is the test of our love for God: Have we turned from sin to God's Son?

"For God so loved the world that he gave his one and only Son, that whoever believes in him shall not perish but have eternal life. For God did not send his Son

into the world to condemn the world, but to save the world through him. (John 3:16-17)

God made him who had no sin to be sin for us, so that in him we might become the righteousness of God. (2 Cor 5:21)

Here is a trustworthy saying that deserves full acceptance: Christ Jesus came into the world to save sinners—of whom I am the worst. (1 Tim 1:15)

So Christ was sacrificed once to take away the sins of many people; and he will appear a second time, not to bear sin, but to bring salvation to those who are waiting for him. (Heb 9:28)

For you know that it was not with perishable things such as silver or gold that you were redeemed from the empty way of life handed down to you from your forefathers, but with the precious blood of Christ, a lamb without blemish or defect. (1 Pet 1:18-19)

He himself bore our sins in his body on the tree, so that we might die to sins and live for righteousness; by his wounds you have been healed. (1 Pet 2:24)

But you know that he appeared so that he might take away our sins. And in him is no sin. (1 John 3:5)

3 (3:6-7) **Sin, Deliverance—Righteousness—Believer, Duty**: there is the proof of deliverance. A person lives, abides in Christ if he has turned from sin. When we accept Jesus Christ as our Savior from sin, we begin to *live in Him*. Remember what *living in Christ* means: to dwell, continue, stay, sojourn, and rest in Christ. It means to live and move and have our being in Christ. We just begin to live and dwell in Christ, all that He is and all that He taught. Note three points.

1. If we live in Christ, we do not continue to sin. If we have really accepted Jesus Christ as our Savior, we love Him because He died for us. Christ paid such an enormous price to take away our sins that we want to please Him. We dare not do anything to hurt Him or cause Him pain; therefore, we do all we can to please Him. The major thing we do is to turn away from sin and begin living in Christ. Our desire is not to walk in sin, but to turn away from sin and to break the habits of sin—all for Him, all because our hearts and lives now belong to Him who has loved us and given Himself for us.

Thought 1. This is the proof of whether or not we love God: Have we accepted Jesus Christ as our Savior from sin? Are we living, abiding, moving, and having our being in Him, in all that He is and in all that He taught? Have we turned away from sin, from practicing and living in sin?

2. If we sin, then we have not seen Christ, neither known Him. This does not mean that we have to be perfect to be saved from sin. The Greek means this: if we continue in sin, if we go on sinning and sinning, then we do not really know Christ. A true believer is still short of God's glory; he still sins. He is still human flesh; therefore, he cannot keep from sinning—not all of the time, not perfectly. But sin is not the dominant focus of his life. He does not keep his mind on the comforts and pleasures and possessions of this life. His focus is Jesus Christ and His mission of righteousness and salvation. He gives of himself, all he is and has, to reach people for Christ and to minister to the desperate needs of the world. He works and labors and then keeps on working and laboring for righteousness and love upon the earth. But note: the person whose focus is still on the world and its pleasures and possessions—the person who continues to sin—that person has not seen Jesus Christ, neither known Him. Once a person sees Jesus Christ, once a person really knows Christ, that person focuses upon and gives his life to Christ. He turns away from sin and turns and follows Jesus Christ. He lives in Christ. He lives and moves and has his being in Christ, in all that Christ taught.

3. We can be deceived about the matter of sin and righteousness. Many think that they are saved and acceptable to God because they have...

- professed Christ
- been baptized
- joined the church
- attended church
- fellowshipped with Christians
- read the Bible
- prayed

They think that if they do these things they can live like they want. They think that they can go ahead and enjoy a few of the world's pleasures and continue to seek after more and more of the world's comforts and possessions. And they think that God will still accept them. But note this verse:

Dear children, do not let anyone lead you astray. He who does what is right is righteous, just as he is righteous. (v.7)

The only person who is acceptable to God is the person who lives righteously, who follows after the righteousness of Jesus Christ. The demand of Jesus Christ is clear.

Then he said to them all: "If anyone would come after me, he must deny himself and take up his cross daily and follow me. (Luke 9:23)

Thought 1. Any person who follows Jesus Christ has to deny himself; he has to die to self. He has to give all he is and has to live righteously. And righteous living does not just mean living pure and clean lives. It means treating other people righteously. It means reaching out and helping all people, giving all we are and have to help them. It means not being unjust by hoarding and keeping more than we need. It means giving and living sacrificially to help those who are dying because they lack the bare necessities of life. It means sacrificing all in order to carry forth the glorious message of salvation from sin, death, and the judgment to come.

Dear children, do not let anyone lead you astray. He who does what is right is righteous, just as he is righteous. (1 John 3:7)

For I tell you that unless your righteousness surpasses that of the Pharisees and the teachers of the law, you will certainly not enter the kingdom of heaven. (Mat 5:20)

Since they did not know the righteousness that comes from God and sought to establish their own, they did not submit to God's righteousness. (Rom 10:3)

When the perishable has been clothed with the imperishable, and the mortal with immortality, then the saying that is written will come true: "Death has been swallowed up in victory." (1 Cor 15:54)

Filled with the fruit of righteousness that comes through Jesus Christ—to the glory and praise of God. (Phil 1:11)

But you, man of God, flee from all this, and pursue righteousness, godliness, faith, love, endurance and gentleness. (1 Tim 6:11)

It teaches us to say "No" to ungodliness and worldly passions, and to live self-controlled, upright and godly lives in this present age, (Titus 2:12)

Since everything will be destroyed in this way, what kind of people ought you to be? You ought to live holy and godly lives (2 Pet 3:11)

No one who lives in him keeps on sinning. No one who continues to sin has either seen him or known him. (1 John 3:6)

Anyone who runs ahead and does not continue in the teaching of Christ does not have God; whoever continues in the teaching has both the Father and the Son. (2 John 1:9)

4 (3:8) **Satan—Jesus Christ, Work of**: there is the great conquest of Christ in deliverance. Note two significant points.

1. The person who sins is *of the devil*. This is a shocking statement to some people, but Jesus Christ put it even more clearly:

You belong to your father, the devil, and you want to carry out your father's desire. He was a murderer from the beginning, not holding to the truth, for there is no truth in him. When he lies, he speaks his native language, for he is a liar and the father of lies. (John 8:44)

What does this mean? Note the words from *the beginning*. This means that Satan was the first person to ever sin. He began sin. He was the first person who ever rebelled against God and disobeyed God. Therefore, every person who sins is akin to Satan. He is following after Satan, in the footsteps of Satan. Morally and spiritually he is the offspring, the child of Satan.

One thing is sure: sin is not of God. God is not the Father of sin and evil and corruption and death. The devil is the father of such things. Therefore when we sin, we are not following after the Father of love and righteousness, we are following after the father of sin and death. Our behavior is not *of God*; it is *of the devil*. It is by sin that we become…

- followers of the devil
- children of the devil
- servants of the devil

It is by sin that we have separated ourselves from God. It is sin that causes us to die and that is going to bring judgment upon us. It is sin that causes the righteousness and justice of God to fall upon us. It is sin that is going to separate the sinner from God for eternity. This is the reason God hates sin so much. God created man to live with Him, and sin has cut man off from God and doomed man

to be cut off forever. But this is the glorious gospel: God is perfect love; He is the sovereign Majesty, the perfect Intelligence and Power of the universe. Therefore, God knows what to do about sin and He has the power to do it. God knows how to save man, and He is able to save man. God knows how to destroy the works of Satan and He is able to do it. This is the discussion of the second point.

2. This was the very purpose for the Son of God coming to earth, that He might destroy the devil's work. The devil's work is destroyed by the death of Jesus Christ. His power, rule, and reign over lives is now destroyed—all by the death of Jesus Christ.

a. Satan's power *to charge men with sin* is now "cast out." Men now have the power to escape the penalty of sin. Christ took the sins of men upon Himself and paid the penalty for their sin. He died for the sins of the world.

He himself bore our sins in his body on the tree, so that we might die to sins and live for righteousness; by his wounds you have been healed. (1 Pet 2:24)
Who will bring any charge against those whom God has chosen? It is God who justifies. (Rom 8:33)

b. Satan's power *to cause death* is now "cast out." Men no longer have to die. Christ died *for man*, became man's substitute in death.

Since the children have flesh and blood, he too shared in their humanity so that by his death he might destroy him who holds the power of death—that is, the devil— and free those who all their lives were held in slavery by their fear of death. (Heb 2:14-15)

c. Satan's power *to cause men to be separated from God* is now cast out. Men no longer have to go to hell. Christ was separated from God *for man* (see note—Mt.27:46-49). Man can now live forever with God.

For Christ died for sins once for all, the righteous for the unrighteous, to bring you to God. He was put to death in the body but made alive by the Spirit, (1 Pet 3:18)
And if the Spirit of him who raised Jesus from the dead is living in you, he who raised Christ from the dead will also give life to your mortal bodies through his Spirit, who lives in you. (Rom 8:11)

d. Satan's power *to enslave men* with the habits of sin and shame is now "cast out." By His death, Christ made it possible for man to be freed from sin. The believer, cleansed by the blood of Christ, becomes a holy temple unto God, a temple fit for the presence and power of God's Spirit. Man can now conquer the enslaving habits of sin by the power of God's Spirit.

Do you not know that your body is a temple of the Holy Spirit, who is in you, whom you have received from God? You are not your own; you were bought at a price. Therefore honor God with your body. (1 Cor 6:19-20)

You, dear children, are from God and have overcome them, because the one who is in you is greater than the one who is in the world. (1 John 4:4)

(See notes—Jn.12:31-33; DEEPER STUDY # 2—12:31; DEEPER STUDY # 1—16:11; notes—Col.2:15; Heb.2:14-16 for more discussion.)

5 (3:9) **New Birth—Sin, Deliverance**: there is the result of deliverance. The believer is free from living in and practicing sin. Note: the verb *to sin* is in the present tense. *To sin* means to continue in sin; to constantly sin; to practice sin; to habitually sin; to live in sin. This needs to be clearly understood. Scripture is not saying that a person reaches sinless perfection while on earth. No person can achieve the perfection of God and His glory. Such is utter nonsense according to Scripture. By his very nature, man is short of God's glory and perfection (see first note of this outline—1 Jn.3:4 for more discussion). What then is the meaning of the words, "no one...born of God will continue to sin" and "he cannot go on sinning"?

A.T. Robertson, the great Greek scholar, says this: "he cannot go on sinning." Robertson adds, "Paul has precisely the same idea in Rom.6:1...'shall we continue in sin'" (*Word Pictures In The New Testament*, Vol.6, p.223). The Amplified New Testament has the correct idea based upon the Greek:

"No one born (begotten) of God [deliberately and knowingly] habitually practices sin, for God's nature abides in him - His principle...remains permanently within him - and he cannot practice sinning because he is born (begotten) of God." (I Jn.3:9)

Once the divine seed or nature of God has been implanted within the believer, the believer cannot go on living in sin. He cannot continue and continue to sin; he cannot practice sin habitually. The divine nature of God will pester and provoke the believer and convict him to the point that he cannot stand it. If he continues on and on in sin, it is clear evidence that he has never been born of God. The genuine believer loves God because of what God has done for him in Christ. God has loved man in the most supreme way possible, by giving up His Son to die for man. Therefore the believer loves God, loves Him with all his heart, and he wants to please God. It is also this that keeps the genuine believer away from sin. Remember what Joseph said when Potiphar's wife tempted him:

No one is greater in this house than I am. My master has withheld nothing from me except you, because you are his wife. How then could I do such a wicked thing and sin against God?" (Gen 39:9)

Note what it is that frees the believer from sin: being born of God, possessing God's seed within him. What is the Seed of God?

⇒ It is the seed of the new birth.

In reply Jesus declared, "I tell you the truth, no one can see the kingdom of God unless he is born again." "How can a man be born when he is old?" Nicodemus asked.

"Surely he cannot enter a second time into his mother's womb to be born!" Jesus answered, "I tell you the truth, no one can enter the kingdom of God unless he is born of water and the Spirit. (John 3:3-5)

⇒ It is the seed of the new creation.

Therefore, if anyone is in Christ, he is a new creation; the old has gone, the new has come! (2 Cor 5:17)

⇒ It is the seed of the new person, the new self.

And to put on the new self, created to be like God in true righteousness and holiness. (Eph 4:24)
And have put on the new self, which is being renewed in knowledge in the image of its Creator. (Col 3:10)

⇒ It is the divine nature.

Through these he has given us his very great and precious promises, so that through them you may participate in the divine nature and escape the corruption in the world caused by evil desires. (2 Pet 1:4)

⇒ It is the imperishable, incorruptible seed of God's Word.

For you have been born again, not of perishable seed, but of imperishable, through the living and enduring word of God. (1 Pet 1:23)

Another way to say the same thing is this: the seed of God within the believer is the Holy Spirit, the very Spirit of God Himself. It is He who helps the believer to conquer sin and to keep from sinning. It is the Spirit of God who stirs the believer to love and focus upon Christ and His mission instead of upon the world and its pleasures and possessions. It is the Spirit of God who stirs the believer not to sin.

William Barclay, in his incisive way of expressing truth, says that John's discussion of sin can be stated in four stages. (Note: we are putting the points in outline form for clarity.)

a. *"The ideal is that in the new age sin is gone for ever.*
b. *"Christians must try to make that true, and, with the help of Christ, they must struggle to avoid individual acts of sin, occasional lapses into that which is wrong, temporary departures from goodness.*
c. *"In point of fact all men do have these lapses, and, when they have them, they must humbly confess them to God, who will always forgive the penitent and the contrite heart.*
d. *"But, in spite of that, no Christian can possibly be a deliberate and a consistent sinner; no Christian can make sin the policy of his life; no Christian can live a life in which sin is dominant and decisive in all his actions. He may have lapses, but he cannot live in sin as the very atmosphere of his life."*

Barclay continues:

"John is not setting before us here a terrifying perfectionism, in which he is demanding a life which is totally and absolutely without sin; but he is demanding a life which is ever on the watch against sin, a life which ever fights the battle of goodness, a life which has never surrendered to sin, a life in which sin is not the permanent state, but only the temporary aberration, a life in which sin is not the normal accepted way, but the abnormal moment of defeat. John is not saying that the man who abides in God cannot sin; but he is saying that the man who abides in God cannot continue to be a consistent and deliberate sinner" (*The Letters of John and Jude*, p.96f).

My dear children, I write this to you so that you will not sin. But if anybody does sin, we have one who speaks to the Father in our defense—Jesus Christ, the Righteous One. He is the atoning sacrifice for our sins, and not only for ours but also for the sins of the whole world. (1 John 2:1-2)

If we claim to have fellowship with him yet walk in the darkness, we lie and do not live by the truth. But if we walk in the light, as he is in the light, we have fellowship with one another, and the blood of Jesus, his Son, purifies us from all sin. If we claim to be without sin, we deceive ourselves and the truth is not in us. If we confess our sins, he is faithful and just and will forgive us our sins and purify us from all unrighteousness. If we claim we have not sinned, we make him out to be a liar and his word has no place in our lives. (1 John 1:6-10)

For everyone born of God overcomes the world. This is the victory that has overcome the world, even our faith. (1 John 5:4)

Since we have these promises, dear friends, let us purify ourselves from everything that contaminates body and spirit, perfecting holiness out of reverence for God. (2 Cor 7:1)

Make every effort to live in peace with all men and to be holy; without holiness no one will see the Lord. (Heb 12:14)

For it is written: "Be holy, because I am holy." (1 Pet 1:16)

Since everything will be destroyed in this way, what kind of people ought you to be? You ought to live holy and godly lives (2 Pet 3:11)

	C. Test 3: Being Marked By Love, 3:10-17	brothers, if the world hates you.	
1 Love reveals one's true nature: Shows that one is either a child of God or of the devil	10 This is how we know who the children of God are and who the children of the devil are: Anyone who does not do what is right is not a child of God; nor is anyone who does not love his brother.	14 We know that we have passed from death to life, because we love our brothers. Anyone who does not love remains in death.	**4 Love is the proof that one has passed from death to life**
2 Love is the message heard from the very beginning	11 This is the message you heard from the beginning: We should love one another.	15 Anyone who hates his brother is a murderer, and you know that no murderer has eternal life in him.	**5 Love does not hate** a. Hate is murder b. Hate exempts one from eternal life
3 Love does not persecute the righteous	12 Do not be like Cain, who belonged to the evil one and murdered his brother. And why did he murder him? Because his own actions were evil and his brother's were righteous.	16 This is how we know what love is: Jesus Christ laid down his life for us. And we ought to lay down our lives for our brothers.	**6 Love is the proof that one understands the love of Christ**
	13 Do not be surprised, my	17 If anyone has material possessions and sees his brother in need but has no pity on him, how can the love of God be in him?	**7 Love has compassion and gives to meet the needs of people**

DIVISION IV

THE PROOF THAT ONE REALLY LOVES GOD: SIX TESTS, 3:1-4:21

C. Test 3: Being Marked by Love, 3:10-17

(3:10-17) **Introduction**: Do we really love God? This is the third test that shows us. Are we marked by love? Is love the chief characteristic of our lives? Do we love one another? Love shows us whether or not we love God. God is love; therefore, if we love God, we are bound to love one another. In fact, since God is love, it is absolutely impossible to love God and not to love one another. The greatest proof of all that we love God is the mark of love. If we have the mark of love upon our lives, if people can clearly see that we love one another, then we love God. But if we have and hold feelings against anyone else, this is clear proof that we do not love God. The great mark of loving God is the mark of loving one another.

1. Love reveals one's true nature: shows that one is either a child of God or of the devil (v.10).
2. Love is the message heard from the very beginning (v.11).
3. Love does not persecute the righteous (v.12-13).
4. Love is the proof that one has passed from death to life (v.14).
5. Love does not hate (v.15).
6. Love is the proof that one understands the love of Christ (v.16).
7. Love has compassion and gives to meet the needs of people (v.17).

1 (3:10) **Love—Devil—Children of God**: love reveals one's true nature; love shows that one is either a child of God or of the devil. Note who it is that is not of God.

⇒ The person who does not live righteously is not of God. The person who does not live a pure and holy life is not of God.

⇒ The person who does not love his brother is not of God. The person who mistreats, abuses, ignores, neglects or takes advantage of his brother is not of God.

This is easily seen: God is holy, righteous, and pure and God is love. Therefore any person who does not live a holy, righteous, and pure life and who does not love could

not be of God. His life stands opposed to all that God stands for. The things that he does are not of God; they are not of the nature of God. Now, of whose nature are they? Whose nature is unholy, unrighteous, impure; and whose nature is unloving? Not God's nature, but the devil's nature. This is not a pleasant thought, but Scripture declares emphatically that we are either a child of God or of the devil. What determines whose child we are? Our lives reveal exactly whose child we are.

⇒ The person who lives a righteous life and who loves his brother takes his nature from God.

⇒ The person who lives an unrighteous life and who mistreats his brother takes his nature from the devil.

We can look at our nature and tell whose child we are. If we live righteous, pure, and holy lives and love one another, we have the nature of God. If we live unrighteous, impure, and unholy lives and mistreat one another, we have the nature of the devil. It is that clear: there is no middle ground. God's nature is not that of unrighteousness and hate. God is righteous and loving; therefore, the person who lives a righteous life and who loves his brother is of God.

Now, note a significant fact: John defines righteousness as love. This is what he is really saying in this verse: the person who does not do righteousness is the person who does not love his brother. Righteousness is love, and unrighteousness is failing to love. This is seen by scanning this passage:

⇒ Note verse 12: Cain did not love his brother so he murdered him and did an unrighteous deed.

⇒ Note verse 14: the proof that we have passed from death to life is our love, our righteous behavior toward our brother.

⇒ Note verse 15: love is not unrighteous acts, hate, or murder.

⇒ Note verse 16: love is the righteous act of God in giving His Son to die for us.

⇒ Note verse 16 again: love is laying down our lives for our brother.

⇒ Note verse 17: love is compassion and giving to meet the needs of our brother.

The point is this: love is action—righteous deeds in action. And righteousness is love—loving deeds in action. This is exactly what John declared earlier.

> **Whoever loves his brother lives in the light, and there is nothing in him to make him stumble. (1 John 2:10)**
> **Love must be sincere. Hate what is evil; cling to what is good. (Rom 12:9)**

This is also what Paul declared in that memorable passage of Romans, a passage that we should live in and preach and teach as long as we live upon earth.

> **Let no debt remain outstanding, except the continuing debt to love one another, for he who loves his fellowman has fulfilled the law. The commandments, "Do not commit adultery," "Do not murder," "Do not steal," "Do not covet," and whatever other commandment there may be, are summed up in this one rule: "Love your neighbor as yourself." Love does no harm to its neighbor. Therefore love is the fulfillment of the law. (Rom 13:8-10)**

How do we know if we really love God? We can look at love and tell. Do we love our brothers? Or, do we hold things within us toward others? Do we think evil thoughts about them? Talk about them? Criticize, murmur, grumble, gossip, or backbite them? Do we do evil against them? This is the nature of the devil—to tear down and destroy—not the nature of God. Therefore, if we do these kinds of things, we are revealing that we are not the children of God, but children of the devil. Love reveals whose child we are.

> **Blessed are the peacemakers, for they will be called sons of God. (Mat 5:9)**
> **Jesus replied: "'Love the Lord your God with all your heart and with all your soul and with all your mind.' This is the first and greatest commandment. And the second is like it: 'Love your neighbor as yourself.' (Mat 22:37-39)**
> **"A new command I give you: Love one another. As I have loved you, so you must love one another. By this all men will know that you are my disciples, if you love one another." (John 13:34-35)**
> **Love must be sincere. Hate what is evil; cling to what is good. (Rom 12:9)**

2 (3:11) **Love**: love is the message heard from the beginning (see note—1 Jn.2:7-8 for discussion. The very same point is discussed.)

3 (3:12-13) **Love—Persecution**: love does not persecute the righteous. The extreme case of persecution is used to illustrate the point—that of murder. Cain committed the very first murder on earth: he killed his own brother Abel (Gen.4:1-15). Why? Because Abel was a believer. Abel believed God, that he was to worship God exactly like God said, by the blood of a sacrificial animal. Cain did not accept such a belief. He felt that if he brought the fruit of his

own hands to God, then God would accept him because of his hard work and because he worshipped and gave offerings to God. God accepted Abel's worship and offering. It was evident in his life, by the way God blessed him and took care of him. But God rejected Cain's offering. Cain did not have a real sense of God's care or blessing upon his life. Therefore, he became jealous and envious of Abel and he killed Abel. The point is twofold.

1. First, love does not persecute the righteous. Cain did not love his brother; therefore, he was of that wicked one, the devil, and he persecuted his brother. A person who truly loves his brother will not persecute him; he will not...

- criticize
- backbite
- censor
- spread rumors
- downgrade
- attack
- abuse
- gossip
- be envious
- stand against
- hurt
- destroy
- murder
- dislike
- oppose
- talk about
- hate

Just think—love means that we will not even dislike another person. We love them, care for them, and reach out to them. We want their fellowship in Christ, longing for them to experience all the richness of life and for them to know all the fullness of Christ and His love. This is the way we know that we love God, if we do not persecute our brother like Cain did.

> **My command is this: Love each other as I have loved you. (John 15:12)**
> **Love must be sincere. Hate what is evil; cling to what is good. (Rom 12:9)**
> **Let no debt remain outstanding, except the continuing debt to love one another, for he who loves his fellowman has fulfilled the law. The commandments, "Do not commit adultery," "Do not murder," "Do not steal," "Do not covet," and whatever other commandment there may be, are summed up in this one rule: "Love your neighbor as yourself." Love does no harm to its neighbor. Therefore love is the fulfillment of the law. (Rom 13:8-10)**
> **We sent Timothy, who is our brother and God's fellow worker in spreading the gospel of Christ, to strengthen and encourage you in your faith, (1 Th 3:2)**
> **Now that you have purified yourselves by obeying the truth so that you have sincere love for your brothers, love one another deeply, from the heart. (1 Pet 1:22)**

2. Second, if we love Christ, then the world will persecute us. (See note, pt.2—1 Jn.3:1 for discussion. Also see notes—1 Pt.4:16; Mt.5:10-12 for more discussion.)

> **"Then you will be handed over to be persecuted and put to death, and you will be hated by all nations because of me. (Mat 24:9)**
> **Blessed are you when men hate you, when they exclude you and insult you and reject your name as evil, because of the Son of Man. "Rejoice in that day and leap for joy, because great is your reward in heaven. For that is how their fathers treated the prophets. (Luke 6:22-23)**

All men will hate you because of me. (Luke 21:17)

If you belonged to the world, it would love you as its own. As it is, you do not belong to the world, but I have chosen you out of the world. That is why the world hates you. (John 15:19)

I have given them your word and the world has hated them, for they are not of the world any more than I am of the world. (John 17:14)

How great is the love the Father has lavished on us, that we should be called children of God! And that is what we are! The reason the world does not know us is that it did not know him. (1 John 3:1)

Do not be surprised, my brothers, if the world hates you. (1 John 3:13)

4 (3:14) **Love—Salvation—Life—Death, Spiritual**: love is the proof that one has passed from death to life. Note two things.

1. The death here is spiritual death and eternal death. Spiritual death speaks of a person who is dead while he still lives (1 Tim.5:6). He is a natural man living in this present world, but he is said to be dead to the Lord Jesus Christ and to God and to spiritual matters.

a. A person who wastes his life in wild living is spiritually dead.

But we had to celebrate and be glad, because this brother of yours was dead and is alive again; he was lost and is found.'" (Luke 15:32)

b. A person who has not partaken of Christ is spiritually dead.

Jesus said to them, "I tell you the truth, unless you eat the flesh of the Son of Man and drink his blood, you have no life in you. (John 6:53)

c. A person who does not have the spirit of Christ is said to be spiritually dead.

You, however, are controlled not by the sinful nature but by the Spirit, if the Spirit of God lives in you. And if anyone does not have the Spirit of Christ, he does not belong to Christ. (Rom 8:9)

d. A person who lives in sin is said to be spiritually dead.

As for you, you were dead in your transgressions and sins, (Eph 2:1)
When you were dead in your sins and in the uncircumcision of your sinful nature, God made you alive with Christ. He forgave us all our sins, (Col 2:13)

e. A person who is separated from the life of God is said to be spiritually dead.

They are darkened in their understanding and separated from the life of God because of the ignorance that is in them due

to the hardening of their hearts. Having lost all sensitivity, they have given themselves over to sensuality so as to indulge in every kind of impurity, with a continual lust for more. (Eph 4:18-19)

f. A person who sleeps in sin is spiritually dead.

For it is light that makes everything visible. This is why it is said: "Wake up, O sleeper, rise from the dead, and Christ will shine on you." (Eph 5:14)

g. A person who lives in sinful pleasure is dead while he lives.

But the widow who lives for pleasure is dead even while she lives. (1 Tim 5:6)

h. A person who does not have the Son of God is dead.

He who has the Son has life; he who does not have the Son of God does not have life. (1 John 5:12)

i. A person who does great religious works but does the wrong works is dead.

"To the angel of the church in Sardis write: These are the words of him who holds the seven spirits of God and the seven stars. I know your deeds; you have a reputation of being alive, but you are dead. (Rev 3:1)

2. Love is the proof that we have passed from death over into life. Love is *not the cause* of our passing over into life; it is *the proof* that we have passed from death to life. Jesus Christ is the One who saves us from death and gives us life. But once He has done this, we love our brothers. And we can know whether or not we have passed from death to life by our love. If we love our brothers—all of them—then we have been saved from death and we have eternal life. If we do not love our brothers, we have not been saved from death and we do not have life. Note what the verse says: we "remain in death." We dwell, live, move, and have our being in death; we have made death our home. We are in the process of dying and we shall die and never receive the life of God, the life that is eternal and that overflows with all the fullness and richness of life. The person who does not love his brother "has not made the passage over"; he is living in an "atmosphere of death" (A. Plummer. *The Pulpit Commentary*, Vol.22, p.74).

5 (3:15) **Love—Hate—Murder**: love does not hate. This should be clearly understood, but it is not. Many people feel that they are acceptable to God and that God will never reject them, yet they have all kinds of negative feelings against others. They have feelings of…

- dislike
- anger
- bitterness
- envy
- jealousy

- disfavor
- sourness
- resentment
- irritability

But note what this verse says: the person who hates his brother is a murderer. Hate is equal to murder; hate is the very same thing as murder. This is exactly what Jesus Christ said:

> **"You have heard that it was said to the people long ago, 'Do not murder, and anyone who murders will be subject to judgment.' But I tell you that anyone who is angry with his brother will be subject to judgment. Again, anyone who says to his brother, 'Raca, ' is answerable to the Sanhedrin. But anyone who says, 'You fool!' will be in danger of the fire of hell. (Mat 5:21-22)**

Anger, bitterness, and contempt are just as serious in God's eyes as murder. Why? Because the person who hates has the very same feelings and spirit that the murderer does—a spirit of anger, bitterness, and contempt. The murderer reacts differently, more violently, but the heart of both the hater and murderer is the same. And God looks and judges by the heart. Some persons can camouflage what is in their heart, but not from God. God knows the heart. The *Pulpit Commentary* has an excellent statement on this point:

> "Love is the only security against hate. And as every one who does not love is potentially a hater, so every hater is potentially a murderer. A murderer is a hater who expresses his hatred in the most emphatic way. A hater who does not murder abstains for various reasons from this extreme way of expressing his hate. But the temper of the two men is the same" (A. Plummer. *The Pulpit Commentary*, Vol.22, p.74).

Note that no murderer has eternal life. The implication is that neither does any person who hates his brother. A person who does not love his brother, who has negative feelings swirling within his heart, who has allowed his heart to become hardened against his brother—that person does not have eternal life dwelling within him. He has death, separation, alienation, division. He has *cut off* fellowship with a brother; he has *put to death* the relationship that exists between him and his brother. Therefore, he will be cut off from God; his relationship with God is put to death.

> **Anyone who claims to be in the light but hates his brother is still in the darkness. (1 John 2:9)**
>
> **Anyone who hates his brother is a murderer, and you know that no murderer has eternal life in him. (1 John 3:15)**
>
> **If anyone says, "I love God," yet hates his brother, he is a liar. For anyone who does not love his brother, whom he has seen, cannot love God, whom he has not seen. And he has given us this command: Whoever loves God must also love his brother. (1 John 4:20-21)**
>
> **Hatred stirs up dissension, but love covers over all wrongs. (Prov 10:12)**

6 (3:16) **Love—Jesus Christ, Love of**: love proves that one understands the love of Christ. Jesus Christ laid down His life for us. And remember when He did it: He died for us...

- when we were still powerless, totally unable to help ourselves or to save ourselves (Ro.5:6).
- when we were ungodly (Ro.5:6).
- when we were sinners (Ro.5:8).
- when we were enemies of God, rebelling, cursing, neglecting, ignoring, denying and rejecting God (Ro.5:10).

Despite all this, Jesus Christ died for us. He took our sins and the guilt for them upon Himself, and He paid the judgment for them. Jesus Christ died for us. Why? Because He loves us; He loves us enough to die for us even when we oppose and do things against Him and stand against Him.

The point is this: if we love God, then we follow His Son, the Lord Jesus Christ. We love people just like He did; we love them even when they oppose and do things against us and stand against us. In fact, love is the proof that we really understand the love of Christ. If we love those who do things against us, then we *know* the love of Christ. But if we do not love those who oppose us, we *do not know* the love of Christ. We can prove whether or not we know the love of Christ by our love for others, even for those who do us evil.

> "Christ died for those who hated Him; and the Christian must confront...the world with a love that is ready even to die for the haters" (A. Plummer. "The Pulpit Commentary," Vol.22, p.74).

> **"As the Father has loved me, so have I loved you. Now remain in my love. (John 15:9)**
>
> **Greater love has no one than this, that he lay down his life for his friends. (John 15:13)**
>
> **Who gave himself for our sins to rescue us from the present evil age, according to the will of our God and Father, (Gal 1:4)**
>
> **And live a life of love, just as Christ loved us and gave himself up for us as a fragrant offering and sacrifice to God. (Eph 5:2)**
>
> **He himself bore our sins in his body on the tree, so that we might die to sins and live for righteousness; by his wounds you have been healed. (1 Pet 2:24)**
>
> **For Christ died for sins once for all, the righteous for the unrighteous, to bring you to God. He was put to death in the body but made alive by the Spirit, (1 Pet 3:18)**
>
> **This is how we know what love is: Jesus Christ laid down his life for us. And we ought to lay down our lives for our brothers. (1 John 3:16)**

7 (3:17) **Love—Ministering**: love has compassion and gives to meet the needs of people. This verse is a question, but the answer is clearly seen. Note the words "material possessions." The meaning is necessities of life, livelihood, the means to sustain life. If we have the bare necessities of life and see a person in need, how can we close our heart against him? How can we shut off feelings for him? How can we keep from helping him and from sharing what we have? If a person does this—if we do this—how can the love of God dwell within us? The answer is clear: the love of God does not exist within a person who does not help those whom he sees in need. No matter what we profess, think, or argue, if we are not actively helping and giving—sacrificially giving—to meet the needs of the desperate and needy of our communities and of the world, we do not love God. God loved us: He gave all that He was and had to save us. Therefore, we must love others: we must give all that we *are and have* to save them. If we do not, how can we say that the love of God dwells in us? For this is exactly what Christ did.

Sell your possessions and give to the poor. Provide purses for yourselves that will not wear out, a treasure in heaven that will not be exhausted, where no thief comes near and no moth destroys. (Luke 12:33)

In everything I did, I showed you that by this kind of hard work we must help the weak, remembering the words the Lord Jesus himself said: 'It is more blessed to give than to receive.'" (Acts 20:35)

Share with God's people who are in need. Practice hospitality. (Rom 12:13)

Therefore, as we have opportunity, let us do good to all people, especially to those who belong to the family of believers. (Gal 6:10)

Command those who are rich in this present world not to be arrogant nor to put their hope in wealth, which is so uncertain, but to put their hope in God, who richly provides us with everything for our enjoyment. Command them to do good, to be rich in good deeds, and to be generous and willing to share. In this way they will lay up treasure for themselves as a firm foundation for the coming age, so that they may take hold of the life that is truly life. (1 Tim 6:17-19)

And do not forget to do good and to share with others, for with such sacrifices God is pleased. (Heb 13:16)

	D. Test 4: Having a Clean Heart, 3:18-24	confidence before God	3 A clean heart is produced by obeying the commandments
1 A clean heart is produced by loving with actions & with words only a. Love assures truth b. Love satisfies conscience	18 Dear children, let us not love with words or tongue but with actions and in truth. 19 This then is how we know that we belong to the truth, and how we set our hearts at rest in his presence.	22 And receive from him anything we ask, because we obey his commands and do what pleases him. 23 And this is his command: to believe in the name of his Son, Jesus Christ, and to love one another as he commanded us.	**4 A clean heart is produced by obeying the supreme commandment of God** a. By believing in God's Son Jesus Christ b. By loving one another
2 A clean heart is produced by God's knowledge a. Knows our need for cleansing & release of conscience b. Assures us	20 Whenever our hearts condemn us. For God is greater than our hearts, and he knows everything. 21 Dear friends, if our hearts do not condemn us, we have	24 Those who obey his commands live in him, and he in them. And this is how we know that he lives in us: We know it by the Spirit he gave us.	**5 A clean heart is produced by the Spirit dwelling within** a. A mutual indwelling b. The Spirit assures that God lives within us

DIVISION IV

THE PROOF THAT ONE REALLY LOVES GOD: SIX TESTS, 3:1-4:21

D. Test 4: Having a Clean Heart, 3:18-24

(3:18-24) **Introduction**: Do we really love God? There are six tests that show us. This is the fourth test: Do we have a clean heart? If our hearts are really clean, then we love God; but if our hearts condemn us, then we do not love God. How then can we have a clean heart?

1. A clean heart is produced by loving with actions and not with words only (v.18-19).
2. A clean heart is produced by God's knowledge (v.20-21).
3. A clean heart is produced by obeying the commandments (v.22).
4. A clean heart is produced by obeying the supreme commandment of God (v.23).
5. A clean heart is produced by the Spirit dwelling within (v.24).

1 (3:18-19) **Heart—Love**: a clean heart is produced by loving with actions and not with words only. Most people have some feelings for a person when they see him, suffering or in need. And most people will talk about and express concern for the needy and suffering. But note this: if the needy and suffering person has done evil against us, then the feelings of many people change. They no longer feel compassion and are no longer ready to reach out and comfort or help. The attitude becomes...

- "He deserves it."
- "He is being paid back."
- "God is judging him for his evil."
- "He made his bed, let him lie in it."
- "He's reaping what he sowed."
- "If he wasn't so lazy, he would find work."
- "He could better himself if he tried."

While this attitude is sweeping through their minds, they still profess to love God and to be caring for people. But note: this is exactly what Scripture is talking about. The love that we are to have is not only the love for friends, but it is the love for one's enemies, the love that loves those who oppose us and do things against us. This is what this exhortation is talking about.

> **"Little children, let us not love [merely] in theory or in speech but in deed and in truth - in practice and in sincerity" (The Amplified New Testament, v.18).**

To love only those who love us is to love only in theory and in speech. It is not loving like God loved; it is not practicing the love of God, the love for those who do evil.

Now note the result: if we love as God loves—if we love those who do evil—then we know we are of the truth. God is truth; He does exactly what should be done. And He loves everyone, even those who do evil. Therefore, if we are to be of the truth, we must also love those who do evil. We must love all those who oppose us and do evil against us and stand against us. When we do, the most wonderful things happen: we bring assurance to our hearts. And note: our hearts are assured *before Him*. This means that we are *accepted by Him*. He accepts us to live forever in His presence. Why? Because we are loving all men even as He loves all men—loving even those who are evil. A clean heart—a heart that is full of assurance, a heart that knows that it is pleasing and acceptable to God—is a heart that loves even as God loves. A clean heart is produced not by loving with words, but by loving with actions.

> **Thought 1.** Oliver Greene gives a good illustration that speaks to all of our hearts:
>
> > "There are occasions when a minister visits widows where there are children in need, and after a pastoral call the minister bows in prayer and asks God to supply the need of that family, when at that time there are hundreds - perhaps thousands - of dollars of God's money in the bank to the credit of the big church with the tall steeple! The parishioners in that church sing, 'O, how I love Jesus!' but they love Him in word only - not in deed and in truth. The Bible admonition is, 'Be ye doers of the Word, and not hearers only, deceiving your own selves' (James 1:22)" (*The Epistles of John*, p.141).

2 (3:20-21) **Heart—Condemnation**: a clean heart is produced by God knowing everything. Note the words, "Whenever our hearts condemn us." Everyone's heart condemns him sometime. Everyone of us knows what it is to sense wrong and condemnation. God has made our hearts sensitive so they will sense wrongdoing. Why? So that we will correct our behavior and not destroy ourselves. God is greater *than our hearts and He knows everything.* This means two things.

1. First, God knows everything about us. He knows when we are good and when we are bad. He knows everything that we do and more. God even knows our thoughts. He knows when we have done wrong and when we rightly or wrongly feel condemned. He knows every little thing that we feel or think. He even knows what we would have done under different circumstances. There is nothing, absolutely nothing, that is hid from God. No cover of darkness, no closed doors, no place off the side of the road, no place in the woods—no secret is unknown to God. Take all the evil we have ever done and all the condemnation we feel and sense—God knows every ounce of heaviness and guilt and condemnation we feel.

> **When I kept silent, my bones wasted away through my groaning all day long. (Psa 32:3)**
>
> **My guilt has overwhelmed me like a burden too heavy to bear. (Psa 38:4)**
>
> **For I know my transgressions, and my sin is always before me. (Psa 51:3)**
>
> **When the people heard this, they were cut to the heart and said to Peter and the other apostles, "Brothers, what shall we do?" (Acts 2:37)**
>
> **As Paul discoursed on righteousness, self-control and the judgment to come, Felix was afraid and said, "That's enough for now! You may leave. When I find it convenient, I will send for you." (Acts 24:25)**
>
> **If I sinned, you would be watching me and would not let my offense go unpunished. (Job 10:14)**
>
> **Surely then you will count my steps but not keep track of my sin. (Job 14:16)**
>
> **Although you wash yourself with soda and use an abundance of soap, the stain of your guilt is still before me," declares the Sovereign LORD. (Jer 2:22)**
>
> **My eyes are on all their ways; they are not hidden from me, nor is their sin concealed from my eyes. (Jer 16:17)**
>
> **Then the Spirit of the LORD came upon me, and he told me to say: "This is what the LORD says: That is what you are saying, O house of Israel, but I know what is going through your mind. (Ezek 11:5)**
>
> **But they do not realize that I remember all their evil deeds. Their sins engulf them; they are always before me. (Hosea 7:2)**
>
> **For I know how many are your offenses and how great your sins. You oppress the righteous and take bribes and you deprive the poor of justice in the courts. (Amos 5:12)**
>
> **He did not need man's testimony about man, for he knew what was in a man. (John 2:25)**

2. Second, God knows how to assure our hearts and how to give us confidence toward Him. God knows how to deliver us from the sense of guilt and condemnation. God knows how to remove *all condemnation* from our hearts. Think about it: all condemnation and all guilt removed forever from our hearts. God knows how to remove it all.

How can God remove all the guilt and condemnation that weighs upon our hearts and lives? By love. By loving us so much that He would give His Son to die for us. When we see God's love for us, when we receive His Son as our Savior, we discover the most wonderful thing.

⇒ Jesus Christ removes the sense of guilt and condemnation; He actually forgives and cleanses us from sin.

⇒ Something else happens as well: we discover that we love everyone just as He loves everyone. Our attitude toward others is actually changed: we love everyone, and we want them to know the love of God just as we have come to know His love.

Our hearts just flow in full assurance and confidence knowing that everything is well with God. There is no more condemnation or guilt. We know that we are forgiven and cleansed through Jesus Christ. We know that we are acceptable to God and our hearts revel in the confidence and assurance of Him.

> **Whoever believes in him is not condemned, but whoever does not believe stands condemned already because he has not believed in the name of God's one and only Son. (John 3:18)**
>
> **"I tell you the truth, whoever hears my word and believes him who sent me has eternal life and will not be condemned; he has crossed over from death to life. (John 5:24)**
>
> **Therefore, there is now no condemnation for those who are in Christ Jesus, (Rom 8:1)**
>
> **Who is he that condemns? Christ Jesus, who died—more than that, who was raised to life—is at the right hand of God and is also interceding for us. (Rom 8:34)**
>
> **If we confess our sins, he is faithful and just and will forgive us our sins and purify us from all unrighteousness. (1 John 1:9)**
>
> **Those who obey his commands live in him, and he in them. And this is how we know that he lives in us: We know it by the Spirit he gave us. (1 John 3:24)**

3 (3:22) **Heart—Commandments**: a clean heart is produced by obeying the commandments of God and doing what pleases God. If a child disobeys his father, he displeases his father. The only way he can please his father is by obeying him. The same is true with God. If we are going to please God, we must obey God.

Note another fact as well. A father cannot reward his child if the child disobeys. The father just cannot grant the child's request, not if he wants to teach him good behavior. Neither can God. The only way we can receive the things we ask is to obey God. He cannot reward our unfaithfulness and disobedience.

This is a great verse of Scripture, for it tells us exactly how to receive the answer to our prayers. In fact, it tells us that we can receive *whatever* we ask, if we will do this one thing: obey God. Just keep His commandments. Obeying God's commandments does two wonderful things for us:

⇒ It gives us everything we ask in prayer.

⇒ It gives us a clean heart, the most wonderful gift we could ever receive.

In my Father's house are many rooms; if it were not so, I would have told you. I am going there to prepare a place for you. (John 14:2)

Jesus replied, "If anyone loves me, he will obey my teaching. My Father will love him, and we will come to him and make our home with him. (John 14:23)

If you remain in me and my words remain in you, ask whatever you wish, and it will be given you. (John 15:7)

If you obey my commands, you will remain in my love, just as I have obeyed my Father's commands and remain in his love. You are my friends if you do what I command. (John 15:10, 14)

But the man who looks intently into the perfect law that gives freedom, and continues to do this, not forgetting what he has heard, but doing it—he will be blessed in what he does. (James 1:25)

You want something but don't get it. You kill and covet, but you cannot have what you want. You quarrel and fight. You do not have, because you do not ask God. When you ask, you do not receive, because you ask with wrong motives, that you may spend what you get on your pleasures. (James 4:2-3)

"Blessed are those who wash their robes, that they may have the right to the tree of life and may go through the gates into the city. (Rev 22:14)

Oh, that their hearts would be inclined to fear me and keep all my commands always, so that it might go well with them and their children forever! (Deu 5:29)

4 (3:23) **Commandments—Believer—Love, Brotherly**: a clean heart is produced by obeying God's supreme commandment. Note that God's supreme commandment has two parts to it. If a person wants a clean heart, he must do these two things above all else.

1. First, he must believe in the *name of God's Son Jesus Christ*. How can a person believe in the name of someone? We can believe a statement or some writing that a person makes. But what does it mean to believe *in the name* of someone? A person's name stands for what he is, for the kind of person he is and for the kind of things he does. Therefore, to believe in the name of Jesus Christ means to believe in all that He stands for and in all that He is. Jesus Christ is the Son of God, the promised Savior and Messiah of the world.

⇒ He is the Son of God who has come to earth to reveal God (see outlines and notes—1 Jn.1:1-5).
⇒ He is the great advocate and sacrifice for man and his sins (see notes—1 Jn.2:1-2).

Believing in the name of the Lord Jesus Christ is the only way a person can ever have a clean heart before God. This is a basic and fundamental fact; it is the foundation of life. No person ever becomes acceptable to God until he believes in the name of God's Son. Obeying this commandment is the very first thing that a person has to do to please God.

2. Second, he must *love all others* (see outline and notes, *Love*—1 Jn.2:7-8; 3:10-17 for discussion).

5 (3:24) **Holy Spirit**: a clean heart is produced by the Holy Spirit dwelling within us. The person who believes in Jesus Christ and loves others dwells in God and God in Him. How do we know that God dwells in us? By the Holy Spirit. This is made abundantly clear: "we know that he lives in us: We know it by the Spirit he gave us."

⇒ Note that we live in God. This means that we take up residence in God, live and walk in Him, live and move and have our being in Him. It means that we make our home in Him.
⇒ Note that God lives in us. This means that He takes up residence in us; lives and moves and has His being within us. It means that God makes a home in our hearts.

Again, how do we know this? By His Spirit which He has given us. The Holy Spirit of God seals and guarantees us, gives us *absolute assurance*. He lives within us, which means that He talks to us, shares with us, leads and guides us, disciplines us, convicts and convinces us. All that is involved in living, the Spirit of God does within us. He is our constant and permanent companion. He never leaves us nor forsakes us. He is always infusing us with the assurance and confidence of God and with His presence and power.

But the Counselor, the Holy Spirit, whom the Father will send in my name, will teach you all things and will remind you of everything I have said to you. (John 14:26)

The Spirit himself testifies with our spirit that we are God's children. Now if we are children, then we are heirs—heirs of God and co-heirs with Christ, if indeed we share in his sufferings in order that we may also share in his glory. (Rom 8:16-17)

Set his seal of ownership on us, and put his Spirit in our hearts as a deposit, guaranteeing what is to come. (2 Cor 1:22)

But when the time had fully come, God sent his Son, born of a woman, born under law, to redeem those under law, that we might receive the full rights of sons. Because you are sons, God sent the Spirit of his Son into our hearts, the Spirit who calls out, "Abba, Father." (Gal 4:4-6)

And you also were included in Christ when you heard the word of truth, the gospel of your salvation. Having believed, you were marked in him with a seal, the promised Holy Spirit, who is a deposit guaranteeing our inheritance until the redemption of those who are God's possession—to the praise of his glory. (Eph 1:13-14)

And do not grieve the Holy Spirit of God, with whom you were sealed for the day of redemption. (Eph 4:30)

Those who obey his commands live in him, and he in them. And this is how we know that he lives in us: We know it by the Spirit he gave us. (1 John 3:24)

	CHAPTER 4 **E. Test 5: Testing the Spirits of False Teachers, 4:1-6**	from God. This is the spirit of the antichrist, which you have heard is coming and even now is already in the world.	
1 Test the spirits of teachers a. Make sure they are born of God b. Because there are many false teachers	Dear friends, do not believe every spirit, but test the spirits to see whether they are from God, because many false prophets have gone out into the world.	4 You, dear children, are from God and have overcome them, because the one who is in you is greater than the one who is in the world.	**3 Test yourselves** a. Are you born of God? b. Have you overcome false teachers?
2 Test the confession of teachers a. The true spirit acknowledges that Jesus Christ has come in the flesh	2 This is how you can recognize the Spirit of God: Every spirit that acknowledges that Jesus Christ has come in the flesh is from God,	5 They are from the world and therefore speak from the viewpoint of the world, and the world listens to them.	**4 Test the followers of teachers** a. False teachers are followed by worldly people b. True teachers are followed by people who know God
b. The false spirit does not acknowledge Jesus	3 But every spirit that does not acknowledge Jesus is not	6 We are from God, and whoever knows God listens to us; but whoever is not from God does not listen to us. This is how we recognize the Spirit of truth and the spirit of falsehood.	

DIVISION IV

THE PROOF THAT ONE REALLY LOVES GOD: SIX TESTS, 3:1-4:21

E. Test 5: Testing the Spirits of False Teachers, 4:1-6

(4:1-6) **Introduction**: this is a critical passage of Scripture. It deals with true and false teachers, in particular with the spirit of truth or error that fills their hearts. This is the fifth test of our love for God. How do we know that we really love God? We can tell by the spirits of the teachers we are following. If we are following the spirit of a true teacher, then it is clear indication that we love God. If we are following the spirit of a false teacher, then it is clear indication that we do not love God. We must test the spirits of teaching throughout the world.

1. Test the spirits of teachers (v.1).
2. Test the confession of teachers (v.2-3).
3. Test yourselves (v.4).
4. Test the followers of teachers (v.5-6).

1 (4:1) **Teaching, False—Evil Spirits**: first, test the spirits of teachers; test them to make sure they are of God. This is a strong charge given to believers. Note the term *Dear friends*. This was John's tender address to the believers of the church. He is definitely addressing believers, and this tells us a significant fact: believers can be misled by the *spirits of false teachers*. What kinds of spirits dwell within a false teacher?

⇒ A false teacher may have a *spirit of light*, especially in industrialized societies. The spirit presents a way of life that seems to be the truth, the very way to live. He presents a way of life that seems to be intelligent and full of knowledge and enlightenment. His way seems to be the way to go, the way that leads to...

- the good life
- progress
- development
- assurance
- satisfaction
- fulfillment
- education
- good feelings
- pleasure
- possessions
- recognition

⇒ A false teacher may have a *spirit of righteousness*. He may preach and teach righteousness, a righteousness that stresses...

- morality
- goodness
- justice
- education
- development
- ministry
- giving
- serving
- helping

⇒ A false teacher may stress *the life and teachings of Jesus Christ*—all the good qualities of life—all the traits that should characterize people. They may tell people to copy the life of Jesus and to focus their hearts upon the good qualities of life, and if they do, God will accept them.

False teachers make one fatal mistake. This is discussed in the next note. The point in this verse is that we must test the spirits of false teachers, test them to make absolutely sure they are of God. Note one other fact: there are "*many false prophets.*" Scripture is not talking about a few, but many. If there were many in the days of John, think how many more there are today. Think how many more religions there are; how many cults have sprung up around Christianity; how many denominations and ministries have sprung up since John wrote these words. Just think of all the churches and pulpits and podiums that are being filled by the teachers of the world. In addition, think how many preachers and teachers claim to be true followers of Christ. There are many, thousands and thousands, of false teachers in the world today. Who are they? This is the discussion of this passage. This is what every person must test in order to keep from being misled.

For such people are not serving our Lord Christ, but their own appetites. By smooth talk and flattery they deceive the minds of naive people. (Rom 16:18)

For such men are false apostles, deceitful workmen, masquerading as apostles of Christ. And no wonder, for Satan himself masquerades as an angel of light. It is not surprising, then, if his servants masquerade

as servants of righteousness. Their end will be what their actions deserve. (2 Cor 11:13-15)

I am astonished that you are so quickly deserting the one who called you by the grace of Christ and are turning to a different gospel— which is really no gospel at all. Evidently some people are throwing you into confusion and are trying to pervert the gospel of Christ. But even if we or an angel from heaven should preach a gospel other than the one we preached to you, let him be eternally condemned! As we have already said, so now I say again: If anybody is preaching to you a gospel other than what you accepted, let him be eternally condemned! (Gal 1:6-9)

While evil men and impostors will go from bad to worse, deceiving and being deceived. (2 Tim 3:13)

2 (4:2-3) **Teachers—Teachers, False**: second, test the confession of teachers. What is it that makes a teacher true or false? Jesus Christ. What a man believes about Jesus Christ makes the teacher true or false. What a man acknowledges about Jesus Christ exposes his spirit, a spirit of truth or a spirit of error. And note what it is about Jesus Christ that exposes a teacher: the incarnation. That is, did Jesus Christ come in the flesh or not?

1. The true Spirit, the Spirit of God Himself, acknowledges that Jesus Christ did come in the flesh, that the incarnation is true. If a teacher has the Spirit of God dwelling in him, then he acknowledges the incarnation, the wonderful truth that God did become Man and did come to earth to save man. The Spirit of God *cannot confess* anything other than the truth; therefore, every teacher who has the Spirit of God will confess the same truth. He cannot confess anything else because the Spirit of God Himself dwells within him. If he acknowledges anything else, then the spirit within him is not the Spirit of God. Now note the acknowledgment in detail, exactly what it is that a true teacher acknowledges: "Jesus Christ has come in the flesh."

   a. The true teacher acknowledges *Jesus*. The name *Jesus* means *Savior*. It is believing that Jesus Christ did come from God to save man, to be the Savior of the world.

   b. The true teacher acknowledges *Christ*. The name *Christ* means *Messiah*, the Anointed One of God. It is believing that Jesus Christ is the promised Messiah of Scripture; that He is the fulfillment of all the prophecies of Scripture; that He is the Anointed Savior sent from God to earth.

   c. The true teacher acknowledges that Jesus Christ is the *Son of God*; that God did send His Son *out of* (ek) heaven, out of the spiritual world and dimension into this world; that God sent His Son in human flesh to save man in fulfillment of Scripture. It means that Jesus Christ fulfilled the Scripture predicting the coming death, resurrection, and exaltation of the Messiah. Simply stated, it means that Jesus Christ is the Son of God who came to earth to save man.

Thought 1. This is the acknowledgment of the true teacher and of every true believer. We must always remember that a true teacher is indwelt by the Spirit of God Himself. Therefore, the true teacher *will al-*

ways acknowledge the incarnation, the wonderful truth that "Jesus Christ has come in the flesh."

Therefore the Lord himself will give you a sign: The virgin will be with child and will give birth to a son, and will call him Immanuel. (Isa 7:14)

For to us a child is born, to us a son is given, and the government will be on his shoulders. And he will be called Wonderful Counselor, Mighty God, Everlasting Father, Prince of Peace. (Isa 9:6)

You will be with child and give birth to a son, and you are to give him the name Jesus. (Luke 1:31)

The Word became flesh and made his dwelling among us. We have seen his glory, the glory of the One and Only, who came from the Father, full of grace and truth. (John 1:14)

For what the law was powerless to do in that it was weakened by the sinful nature, God did by sending his own Son in the likeness of sinful man to be a sin offering. And so he condemned sin in sinful man, (Rom 8:3)

But made himself nothing, taking the very nature of a servant, being made in human likeness. (Phil 2:7)

Beyond all question, the mystery of godliness is great: He appeared in a body, was vindicated by the Spirit, was seen by angels, was preached among the nations, was believed on in the world, was taken up in glory. (1 Tim 3:16)

Since the children have flesh and blood, he too shared in their humanity so that by his death he might destroy him who holds the power of death—that is, the devil— and free those who all their lives were held in slavery by their fear of death. (Heb 2:14-15)

This is how you can recognize the Spirit of God: Every spirit that acknowledges that Jesus Christ has come in the flesh is from God, (1 John 4:2)

"Whoever acknowledges me before men, I will also acknowledge him before my Father in heaven. (Mat 10:32)

"I tell you, whoever acknowledges me before men, the Son of Man will also acknowledge him before the angels of God. (Luke 12:8)

And every tongue confess that Jesus Christ is Lord, to the glory of God the Father. (Phil 2:11)

No one who denies the Son has the Father; whoever acknowledges the Son has the Father also. (1 John 2:23)

If anyone acknowledges that Jesus is the Son of God, God lives in him and he in God. (1 John 4:15)

2. The false spirit denies that Jesus Christ is from God. He denies the incarnation. He does not believe that God took on human flesh and became a man.

   a. The false teacher does not believe that Jesus Christ is the Savior of the world. He may accept Jesus Christ as a great teacher and a great religious leader, perhaps the greatest, but he does not believe that Jesus Christ is *the Savior*. He believes there are other ways to God, that other people who believe in God will be as acceptable to God as a follower of Jesus Christ.

b. The false teacher does not believe that Jesus is the Christ, the promised Messiah and Anointed One from God. He does not believe the Scriptures are the inspired Word of God. He accepts them only as the writings of great religious people of the past; therefore, there are no prophetic promises of a Messiah, no promise of a coming Savior. To the false teacher, Jesus Christ is only a great religious teacher, only one way to reach God. He is not *the Anointed One* sent from God to save all men. He is not the only way to God.

c. The false teacher does not believe Jesus Christ has *come from God*. He does not believe Jesus Christ is the Son of God, that Jesus Christ came out of heaven, out from the spiritual world and dimension. He does not believe that God sent His Son into the world in human flesh as a man. Again, the false teacher believes that Jesus Christ is only a man just like all other men—a great man, perhaps the greatest, perhaps the man who got closer to God than any other man. Nevertheless, to the false teacher Jesus Christ was only a man who taught us how to worship and serve God. The false teacher would say...

- that Jesus Christ was not sinless. He lived close to God, but no man can achieve sinlessness.
- that Jesus Christ died, but not as a substitute for man's sins. He died as a great martyr showing us how we should face death and how we should be willing to die for the great cause of righteousness.
- that the resurrection of Jesus Christ did not take place. It is only a picture of the spiritual truth that man can live in God's presence.

Now, note the fatal mistake of the false teachers: to deny that Jesus Christ is not from God is to deny that man can ever be saved beyond this world. Why? Because man can never know for sure that God exists nor how to reach God if He does exist. No person has ever seen God or heaven, and they never will, not by physical and material technology. The physical world cannot penetrate or cross over into the spiritual world, no matter what some persons may claim. If man is ever to know God and the spiritual world, then God has to come to earth and reveal the truth to us. There is no other way. Therefore, to deny that God sent His Son into the world is to deny that we can ever be saved.

There is another fact that needs to be noted as well, that of perfection. God is perfect and man is imperfect. Therefore, God could never let man penetrate or cross over into perfection. Why? Because man's imperfection would affect the perfect world of God. Heaven would no longer be heaven; it would no longer be perfect if God allowed imperfect beings to enter it. No matter what some people may claim about penetrating heaven, they have not. Imperfection just cannot cross over into perfection. The fatal mistake of false teachers is just that, *fatal*—fatal and eternally dooming. The consequences of denying the incarnation of Jesus Christ are terrible. If Jesus Christ is not from God, then it means...

- that God has not loved us enough to reveal Himself to us (1 Jn.1:2).
- that God has not loved us enough to send us the Word of life (1 Jn.1:1).
- that God has not loved us enough to show us eternal life (1 Jn.1:2).
- that there is no eternal life (1 Jn.1:2).
- that there is no fellowship with God, not for sure (1 Jn.1:3).
- that the message of hope and of Scripture are not true, not for sure (1 Jn.1:3).
- that there is no joy beyond this life, not for sure, no fullness of joy (1 Jn.1:4).
- that Jesus Christ is not our Advocate (1 Jn.2:2).
- that there is no forgiveness of sin (1 Jn.1:9; 2:2).
- that there is no perfect sacrifice for sin (1 Jn.2:2).

On and on the list could go, but the point is clearly seen. The false teacher destroys the hope of salvation and of eternity with God. We are left without hope and without God in this world unless God has loved us, loved us so much that He sent His Son Jesus Christ into the world. Jesus Christ is the crux of the message of the gospel. Note that the spirit of the false teacher is the spirit of antichrist (see outline and notes—1 Jn.2:18-23). If a teacher confesses that Jesus Christ has come in the flesh, he is a true teacher. If not, he is a false teacher who promotes the very spirit of antichrist. "Dear friends, do not believe every spirit, but test the spirits" (v.1).

But whoever disowns me before men, I will disown him before my Father in heaven. (Mat 10:33)

If anyone is ashamed of me and my words in this adulterous and sinful generation, the Son of Man will be ashamed of him when he comes in his Father's glory with the holy angels." (Mark 8:38)

But there were also false prophets among the people, just as there will be false teachers among you. They will secretly introduce destructive heresies, even denying the sovereign Lord who bought them— bringing swift destruction on themselves. if this is so, then the Lord knows how to rescue godly men from trials and to hold the unrighteous for the day of judgment, while continuing their punishment. (2 Pet 2:1, 9)

Who is the liar? It is the man who denies that Jesus is the Christ. Such a man is the antichrist—he denies the Father and the Son. (1 John 2:22)

I am astonished that you are so quickly deserting the one who called you by the grace of Christ and are turning to a different gospel— which is really no gospel at all. Evidently some people are throwing you into confusion and are trying to pervert the gospel of Christ. But even if we or an angel from heaven should preach a gospel other than the one we preached to you, let him be eternally condemned! As we have already said, so now I say again: If anybody is preaching to you a gospel other than what you accepted, let him be eternally condemned! (Gal 1:6-9)

Anyone who breaks one of the least of these commandments and teaches others to do the same will be called least in the kingdom of heaven, but whoever practices and teaches these commands will be called great in the kingdom of heaven. (Mat 5:19)

They worship me in vain; their teachings are but rules taught by men.'" (Mat 15:9)

They want to be teachers of the law, but they do not know what they are talking about or what they so confidently affirm. (1 Tim 1:7)

The Spirit clearly says that in later times some will abandon the faith and follow deceiving spirits and things taught by demons. Such teachings come through hypocritical liars, whose consciences have been seared as with a hot iron. (1 Tim 4:1-2)

If anyone teaches false doctrines and does not agree to the sound instruction of our Lord Jesus Christ and to godly teaching, (1 Tim 6:3)

For the time will come when men will not put up with sound doctrine. Instead, to suit their own desires, they will gather around them a great number of teachers to say what their itching ears want to hear. They will turn their ears away from the truth and turn aside to myths. (2 Tim 4:3-4)

For there are many rebellious people, mere talkers and deceivers, especially those of the circumcision group. They must be silenced, because they are ruining whole households by teaching things they ought not to teach—and that for the sake of dishonest gain. (Titus 1:10-11)

But there were also false prophets among the people, just as there will be false teachers among you. They will secretly introduce destructive heresies, even denying the sovereign Lord who bought them—bringing swift destruction on themselves. (2 Pet 2:1)

3 (4:4) **Believers**: third, test yourselves. How? There are two ways.

1. Ask yourself if you are *from God*; that is, have you been born of God? (See note—1 Jn.2:29 for discussion.)

2. Ask yourself if you are overcoming the spirits of false teachers? The Spirit of God is in you, and He is far greater than the evil spirits of false teachers. He enables you to conquer false teachers. Therefore, if you are following a teacher who denies the incarnation, that the Son of God has come in the flesh, then you are *not from God*. You are not born of God. But if you have rejected the teachings of men who deny the incarnation of Jesus Christ, then you are born of God.

Thought 1. Many false teachers are persuasive. They are very personable, attractive, and appealing—full of charisma. Their ideas and teachings sound reasonable and appealing. But if a person has been truly born of God, he has the Holy Spirit to help him see the error of the teaching. And note the words "you have overcome them." The Spirit of God does not fail. Therefore, if a person is following some strange teaching about Jesus Christ, he is most likely not *born of God*. Those who are truly *born of God* acknowledge that Jesus Christ is the Son of God who has come in the flesh. They confess...

• the incarnation
• the righteousness and sinlessness of Jesus Christ

• the death, burial, and resurrection of Jesus Christ
• the ascension and exaltation of Jesus Christ

The Spirit of truth. The world cannot accept him, because it neither sees him nor knows him. But you know him, for he lives with you and will be in you. (John 14:17)

But the Counselor, the Holy Spirit, whom the Father will send in my name, will teach you all things and will remind you of everything I have said to you. (John 14:26)

But when he, the Spirit of truth, comes, he will guide you into all truth. He will not speak on his own; he will speak only what he hears, and he will tell you what is yet to come. (John 16:13)

You, however, are controlled not by the sinful nature but by the Spirit, if the Spirit of God lives in you. And if anyone does not have the Spirit of Christ, he does not belong to Christ. (Rom 8:9)

Because those who are led by the Spirit of God are sons of God. (Rom 8:14)

We have not received the spirit of the world but the Spirit who is from God, that we may understand what God has freely given us. This is what we speak, not in words taught us by human wisdom but in words taught by the Spirit, expressing spiritual truths in spiritual words. (1 Cor 2:12-13)

Don't you know that you yourselves are God's temple and that God's Spirit lives in you? (1 Cor 3:16)

As for you, the anointing you received from him remains in you, and you do not need anyone to teach you. But as his anointing teaches you about all things and as that anointing is real, not counterfeit—just as it has taught you, remain in him. (1 John 2:27)

Those who obey his commands live in him, and he in them. And this is how we know that he lives in us: We know it by the Spirit he gave us. (1 John 3:24)

We know that we live in him and he in us, because he has given us of his Spirit. (1 John 4:13)

4 (4:5-6) **Teachers—Teachers, False**: fourth, test the followers of teachers. We can look at the people who follow teachers and tell whether a teacher is false or not.

1. False teachers are followed by people who are worldly. Note the three things said:
   a. False teachers are from the world. They have only a natural birth; they have never been born of God, never been spiritually born. The Spirit of God, the divine nature of God, is not dwelling within their hearts.
   b. False teachers speak from the viewpoint of the world. What does this mean? It means they teach a worldly or human approach to God:
   ⇒ that man reaches God by being good and doing good.
   ⇒ that man becomes acceptable to God by living a religious life and by doing religious things

such as being confirmed, baptized, going to church, confessing, and keeping the rituals and ceremonies.

⇒ that man secures God's approval by combining his spirit with God's Spirit through communion and through righteous deeds.

Note: such approaches to God center and focus upon man and what he does. They are centered in the world, not in God and what God has done to save man. Man saves himself, not God through His Son Jesus Christ.

c. The world listens to false teachers. The message of false teachers appeals to man. For if the Son of God has not come to earth, then there is no absolute and infallible rule to govern man. Therefore, we are somewhat free to find our own way to God the best we can. If we stumble here and there, it will not matter that much. God will understand, for He has left us to find our own way. This teaching, of course, tends…

* to excuse sin
* to exalt man as his own savior
* to stress ego and self-image over the power of God and His Spirit
* to give man the right to gain personal authority and power over others
* to give man the right to focus upon success, position, money, pleasures, and possessions
* to stress man and his inner power [will] over God's power
* to exalt man and his importance over God
* to focus upon the discipline and control of the flesh (sinful nature) over the power of God's Spirit

To some who were confident of their own righteousness and looked down on everybody else, Jesus told this parable: (Luke 18:9)

Jesus said to them, "If God were your Father, you would love me, for I came from God and now am here. I have not come on my own; but he sent me. Why is my language not clear to you? Because you are unable to hear what I say. (John 8:42-43)

Can any of you prove me guilty of sin? If I am telling the truth, why don't you believe me? He who belongs to God hears what God says. The reason you do not hear is that you do not belong to God." (John 8:46-47)

For since the creation of the world God's invisible qualities—his eternal power and divine nature—have been clearly seen, being understood from what has been made, so that men are without excuse. For although they knew God, they neither glorified him as God nor gave thanks to him, but their thinking became futile and their foolish hearts were darkened. Although they claimed to be wise, they became fools (Rom 1:20-22; cp. v.18-32)

For the message of the cross is foolishness to those who are perishing, but to us who are being saved it is the power of God. For it is written: "I will destroy the wisdom of the wise; the in-telligence of the intelligent I will frustrate." Where is the wise man? Where is the scholar? Where is the philosopher of this age? Has not God made foolish the wisdom of the world? For since in the wisdom of God the world through its wisdom did not know him, God was pleased through the foolishness of what was preached to save those who believe. (1 Cor 1:18-21; cp. 1 Cor.3.19-21)**

The man who thinks he knows something does not yet know as he ought to know. (1 Cor 8:2)

So, if you think you are standing firm, be careful that you don't fall! (1 Cor 10:12)

If anyone thinks he is something when he is nothing, he deceives himself. (Gal 6:3)

Do not be wise in your own eyes; fear the LORD and shun evil. (Prov 3:7)

Many a man claims to have unfailing love, but a faithful man who can find? (Prov 20:6)

He who trusts in himself is a fool, but he who walks in wisdom is kept safe. (Prov 28:26)

Woe to those who are wise in their own eyes and clever in their own sight. (Isa 5:21)

"Now then, listen, you wanton creature, lounging in your security and saying to yourself, 'I am, and there is none besides me. I will never be a widow or suffer the loss of children.' Both of these will overtake you in a moment, on a single day: loss of children and widowhood. They will come upon you in full measure, in spite of your many sorceries and all your potent spells. You have trusted in your wickedness and have said, 'No one sees me.' Your wisdom and knowledge mislead you when you say to yourself, 'I am, and there is none besides me.' (Isa 47:8-10)

But you have planted wickedness, you have reaped evil, you have eaten the fruit of deception. Because you have depended on your own strength and on your many warriors, (Hosea 10:13)

The pride of your heart has deceived you, you who live in the clefts of the rocks and make your home on the heights, you who say to yourself, 'Who can bring me down to the ground?' Though you soar like the eagle and make your nest among the stars, from there I will bring you down," declares the LORD. (Oba 1:3-4)

2. True teachers are followed by people who know God. They know and acknowledge that Jesus Christ, the Son of God, has come in the flesh. Therefore, they follow the teacher who proclaims…

- the incarnation of God, that is, the virgin birth, that Jesus Christ has come in the flesh.
- the righteousness of Jesus Christ, that He did live a sinless life when He was upon earth and thereby secured righteousness for man.
- the death of Jesus Christ, that He died for man's sins, that He was the perfect sacrifice for sin, wholly and perfectly acceptable to God.
- the resurrection of Jesus Christ, that He arose and conquered death for all men and made it possible for man to live a new life, a new life that conquers all the forces of evil and that infuses into man the seed of eternal life.

Note what the verse says: those who *know God* are the followers of the true teacher, but those who *are not from God* do not hear the true teacher. This is the way we know the spirit of truth and the spirit of error.

Thought 1. We can tell a true teacher by the people who follow him. Our task is to look at the followers of any teacher. What kind of life do they live—a worldly or righteous life? (See outlines and notes—1 Jn.2:15-17; 1 Jn.2:29; 3:4-9 for more discussion.)

The seed that fell among thorns stands for those who hear, but as they go on their way they are choked by life's worries, riches and pleasures, and they do not mature. (Luke 8:14)

Jesus answered, "My teaching is not my own. It comes from him who sent me. If anyone chooses to do God's will, he will find out whether my teaching comes from God or whether I speak on my own. (John 7:16-17)

To the Jews who had believed him, Jesus said, "If you hold to my teaching, you are really my disciples. (John 8:31)

The Spirit of truth. The world cannot accept him, because it neither sees him nor knows him. But you know him, for he lives with you and will be in you. (John 14:17)

"When the Counselor comes, whom I will send to you from the Father, the Spirit of truth who goes out from the Father, he will testify about me. (John 15:26)

But when he, the Spirit of truth, comes, he will guide you into all truth. He will not speak on his own; he will speak only what he hears, and he will tell you what is yet to come. (John 16:13)

We have not received the spirit of the world but the Spirit who is from God, that we may understand what God has freely given us. (1 Cor 2:12)

We are from God, and whoever knows God listens to us; but whoever is not from God does not listen to us. This is how we recognize the Spirit of truth and the spirit of falsehood. (1 John 4:6)

1 Proves that we are born of God & know God	F. Test 6: Loving One Another, 4:7-21	the world.	did send Christ to be the Savior

7 Dear friends, let us love one another, for love comes from God. Everyone who loves has been born of God and knows God.
8 Whoever does not love does not know God, because God is love.
9 This is how God showed his love among us: He sent his one and only Son into the world that we might live through him.
10 This is love: not that we loved God, but that he loved us and sent his Son as an atoning sacrifice for our sins.
11 Dear friends, since God so loved us, we also ought to love one another.
12 No one has ever seen God; but if we love one another, God lives in us and his love is made complete in us.
13 We know that we live in him and he in us, because he has given us of his Spirit.
14 And we have seen and testify that the Father has sent his Son to be the Savior of the world.
15 If anyone acknowledges that Jesus is the Son of God, God lives in him and he in God.
16 And so we know and rely on the love God has for us. God is love. Whoever lives in love lives in God, and God in him.
17 In this way, love is made complete among us so that we will have confidence on the day of judgment, because in this world we are like him.
18 There is no fear in love. But perfect love drives out fear, because fear has to do with punishment. The one who fears is not made perfect in love.
19 We love because he first loved us.
20 If anyone says, "I love God," yet hates his brother, he is a liar. For anyone who does not love his brother, whom he has seen, cannot love God, whom he has not seen.
21 And he has given us this command: Whoever loves God must also love his brother.

1 Proves that we are born of God & know God

2 Proves that we see God's love
a. God's love is seen in one supreme act: He sent His Son
b. God's way of saving man
c. The conclusion: We should, therefore, love one another

3 Proves that God's Spirit is within us
a. God is not known by sight
b. God is known only by love—maturing love
c. Conclusion: Mature love proves that God's Spirit is within us

4 Proves that our testimony confession are true
a. The great testimony: God

b. The great promise: The person who acknowledges Christ lives in God & God in him
c. The great confession: We do know & believe the love of God

5 Proves that God is going to deliver us from judgment

6 Proves that God delivers us from fear

7 Proves that we love God
a. The basis: His love
b. The illustration: A false profession
c. The commandment: God commands love

DIVISION IV

THE PROOF THAT ONE REALLY LOVES GOD: SIX TESTS, 3:1-4:21

F. Test 6: Loving One Another, 4:7-21

(4:7-21) **Introduction**: Do we really love God? This is the sixth test, the one sure way to measure whether or not we love God: Do we love one another? Do we really love our neighbors, all of our fellow men? No matter who they are, do we love them? If we love our fellow man, this proves that we love God. Loving one another proves seven things.

1. Loving one another proves that we are born of God and know God (v.7-8).
2. Loving one another proves that we see God's love (v.9-11).
3. Loving one another proves that God's Spirit is within us (v.12-13).
4. Loving one another proves that our testimony and confession are true (v.14-16).
5. Loving one another proves that God is going to deliver from judgment (v.17).
6. Loving one another proves that God delivers us from fear (v.18).
7. Loving one another proves that we love God (v.19-21).

1 (4:7-8) **Love—New Birth**: loving one another proves that we are born of God and that we know God. Note two things.

1. God is love; His very nature is love (v.7). Therefore, if a person loves God, he becomes a loving person; he takes on the very nature of God. If a person really loves God, then he does what God does: he loves everyone. Note exactly what the verse says. When we love one another, people see two things:

⇒ People see that we are born of God. They see that we have the nature of God, that God has put His divine nature into us. How do they see God's nature in us? By our love. They see us doing the very same thing that God does—loving people. They see us loving everyone: the rich and poor, healthy and suffering, deserving and undeserving, acceptable and unacceptable, good and bad. They see us loving everyone, no matter who they are.

⇒ People see that we know God. They see that we have been talking to God and learning about God; that we are doing what God says, carrying out His instructions. They see that we know God, fellowship and commune with Him; that we are living godly lives, and that we are actually taking on the very nature of God. How do they see all this? By our love. They see that we are loving and caring just as God is loving and caring.

2. But note a significant fact: the person who does not love others reveals something as well: he does not know God (v.8). Who is this person? Who is it that does not know God? The person who...

- lives selfishly
- hoards and banks
- discriminates
- is prejudiced
- elevates himself
- steals
- neglects others
- abuses

- criticizes
- backbites
- gossips
- curses
- gets angry
- hates
- murders

This person does not know God. God is love and this person is not loving. He is not living like God lives; he is not demonstrating love for other people, not showing concern and care and not helping and ministering to people's needs. He is not blessing other people; he is causing hurt and pain and destroying them. And this is not God's nature; God is love. God blesses people; He does not hurt and destroy them.

> **And the second is like it: 'Love your neighbor as yourself.' (Mat 22:39)**
> **By this all men will know that you are my disciples, if you love one another." (John 13:35)**
> **My command is this: Love each other as I have loved you. (John 15:12)**
> **Love must be sincere. Hate what is evil; cling to what is good. (Rom 12:9)**
> **May the Lord make your love increase and overflow for each other and for everyone else, just as ours does for you. (1 Th 3:12)**
> **Now that you have purified yourselves by obeying the truth so that you have sincere love for your brothers, love one another deeply, from the heart. (1 Pet 1:22)**

2 (4:9-11) **God, Love of—Jesus Christ, Death—Propitiation**: loving one another proves that we see God's love.

1. Note God's love (v.9). In fact this is the very way that we know that God is love. If someone asks, "How do we know that God is love? The world is full of so much evil and bad, how can we be sure God loves us?" Note the Scripture: this is the way God revealed that He loves us. "God sent his one and only Son into the world that we might live through him." The world is full of evil and bad. Men commit all kinds of evil, and in addition to this they…

- curse God
- ignore God
- neglect God
- disobey God
- disbelieve God

- reject God
- rebel against God
- deny God
- oppose God

But this is the glorious love of God. God still loves man and still wants to help and to take care of man. Man has the most serious problem imaginable: not only is he engulfed with all the evil of the world, but he dies and ceases to be on this earth. He lives at most for just a few short years and then he is gone forever from the earth. But as stated, God is love and He has proven His love. He has sent His only Son into the world so that man might live through Him.

2. Note how we know the love of God:fcy by salvation. We know that God loves us because God saves man. How can we live through Christ? How does God give us life through Christ? By sending Christ to be the propitiation, the atoning sacrifice for our sins (v.10. See note, pt.2—1 Jn.2:1-2; DEEPER STUDY # 1—1 Jn.2:2 for discussion.)

3. The conclusion is compelling: "Dear friends, if God so loved us, we also ought to love one another" (v.11). If God loved us when we opposed and did things against Him, when we disobeyed and ignored Him, then there is no person we should not love. If God went to such great lengths to give His very own Son to die for us, then we should go to the same length to love one another. We are to love those who…

- oppose us
- do things against us
- ignore us
- distrust us

- curse us
- reject us
- persecute us
- kill us

No matter who the person is, God loves him and has shown in the most supreme way possible that He loves him. Therefore, we are to love that person and demonstrate our love for him. We are to sacrifice ourselves and try to bring life to him. This we do by loving him, by showing him there is a better way, the way of love.

3 (4:12-13) **Love—Holy Spirit—Indwelling Presence**: loving one another proves that God's Spirit is within us.

1. God is not known by sight (v.12). No person has ever seen God face to face. No person has ever penetrated the spiritual world and crossed over into heaven and seen God. No matter what some claim, Scripture is clear—no person has ever seen God. Even Jesus Christ Himself declared the same fact:

> **No one has ever seen God, but God the One and Only, who is at the Father's side, has made him known. (John 1:18)**

2. How then can we know God (v.12)? God is known only by love, only by His Spirit who dwells within believers. When a person believes in the love of God, that God loves us so much that He gave His Son to die for our sins, it pleases God supremely. God is perfectly pleased, for God loves His Son with a perfect love. Therefore, when a person honors God's Son by believing in Christ, God takes that person and puts His Spirit into the person. God actually implants His divine nature, the Holy Spirit, into the life of the believer. He does this so that His Son, the Lord Jesus Christ, will have many followers, followers who will honor Christ by living and loving just as He lived and loved.

Simply stated, we know God by love. If we love God, then we accept what God has done for us in Christ. When we accept Christ, God puts His Spirit in us. It is that simple. We simply know God by loving Him, loving Him for all that He has done for us in Christ. And when we love Him and love His Son, God just floods our being with His precious Holy Spirit.

Now note what happens when God begins to live and dwell in us (v.12). We love one another and God's love becomes perfected, that is, complete and fulfilled in us. We just grow and grow in love. We mature more and more, ever completing and perfecting the love of God upon earth.

3. Note one other thing: How do we know that we live in God and He in us (v.13)? By the Holy Spirit whom He has given to us. If we have the Holy Spirit living and dwelling in us, He bears witness with our spirit. It is impossible for God to be living within the body and life of a person and the person not know it. It is the Spirit of God who tells us that we have been saved and are in God and God in us.

Thought 1. If a person does not have the witness of God's Spirit within him, he needs to evaluate his conversion. The likelihood is that he has never been saved. Even if he is temporarily in a backslidden state, the Holy Spirit is convicting and bugging him to repent and turn back to God.

> But I tell you the truth: It is for your good that I am going away. Unless I go away, the Counselor will not come to you; but if I go, I will send him to you. When he comes, he will convict the world of guilt in regard to sin and righteousness and judgment: in regard to sin, because men do not believe in me; in regard to righteousness, because I am going to the Father, where you can see me no longer; and in regard to judgment, because the prince of this world now stands condemned. (John 16:7-11)

> And if the Spirit of him who raised Jesus from the dead is living in you, he who raised Christ from the dead will also give life to your mortal bodies through his Spirit, who lives in you. (Rom 8:11)

> The Spirit himself testifies with our spirit that we are God's children. (Rom 8:16)

> Because you are sons, God sent the Spirit of his Son into our hearts, the Spirit who calls out, "Abba, Father." (Gal 4:6)

> Those who obey his commands live in him, and he in them. And this is how we know that he lives in us: We know it by the Spirit he gave us. (1 John 3:24)

> We know that we live in him and he in us, because he has given us of his Spirit. (1 John 4:13)

> This is the one who came by water and blood—Jesus Christ. He did not come by water only, but by water and blood. And it is the Spirit who testifies, because the Spirit is the truth. (1 John 5:6)

4 (4:14-16) **Testimony—Confession—Love**: loving one another proves that our testimony and confession are true. This is the great testimony of John. But note how it is the testimony of every genuine believer as well.

1. There is John's declaration: that he and the early believers had seen and testified that the Father sent His Son to be the Savior of the world (v.14. See outline and notes—1 Jn.1:1-5 for discussion.)

2. There is the great promise to the whole human race: "If anyone acknowledges that Jesus is the Son of God, God lives in him and he in God." (v.15. See note—1 Jn.4:2-3 for discussion. Apply what is said about teachers to every person. Also see note, *Jesus Christ, Deity*—1 Jn.1:1 for more discussion.)

3. There is the great testimony and confession of John himself and the early believers: "and so we know and rely on the love that God has for us" (v.16). What is it that they knew and believed? Three things, and all three are critical. Note them closely.

   a. "God is love." God has sent His Son to be the Savior of the world. This is the way we know that God is love.

   b. Believers must love. They must live in love, love one another with all their hearts.

   c. Loving one another is the way we can tell that we are saved. If we live in love, then we live in God and God in us. The way we know that we live in God and God in us is by our love. If we love one another, then we are demonstrating the nature of God. If we are *not loving* one another, then we are demonstrating that we *do not have* the nature of God. Loving one another shows whether or not God is in us.

   ⇒ God is love; therefore, if we have the nature of God, we are loving people—all people—just as God loves them.

   ⇒ God is love, therefore, if we are *not loving* people, we *do not have* the nature of God. We *are not saved* no matter what we claim. The proof that we are saved, that we have the nature of God, is loving others.

> Then they asked him, "What must we do to do the works God requires?" Jesus answered, "The work of God is this: to believe in the one he has sent." (John 6:28-29)

> That if you confess with your mouth, "Jesus is Lord," and believe in your heart that God raised him from the dead, you will be saved. For it is with your heart that you believe and are justified, and it is with your mouth that you confess and are saved. (Rom 10:9-10)

> And every tongue confess that Jesus Christ is Lord, to the glory of God the Father. (Phil 2:11)

> No one who denies the Son has the Father; whoever acknowledges the Son has the Father also. (1 John 2:23)

> Dear children, let us not love with words or tongue but with actions and in truth. This then is how we know that we belong to the truth, and how we set our hearts at rest in his presence (1 John 3:18-19)

> We are from God, and whoever knows God listens to us; but whoever is not from God does not listen to us. This is how we recognize the Spirit of truth and the spirit of falsehood. Dear friends, let us love one another, for love comes from God. Everyone who loves has been born of God and knows God. Whoever does not love does not know God, because God is love. (1 John 4:6-8)

> If anyone acknowledges that Jesus is the Son of God, God lives in him and he in God. (1 John 4:15)

5 (4:17) **Assurance—Judgment—Boldness—Love**: loving one another proves that God is going to deliver us from judgment. Judgment is coming—a day of universal judgment when all persons will be brought before the great Judge Himself, the Lord Jesus Christ. This is the clear declaration of Scripture:

> But I tell you that men will have to give account on the day of judgment for every

careless word they have spoken. (Mat 12:36)

For the Son of Man is going to come in his Father's glory with his angels, and then he will reward each person according to what he has done. (Mat 16:27)

"When the Son of Man comes in his glory, and all the angels with him, he will sit on his throne in heavenly glory. All the nations will be gathered before him, and he will separate the people one from another as a shepherd separates the sheep from the goats. (Mat 25:31-32)

You, then, why do you judge your brother? Or why do you look down on your brother? For we will all stand before God's judgment seat. (Rom 14:10)

For we must all appear before the judgment seat of Christ, that each one may receive what is due him for the things done while in the body, whether good or bad. (2 Cor 5:10)

Since you know that you will receive an inheritance from the Lord as a reward. It is the Lord Christ you are serving. Anyone who does wrong will be repaid for his wrong, and there is no favoritism. (Col 3:24-25)

Just as man is destined to die once, and after that to face judgment, (Heb 9:27)

Since you call on a Father who judges each man's work impartially, live your lives as strangers here in reverent fear. (1 Pet 1:17)

If this is so, then the Lord knows how to rescue godly men from trials and to hold the unrighteous for the day of judgment, while continuing their punishment. (2 Pet 2:9)

By the same word the present heavens and earth are reserved for fire, being kept for the day of judgment and destruction of ungodly men. (2 Pet 3:7)

Enoch, the seventh from Adam, prophesied about these men: "See, the Lord is coming with thousands upon thousands of his holy ones to judge everyone, and to convict all the ungodly of all the ungodly acts they have done in the ungodly way, and of all the harsh words ungodly sinners have spoken against him." (Jude 1:14-15)

And I saw the dead, great and small, standing before the throne, and books were opened. Another book was opened, which is the book of life. The dead were judged according to what they had done as recorded in the books. (Rev 20:12)

But note the most wonderful thing: we can be delivered from judgment. We can face the great day of judgment boldly without dread and fear. How? By living a life of love, by loving one another completely. In fact, the fruit of love is having boldness in the day of judgment. If we love completely—if we allow our love to be complete and fulfilled—if we allow love to *live itself out* through us—then we will have boldness in the day of judgment. God will give us assurance that we shall not be judged, but on the contrary, we shall be rewarded.

How, then, is it possible to complete our love while on earth? By living in the world just as Jesus lived. Even as He was in the world, so we are to be in the world. That is, Jesus Christ loved when He was in the world; He walked in love. Therefore, we are to love one another while in the world. We are to bear witness and proclaim the love of God and love one another just as Christ did. This is to be the consuming passion of our lives. The more we love, the more we grow and become completed in love; and the more we grow and become completed in love, the more assurance and boldness we have about the future judgment. The more we love, the more assurance God gives us that we shall not be judged in that day.

Thought 1. Most people, even believers, are wrong in their ideas about the return of Christ. He is Judge as well as Savior. And believers are to be judged at the judgment seat of Christ. Some will be weeping even as others will be joyful. It all depends upon how we have lived, what we have done in our bodies and in our works for Him.

For we must all appear before the judgment seat of Christ, that each one may receive what is due him for the things done while in the body, whether good or bad. (2 Cor 5:10)

The only way to be assured of deliverance from judgment, of having boldness to stand with uplifted face, is to live a life of love—to love everyone more and more while on earth.

In him and through faith in him we may approach God with freedom and confidence. (Eph 3:12)

Let us then approach the throne of grace with confidence, so that we may receive mercy and find grace to help us in our time of need. (Heb 4:16)

That is why I am suffering as I am. Yet I am not ashamed, because I know whom I have believed, and am convinced that he is able to guard what I have entrusted to him for that day. (2 Tim 1:12)

Let us draw near to God with a sincere heart in full assurance of faith, having our hearts sprinkled to cleanse us from a guilty conscience and having our bodies washed with pure water. Let us hold unswervingly to the hope we profess, for he who promised is faithful. And let us consider how we may spur one another on toward love and good deeds. Let us not give up meeting together, as some are in the habit of doing, but let us encourage one another—and all the more as you see the Day approaching. (Heb 10:22-25)

We know that we have come to know him if we obey his commands. The man who says, "I know him," but does not do what he commands is a liar, and the truth is not in him. But if anyone obeys his word, God's love is truly made complete in him. This is how we know we are in him: (1 John 2:3-5)

Dear children, let us not love with words or tongue but with actions and in truth. This then is how we know that we belong to the truth, and how we set our hearts at rest in his presence whenever our hearts condemn us. For God is greater than our hearts, and he knows everything. Dear friends, if our hearts do not condemn us, we have confidence before God and receive from him anything we ask, because we obey his commands and do what pleases him. (1 John 3:18-22)

We know that we live in him and he in us, because he has given us of his Spirit. (1 John 4:13)

In this way, love is made complete among us so that we will have confidence on the day of judgment, because in this world we are like him. (1 John 4:17)

And this is the testimony: God has given us eternal life, and this life is in his Son. He who has the Son has life; he who does not have the Son of God does not have life. I write these things to you who believe in the name of the Son of God so that you may know that you have eternal life. (1 John 5:11-13)

6 (4:18) **Fear—Fearlessness—Love:** loving one another proves that God delivers us from fear. This is an excellent verse on fear and how to conquer fear. Note the four things said.

1. There is no fear in love. If we really love someone, there is no need to fear him. In fact, we will not fear him. If we love the person, sacrificially give him our very best, then we have done all we can. Our lives and what we have done are in God's hands. We will rest assured that we can do no more. A peace, an assurance, will sweep over our soul. Note this, for it is the promise of God: when we really love someone, really give sacrificially all that we can, God will give us a peace and an assurance of soul that erases all fear. Our souls will know no fear, only peace and assurance of God's care. This is the promise of God even if some people react against us and persecute us and martyr us. God will give us such a deep sense of His presence—so deep that we will be flooded with peace and assurance. This is what Peter calls "the Spirit of glory and of God" that rests upon the believer when he is reproached.

If you are insulted because of the name of Christ, you are blessed, for the Spirit of glory and of God rests on you. (1 Pet 4:14)

2. Perfect love drives out fear. This is critical to note, for only a love that is growing and growing will be blessed by God. A believer cannot love one person and hold feelings against another person. This is not love. True love is impartial. A person who really loves loves everyone. There is no such thing as a heart filled with love and hate. The two are incompatible. Therefore, the only believer who knows the peace and assurance of God is the believer who is being completed in love, the believer who is growing and growing in love, fulfilling and completing his love.

3. Fear has punishment; that is, it thinks about and expects punishment or suffering or loss. A person feels that something is going to happen to him. Such feelings, of course, cause all kinds of disturbance and problems for people, all to varying degrees. People fear all kinds of things:

⇒ suffering   ⇒ economic slump
⇒ divorce   ⇒ the future
⇒ loss of health   ⇒ God and His judgment
⇒ loss of a loved one   ⇒ loss of a job
⇒ loss of wealth   ⇒ heights, darkness ,etc.

Fear causes anxiety, dread, alarm, fright, panic, and terror. It causes all kinds of unpleasant emotions, phobias, neurosis, and even the more serious psychotic disorders. The torment of fear is one of the worst problems faced by man.

4. Fear means that a person is not made perfect in love.
⇒ The person is not fully grasping (perfected) the love and care of God for him (see note—1 Jn.4:9-11 for more discussion).
⇒ The person is not loving other people like he should; he is not growing more and more in love. His eyes are upon himself, not upon God and others like they should be.

In summary, fear can be driven out only by the perfect love of God. The more we know of God's love and care and the more we love other people, the more fear is conquered in our lives. The reason is clearly seen in the promises of God. God loves us so much that He will take care of us through all the trials and temptations of life, no matter what they are.

⇒ There is no need to fear people, the evil that they can do to us; God will strengthen and deliver us even through death.

At my first defense, no one came to my support, but everyone deserted me. May it not be held against them. But the Lord stood at my side and gave me strength, so that through me the message might be fully proclaimed and all the Gentiles might hear it. And I was delivered from the lion's mouth. The Lord will rescue me from every evil attack and will bring me safely to his heavenly kingdom. To him be glory for ever and ever. Amen. (2 Tim 4:16-18)

Even though I walk through the valley of the shadow of death, I will fear no evil, for you are with me; your rod and your staff, they comfort me. (Psa 23:4)

The LORD is with me; I will not be afraid. What can man do to me? (Psa 118:6)

So we say with confidence, "The Lord is my helper; I will not be afraid. What can man do to me?" (Heb 13:6)

⇒ There is no need to fear judgment. God delivers us from judgment.

Who is he that condemns? Christ Jesus, who died—more than that, who was raised to life—is at the right hand of God and is also interceding for us. Who shall separate us from the love of Christ? Shall trouble or hardship or persecution or famine or nakedness or danger or sword? (Rom 8:34-35)

⇒ There is no need to fear the dark or the enemies of the dark. God will take care of us.

What if some did not have faith? Will their lack of faith nullify God's faithfulness? Not at all! Let God be true, and every man a liar. As it is written: "So that you may be proved right when you speak and prevail

when you judge." But if our unrighteousness brings out God's righteousness more clearly, what shall we say? That God is unjust in bringing his wrath on us? (I am using a human argument.) (Rom 3:3-5)

You will not fear the terror of night, nor the arrow that flies by day, (Psa 91:5)

When you lie down, you will not be afraid; when you lie down, your sleep will be sweet. (Prov 3:24)

⇒ There is no need to fear not having food to eat or clothing.

So do not worry, saying, 'What shall we eat?' or 'What shall we drink?' or 'What shall we wear?' For the pagans run after all these things, and your heavenly Father knows that you need them. But seek first his kingdom and his righteousness, and all these things will be given to you as well. (Mat 6:31-33)

7 (4:19-21) **Love**: loving one another proves that we love God. How do we know that we love God? There are three ways.

1. We know that we love God because we know God's love for us (v.19). He loves us and we have seen His love; therefore, we love Him. (See note—1 Jn.4:9-11 for more discussion.)

2. We know that we love God because we do not hate our brother. If we love God, it is impossible to hold feelings against our brother. Why? Because God is love. If we have the nature of God in us, then we love our brothers. Note how strong this verse states the fact.

If anyone says, "I love God," yet hates his brother, he is a liar. For anyone who does not love his brother, whom he has seen, cannot love God, whom he has not seen. (v.20)

We cannot see God, but we can see our brothers. It is far easier to love someone in this world whom we can see than it is to love someone whom we cannot see. Therefore, if we say that we love God and hate those whom we see, we are lying.

3. We know that we love God because we obey His commandment. What is His commandment? If we love God, we are to love our brothers also.

"A new command I give you: Love one another. As I have loved you, so you must love one another. By this all men will know that you are my disciples, if you love one another." (John 13:34-35)

Again Jesus said, "Simon son of John, do you truly love me?" He answered, "Yes, Lord, you know that I love you." Jesus said, "Take care of my sheep." (John 21:16)

We know that we have passed from death to life, because we love our brothers. Anyone who does not love remains in death. Anyone who hates his brother is a murderer, and you know that no murderer has eternal life in him. This is how we know what love is: Jesus Christ laid down his life for us. And we ought to lay down our lives for our brothers. If anyone has material possessions and sees his brother in need but has no pity on him, how can the love of God be in him? (1 John 3:14-17)

And this is his command: to believe in the name of his Son, Jesus Christ, and to love one another as he commanded us. (1 John 3:23)

	CHAPTER 5	2 This is how we know that we love the children of God: by loving God and carrying out his commands.	2 Proof 2: Loving God & Obeying His commandments
	V. THE PROOF THAT ONE REALLY BELIEVES IN GOD: FOUR TESTS, 5:1-21		a. Proves one's love for God's children
		3 This is love for God: to obey his commands. And his commands are not burdensome,	b. Proves one's love for God
	A. Test 1: Being Born Again,*DS1* 5:1-5	4 For everyone born of God overcomes the world. This is the victory that has overcome the world, even our faith.	3 Proof 3: Conquering the world
1 Proof 1: Believing Jesus is the Christ	Everyone who believes that Jesus is the Christ is born of God, and everyone who loves the father loves his child as well.		a. Proves one's faith
a. Proves one's love for God		5 Who is it that overcomes the world? Only he who believes that Jesus is the Son of God.	b. Proves one really believes Jesus is the Son of God
b. Proves one's love for other believers			

DIVISION V

THE PROOF THAT ONE REALLY BELIEVES IN GOD: FOUR TESTS, 5:1-21

A. Test 1: Being Born Again, 5:1-5

(5:1-5) **Introduction**: practically every person claims that he believes in God. Few people claim to be atheistic or agnostic. Most people claim to believe in God and claim to have some idea in their minds about what God is like. But note this: people's beliefs and ideas differ. Quickly think across the world at the different beliefs and ideas of God, the beliefs and ideas of the Muslims, the Buddhists, the Jews, the Hindus, the Christians and so on. In reality, there are just about as many ideas about God as there are people upon earth, for every person has his own mind, and within his mind his own idea of God. This fact brings about a critical question: Who is right? Whose belief and idea of God is correct? One thing is sure: if God really exists, then it is of utmost importance that we be correct in what we believe and think about Him. For someday we shall all stand before Him and give an account to Him.

How can we tell if we believe in God, if our beliefs and concepts of God are accurate? How can we tell if we really believe in the *only living and true God*? This is the discussion of this last chapter of First John. There are four tests that will show us. The first test is basic: Have we been born of God? If we have been born of God, then we definitely believe in God. God would not have given His divine nature to a person who does not believe in Him. Therefore, if we have the divine nature of God, if we have been truly born again, then we believe in God, in the living and true God. But how can we tell if we have been born of God? There are three proofs.

1. Proof 1: believing Jesus is the Christ (v.1).
2. Proof 2: Loving God and obeying His commandments (v.2-3).
3. Proof 3: conquering the world (v.4-5).

DEEPER STUDY # 1
(5:1-5) **New Birth—Born Again—New Creation—Regeneration**: being born of God means a spiritual birth, a rebirth of one's spirit, a new life, a renewed soul, a regenerated spirit. It is the regeneration and renewal of one's spirit and behavior (2 Cor.5:17). It is the endowment of a new life, of a godly nature (2 Pt.1:4). The new birth is so radical a change in a person's life that it can be described only as being *born again*. Something so wonderful happens to the soul that it is just like a *new birth*. It is a spiritual birth, a birth beyond the grasp of man's hands and efforts.

It is so radical, so life-changing, and so wonderful that it can be wrought only by the love and power of God Himself.

The New Testament teaching on the new birth is rich and full.

1. The new birth is a necessity. A person will never see (Jn.3:3) nor ever enter (Jn.3:5) the Kingdom of God unless he is born again (Jn.3:7).
2. The new birth is a spiritual birth, the birth of a new power and spirit in life. It is not reformation of the old nature (Ro.6:6). It is the actual creation of a new birth within—spiritually (Jn.3:5-6; cp. Jn.1:12-13; 2 Cor.5:17; Eph.2:10; 4:24). (See notes—Eph.1:3; 4:17; DEEPER STUDY # 3—4:24.) A person is spiritually born again:
   a. By water, even the Spirit (see DEEPER STUDY # 2—Jn.3:5).
   b. By the will of God (Jas.1:18).
   c. By imperishable, incorruptible seed, even through the Word of God (1 Pt.1:23).
   d. By God from above (1 Pt.1:3). The words new birth (anagennao) in the phrase "given us new birth" can mean given a new birth from *above*. (Cp. Jn.1:12-13.)
   e. By Christ, who gives both the *power and right* to be born again (Jn.1:12-13).
3. The new birth is a definite experience, a real experience. A person experiences the new birth:
   a. By believing that Jesus is the Christ, the Son of God (1 Jn.5:1; cp. Jn.3:14-15).
   b. By the gospel as it is shared by believers (1 Cor.4:15; Phile.10).
   c. By the Word of God (1 Pt.1:23), or by the Word of Truth (Jas.1:18).
4. The new birth is a changed life, a totally new life. A person proves that he is born again:
   a. By doing righteous acts (1 Jn.2:29; cp. Eph.2:10; 4:24).
   b. By not practicing sin (1 Jn.3:9; 5:18).
   c. By loving other believers (1 Jn.4:7).
   d. By overcoming the world (1 Jn.5:4).
   e. By keeping himself (1 Jn.5:18).
   f. By possessing the divine seed or nature (1 Jn.3:9; 1 Pt.1:23; 2 Pt.1:14; cp. Col.1:27).

1 (5:1) **New Birth—Belief**: the first proof of the new birth is this: believing that Jesus is the *Christ*. The word *Christ* means *Messiah* or *Anointed One*. Jesus Christ is the Son of God anointed to be the Savior of the world. He was anointed by God for a very special mission, the mission of coming to earth to save man and to give man eternal life (see notes—1 Jn.2:1-2; DEEPER STUDY # 1—2:2; notes—3:23; 4:2-3; 4:9-11 for more discussion). The person who believes that Jesus is the *Anointed One* of God, that He was sent into the world to save man, that person is given a new birth by God.

⇒ He is "born of God."

> Everyone who believes that Jesus is the Christ is born of God, and everyone who loves the father loves his child as well. (1 John 5:1)

⇒ He is "born again."

> In reply Jesus declared, "I tell you the truth, no one can see the kingdom of God unless he is born again." "How can a man be born when he is old?" Nicodemus asked. "Surely he cannot enter a second time into his mother's womb to be born!" Jesus answered, "I tell you the truth, no one can enter the kingdom of God unless he is born of water and the Spirit. (John 3:3-5)

⇒ He is made into "a new creation."

> Therefore, if anyone is in Christ, he is a new creation; the old has gone, the new has come! (2 Cor 5:17)

⇒ He is made into "a new person, a new self."

> And to put on the new self, created to be like God in true righteousness and holiness. (Eph 4:24)
> And have put on the new self, which is being renewed in knowledge in the image of its Creator. (Col 3:10)

Note two significant facts.

1. A person who is "born of God" loves God. He cannot help loving God, for God does this most wonderful thing for him. God recreates him into a new creature who will live forever in God's presence. When we really think about what God has done for us in Christ, that God sacrificed His Son to save us, our hearts just flood with love for God.

Thought 1. We should often get alone and meditate on the great love of God. The very thought that God sacrificed His Son to bear our sins is enough to break us in humble adoration. But we must take time to get alone and study the Scriptures that cover God's love and sacrifice. We must take time to meditate upon the great truth in order to see and understand it in all its depth and meaning.

> "As the Father has loved me, so have I loved you. Now remain in my love. (John 15:9)

> No, the Father himself loves you because you have loved me and have believed that I came from God. (John 16:27)

> For Christ's love compels us, because we are convinced that one died for all, and therefore all died. (2 Cor 5:14)

> I have been crucified with Christ and I no longer live, but Christ lives in me. The life I live in the body, I live by faith in the Son of God, who loved me and gave himself for me. (Gal 2:20)

> Grace [God's salvation] to all who love our Lord Jesus Christ with an undying love. (Eph 6:24)

> Though you have not seen him, you love him; and even though you do not see him now, you believe in him and are filled with an inexpressible and glorious joy, (1 Pet 1:8)

> Keep yourselves in God's love as you wait for the mercy of our Lord Jesus Christ to bring you to eternal life. (Jude 1:21)

> Love the LORD your God with all your heart and with all your soul and with all your strength. (Deu 6:5)

2. A person who loves God will love other believers as well. Note why: because God has given other believers a spiritual birth as well. They are our brothers and sisters in Christ. They too have been born of God and made into new creatures. We are all of the family of God; God is our Father who has given birth to us all. Therefore, we are brothers and sisters of one another. We share…

- the same God
- the same Father
- the same rebirth
- the same divine nature
- the same adoption

The point is that we love one another. If we have truly been "born of God" and love God, then we love the whole family of God. We love all those who have been *born of God*; we love all our brothers and sisters in Christ.

Thought 1. True believers love one another. There are no believers who do not love their brothers and sisters in Christ. How can we say this? Because a true believer has the nature of God, and God is love. If a person has the nature of God (been born of God), then he loves: he loves the family of God. Differences do not matter, differences of…

- opinion
- color
- class
- neighborhood
- position
- race
- denomination
- social status

Nothing keeps us from loving one another if we have truly been born of God. The person who is born of God loves God, and he loves all those who love God. He loves his brothers and sisters in the Lord.

> "A new command I give you: Love one another. As I have loved you, so you must love one another. By this all men will know that you are my disciples, if you love one another." (John 13:34-35)

> My command is this: Love each other as I have loved you. (John 15:12)

> May the Lord make your love increase and overflow for each other and for every-

one else, just as ours does for you. (1 Th 3:12)

Now that you have purified yourselves by obeying the truth so that you have sincere love for your brothers, love one another deeply, from the heart. (1 Pet 1:22)

This is how we know what love is: Jesus Christ laid down his life for us. And we ought to lay down our lives for our brothers. (1 John 3:16)

2 (5:2-3) **Commandments—Love:** the second proof of the new birth is obedience. The person who is born of God loves God and obeys His commandments.

⇒ Do we really believe God? Yes, if we obey His commandments. No, if we do not obey His commandments. The person who *really believes* God, who *really casts himself* upon God and relies upon God, does what God says. He depends upon God's Word; he believes that God's Word works. Therefore, he obeys God.

⇒ Do we really love God (v.2)? Yes, if we obey His commandments. No, if we do not obey His commandments. If we really love God, really care for Him, then we want to please Him. We want to do what He says. Therefore, the person who really loves God is the person who obeys His commandments.

Now note what these two verses say:

1. Our obedience and love for God prove that we love the children of God. God commands us to love our brothers and sisters in Christ; therefore, if we obey God, we *must* love them. If we love God, then we obey Him and love one another.

Thought 1. A person has no choice; this is not an optional commandment. If a person is going to love God…
- he must obey God.
- he must obey by loving the other children of God—all of them no matter who they are.

2. Our obedience to God proves our love for God (v.3). In fact, this is the love of God, that we obey His commandment. Obeying God's commandment proves…
- that we *love* God
- that we *are loving* God
- that we *possess love* for God
- that we *lift up our hearts in love* to God

There is no other way to show God that we love Him except by doing what He says. Note: some people feel that God's commandments are grievous, a real burden. They feel that the commandments of Scripture restrict them too much, and keep a person from the pleasures and possessions of the world. They feel that to be a Christian disallows a person from having fun and enjoying life. To them the demands of God are just too large a price to pay, that demanding all one is and has is too much to ask of a person. But the exact opposite is true: Scripture declares that God's commandments are not grievous. They are not too large a burden for men to carry. How could this be, for there is no question: God demands the total allegiance of all one is and has.

⇒ Jesus Christ gives rest to the soul. All the restlessness, disturbance, distress, pain, and suffering that man experiences in this world is replaced by peace when a person turns his life over to God and begins to love and obey God.

"Come to me, all you who are weary and burdened, and I will give you rest. Take my yoke upon you and learn from me, for I am gentle and humble in heart, and you will find rest for your souls. For my yoke is easy and my burden is light." (Mat 11:28-30)

⇒ Jesus Christ never allows a trial or temptation to come upon a person beyond what the person can bear. Christ always provides the strength or the way to escape.

No temptation has seized you except what is common to man. And God is faithful; he will not let you be tempted beyond what you can bear. But when you are tempted, he will also provide a way out so that you can stand up under it. (1 Cor 10:13)

Now when I went to Troas to preach the gospel of Christ and found that the Lord had opened a door for me, (2 Cor 2:12)

Now to him who is able to do immeasurably more than all we ask or imagine, according to his power that is at work within us, (Eph 3:20)

For God did not give us a spirit of timidity, but a spirit of power, of love and of self-discipline. (2 Tim 1:7)

⇒ Jesus Christ gives a person the greatest hope in all the world; He gives us the greatest promises of reward. Therefore, when a person keeps his eyes upon the hope, the commandments of God become light and easy to bear.

In my Father's house are many rooms; if it were not so, I would have told you. I am going there to prepare a place for you. And if I go and prepare a place for you, I will come back and take you to be with me that you also may be where I am. (John 14:2-3)

It teaches us to say "No" to ungodliness and worldly passions, and to live self-controlled, upright and godly lives in this present age, while we wait for the blessed hope—the glorious appearing of our great God and Savior, Jesus Christ, (Titus 2:12-13)

So that, having been justified by his grace, we might become heirs having the hope of eternal life. (Titus 3:7)

⇒ God gives all true believers His Spirit, and the Spirit gives all the assurance, confidence, and security, and all the love, joy, and peace that one could ever need or want. The believer is filled with life and all the real and meaningful things of life. Therefore, the believer never thinks of God's commandments as being burdensome. They are a joy to him, for they bring abundant life to him.

But the fruit of the Spirit is love, joy, peace, patience, kindness, goodness, faithfulness, gentleness and self-control. Against such things there is no law. (Gal 5:22-23)

We have not received the spirit of the world but the Spirit who is from God, that we may understand what God has freely given us. (1 Cor 2:12)

"If you love me, you will obey what I command. And I will ask the Father, and he will give you another Counselor to be with you forever— the Spirit of truth. The world cannot accept him, because it neither sees him nor knows him. But you know him, for he lives with you and will be in you. I will not leave you as orphans; I will come to you. (John 14:15-18)

But the Counselor, the Holy Spirit, whom the Father will send in my name, will teach you all things and will remind you of everything I have said to you. Peace I leave with you; my peace I give you. I do not give to you as the world gives. Do not let your hearts be troubled and do not be afraid. (John 14:26-27)

⇒ God gives the true believer fellowship with Himself and with Christ, then He floods the heart of the believer with joy.

I have told you this so that my joy may be in you and that your joy may be complete. (John 15:11)

We write this to make our joy complete. (1 John 1:4)

3 (5:4-5) **Faith—New Birth—Victory—World**: the third proof of the new birth is this—we are overcoming the world. These two verses are two of the great verses of Scripture, verses that should be memorized and lived by every believer. Note that the same point is being made in every statement; the very same thing is being said three times. What emphasis! The point is to be understood and followed.

⇒ The person who is *born of God* overcomes the world.
⇒ The victory that overcomes the world is our *faith*.
⇒ The person who overcomes the world is the person who *believes* that Jesus Christ is the Son of God.

Who is it that is *born of God*? It is the person who *believes* that Jesus Christ is the Son of God. The world is overcome by faith. Victory is gained over the world by faith in Jesus Christ, by believing that Jesus Christ is the Son of God.

Now note: the one thing that man needs is victory over the world. Why? Because the world is full of...

- suffering
- disease
- accidents
- corruption
- hate
- bitterness
- immorality
- destroyed families
- wickedness
- drugs
- drunkenness
- envy

- murder
- war
- arguments
- backbiters
- pride
- arrogance
- hunger
- homelessness
- pain
- hurt
- selfishness
- greed

Then there is the most fatal blow of all: corruption and death. Without exception we are all corrupt and we all die. The one thing that man needs above all else is victory over the world with all its corruption and death. How then can he triumph and conquer the world? How can he overcome the world? By believing that Jesus Christ is the Son of God. When a person believes that Jesus Christ is the Son of God, God gives him a new heart. He is "born of God"— *spiritually born of God*. It is his faith that overcomes the world. What does this mean?

⇒ It means that God gives the believer victory over all the trials and temptations of life.

"I have told you these things, so that in me you may have peace. In this world you will have trouble. But take heart! I have overcome the world." (John 16:33)

No temptation has seized you except what is common to man. And God is faithful; he will not let you be tempted beyond what you can bear. But when you are tempted, he will also provide a way out so that you can stand up under it. (1 Cor 10:13)

The Lord will rescue me from every evil attack and will bring me safely to his heavenly kingdom. To him be glory for ever and ever. Amen. (2 Tim 4:18)

If this is so, then the Lord knows how to rescue godly men from trials and to hold the unrighteous for the day of judgment, while continuing their punishment. (2 Pet 2:9)

⇒ It means that God gives the believer victory over all the forces and difficulties of life.

Who shall separate us from the love of Christ? Shall trouble or hardship or persecution or famine or nakedness or danger or sword? No, in all these things we are more than conquerors through him who loved us. For I am convinced that neither death nor life, neither angels nor demons, neither the present nor the future, nor any powers, neither height nor depth, nor anything else in all creation, will be able to separate us from the love of God that is in Christ Jesus our Lord. (Rom 8:35, 37-39)

But thanks be to God, who always leads us in triumphal procession in Christ and through us spreads everywhere the fragrance of the knowledge of him. (2 Cor 2:14)

The LORD is my strength and my shield; my heart trusts in him, and I am helped. My heart leaps for joy and I will give thanks to him in song. (Psa 28:7)

So do not fear, for I am with you; do not be dismayed, for I am your God. I will strengthen you and help you; I will uphold you with my righteous right hand. (Isa 41:10)

But now, this is what the LORD says— he who created you, O Jacob, he who formed you, O Israel: "Fear not, for I have redeemed you; I have summoned you by name; you are mine. When you pass through the waters, I will be with you; and when you pass through the rivers, they will not sweep over you. When you walk through the fire, you will not be burned; the flames will not set you ablaze. (Isa 43:1-2)

⇒ It means that God gives the believer victory over sin.

For we know that our old self was crucified with him so that the body of sin might be done away with, that we should no longer be slaves to sin— because anyone who has died has been freed from sin. Now if we died with Christ, we believe that we will also live with him. (Rom 6:6-8)

In the same way, count yourselves dead to sin but alive to God in Christ Jesus. Therefore do not let sin reign in your mortal body so that you obey its evil desires. Do not offer the parts of your body to sin, as instruments of wickedness, but rather offer yourselves to God, as those who have been brought from death to life; and offer the parts of your body to him as instruments of righteousness. For sin shall not be your master, because you are not under law, but under grace. (Rom 6:11-14)

But now that you have been set free from sin and have become slaves to God, the benefit you reap leads to holiness, and the result is eternal life. (Rom 6:22)

He himself bore our sins in his body on the tree, so that we might die to sins and live for righteousness; by his wounds you have been healed. (1 Pet 2:24)

⇒ It means that God gives the believer victory over death.

"I tell you the truth, whoever hears my word and believes him who sent me has eternal life and will not be condemned; he has crossed over from death to life. (John 5:24)

Since the children have flesh and blood, he too shared in their humanity so that by his death he might destroy him who holds the power of death—that is, the devil— and free those who all their lives were held in slavery by their fear of death. (Heb 2:14-15)

⇒ It means that God gives the believer victory over judgment.

"For God so loved the world that he gave his one and only Son, that whoever believes in him shall not perish but have eternal life. For God did not send his Son into the world to condemn the world, but to save the world through him. Whoever believes in him is not condemned, but whoever does not believe stands condemned already because he has not believed in the name of God's one and only Son. (John 3:16-18)

But God demonstrates his own love for us in this: While we were still sinners, Christ died for us. Since we have now been justified by his blood, how much more shall we be saved from God's wrath through him! For if, when we were God's enemies, we were reconciled to him through the death of his Son, how much more, having been reconciled, shall we be saved through his life! (Rom 5:8-10)

⇒ It means that God gives the believer victory over fear and despair and fills him with love, joy, and peace.

Peace I leave with you; my peace I give you. I do not give to you as the world gives. Do not let your hearts be troubled and do not be afraid. (John 14:27)

"I have told you these things, so that in me you may have peace. In this world you will have trouble. But take heart! I have overcome the world." (John 16:33)

For if, when we were God's enemies, we were reconciled to him through the death of his Son, how much more, having been reconciled, shall we be saved through his life! Not only is this so, but we also rejoice in God through our Lord Jesus Christ, through whom we have now received reconciliation. (Rom 5:10-11)

But the fruit of the Spirit is love, joy, peace, patience, kindness, goodness, faithfulness, gentleness and self-control. Against such things there is no law. (Gal 5:22-23)

Be self-controlled and alert. Your enemy the devil prowls around like a roaring lion looking for someone to devour. Resist him, standing firm in the faith, because you know that your brothers throughout the world are undergoing the same kind of sufferings. And the God of all grace, who called you to his eternal glory in Christ, after you have suffered a little while, will himself restore you and make you strong, firm and steadfast. (1 Pet 5:8-10)

⇒ It means that God gives the believer victory over Satan and all other spiritual forces.

Put on the full armor of God so that you can take your stand against the devil's schemes. For our struggle is not against flesh and blood, but against the rulers, against the authorities, against the powers of this dark world and against the spiritual forces of evil in the heavenly realms. Therefore put on the full armor of God, so that when the day of evil comes, you may be able to stand your ground, and after you have done everything, to stand. (Eph 6:11-13)

And having disarmed the powers and authorities, he made a public spectacle of them, triumphing over them by the cross. (Col 2:15)

		water only, but by water and blood. And it is the Spirit who testifies, because the Spirit is the truth.	b. To come by blood (the cross & death)
B. Test 2: Believing the Testimony About Christ: That He is the Son of God (Part I), 5:6-8		7 For there are three that testify:	**2 There is the testimony of the Holy Spirit**
			3 There are the witnesses[DS1]
1 There is the mission of Jesus Christ	6 This is the one who came by water and blood—Jesus Christ. He did not come by	8 The Spirit, the water and the blood; and the three are in agreement.	a. The Holy Spirit
a. To come by water (baptism)			b. The water (baptism) of Christ
			c. The blood of Christ

DIVISION V

THE PROOF THAT ONE REALLY BELIEVES IN GOD: FOUR TESTS, 5:1-21

B. Test 2: Believing the Testimony About Christ: That He is the Son of God (Part I), 5:6-8

(5:6-8) Introduction: Do we really believe in God? There are four tests that will show us. The second test is striking: Do we believe the witness about Christ? There are several witnesses to Christ, strong witnesses.

The question arises: Is Jesus *the Christ*, the true Messiah, the promised Messiah of the Old Testament prophecies? Is Jesus Christ really the Savior of men, the One sent by God to earth to save men and to give them life? Is Jesus Christ really, beyond any question, the Son of God? There are very strong witnesses that emphatically declare, "Yes!" If a person believes these witnesses, then he believes in God. If he does not accept the witnesses to Jesus Christ, then he does not believe in God, not in the true and living God. Whatever *god* the person believes in, that *god* is a *god* of his own imagination. Why do we say this? Because God, the true and living God, loves man—loves him so much that He has sent His Son into the world to save man. And in addition to this glorious demonstration of love, God has given witness after witness that His Son has come into the world. All men are, therefore, without excuse if they reject the witnesses to Jesus Christ. The task of man is to receive the testimony of the witnesses, to believe the testimony about His Son, the Lord Jesus Christ.

1. There is the mission of Jesus Christ (v.6).
2. There is the testimony of the Holy Spirit (v.6).
3. There are the testimony of heaven (v.7-8).

1 (5:6) **Jesus Christ, Mission**: there is the mission of Jesus Christ. Note how John declares the mission of Christ:

> **"This is the one who came by water and blood Jesus Christ. He did not come by water only, but by water and blood" (v.6).**

This may seem like a strange way to state the mission of Christ, to say that Jesus "came by water [His baptism] and blood [His death]." But remember what has just been said in verse 5: a person must "believe that Jesus is the Son of God." Here in verse 6 John is declaring that beyond any question Jesus Christ is the Son of God. He was declared to be the Son of God...

• by His baptism, by the water.
• by His death, by the blood.

Both the water (His baptism) and the blood (His death) declare Him to be the Son of God. Both are extremely important.

1. The baptism of Jesus Christ is a great witness to Jesus Christ. It launched His mission upon earth. Two things happened at the baptism that were most unusual.

a. The Spirit of God came upon Christ in the form of a dove. Remember that John the Baptist was to be the forerunner of the Messiah. In order to point to the Messiah, John had to know who the Messiah was and to know beyond any question. Therefore, God told John that He would give him a sign, the sign of a dove. God would cause the Spirit of God to come upon His Son in the form of a dove. By this sign John would know the Messiah.

Then John gave this testimony: "I saw the Spirit come down from heaven as a dove and remain on him. I would not have known him, except that the one who sent me to baptize with water told me, 'The man on whom you see the Spirit come down and remain is he who will baptize with the Holy Spirit.' I have seen and I testify that this is the Son of God." (John 1:32-34)

Note how emphatic John is. He states the glorious truth as forcefully as he can: "I have seen, and I testify that this is the Son of God." The water, the baptism of Jesus Christ, declares emphatically that Jesus is the Son of God.

b. The *voice of God* proclaimed Jesus Christ to be the Son of God.
⇒ Matthew testifies that God's voice called Jesus Christ His Son.

And a voice from heaven said, "This is my Son, whom I love; with him I am well pleased." (Mat 3:17)

⇒ Mark testifies that God's voice called Jesus Christ His Son.

And a voice came from heaven: "You are my Son, whom I love; with you I am well pleased." (Mark 1:11)

⇒ Luke testifies that God's voice called Jesus Christ His Son.

And the Holy Spirit descended on him in bodily form like a dove. And a voice came from heaven: "You are my Son, whom I love; with you I am well pleased." (Luke 3:22)

2. The blood of Jesus Christ, His death and cross, declares Him to be the Son of God. It is by His death and cross that our sins are forgiven. He bore our sins upon the cross, took our judgment and suffered the punishment for

us. This is what He was doing upon the cross. And this is the glorious gospel. Since Jesus Christ took our sins and died for them, sin is removed from us. Christ has taken them off of us. We are free of sin; therefore, we become acceptable to God. Through the death of Jesus Christ, we are able to stand righteous and perfect before God. We are able to stand before God being free of sin, free because Jesus Christ took our sins and bore the judgment for them.

Now note: only the Son of God could do this; only the Son of God could die for man's sins. Why? Because God is perfect; He can accept only perfection. He can accept only the Ideal and Perfect Man. This is the reason God's Son had to come to earth and live as a Man. He had to come and live a sinless life; He had to secure the perfect and ideal righteousness; He had to become the Ideal and Perfect Man. By becoming such, He could then offer Himself as the perfect Sacrifice for man's sins. God would accept His sacrifice because it was the sacrifice of the Perfect and Ideal Man. It was the ideal that could cover and stand for every man.

This is the point: the blood of Jesus Christ, His cross and death, declare Him to be the Son of God who takes away the sins of the world. This is exactly what witness after witness declares.

> **This is my blood of the covenant, which is poured out for many for the forgiveness of sins. (Mat 26:28)**
>
> **Keep watch over yourselves and all the flock of which the Holy Spirit has made you overseers. Be shepherds of the church of God, which he bought with his own blood. (Acts 20:28)**
>
> **Since we have now been justified by his blood, how much more shall we be saved from God's wrath through him! (Rom 5:9)**
>
> **How much more, then, will the blood of Christ, who through the eternal Spirit offered himself unblemished to God, cleanse our consciences from acts that lead to death, so that we may serve the living God! (Heb 9:14)**
>
> **For you know that it was not with perishable things such as silver or gold that you were redeemed from the empty way of life handed down to you from your forefathers, but with the precious blood of Christ, a lamb without blemish or defect. (1 Pet 1:18-19)**
>
> **But if we walk in the light, as he is in the light, we have fellowship with one another, and the blood of Jesus, his Son, purifies us from all sin. (1 John 1:7)**
>
> **And from Jesus Christ, who is the faithful witness, the firstborn from the dead, and the ruler of the kings of the earth. To him who loves us and has freed us from our sins by his blood, (Rev 1:5)**
>
> **I answered, "Sir, you know." And he said, "These are they who have come out of the great tribulation; they have washed their robes and made them white in the blood of the Lamb. (Rev 7:14)**
>
> **And are justified freely by his grace through the redemption that came by Christ Jesus. God presented him as a sacrifice of atonement, through faith in his blood. He did this to demonstrate his justice, because in**

> **his forbearance he had left the sins committed beforehand unpunished— (Rom 3:24-25)**
>
> **You see, at just the right time, when we were still powerless, Christ died for the ungodly. (Rom 5:6)**
>
> **For what I received I passed on to you as of first importance : that Christ died for our sins according to the Scriptures, (1 Cor 15:3)**
>
> **And he died for all, that those who live should no longer live for themselves but for him who died for them and was raised again. (2 Cor 5:15)**
>
> **Christ redeemed us from the curse of the law by becoming a curse for us, for it is written: "Cursed is everyone who is hung on a tree." (Gal 3:13)**
>
> **In him we have redemption through his blood, the forgiveness of sins, in accordance with the riches of God's grace (Eph 1:7)**
>
> **In whom we have redemption, the forgiveness of sins. (Col 1:14)**
>
> **Who gave himself for us to redeem us from all wickedness and to purify for himself a people that are his very own, eager to do what is good. (Titus 2:14)**
>
> **He did not enter by means of the blood of goats and calves; but he entered the Most Holy Place once for all by his own blood, having obtained eternal redemption. The blood of goats and bulls and the ashes of a heifer sprinkled on those who are ceremonially unclean sanctify them so that they are outwardly clean. How much more, then, will the blood of Christ, who through the eternal Spirit offered himself unblemished to God, cleanse our consciences from acts that lead to death, so that we may serve the living God! (Heb 9:12-14)**
>
> **And they sang a new song: "You are worthy to take the scroll and to open its seals, because you were slain, and with your blood you purchased men for God from every tribe and language and people and nation. (Rev 5:9)**

2 (5:6) **Holy Spirit**: there is the testimony of the Holy Spirit that declares Jesus Christ to be the Son of God. This is what the gospel is—what has happened upon the world scene of human history:

⇒ God Himself has sent His Son into the world to save man from sin and death and condemnation.

⇒ Jesus, the carpenter from Nazareth, is actually the Son of God. He lived a sinless life—was the Perfect and Ideal Man who could die as the perfect sacrifice for the sins of men. And this He did when He died on the cross. He freed us from sin; therefore, we are now acceptable to God.

⇒ But note: we have to do something. We have to believe in God's Son. Unless we honor Him by believing in Him, God does not accept us. We still carry our sins and their guilt and condemnation ourselves. This means we stand condemned by God and shall never be allowed to live with Him.

This is the glorious gospel. But how can God get men to listen? How can He stir men to believe in Christ? There is only one way. He must put His Spirit upon earth to work within the hearts of men. This is the point of what is now said:

It is the Spirit who testifies, because the Spirit is the truth. (v.6)

Note: the Spirit of God is truth. He testifies because He is the truth. He can do nothing else but declare the truth. Jesus Christ is the Son of God sent into the world to save men; therefore, the Spirit of God must declare the truth. This is exactly what Jesus Christ promised.

The Spirit of truth. The world cannot accept him, because it neither sees him nor knows him. But you know him, for he lives with you and will be in you. (John 14:17)

"When the Counselor comes, whom I will send to you from the Father, the Spirit of truth who goes out from the Father, he will testify about me. (John 15:26)

"I have much more to say to you, more than you can now bear. But when he, the Spirit of truth, comes, he will guide you into all truth. He will not speak on his own; he will speak only what he hears, and he will tell you what is yet to come. He will bring glory to me by taking from what is mine and making it known to you. All that belongs to the Father is mine. That is why I said the Spirit will take from what is mine and make it known to you. (John 16:12-15)

We are from God, and whoever knows God listens to us; but whoever is not from God does not listen to us. This is how we recognize the Spirit of truth and the spirit of falsehood. (1 John 4:6)

How does the Spirit testify and bear witness in the world? Scripture says several ways.

⇒ The Holy Spirit testifies and bears witness by *convicting* the world of sin, righteousness, and judgment.

But I tell you the truth: It is for your good that I am going away. Unless I go away, the Counselor will not come to you; but if I go, I will send him to you. When he comes, he will convict the world of guilt in regard to sin and righteousness and judgment: in regard to sin, because men do not believe in me; in regard to righteousness, because I am going to the Father, where you can see me no longer; and in regard to judgment, because the prince of this world now stands condemned. (John 16:7-11)

⇒ The Holy Spirit testifies by quickening, giving life to men when they are willing to believe in Christ.

The Spirit gives life; the flesh counts for nothing. The words I have spoken to you are spirit and they are life. (John 6:63)

He has made us competent as ministers of a new covenant—not of the letter but of the Spirit; for the letter kills, but the Spirit gives life. (2 Cor 3:6)

⇒ The Holy Spirit testifies and bears witness by giving the believer assurance and guaranteeing his salvation.

Set his seal of ownership on us, and put his Spirit in our hearts as a deposit, guaranteeing what is to come. (2 Cor 1:22)

And you also were included in Christ when you heard the word of truth, the gospel of your salvation. Having believed, you were marked in him with a seal, the promised Holy Spirit, who is a deposit guaranteeing our inheritance until the redemption of those who are God's possession—to the praise of his glory. (Eph 1:13-14)

And do not grieve the Holy Spirit of God, with whom you were sealed for the day of redemption. (Eph 4:30)

Those who obey his commands live in him, and he in them. And this is how we know that he lives in us: We know it by the Spirit he gave us. (1 John 3:24)

⇒ The Holy Spirit testifies by bearing witness with the heart of believers, assuring them that they are children of God.

The Spirit himself testifies with our spirit that we are God's children. (Rom 8:16)

Because you are sons, God sent the Spirit of his Son into our hearts, the Spirit who calls out, "Abba, Father." (Gal 4:6)

Those who obey his commands live in him, and he in them. And this is how we know that he lives in us: We know it by the Spirit he gave us. (1 John 3:24)

We know that we live in him and he in us, because he has given us of his Spirit. (1 John 4:13)

This is the one who came by water and blood—Jesus Christ. He did not come by water only, but by water and blood. And it is the Spirit who testifies, because the Spirit is the truth. (1 John 5:6)

⇒ The Holy Spirit testifies by teaching the believer about Christ.

But the Counselor, the Holy Spirit, whom the Father will send in my name, will teach you all things and will remind you of everything I have said to you. (John 14:26)

This is what we speak, not in words taught us by human wisdom but in words taught by the Spirit, expressing spiritual truths in spiritual words. (1 Cor 2:13)

⇒ The Holy Spirit testifies by living within the believer and making his body a holy temple for God.

Don't you know that you yourselves are God's temple and that God's Spirit lives in you? (1 Cor 3:16)

Do you not know that your body is a temple of the Holy Spirit, who is in you, whom you have received from God? You are not your own; you were bought at a

price. Therefore honor God with your body. (1 Cor 6:19-20)

Guard the good deposit that was entrusted to you—guard it with the help of the Holy Spirit who lives in us. (2 Tim 1:14)

⇒ The Holy Spirit testifies by showing believers things to come.

But when he, the Spirit of truth, comes, he will guide you into all truth. He will not speak on his own; he will speak only what he hears, and he will tell you what is yet to come. (John 16:13)

⇒ The Holy Spirit testifies by giving believers the power to witness.

I am going to send you what my Father has promised; but stay in the city until you have been clothed with power from on high." (Luke 24:49)

But you will receive power when the Holy Spirit comes on you; and you will be my witnesses in Jerusalem, and in all Judea and Samaria, and to the ends of the earth." (Acts 1:8)

For God did not give us a spirit of timidity, but a spirit of power, of love and of self-discipline. So do not be ashamed to testify about our Lord, or ashamed of me his prisoner. But join with me in suffering for the gospel, by the power of God, (2 Tim 1:7-8)

⇒ The Holy Spirit testifies by proclaiming the things of God through believers.

We have not received the spirit of the world but the Spirit who is from God, that we may understand what God has freely given us. This is what we speak, not in words taught us by human wisdom but in words taught by the Spirit, expressing spiritual truths in spiritual words. (1 Cor 2:12-13)

For the Holy Spirit will teach you at that time what you should say." (Luke 12:12)

As for you, the anointing you received from him remains in you, and you do not need anyone to teach you. But as his anointing teaches you about all things and as that anointing is real, not counterfeit—just as it has taught you, remain in him. (1 John 2:27)

⇒ The Holy Spirit testifies by leading and guiding the believer.

But when he, the Spirit of truth, comes, he will guide you into all truth. He will not speak on his own; he will speak only what he hears, and he will tell you what is yet to come. (John 16:13)

Because those who are led by the Spirit of God are sons of God. (Rom 8:14)

For this God is our God for ever and ever; he will be our guide even to the end. (Psa 48:14)

You guide me with your counsel, and afterward you will take me into glory. (Psa 73:24)

Whether you turn to the right or to the left, your ears will hear a voice behind you, saying, "This is the way; walk in it." (Isa 30:21)

⇒ The Holy Spirit testifies by choosing believers for special ministry and gifting them for that ministry.

You did not choose me, but I chose you and appointed you to go and bear fruit—fruit that will last. Then the Father will give you whatever you ask in my name. (John 15:16)

While they were worshiping the Lord and fasting, the Holy Spirit said, "Set apart for me Barnabas and Saul for the work to which I have called them." (Acts 13:2)

There are different kinds of gifts, but the same Spirit. There are different kinds of service, but the same Lord. There are different kinds of working, but the same God works all of them in all men. Now to each one the manifestation of the Spirit is given for the common good. To one there is given through the Spirit the message of wisdom, to another the message of knowledge by means of the same Spirit, to another faith by the same Spirit, to another gifts of healing by that one Spirit, to another miraculous powers, to another prophecy, to another distinguishing between spirits, to another speaking in different kinds of tongues, and to still another the interpretation of tongues. All these are the work of one and the same Spirit, and he gives them to each one, just as he determines. (1 Cor 12:4-11)

⇒ The Holy Spirit testifies by making alive the mortal bodies of believers at death.

And if the Spirit of him who raised Jesus from the dead is living in you, he who raised Christ from the dead will also give life to your mortal bodies through his Spirit, who lives in you. (Rom 8:11)

3 (5:8) **Witnessing**: there are the witnesses that declare Jesus Christ to be the Son of God. Note that all three of these witnesses agree; they have only one message that they declare—Jesus Christ is the Son of God. Therefore, man must believe that "Jesus is the Son of God" (1 Jn.5:5). This is the only way that we can overcome and conquer the sin and death and condemnation of this world. Belief in Jesus Christ as the Son of God is the only way man can dwell forever with God.

1. There is the agreement of the Spirit (see note 2, *Holy Spirit*—1 Jn.5:6 for discussion).

2. There is the agreement of the water or baptism of Jesus Christ (see note 1, *Jesus Christ, Mission*, pt.1—1 Jn.5:6 for discussion).

3. There is the agreement of the blood or cross and death of Jesus Christ (see note above, pt.2—1 Jn.5:6 for discussion).

DEEPER STUDY # 1

(5:7) Witnessing—Testifying—The Word—God: Most scholars and most translations, almost without exception, agree that verse 7 was added by some copyist long after John wrote this epistle. Checking almost any translation of the Scripture will show that most Bibles omit the verse. The verse does not seem to be in any of the authentic Greek manuscripts before the sixteenth century. William Barclay gives an excellent discussion for the position that omits the verse. Matthew Henry gives an excellent discussion for the position that maintains the verse. Referring to these two commentators will give the two varying positions.) We are including commentary for those who follow the position of Matthew Henry, that the verse should read as follows:

> (v.7) "For there are three that testify in heaven: The Father, the Word and the Holy Spirit, and these three are one.
> (v.8) "And there are three that testify on earth, the Spirit, the water, and the blood: and these three agree in one."

There are three witnesses in heaven. There are three Persons who testify that Jesus Christ is the Son of God. Note what the scripture says: "for there are three that testify."

1. There is the Father. How does the Father bear witness that Jesus Christ is the Son of God? There are primarily two ways.

a. The Father is behind everything: the whole plan of redemption is His plan and work. It is His Son who came to earth to make salvation possible. It is also His Spirit who is working upon earth convicting and trying to get men to repent and to trust the Son of God for salvation. The Father is bearing witness to His Son through everything that is happening in the hearts and lives of believers and in the life of the church.

b. The Father bore dynamic witness to Christ when Christ was upon the earth.

⇒ He proclaimed Christ to be His Son at the baptism of Christ.

> **And a voice from heaven said, "This is my Son, whom I love; with him I am well pleased." (Mat 3:17)**

⇒ He proclaimed Christ to be His Son by giving Him the Holy Spirit without measure so that Christ could *speak the Word of God.*

> **For the one whom God has sent speaks the words of God, for God gives the Spirit without limit. (John 3:34)**

⇒ He proclaimed Christ to be His Son by enabling Him to do the very *miracles of God.*

> **Do not believe me unless I do what my Father does. But if I do it, even though you do not believe me, believe the miracles, that you may know and understand that the Father is in me, and I in the Father." (John 10:37-38)**

He proclaimed Christ to be His Son by causing the very glory of God to shine through His person at the transfiguration.

> **While he was still speaking, a bright cloud enveloped them, and a voice from the cloud said, "This is my Son, whom I love; with him I am well pleased. Listen to him!" (Mat 17:5)**

⇒ He proclaimed Christ to be His Son by raising Him from the dead.

> **In regard to righteousness, because I am going to the Father, where you can see me no longer; (John 16:10)**
> **And who through the Spirit of holiness was declared with power to be the Son of God by his resurrection from the dead: Jesus Christ our Lord. (Rom 1:4)**

2. There is the witness of the Word, the Lord Jesus Christ Himself. The Word, of course, refers to Jesus Christ. John declares this in both his Gospel and Epistle.

> **In the beginning was the Word, and the Word was with God, and the Word was God. (John 1:1)**
> **That which was from the beginning, which we have heard, which we have seen with our eyes, which we have looked at and our hands have touched—this we proclaim concerning the Word of life. (1 John 1:1)**

How does Christ as the Word testify? What does it mean to say that the Word testifies in heaven? Remember what a word is: the expression of an idea, a thought, an image in the mind of a person. God had an idea, a thought, an image; that is, He had a message, a word that He wanted to say to the world. But He wanted to say it in person. Therefore, He sent His Son into the world to speak the Word of God. As the Son of God, Jesus Christ had the very nature of God. By nature He was perfect even as God the Father is perfect. He was God the Son sent to earth by God the Father. This means that everything Jesus Christ did was perfect. He was the very embodiment of God Himself. He was the very revelation of God. Jesus Christ was everything that God wanted to say to man; He was the very Word of God.

This glorious fact means the most wonderful thing: it means that the Word of God has come to earth in the person of Jesus Christ. Everything that Jesus Christ said and did is the very thought and idea of God. Jesus Christ is the very Word that God wanted to say to man. Jesus Christ, the Word of God, bears witness to Himself. We can look at His words and deeds and see that He is the Son of God. We can look at the *picture of God*—the image, the idea, the expression of God—that Jesus Christ painted, and we can tell that He is the Son of God. All that He said, did, and was is the *perfect picture* of God. It is the *perfect description*, the *perfect Word* of God. The Word, Jesus Christ Himself, testifies that He is the Son of God.

3. There is the Holy Spirit (see note 2, *Holy Spirit—1 Jn.5:6* for discussion).

	C. Test 3: Believing the Testimony About Christ: That He is the Son of God (Part II), 5:9-15	God has given us eternal life, and this life is in his Son. 12 He who has the Son has life; he who does not have the Son of God does not have life.	clearly stated 1) God has given eternal life in His Son[DS1] 2) He who has the Son has life, & he who does not have the Son does not have life
1 There is the testimony of God Himself a. God's testimony is greater than any testimony of man b. God's testimony lives within the heart of the believer c. God's testimony is rejected by unbelievers	9 We accept man's testimony, but God's testimony is greater because it is the testimony of God, which he has given about his Son. 10 Anyone who believes in the Son of God has this testimony in his heart. Anyone who does not believe God has made him out to be a liar, because he has not believed the testimony God has given about his Son.	13 I write these things to you who believe in the name of the Son of God so that you may know that you have eternal life. 14 This is the confidence we have in approaching God: that if we ask anything according to his will, he hears us. 15 And if we know that he hears us—whatever we ask— we know that we have what we asked of him.	**2 There is the testimony of John** a. A person can be assured of eternal life b. A person can be assured of answered prayer 1) If we are in Christ 2) If we ask according to Christ's will 3) If we know that Christ hears prayer
d. God's testimony is	11 And this is the testimony:		

DIVISION V

THE PROOF THAT ONE REALLY BELIEVES IN GOD: FOUR TESTS, 5:1-21

C. Test 3: Believing the Testimony About Christ: That He is the Son of God (Part II), 5:9-15

(5:9-15) Introduction: Do we really believe in God? We can tell by testing ourselves, by asking this one question: Do we believe the testimonies about Christ? This passage covers two dynamic testimonies.

1. There is the testimony of God Himself (v.9-12).
2. There is the testimony of John (v.13-15).

1 (5:9-12) **Testimonies—Eternal Life**: there is the testimony of God. Note four significant points.

1. God's testimony is greater, far greater than the testimony of men (v.9). We believe the testimony of men, we accept what they say as true.

⇒ Spouses believe the word of one another.
⇒ Children believe the word of parents and teachers.
⇒ Businessmen believe the word of employers.
⇒ Juries believe the testimony of testimonies.

We all accept reports of the news media and the word of friends every day. This being so, how much greater is the testimony of God. Men interpret facts; they sometimes exaggerate and twist the facts. We are never completely free of personal opinion and interests. And some men even lie and deceive when sharing with us. But not God. God never exaggerates or twists the facts; He never lies or deceives. What God says is always true; it is the plain and simple truth. Therefore, God's record about His Son should be believed. Every human being should believe God's record of His Son. What is that testimony? Note what the verse says: "It is the testimony of God which He has *given about His Son.*" The testimony is that Jesus Christ is *His Son.* Jesus Christ is the Son of God whom God sent into the world to save man. It is this that we should believe.

2. God's testimony lives within the heart of the believer (v.10). When a person believes in the Son of God, God *implants the testimony of God* within him. What is that testimony? It is the *Spirit of God Himself.* The Holy Spirit seals and guarantees the believer, gives him assurance that Jesus Christ has saved him from sin, death, and condemnation and has made him acceptable to God.

Yet to all who received him, to those who believed in his name, he gave the right to become children of God— children born not of natural descent, nor of human decision or a husband's will, but born of God. (John 1:12-13)

From the fullness of his grace we have all received one blessing after another. For the law was given through Moses; grace and truth came through Jesus Christ. No one has ever seen God, but God the One and Only, who is at the Father's side, has made him known. (John 1:16-18)

The Spirit himself testifies with our spirit that we are God's children. Now if we are children, then we are heirs—heirs of God and co-heirs with Christ, if indeed we share in his sufferings in order that we may also share in his glory. (Rom 8:16-17)

Now it is God who makes both us and you stand firm in Christ. He anointed us, set his seal of ownership on us, and put his Spirit in our hearts as a deposit, guaranteeing what is to come. (2 Cor 1:21-22)

But when the time had fully come, God sent his Son, born of a woman, born under law, to redeem those under law, that we might receive the full rights of sons. Because you are sons, God sent the Spirit of his Son into our hearts, the Spirit who calls out, "Abba, Father." (Gal 4:4-6)

And you also were included in Christ when you heard the word of truth, the gospel of your salvation. Having believed, you were marked in him with a seal, the promised Holy Spirit, who is a deposit guaranteeing our inheritance until the redemption of those who are God's possession—to the praise of his glory. (Eph 1:13-14)

And do not grieve the Holy Spirit of God, with whom you were sealed for the day of redemption. (Eph 4:30)

Those who obey his commands live in him, and he in them. And this is how we know that he lives in us: We know it by the Spirit he gave us. (1 John 3:24)

We know that we live in him and he in us, because he has given us of his Spirit. (1 John 4:13)

This is the one who came by water and blood—Jesus Christ. He did not come by water only, but by water and blood. And it is the Spirit who testifies, because the Spirit is the truth. (1 John 5:6)

3. God's testimony is rejected by unbelievers (v.10b). This is strong language, but the person who does not believe that Jesus Christ is the Son of God makes God a liar. How could this be? Note the verse: because he does not believe the record that God gave of His Son. God has given testimony after testimony that Jesus Christ is His Son:

⇒ the testimony of the life of Christ, His miracles and words.
⇒ the testimony of the baptism of Christ.
⇒ the testimony of the blood, the cross and death, of Jesus Christ.
⇒ the testimony of the resurrection.
⇒ the testimony of the Scriptures.
⇒ the testimony of the Holy Spirit that convicts the human heart.
⇒ the testimony of believers who have experienced the power of Christ in their lives.

If a person does not believe the testimony of God—all the great testimonies that God has given—if a person does not believe that God has sent His Son into the world to save man—then that person is in effect saying that *the record is a lie*. But note: God did send His Son, and God has testified to the truth. Therefore, to disbelieve the record is to say that God is lying; it is to call God a liar, for God did send Christ.

"For God so loved the world that he gave his one and only Son, that whoever believes in him shall not perish but have eternal life. For God did not send his Son into the world to condemn the world, but to save the world through him. Whoever believes in him is not condemned, but whoever does not believe stands condemned already because he has not believed in the name of God's one and only Son. (John 3:16-18)

Whoever believes in the Son has eternal life, but whoever rejects the Son will not see life, for God's wrath remains on him." (John 3:36)

I told you that you would die in your sins; if you do not believe that I am the one I claim to be, you will indeed die in your sins." (John 8:24)

When he comes, he will convict the world of guilt in regard to sin and righteousness and judgment: in regard to sin, because men do not believe in me; (John 16:8-9)

4. God's testimony is clearly stated. Note how clearly and simply it is stated:

And this is the testimony: God has given us eternal life, and this life is in his Son. He who has the Son has life; he who does not have the Son of God does not have life. (v.11-12)

a. God has given us eternal life in His Son. The one thing man wants is to live forever. He does not want to die. But note: to live forever in a corruptible world such as ours would not necessarily be a good thing. This is a world of evil and corruption and death. Therefore, what we have now is not *real life*. It is not what life was meant to be. The life that God gives, eternal life, is the life that man was meant to live (see note, *Life*—1 Jn.5:11 for a discussion on what life is and how it comes through Jesus Christ).

b. The person who has the Son has life, but the person who does not have the Son does not have life. Why is this so? Because Jesus Christ is *the righteous One*. He is the Son of God who came to earth and lived a sinless life as Man. He is the One who secured the *perfect and ideal righteousness* for man. Therefore, Jesus Christ is the *only Person* who has the right to stand before God. Why? Because God is perfect, and only a perfect person can stand in God's presence. This is the reason man must approach God through Jesus Christ: He and He alone is perfect and righteous. He and He alone has the right to stand in the court of God as the Advocate or attorney to represent man. There is no other righteousness, no other goodness that is acceptable to God; only the perfect and ideal righteousness of Christ has been approved to stand as the advocate in the court of heaven.

This means a most wonderful thing. God will never turn down a person who has Jesus Christ as his advocate. The person who has Jesus Christ to approach God for him will never be turned down, for Jesus Christ has the right to stand as the advocate before God in the court of heaven. (See note—1 Jn.2:1-2; DEEPER STUDY # 1—2:2 for more discussion.)

DEEPER STUDY # 1

(5:11) **Life—Eternal Life**: life is one of the great words of the Scriptures. The word "life" (zoe) and the verb "to live" or "to have life" (zen) have a depth of meaning. (See DEEPER STUDY # 2—Jn.1:4; DEEPER STUDY # 1—17:2-3.)

1. Life is the energy, the force, the power of being.

Jesus answered, "I am the way and the truth and the life. No one comes to the Father except through me. (John 14:6)

Now this is eternal life: that they may know you, the only true God, and Jesus Christ, whom you have sent. (John 17:3)

2. Life is the opposite of perishing. It is deliverance from condemnation and death. It is the stopping or cessation of deterioration, decay, and corruption.

"For God so loved the world that he gave his one and only Son, that whoever believes in him shall not perish but have eternal life. (John 3:16)

"I tell you the truth, whoever hears my word and believes him who sent me has eternal life and will not be condemned; he has crossed over from death to life. and come out—those who have done good will rise to live, and those who have done evil will rise to be condemned. (John 5:24, 29)

I give them eternal life, and they shall never perish; no one can snatch them out of my hand. (John 10:28)

3. Life is eternal (aionios). It is forever. It is the very life of God Himself (Jn.17:3). However, eternal life does not refer just to duration. Living forever would be a curse for some persons. The idea of eternal life is also quality, a certain kind of life, a life that consistently knows love, joy, peace, power, and responsibility.

The thief comes only to steal and kill and destroy; I have come that they may have life, and have it to the full. (John 10:10)

4. Life is satisfaction.

Then Jesus declared, "I am the bread of life. He who comes to me will never go hungry, and he who believes in me will never be thirsty. (John 6:35)

5. Life is security and enjoyment.

The thief comes only to steal and kill and destroy; I have come that they may have life, and have it to the full. (John 10:10)

6. Life is found only in God. God is the source and author of life, and it is God who has appointed Jesus Christ to bring life to man. Jesus Christ gives the very life of God Himself to believers.

For as the Father has life in himself, so he has granted the Son to have life in himself. (John 5:26)
Do not work for food that spoils, but for food that endures to eternal life, which the Son of Man will give you. On him God the Father has placed his seal of approval." For my Father's will is that everyone who looks to the Son and believes in him shall have eternal life, and I will raise him up at the last day." (John 6:27, 40)
I give them eternal life, and they shall never perish; no one can snatch them out of my hand. (John 10:28)
I in them and you in me. May they be brought to complete unity to let the world know that you sent me and have loved them even as you have loved me. (John 17:23)

7. Life has now been revealed. It has been unveiled and is clearly seen in Jesus Christ. Jesus Christ shows man what life is.

In him was life, and that life was the light of men. The light shines in the darkness, but the darkness has not understood it. (John 1:4-5)

For as the Father has life in himself, so he has granted the Son to have life in himself. (John 5:26)
The life appeared; we have seen it and testify to it, and we proclaim to you the eternal life, which was with the Father and has appeared to us. (1 John 1:2)

Note: God gives us life through His Son, the Lord Jesus Christ. Life only comes to a man by believing in Jesus Christ. A man outside Jesus Christ only exists. He merely has an animalistic existence. Real life is found only in God. This is to be expected and it is logically true, for God is the Creator of life. As the Creator of life, He alone knows what life really is and what it is supposed to be (Jn.3:36; 5:24; 6:47). This is the reason He sent His Son, the Lord Jesus Christ into the world: to show man what life is. When a person looks at Jesus Christ he sees exactly what life is, exactly what it involves (cp. Gal.5:22-23):

⇒ love   ⇒ goodness
⇒ joy   ⇒ faithfulness
⇒ peace   ⇒ gentleness
⇒ patience   ⇒ self-control
⇒ kindness

2 (5:13-15) **Witnessing—Assurance—John the Apostle**: there is the witness of John himself. John bears testimony to two glorious things.

1. He declares that a believer can be assured of eternal life. And note the force of his declaration: we can *know*, that is, be perfectly *assured by experience*, that we have eternal life. We can experience eternal life and all that life was ever meant to be, and we can experience it now upon earth as well as in the future throughout all of eternity. We can *know by experience* that we have eternal life, know beyond a shadow of doubt, know absolutely and perfectly. How? John says there are three ways.

a. We receive eternal life by heeding the Scripture. John emphatically declares that he has written his Epistle so that we can have eternal life and *know that we have it*.

b. We receive eternal life by believing in the name of Jesus Christ. Only the person who believes on the name of the Son has eternal life.

c. We receive eternal life by continuing to believe in the name of Jesus Christ. Note: John is writing to believers, and he says that he has written so that believers "may believe on the name of the Son of God [Jesus Christ]." Do believers not already believe in Christ? Yes, but John is saying that we must continue to believe; we must endure in our belief, keep on believing and believing until the Lord takes us home. There is no such thing as a person believing and then ceasing to believe and then receiving eternal life. If a person forsakes Christ, it is clear evidence that he never received eternal life in the first place. If a person really knows the Son of God and has received eternal life, it is almost impossible for him to turn away from Christ for too long. Experiencing Christ and life is too wonderful. If a person happens to turn back for too long, to the point that he will not return to Christ, then God will go ahead and take him on home (see DEEPER STUDY # 1—1 Jn.5:16 for more discussion).

The point is this: we must believe in the name of God's Son and keep on believing. We must persevere and endure in our belief.

> **All men will hate you because of me, but he who stands firm to the end will be saved. (Mat 10:22)**

> **Jesus answered, "My teaching is not my own. It comes from him who sent me. If anyone chooses to do God's will, he will find out whether my teaching comes from God or whether I speak on my own. (John 7:16-17)**

> **To the Jews who had believed him, Jesus said, "If you hold to my teaching, you are really my disciples. Then you will know the truth, and the truth will set you free." (John 8:31-32)**

> **Because our gospel came to you not simply with words, but also with power, with the Holy Spirit and with deep conviction. You know how we lived among you for your sake. (1 Th 1:5)**

> **That is why I am suffering as I am. Yet I am not ashamed, because I know whom I have believed, and am convinced that he is able to guard what I have entrusted to him for that day. (2 Tim 1:12)**

> **See to it, brothers, that none of you has a sinful, unbelieving heart that turns away from the living God. (Heb 3:12)**

> **Let us, therefore, make every effort to enter that rest, so that no one will fall by following their example of disobedience. (Heb 4:11)**

> **Let us draw near to God with a sincere heart in full assurance of faith, having our hearts sprinkled to cleanse us from a guilty conscience and having our bodies washed with pure water. Let us hold unswervingly to the hope we profess, for he who promised is faithful. (Heb 10:22-23)**

> **We know that we have come to know him if we obey his commands. (1 John 2:3)**

2. John declares that a believer can be assured of answered prayer.

> **This is the confidence we have in approaching God: that if we ask anything according to his will, he hears us. And if we know that he hears us—whatever we ask—we know that we have what we asked of him. (1 John 5:14-15)**

This is a great passage on prayer. The very basis of prayer is covered. Note exactly what is said.

a. We can have confidence that God hears our prayers if we approach Him (v.14). We can approach God in Christ and in Christ alone. Christ alone is the *righteous One*, the only *perfect Person*; therefore He alone has the right to stand before God. Any person who wishes to approach God must come in the name of Jesus Christ. (See note—1 Jn.2:1-2 for more discussion.) A person must believe in the name of the Son of God and approach God in His name. The name of Jesus Christ is the only acceptable name to God, the only name that can receive anything from God.

b. We can have confidence that God hears our prayer if we ask according to His will (v.14). God has revealed His will in His Word. His will for us includes all the great things of life.

⇒ It is the will of God for us to experience the fruit of the spirit.

> **But the fruit of the Spirit is love, joy, peace, patience, kindness, goodness, faithfulness, gentleness and self-control. Against such things there is no law. (Gal 5:22-23)**

⇒ It is the will of God for us to have the provisions and necessities of life.

> **So do not worry, saying, 'What shall we eat?' or 'What shall we drink?' or 'What shall we wear?' For the pagans run after all these things, and your heavenly Father knows that you need them. But seek first his kingdom and his righteousness, and all these things will be given to you as well. Therefore do not worry about tomorrow, for tomorrow will worry about itself. Each day has enough trouble of its own. (Mat 6:31-34)**

⇒ It is the will of God for us to be protected and delivered through all the trials and temptations of life.

> **No temptation has seized you except what is common to man. And God is faithful; he will not let you be tempted beyond what you can bear. But when you are tempted, he will also provide a way out so that you can stand up under it. (1 Cor 10:13)**

> **So we say with confidence, "The Lord is my helper; I will not be afraid. What can man do to me?" (Heb 13:6)**

> **So do not fear, for I am with you; do not be dismayed, for I am your God. I will strengthen you and help you; I will uphold you with my righteous right hand. (Isa 41:10)**

⇒ It is the will of God for us to be delivered from sin, death, condemnation, and the fear of death.

> **"I tell you the truth, whoever hears my word and believes him who sent me has eternal life and will not be condemned; he has crossed over from death to life. (John 5:24)**

> **Since the children have flesh and blood, he too shared in their humanity so that by his death he might destroy him who holds the power of death— that is, the devil— and free those who all their lives were held in slavery by their fear of death. (Heb 2:14-15)**

⇒ It is the will of God for us to be delivered through severe persecution and trouble, to be delivered *into the very presence of God*.

When they heard this, they were furious and gnashed their teeth at him. But Stephen, full of the Holy Spirit, looked up to heaven and saw the glory of God, and Jesus standing at the right hand of God. "Look," he said, "I see heaven open and the Son of Man standing at the right hand of God." (Acts 7:54-56)

The Lord will rescue me from every evil attack and will bring me safely to his heavenly kingdom. To him be glory for ever and ever. Amen. (2 Tim 4:18)

We could go on and on listing the glorious promises that God makes to us, promises that should fill our prayers as we face the various events and difficulties of life. The point is this: we can boldly know that God will hear us when we pray according to His will.

c. We can have confidence that God hears our prayers if we know that He hears (v.15). We have to know that He hears if we wish to receive what we ask. It is foolish to waste time asking God unless we believe that He will hear us. We must have confidence in God, believe that He loves us and will do what He promises for us. This is the declaration of Scripture time and again.

If you believe, you will receive whatever you ask for in prayer." (Mat 21:22)

Therefore I tell you, whatever you ask for in prayer, believe that you have received it, and it will be yours. (Mark 11:24)

If you remain in me and my words remain in you, ask whatever you wish, and it will be given you. (John 15:7)

And without faith it is impossible to please God, because anyone who comes to him must believe that he exists and that he rewards those who earnestly seek him. (Heb 11:6)

And receive from him anything we ask, because we obey his commands and do what pleases him. (1 John 3:22)

This is the confidence we have in approaching God: that if we ask anything according to his will, he hears us. (1 John 5:14)

	D. Test 4: Living Free of Sin, 5:16-21	to sin; the one who was born of God keeps him safe, and the evil one cannot harm him.	c. Result: Untouched by Satan
1 By praying for a sinning brother[DS1] a. The brother is seen visibly sinning b. One exception to praying for he sinning brother: If he commits the *sin that leads to death*	16 If anyone sees his brother commit a sin that does not lead to death, he should pray and God will give him life. I refer to those whose sin does not lead to death. There is a sin that leads to death. I am not saying that he should pray about that.	19 We know that we are children of God, and that the whole world is under the control of the evil one. 20 We know also that the Son of God has come and has given us understanding, so that we may know him who is true. And we are in him who is true—even in	**3 By knowing that one is born of God & that the world is under the power of Satan** **4 By receiving the spiritual understanding that is given by Christ** a. To know God who is true
2 By keeping oneself from sin a. By knowing all wrongdoing is sin b. By the new birth & the keeping power of God's Son	17 All wrongdoing is sin, and there is sin that does not lead to death. 18 We know that anyone born of God does not continue	his Son Jesus Christ. He is the true God and eternal life. 21 Dear children, keep yourselves from idols.	b. To know we are in God & in His Son, the Lord Jesus Christ c. To know that knowing God is eternal life **5 By keeping oneself from idols**

DIVISION V

THE PROOF THAT ONE REALLY BELIEVES IN GOD: FOUR TESTS, 5:1-21

D. Test 4: Living Free of Sin, 5:16-21

(5:16-21) **Introduction**: Do we really believe in God? There are four tests that will clearly show us. This is the fourth and final test: Are we living free of sin or not? If we live in sin, it is clear proof we do not believe in God. But if we live in righteousness, live a life that is free of sin, then this is clear proof that we do believe in God. The person who wants to be acceptable to God must live a life of righteousness. He must live for God. No person should ever think that he can live a life of sin and be acceptable to God. The test of whether or not we believe God is the test of sin: Are we living in sin or not? This passage discusses the great subject of how to live free of sin.

1. By praying for a sinning brother (v.16).
2. By keeping oneself from sin (v.17-18).
3. By knowing that one is born of God and that the world is under the power of Satan (v.19).
4. By receiving the spiritual understanding that is given by Christ (v.21).
5. By keeping oneself from idols (v.21).

1 (5:16) **Sin—Prayer—Judgment**: How do we live free of sin? First, by praying for sinning brothers. If we are praying for believers who are living in sin, then we are concerned about sin, about living righteous lives. Scripture is clear: we are to pray for sinning brothers. But note: there is one time when we are not to pray for a sinning brother. When? When he has committed a "sin that leads to death" (see DEEPER STUDY # 1, *Sin*—1 Jn.5:16 for discussion).

DEEPER STUDY # 1
(5:16) **Sin—Believer's Judgment**: this is a difficult passage. It is one of those passages where there are almost as many different interpretations as there are words in the passage. The one thing that is clear is this: this passage is a severe warning. It is a warning so severe that one must walk ever so righteously; one must trust the Lord Jesus Christ to grant the power to overcome sin.

There are several passages of Scripture that issue a severe warning and speak of the sinful behavior of believers...

- sinful behavior that causes loss of all reward by fire—a loss so great one is stripped as much as a burned-out building. It is the loss of all except the bare salvation of oneself (1 Cor.3:11-15, esp.v.15).
- sinful behavior that destroys the flesh [sinful nature] so that the Spirit may be saved (1 Cor.5:5).
- sinful behavior that can cause a person to become disqualified (1 Cor.9:27).
- sinful behavior that causes death for a believer (1 Cor.11:29-30, esp. v.30; 1 Jn.5:16).
- sinful behavior that merits no escape (Heb.2:1-3; 12:25f).
- sinful behavior that prohibits a person from ever repenting again (Heb.6:4f).
- sinful behavior that causes a person to miss God's rest (Heb.4:1f).
- sinful behavior that prohibits any future sacrifice for sins and merits terrible punishment (Heb. 10:26f).
- sinful behavior that entangles a person in the corruption of the world after he has come to the knowledge of the Lord Jesus Christ (2 Pt.2:20).
- sinful behavior that leads to death (1 Jn.5:16).

There are basically two positions on the "sin that leads to death" that need to be looked at and studied.

1. The first position sees the *sin that leads to death* as being spiritual and eternal death. Some who hold this position believe that it can be committed only by a person who makes a *false profession*; others think that it can be committed by *genuine believers*. Note these facts.

a. First, note the word *brother*. The word *brother* means either true believers or professing believers who commit the *sin that leads to death*. The person who commits the sin that leads to death is a *church member*.

b. Second, note that the words life and death must correspond. If it is spiritual and eternal life that God gives to a person, then the sin that leads to death has to be referring to spiritual and eternal death. (The Greek scholar Marvin Vincent points this out. *Word Studies In The New Testament*, Vol.1, p.371.) Note what the verse is saying:

God will give him life. (v. 16)

What kind of life is John talking about? Physical or spiritual life? The context points strongly to spiritual and eternal life. This has been the whole discussion of this passage: for example...

He who has the Son has life; he who does not have the Son of God does not have life. (v. 12)

Again, if the life that God gives is spiritual and eternal life, then the *sin that leads to death* must correspond; it must mean the opposite, that is, spiritual and eternal death. Note what the full verse says:

If anyone sees his brother commit a sin that does not lead to death, he should pray and God will give him life. I refer to those whose sin does not lead to death. There is a sin that leads to death. I am not saying that he should pray about that. (v. 16)

c. Third, does this mean that a believer can commit sin to the point that he is doomed to spiritual and eternal death? If so, what do we do with passages of Scripture where *God assures Christ* that He will never lose a single brother who genuinely believes in Him? Passages and promises such as these...

- God will allow no genuine believer to be snatched out of His hand.

    I give them eternal life, and they shall never perish; no one can snatch them out of my hand. My Father, who has given them to me, is greater than all ; no one can snatch them out of my Father's hand. (John 10:28-29)

- God has predestinated believers to the image of Christ so that Christ will have many brothers.

    For those God foreknew he also predestined to be conformed to the likeness of his Son, that he might be the firstborn among many brothers. (Rom 8:29)

- God will perform the work of salvation and growth until the day of Jesus Christ.

    Being confident of this, that he who began a good work in you will carry it on to completion until the day of Christ Jesus. (Phil 1:6)

- God shields the believer by His power.

    Who through faith are shielded by God's power until the coming of the salvation that is ready to be revealed in the last time. (1 Pet 1:5)
    That is why I am suffering as I am. Yet I am not ashamed, because I know whom I have believed, and am convinced that he is able to guard what I

have entrusted to him for that day. (2 Tim 1:12)

To him who is able to keep you from falling and to present you before his glorious presence without fault and with great joy— to the only God our Savior be glory, majesty, power and authority, through Jesus Christ our Lord, before all ages, now and forevermore! Amen. (Jude 1:24-25)

To repeat the question above, does the *sin that leads to* death mean that a believer can commit sin to the point that he is doomed to spiritual and eternal death?

⇒ Once a person is *born again* by the Spirit of God, can he be *unborn*?
⇒ Once a person receives the divine nature of God, once the divine nature has been incorporated into the fiber of his being, can the divine nature be taken away and unincorporated? (Cp. 2 Pt.1:4.)
⇒ Once a person has been given the imperishable, incorruptible seed and nature, can he again become perishable, corruptible? (Cp. 1 Pt.1:23; 1 Pt.1:3-4.)
⇒ Once a person has been created into *a new creation* in Christ, can he become the *old creation* again? (Cp. 2 Cor.5:17.)
⇒ Once a person is transformed from the *old person, the old self* into the *new person, the new self*, can he be re-transformed and changed back into the *old person, the old person*? (Cp. Eph.4:22-24.)
⇒ Once the Spirit of God enters a person's life and turns the person's body into a *holy temple*, does the Spirit ever leave a person? (Cp. Jn.14:16-17; 1 Cor.3:16-17; 6:19-20.)
⇒ Once our Lord Jesus Christ Himself has entered the life of a person, does God ever lose the life to such a point that His Son has to leave the life? (Cp. Jn.14:16-18; 14:20; 17:23; Gal.2:20; Col.1:27; Rev.3:20.)

Now note: all this would have to be possible and would have to happen if the *sin that leads to death* refers to a genuine believer. Does the *sin that leads to death* refer...

- to a genuine believer or to a professing believer?
- to a person who looks like a brother but is a false believer?

John himself refers to some *professing believers* who had committed the terrible sin of denying Christ. He calls them antichrists (plural), persons who had been in the church and who had professed Christ, but who had turned away from Christ and stood opposed to Him.

Note that these persons had been in the church, but they had forsaken Christ and had left the church. Picture the scene: there would still be friends and perhaps family members in the church who loved them and cared for them and who wanted them to be led back to Christ and His church. Therefore, they would be praying for them to return. But note: their sin is so great that

John does not encourage people to pray for them. He does not forbid it, but he does not encourage it. He simply says: "I am not saying that he [the true believer, the loved one] should pray about that [the sin that leads to death]."

Note what John says about these whom he calls antichrists:

Dear children, this is the last hour; and as you have heard that the antichrist is coming, even now many antichrists have come. This is how we know it is the last hour. They went out from us, but they did not really belong to us. For if they had belonged to us, they would have remained with us; but their going showed that none of them belonged to us. (1 John 2:18-19)

d. Now what is the *sin that leads to death*? Marvin Vincent (the Greek scholar) says that it is "the tendency...to cut the bond of fellowship with Christ....[it is] whatever breaks the fellowship with the soul and Christ, and, by consequence, with the individual and the body of believers...for there is no life apart from Christ." He says that the sin arises from the character of a person who is "alien from God." That is, the person never knew God, not really. His profession was false to begin with (*Word Studies In The New Testament*, Vol.1, p.371). Kenneth Wuest, who is also a Greek scholar, says,

"'The sin that leads to death' refers in the context in which John is writing, to the denial of the Incarnation...it would be committed by those whom John designates as antichrists, who did not belong to the true Christian body of believers, but were unsaved" (*In These Last Days*. "Word Studies in the Greek New Testament," Vol.4. Grand Rapids, MI: Eerdmans, 1946, p.181).

Kenneth Wuest also quotes the Greek scholar Henry Alford of the *Alford Greek Testament* as saying:

"There are those who have gone out from us, not being of us (2:19), who are called antichrists, who not only 'have not' Christ, but are Christ's enemies, denying the Father and the Son (2:22), whom we are not even to receive into our houses nor to greet (II John 10, 11). These seem to be the persons pointed out here, and this is the sin, namely, the denial that Jesus is the Christ, the incarnate Son of God. This alone of all sins bears upon it the stamp of severance from Him who is the Life itself. As the confession of Christ, with the mouth and in the heart, is salvation unto life (Rom.10:9), so denial of Christ with the mouth and in the heart, is sin that leads to death" (*In These Last Days*. "Word Studies in the Greek New Testament," Vol.4, p.181).

A.T. Robertson, another Greek scholar, says:
"John conceives of a sin that is deadly enough to be called unto death'....There is a distinction in Heb.10:26 between sinning willfully after full knowledge and sins of ignorance (Heb.5:2). Jesus spoke of the unpardonable sin (Mk.3:29; Mt.12:32; Lk.12:10), which was attributing to the devil the manifest work of the Holy Spirit. It is possible that John has this idea in mind when he applies it to those who reject Jesus Christ as God's Son and set themselves up as antichrists" (*Word Pictures In The New Testament*, Vol.6, p.243f).

William Barclay says that the Greek for "sin that leads to death" (harmatia pros thanaton) means "the sin which is going towards death, the sin whose end is death, the sin which, if continued in, must finish in death" (*The Letters of John and Jude*, p.142). He says that the sin is...
- persistent sin
- obstinate sin
- deliberate sin
- cold-blooded sin
- wide open sin
- purposeful sin

He says that the *sin that leads to death* is committed by a man...
- who persists in sin
- who rejoices in sin
- who never thinks of temptation as a sin
- who has no regret for sinning
- who glories in his sin
- who boasts in his sin
- who is proud of his sin
- who is proud that he knows how to get away with his sin
- who delights in sin

In his usual descriptive way, William Barclay describes the person who commits the *sin that leads to death*:

"Now in life it is a fact of experience that there are two kinds of sinners....So long as a man in his heart of hearts hates sin and hates himself for sinning, so long as he knows that he is sinning, he is never beyond repentance, and, therefore, never beyond forgiveness; but once a man begins to revel in sin, and to make sin the deliberate policy of his life, and loses all sense of the terror and the awfulness of sin, and also the feeling of self-disgust, he is on the way to death, for he is on the way to a state where the idea of repentance will not, and cannot enter his head.

"The sin that leads to death is the state of the man who has listened to sin so often, and refused to listen to God so often, that he has come to a state when he loves his sin, and when he regards sin as the most profitable thing in the world" (*The Letters of John and Jude*, p.142).

The conclusion of this interpretation would be one of two conclusions:

First, there are some who conclude that the sin that leads to death refers to a professing believer, a person who makes a profession only, a false profession. Therefore, he was never really converted...

- never born again
- never indwelt by the Holy Spirit
- never filled with the divine nature
- never indwelt by Christ
- never made into a new man
- never created into a new creature
- never filled with the incorruptible nature

Because of this, the person is easily led back into the world and into sin. He leaves the fellowship of believers and of the church and returns to the possessions and pleasures of the world. He stands opposed to Christ, not really believing that Jesus Christ is the Son of God.

Second, there are others who conclude that the sin that leads to death refers to genuine believers. The person who commits the sin that leads to death was genuinely converted, but he now becomes unconverted.

⇒ He loses his *new birth*; he is no longer born again.
⇒ He loses his *divine nature*; it is taken from him.
⇒ He loses the *Holy Spirit*; the Holy Spirit leaves the body of the believer and turns the body back into a temple for sin and death.
⇒ He loses the *new person, the new self*; his new self is re-transformed back into the old self.
⇒ He loses the creation of the *new creation*; he is recreated back into the old creation.
⇒ He loses the indwelling presence of Christ; God loses the sinner to the point that Christ has to leave him.

Now note: as stated in the beginning, if the life that God gives is spiritual and eternal life, then the sin that leads to death has to be spiritual and eternal death. Therefore, the person who commits the sin is either a genuine believer or only a professing believer, a person making a false profession. John does call the person a *brother*. Therefore, we can say that this means he is definitely a genuine believer. Or, we can say that every professing believer in the church *looks* like a brother to us, but many are not. They are making a false profession, and very practically, we cannot always tell who is a genuine brother and who is a false brother. We can say that John knew this as well as we do; therefore, he is calling every church member a brother, but making it clear that some are making a false profession. They are committing *sin that leads to death*. Whatever position we take, we must make sure that we are taking it because we are convinced that it is the teaching of God's Word. We must never hold a position because of such things as denomination, church, friends, teachers, or education. We must study the Word and let the Word interpret and speak for itself. And where there are difficult passages, we must come to the best conclusion we can under the guidance of the Holy Spirit. There is no question that the warnings of Scripture given to believers are some of the most difficult passages to interpret in all of Scripture. Perhaps God has deliberately made them this way to warn us how terrible sin is, that we must watch and guard against sin—that sin points to a false profession—that sin can and does lead to severe consequences—that we must be careful to make our profession sure and steadfast—that we can not deliberately and willfully sin and be obstinate and hardened in sin, not without suffering the most severe consequences.

2. The second position sees the sin that leads to death as referring to physical death. Briefly stated, these commentators say that the person is a genuine believer who falls into sin so deeply that he has to be severely disciplined by God and taken on home to be with Him. They look at the passage dealing with the sinful behavior of believers and say that a believer can continue in sin and can practice sin, and that there is no question about this. The believer still has freedom of choice.

And despite the tug and the pull of the Holy Spirit within, every honest believer knows what it is to succumb and give in to sin. Most believers even know what it is to practice sin for awhile without repentance. It is only the patience of God that convicts and that leads to repentance.

This position would say this: perhaps it is possible for a believer to continue in sin so long that he reaches a point of no return (see note—Acts 5:5-6). He is so rooted and imbedded in sin that God knows he will never repent. Now if such is possible, only God could know it. Only God can know the heart of a man to such a point that He knows the future of the man. If a man reaches that point of no repentance, his testimony and service on earth is forever ruined and forever useless. In fact, he has brought disrepute and dishonor to the name of Christ. He has harmed the Lord's cause, and so long as he is on earth, he will continue to add to the sin of the world and to heap abuse upon the name of Christ. His very purpose for living upon the earth as a Christian is lost and gone forever. The desire to return to the Lord and to live for Him, and to witness to His saving grace will never be aroused in his heart again. God knows this. But despite all this, God still loves him. And God has determined, for Christ's sake, that His purpose will be fulfilled in every single believer (Ro.8:29). Not a single believer shall be snatched out of His hand (Jn.10:28). Thus, God takes the believer on to be with Him. God goes ahead and unites the believer with Christ, His dear Son (cp. 1 Cor.11:29-30).

There are several examples in Scripture that seem to be warning and speaking to men about the same sinful behavior. There is the example...

- of Moses' death (Dt.32:48-52).
- of Israel and the golden calf (Gen.32:1-35).
- of the man who gathered sticks on the Sabbath right after the Sabbath was instituted (Num. 15:32-36).
- of Nadab and Abihu (Lev.10:1-2).
- of Korah (Num.16:31-34).
- of Achan (Josh.7:16-26).
- of Uzziah (2 Sam.6:1-7).
- of Ananias and Sapphira (Acts 5:1-11).
- of the man who had slipped into a shameful immoral sin (1 Cor.5:1-5).
- of some who had slipped into sin and were mocking God by partaking of the Lord's Supper without repenting (1 Cor.11:27-30).

Oliver Greene says:

"What IS 'the sin unto death?' The best place to find the answer is in Paul's letter to the church at Corinth. If you will study the eleventh chapter of 1 Corinthians in its entirety, you will find that some of the believers were grievously misbehaving at the Lord's table, making gluttons of themselves and drinking until they became intoxicated....'FOR THIS CAUSE many are weak and sickly among you, AND MANY SLEEP (are dead).'

"Paul also warned the Corinthian Christians that if they would judge themselves, repent of their misbehaving in the house of God and straighten up, God would not be forced to judge them; but if they did not judge themselves, God would have no alternative but to judge and chasten them, that they should 'not be condemned with the world' (1 Cor.11:32).

"The 'sin unto death' therefore is continually rebelling against light. When a believer knows what he should do, when he is convicted that he should do it, and yet he refuses to obey the Holy Spirit and the Word of God, he is in danger of committing the sin unto death.

"We have another instance of this in 1 Corinthians 5:1-5, when immorality was found in the church. A young man had taken his father's wife and was guilty of fornication. There are those who will not agree that this young man was saved and had committed the sin unto death, but Paul clearly told the other believers in the church what action they should take in the matter:

"'In the name of our Lord Jesus Christ, when ye are gathered together, and my spirit, with the power of Lord Jesus Christ, to deliver such an one unto satan, for the destruction of the flesh, that the spirit may be saved in the day of the lord Jesus' (1 Cor.5:4, 5).

"Beloved, it is clear that the sin that leads to death has nothing to do with the salvation of the soul; it has to do with the destruction of the body. Such a person will 'suffer loss, but he himself shall be saved; yet so as by fire' (1 Cor.3:12-15). All reward is lost, and such a one will stand before God empty handed. What that will mean, I confess I do not know; but according to the passage from 1 Corinthians, the person who loses his reward will 'suffer loss' - not loss of soul and spirit, but loss of eternal reward" (*The Epistles of John*, p.211).

Oliver Greene gives an excellent illustration in the life of Abraham:

"But 'there IS a sin unto death,' and when a believer has committed that sin there is no point in praying for him. In the life of Abraham we find an illustration of a time when it was useless to pray. In Genesis 18:20-30 God revealed to Abraham that He was going to destroy Sodom and Gomorrah. Abraham knew that his nephew Lot and his family were living in Sodom, so he drew near to God and asked, 'Wilt thou also destroy the righteous with the wicked? Peradventure there be fifty righteous within the city: wilt thou also destroy and not spare the place for the fifty righteous that are therein?' The Lord replied, 'If I find in Sodom fifty righteous within the city, then I will spare all the place for their sakes.' But there could not be fifty righteous men found in all of Sodom - and Abraham continued to pray until the number was reduced to ten - just ten righteous people in the great city of Sodom. And the Lord said, I will not destroy it for ten's sake.' But God knew that ten righteous ones could not be found in the city, and verse 33 tells us that 'THE LORD WENT HIS WAY, as soon as He had left communing with Abraham.'

"With God there is a stopping place, a limit; and Abraham had reached that limit in his intercession for Sodom. God ceased communing with him and left him. What God actually said in departing was, 'Abraham, there is no need to pray any longer. There is no need for you to make further request. Pray no more for Sodom, for that city must be destroyed!' When a city or an individual has committed such sin, there is no reason for any Christian to pray for that city or that individual.

"There are times when we should no longer pray for certain people, there are times when we should no longer witness to certain people. Concerning things spiritual Jesus said, 'Give not that which is holy unto the dogs, neither cast ye your pearls before swine, lest they trample them under their feet, and turn again and rend you' (Matt.7:6)" (*The Epistles of John*, p.210f).

Thought 1. Whatever our position, we must always remember this: the answer to sin is repentance and confession. As long as a person is still alive, he can repent and confess his sin and God will forgive him and restore him into the fellowship of His dear Son. As long as we are living, there is still hope; there is assurance of forgiveness and cleansing if we will only repent and confess.

I tell you, no! But unless you repent, you too will all perish. (Luke 13:3)

Repent, then, and turn to God, so that your sins may be wiped out, that times of refreshing may come from the Lord, (Acts 3:19)

Repent of this wickedness and pray to the Lord. Perhaps he will forgive you for having such a thought in your heart. (Acts 8:22)

In him we have redemption through his blood, the forgiveness of sins, in accordance with the riches of God's grace (Eph 1:7)

If we confess our sins, he is faithful and just and will forgive us our sins and purify us from all unrighteousness. (1 John 1:9)

Let the wicked forsake his way and the evil man his thoughts. Let him turn to the LORD, and he will have mercy on him, and to our God, for he will freely pardon. (Isa 55:7)

2 (5:17-18) **Unrighteousness—Sin—Wrongdoing**: How do we live free of sin? By keeping ourselves free from sin. Two things are essential in order to live free of sin.

1. We must know that *all wrongdoing* is sin. Too many people think too lightly of some sins. They rank sins, feeling that some sins are not so bad and are more acceptable to God. They feel that...

- some sins are small; others are big.
- some sins are white; others are black.
- some sins are more permissible; others are less permissible.
- some sins are more acceptable; others are less acceptable.

But note what Scripture says: *"all wrongdoing is sin."* There is not a single act of wrongdoing that is not sin. There is only one sin that is ranked as a *sin that leads to death*. As seen above, that sin is either apostasy, denying that Jesus Christ is the Son of God, or else obstinate and persistent sin that just refuses to repent. This is the ultimate sin, the unpardonable sin. But God does not list this sin to say that we can commit all the other sins and get away with them. He tells us about the *sin that leads to death* in order to warn us that we can sin too much. We can turn away from Christ too often, so often that we become engulfed and encrusted with sin—so hardened that we cannot break away. We doom ourselves if we continue to sin. All wrongdoing is sin; no matter how small and white or how permissible and acceptable we may think the act of wrongdoing is, it is sin to God. And if we persist in it, we are moving toward becoming so engulfed and encrusted in it that we border on the *sin that leads to death*.

The point is this: the way we live free of sin is to know that all wrongdoing is sin. There is not an act of wrongdoing that is not sin. No matter what we think, no matter how we may rank sin, there is no rank of sin with God. Sin is sin; wrongdoing is wrongdoing. We must repent and forsake all sin—know that all wrongdoing is sin—if we are to live free of sin.

> **The wrath of God is being revealed from heaven against all the godlessness and wickedness of men who suppress the truth by their wickedness, (Rom 1:18)**
>
> **Do not offer the parts of your body to sin, as instruments of wickedness, but rather offer yourselves to God, as those who have been brought from death to life; and offer the parts of your body to him as instruments of righteousness. (Rom 6:13)**
>
> **But the man who has doubts is condemned if he eats, because his eating is not from faith; and everything that does not come from faith is sin. (Rom 14:23)**
>
> **Anyone, then, who knows the good he ought to do and doesn't do it, sins. (James 4:17)**
>
> **They will be paid back with harm for the harm they have done. Their idea of pleasure is to carouse in broad daylight. They are blots and blemishes, reveling in their pleasures while they feast with you. (2 Pet 2:13)**
>
> **Everyone who sins breaks the law; in fact, sin is lawlessness. (1 John 3:4)**

2. We must be born of God and put ourselves under the keeping power of God's Son, the Lord Jesus Christ (v.18). This is a difficult verse. Looking at several translations will help us to see what it is saying.

⇒ The New American Standard says:

> **"We know that no one who is born of God sins; but He [the Son of God] who was born of God keeps him and the evil one does not touch him."**

⇒ Williams says:

> **"We know that no one who is born of God makes a practice of sinning, but the Son who was born of God continues to keep him, and the evil one cannot touch him."**

⇒ The Amplified New Testament says:

> **"We know [absolutely] that anyone born of God does not [deliberately and knowingly] practise committing sin, but the One Who was begotten of God carefully watches over and protects him - Christ's divine presence within him preserves him against the evil - and the wicked one does not lay hold (get a grip) on him or touch [him]."**

Every person has sinned and is guilty of sin. We have all ignored God, neglected God, disbelieved God, disobeyed God, rebelled against God, and rejected God. Therefore, we are unacceptable to God. We are alienated and separated from God. We cannot live in God's presence. God is perfect, and no imperfect person can live in His presence.

But this is the glorious gospel. God sent His Son into the world to save man. Jesus Christ took our sins upon Himself and bore the guilt and judgment for them. Our sins are taken off of us, removed from us. Jesus Christ took them off. Therefore, we are free of sin. When we really believe in Jesus Christ, God counts the death of Christ for us. He counts our sins as having been paid by Christ. He counts us as being free of sin; He counts us as righteous. Therefore, we are acceptable to Him. But remember: it is all through Christ.

Now note this: when this happens, when we truly believe in Christ and we become free of sin, God does a most wonderful thing for us.

⇒ He recreates our spirit, causes us to be born again.

> **In reply Jesus declared, "I tell you the truth, no one can see the kingdom of God unless he is born again." Jesus answered, "I tell you the truth, no one can enter the kingdom of God unless he is born of water and the Spirit. (John 3:3, 5)**
>
> **For you have been born again, not of perishable seed, but of imperishable, through the living and enduring word of God. (1 Pet 1:23)**

⇒ He makes us into a new creation.

> **Therefore, if anyone is in Christ, he is a new creation; the old has gone, the new has come! (2 Cor 5:17)**

⇒ He recreates us into a new person, a new self.

And to put on the new self, created to be like God in true righteousness and holiness. (Eph 4:24)

And have put on the new self, which is being renewed in knowledge in the image of its Creator. (Col 3:10)

In the words of this verse, we are *born of God* (v.18). This is the way we keep ourselves from sin: being born of God. By being born of God, all of our past sins are removed from us. We are not guilty of a single sin because of Jesus Christ. Because Jesus Christ took our sins upon Himself, we are freed of sin. We stand acceptable to God.

But note: What about the sins we commit now and the sins we have committed since we first believed in Christ? How can we live free of them? Again, by the keeping power of God's Son. If we genuinely confess our sins, if we are sincere, if we struggle and struggle against sin, if we keep coming to Jesus Christ for the forgiveness of sins, then the blood of Jesus Christ continues to cleanse us from sin. Jesus Christ is eternal; He is the Ideal and Perfect Man, the Ideal Man who made the perfect sacrifice for sins. Therefore, His perfect sacrifice stands for and covers sin forever and ever.

The point is the most striking and wonderful news in all the world: we can be free of sin through Jesus Christ. All we have to do is cast ourselves upon Him *continually*. When we do this, He purifies us from sin continually (1 Jn.1:9).

The word "keep" (tereo) means to keep a watchful eye over. Jesus Christ keeps His eye upon those who truly trust Him. He knows who they are, for they are...

- always coming to Him
- always walking with Him
- always fellowshipping and communing with Him
- always praying, praising, and confessing their shortcomings and sins

Note that the wicked one does not touch the genuine believer. This does not mean that the believer never sins. The word "harm" (hapto) means to lay hold of, grasp, and grip. The idea is that Satan cannot touch the believer to harm him. The genuine believer is under the keeping power of Jesus Christ; his sins are covered under the blood of Jesus Christ.

Peter replied, "Repent and be baptized, every one of you, in the name of Jesus Christ for the forgiveness of your sins. And you will receive the gift of the Holy Spirit. (Acts 2:38)

"Therefore, my brothers, I want you to know that through Jesus the forgiveness of sins is proclaimed to you. (Acts 13:38)

In him we have redemption through his blood, the forgiveness of sins, in accordance with the riches of God's grace (Eph 1:7)

In fact, the law requires that nearly everything be cleansed with blood, and without the shedding of blood there is no forgiveness. (Heb 9:22)

But if we walk in the light, as he is in the light, we have fellowship with one another, and the blood of Jesus, his Son, purifies us from all sin. (1 John 1:7)

If we confess our sins, he is faithful and just and will forgive us our sins and purify us from all unrighteousness. (1 John 1:9)

And from Jesus Christ, who is the faithful witness, the firstborn from the dead, and the ruler of the kings of the earth. To him who loves us and has freed us from our sins by his blood, (Rev 1:5)

3 (5:19) **World—Satan**: How do we live free of sin? By knowing that we are born of God and that the whole world is under the power of the evil one. What does this mean? How is the world under the power of Satan?

⇒ It means that Satan has *brought corruption and deterioration to the world*. The world is passing away. The world is corruptible and deteriorating and will eventually be destroyed. Therefore, do not become attached to the world; be attached to God and to heaven. Do not love the world so much that you desire to stay here more than you desire to be with God and in heaven.

⇒ It means that Satan has *affected the governments and societies of the world*. He has corrupted the hearts and minds, laws and rules of man. No government and no set of laws are perfect in governing the nations and societies of the earth. Therefore, believers must respect and be loyal to the good, but reject and stand against the bad. Believers must not love any organization more than they love God, not to the point that they are more attached to the systems of man's organizations than they are to God and heaven.

⇒ It means that Satan has *injected and infected the world with sin and with lust, evil, pride, and rebellion against God*. The world is full of sinful people, people who are evil and full of lust and pride; it is full of people who are in rebellion against God. Do not love this sinful system of the world.

The world is not as God created it, neither the earth and heavens nor the people in them. They have all been corrupted in their very nature: they are aging, deteriorating, and passing away. And man himself has rebelled against God, become disobedient and unbelieving. He curses and rejects God with ever so many breaths, and he lives a selfish life, doing what he wants and seeking the pleasures and passions of the world. The end result is death and doom, utter destruction for both himself and his world.

The point is this: How does the believer live free of sin? How does he conquer and live victoriously over sin? By knowing that the world is in opposition to God, that it lies under the power of the wicked one. When the believer knows this, then he knows that he must not touch the world. He must separate himself from the worldliness of the world and live for God, for he is born of God.

If you belonged to the world, it would love you as its own. As it is, you do not belong to the world, but I have chosen you out of the world. That is why the world hates you. (John 15:19)

With many other words he warned them; and he pleaded with them, "Save yourselves from this corrupt generation." (Acts 2:40)

Therefore, I urge you, brothers, in view of God's mercy, to offer your bodies as living sacrifices, holy and pleasing to God—this is your spiritual act of worship. Do not conform any longer to the pattern of this world, but be transformed by the renewing of your mind. Then you will be able to test and approve what God's will is—his good, pleasing and perfect will. (Rom 12:1-2)

"Therefore come out from them and be separate, says the Lord. Touch no unclean thing, and I will receive you." "I will be a Father to you, and you will be my sons and daughters, says the Lord Almighty." (2 Cor 6:17-18)

Have nothing to do with the fruitless deeds of darkness, but rather expose them. (Eph 5:11)

In the name of the Lord Jesus Christ, we command you, brothers, to keep away from every brother who is idle and does not live according to the teaching you received from us. (2 Th 3:6)

Do not love the world or anything in the world. If anyone loves the world, the love of the Father is not in him. For everything in the world—the cravings of sinful man, the lust of his eyes and the boasting of what he has and does—comes not from the Father but from the world. (1 John 2:15-16)

4 (5:20) **Knowledge—Assurance**: How do we live free of sin? By receiving the spiritual understanding that is given by Christ. Note: the understanding being spoken about is the spiritual understanding that is given by Christ and by Christ alone. Understanding other areas of life will not deliver us from sin. Deliverance from sin is not found in understanding…

- emotion
- behavior
- psychology
- medicine
- sociology
- education
- philosophy
- religion

All of these are important and have their place in society, but there is only one understanding that can deliver us from sin: the spiritual understanding that Jesus Christ gives. The human mind has to be enlightened to understand who Christ is. Our minds have to be quickened to receive Christ as our Savior from sin, quickened by Christ Himself.

Jesus Christ gives us spiritual understanding so that we can know three things.

1. Jesus Christ gives us the knowledge of God, to know that God is true: that God does exist; that God is behind all things; that God is the Maker and Creator of all things—both heaven and earth and all that is therein.

2. Jesus Christ gives us the knowledge that we are in God and in His Son, the Lord Jesus Christ; that we have been born of God; that God has placed us in Him and in His Son; that we live, move, and have our being in God and in Christ; that we are secure forever and ever in God and His dear Son because we are in the very divine nature of God Himself.

3. Jesus Christ gives us the knowledge that we know the true God who lives eternally: that we are in Him; that we have eternal life; that we will never die, but will live with God forever and ever.

Jesus answered, "My teaching is not my own. It comes from him who sent me. If anyone chooses to do God's will, he will find out whether my teaching comes from God or whether I speak on my own. (John 7:16-17)

To the Jews who had believed him, Jesus said, "If you hold to my teaching, you are really my disciples. Then you will know the truth, and the truth will set you free." (John 8:31-32)

Now this is eternal life: that they may know you, the only true God, and Jesus Christ, whom you have sent. (John 17:3)

But let him who boasts boast about this: that he understands and knows me, that I am the LORD, who exercises kindness, justice and righteousness on earth, for in these I delight," declares the LORD. (Jer 9:24)

Let us acknowledge the LORD; let us press on to acknowledge him. As surely as the sun rises, he will appear; he will come to us like the winter rains, like the spring rains that water the earth." (Hosea 6:3)

5 (5:21) **Idolatry**: How do we live free of sin? By keeping ourselves from idols. This exhortation closes the Epistle of First John. Note the tenderness with which John speaks: he calls the believers "dear children." He is the aged and faithful minister who has served God for decade after decade. He has served God by reaching people for Christ and by building up the believers of the Lord's church. He loves every believer, loves them ever so dearly. He counts them as his *dear children* in the faith.

Note another fact as well: this exhortation is directed to believers. It is believers who must guard and keep themselves from idols. What does John mean?

An idol is anything that takes first place in a person's life, anything that a person puts before God. An idol is anything that consumes man's focus and concentration, that consumes his energy and efforts more than God. A person can make an idol out of anything in this world; a person can take anything and worship it before God; he can allow it to consume his mind and thoughts and life:

⇒ houses	⇒ money
⇒ lands	⇒ comfort
⇒ job	⇒ television
⇒ position	⇒ sex
⇒ wives	⇒ food
⇒ children	⇒ power
⇒ cars	⇒ possessions
⇒ boats	⇒ pleasures
⇒ sports	⇒ recreation

Dear children, keep yourselves from idols. [Set God before your face; look full into His wonderful face. Follow after Him with all the diligence you can arouse, for your life, all the fulness of life—all the meaning, purpose, and significance of life—all the love and joy and peace of life—all the assurance and confidence and security of life—it is all found in the worship of God, in the worship of our Lord and Savior Jesus Christ.] (1 John 5:21)

Then he said to them, "Watch out! Be on your guard against all kinds of greed; a man's life does not consist in the abundance of his possessions." (Luke 12:15)

Although they claimed to be wise, they became fools and exchanged the glory of

the immortal God for images made to look like mortal man and birds and animals and reptiles. (Rom 1:22-23)

But among you there must not be even a hint of sexual immorality, or of any kind of impurity, or of greed, because these are improper for God's holy people. (Eph 5:3)

Put to death, therefore, whatever belongs to your earthly nature: sexual immorality, impurity, lust, evil desires and greed, which is idolatry. (Col 3:5)

Do not be hasty in the laying on of hands, and do not share in the sins of others. Keep yourself pure. (1 Tim 5:22)

Religion that God our Father accepts as pure and faultless is this: to look after orphans and widows in their distress and to keep oneself from being polluted by the world. (James 1:27)

Dear children, keep yourselves from idols. (1 John 5:21)

Keep yourselves in God's love as you wait for the mercy of our Lord Jesus Christ to bring you to eternal life. (Jude 1:21)

"You shall not make for yourself an idol in the form of anything in heaven above or on the earth beneath or in the waters below. (Exo 20:4)

Be careful, or you will be enticed to turn away and worship other gods and bow down to them. (Deu 11:16)

"I am the LORD; that is my name! I will not give my glory to another or my praise to idols. (Isa 42:8)

THE

OUTLINE & SUBJECT INDEX

REMEMBER: When you look up a subject and turn to the Scripture reference, you have not only the Scripture, you have *an outline and a discussion* (commentary) of the Scripture and subject.

This is one of the *GREAT VALUES* of **The Preacher's Outline & Sermon Bible**®. Once you have all the volumes, you will have not only what all other Bible indexes give you, that is, a list of all the subjects and their Scripture references, *BUT* you will also have…

- An outline of *every* Scripture and subject in the Bible.
- A discussion (commentary) on every Scripture and subject.
- Every subject supported by other Scriptures or cross references.

DISCOVER THE GREAT VALUE for yourself. Quickly glance below to the very first subject of the Index of First John. It is:

> **ABIDE - ABIDING**
> Duty to **a**. In the walk and life of Christ. 2:6; 3:23-24

Turn to the reference. Glance at the Scripture and outline of the Scripture, then read the commentary. You will immediately see the GREAT VALUE of the INDEX of **The Preacher's Outline & Sermon Bible**®.

OUTLINE AND SUBJECT INDEX

ABIDE - ABIDING (See **CONTINUE - CONTINUING**)
Duty to **a**. In the walk and life of Christ. 2:6; 3:23-24
Proof of.
    Faithfulness. 2:17
    How one knows God **a**. within. 3:24
    One is born again. 2:28-29
    One's love. 4:12-16
    Righteousness. 2:29
Results of **a**.
    Confident. 2:28-29
    Keeps one from sin. 3:6
    Power. 2:24; 2:27
    Unashamedness. 2:28
Source of **a**.
    A Christ-like walk. 2:6
    Holy Spirit. 2:27; 3:24
    Loving one another. 4:12-16
    Obedience and discipline. 2:5-6; 2:17; 3:24
    The gospel. 2:27
Things that are to **a**.
    The believer himself. 2:5-6; 2:17; 2:24; 2:28
    The believer's anointing. 2:27
    The gospel. 2:24
    The obedient. 2:17

ADOPTED - ADOPTION
How one is **a**. Through God's love. 3:1-2
Meaning. To become a child of God. 3:1-2
Proof of **a**.
    Being different from the world. 3:1; 3:10-17
    Purifying self. 3:2-3
Results of **a**.
    Conformity to Christ's image. 3:2
    Righteousness. 3:2-3; 3:10-17
Stages of **a**.
    Future: To be conformed to Christ. 3:2
    Present: Accepted as children. 3:2

ADVOCATE
Discussed. 2:1-2

ANOINTED
Of believers.
    By the Holy Spirit. 2:20; 2:27
    Occurs when saved. 2:20; 2:27
Source. Salvation. 2:20; 2:27

ANOINTING
Equips the believer. 2:20; 2:27
Source. The Holy One. 2:20

ANTICHRIST
Described. Antichrist. 2:18
Duty.
    To guard against. 2:18-23; 4:1-6
    To watch for. 2:18
Identity - Titles.
    Is a man, a real person, not some force or spirit of evil. 2:18
    Many **a**. - now. 2:18-23; 4:1-6
Methods used by. Denying Christ's incarnation. 2:22; 4:1-6
Warning against. Discussed. (See **ANTICHRIST**, Discussed) 2:18-12; 4:1-6
When **a**. comes. (See **ANTICHRIST**, Discussed)
    In the last time. 2:18

APOSTASY
Deliverance found in. Testing the spirit of teachers. 4:1-6
Described as.
    A time existing now. 4:2-3
    Going out into the world. 4:1, cp. 2:18-19
Discussed. 2:18-23; 4:1-6
Marks of - Characteristics of.
    Denying the incarnation. 2:22-23, cp. 18-19; 4:2-3
    Out in the world. 4:1, cp. 2:18-19
Source of. False prophets and teachers. 2:18-23; 4:1-6

ASHAMED (See **UNASHAMED**)

ASSURANCE
Needed in.
    Being untouched by Satan. 5:18
    Dealing with sin. 5:16-21

Prayer. 5:14-15
Receiving eternal life. 5:13
Of the believer.
    Discussed. 5:16
    Kept by the keeping power of Christ. 5:17-18
    Source. Jesus Christ. New birth. 5:20
Of eternal life. Discussed. 5:9-12; 5:13-15
Of what. Of deliverance from judgment. 4:17
Proves.
    That one really knows God. 2:3-29
    That one really loves God. 3:1-4:21
Source - Comes by.
    Being born of God. 5:18
    Clean heart. 3:18-24; 4:16-18
    God. 4:17
    Keeping one's self. 5:18
    Knowing Satan cannot touch. 5:18
    Loving one another. 4:7-21
    The Holy Spirit. 3:24; 4:13

ASTRAY
Meaning. 2:26

ATONING SACRIFICE
Discussed. 2:1-2; 2:2
Source. Sacrifice and death of Christ. 4:9-11

BELIEVE - BELIEF (See **FAITH**)
Importance of. 5:9-15
Proof of. Four proofs. 5:1-21
Results.
    Conquers the world. 5:4-5
    Proves one's love for God. 5:2-3
    Puts a witness within. 5:6-12
Source of.
    God's command - belief in Christ. 3:23-24
    The Scriptures. 5:13

BELIEVER - BELIEVERS
Duty.
    Not to continue in sin. 3:6-7; 3:9
    Of different stages of growth. 2:12-13
    Of mature believers. 2:12-13

INDEX

INDEX

WALK, SPIRITUAL
Duty. To walk as Christ walked. 2:6

WITNESS - WITNESSING
Discussed.
Word of God and of John the Apostle. 5:9-15
Word of heaven and earth. 5:6-8

WORD, THE
Mission.
To testify that God has saved the world. 5:6-8
To reveal God. 1:1

WORKS, LEGALISTIC (See **LAW; LIBERTY**)
Need. Do the work of God; believe in Christ. 3:23

WORLD
Duty. Not to love the world. 2:15-17
Fact. Under the power of Satan. 5:19
How to overcome.
By believing that Jesus Christ is the Son of God. 5:4-5
By faith. 5:4-5
Meaning. 2:15; 5:19
Nature of. Under the contol of the evil one. 5:19

WORLDLINESS
Defined.
Love for the **w**. 2:15-17
What **w**. is. 2:15-17
Deliverance from.
By not loving the world. 2:15-17
How to conquer. 5:4-5
Nature.
Evil. 5:19
Hatred of believers. 3:12-13
Lost. 2:15-16
Pride. 2:15-16
Sinful. 2:2
Struggles against man. 5:4-5

WRONGDOING
Described. As sin. All **w**. is sin. 5:17-18

SECOND

JOHN

2 JOHN

INTRODUCTION

AUTHOR: John, the Apostle (see I John, Introductory Notes).

DATE: Probably A.D. 85-95 (see I John, Introductory Notes).

TO WHOM WRITTEN: "To the chosen lady (2 Jn.1:1).

Is the "chosen lady" an individual who was very dear to John, or is she a church who is symbolically referred to as the "chosen lady"? Opinions vary. Either conclusion does not affect the message. However, when all the facts are considered, the evidence points heavily toward the chosen lady being a very precious lady who loved the Lord with all her heart. Remember: there were no church buildings in that day. The church met in the homes of faithful believers who had homes large enough to handle the crowd. There is a good possibility that the church met in this dear lady's home. Wuest says that the Greek word "lady" (kuria) means Martha (*In These Last Days*, Vol.4, p.199). She apparently lived near Ephesus.

PURPOSE: John's purpose for writing the letter was twofold.

1. To exhort the lady to love all believers no matter what they did. Apparently, she had taken a stand for Christ against false teachers, and some in the church were criticizing, backbiting, and turning against her. She needed to love them despite their rotten and ungodly behavior. (See note and DEEPER STUDY # 1, *Love*—2 Jn.5.)

2. To exhort the lady to continue to stand against false teachers and not to let them into her home. The church was probably meeting in her home; therefore, the importance of refusing hospitality to false teachers could not be overstressed. (What a lesson for today!) (see outline and notes—2 Jn.7-13).

SPECIAL FEATURES:

1. II John is "A General Epistle." That is, it is not written to a specific church. It is a highly personal letter written from the heart of a tender pastor who deeply loves this dear lady in the Lord.

2. II John is "An Epistle Governing Traveling Ministers such as Prophets, Teachers, Evangelists, and Missionaries." After the apostles died off, a clash arose over the ministers of local churches and the traveling ministers. There were some false ministers who had begun to fill the pulpits of the local churches and others who had begun to travel about taking advantage of the Christians who were kind enough to provide them food and lodging during their ministry and stay (II John 10). Because of this abuse, some within the churches arose and began to oppose all *traveling ministers* (Diotrephes of III John is an example of this). John writes the chosen lady to warn her of false teachers. But on the other hand, he writes Gaius to encourage him to receive the *true prophets* (III John). III John shows that the conflict had become so heated that Diotrephes was even trying to have church members expelled if they accepted the traveling minister (cp. III John).

3. II John is "An Epistle Combating False Teachers and Their Doctrinal Errors." (See I John, Purpose, Introduction for a discussion of the error.)

OUTLINE OF 2 JOHN

THE PREACHER'S OUTLINE & SERMON BIBLE® is *unique*. It differs from all other Study Bibles & Sermon Resource Materials in that every Passage and Subject is outlined right beside the Scripture. When you choose any *Subject* below and turn to the reference, you have not only the Scripture, but you discover the Scripture and Subject *already outlined for you—verse by verse.*

For a quick example, choose one of the subjects below and turn over to the Scripture, and you will find this marvelous help for faster, easier, and more accurate use.

In addition, every point of the Scripture and Subject is *fully developed in a Commentary with supporting Scripture* at the bottom of the page. Again, this arrangement makes sermon preparation much easier and faster.

Note something else: The Subjects of SECOND JOHN have titles that are both Biblical and *practical*. The practical titles sometimes have more appeal to people. This *benefit* is clearly seen for use on billboards, bulletins, church newsletters, etc.

A suggestion: For the quickest overview of SECOND JOHN, first read *all the major titles* (I, II, III, etc.), then come back and read the subtitles.

OUTLINE OF 2 JOHN

GREETING: THE ELECT OR CHOSEN LADY, 1-4

I.   THE COMMANDMENT OF LOVE, 5-6

II.   THE WARNING AGAINST DECEIVERS AND FALSE TEACHERS, 7-13

	GREETING: THE ELECT OR CHOSEN LADY, 1-4	forever:	who lives within
1 She was elect, chosen by God **2 She was loved in the truth** a. Believers *loved her in the truth* b. Believers loved her because of the truth (Christ)	The elder, To the chosen lady and her children, whom I love in the truth—and not I only, but also all who know the truth— 2 Because of the truth, which lives in us and will be with us	3 Grace, mercy and peace from God the Father and from Jesus Christ, the Father's Son, will be with us in truth and love. 4 It has given me great joy to find some of your children walking in the truth, just as the Father commanded us.	**3 She lived in truth & love** a. Experiencing grace^DS1 b. Experiencing mercy c. Experiencing peace **4 She had children who walked in the truth**

GREETING: THE ELECT OR CHOSEN LADY, 1-4

(v.1-4) Introduction: this is a soft and tender exhortation to a Christian mother and her children. It is a beautiful exhortation, yet it is a strong challenge. The elect lady is taken by some to refer to a church and by others to refer to a particular lady in the local church (see *To Whom Written*—Introduction 2 John). After looking at all the arguments for both positions, it seems far more natural to take the address as referring to a dear lady who loved the Lord with all her heart. There is a possibility that she had written John about the problem of false teaching that had infiltrated the church. Remember: there were no church buildings in that day and time; therefore, believers met in the homes of committed members. There is a good possibility that the church met in the home of this dear lady (cp. v.10). Whatever the case, John was writing her as a dear friend and warning her against the false teaching. This first section deals solely with the lady and her children. She is *the elect or chosen lady*.

1. She was elect, chosen by God (v.1).
2. She was loved in the truth (v.1-2).
3. She lived in truth and love (v.3).
4. She had children who walked in the truth (v.4).

1 (v.1) **Election**: she was elect. *Elect* means to be chosen by God. It means to be one of God's *holy and dearly loved* followers. This is exactly what Paul said about believers: he said they were "God's chosen people, holy and dearly loved." (Col. 3:12). This dear mother was chosen by God to be one of His elect, one of His *holy and dearly loved* followers.

1. She was elected to be holy. The word "holy" (hagios) means separated or set apart. God had called this dear mother out of the world and away from the old life that it offered, the old life of sin and death. She was elected to be holy, to have nothing to do with the worldly pleasures and possessions of the world. She was to be separated and set apart unto God Himself and the new life He offers, the new life of righteousness and eternity.

2. She was chosen to be one of the *dearly loved* followers of God. God had called her to turn away from the old life...

- that had been disobedient to God.
- that had ignored and neglected God.
- that had disbelieved God.
- that had rebelled against and rejected God.
- that had cursed God.

God had chosen her to be His elect, one of His dear followers. She was chosen to be *holy and dearly loved* before Him; to receive His love in Christ Jesus and to allow Him to shower His love upon her and her children. She was elected to follow God with all her heart and life; elected to live a holy life, a life as one of God's dearly loved children.

Therefore, I urge you, brothers, in view of God's mercy, to offer your bodies as living sacrifices, holy and pleasing to God—this is your spiritual act of worship. Do not conform any longer to the pattern of this world, but be transformed by the renewing of your mind. Then you will be able to test and approve what God's will is—his good, pleasing and perfect will. (Rom 12:1-2)

"Therefore come out from them and be separate, says the Lord. Touch no unclean thing, and I will receive you." "I will be a Father to you, and you will be my sons and daughters, says the Lord Almighty." (2 Cor 6:17-18)

Have nothing to do with the fruitless deeds of darkness, but rather expose them. (Eph 5:11)

Therefore, as God's chosen people, holy and dearly loved, clothe yourselves with compassion, kindness, humility, gentleness and patience. (Col 3:12)

Paul, a servant of God and an apostle of Jesus Christ for the faith of God's elect and the knowledge of the truth that leads to godliness— (Titus 1:1)

Who have been chosen according to the foreknowledge of God the Father, through the sanctifying work of the Spirit, for obedience to Jesus Christ and sprinkling by his blood: Grace and peace be yours in abundance. (1 Pet 1:2)

Do not love the world or anything in the world. If anyone loves the world, the love of the Father is not in him. For everything in the world—the cravings of sinful man, the lust of his eyes and the boasting of what he has and does—comes not from the Father but from the world. (1 John 2:15-16)

2 (v.1-2) **Truth—Love**: she was loved in the truth. Note two significant points.

1. This tells us how we should love one another. We are to love just as John and all the early believers loved—*"in the truth."* What does this mean?

⇒ It means that we are to love one another in Jesus Christ. Jesus Christ said that He is the truth.

Jesus answered, "I am the way and the truth and the life. No one comes to the Father except through me. (John 14:6)

Jesus Christ is the truth, the very ideal of humanity, the Ideal and Perfect Man. All that a person should be, all that God wants a person to be—it is all wrapped up in Jesus Christ. Jesus Christ embraces the ideal and perfect truth; He is the very embodiment of truth; He is the very life that a man should live.

⇒ But note: Jesus Christ also said that the Word of God is truth.

Sanctify them by the truth; your word is truth. (John 17:17)

All that a person should be is also written out for man in the Word of God. God's Word spells out the perfect and ideal man, just what God wants a person to be. The Word of God itself is the truth.

How are we to love one another? *In the truth.* We are to love one another in the Lord Jesus Christ and in the Word of God. This is significant, for it means that we are to love one another as Jesus Christ loved and as the Word of God instructs us. Note: this is a love that is entirely different from the love that is displayed in the world. The world's love focuses upon...

- infatuation and passion
- feelings and sentimentality
- personal pleasure and gratification
- loving those who love us

But the love of Jesus Christ and of the Word of God is a different love. It is the love that *gives sacrificially,* that helps people even if they are unlovely and unattractive. It is the love that reaches out to people even when they do not deserve it. The love of Christ loves everyone no matter who they are or what they have done. The love that we are to have is the love of Christ, the love that knows this fact: Christ loved us and gave Himself for us even when we did not deserve it. It is the love that tells us this: we must do as He did, love a person regardless of who he is.

Thought 1. This means a most wonderful thing. It means that no matter who we are, no matter what we have done, no matter how terrible we have been, we are loved by Christ. But, in addition to Christ, it means that there are others, a multitude of people, who love us. All of God's elect, all of His holy and beloved followers, love us. No matter how unloved we may feel, how lonely and empty, there is a multitude of people who love us just as Christ loves us.

⇒ The lonely and empty just need to get up and go to church and be around God's holy and beloved people. And God's dear people need to get out into the community more and more to reach the lonely and empty.

2. This tells us why we are to love one another. We are to love "because of the truth," that is, for the sake of the Lord Jesus Christ and of the Word of God. John and the early believers loved this dear lady "because of the truth." That is, they loved her for the sake of Christ, because they loved Him and they wanted to please Him. Jesus Christ had come to earth to show us that God loves us and to show us that we should love one another. Therefore, nothing pleases Christ any more than our loving one another. If we wish to please Him, we must love one another; we must love just like the Word of God says to love.

Note: the truth dwells in us and shall be with us forever. This is the indwelling presence of the Lord Jesus Christ, of His Holy Spirit within us. If we know Christ, really know Him, then He lives within our hearts. The truth dwells within us and shall be with us forever. Jesus Christ is within us to help us to love as He loved.

Thought 1. This means a great thing to the lonely and empty, to all those who feel unloved. They can know this: genuine believers will love them. Genuine believers will embrace and care for them and do all they can to ease their hurt and pain. The lonely and empty just need to get up and go find a church of true believers.

"A new command I give you: Love one another. As I have loved you, so you must love one another. By this all men will know that you are my disciples, if you love one another." (John 13:34-35)

"As the Father has loved me, so have I loved you. Now remain in my love. (John 15:9)

My command is this: Love each other as I have loved you. (John 15:12)

Love must be sincere. Hate what is evil; cling to what is good. (Rom 12:9)

And live a life of love, just as Christ loved us and gave himself up for us as a fragrant offering and sacrifice to God. (Eph 5:2)

May the Lord make your love increase and overflow for each other and for everyone else, just as ours does for you. (1 Th 3:12)

Now that you have purified yourselves by obeying the truth so that you have sincere love for your brothers, love one another deeply, from the heart. (1 Pet 1:22)

This is how we know what love is: Jesus Christ laid down his life for us. And we ought to lay down our lives for our brothers. (1 John 3:16)

3 (v.3) **Grace—Mercy—Peace:** she lived in truth and love with other believers. This is a declaration of fact not a prayer. John says that the grace, mercy, and peace of God and of Christ are with believers. There is no question about it: a true believer knows the grace, mercy, and peace of God and of Christ. The idea is this: believers know the *fullness of God and of Christ* in truth and love. God and Christ flood their hearts and lives with all the fullness of life—with grace, mercy, and peace.

1. Grace means the undeserved and unmerited favor and blessings of God; the depth and richness of the heart and mind of God; the kindness and love that dwells within the very nature of God. God's grace covers all of life. (See DEEPER STUDY # 1, *Grace*—2 John v.3 for more discussion.)

2. Mercy means feelings of pity, compassion, affection, and kindness. It is a desire to succor; to tenderly draw unto oneself and to care for. Two things are essential in order to have mercy: seeing a need and being able to meet that need. God sees our need and feels for us (Eph.2:1-3). Therefore, He acts; He has mercy upon us...

- God withholds His judgment.
- God provides a way for us to be saved.

Mercy arises from a heart of love: God has mercy upon us because He loves us. His mercy has been demonstrated in two great ways:

⇒ God has withheld His judgment from us—withheld it even when we deserve it.

⇒ God has provided a way for us to be saved through the Lord Jesus Christ.

When Jesus Christ died, He died for our sins. He took our sins upon Himself and bore the judgment of sin for us. Therefore, if we trust Christ as our Savior, God *does not count* sin against us. Instead, He *counts the righteousness* of Christ for us. We become acceptable to God through the righteousness of Christ. The great mercy of God is this:

⇒ He allowed Christ, His very own Son, to die for us. He actually allowed His own Son to bear the punishment of our sins for us.

⇒ He loves us so much that He will forgive our sins if we will only trust Christ.

The point is this: the true believer is a person upon whom God and Christ have poured out their mercy. It is not that believers *are going to* experience the mercy of God, they have *already received* the mercy of God.

> **But because of his great love for us, God, who is rich in mercy, made us alive with Christ even when we were dead in transgressions—it is by grace you have been saved. (Eph 2:4-5)**
>
> **But when the kindness and love of God our Savior appeared, he saved us, not because of righteous things we had done, but because of his mercy. He saved us through the washing of rebirth and renewal by the Holy Spirit, (Titus 3:4-5)**

3. Peace means to be bound, joined, and woven together. It means to be assured, confident, and secure in the love and care of God. It means to have a sense, a consciousness, a knowledge that God will…

- provide
- guide
- strengthen
- sustain
- deliver
- encourage
- save
- give life, real life both now and forever

A person can experience true peace only as he comes to know Jesus Christ. Only Christ can bring peace to the human heart, the kind of peace that brings deliverance and assurance to the human soul.

> **Peace I leave with you; my peace I give you. I do not give to you as the world gives. Do not let your hearts be troubled and do not be afraid. (John 14:27)**
>
> **"I have told you these things, so that in me you may have peace. In this world you will have trouble. But take heart! I have overcome the world." (John 16:33)**
>
> **Therefore, since we have been justified through faith, we have peace with God through our Lord Jesus Christ, (Rom 5:1)**
>
> **The mind of sinful man is death, but the mind controlled by the Spirit is life and peace; (Rom 8:6)**
>
> **But the fruit of the Spirit is love, joy, peace, patience, kindness, goodness, faithfulness, gentleness and self-control. Against such things there is no law. (Gal 5:22-23)**
>
> **I will lie down and sleep in peace, for you alone, O LORD, make me dwell in safety. (Psa 4:8)**

Note one other significant point: Jesus Christ is said to be the Son of the Father. This is a clear declaration that Jesus Christ is God, that He possesses the very nature of God

the Father. Note also that grace, mercy, and peace come from Jesus Christ as well as from the Father. The Son is said to be equal with the Father.

DEEPER STUDY # 1

(v.3) **Grace**: (charis): the favor and blessings of God; the undeserved and unmerited favor and blessings of God; the depth and richness of the heart and mind of God; the kindness and love that dwells within the very nature of God. God's grace covers all of life.

1. Grace means the kindness and love that God freely gives to those who *have acted against Him*. It is the favor of God showered upon men who do not deserve His favor, men who are…

- "powerless" (Ro.5:6).
- "ungodly" (Ro.5:6).
- "sinners" (Ro.5:8).
- "enemies" (Ro.5:10).

No other word so expresses the depth and richness of the heart and mind of God. This is the distinctive difference between God's grace and man's grace. Whereas man sometimes does favors for his friends and thereby can be said to be gracious, God has done a thing unheard of among men. God has favored man with an unbelievable gift: God has given His very own Son to die for His enemies (Ro.5:8-10). (See notes—Jn.21:15-17; Eph.2:8-10.)

a. God's grace is not earned. It is something completely undeserved and unmerited.

> **For it is by grace you have been saved, through faith—and this not from yourselves, it is the gift of God— not by works, so that no one can boast. (Eph 2:8-9)**
>
> **But when the kindness and love of God our Savior appeared, he saved us, not because of righteous things we had done, but because of his mercy. He saved us through the washing of rebirth and renewal by the Holy Spirit, (Titus 3:4-5)**

b. God's grace is the free gift of God. God extends His grace out toward man.

> **And are justified freely by his grace through the redemption that came by Christ Jesus. (Rom 3:24)**
>
> **But because of his great love for us, God, who is rich in mercy, made us alive with Christ even when we were dead in transgressions—it is by grace you have been saved. (Eph 2:4-5)**
>
> **For the grace of God that brings salvation has appeared to all men. It teaches us to say "No" to ungodliness and worldly passions, and to live self-controlled, upright and godly lives in this present age, while we wait for the blessed hope—the glorious appearing of our great God and Savior, Jesus Christ, who gave himself for us to redeem us from all wickedness and to purify for himself a people that are his very own, eager to do what is good. (Titus 2:11-14)**

c. God's grace is the only way man can be saved.

> **But the gift is not like the trespass. For if the many died by the trespass of the one man, how much more did God's grace and**

the gift that came by the grace of the one man, Jesus Christ, overflow to the many! (Rom 5:15)

I always thank God for you because of his grace given you in Christ Jesus. (1 Cor 1:4)

For you know the grace of our Lord Jesus Christ, that though he was rich, yet for your sakes he became poor, so that you through his poverty might become rich. (2 Cor 8:9)

Whom he poured out on us generously through Jesus Christ our Savior, so that, having been justified by his grace, we might become heirs having the hope of eternal life. (Titus 3:6-7)

2. Grace means all the favors and gifts of God. It means all the good and perfect gifts of God, all the good and beneficial things He gives us and does for us, whether physical, material, or spiritual (Jas.1:17).

In him we have redemption through his blood, the forgiveness of sins, in accordance with the riches of God's grace (Eph 1:7)

In order that in the coming ages he might show the incomparable riches of his grace, expressed in his kindness to us in Christ Jesus. (Eph 2:7)

And my God will meet all your needs according to his glorious riches in Christ Jesus. (Phil 4:19)

Nor to devote themselves to myths and endless genealogies. These promote controversies rather than God's work—which is by faith. (1 Tim 1:4)

4 (v.4) **Truth—Commandment**: she had children who walked in truth. Remember John is some distance away from this dear friend of his, so far away that he is writing instead of visiting her. Note that some of her children had been in the city where John was, and John had seen them and noted that they were walking in Christ. In fact, John says they were a dynamic testimony of the truth. They were walking in Christ, walking just as we have been commanded to walk, walking just as the Word of God says we are to walk. Why were the children in the city where John was?

⇒ Were they there on business? Traveling salesmen? Businessmen or women? Visiting relatives or friends? Vacationing? Sight-seeing? Away at some university?

We are not told. All we know is that John saw them someplace in the city and apparently was able to observe their lives long enough to note that they walked faithfully in Christ.

Thought 1. Note several strong lessons for us.
1) What a dynamic witness the mother had been to her children! She had reared them to know the Lord and to live in His Word.
2) No matter where we are, at work or at play, we are to live for Christ. No matter where we travel, we should do as this dear mother's children did: walk in Christ and maintain a dynamic testimony for Christ.

Then he said to them all: "If anyone would come after me, he must deny himself and take up his cross daily and follow me. (Luke 9:23)

Do not conform any longer to the pattern of this world, but be transformed by the renewing of your mind. Then you will be able to test and approve what God's will is—his good, pleasing and perfect will. (Rom 12:2)

Therefore, if anyone is in Christ, he is a new creation; the old has gone, the new has come! (2 Cor 5:17)

So then, just as you received Christ Jesus as Lord, continue to live in him, (Col 2:6)

Endure hardship with us like a good soldier of Christ Jesus. No one serving as a soldier gets involved in civilian affairs—he wants to please his commanding officer. (2 Tim 2:3-4)

Whoever claims to live in him must walk as Jesus did. (1 John 2:6)

Do not love the world or anything in the world. If anyone loves the world, the love of the Father is not in him. For everything in the world—the cravings of sinful man, the lust of his eyes and the boasting of what he has and does—comes not from the Father but from the world. (1 John 2:15-16)

	I. THE COMMANDMENT OF LOVE, .5-6
1 Love is not a new commandment*DS1*	5 And now, dear lady, I am not writing you a new command but one we have had from the beginning. I ask that we love one another.
2 Love is a behavior—a way of life—a walk	6 And this is love: that we walk in obedience to his commands. As you have heard from the beginning, his command is that you walk in love.

DIVISION I

THE COMMANDMENT OF LOVE, 5-6

(v.5-6) **Introduction**: note the word "ask" (eroto). It means to urge, beg, and entreat. It has the idea of urgency and necessity. What John is now saying is urgent; it is an absolute necessity. What is it? Love—we must love one another. Love is not an option for believers: believers must love one another. Two things are said.

1. Love is not a new commandment (v.5).
2. Love is a behavior—a way of life—a walk (v.6).

1 (v.5) **Love**: love is not a new commandment. It is the old commandment, the very same commandment that we had from the beginning. Note how John immediately brings up the subject of love. This tells us something: the dear friend of John was having problems with some people. Some people were mistreating her Lord and her. We know from the next passage that there were some false teachers who wanted to teach in her church or else they wanted to use her house for some purpose:

⇒ to visit her and talk to her about their beliefs
⇒ to room and board in her house
⇒ to use her house for a church or study group or church social function

Apparently she had refused to grant the request, and as a result, she was being criticized. Whatever the case was, she had actually refused to open her home to some false teachers or else John was instructing her not to welcome them (cp. v.7-11). In either case, the dear lady was under attack by some in the church. She was being...

- criticized
- murmured against
- talked about
- hurt
- mistreated
- abused

Now note John's exhortation to her: love them. "We must love one another. No matter what they say about you; no matter how they mistreat you; no matter how they hurt you—love them."

The point is this: love is the very first commandment that man ever received from God, and it is the very first commandment that we ever received from Christ. It is even the first commandment that we receive when we become a believer. Love is the first commandment of the church itself.

⇒ God had said from the beginning that we are to love our neighbor.

"'Do not seek revenge or bear a grudge against one of your people, but love your neighbor as yourself. I am the LORD. (Lev 19:18)

⇒ Jesus Christ proclaimed that love would be the distinctive mark of His followers, the very mark that would show the world that a person was a true follower of His.

By this all men will know that you are my disciples, if you love one another." (John 13:35)

Now note another fact about this dear lady of God: she was being exhorted to love those who were mistreating her. She was not being told...

- to love her friend but not her enemy.
- to love the good but not the bad.
- to love the righteous but not the sinner.
- to love the acceptable but not the unacceptable.
- to love the friendly but not the abusive.
- to love the kind but not the criticizer.

This is a totally new concept of love. Man has always felt that he was to love his friends. He has always felt free to take others, especially those who had mistreated him, and...

- mistreat them
- ignore them
- criticize them
- hate them
- strike back at them
- neglect them
- be unkind to them
- hurt them

But John says, "no!" He instructs this dear friend to love those who mistreated her. How? How can we possibly love those who mistreat us? There is only one way: we must love as God loves. We must possess the love of God within our hearts and lives. (See DEEPER STUDY # 1, Love—2 Jn.5 for more discussion.)

DEEPER STUDY # 1

(v.5) **Love**: the Greek word used for "love" is *agape*. The meaning of *agape love* is more clearly seen by contrasting it with the various kinds of love. There are essentially four kinds of love. Whereas the English language has only the word *love* to describe all the affectionate experiences of men, the Greek language had a different word to describe each kind of love.

1. There is *passionate love* or *eros love*. This is the physical love between sexes; the patriotic love of a person for his nation; the ambition of a person for power, wealth, or fame. Briefly stated, *eros love* is the base love of a man that arises from his own inner passion. Sometimes *eros love* is focused upon good and other times it is focused

317

upon bad. It should be noted that *eros love* is never used in the New Testament.

2. There is *affectionate love* or *storge love*. This is the kind of love that exists between parent and child and between loyal citizens and a trustworthy ruler. *Storge love* is also not used in the New Testament.

3. There is an *endearing love*, the love that cherishes. This is *phileo love*, the love of a husband and wife for each other, of a brother for a brother, of a friend for the dearest of friends. It is the love that cherishes, that holds someone or something ever so dear to one's heart.

4. There is *selfless and sacrificial love* or *agape love*. Agape love is the love of the mind, of the reason, of the will. It is the love that goes so far...

- that it loves a person even if he does not deserve to be loved.
- that it actually loves the person who is utterly unworthy of being loved.

Note four significant points about agape love.

a. Selfless or agape love is the love of God, the very love possessed by God Himself. It is the love demonstrated in the cross of Christ.

⇒ It is the love of God for the *ungodly*.

> **You see, at just the right time, when we were still powerless, Christ died for the ungodly. (Rom 5:6)**

⇒ It is the love of God for *unworthy sinners*.

> **But God demonstrates his own love for us in this: While we were still sinners, Christ died for us. (Rom 5:8)**

⇒ It is the love of God for *undeserving enemies*.

> **For if, when we were God's enemies, we were reconciled to him through the death of his Son, how much more, having been reconciled, shall we be saved through his life! (Rom 5:10)**

b. Selfless or agape love is a gift of God. It can be experienced only if a person knows God *personally*—only if a person has received the love of God into his heart and life. Agape love has to be shed abroad (poured out, flooded, spread about) by the Spirit of God within the heart of a person.

> **And hope does not disappoint us, because God has poured out his love into our hearts by the Holy Spirit, whom he has given us. (Rom 5:5)**

c. Selfless or agape love is the greatest thing in all of life according to the Lord Jesus Christ.

> **"The most important one," answered Jesus, "is this: 'Hear, O Israel, the Lord our God, the Lord is one. Love the Lord your God with all your heart and with all your soul and with all your mind and with all your strength.' The second is this: 'Love your neighbor as yourself.' There is no commandment greater than these." (Mark 12:29-31)**

d. Selfless or agape love is the greatest possession and gift in human life according to the Scripture (1 Cor.13:1-13).

> **And now these three remain: faith, hope and love. But the greatest of these is love. (1 Cor 13:13)**

2 (v.6) **Love—Obedience—Believer, Life and Walk**: love is a behavior, a way of life, a walk; it is obeying God's commandments. Note the phrase: *"This is love."* Love is obedience, that is, the only way we can show that we love God is by doing what pleases Him. When we love someone, we want to do things that please him or her. We want their acceptance and approval; we want them to love us in return. Therefore, we are careful to do things that will please them and win their favor and love. The same is true with us and God. If we love God, we do those things that please Him. We keep His commandments. What is His commandment? "His command is"—the *great commandment*—the commandment that you have heard from the beginning: "that you walk in love." How does a believer walk in love? He walks upon earth just like Jesus Christ walked: he loves everyone. He does the great acts of love, and the great acts of love are clearly spelled out by Scripture in 1 Cor.13:4-7. This great passage gives the very behavior that is to characterize the believer, the very way the believer is to live among others. This is what loving others means.

1. Love is patient (makrothumei) with people. The word always refers to being patient with people, not with circumstances (William Barclay. *The Letters to the Corinthians.* "The Daily Study Bible." Philadelphia, PA: The Westminister Press, 1954, p.133).

Love is patient a long, long time...

- no matter the evil and injury done by a person.
- no matter the neglect or ignoring by a loved one.

Love is patient a long, long time without resentment, anger, or seeking revenge. Love controls itself in order to win the person and to help him to live, work, and serve as he should.

> **But the fruit of the Spirit is love, joy, peace, patience, kindness, goodness, faithfulness, (Gal 5:22)**
> **Being strengthened with all power according to his glorious might so that you may have great endurance and patience, and joyfully (Col 1:11)**
> **Preach the Word; be prepared in season and out of season; correct, rebuke and encourage—with great patience and careful instruction. (2 Tim 4:2)**

2. Love is kind (chresteuetai): courteous, good, helpful, useful, giving, showing and showering favors. Love does not resent evil; it does not revel in the hurt and neglect. Love reaches out in kindness: in helpfulness, in giving, and in showering favors upon the person who neglects or hurts oneself.

> **Be devoted to one another in brotherly love. Honor one another above yourselves. (Rom 12:10)**
> **Be kind and compassionate to one another, forgiving each other, just as in Christ God forgave you. (Eph 4:32)**

3. Love does not envy (zeloi): is not jealous; does not have feelings against others because of what they have, such as gifts, position, friends, recognition, possessions, popularity, abilities. Love does not begrudge or attack or downplay the abilities and success of others. Love shares and joys and rejoices in the experience and good of others.

> Let us not become conceited, provoking and envying each other. (Gal 5:26)
> Of David. Do not fret because of evil men or be envious of those who do wrong; (Psa 37:1)
> Do not envy a violent man or choose any of his ways, (Prov 3:31)
> A heart at peace gives life to the body, but envy rots the bones. (Prov 14:30)
> Do not let your heart envy sinners, but always be zealous for the fear of the LORD. (Prov 23:17)

4. Love does not boast (peopereuetai): is not boastful; does not brag nor seek recognition, honor, or applause from others. On the contrary, love seeks to give: to recognize, to honor, to applaud the other person.

> For by the grace given me I say to every one of you: Do not think of yourself more highly than you ought, but rather think of yourself with sober judgment, in accordance with the measure of faith God has given you. (Rom 12:3)
> Be devoted to one another in brotherly love. Honor one another above yourselves. (Rom 12:10)
> Do nothing out of selfish ambition or vain conceit, but in humility consider others better than yourselves. (Phil 2:3)

5. Love is not proud (phusioutai): prideful, arrogant, conceited; does not think nor act as though oneself is better or above others. Love is modest and humble and recognizes and honors others.

> Therefore, whoever humbles himself like this child is the greatest in the kingdom of heaven. (Mat 18:4)
> But when you are invited, take the lowest place, so that when your host comes, he will say to you, 'Friend, move up to a better place.' Then you will be honored in the presence of all your fellow guests. (Luke 14:10)
> But you are not to be like that. Instead, the greatest among you should be like the youngest, and the one who rules like the one who serves. (Luke 22:26)
> Young men, in the same way be submissive to those who are older. All of you, clothe yourselves with humility toward one another, because, "God opposes the proud but gives grace to the humble." (1 Pet 5:5)

6. Love is not rude (aschemonei): unbecomingly, rudely, indecently, unmannerly, disgracefully. Love does nothing to shame oneself. Love is orderly and controlled; and it behaves and treats all persons with respect, honoring and respecting who they are.

> So that you may be able to discern what is best and may be pure and blameless until the day of Christ, (Phil 1:10)
> For you yourselves know how you ought to follow our example. We were not idle when we were with you, (2 Th 3:7)

7. Love is not self-seeking: is not selfish; does not insist upon its own rights (Williams). Love is not focused upon who one is nor upon what one has done. Love seeks to serve, not have others serving oneself. Love is acknowledging others, not insisting that others acknowledge oneself; it is giving to others, not insisting that others give to oneself.

> Nobody should seek his own good, but the good of others. (1 Cor 10:24)
> Each of you should look not only to your own interests, but also to the interests of others. (Phil 2:4)

8. Love is not easily angered (paroxunetai): not easily angered; not ready to take offense; not quick tempered; not "touchy" (Phillips, as quoted by Leon Morris. *The First Epistle of Paul to the Corinthians.* "The Tyndale Bible Commentaries," ed. by RVG Tasker. Grand Rapids, MI: Eerdmans, 1958, p.184). It is not easily aroused to anger; does not become "exasperated" (Barclay). Love controls the emotions, and never becomes angry without a cause (Ro.12:18).

> But now you must rid yourselves of all such things as these: anger, rage, malice, slander, and filthy language from your lips. (Col 3:8)
> My dear brothers, take note of this: Everyone should be quick to listen, slow to speak and slow to become angry, (James 1:19)
> Refrain from anger and turn from wrath; do not fret—it leads only to evil. (Psa 37:8)
> Better a patient man than a warrior, a man who controls his temper than one who takes a city. (Prov 16:32)
> A man's wisdom gives him patience; it is to his glory to overlook an offense. (Prov 19:11)
> Do not be quickly provoked in your spirit, for anger resides in the lap of fools. (Eccl 7:9)

9. Love keeps no record of wrongs (logizetai to kakon): does not consider the wrong suffered; is not resentful; does not hold the evil done to oneself. Love suffers the evil done to it and forgets it.

> But I tell you, Do not resist an evil person. If someone strikes you on the right cheek, turn to him the other also. (Mat 5:39)
> Do not repay anyone evil for evil. Be careful to do what is right in the eyes of everybody. (Rom 12:17)
> Make sure that nobody pays back wrong for wrong, but always try to be kind to each other and to everyone else. (1 Th 5:15)

Do not repay evil with evil or insult with insult, but with blessing, because to this you were called so that you may inherit a blessing. (1 Pet 3:9)

10. Love does not delight in evil (adikia): unrighteousness, evil, wrong-doing. Love does not take pleasure in the unrighteousness and sin of others; it does not feed upon sin and wrong, nor does it pass along the stories of sin and wrong. Man's nature is too often fed the tragedy of evil, whether personal sin or natural disaster (cp. the daily news reports and most subjects of conversation between so many people).

"Why do you look at the speck of sawdust in your brother's eye and pay no attention to the plank in your own eye? (Mat 7:3)
We who are strong ought to bear with the failings of the weak and not to please ourselves. (Rom 15:1)
Brothers, if someone is caught in a sin, you who are spiritual should restore him gently. But watch yourself, or you also may be tempted. (Gal 6:1)
Above all, love each other deeply, because love covers over a multitude of sins. (1 Pet 4:8)

11. Love rejoices with the truth: rejoices when the truth is known and when it prevails; rejoices when others are recognized and promoted for who they are and for what they have contributed. Love rejoices when the truth is rooted and grounded in a person and among the people of the world. Note that love never covers nor hides the truth; love is courageous in that it faces the truth.

Therefore each of you must put off falsehood and speak truthfully to his neighbor, for we are all members of one body. (Eph 4:25)
Stand firm then, with the belt of truth buckled around your waist, with the breastplate of righteousness in place, (Eph 6:14)
These are the things you are to do: Speak the truth to each other, and render true and sound judgment in your courts; (Zec 8:16)
True instruction was in his mouth and nothing false was found on his lips. He walked with me in peace and uprightness, and turned many from sin. (Mal 2:6)

12. Love always protects: the word protects (stegei) means both to cover all things and to bear up under all things. Love does both: it stands up under the weight and onslaught of all things and it covers up the faults of others. It has no pleasure in exposing the wrong and weaknesses of others. Love bears up under any neglect, abuse, ridicule—anything that is thrown against it.

Be completely humble and gentle; be patient, bearing with one another in love. Make every effort to keep the unity of the Spirit through the bond of peace. (Eph 4:2-3)
And masters, treat your slaves in the same way. Do not threaten them, since you know that he who is both their Master and

yours is in heaven, and there is no favoritism with him. (Eph 6:9)
Bear with each other and forgive whatever grievances you may have against one another. Forgive as the Lord forgave you. (Col 3:13)

13. Love always trusts: is "completely trusting" (Barclay); "always eager to believe the best" (Moffatt, as quoted by Leon Morris); is "ever ready to believe the best" (Amplified New Testament). Love sees and understands the circumstances and accepts and forgives and believes the very best about a person.

If he sins against you seven times in a day, and seven times comes back to you and says, 'I repent,' forgive him." (Luke 17:4)
Be kind and compassionate to one another, forgiving each other, just as in Christ God forgave you. (Eph 4:32)
Bear with each other and forgive whatever grievances you may have against one another. Forgive as the Lord forgave you. (Col 3:13)

14. Love always hopes: it "never ceases to hope" (Barclay); it expects the good to eventually triumph and to gain the victory; it refuses to accept failure; it always hopes for the best and for the ultimate triumph of the good—no matter how fallen or how tragic the fall or how difficult gaining the victory may seem.

For in this hope we were saved. But hope that is seen is no hope at all. Who hopes for what he already has? (Rom 8:24)
For everything that was written in the past was written to teach us, so that through endurance and the encouragement of the Scriptures we might have hope. (Rom 15:4)
May our Lord Jesus Christ himself and God our Father, who loved us and by his grace gave us eternal encouragement and good hope, encourage your hearts and strengthen you in every good deed and word. (2 Th 2:16-17)
Everyone who has this hope in him purifies himself, just as he is pure. (1 John 3:3)

15. Love always perseveres: the word endures (huopmenei) is a military word meaning to stand against the attack of an enemy. Love actively fights and endures all attacks. Love is strong, full of fortitude and fight, and it struggles against any and every assault to buckle in to being unloving. Love conquers and triumphs—always—because it endures all things. No matter what attacks love, named or unnamed, it endures the attack and continues to love.

All men will hate you because of me, but he who stands firm to the end will be saved. (Mat 10:22)
Therefore, my dear brothers, stand firm. Let nothing move you. Always give yourselves fully to the work of the Lord, because you know that your labor in the Lord is not in vain. (1 Cor 15:58)

Let us not become weary in doing good, for at the proper time we will reap a harvest if we do not give up. (Gal 6:9)

Blessed is the man who perseveres under trial, because when he has stood the test, he will receive the crown of life that God has promised to those who love him. (James 1:12)

As you know, we consider blessed those who have persevered. You have heard of Job's perseverance and have seen what the Lord finally brought about. The Lord is full of compassion and mercy. (James 5:11)

I am coming soon. Hold on to what you have, so that no one will take your crown. (Rev 3:11)

Thought 1. The point is well made: the dear friend of John was to walk in love no matter how others treated her. She was to love even as God's Son had loved when He was upon earth. So are we.

	II. THE WARNING A-GAINST DECEIVERS & FALSE TEACHERS, 7-13	have God; whoever continues in the teaching has both the Father and the Son.	a. If you do not continue, you do not have God
			b. If you continue, you possess God & Christ
		10 If anyone comes to you and does not bring this teaching, do not take him into your house or welcome him.	**4 Do not receive a deceiver; do not compromise: Guard your testimony**
1 Guard against deceivers a. They deny that Christ has come in the flesh b. They are antichrists	7 Many deceivers, who do not acknowledge Jesus Christ as coming in the flesh, have gone out into the world. Any such person is the deceiver and the antichrist.	11 Anyone who welcomes him shares in his wicked work.	a. He deceives & misleads b. You share in his evil
2 Watch yourself: Do not lose the things already worked in you—receive a full reward	8 Watch out that you do not lose what you have worked for, but that you may be rewarded fully.	12 I have much to write to you, but I do not want to use paper and ink. Instead, I hope to visit you and talk with you face to face, so that our joy may be complete.	**5 Conclusion: Much exhortation is needed** a. Writing was inadequate; therefore, John planned a visit
3 Do not go too far: Stay in the teaching of Christ—prove your salvation	9 Anyone who runs ahead and does not continue in the teaching of Christ does not	13 The children of your chosen sister send their greetings.	b. Christian greetings were sent by relatives

DIVISION II

THE WARNING AGAINST DECEIVERS AND FALSE TEACHERS, v.7-13

(v.7-13) **Introduction**: one of the greatest problems faced by believers is false teaching. False teaching abounds everywhere. No matter which direction we turn, there are deceivers and impostors who go by the name of Christian, by the name of our Lord Jesus Christ; yet they are anything but followers of Him. But their teaching is so insidious, and it contains enough of the truth that millions are ensnared by their seduction. This is the importance of this passage: it is a *warning against deceivers or false teachers*.

1. Guard against deceivers (v.7).
2. Watch yourself: do not lose the things already worked in you—receive a full reward (v.8).
3. Do not go too far: stay in the teaching of Christ—prove your salvation (v.9).
4. Do not receive a deceiver; do not compromise: guard your testimony (v.10-11).
5. Conclusion: much exhortation is needed (v.12-13).

1 (v.7) **Teachers, False—Deceivers—Antichrist**: first, guard against deceivers. A deceiver is an impostor, a person who claims to be a follower of Christ, but he is not—not really. He does not live like Christ taught us to live, and he does not believe the truth about Christ. He lives and teaches something entirely different than what Christ lived and taught. Note three significant facts.

1. There are many deceivers in the world. There were many in the days of John and the elect lady, and there have been many ever since. Deceivers are in every area of society—in our factories and plants, schools and universities, clubs and recreational halls, offices and businesses, and even in our churches and religious societies.

Some are businessmen; others are employees. Some are teachers; others are students. Some are ministers; others are laymen. Deceivers are everywhere, impostors who claim to be Christian, but they do not live for Christ nor do they believe what Christ taught. By their lives and by their beliefs and teachings, they deceive people. Through everyday conversation and sharing and from the teaching positions of the world, they ensnare people into the net of their false beliefs.

2. Note who a deceiver is: he is a person who denies that Jesus Christ has come in the flesh. That is, he denies that Jesus Christ is the Son of God.

⇒ He *denies the deity* of Jesus Christ: that He is the Son of God who came *out of* (ek) heaven, out from the spiritual world and dimension into this world; who came through the womb of a virgin as the God-Man to save the world.

⇒ He *denies that Jesus Christ is the sinless Son of God* who lived a perfect and righteous life and thereby secured the ideal and perfect righteousness for man.

⇒ He *denies the death and resurrection* of Jesus Christ: that He died as the sacrifice for man's sins and that He arose from the dead to conquer death for man.

⇒ He *denies the Lordship* of Jesus Christ: that He is truly the Son of God seated at the right hand of God as the Lord and God of the universe.

⇒ He *denies the return of Jesus Christ to earth*: that He is coming again to execute judgment upon the earth.

Any person can be a deceiver. No matter who we are, if we do not believe that God's Son, the Lord Jesus Christ, has come in the flesh, then we deceive people and mislead them. We ensnare them into false belief and doom them to be separated from God forever. How? By teaching them that they can be good enough on their own to become acceptable to God; that they can do enough good and be religious enough to make God accept them. But this is false teaching, for God is perfect and He can accept only perfection. No person is perfect; therefore, all persons are doomed if they present only their own goodness to God. Their goodness is not perfection. We have all committed some sins, and we are all short of God's glory. We all stand guilty before God. Therefore, there has to be a perfect sacrifice for our sins. This is the glorious news about Jesus Christ, the Son of God. He came to earth to live a sinless life and to become the Perfect and Ideal Man. This He did so that He could be the *perfect and ideal sacrifice* for our sins. Jesus Christ has taken our sins upon Himself and borne the punishment for them. Therefore, sin is taken care of. Sin can be removed from us, and God can accept us in Christ as sinless and perfect.

This is the point: this is the reason that God had to send His Son into the world. If we deny Jesus Christ, if we do not trust Jesus Christ as the perfect sacrifice for our sins, then we are doomed—doomed because we still bear our sins. And God cannot allow a single sinner to contaminate and dirty the perfection of heaven. Sin has to be removed before God can ever accept us and allow us to live in His presence.

Therefore, any person who denies that Jesus Christ has come in the flesh is a deceiver. He is denying what God has done. And most tragic of all: he leads other people astray.

Note one other fact about this verse of Scripture. The words "Jesus Christ as coming in the flesh" is in the present tense. That is, the deceiver denies that God or the Son of God could ever come to earth.

⇒ He denies that God's Son came the first time; denies that Jesus the carpenter was the Son of God.

⇒ He denies that the Son of God is ever coming; denies a second coming or any other coming of the Son of God to earth.

The deceiver just does not believe that God could or would ever come to earth. He does not believe that God could become a man, or else that He ever would become a man. And if God could come to earth, the deceiver sees no need for such an act—for to him man is capable of becoming good enough to secure God's approval and acceptance on his own.

3. Note that the deceiver is called an antichrist; that is, he is a forerunner of the antichrist (see note—1 Jn.2:18 for discussion).

Thought 1. The warning has been sounded. We must guard against deceivers and false teachers.

> "Watch out for false prophets. They come to you in sheep's clothing, but inwardly they are ferocious wolves. By their fruit you will recognize them. Do people pick grapes from thornbushes, or figs from thistles? Likewise every good tree bears good fruit, but a bad tree bears bad fruit. A good tree cannot bear bad fruit, and a bad tree cannot bear good fruit. Every tree that does not bear good fruit is cut down and thrown into the fire. Thus, by their fruit you will recognize them. "Not everyone who says to me, 'Lord, Lord,' will enter the kingdom of heaven, but only he who does the will of my Father who is in heaven. Many will say to me on that day, 'Lord, Lord, did we not prophesy in your name, and in your name drive out demons and perform many miracles?' Then I will tell them plainly, 'I never knew you. Away from me, you evildoers!' (Mat 7:15-23)

> For such men are false apostles, deceitful workmen, masquerading as apostles of Christ. And no wonder, for Satan himself masquerades as an angel of light. It is not surprising, then, if his servants masquerade as servants of righteousness. Their end will be what their actions deserve. (2 Cor 11:13-15)

> They want to be teachers of the law, but they do not know what they are talking about or what they so confidently affirm. (1 Tim 1:7)

> The Spirit clearly says that in later times some will abandon the faith and follow deceiving spirits and things taught by demons. Such teachings come through hypocritical liars, whose consciences have been seared as with a hot iron. (1 Tim 4:1-2)

> If anyone teaches false doctrines and does not agree to the sound instruction of our Lord Jesus Christ and to godly teaching, he is conceited and understands nothing. He has an unhealthy interest in controversies and quarrels about words that result in envy, strife, malicious talk, evil suspicions and constant friction between men of corrupt mind, who have been robbed of the truth and who think that godliness is a means to financial gain. (1 Tim 6:3-5)

> For the time will come when men will not put up with sound doctrine. Instead, to suit their own desires, they will gather around them a great number of teachers to say what their itching ears want to hear. They will turn their ears away from the truth and turn aside to myths. (2 Tim 4:3-4)

> But there were also false prophets among the people, just as there will be false teachers among you. They will secretly introduce destructive heresies, even denying the sovereign Lord who bought them—bringing swift destruction on themselves. (2 Pet 2:1)

> "From the least to the greatest, all are greedy for gain; prophets and priests alike, all practice deceit. (Jer 6:13)

> "Both prophet and priest are godless; even in my temple I find their wickedness," declares the LORD. (Jer 23:11)

> "My people have been lost sheep; their shepherds have led them astray and caused them to roam on the mountains. They wandered over mountain and hill and forgot their own resting place. (Jer 50:6)

> But if the watchman sees the sword coming and does not blow the trumpet to warn the people and the sword comes and takes the life of one of them, that man will be taken away because of his sin, but I will hold the watchman accountable for his blood.' (Ezek 33:6)

2 (v.8) **Watch—Believers, Duty**: second, watch yourself so that you will receive a full reward. Remember: John is writing to a dear mother and her children. False teaching was so rampant that the family unit itself needed to be on guard. The family needed to consider what teachers they were listening to and sitting under. Note why: lest they lose the reward for the good works they had already worked. Believers are to be rewarded for their good works, for their labor for Christ. But there is danger that they can lose their reward. What is that danger? Heeding false teaching. If we heed false teaching, we will lose our reward.

Thought 1. No matter how much charisma a teacher may have, no matter how much we may like him, no matter how persuasive he may be—we must not listen to him, not if he is denying that God's Son, the Lord Jesus Christ, has come to earth as a Man. If we are led astray, we will lose our reward.

And that you, O Lord, are loving. Surely you will reward each person according to what he has done. (Psa 62:12)

"I the LORD search the heart and examine the mind, to reward a man according to his conduct, according to what his deeds deserve." (Jer 17:10)

For the Son of Man is going to come in his Father's glory with his angels, and then he will reward each person according to what he has done. (Mat 16:27)

For we must all appear before the judgment seat of Christ, that each one may receive what is due him for the things done while in the body, whether good or bad. (2 Cor 5:10)

Since you call on a Father who judges each man's work impartially, live your lives as strangers here in reverent fear. (1 Pet 1:17)

And I saw the dead, great and small, standing before the throne, and books were opened. Another book was opened, which is the book of life. The dead were judged according to what they had done as recorded in the books. (Rev 20:12)

"Behold, I am coming soon! My reward is with me, and I will give to everyone according to what he has done. (Rev 22:12)

3 (v.9) **Salvation—Teaching, False**: third, continue in the teaching of Christ. The person who does not continue in the teachings of Christ does not have or possess God. The Greek words are *pas ho proagon*. They mean to transgress against God by going too far, by trying to move out ahead of Christ. There are many teachers, ministers and laymen alike, who would like to be progressive and creative, to come up with a novel idea, to make some advancement in thought. They want people to recognize and approve them; therefore, they try to impress people. In so doing, they go beyond Christ and what He taught. They twist or branch off from the teachings of Christ. John warns against this: if a person does not stay in the teachings of Christ, then he does not have God. He is not saved; he is not truly born of God. The only person who is born of God is the person who stays in the teachings of Christ. This does not mean that believers are not to be creative and thoughtful. It means that we must not move out beyond Christ and what He taught.

Thought 1. Note: it is the *teachings of Christ* that we are to follow, not *teachings about* Christ. As A.T. Robertson says in his *Word Pictures In The New Testament* (Vol.6, p.254), our standard is to be Christ. We must be progressive and seek after progress, but it should be toward Christ, not away from Him. What are the teachings of Christ? The following verses give us the teaching of Christ.

The Word became flesh and made his dwelling among us. We have seen his glory, the glory of the One and Only, who came from the Father, full of grace and truth. (John 1:14)

Just as Moses lifted up the snake in the desert, so the Son of Man must be lifted up, that everyone who believes in him may have eternal life. (John 3:14-15)

That all may honor the Son just as they honor the Father. He who does not honor the Son does not honor the Father, who sent him. (John 5:23)

Then Jesus declared, "I am the bread of life. He who comes to me will never go hungry, and he who believes in me will never be thirsty. (John 6:35)

Yet there are some of you who do not believe." For Jesus had known from the beginning which of them did not believe and who would betray him. He went on to say, "This is why I told you that no one can come to me unless the Father has enabled him." From this time many of his disciples turned back and no longer followed him. "You do not want to leave too, do you?" Jesus asked the Twelve. Simon Peter answered him, "Lord, to whom shall we go? You have the words of eternal life. (John 6:64-68)

Jesus answered, "My teaching is not my own. It comes from him who sent me. If anyone chooses to do God's will, he will find out whether my teaching comes from God or whether I speak on my own. (John 7:16-17)

I and the Father are one." (John 10:30)

He who hates me hates my Father as well. (John 15:23)

Now this is eternal life: that they may know you, the only true God, and Jesus Christ, whom you have sent. (John 17:3)

Jesus did many other miraculous signs in the presence of his disciples, which are not recorded in this book. But these are written that you may believe that Jesus is the Christ, the Son of God, and that by believing you may have life in his name. (John 20:30-31)

4 (v.10-11) **Hospitality**: fourth, do not receive a deceiver or false teacher nor wish him well. Remember: most churches of that day and time met in the homes of prominent members (cp. Ro.16:5; Col.4:15). It is likely that the church was meeting in the home of this dear lady and her children. If not, then she had apparently refused to provide room and board or to welcome some false teachers into her home. The charge is strong and its meaning is perfectly clear. False teachers are not to be allowed in the church nor in our homes. There is no greater danger to a church or a home than the threat of false teachers. False teachers doom the souls of people, shut them off from Christ. And any person who is shut off from Christ is not acceptable to God. Therefore, the church and the members of our families must be protected at all costs from false teachers. Note: we are not to encourage the false teacher at all; not to welcome him. If we encourage him, God counts us as a participant in his evil deeds. This means, of course, that we do not support deceivers and false teachers...

* by allowing them to be around our children or young people.
* by allowing them to be around believers where they can share their ideas.
* by allowing them to teach in our churches.
* by attending their meetings.
* by supporting them financially.
* by showing any encouragement whatsoever to them.

Any person who denies Jesus Christ is the most dangerous person alive, for he can doom our children and loved ones and even doom us. Jesus Christ is God's Son, and God loves His Son with a divine jealousy and vengeance over how men treat Him. No matter what we may feel or think, God is both loving and just, and His justice must be executed the same as His love has been demonstrated. The point is this: God's justice stands more against those who teach that Jesus Christ is not His Son than against anyone else.

> "Do not give dogs what is sacred; do not throw your pearls to pigs. If you do, they may trample them under their feet, and then turn and tear you to pieces. (Mat 7:6)
> "Watch out for false prophets. They come to you in sheep's clothing, but inwardly they are ferocious wolves. By their fruit you will recognize them. Do people pick grapes from thornbushes, or figs from thistles? Likewise every good tree bears good fruit, but a bad tree bears bad fruit. A good tree cannot bear bad fruit, and a bad tree cannot bear good fruit. Every tree that does not bear good fruit is cut down and thrown into the fire. Thus, by their fruit you will recognize them. "Not everyone who says to me, 'Lord, Lord,' will enter the kingdom of heaven, but only he who does the will of my Father who is in heaven. Many will say to me on that day, 'Lord, Lord, did we not prophesy in your name, and in your name drive out demons and perform many miracles?' Then I will tell them plainly, 'I never knew you. Away from me, you evildoers!' (Mat 7:15-23)
> "Therefore come out from them and be separate, says the Lord. Touch no unclean thing, and I will receive you." "I will be a Father to you, and you will be my sons and daughters, says the Lord Almighty." (2 Cor 6:17-18)
> I am astonished that you are so quickly deserting the one who called you by the grace of Christ and are turning to a different gospel— which is really no gospel at all. Evidently some people are throwing you into confusion and are trying to pervert the gospel of Christ. But even if we or an angel from heaven should preach a gospel other than the one we preached to you, let him be eternally condemned! As we have already said, so now I say again: If anybody is preaching to you a gospel other than what

you accepted, let him be eternally condemned! (Gal 1:6-9)
> Have nothing to do with the fruitless deeds of darkness, but rather expose them. (Eph 5:11)

5 (v.12-13) **Conclusion**: much exhortation is needed by believers. John had much that needed to be said to this dear lady and her children. But it would be better to say it to them face to face. Therefore, John planned a trip to visit her and the other believers in the area.

> **Thought 1.** Note how important the gospel is even for believers—so important that John would plan a special trip to share the glorious teachings of Jesus Christ. And remember: John was already an elderly man.

Note that the elect or chosen lady had a sister. The final words are greetings from the children of the sister. This is significant: it shows how the gospel had spread throughout the whole family. First one sister was reached for Christ, then the other sister, and then the children of both families. When we surrender our lives to Jesus Christ, our duty is to do all we can to reach our families for Christ, all our brothers and sisters and their families.

> For we cannot help speaking about what we have seen and heard." (Acts 4:20)
> You will be his witness to all men of what you have seen and heard. (Acts 22:15)
> It is written: "I believed; therefore I have spoken." With that same spirit of faith we also believe and therefore speak, (2 Cor 4:13)
> So do not be ashamed to testify about our Lord, or ashamed of me his prisoner. But join with me in suffering for the gospel, by the power of God, (2 Tim 1:8)
> And the things you have heard me say in the presence of many witnesses entrust to reliable men who will also be qualified to teach others. (2 Tim 2:2)
> These, then, are the things you should teach. Encourage and rebuke with all authority. Do not let anyone despise you. (Titus 2:15)
> But in your hearts set apart Christ as Lord. Always be prepared to give an answer to everyone who asks you to give the reason for the hope that you have. But do this with gentleness and respect, (1 Pet 3:15)

THE
OUTLINE & SUBJECT INDEX

REMEMBER: When you look up a subject and turn to the Scripture reference, you have not only the Scripture, you have *an outline and a discussion* (commentary) of the Scripture and subject.

This is one of the *GREAT VALUES* of **The Preacher's Outline & Sermon Bible**®. Once you have all the volumes, you will have not only what all other Bible indexes give you, that is, a list of all the subjects and their Scripture references, *BUT* you will also have...

- An outline of *every* Scripture and subject in the Bible.
- A discussion (commentary) on every Scripture and subject.
- Every subject supported by other Scriptures or cross references.

DISCOVER THE GREAT VALUE for yourself. Quickly glance below to the very first subject of the Index of Second John. It is:

ABIDE - ABIDING
  Duty. To abide, continue in the teaching of Christ. 9

Turn to the reference. Glance at the Scripture and outline of the Scripture, then read the commentary. You will immediately see the GREAT VALUE of the INDEX of **The Preacher's Outline & Sermon Bible**®.

OUTLINE AND SUBJECT INDEX

ABIDE - ABIDING
  Duty. To abide, continue in the teaching of Christ. 9
  Proves. One has God. 9
  Source of **a**. The truth. 2

ANTICHRISTS
  Discussed. 7-13
  Identity.
    A deceiver. 7
    Many **a**. - now. 7
  Methods used by. Denying Christ's incarnation. 7
  Warning against. Discussed. 7-13

BELIEVER
  Duty.
    To guard against false teaching. 7-13
    To love one another. 5-6
    To walk in the truth. 4
  Example. The elect lady. 1, 4

BELOVED (See **DEARLY LOVED**)

CHILDREN
  Duty. To walk in Christ no matter where they are. 4

CHURCH
  Duty. To guard against false teachers. 10-11

COMMANDS
  Greatest **c**. Discussed. 5-6
  Of God. Duty. To obey. 5-6

CONFESS - CONFESSION
  Meaning. **C**. the incarnation: that God's Son, Jesus Christ, as coming in the flesh. 7

DEARLY LOVED
  Meaning. 1

DECEIVE - DECEPTION
  Message of **d**. Deny Jesus has come in the flesh. 7

Warning against.
    Fourfold warning. 7-13
    Not to be received in home or church. 10-11
    Strong **d**. in the last days. 7
  Who deceives. Antichrist. 7

DENY - DENIAL
  Of Jesus Christ. Discussed. 7-13

DOCTRINE
  Of Christ.
    Are to guard. 7-11
    Discussed. 7-13

ELECT - ELECTION
  Meaning. 1

EMPTY - EMPTINESS
  Fact. The **e**. are loved by Jesus Christ and by genuine believers. 1-2

FAMILIES
  Duty. To guard against false teachers. 10-11

GRACE
  Meaning. 3

HOLY
  Meaning. 1

HOSPITALITY
  Who to receive. Not false teachers. 10-11

JESUS CHRIST
  Deity. Denial of. 7-13
  Incarnation. (See **JESUS CHRIST**, Origin and Nature, Deity, Humanity)
    Belief in is essential. 7, 10-11
    Some deny that God's Son, Jesus Christ, as coming in the flesh. 7
  Names - Titles. Truth, The. 1-2

LADY, THE ELECT
  Discussed. 1-4

LONELY
  Fact. Are loved by Jesus Christ and by genuine believers. 1-2

LOVE
  Acts of. 5-6
  Discussed. 5-6
    Great command of. 5-6
  Duty.
    To love those who criticize and mistreat. 5
    To love another in the truth (in Christ and in the Word of God). 1-2
  Meaning. 5

MERCY
  Meaning. 3

MOTHER
  Duty.
    To live as the holy and dearly loved, chosen person of the Lord. 1-4
    To rear children in the truth. 1-4

OBEDIENCE
  Duty. To obey the command of God. 4
  Results. Proves one's love. 6

PEACE
  Meaning. 3

REWARD
  Described - Identified as. A full reward. 8
  Duty. To watch so that we will not lose our **r**. 8

TEACHERS, FALSE
  Described as.
    Antichrist. 7
    Deceiver. 7
  Message of. Deny the incarnation, that God's Son, Jesus Christ, as coming in the flesh. 7
  Warning against. Not to be welcomed in one's home. 10-11

TEACHING
  Message. Doctrine and teachings of Christ. 9-11

INDEX

TRUTH
  Discussed. 1-2
  Duty. To walk in the **t**. 4
  Meaning. Jesus Christ is truth and the
    Word of God is truth. 1-2

UNLOVED, THE
  Fact. Are loved by Jesus Christ and by
    genuine believers. 1-2

WOMEN
  The chosen lady of 2 John. 1-4

WORD OF GOD
  Described. Truth, The. 1-2

THIRD

JOHN

3 JOHN

INTRODUCTION

AUTHOR: John, the Apostle (see I John, Introductory Notes).

DATE: Probably A.D. 85-95 (see I John, Introductory Notes).

TO WHOM WRITTEN: "To my dear friend Gaius" (3 Jn.1). (See outline and notes—3 Jn.1-8 for a discussion of Gaius.)

PURPOSE: To warn against rejecting true ministers and spiritual leadership. (See Introduction, Special Features, pt.2—II John for more discussion.)

SPECIAL FEATURES:

1. III John is "A General Epistle." That is, it is not written to a specific church. It is written from a pastor whose leadership and authority have been unduly rejected (3 Jn.9).

He now appeals to another leader to hear and receive his instructions.

2. III John is "An Epistle Governing Traveling Ministers such as Prophets, Teachers, Evangelists, and Missionaries." After the apostles died off, a clash arose over the ministers of local churches and the traveling ministers. There were some false ministers who had begun to fill the pulpits of the local churches and others who had begun to travel about taking advantage of the Christians who were kind enough to provide them food and lodging during their ministry and stay (II John 10). Because of this abuse, some within the churches arose and began to oppose all *traveling ministers* (Diotrephes of III John is an example of this). In II John, John writes the elect or chosen lady to warn her of false teachers. But on the other hand, he writes Gaius to encourage him to receive the *true prophets* (III John). III John shows that the conflict had become so heated that Diotrephes was even trying to have church members expelled if they accepted the traveling minister.

OUTLINE OF 3 JOHN

THE PREACHER'S OUTLINE & SERMON BIBLE® is *unique*. It differs from all other Study Bibles & Sermon Resource Materials in that every Passage and Subject is outlined right beside the Scripture. When you choose any *Subject* below and turn to the reference, you have not only the Scripture, but you discover the Scripture and Subject *already outlined for you—verse by verse*.

For a quick example, choose one of the subjects below and turn over to the Scripture, and you will find this marvellous help for faster, easier, and more accurate use.

In addition, every point of the Scripture and Subject is *fully developed in a Commentary with supporting Scripture* at the bottom of the page. Again, this arrangement makes sermon preparation much easier and faster.

Note something else: The Subjects of THIRD JOHN have titles that are both Biblical and *practical*. The practical titles sometimes have more appeal to people. This *benefit* is clearly seen for use on billboards, bulletins, church newsletters, etc.

A suggestion: For the quickest overview of THIRD JOHN, first read *all the major titles* (I, II, III, etc.), then come back and read the subtitles.

OUTLINE OF 3 JOHN

I. **THE SPIRITUAL AND BELOVED LEADER: GAIUS, A MAN WHO HELPED MUCH, 1-8**

II. **THE DIVISIVE CHURCH LEADER AND THE GODLY MINISTER, 9-14**

3 JOHN

	I. THE SPIRITUAL & BELOVED LEADER: GAIUS, A MAN WHO HELPED MUCH, 1-8	hear that my children are walking in the truth.	4 He helped Christian believers & strangers
1 He was a dear friend	The elder, To my dear friend Gaius, whom I love in the truth.	5 Dear friend, you are faithful in what you are doing for the brothers, even though they are strangers to you.	a. He was a dynamic example before the whole church
2 He prospered spiritually despite ill health	2 Dear friend, I pray that you may enjoy good health and that all may go well with you, even as your soul is getting along well.	6 They have told the church about your love. You will do well to send them on their way in a manner worthy of God.	b. He should continue to minister & show hospitality
3 He walked in the truth	3 It gave me great joy to have some brothers come and tell about your faithfulness to the truth and how you continue to walk in the truth.	7 It was for the sake of the Name that they went out, receiving no help from the pagans.	1) Because traveling ministers go forth for Christ without regular income
a. He had the testimony of walking in the truth		8 We ought therefore to show hospitality to such men so that we may work together for the truth.	2) Because we need to be fellow-workers in the truth
b. He brought joy to believers	4 I have no greater joy than to		

DIVISION I

THE SPIRITUAL AND BELOVED LEADER: GAIUS, A MAN WHO HELPED MUCH, v.1-8

(v.1-8) **Introduction**: leadership within the church is critical. Church leaders are chosen to lead people to Jesus Christ. Therefore how leaders live and behave is of critical importance: their lives affect the lives of the whole church. Their behavior often determines the growth of believers and whether or not the church has a dynamic ministry for Christ. This is what the letter of Third John is all about, leadership within the church. Three leaders are seen, two were godly men and one was a troublemaker. The first leader was Gaius. He is a picture of the spiritual and beloved leader, a man who took the lead within the church by reaching out and helping all those who needed help.

1. He was a dear friend (v.1).
2. He prospered spiritually—despite ill health (v.2).
3. He walked in the truth (v.3-4).
4. He helped Christian believers and strangers (v.5-8).

1 (v.1) **Gaius—A Dear Friend**: he was a dear friend. Note that John calls Gaius *dear friend* four times (v.1, 2, 5, 11). Gaius was dear to the heart of John. He was deeply loved. Why? Apparently they were close friends, but their friendship was not the main reason for their bond. The main reason for their close bond was Christ. Gaius had trusted Jesus Christ as his Savior and was faithful to the call God had given him. He was a leader in the church and he did his job well. He lived for Christ and performed his functions for the sake of Christ and the church (see note 2, *Truth*—2 Jn.1-2 for more discussion). John loved Gaius because he was both a dear friend and a great servant of Christ.

> "A new command I give you: Love one another. As I have loved you, so you must love one another. By this all men will know that you are my disciples, if you love one another." (John 13:34-35)
>
> "As the Father has loved me, so have I loved you. Now remain in my love. (John 15:9)
>
> My command is this: Love each other as I have loved you. (John 15:12)

> Love must be sincere. Hate what is evil; cling to what is good. (Rom 12:9)
>
> And live a life of love, just as Christ loved us and gave himself up for us as a fragrant offering and sacrifice to God. (Eph 5:2)
>
> May the Lord make your love increase and overflow for each other and for everyone else, just as ours does for you. (1 Th 3:12)
>
> Now that you have purified yourselves by obeying the truth so that you have sincere love for your brothers, love one another deeply, from the heart. (1 Pet 1:22)
>
> This is how we know what love is: Jesus Christ laid down his life for us. And we ought to lay down our lives for our brothers. (1 John 3:16)

2 (v.2) **Gaius—Prosperity—Health**: he prospered spiritually despite ill health. Gaius was apparently a man who suffered some illness or disease or was at least subject to being sick a lot. His health crosses John's mind, and John wants him to know that he is thinking and praying for his health just as he is praying for his soul to prosper. Note two things.

1. Gaius' soul did prosper. John actually says that it "is getting along well." The idea is that he was growing spiritually, growing stronger and stronger in Christ and in the fruit of the Spirit. He experienced the fullness of God day by day...

- love
- joy
- peace
- patience
- kindness
- goodness
- faithfulness
- gentleness
- self-control

Gaius, the church leader, prospered in that he experienced both abundant and eternal life. He knew God's care and guidance every day of his life.

2. John prayed for Gaius to enjoy good health and that all would go well with him. In this case, John was wanting

Gaius to be prosperous and fulfilled and satisfied in all of life...

- in his home
- in his work
- in his relationships
- in his leadership
- in his church
- in whatever he undertook

Thought 1. We should be praying for one another—for all believers—to be prosperous and fulfilled and satisfied in all that we undertake. We should be praying for success and joy in all of life. But remember: success does not mean money as much as it means joy, fulfillment, and satisfaction. Nothing can ever take the place of peace of heart and mind. And peace comes only through Jesus Christ.

> **For physical training is of some value, but godliness has value for all things, holding promise for both the present life and the life to come. (1 Tim 4:8)**
> **But godliness with contentment is great gain. For we brought nothing into the world, and we can take nothing out of it. But if we have food and clothing, we will be content with that. (1 Tim 6:6-8)**
> **This is a trustworthy saying. And I want you to stress these things, so that those who have trusted in God may be careful to devote themselves to doing what is good. These things are excellent and profitable for everyone. (Titus 3:8)**
> **Keep your lives free from the love of money and be content with what you have, because God has said, "Never will I leave you; never will I forsake you." (Heb 13:5)**
> **He is like a tree planted by streams of water, which yields its fruit in season and whose leaf does not wither. Whatever he does prospers. (Psa 1:3)**
> **Carefully follow the terms of this covenant, so that you may prosper in everything you do. (Deu 29:9)**

3 (3-4) **Truth—Gaius**: he walked in the truth. Note two significant facts.

1. Gaius, the church leader, had a strong testimony among the believers of the church. Some of the believers had visited the city where John was and shared the testimony of Gaius with John. What they shared was this: Gaius *walked in the truth*. This means that he walked in the truth of Jesus Christ and in the truth of God's Word.

⇒ Jesus Christ said that He is the truth.

> **Jesus answered, "I am the way and the truth and the life. No one comes to the Father except through me. (John 14:6)**

Jesus Christ is the truth, the very ideal of humanity, the Ideal and Perfect Man. Jesus Christ is everything that a person should be, all that God wants a person to be. Therefore, Gaius walked in Jesus Christ. He patterned his life after the truth, after Jesus Christ Himself.

⇒ Jesus Christ also said that the Word of God is truth.

> **Sanctify them by the truth; your word is truth. (John 17:17)**

All that a person should be is also written out in the Word of God. God's Word spells out the ideal and perfect person, just what God wants a person to be. Therefore, Gaius obeyed the Word of God. He walked in the truth of God's Word and lived as God's Word says to live.

2. Gaius brought joy to the hearts of believers. Not only were the believers joying in the testimony of Gaius, but John himself joyed in Gaius as well. But note again: he was not joying in Gaius' friendship, although he was bound to be thankful for a friend as close as Gaius. John was joyful over the Christian life Gaius was living, over the fact that Gaius walked in the truth.

Note another significant fact: Gaius was apparently standing firm in the truth despite severe opposition from another church leader and a clique that the divisive leader had drawn around him (v.9-11).

Thought 1. What a man Gaius must have been! It is difficult enough to stand against the normal temptations and trials of life, but when fellow believers begin to attack us, it makes standing up for the truth even more difficult. The tendency is to back off and just keep silent and let things run their course. But note Gaius. He stood up for the truth of Christ and of God's Word. He stood against those within the church who were not following the truth and were damaging and destroying the church by their divisiveness.

> **Then he said to them all: "If anyone would come after me, he must deny himself and take up his cross daily and follow me. (Luke 9:23)**
> **Do not conform any longer to the pattern of this world, but be transformed by the renewing of your mind. Then you will be able to test and approve what God's will is—his good, pleasing and perfect will. (Rom 12:2)**
> **Therefore, if anyone is in Christ, he is a new creation; the old has gone, the new has come! (2 Cor 5:17)**
> **So then, just as you received Christ Jesus as Lord, continue to live in him, (Col 2:6)**
> **Endure hardship with us like a good soldier of Christ Jesus. No one serving as a soldier gets involved in civilian affairs—he wants to please his commanding officer. (2 Tim 2:3-4)**
> **Whoever claims to live in him must walk as Jesus did. (1 John 2:6)**
> **Do not love the world or anything in the world. If anyone loves the world, the love of the Father is not in him. For everything in the world—the cravings of sinful man, the lust of his eyes and the boasting of what he has and does—comes not from the Father but from the world. (1 John 2:15-16)**

4 (5-8) **Gaius—Ministering—Hospitality—Benevolence**: he helped Christian believers and strangers. This tells us why John was writing to Gaius and the church. There were some in the church who did not like the idea of traveling ministers visiting and holding meetings in their church. They were opposed to any kind of minister or ministry that was not settled within the church itself. They did not, therefore, want the traveling evangelists, missionaries, prophets, and teachers preaching and teaching in their church. They saw no use for their ministry. They felt...

- that believers could learn all they needed to know from their own ministers and from others in the settled ministry.
- that they did not need help in reaching out to the lost.
- that they could carry out the mission of Christ without the help of traveling ministers.

This will be seen when the opposition is discussed in the next passage and outline. For now, note three significant points.

1. Gaius was doing all he could to help the traveling ministers. He was opening his home and supporting them—so much so that he had a strong testimony in the ministry of hospitality. Note that he even opened his home to strangers in order to reach and grow them in Christ.

2. Gaius is to continue to receive and support the traveling ministers (v.6b). Note: it is said that this is exactly what God Himself would do. Gaius is told this is the godly way, the godly thing to do. That is, it is exactly what God would do; therefore, it is what the church leader is to do. There are two strong reasons why.

a. Traveling ministers should be received and supported as they go forth for Christ. They have dedicated their lives to serve Christ by reaching the lost and growing believers, and the church needs their ministry. In addition, they have made the commitment by faith, without receiving a regular income.

b. Traveling ministers should be received and supported because we need to be fellow-workers in the truth. There is no question: they are workers in the truth. Traveling evangelists, missionaries, prophets, and teachers alike are carrying the gospel of truth across the world. The only question is: Are we in the local church going to be fellow workers with them? John says that it is the very thing that God Himself would do. Therefore, we in the local church must labor with all those who walk in the truth of Jesus Christ and the Word of God. We must labor with all those chosen by God to carry forth the Word of truth, the Word of His dear Son, the Lord Jesus Christ.

Thought 1. Gaius is a dynamic example for the leaders of the local church. All Christian leaders are to...

- open their homes to strangers: college students who are away from home, single parents with children, the homeless, the needy, the hungry, foreigners, and all others.
- open their homes in supporting the traveling evangelists and teachers who are faithfully serving our Lord Jesus.
- open their homes to the various ministries of the church such as Bible Study groups, youth meetings and fellowships.

> **Share with God's people who are in need. Practice hospitality. (Rom 12:13)**
>
> **Now the overseer must be above reproach, the husband of but one wife, temperate, self-controlled, respectable, hospitable, able to teach, (1 Tim 3:2)**
>
> **No widow may be put on the list of widows unless she is over sixty, has been faithful to her husband, (1 Tim 5:9)**
>
> **Rather he must be hospitable, one who loves what is good, who is self-controlled, upright, holy and disciplined. (Titus 1:8)**
>
> **Do not forget to entertain strangers, for by so doing some people have entertained angels without knowing it. (Heb 13:2)**
>
> **Offer hospitality to one another without grumbling. (1 Pet 4:9)**
>
> **And is well known for her good deeds, such as bringing up children, showing hospitality, washing the feet of the saints, helping those in trouble and devoting herself to all kinds of good deeds. (1 Tim 5:10)**

	II. THE DIVISIVE CHURCH LEADER & THE GODLY MINISTER, 9-14	Anyone who does what is good is from God. Anyone who does what is evil has not seen God.	f. He was not to be followed because he was evil
1 The divisive church leader	9 I wrote to the church, but Diotrephes, who loves to be first, will have nothing to do with us.	12 Demetrius is well spoken of by everyone—and even by the truth itself. We also speak well of him, and you know that our testimony is true.	**2 The godly leader who stands in the truth**
a. He loved to be the first, the preeminence			a. A man of testimony
b. He rejected ministerial leadership	10 So if I come, I will call attention to what he is doing, gossiping maliciously about us. Not satisfied with that, he refuses to welcome the brothers. He also stops those who want to do so and puts them out of the church.		b. A man of the truth
c. He talked about, criticized, & censored the minister			c. A man highly esteemed by other leaders
d. He opposed those who supported the minister		13 I have much to write you, but I do not want to do so with pen and ink.	**3 Conclusion: The problem in the church was so severe that a personal visit was needed by the minister John**
e. He had to be disciplined	11 Dear friend, do not imitate what is evil but what is good.	14 I hope to see you soon, and we will talk face to face. Peace to you. The friends here send their greetings. Greet the friends there by name.	

DIVISION II

THE DIVISIVE CHURCH LEADER AND THE GODLY MINISTER, 9-14

(v.9-14) **Introduction**: a divisive leader is one of the most serious problems that ever confronts a church. When a church has within its ranks a divisive leader, the very life and ministry of the church are threatened. A divisive leader always carries a church through one of its most traumatic experiences. He usually gathers others around him into a clique of opposition, and when he goes this far, he becomes much more of a threat to the life of the church. This is the very reason that Third John was written. There was a divisive leader in the church who was causing serious problems. In writing, John covers the traits of the divisive leader and he tells us how to handle him.

1. The divisive church leader (v.9-11).
2. The godly leader who stands in the truth (v.12).
3. Conclusion: the problem in the church was so severe that a personal visit was needed by the minister John (v.13-14).

2 (9-11) **Divisive Church Leaders—Diotrephes—Discipline**: there is the divisive church leader, a man called Diotrephes. Who was he? All we know is what is said here, for this is the only time he is mentioned in Scripture. But a great deal is given here. We can tell that he was a prominent leader in the church. Note: he had enough authority to reject John's letter, and remember John was not only an apostle, but one of the three closest apostles to Christ (v.9). He also had enough authority to stop traveling ministers from holding meetings in the church, ministers such as evangelists, teachers, and prophets (v.10). He even had the authority to force people out of the church (v.10).

All this points to his being a minister or one of the highest lay officials in the church such as a deacon. What an enormous opportunity and privilege he had! Holding such a high call in the church, he could have been a dynamic example of what a believer should be—an example of love, care, ministry, outreach, evangelism, and of purity of life. But the legacy he has left behind is a far cry from being a testimony. His legacy is division; he was a divisive leader. Imagine! After his death, the major thing remembered about him is that he was the person who caused division in the church. Six things are said about him.

1. Diotrephes, the divisive leader, loved recognition. He loved to be preeminent, to be first in the church (v.9).

⇒ He wanted people recognizing him as the most important leader in the church.
⇒ He wanted people coming to him for advice and counsel.
⇒ He wanted people seeking his opinion first before they went to others.
⇒ He wanted all new ideas and ministries and programs to be brought to him first.
⇒ He wanted to sit in on all major discussions and meetings.
⇒ He wanted to have the major say-so in all decisions.
⇒ He wanted the right to approve or disapprove who did what in the church.

On and on the list could go. This church leader wanted to be first, to have the recognition and preeminence in the church.

Thought 1. A.T. Robertson shares a personal experience that is most interesting and that should speak to all of our hearts about how insidious the desire to be first can be:

"He [Diotrephes] may have been an elder (bishop) or deacon, but clearly desired to rule the whole church. Some forty years ago I wrote an article on Diotrephes for a denominational paper. The editor told me that twenty-five deacons stopped the paper to show their resentment against being personally attacked in the paper" (*Word Pictures In The New Testament*, Vol.6, p.263).

For whoever exalts himself will be humbled, and whoever humbles himself will be exalted. (Mat 23:12)
Also a dispute arose among them as to which of them was considered to be greatest. (Luke 22:24)
How can you believe if you accept praise from one another, yet make no

effort to obtain the praise that comes from the only God ? (John 5:44)

Live in harmony with one another. Do not be proud, but be willing to associate with people of low position. Do not be conceited. (Rom 12:16)

Do nothing out of selfish ambition or vain conceit, but in humility consider others better than yourselves. Each of you should look not only to your own interests, but also to the interests of others. (Phil 2:3-4)

Not lording it over those entrusted to you, but being examples to the flock. (1 Pet 5:3)

Pride goes before destruction, a haughty spirit before a fall. (Prov 16:18)

A friend loves at all times, and a brother is born for adversity. (Prov 17:17)

It is not good to eat too much honey, nor is it honorable to seek one's own honor. (Prov 25:27)

A greedy man stirs up dissension, but he who trusts in the LORD will prosper. (Prov 28:25)

Woe to those who are wise in their own eyes and clever in their own sight. (Isa 5:21)

You said in your heart, "I will ascend to heaven; I will raise my throne above the stars of God; I will sit enthroned on the mount of assembly, on the utmost heights of the sacred mountain. I will ascend above the tops of the clouds; I will make myself like the Most High." (Isa 14:13-14)

Though you soar like the eagle and make your nest among the stars, from there I will bring you down," declares the LORD. (Oba 1:4)

Thought 2. Oliver Greene makes a very practical comment that needs to be heeded by all church leaders who desire to be preeminent in the church.

"Greek authorities tell us that the phrase here translated 'who loveth to have the preeminence' [who loves to be first] is only one word in the Greek, and it is not found anywhere else in the New Testament. The meaning is simply 'one who loves to be first,' one who will rule or ruin. But there ARE no rulers or lords in God's Church. Pastors, deacons, church leaders are not to be 'lords over God's heritage' (1 Pet.5:3)" (*The Epistles of John*, p.254).

2. Diotrephes, the divisive leader, rejected ministerial leadership. Note: John had written some previous letter to the church. Again remember that this is John the apostle, one of the men who had walked with Jesus Himself. But this did not matter to this divisive leader. He rejected John's authority as a minister of God. In fact, he totally rejected the minister's authority. He would not even allow John's letter to be read before the church. This is the very

reason John has addressed this letter to Gaius. Diotrephes had destroyed John's former letter to the church; therefore, this time John sends the letter to Gaius, who is another leader in the church.

Thought 1. When a person wants his own way in the church, authority matters little. In fact, this is usually the way we can tell whether or not a person is wanting to be recognized: if he is rejecting the appointed authority in the church.

Do nothing out of selfish ambition or vain conceit, but in humility consider others better than yourselves. Each of you should look not only to your own interests, but also to the interests of others. (Phil 2:3-4)

3. Diotrephes criticized, talked about, and censored the minister. And note: he used malicious words; he was bitter and divisive against the minister John. He went about *overflowing with talk* and rattling on about the matter, talking against and letting the members know that he opposed the minister.

But I tell you that men will have to give account on the day of judgment for every careless word they have spoken. (Mat 12:36)

Get rid of all bitterness, rage and anger, brawling and slander, along with every form of malice. (Eph 4:31)

The tongue also is a fire, a world of evil among the parts of the body. It corrupts the whole person, sets the whole course of his life on fire, and is itself set on fire by hell. (James 3:6)

Brothers, do not slander one another. Anyone who speaks against his brother or judges him speaks against the law and judges it. When you judge the law, you are not keeping it, but sitting in judgment on it. (James 4:11)

Therefore, rid yourselves of all malice and all deceit, hypocrisy, envy, and slander of every kind. (1 Pet 2:1)

For I hear the slander of many; there is terror on every side; they conspire against me and plot to take my life. (Psa 31:13)

Whoever slanders his neighbor in secret, him will I put to silence; whoever has haughty eyes and a proud heart, him will I not endure. (Psa 101:5)

He who conceals his hatred has lying lips, and whoever spreads slander is a fool. (Prov 10:18)

Like clouds and wind without rain is a man who boasts of gifts he does not give. (Prov 25:14)

4. Diotrephes opposed those who stood behind the minister. The issue within the church was whether or not to support traveling ministers such as evangelists, prophets, missionaries, and teachers. Some in the church led by Diotrephes felt that the only legitimate ministers were ministers of local churches. They felt that ministers such as traveling evangelists, prophets, missionaries, and outside teachers were not needed, that the church did not need their help to mature the believers nor to reach out to the lost.

But note: the minister John knew better. He knew that the Lord Jesus Christ had called and appointed specific officers for His church. He knew that believers needed the help of many ministers with very special gifts, ministers who could help the believers grow and carry out their own ministry. John knew that evangelists and missionaries could help the church reach out to reap the lost and stir believers to be more outreach minded. John knew that teachers and prophets could help believers of the local church grow, help them by giving them a different personality, voice, and perspective of God's Word and Christian growth.

As stated, the divisive leader, Diotrephes, opposed John the minister. He was so strong in his opposition that he was publicly opposing those who stood behind the minister. He was even driving some of them out and away from the church.

5. Diotrephes had to be disciplined. He was destroying the church. He had opposed the minister John so much that some believers had already left the church. He was disturbing every facet of church life:

⇒ affecting the testimony of the church before the world.
⇒ affecting the fellowship among believers.
⇒ affecting the spirit and enthusiasm of the believers, causing gloom and a disheartened spirit to set in.
⇒ affecting young and immature believers.
⇒ affecting the church's outreach into the community.
⇒ affecting the ministries and programs of the church. Few felt like participating.
⇒ affecting the reaching of the lost. Outsiders looked upon the church as being hypocritical.
⇒ affecting the offerings of the church.

This and so much more is what always happens when a divisive leader stirs up trouble within a church. This is the reason why a divisive leader must always be disciplined. Note: John says that he will deal with Diotrephes when he visits the church (v.9). The idea is that he, as the minister of God, is going to lead the church to discipline him. Jesus Christ instructs us how to handle discipline in the church, and no doubt, this is what John meant (see outline and notes—Mt.18:15-20 for discussion on church discipline).

> "If your brother sins against you, go and show him his fault, just between the two of you. If he listens to you, you have won your brother over. But if he will not listen, take one or two others along, so that 'every matter may be established by the testimony of two or three witnesses.' If he refuses to listen to them, tell it to the church; and if he refuses to listen even to the church, treat him as you would a pagan or a tax collector. (Mat 18:15-17)
> Jesus said to his disciples: "Things that cause people to sin are bound to come, but woe to that person through whom they come. It would be better for him to be thrown into the sea with a millstone tied around his neck than for him to cause one of these little ones to sin. So watch yourselves. "If your brother sins, rebuke him, and if he repents, forgive him. (Luke 17:1-3)
> Those who sin are to be rebuked publicly, so that the others may take warning. (1 Tim 5:20)
> Preach the Word; be prepared in season and out of season; correct, rebuke and

encourage—with great patience and careful instruction. (2 Tim 4:2)
> This testimony is true. Therefore, rebuke them sharply, so that they will be sound in the faith (Titus 1:13)
> These, then, are the things you should teach. Encourage and rebuke with all authority. Do not let anyone despise you. (Titus 2:15)
> Warn a divisive person once, and then warn him a second time. After that, have nothing to do with him. (Titus 3:10)

6. Diotrephes was not to be followed. This is a strong warning issued by the minister John: do not imitate what is evil, but imitate what is good. A divisive leader is not to be imitated. He may be a leader—he may be the first leader in the church, but he is not to be imitated if he is divisive and bucking against the authority of the minister and other leaders of the church. No matter who he is, no matter what his position, his leadership is to be rejected if he begins to sow seeds of divisiveness. His evil is not to be imitated. Note why. The reason is shocking: a divisive person does evil, and the person who does what is evil is not born of God. No matter what the divisive person claims, no matter how great a leader he is in the church, no matter how long he has been in the church—the divisive person is not born of God. How could he be? For God is good, and only the person who does good is born of God.

> Love must be sincere. Hate what is evil; cling to what is good. (Rom 12:9)
> Avoid every kind of evil. (1 Th 5:22)
> Make every effort to live in peace with all men and to be holy; without holiness no one will see the Lord. See to it that no one misses the grace of God and that no bitter root grows up to cause trouble and defile many. (Heb 12:14-15)
> And do not forget to do good and to share with others, for with such sacrifices God is pleased. (Heb 13:16)
> He must turn from evil and do good; he must seek peace and pursue it. (1 Pet 3:11)
> All wrongdoing is sin, and there is sin that does not lead to death. (1 John 5:17)
> Turn from evil and do good; seek peace and pursue it. (Psa 34:14)

2 (v.12) **Minister—Demetrius**: there is the godly leader who stands in the truth. Who is Demetrius? What is said here in this verse is all we know.

⇒ He could be a leader in the church who stood toe to toe with Diotrephes. If so, then John is telling Gaius to lead the church in supporting him.
⇒ Most likely he is the minister and messenger John is sending to the church to deliver this third letter of John, a minister who is to help straighten out the division in the church.

Whatever the case, Demetrius stands as a dynamic example of a godly leader, of just what a leader in the church should be. Note three strong facts about him.

1. Demetrius had a strong testimony among all believers. Few leaders have a dynamic testimony among all, but this church leader did. He was held in the highest esteem by God's people. They respected him every so highly.

2. Demetrius had a strong testimony for walking in the truth (see note, *Truth*—3 Jn.3-4 for discussion).

3. Demetrius was highly esteemed by other leaders. Note: John says we also bear record to the testimony of Demetrius, and then he strongly affirms the fact: he declares that his own testimony is trustworthy. What he is saying about the character of Demetrius is true. Demetrius is a godly servant of the Lord no matter what any divisive leader says. This emphasis points rather strongly toward Demetrius being one of the traveling evangelists or teachers serving with John. There is a possibility that he was one of those who had been opposed by Diotrephes and not allowed to teach in the church.

Whatever the case, Demetrius is a dynamic example of what church leaders should be. Note that he is not a cowardly man. He is willing to personally deliver the letter of Third John to Gaius and the church and to deal with the problems of the division.

Thought 1. This is to be the testimony of all church leaders. A life that is rooted and grounded in Christ is the very purpose for which God calls church leaders.

> **A good name is more desirable than great riches; to be esteemed is better than silver or gold. (Prov 22:1)**

> **Brothers, choose seven men from among you who are known to be full of the Spirit and wisdom. We will turn this responsibility over to them (Acts 6:3)**

> **The brothers at Lystra and Iconium spoke well of him. (Acts 16:2)**

> **First, I thank my God through Jesus Christ for all of you, because your faith is being reported all over the world. (Rom 1:8)**

> **Everyone has heard about your obedience, so I am full of joy over you; but I want you to be wise about what is good, and innocent about what is evil. (Rom 16:19)**

> **And we are sending along with him the brother who is praised by all the churches for his service to the gospel. (2 Cor 8:18)**

> **Demetrius is well spoken of by everyone—and even by the truth itself. We also speak well of him, and you know that our testimony is true. (3 John 1:12)**

3 (13-14) **Conclusion**: the problem in the church was severe, so severe that John planned to visit the church and to visit it soon. He would write no more. He had much to say to Gaius and the believers, but he needed to say it face to face, not in a letter. Note the minister's closing remarks:

⇒ He wishes *peace* upon them; this was the very thing Gaius and the church needed.

⇒ He sends greetings from mutual friends: this was saying to Gaius and the believers that they were not being rejected by other churches and believers. They were not being frowned upon because they were unable to handle the division and to discipline the divisive leader.

⇒ He asks Gaius to greet his friends by name for him.

THE
OUTLINE & SUBJECT INDEX

REMEMBER: When you look up a subject and turn to the Scripture reference, you have not only the Scripture, you have *an outline and a discussion* (commentary) of the Scripture and subject.

This is one of the *GREAT VALUES* of **The Preacher's Outline & Sermon Bible**®. Once you have all the volumes, you will have not only what all other Bible indexes give you, that is, a list of all the subjects and their Scripture references, *BUT* you will also have…

- An outline of *every* Scripture and subject in the Bible.
- A discussion (commentary) on every Scripture and subject.
- Every subject supported by other Scriptures or cross references.

DISCOVER THE GREAT VALUE for yourself. Quickly glance below to the very first subject of the Index of Third John. It is:

AMBITION - AMBITIOUS
    Duty.
        Not to love the preeminence, the desire to be
        first. 9-11

Turn to the reference. Glance at the Scripture and outline of the Scripture, then read the commentary. You will immediately see the GREAT VALUE of the INDEX of **The Preacher's Outline & Sermon Bible**®.

OUTLINE AND SUBJECT INDEX

AMBITION - AMBITIOUS
Duty.
    Not to love the preeminence, the desire to be first. 9-11
    To rebuke evil **a**. 10
Evil **a**. Causes. Loving the preeminence. 9
Examples of evil **a**. Diotrephes: loving the preeminence. 9-11

BELIEVERS
Example - Illustration.
    A godly minister. 12
    A haughty outspoken leader. 9-11
    A spiritual leader. 1-8

CHURCH DISCIPLINE
A divisive leader needing rebuke. 10

DEMETRIUS
Godly church leader. 12

DIOTREPHES
Divisive church leader. 9-11

DIVISION
Caused by. Divisive church leaders. 9-11
Results. Discussed. 9-11

EVANGELISTS
Duty toward. To welcome and support. 3-4, 5-8

GAIUS
A beloved leader in the church. 1-8
The recipient of 3 John. 1

GIFTS, SPIRITUAL
Example of. Gift of helps. 5-8

HOSPITALITY
Duty.
    To have a strong testimony in **h**. 3-4, 5-8
    To welcome evangelists, prophets, traveling ministers. 3-4, 5-8
Example of. 5-8

MINISTERING
Duty. To minister faithfully to all in need, even to strangers. 5-8
Ministers. Duty toward. To welcome if they are traveling **m**., evangelists, missionaries, prophets, and teachers. 3-4, 5-8

MINISTERS
Duty. To welcome traveling **m**., evangelists, prophets, teachers, and missionaries. 3-4, 5-8

MISSIONARIES
Duty toward. To welcome if they are traveling **m**., evangelists, teachers. 3-4, 5-8

PRIDE
Caused by. Loving the preeminence, the desire to be first. 9-11

SERVE - SERVICE (See **BELIEVER; MINISTER; MINISTRY**)
Example. A man who helps much. 5-8

TESTIMONY
Duty. To have a strong **t**. in ministering. 3-4, 5-8
Example. A messenger with a good report. 12

TRUTH
Duty. To walk in the **t**. 3-4
Meaning. Is both Jesus Christ and the Word of God. 3-4

JUDE

JUDE

INTRODUCTION

AUTHOR: Jude, the brother of James and the half-brother of Jesus Christ Himself (cp. Mt.13:55; Mk.6:3). This is the traditional view, and there is nothing of substance to argue against it. Jude was slow in being accepted into the canon as Scripture. It was not fully accepted until about A.D. 350. This was probably due to Jude's quoting some apocryphal books (cp. Jude 9, 14-15). The apocryphal books were written between the Old Testament and the New Testament and have never been counted as Scripture by most believers. Eventually Jude proved itself as Scripture and was fully accepted by the church. As stated, it is mentioned by the middle of the third century (A.D. 350).

DATE: Uncertain. Somewhere between A.D. 67-90.

There is no clear indication when the epistle was written. However, there are some factors that point toward a date somewhere between the middle 70's and 80's.

1. Jude refers to a body of beliefs that had been formulated by the church (Jude 3). The church most likely would not formulate a creed of beliefs until after the apostles had begun to die off. As far as is known, all of the apostles had gone on to be with the Lord by the late 60's except for John.

2. Jude challenges the believers to remember the words of the apostles—as though most of the apostles had already passed on and there was a need to look way back over the early years of church history (Jude 17-19).

3. Jude and Peter deal with the same subject of false teachers, and they make many of the same points. Because of this it looks as though II Peter made use of Jude or Jude made use of II Peter. Peter probably had access to Jude, incorporating the short book primarily into the second chapter. It is unlikely that Jude would have had access to II Peter and made use of only the second chapter.

TO WHOM WRITTEN: "To those who have been called...chosen...and kept" (Jude 1).

Jude wrote to a specific people in a particular situation. This is seen in his calling them "dear friends" and speaking so directly to them as though he knows them in a most personal way (Jude 3-5, 17-18, 20). But their identity is nowhere given.

PURPOSE: "To write and urge you to contend for the faith" (Jude 3-4).

Jude states explicitly that he set out to write about "our common salvation." But all of a sudden, he changed his epistle to combat false teachers and their apostasy. The false teaching was the same false teaching that John, Paul, and Peter had to combat, that of Gnosticism. (See Introduction, Purpose—I John and Colossians for a discussion of the false teaching. Also see Col.1:15 for more discussion.)

SPECIAL FEATURES:

1. Jude is "The Last General Epistle." That is, it is not written to a particular church so far as we know

2. Jude is "An Epistle of Triads." That is, the author writes in sets of three. For example, he uses three historic examples of judgments (Jude 5-7), and three great rebels of the Old Testament (Jude 11). Verse one alone has two sets of triads, verse two one set. There are many others easily spotted as one reads the book.

3. Jude is "An Epistle Written to Combat False Teachers and Their Apostasy." (See Purpose, Introduction—I John for discussion.)

4. Jude is "The Epistle that Covers the Terrible Characteristics and Judgments of False Teachers" (Jude 3-16).

5. Jude is "The Epistle that Tells Believers How to Combat False Teaching" (Jude 17-23).

6. Jude is "An Epistle that Stresses Mercy and Rescue." Believers are to do all they can to save those polluted and contaminated by false teaching (Jude 22-23).

7. Jude is "The Epistle with the Reassuring Doxology." No more reassuring words could be chosen to close a letter than the words of Jude 24-25. Of all the closing words of the epistles, these are probably the best known.

THE PREACHER'S OUTLINE & SERMON BIBLE® is *unique*. It differs from all other Study Bibles & Sermon Resource Materials in that every Passage and Subject is outlined right beside the Scripture. When you choose any *Subject* below and turn to the reference, you have not only the Scripture, but you discover the Scripture and Subject *already outlined for you—verse by verse.*

For a quick example, choose one of the subjects below and turn over to the Scripture, and you will find this marvelous help for faster, easier, and more accurate use.

In addition, every point of the Scripture and Subject is *fully developed in a Commentary* with supporting Scripture at the bottom of the page. Again, this arrangement makes sermon preparation much easier and faster.

Note something else: The Subjects of JUDE have titles that are both Biblical and *practical*. The practical titles sometimes have more appeal to people. This *benefit* is clearly seen for use on billboards, bulletins, church newsletters, etc.

A suggestion: For the quickest overview of JUDE, first read *all the major titles* (I, II, III, etc.), then come back and read the subtitles.

OUTLINE OF JUDE

I. **THE DESCRIPTION OF TRUE BELIEVERS, 1-2**

II. **THE WARNINGS AGAINST APOSTASY: THE CHARACTERISTICS AND JUDGMENT OF FALSE TEACHERS, 3-16**

III. **THE EXHORTATION TO BELIEVERS, 17-25**

	I. THE DESCRIPTION OF TRUE BELIEVERS, 1-2
1 There is the picture of the true minister	Jude, a servant of Jesus Christ and a brother of James, To those who have been called, who are loved by God the Father and kept by Jesus Christ:
2 There is the picture of the true believer a. He is called b. He is loved by God c. He is kept by Jesus Christ d. He receives mercy, peace, & love	2 Mercy, peace and love be yours in abundance.

DIVISION I

THE DESCRIPTION OF TRUE BELIEVERS, 1-2

(v.1-2) **Introduction**: How can we tell whether or not a person is a true minister of God? How can we tell whether or not a person is a true believer? This is the discussion of this passage. Remember: Jude was the brother of our Lord. At first, he did not believe in Jesus Christ. But some time after the resurrection of Christ, he gave his heart to the Lord and surrendered his life to preach the gospel. Here we see him sitting down and writing to the believers of the first century. And in writing, he wastes no time: right from the start he describes himself as a true minister of Jesus Christ and his readers as true believers of Christ. Consequently, in his opening remark we have a picture by which we can measure ourselves, the picture of a true minister and of a true believer.

1. There is the picture of the true minister (v.1).
2. There is the picture of the true believer (v.1-2).

1 (v.1) **Minister—Servant—Humility**: there is the picture of the true minister. Who is he? Jude says two simple things about himself.

1. He says that he is "a servant of Jesus Christ." This is amazing, for as stated above, Jude was the brother of Jesus, the carpenter from Nazareth (Mt.13:55; Mk.6:3; cp. Jn.7:1-5, esp. v.5). At first he did not believe that Jesus was the Christ, the Anointed One of God, the Son of God who was to come to earth as the Savior of the world. But note what Jude says here: he says that he is "a servant of *Jesus Christ*." He now believes that his brother Jesus is the Messiah, the *Anointed One* of God. He believes that his brother Jesus is the Son of God who came into the world to save man. He believes that his brother Jesus can save him from sin, death, and judgment; he believes that his brother Jesus can make him acceptable to God. What an enormous turnaround! What a testimony for our Lord Jesus Christ!

Note what else Jude says: he says he is a servant of Jesus Christ (see note, *Servant*—2 Pt.1:1 for discussion).

> Whoever serves me must follow me; and where I am, my servant also will be. My Father will honor the one who serves me. (John 12:26; cp. Ro.12:1; 1 Cor.15:58)
> Obey them not only to win their favor when their eye is on you, but like slaves of Christ, doing the will of God from your heart. Serve wholeheartedly, as if you were serving the Lord, not men, (Eph 6:6-7)
> Whatever you do, work at it with all your heart, as working for the Lord, not for men, since you know that you will receive an inheritance from the Lord as a reward. It is the Lord Christ you are serving. (Col 3:23-24)
> Therefore, since we are receiving a kingdom that cannot be shaken, let us be thankful, and so worship God acceptably with reverence and awe, (Heb 12:28)
> Worship the LORD your God, and his blessing will be on your food and water. I will take away sickness from among you, (Exo 23:25)
> And now, O Israel, what does the LORD your God ask of you but to fear the LORD your God, to walk in all his ways, to love him, to serve the LORD your God with all your heart and with all your soul, (Deu 10:12)
> Serve the LORD with fear and rejoice with trembling. (Psa 2:11)
> Worship the LORD with gladness; come before him with joyful songs. (Psa 100:2)

2. Jude says that he is the brother of James. Who is James? What James would be so famous and well known that all the believers of the first century would know him by his first name? There was only one such James, the James who was the Lord's brother, the James who was the pastor of the great Jerusalem church, the mother church of Christianity.

Note this fact: Jude identifies himself by referring to James. Believers all over the world knew James, but few knew Jude. Therefore, he must identify himself so that his audience will receive his exhortation. He is simply Jude "A servant of Jesus Christ and a brother of James." Note the *humility* of this man! The only claim he has is that he is a slave to Jesus Christ and the brother of a famous man. He could have easily been jealous of his famous brother, resentful of the fact that he had to live under the shadow of his brother, resentful that he had to use his brother's name to get a hearing from believers. But Jude was not jealous or resentful. He was a true minister of God: he walked humbly among the believers of the world, humbly before God, ever so thankful that God had called him to serve His Son the Lord Jesus Christ, thankful for whatever call God gave him.

Thought 1. The true minister of God has two very basic traits.

1) The trait of being a servant and slave of Jesus Christ. And remember: Christ means Messiah, the *Anointed One* of God, the Son of God whom God sent into the world to save men. This is the most basic belief of a true follower of Jesus Christ. Therefore, every true minister of the gospel makes this belief the basis of his life and ministry. He is a true minister because he is a servant and slave of *Jesus Christ*.

2) The trait of humility. The true minister walks humbly among believers and before God. No matter how low God's call is to him, he is thankful for the very fact that God called him. He is, after all, the servant and slave who is available to do the bidding of his Master.

Thought 2. The fact that Jude was a brother of our Lord is glorious evidence that Jesus Christ is exactly who He claimed to be. It is touching when we realize that Jude had lived as the half-brother to Jesus for years. Day in and day out, hour by hour, month by month, and year by year Jude had played, eaten, worked, slept, and gone to school with Jesus. He had roamed the surrounding hills with Jesus as a boy and seen Him play with other children and relate to the neighbors and adults of their neighborhood. Jude had seen how his brother received and responded to adult instruction, teaching, and supervision. He had also probably seen Jesus take over the head of the household when their father, Joseph, had died.

> **After the Lord Jesus had spoken to them, he was taken up into heaven and he sat at the right hand of God. (Mark 16:19)**

> **But from now on, the Son of Man will be seated at the right hand of the mighty God." (Luke 22:69)**

> **"The one who comes from above is above all; the one who is from the earth belongs to the earth, and speaks as one from the earth. The one who comes from heaven is above all. (John 3:31)**

> **"Therefore let all Israel be assured of this: God has made this Jesus, whom you crucified, both Lord and Christ." (Acts 2:36)**

> **God exalted him to his own right hand as Prince and Savior that he might give repentance and forgiveness of sins to Israel. (Acts 5:31)**

> **That if you confess with your mouth, "Jesus is Lord," and believe in your heart that God raised him from the dead, you will be saved. (Rom 10:9)**

> **For this very reason, Christ died and returned to life so that he might be the Lord of both the dead and the living. (Rom 14:9)**

> **Yet for us there is but one God, the Father, from whom all things came and for whom we live; and there is but one Lord, Jesus Christ, through whom all things came and through whom we live. (1 Cor 8:6)**

> **And his incomparably great power for us who believe. That power is like the working of his mighty strength, which he exerted in Christ when he raised him from the dead and seated him at his right hand in the heavenly realms, (Eph 1:19-20)**

> **Who, being in very nature God, did not consider equality with God something to be grasped, but made himself nothing, taking the very nature of a servant, being made in human likeness. And being found in appearance as a man, he humbled himself and became obedient to death— even death on a cross! Therefore God exalted him to the highest place and gave him the name that is above every name, that at the name of Jesus every knee should bow, in heaven and on earth and under the earth, and every tongue confess that Jesus Christ is Lord, to the glory of God the Father. (Phil 2:6-11)**

> **In a loud voice they sang: "Worthy is the Lamb, who was slain, to receive power and wealth and wisdom and strength and honor and glory and praise!" (Rev 5:12)**

2 (1-2) **Believers—Loved—Kept—Called**: there is the picture of a true believer. Who were these believers? If Jude was writing to a particular church or group of churches, he does not name the church or churches. This points toward him writing to all the believers of the first century. Apparently the fact that Jude and James were brothers of the Lord Jesus Christ carried a lot of weight with the believers of their day. When they spoke, it made the believers stand up and take notice, for they had lived with Jesus day by day before His ministry and had experienced dramatic conversions from unbelief to staunch belief. This fact probably points to Jude writing to a wider audience. What he was writing was to be circulated among all the churches among all believers. In these opening words, Jude pictures just who a believer is. We can actually measure ourselves against his description and tell whether or not we are a believer.

1. Believers are the "*called*" (kletois). This means several things.

   a. It means that believers are the persons who have responded to the call of the gospel. God calls man to accept the gospel. He tugs and pulls at the heart strings, convicts and convinces man to accept Jesus Christ as His Son, but man has to respond to the call of God. God cannot make the decision for man. The believer is a person who has genuinely accepted the call of God. God summoned him, called him, and the believer responded. He became a believer, a person who truly believed in Jesus Christ.

   > **"So the last will be first, and the first will be last." (Mat 20:16; cp. Mt.22:14)**

   > **And you also are among those who are called to belong to Jesus Christ. To all in Rome who are loved by God and called to be saints: Grace and peace to you from God our Father and from the Lord Jesus Christ. (Rom 1:6-7)**

   > **To the church of God in Corinth, to those sanctified in Christ Jesus and called to be holy, together with all those everywhere who call on the name of our Lord Jesus Christ—their Lord and ours: (1 Cor 1:2)**

But we preach Christ crucified: a stumbling block to Jews and foolishness to Gentiles, but to those whom God has called, both Jews and Greeks, Christ the power of God and the wisdom of God. (1 Cor 1:23-24)

Who has saved us and called us to a holy life—not because of anything we have done but because of his own purpose and grace. This grace was given us in Christ Jesus before the beginning of time, (2 Tim 1:9)

b. It means that a believer has been called to be a *saint*, that is, to live a life of holiness. The word "saint" (hagios) means holy one or holiness. The believer is called to be holy and pure and righteous just as God is.

To all in Rome who are loved by God and called to be saints: Grace and peace to you from God our Father and from the Lord Jesus Christ. (Rom 1:7)

To the church of God in Corinth, to those sanctified in Christ Jesus and called to be holy, together with all those everywhere who call on the name of our Lord Jesus Christ—their Lord and ours: (1 Cor 1:2)

But just as he who called you is holy, so be holy in all you do; (1 Pet 1:15)

c. It means that the believer is called to have a heavenly hope. He is called to an eternal hope, the hope of living forever with God. He is called to be perfected and conformed to the image of the Lord Jesus Christ forever.

There is one body and one Spirit— just as you were called to one hope when you were called— (Eph 4:4)

Therefore, holy brothers, who share in the heavenly calling, fix your thoughts on Jesus, the apostle and high priest whom we confess. (Heb 3:1)

I press on toward the goal to win the prize for which God has called me heavenward in Christ Jesus. (Phil 3:14)

d. It means that the believer is appointed to a very special task and duty while on earth. He is called to serve Jesus Christ.

Paul, a servant of Christ Jesus, called to be an apostle and set apart for the gospel of God— (Rom 1:1)

Paul, called to be an apostle of Christ Jesus by the will of God, and our brother Sosthenes, (1 Cor 1:1)

Each one should remain in the situation which he was in when God called him. Were you a slave when you were called? Don't let it trouble you—although if you can gain your freedom, do so. For he who was a slave when he was called by the Lord is the Lord's freedman; similarly, he who was a free man when he was called is Christ's slave. You were bought at a price; do not become slaves of men. Brothers, each man, as responsible to God, should remain in the situation God called him to. (1 Cor 7:20-24)

2. Believers are loved by God. That is, believers are *beloved* in God the Father. God holds them ever so close to His heart. They have accepted His Son, the Lord Jesus Christ; honored Him by believing in Him. Therefore, God loves the believer with a very special love, the love that accepts the believer and gives him the right to live in God's presence forever and ever. Note: the Greek text here is uncertain. Some have the word *sanctified* (hagios) instead of *beloved*. The sanctified person is a person who has turned away from sin and set his life apart to follow God. He is a person who is set apart unto God, a person separated from the world and its possessions and pleasures, a person who is dedicated to following God, a person who has given *all he is and has* to God. (See DEEPER STUDY # 1, *Sanctification—* 1 Pt.1:15-16 for more discussion.)

3. Believers are "kept by Jesus Christ." The word "kept" (teteremenois) means to be kept; to be guarded and watched after. God keeps the believer, guards and watches over him. The believer is a person...

- who is watched over by God.
- who is guided and directed by God day by day.
- who is strengthened by God to walk through all the trials and temptations of life.
- who is protected from all the enemies of life, even death.
- who is to be escorted into heaven quicker than the blink of an eye when the time comes for him to leave this world.
- who is given life, both abundant and eternal.
- who is given assurance of God's presence and love through all of life.

The true believer is a person who is kept by God. He is a person who is looked after and cared for by God. But note: it is *by Jesus Christ* that God keeps a person. The believer is a person who has placed his life into Jesus Christ; he is a person who is *trusting* Jesus Christ to save him. It is the true believer in Jesus Christ whom God keeps.

4. The believer is a person who has received the mercy and peace and love of God.

a. He has received the mercy of God (see note, *Mercy*—2 Jn.3 for discussion).

b. He has received the peace of God (see note, *Peace*—2 Jn.3 for discussion).

c. He has received the love of God (see DEEPER STUDY # 1, *Love*—2 Jn.5 for discussion).

	II. THE WARNINGS AGAINST APOSTASY: THE CHARACTERIS-TICS & JUDGMENT OF FALSE TEACHERS, 3-16	with the devil about the body of Moses, did not dare to bring a slanderous accusation against him, but said, "The Lord rebuke you!"
		10 Yet these men speak abusively against whatever they do not understand; and what things they do understand by instinct, like unreasoning animals—these are the very things that destroy them.
1 False teachers are to be opposed by believers	3 Dear friends, although I was very eager to write to you about the salvation we share, I felt I had to write and urge you to contend for the faith that was once for all entrusted to the saints.	
2 They creep into the church secretly	4 For certain men whose condemnation was written about long ago have secretly slipped in among you. They are godless men, who change the grace of our God into a license for immorality and deny Jesus Christ our only Sovereign and Lord.	
3 They are ordained, marked for to judgment		
4 They are ungodly		
5 They are immoral		
6 They deny the Lord God		
7 They are sure to be judged	5 Though you already know all this, I want to remind you that the Lord delivered his people out of Egypt, but later destroyed those who did not believe.	
a. The unbelievers in Israel were judged		
b. The rebellious angels were judged	6 And the angels who did not keep their positions of authority but abandoned their own home—these he has kept in darkness, bound with everlasting chains for judgment on the great Day.	
c. Sodom & Gomorrah were judged	7 In a similar way, Sodom and Gomorrah and the surrounding towns gave themselves up to sexual immorality and perversion. They serve as an example of those who suffer the punishment of eternal fire.	
8 They are filthy dreamers	8 In the very same way, these dreamers pollute their own bodies, reject authority and slander celestial beings.	
9 They reject authority		
10 They scoff at spiritual beings		
a. They do that which even the highest angel would not do	9 But even the archangel Michael, when he was disputing	

		b. They make a terrible, foolish mistake: They speak about things they know nothing about
11 Woe to them! They have taken the way of Cain; they have rushed for profit into Balaam's error; they have been destroyed in Korah's rebellion.		**11 They go after the way of Cain: Unbelief**
		12 They go after the way of Balaam: Going astray
12 These men are blemishes at your love feasts, eating with you without the slightest qualm—shepherds who feed only themselves. They are clouds without rain, blown along by the wind; autumn trees, without fruit and uprooted—twice dead.		**13 They go after the way of Korah: Rebellion**
		14 They are blemishes upon the fellowship of the church
		15 They are filled with emptiness & instability
13 They are wild waves of the sea, foaming up their shame; wandering stars, for whom blackest darkness has been reserved forever.		**16 They teach things that are shameful**
		17 They wander about as a falling star that quickly passes into eternal darkness
14 Enoch, the seventh from Adam, prophesied about these men: "See, the Lord is coming with thousands upon thousands of his holy ones		**18 They are doomed to be judged by the Lord Jesus Christ Himself**
15 To judge everyone, and to convict all the ungodly of all the ungodly acts they have done in the ungodly way, and of all the harsh words ungodly sinners have spoken against him."		a. To be judged for all ungodly acts
		b. To be judged for all defiant & harsh words spoken against Christ
16 These men are grumblers and faultfinders; they follow their own evil desires; they boast about themselves and flatter others for their own advantage.		**19 They are grumblers and faultfinders**
		20 They follow their lusts
		21 They use showy words but they are empty
		22 They flatter people for personal gain

DIVISION II

THE WARNINGS AGAINST APOSTASY: THE CHARACTERISTICS AND JUDGMENT OF FALSE TEACHERS, 3-16

(v.3-16) **Introduction**: there is a terrible danger facing believers, a horrifying danger that always lies right over the horizon. What is it? The danger of false teaching. If a believer swallows false teaching, he dooms himself. Any person who denies that God sent His Son into the world to save man—who denies that Jesus Christ is the Son of God and the Savior of the world—will never be accepted by God. He is doomed to spend eternity cut off from God. Why? Because he has not believed in the name of God's Son. Time and time again, God warns believers of apostasy. This is the very reason for the books of Jude and Second Peter being written. Strong warnings against false teachers are also issued by Paul in Galatians, Colossians, Thessalonians, Timothy, and Titus. There are severe warnings all throughout Hebrews. And Christ Himself gave strong warnings time and again throughout all the gospels. (See *Teachers, False*—Master Subject Index.)

No matter who the person is—no matter how well liked and influential and attractive his teachings may be—if he denies Jesus Christ and God's Word, he is a false teacher.

Here is the thrust of the letter of Jude, the very purpose for which Jude writes. Here is one of the most horrifying pictures in all the Bible, a picture of the characteristics and judgment of false teachers. (Note: this passage may need to be divided into several sections. It is combined into one outline because it all applies to the same subject. A suggested division would be Jude 3-7, 8-11, 12-16.)

1. False teachers are to be opposed by believers (v.3).
2. They creep into the church secretly (v.4).
3. They are destined to judgment (v.4).
4. They are ungodly (v.4).
5. They are immoral (v.4).
6. They deny the Lord God (v.4).
7. They are sure to be judged (v.5-7).
8. They are filthy dreamers (v.8).
9. They reject authority (v.8).
10. They scoff at spiritual beings (v.8-10).
11. They go after the way of Cain, of unbelief (v.11).
12. They go after the way of Balaam, of going astray (v.11).
13. They go after the way of Korah, of rebellion (v.11).
14. They are blemishes upon the fellowship of the church (v.12).
15. They are filled with emptiness and instability (v.12).
16. They teach things that are shameful (v.13).
17. They wander about as a falling star that quickly passes into eternal darkness (v.13).
18. They are doomed to be judged by the Lord Jesus Christ Himself (v.14-15).
19. They are grumblers and faultfinders (v.16).
20. They follow their lusts (v.16).
21. They use showy words but they are empty (v.16).
22. They flatter people for personal gain (v.16).

1 (v.3) **Believers**: believers are to contend for the faith against false teachers. Note that Jude had planned to write the believers, but he had never planned to write this particular letter. He had planned to write about the great subject of salvation. But he was not able to. The believers were being attacked, but not by persecutors. They were being attacked by false teachers and their false beliefs. Jude is forced to snatch up his pen to expose the heretical teachers. He was forced to warn believers of the horrible danger of apostasy. He wanted to write a pastoral letter, to encourage them to grow in Christ, but now he must warn them and exhort them: they must go to war, to spiritual war. They must earnestly contend and fight for the faith. They must be diligent and strive unceasingly in the fight against false teaching. They must not buckle under any whatsoever in standing up for the faith that has been delivered to the saints. The faith must not be twisted, added to, or taken away from. It must be kept pure and free from all error. Note why: certain men had *secretly slipped into the church* and were teaching false doctrine. The characteristics and judgment of false teachers show how horrible false teaching is to God. He considers false teachers to be the worst of all men upon earth, and He issues the most severe warning to them, warnings that far exceed the warnings to other men (cp. Mt.5:19; 18:6; 23:13-16; Gal.1:6-9; 2 Pt.2:20-22).

2 (v.4) **Teachers, False**: false teachers creep into the church secretly. They are *not God-called* teachers. They choose to teach in the church as a profession or as a way to serve people and to teach the morals and virtues of this world. The idea is that they entered the church unnoticed. They did not believe in Jesus Christ, that He is the Son of God who came to earth to save man. Therefore, they did not belong in the church. But they joined it for the benefit and opportunities it brought them. They accepted the teachings of Christ, believed that He was a great religious leader, but they denied His deity.

> **The Spirit clearly says that in later times some will abandon the faith and follow deceiving spirits and things taught by demons. Such teachings come through hypocritical liars, whose consciences have been seared as with a hot iron. (1 Tim 4:1-2)**
> **They claim to know God, but by their actions they deny him. They are detestable, disobedient and unfit for doing anything good. (Titus 1:16)**
> **For such people are not serving our Lord Christ, but their own appetites. By smooth talk and flattery they deceive the minds of naive people. (Rom 16:18)**
> **For such men are false apostles, deceitful workmen, masquerading as apostles of Christ. And no wonder, for Satan himself masquerades as an angel of light. It is not surprising, then, if his servants masquerade as servants of righteousness. Their end will be what their actions deserve. (2 Cor 11:13-15)**

3 (v.4) **Teachers, False—Judgment**: false teachers are destined to judgment. They reject Jesus Christ; therefore, judgment is waiting for them. God has ordained from the beginning of time that all unbelievers shall be judged. And both Jesus Christ and Scripture teach that the judgment for false teachers is to be far more severe than for other persons.

> **Anyone who breaks one of the least of these commandments and teaches others to do the same will be called least in the kingdom of heaven, but whoever practices and teaches these commands will be called great in the kingdom of heaven. (Mat 5:19)**
> **But if anyone causes one of these little ones who believe in me to sin, it would be better for him to have a large millstone hung around his neck and to be drowned in the depths of the sea. (Mat 18:6)**
> **I am astonished that you are so quickly deserting the one who called you by the grace of Christ and are turning to a different gospel— which is really no gospel at all. Evidently some people are throwing you into confusion and are trying to pervert the gospel of Christ. But even if we or an angel from heaven should preach a gospel other than the one we preached to you, let him be eternally condemned! As we have already said, so now I say again: If anybody is preaching to you a gospel other than what you accepted, let him be eternally condemned! (Gal 1:6-9)**
> **If they have escaped the corruption of the world by knowing our Lord and Savior Jesus Christ and are again entangled in it and overcome, they are worse off at the end**

than they were at the beginning. It would have been better for them not to have known the way of righteousness, than to have known it and then to turn their backs on the sacred command that was passed on to them. Of them the proverbs are true: "A dog returns to its vomit," and, "A sow that is washed goes back to her wallowing in the mud." (2 Pet 2:20-22)

4 (v.4) **Teachers, False—Ungodly**: false teachers are ungodly. They do not live like God; they are different from God. They have a different lifestyle than what God would have if He was walking upon earth. God is perfect, moral, pure, just, and loving. But false teachers are not moral, pure, just, or loving. They are deceptive, leading people away from the love and purity of God, the love and purity revealed in His Son, the Lord Jesus Christ. They do not teach the truth of God's love and purity demonstrated in Christ. They profane God and the truth of His love and godliness.

> The wrath of God is being revealed from heaven against all the godlessness and wickedness of men who suppress the truth by their wickedness, (Rom 1:18)
> And, "If it is hard for the righteous to be saved, what will become of the ungodly and the sinner?" (1 Pet 4:18)
> For if God did not spare angels when they sinned, but sent them to hell, putting them into gloomy dungeons to be held for judgment; if he did not spare the ancient world when he brought the flood on its ungodly people, but protected Noah, a preacher of righteousness, and seven others; (2 Pet 2:4-5)
> By the same word the present heavens and earth are reserved for fire, being kept for the day of judgment and destruction of ungodly men. (2 Pet 3:7)
> For certain men whose condemnation was written about long ago have secretly slipped in among you. They are godless men, who change the grace of our God into a license for immorality and deny Jesus Christ our only Sovereign and Lord. (Jude 1:4)

5 (v.4) **Grace—Debauchery**: they turn the grace of God into a license for immorality (aselgeian). (See note, *False Teachers*—2 Pt.2:19 for how false teachers turn the grace of God into the enslavement of sin. Also see note, pt.1—1 Pt.4:3 for meaning of immorality).

6 (v.4) **Denial**: false teachers deny the only Lord God, that is, our Lord Jesus Christ. (See note, *False Teachers*—1 Jn.4:2-3 for discussion.)

7 (v.5-7) **Judgment**: false teachers are to be judged and condemned. Jude speaks directly to the false teachers and to all who follow after them: "Remember the judgment of God. You once knew that God judged unbelief. I am reminding you that He does." Jude recalls three examples.

1. There was the example of Israel right after they were delivered from Egyptian slavery. God judged and punished all the unbelievers of Israel. What happened to most of the believers of Israel is tragic. There were over six-hundred thousand men alone who broke away from the enslavements of Egypt and began the journey to the promised land. This means that including the women and children there were well over two million who stepped out to follow God to the promised land (cp. Ex.12:37; Num.1:46). But the critical question is this:

⇒ How many remained faithful to God through the wilderness journey? How many actually turned away from the fleshly desires aroused by the delicious foods, drinks, and bodily stimulations of Egypt and the world? How many actually disciplined their bodies, subjected their desires, and kept their eyes and hearts upon the promised land? How many were faithful and steadfast, unmoveable and always abounding in the work of the Lord until they reached the promised land? Remember over two million began the journey: How many entered the promised land? *Only two! Caleb and Joshua*. Caleb and Joshua alone remained faithful to God. Only two did not sin and displease God. Everyone else, over two to three million, perished in the wilderness. They were scattered (katastronnumi), corpses all over the wilderness or desert (cp. 1 Cor. 10:5). Why? Because they did not please God.

> "The LORD was very angry with your forefathers. Therefore tell the people: This is what the LORD Almighty says: 'Return to me,' declares the LORD Almighty, 'and I will return to you,' says the LORD Almighty. (Zec 1:2-3)
> But I am very angry with the nations that feel secure. I was only a little angry, but they added to the calamity.' (Zec 1:15)

Jude says that what happened to Israel is going to happen to the false teachers and to all who follow their teachings. The doom that fell upon the unbelievers of Israel will fall upon anyone who forsakes Christ. What were the sins of Israel that brought judgment upon them?

a. There was the sin of lust. We must not lust after evil things as they lusted. They lusted and craved for the delicious foods of Egypt (Num.11:4f). As a result of the lust, a plague broke out among the people and killed many of them. In fact, so many died that the place became known as Kibroth Hattaarah—"the grave of greediness or of lust" (Num.11:34).

The lust of those believers is a strong warning to us: we must "set our hearts on evil things" (1 Cor. 10:6), the pleasures and possessions of the world.

> But the worries of this life, the deceitfulness of wealth and the desires for other things come in and choke the word, making it unfruitful. (Mark 4:19)
> All of us also lived among them at one time, gratifying the cravings of our sinful nature and following its desires and thoughts. Like the rest, we were by nature objects of wrath. (Eph 2:3)
> That each of you should learn to control his own body in a way that is holy and

honorable, not in passionate lust like the heathen, who do not know God; (1 Th 4:4-5)

Flee the evil desires of youth, and pursue righteousness, faith, love and peace, along with those who call on the Lord out of a pure heart. (2 Tim 2:22)

Then, after desire has conceived, it gives birth to sin; and sin, when it is full-grown, gives birth to death. (James 1:15)

You want something but don't get it. You kill and covet, but you cannot have what you want. You quarrel and fight. You do not have, because you do not ask God. (James 4:2)

Dear friends, I urge you, as aliens and strangers in the world, to abstain from sinful desires, which war against your soul. (1 Pet 2:11)

Do not love the world or anything in the world. If anyone loves the world, the love of the Father is not in him. For everything in the world—the cravings of sinful man, the lust of his eyes and the boasting of what he has and does—comes not from the Father but from the world. (1 John 2:15-16)

b. There was the sin of idolatry. When Moses was on Mount Sinai receiving the law, the people became restless waiting for the Word of God. Therefore, they decided to go ahead and create their own form of worship (cp. Ex.32:1f). It should be noted that the people were actually dedicating their worship to God Himself.

When Aaron saw this, he built an altar in front of the calf and announced, "Tomorrow there will be a festival to the LORD." (Exo 32:5)

The point to see is this: the image of the golden calf was only to help them picture and imagine God. They felt the need for some image to help them in their worship of Jehovah. Note the reference to eating, drinking, and playing (immoral play). Such behavior often accompanies idolatry, the worship of a self-made god created by a person's own mind.

c. There was the sin of sexual immorality. This was a gross sin of some of the believers of Israel. Over twenty thousand of them committed immorality with their neighbors and as a result they were judged and condemned to destruction, banned from the promised land (cp. Num.25:1-9). (See notes—1 Cor.5:9-10; 6:9 for discussion.)

In the same way the men also abandoned natural relations with women and were inflamed with lust for one another. Men committed indecent acts with other men, and received in themselves the due penalty for their perversion. (Rom 1:27)

Do you not know that the wicked will not inherit the kingdom of God? Do not be deceived: Neither the sexually immoral nor idolaters nor adulterers nor male prostitutes nor homosexual offenders (1 Cor 6:9)

The acts of the sinful nature are obvious: sexual immorality, impurity and debauchery; and envy; drunkenness, orgies,

and the like. I warn you, as I did before, that those who live like this will not inherit the kingdom of God. (Gal 5:19, 21)

Having lost all sensitivity, they have given themselves over to sensuality so as to indulge in every kind of impurity, with a continual lust for more. (Eph 4:19)

But among you there must not be even a hint of sexual immorality, or of any kind of impurity, or of greed, because these are improper for God's holy people. (Eph 5:3)

It is God's will that you should be sanctified: that you should avoid sexual immorality; (1 Th 4:3)

For certain men whose condemnation was written about long ago have secretly slipped in among you. They are godless men, who change the grace of our God into a license for immorality and deny Jesus Christ our only Sovereign and Lord. In a similar way, Sodom and Gomorrah and the surrounding towns gave themselves up to sexual immorality and perversion. They serve as an example of those who suffer the punishment of eternal fire. (Jude 1:4, 7)

d. There was the sin of tempting God (cp. Heb. 3:9f). The word "tempt" (peirazo) means to try the Lord's patience; to see how far a person can go; to test the patience of Christ. The believers of Israel...
- often felt that God and His leader Moses *demanded and expected too much*.
- often longed for the things of the flesh which they had formerly known in Egypt (the world).

They became discontent with the things God provided, and longed to return to Egypt (the world). Therefore, many of them perished in the wilderness and were not allowed to enter the promised land.

Thought 1. Believers often feel that God expects too much and that they are missing out on something in the world. They often feel that God will forgive them...
- even if they do look.
- even if they do taste.
- even if they do touch.
- even if they do slip a little.
- even if they do hold back a little.

Now listen, you who say, "Today or tomorrow we will go to this or that city, spend a year there, carry on business and make money." (James 4:13)

Do not test the LORD your God as you did at Massah. (Deu 6:16)

e. There was the sin of murmuring and complaining and grumbling. Some of the believers in Israel were always complaining and murmuring against God and Moses (cp. Num.14:2, 36; 16:11, 41). The result was judgment and punishment by the destroyer, that is, an angel sent by God to execute judgment. They perished in the wilderness and never saw the promised land. (Cp. Ex.14:11; 15:24; 16:2; 17:3; Num.11:1; 14:27; 20:3; 21:5.)

Thought 1. How many believers grumble and gripe? How many become dissatisfied...

- with the direction God gives through His leaders?
- with the food God gives through His leaders?
- with the way God guides through His leaders?
- with the words God gives to His leaders?

How many voice their complaints to others? The warning is clear to the believers of God's church.

> And do not grumble, as some of them did—and were killed by the destroying angel. (1 Cor 10:10)
>
> Do everything without complaining or arguing, (Phil 2:14)
>
> These men are grumblers and fault-finders; they follow their own evil desires; they boast about themselves and flatter others for their own advantage. (Jude 1:16)
>
> So the people grumbled against Moses, saying, "What are we to drink?" (Exo 15:24)
>
> I remembered you, O God, and I groaned; I mused, and my spirit grew faint. Selah (Psa 77:3)
>
> A man's own folly ruins his life, yet his heart rages against the LORD. (Prov 19:3)
>
> Why should any living man complain when punished for his sins? (Lam 3:39)

2. There was the example of the rebellious angels (see note—2 Pt.2:3-9 for discussion).

3. There was Sodom and Gomorrah (see note, pt.3—2 Pt.2:3-9 for discussion).

8 (v.8) **Teachers, False—Dreams—Thoughts, Evil**: false teachers are filthy dreamers who defile their body. This means two things.

1. It means that false teachers engage in the pleasures of the world: the lust of the eyes and the lust of the flesh, the cravings of sinful desires. They do not struggle to keep their thoughts clean and pure. They *dream and covet* after the positions, possessions, and things of the world. They look at the opposite sex, perhaps pornographic books, films, and bodies not dressed as much as they should be. The result is *thoughts and dreams* of success, grandeur, personal recognition and honor, and sexual misbehavior. False teachers defile the flesh through such dreams.

2. It means that the false teachers sometimes claim to have *visions and dreams* from the Lord that are not from Him. They use their visions and dreams to secure the following and loyalty of people.

> Knowing their thoughts, Jesus said, "Why do you entertain evil thoughts in your hearts? (Mat 9:4)
>
> For out of the heart come evil thoughts, murder, adultery, sexual immorality, theft, false testimony, slander. (Mat 15:19)
>
> For although they knew God, they neither glorified him as God nor gave thanks to him, but their thinking became futile and their foolish hearts were darkened. (Rom 1:21)
>
> The LORD saw how great man's wickedness on the earth had become, and that every inclination of the thoughts of his heart was only evil all the time. (Gen 6:5)
>
> The LORD knows the thoughts of man; he knows that they are futile. (Psa 94:11)
>
> A heart that devises wicked schemes, feet that are quick to rush into evil, (Prov 6:18)
>
> For he is the kind of man who is always thinking about the cost. "Eat and drink," he says to you, but his heart is not with you. (Prov 23:7)
>
> He said to me, "Son of man, have you seen what the elders of the house of Israel are doing in the darkness, each at the shrine of his own idol? They say, 'The LORD does not see us; the LORD has forsaken the land.'" (Ezek 8:12)

9 (v.8) **Teachers, False—Authority, Rejection of**: false teachers reject authority (see note, *False Teachers—2 Pt.2:10* for discussion).

10 (v.8-10) **Teachers, False—Spiritual World**: false teachers scoff at the idea of angels and of spiritual beings, in particular of Satan and other fallen angels. This is definitely the meaning of this trait: the illustration shows this (v.9-10). False teachers speak against, doubt, and question spiritual beings such as angels and the cherubim and seraphim. They ridicule the ideas of Christ and angels and other spiritual beings living in a spiritual world. They question whether there are beings in a spiritual world who are living and functioning just as we are in this world.

⇒ The idea of another dimension of being, of a spiritual world that is as real and alive as the physical world is questioned.

⇒ The idea of levels of authority, of principalities and powers and rulers in a spiritual world is mocked.

⇒ The idea of Christ being exalted to the right hand of God and of believers someday ruling and serving and ministering for Christ in a new heavens and earth is doubted and often ridiculed.

But note two things.

1. False teachers do that which even the highest angel would not dare do. Even Michael himself, one of the highest if not the highest angel in heaven, would not rebuke the devil. This is a strong warning to the false teachers. The angels themselves do not dare rail and mock the principalities and powers of the spiritual world.

> For our struggle is not against flesh and blood, but against the rulers, against the authorities, against the powers of this dark world and against the spiritual forces of evil in the heavenly realms. (Eph 6:12)
>
> For by him all things were created: things in heaven and on earth, visible and invisible, whether thrones or powers or rulers or authorities; all things were created by him and for him. (Col 1:16)
>
> And having disarmed the powers and authorities, he made a public spectacle of them, triumphing over them by the cross. (Col 2:15)

2. False teachers make a terrible, foolish mistake. They are like brute beasts who have no understanding. They are speaking of things they do not understand. No person knows what the spiritual world is like, for no person has ever been there. There is only one Person who has ever been there, and that is the Person who came to earth from the other world, the Lord Jesus Christ. He alone knows what the other world is like. This is the very reason He came to earth: to bring the Word of God and the promise of heaven to us. We either believe Him or not. It is that simple. But note this: the Word of God is the prophecy and record concerning the Lord Jesus Christ. If a person does not believe Christ, then he has no right to claim to be a follower and minister of Christ. He should not abuse the Word of God through hypocrisy. When he does, he is as a brute beast, speaking about things he knows nothing about. And note what the Scripture says about him:

⇒ He is like an unreasoning animal made to be taken and destroyed (v.10).
⇒ He shall utterly perish in his own corruption. That is, in trying to pollute the Word of God and Christ, he destroys lives; therefore, he shall be utterly destroyed. His own corruption shall destroy him.

> **But if your eyes are bad, your whole body will be full of darkness. If then the light within you is darkness, how great is that darkness! (Mat 6:23)**
>
> **This is the verdict: Light has come into the world, but men loved darkness instead of light because their deeds were evil. (John 3:19)**
>
> **For, "Everyone who calls on the name of the Lord will be saved." (Rom 10:13)**
>
> **The god of this age has blinded the minds of unbelievers, so that they cannot see the light of the gospel of the glory of Christ, who is the image of God. (2 Cor 4:4)**
>
> **They are darkened in their understanding and separated from the life of God because of the ignorance that is in them due to the hardening of their hearts. (Eph 4:18)**
>
> **If we claim to have fellowship with him yet walk in the darkness, we lie and do not live by the truth. (1 John 1:6)**
>
> **"My people are fools; they do not know me. They are senseless children; they have no understanding. They are skilled in doing evil; they know not how to do good." (Jer 4:22)**

11 (v.11) **Teachers, False—Cain**: false teachers go after the way of Cain, the way of unbelief and lack of godly love. Cain committed the very first murder on earth: he killed his own brother Abel (Gen.4:1-15). Why? Because Abel was a believer. Abel believed God, that he was to worship God exactly like God said, by the blood of a sacrificial animal. Cain did not accept such a belief. He felt that if he brought the fruit of his own hands to God, then God would accept him because of his hard work and because he worshipped and gave offerings to God. God accepted Abel's worship and offering. It was evident in his life by the way God blessed him and took care of him. But God rejected Cain's offering. Cain did not have a real sense of God's care or blessing upon his life. Therefore, he

became jealous and envious of Abel, and he killed Abel. Three things are being said about false teachers.

1. False teachers do not believe God—that a person has to worship God exactly like God says, by the blood of Jesus Christ. They do not accept Jesus Christ as the perfect sacrifice for man's sins. They believe like Cain did, that they can become acceptable to God by the works of their own hands, by being good and doing good.

2. False teachers do not love like God says to love. God says that we must love one another in the *love of Christ*. What is the love of Christ? It is the love that loves so much that it will sacrifice one's life for the other person, even if the other person is an enemy. (See note, *Love*—1 Jn.3:1 for more discussion.)

3. False teachers shall be destroyed. Note the word "woe." It means grief or denunciation (Kenneth Wuest. *In These Last Days*, Vol.4, p.248). All false teachers shall be doomed to an eternity of grief and denunciation or judgment.

12 (v.11) **Teachers, False—Balaam**: false teachers walk in the way of Balaam, the way that forsakes the life of God and leads to destruction (see note, *False Teachers*—2 Pt.2:15 for discussion).

13 (v.11) **Teachers, False—Korah**: false teachers walk after the way of Korah, the way of rebellion and rejection of authority (cp. Num.16:1-35). Korah was the man who rebelled against the leadership of Moses and Aaron. Korah wanted a higher position of leadership among the people; therefore, he rebelled against Moses and Aaron. He wanted to serve where he had no right to serve. As a result he was judged and doomed.

The point is this: false teachers follow the way of rebellion and rejection of authority. They rebel against and reject the authority of God and of the ministers God has appointed and placed in His church. And most of all they rebel and reject the supreme authority of Christ, the Lord Himself. They reject His deity, that He has purchased the church through His sacrificial death. They rebel against the very authority of God Himself. They choose to go their own way and do their own thing. They use the church and believers for their own ends.

> **For this people's heart has become calloused; they hardly hear with their ears, and they have closed their eyes. Otherwise they might see with their eyes, hear with their ears, understand with their hearts and turn, and I would heal them.' (Acts 28:27)**
>
> **They are darkened in their understanding and separated from the life of God because of the ignorance that is in them due to the hardening of their hearts. (Eph 4:18)**
>
> **The Spirit clearly says that in later times some will abandon the faith and follow deceiving spirits and things taught by demons. Such teachings come through hypocritical liars, whose consciences have been seared as with a hot iron. (1 Tim 4:1-2)**
>
> **But encourage one another daily, as long as it is called Today, so that none of you may be hardened by sin's deceitfulness. (Heb 3:13)**
>
> **A man who remains stiff-necked after many rebukes will suddenly be destroyed—without remedy. (Prov 29:1)**

"You stiff-necked people, with uncircumcised hearts and ears! You are just like your fathers: You always resist the Holy Spirit! (Acts 7:51)

This is especially true of those who follow the corrupt desire of the sinful nature and despise authority. Bold and arrogant, these men are not afraid to slander celestial beings; (2 Pet 2:10)

This is what the Sovereign LORD, the Holy One of Israel, says: "In repentance and rest is your salvation, in quietness and trust is your strength, but you would have none of it. (Isa 30:15)

"We will not listen to the message you have spoken to us in the name of the LORD! (Jer 44:16)

"But they refused to pay attention; stubbornly they turned their backs and stopped up their ears. (Zec 7:11)

14 (v.12) **Teachers, False—Pleasure Seeking**: false teachers are *blemishes* upon the fellowship of the church. The Greek word for "blemishes" (spilas) can mean *submerged rocks or hidden reefs* that can wreck a ship. False teachers are reefs within the church which can wreck the fellowship of the church. Translators differ as to which meaning Jude intended. Perhaps he meant both, for both are certainly true.

The *love feasts* referred to were called *love feasts* by the early church. They were fellowship meals that the church celebrated after the services on the Lord's Day. Each family brought what food they could. This, of course, meant that the wealthy brought plenty and the poor brought little or nothing. Remember that many of the believers were slaves in that day, so some of them would not be able to bring any food whatsoever. Some churches had the most joyful fellowship around the love feasts. It provided a time when the believers could share the warmth of their hearts and grow in fellowship together. It was a time when the Holy Spirit could draw the hearts of believers together in love and joy and care and sharing. It was a time that the Holy Spirit could use to bind believers together in feelings for one another and in warmth and tenderness.

The point is this: fellowship among believers is a most wonderful time, a unique opportunity to grow and share together. But when false teachers are present, the scene is entirely different.

⇒ False teachers are spots or blemishes upon the fellowship of believers. They dirty and soil the name of Christ and the testimony of the church. They profess to be believers and are even teachers of God's Word, but they are not pure. Their false teaching disturbs genuine believers and causes division within the fellowship of the church. Those who are not rooted in Christ and in God's Word follow and support the false teacher; those who are rooted in Christ and in God's Word reject the false teacher. False teachers always spot and dirty the fellowship of the church because they cause division among the people and destroy the Spirit of Christ among them.

⇒ False teachers are reefs or submerged rocks that wreck the fellowship of the church. Their teaching is often injected into the church quietly and insidiously, completely unknown to the general membership. Therefore, the fellowship is subject to being shipwrecked upon the reefs of false teaching.

Note that the false teachers feed themselves—that is, they fellowship with believers—without fear. There is no fear of God nor thought about the damage they are doing to the fellowship of the church. Their interest is to boost themselves forward; to be recognized as an excellent teacher or preacher, a person of unusual gifts, a teacher with new insights, a teacher who is progressive, who is a notch above others.

Thought 1. The fellowship of believers is spiritual. It is not a social fellowship based upon emotional feelings for one another. It is fellowship wrought by the Spirit of God. Feelings are involved; but beyond that there is godly love, joy, peace, and purpose, meaning, and significance—all centered around Jesus Christ. When false teaching is present, all this is disrupted. Therefore, false teaching must never be allowed in the true church. But when the mature believers become aware of it, *in Christ* they are forced to reject it and to make it known.

For where two or three come together in my name, there am I with them." (Mat 18:20)

In the same way, on the outside you appear to people as righteous but on the inside you are full of hypocrisy and wickedness. (Mat 23:28)

Meanwhile, when a crowd of many thousands had gathered, so that they were trampling on one another, Jesus began to speak first to his disciples, saying: "Be on your guard against the yeast of the Pharisees, which is hypocrisy. (Luke 12:1)

They asked each other, "Were not our hearts burning within us while he talked with us on the road and opened the Scriptures to us?" (Luke 24:32)

"Their throats are open graves; their tongues practice deceit." "The poison of vipers is on their lips." (Rom 3:13)

God, who has called you into fellowship with his Son Jesus Christ our Lord, is faithful. (1 Cor 1:9)

Such teachings come through hypocritical liars, whose consciences have been seared as with a hot iron. (1 Tim 4:2)

They claim to know God, but by their actions they deny him. They are detestable, disobedient and unfit for doing anything good. (Titus 1:16)

We proclaim to you what we have seen and heard, so that you also may have fellowship with us. And our fellowship is with the Father and with his Son, Jesus Christ. (1 John 1:3)

Here I am! I stand at the door and knock. If anyone hears my voice and opens the door, I will come in and eat with him, and he with me. (Rev 3:20)

15 (v.12) **Teacher, False—Emptiness—Instability**: false teachers are filled with emptiness and instability. Two illustrations are given.

⇒ They are like clouds that offer rain to the farmer, but when the clouds arrive, they are driven away by the rushing winds of the storm.

⇒ They are like fruit trees that seem to be flourishing and that promise fruit, but when harvest comes there is no fruit.

This is a picture of false teachers offering hope to people, but their hope is empty and unstable—just as empty and unstable as the world's fleeting clouds of hope and unbearing promise of fruit. The false teachers cannot water the seed of God's Word in people's hearts, nor can their teaching bear fruit within people. The opinions of false teachers cannot help people in facing the trials and temptations of life, nor can they prepare people to face eternity that lies just over the horizon. In dealing with eternity—with God, Christ, and the Holy Scripture—the false teacher is nothing more than a cloud without water and a tree without fruit. He may sound like he offers hope, security, and fullness of life; but his message is unstable and empty and will leave a person hopeless when he meets God face to face.

> So I tell you this, and insist on it in the Lord, that you must no longer live as the Gentiles do, in the futility of their thinking. (Eph 4:17)
>
> In the morning you will say, "If only it were evening!" and in the evening, "If only it were morning!"—because of the terror that will fill your hearts and the sights that your eyes will see. (Deu 28:67)
>
> Yet when I surveyed all that my hands had done and what I had toiled to achieve, everything was meaningless, a chasing after the wind; nothing was gained under the sun. (Eccl 2:11)
>
> All his days his work is pain and grief; even at night his mind does not rest. This too is meaningless. (Eccl 2:23)
>
> Why spend money on what is not bread, and your labor on what does not satisfy? Listen, listen to me, and eat what is good, and your soul will delight in the richest of fare. (Isa 55:2)
>
> But the wicked are like the tossing sea, which cannot rest, whose waves cast up mire and mud. (Isa 57:20)
>
> "Watch out for false prophets. They come to you in sheep's clothing, but inwardly they are ferocious wolves. By their fruit you will recognize them. Do people pick grapes from thornbushes, or figs from thistles? Likewise every good tree bears good fruit, but a bad tree bears bad fruit. A good tree cannot bear bad fruit, and a bad tree cannot bear good fruit. Every tree that does not bear good fruit is cut down and thrown into the fire. Thus, by their fruit you will recognize them. "Not everyone who says to me, 'Lord, Lord,' will enter the kingdom of heaven, but only he who does the will of my Father who is in heaven. (Mat 7:15-21)

16 (v.13) **Teachers, False—Shame**: false teachers teach things that are shameful and ugly and repulsive and that do not belong within the church. The picture is that of sea waves that rage and foam under the fierce winds of a storm. After the storm quietens down, there is all kinds of debris strung along the shoreline, debris such as driftwood, seaweed, scum, and all kinds of litter. The sight is ghastly and ugly and repulsive. The sight is shameful. Thus it is with false teachers. They foam out their teaching that leaves a ghastly scene upon the church. What they teach is shameful; it brings shame upon the name of Christ and shame upon the name of the church. Their teaching is a disgrace, ugly, and repulsive. It is nothing more than useless debris that does not belong in the church of the Lord Jesus Christ.

> "Why do you call me, 'Lord, Lord,' and do not do what I say? (Luke 6:46)
>
> You, then, who teach others, do you not teach yourself? You who preach against stealing, do you steal? (Rom 2:21)
>
> You who brag about the law, do you dishonor God by breaking the law? As it is written: "God's name is blasphemed among the Gentiles because of you." (Rom 2:23-24)
>
> They claim to know God, but by their actions they deny him. They are detestable, disobedient and unfit for doing anything good. (Titus 1:16)
>
> Out of the same mouth come praise and cursing. My brothers, this should not be. (James 3:10)
>
> Many will follow their shameful ways and will bring the way of truth into disrepute. (2 Pet 2:2)
>
> So I continued, "What you are doing is not right. Shouldn't you walk in the fear of our God to avoid the reproach of our Gentile enemies? (Neh 5:9)
>
> The wise inherit honor, but fools he holds up to shame. (Prov 3:35)
>
> When pride comes, then comes disgrace, but with humility comes wisdom. (Prov 11:2)
>
> I will bring upon you everlasting disgrace—everlasting shame that will not be forgotten." (Jer 23:40)

17 (v.13) **Teachers, False—Wanderers—Lost**: false teachers wander about as a falling star that passes into eternal darkness. This is the picture of a shooting star that shoots its light across the sky ever so quickly, but then it is gone forever into the darkness. The light promised by false teachers does not last nor can it last, for it is only of the earth; and all things of the earth disappear through age, change, deterioration, decay, and death—disappear into the eternal abyss of darkness ever so quickly.

False teachers wander about grasping for light after light, truth after truth, idea after idea, help after help. But nothing meets the desperate need of man for life—for love, joy, peace, fulfillment, completeness and satisfaction. The reason is ever so clear: life in all of its fullness is found only in Christ, the One who revealed the life of God to us.

> I have strayed like a lost sheep. Seek your servant, for I have not forgotten your commands. (Psa 119:176)
>
> A man who strays from the path of understanding comes to rest in the company of the dead. (Prov 21:16)
>
> Like a bird that strays from its nest is a man who strays from his home. (Prov 27:8)

Now they grope through the streets like men who are blind. They are so defiled with blood that no one dares to touch their garments. (Lam 4:14)

For you were like sheep going astray, but now you have returned to the Shepherd and Overseer of your souls. (1 Pet 2:25)

They have left the straight way and wandered off to follow the way of Balaam son of Beor, who loved the wages of wickedness. (2 Pet 2:15)

They are wild waves of the sea, foaming up their shame; wandering stars, for whom blackest darkness has been reserved forever. (Jude 1:13)

18 (v.14-15) **Teachers, False—Judgment**: false teachers are doomed. They are to be judged by the Lord Jesus Christ Himself. The Lord Jesus Christ is returning to earth to judge false teachers. He is coming with ten thousands of His holy ones. The words "ten thousands" means thousands multiplied by thousands, multitudes and myriads—an unlimited number of holy beings. He is coming to judge the world, but note: the present passage is talking specifically about the judgment of false teachers, the judgment of all those who have taught something other than the fact that Jesus Christ is the Son of God sent into the world to save men. False teachers will be judged for two things.

1. They will be judged for all their *ungodly acts*. All the acts that did not center around Jesus Christ as God's Son shall bring judgment upon the false teachers.

And that you, O Lord, are loving. Surely you will reward each person according to what he has done. (Psa 62:12)

"I the LORD search the heart and examine the mind, to reward a man according to his conduct, according to what his deeds deserve." (Jer 17:10)

For the Son of Man is going to come in his Father's glory with his angels, and then he will reward each person according to what he has done. (Mat 16:27)

For we must all appear before the judgment seat of Christ, that each one may receive what is due him for the things done while in the body, whether good or bad. (2 Cor 5:10)

Since you call on a Father who judges each man's work impartially, live your lives as strangers here in reverent fear. (1 Pet 1:17)

And I saw the dead, great and small, standing before the throne, and books were opened. Another book was opened, which is the book of life. The dead were judged according to what they had done as recorded in the books. (Rev 20:12)

"Behold, I am coming soon! My reward is with me, and I will give to everyone according to what he has done. (Rev 22:12)

If this is so, then the Lord knows how to rescue godly men from trials and to hold the unrighteous for the day of judgment, while continuing their punishment. (2 Pet 2:9)

By the same word the present heavens and earth are reserved for fire, being kept for the day of judgment and destruction of ungodly men. (2 Pet 3:7)

2. They will be judged for all the *untrue, harsh, and defiant words* spoken against Christ.

You brood of vipers, how can you who are evil say anything good? For out of the overflow of the heart the mouth speaks. (Mat 12:34)

"Their throats are open graves; their tongues practice deceit." "The poison of vipers is on their lips." (Rom 3:13)

The tongue also is a fire, a world of evil among the parts of the body. It corrupts the whole person, sets the whole course of his life on fire, and is itself set on fire by hell. (James 3:6)

Not a word from their mouth can be trusted; their heart is filled with destruction. Their throat is an open grave; with their tongue they speak deceit. (Psa 5:9)

His mouth is full of curses and lies and threats; trouble and evil are under his tongue. (Psa 10:7)

The words of his mouth are wicked and deceitful; he has ceased to be wise and to do good. (Psa 36:3)

Note: Jude says that Enoch prophesied these things and then he gives the prophecy of Enoch. Jude is referring to the apocryphal book of Enoch.

William Barclay has an excellent statement on this that is worthy of our note:

"Are we then to regard Enoch as sacred Scripture, since Jude uses it exactly as he would have used one of the prophets? Or, are we to take the view of which Jerome speaks? Are we to say that Jude cannot be Scripture, because Jude makes the mistake of using as Scripture a book which is, in fact, not Scripture?

"We need waste not time at all upon this debate. The fact is that Jude, a pious Jew, knew and loved the Book of Enoch and had grown up in a circle and a sphere where the Book of Enoch was regarded with respect, and even reverence; and he takes his quotation from it perfectly naturally, knowing that his readers would recognize it, and that they would respect it. Jude is simply doing what all the New Testament writers do, and which every writer must do in every age, he is speaking to men in language which they recognized and understood" (*The Letters of John and Jude*, p.231).

19 (v.16) **Teachers, False—Grumbling—Complaining**: false teachers are grumblers and faultfinders. They do not have the peace of God in their hearts; therefore, they are not content with their lot in life. They are often dissatisfied with their...

- employment
- position
- income
- students
- trials
- recognition
- honor
- spouse

- family
- temptations
- sufferings
- hardship
- lack of eternal assurance and security
- friends

There is just a general dissatisfaction with life; therefore, they often complain and find fault. They do not have Christ to guide and help them through life, for they have rejected Him as the Son of God. Consequently they have to plough through life all alone without the hand of God to look after them.

> **A man's own folly ruins his life, yet his heart rages against the LORD. (Prov 19:3)**
>
> **Why should any living man complain when punished for his sins? (Lam 3:39)**
>
> **"Stop grumbling among yourselves," Jesus answered. (John 6:43)**
>
> **And do not grumble, as some of them did—and were killed by the destroying angel. (1 Cor 10:10)**
>
> **Do everything without complaining or arguing, (Phil 2:14)**
>
> **I am not saying this because I am in need, for I have learned to be content whatever the circumstances. (Phil 4:11)**
>
> **But godliness with contentment is great gain. (1 Tim 6:6)**
>
> **Keep your lives free from the love of money and be content with what you have, because God has said, "Never will I leave you; never will I forsake you." (Heb 13:5)**
>
> **Better a little with the fear of the LORD than great wealth with turmoil. (Prov 15:16)**
>
> **Yet when I surveyed all that my hands had done and what I had toiled to achieve, everything was meaningless, a chasing after the wind; nothing was gained under the sun. (Eccl 2:11)**
>
> **He feeds on ashes, a deluded heart misleads him; he cannot save himself, or say, "Is not this thing in my right hand a lie?" (Isa 44:20)**

20 (v.16) **Teachers, False—Lust**: false teachers follow their own lusts or desires. They live after the flesh (sinful nature), in the lusts of the flesh. They ignore the spirit and follow the passions of the flesh (sinful nature). They indulge and gratify the flesh. They teach their false doctrine for personal gain. They desire…

- to live like they want.
- to do away with godly restraints and demands.
- to gain recognition and honor and a following.
- to gain a livelihood and security.

As stated, the flesh (sinful nature) desires these things and there is nothing wrong with them: a person needs recognition to feel that he is meaningful and significant. He also needs freedom and a livelihood. But when a person seeks more and more of these, when he takes the desires of the flesh and begins to lust and lust after the desires, they become harmful and sinful.

⇒ One helping of food is good; two helpings are damaging to the body.

⇒ Some recognition is good; too much leads to pride and arrogance or indulgent selfishness.

⇒ Being free to secure the necessities of life is right, but trying to seek them without law leads to sinful transgression and lawlessness. As an example, we have all seen scenes of a community without law, all the looting and evil that runs rampant.

The point is this: false teachers walk after the flesh, not the spirit. They follow their own desires. They are teaching in order to satisfy the flesh (sinful nature), to please people and to gain recognition, security, or livelihood. They teach a false doctrine in order to do away with the Lordship of Christ, for the Lordship of Christ demands the sacrifice of all one is and has. They want to live like they want, to do their own thing; therefore, they try to do away with the demands of God as much as they can. Again, false teachers walk after the flesh, not the spirit. They follow their own desires.

> **For, as I have often told you before and now say again even with tears, many live as enemies of the cross of Christ. Their destiny is destruction, their god is their stomach, and their glory is in their shame. Their mind is on earthly things. (Phil 3:18-19)**
>
> **Dear friends, I urge you, as aliens and strangers in the world, to abstain from sinful desires, which war against your soul. (1 Pet 2:11)**
>
> **As a result, he does not live the rest of his earthly life for evil human desires, but rather for the will of God. (1 Pet 4:2)**
>
> **First of all, you must understand that in the last days scoffers will come, scoffing and following their own evil desires. (2 Pet 3:3)**
>
> **They said to you, "In the last times there will be scoffers who will follow their own ungodly desires." (Jude 1:18)**

21 (v.16) **Teachers, False—Preaching**: false teachers speak showy words, great boasting words, but they are empty (see note, *False Teachers*—2 Pt.2:18 for discussion).

22 (v.16) **Teachers, False—Flattery**: false teachers flatter people to gain some advantage. False teachers are serving under the umbrella of Christianity…

- to gain a livelihood
- to serve mankind
- to stress morality
- to gain an image
- to have a respectable profession

But they reject Jesus Christ as the Son of God. They know nothing about God's call to the ministry. Therefore, they are left on their own. They have to depend upon other people for acceptance and security, for they know little about the provision and security of God. Consequently, they have to depend upon people. Therefore, they butter up to people, flatter them, and try to win their support and favor. And note: there is all the difference in the world between loving people and flattering them in order to assure one's place and security. As the occasion arises, false teachers flatter, hoping to get what they want. Note how this leads to partiality and favoritism within the church.

> **"'Do not pervert justice; do not show partiality to the poor or favoritism to the great, but judge your neighbor fairly. (Lev 19:15)**
>
> **He would surely rebuke you if you secretly showed partiality. (Job 13:10)**

"So I have caused you to be despised and humiliated before all the people, because you have not followed my ways but have shown partiality in matters of the law." (Mal 2:9)

I charge you, in the sight of God and Christ Jesus and the elect angels, to keep these instructions without partiality, and to do nothing out of favoritism. (1 Tim 5:21)

Have you not discriminated among yourselves and become judges with evil thoughts? (James 2:4)

I will show partiality to no one, nor will I flatter any man; (Job 32:21)

May the LORD cut off all flattering lips and every boastful tongue (Psa 12:3)

A gossip betrays a confidence; so avoid a man who talks too much. (Prov 20:19)

Whoever says to the guilty, "You are innocent"— peoples will curse him and nations denounce him. (Prov 24:24)

He who rebukes a man will in the end gain more favor than he who has a flattering tongue. (Prov 28:23)

Whoever flatters his neighbor is spreading a net for his feet. (Prov 29:5)

My brothers, as believers in our glorious Lord Jesus Christ, don't show favoritism. Suppose a man comes into your meeting wearing a gold ring and fine clothes, and a poor man in shabby clothes also comes in. If you show special attention to the man wearing fine clothes and say, "Here's a good seat for you," but say to the poor man, "You stand there" or "Sit on the floor by my feet," have you not discriminated among yourselves and become judges with evil thoughts? (James 2:1-4)

	III. THE EXHORTATION TO BELIEVERS, 17-25	of our Lord Jesus Christ to bring you to eternal life.	d. By waiting for the mercy of Christ, His return
1 Remember: There shall be mockers a. Who were predicted by the apostles b. Who follow their passions	17 But, dear friends, remember what the apostles of our Lord Jesus Christ foretold. 18 They said to you, "In the last times there will be scoffers who will follow their own ungodly desires."	22 Be merciful to those who doubt; 23 Snatch others from the fire and save them; to others show mercy, mixed with fear—hating even the clothing stained by corrupted flesh.	**3 Be compassionate & reclaim people** a. The doubting b. The lost c. A caution: Must guard against becoming polluted
c. Who cause divisions d. Who are worldly minded e. Reason: They do not have the Spirit **2 Build up yourselves** a. By building upon your "most holy faith" b. By praying c. By keeping yourselves in the love of God	19 These are the men who divide you, who follow mere natural instincts and do not have the Spirit. 20 But you, dear friends, build yourselves up in your most holy faith and pray in the Holy Spirit. 21 Keep yourselves in God's love as you wait for the mercy	24 To him who is able to keep you from falling and to present you before his glorious presence without fault and with great joy— 25 To the only God our Savior be glory, majesty, power and authority, through Jesus Christ our Lord, before all ages, now and forevermore! Amen.	**4 Walk in the power of God** a. God is able to keep you from falling b. God makes you blameless c. God infuses you with unspeakable joy d. God is the only God & Savior e. God alone dwells in glory & majesty, power & authority

DIVISION III

THE EXHORTATION TO BELIEVERS, 17-25

(v.17-25) **Introduction**: Jude has just covered the terrible danger that is facing believers, the horrifying danger of false teachers. And they are within the church. This makes the danger even more terrible, for it means that there are people within the church who do not believe...

- that Jesus Christ is the Son of God who came to earth to save man.
- that Jesus Christ is the sinless Son of God.

There are false teachers within the church, people who claim to be followers of Christ, but they are not. They are people who teach...

- that Jesus Christ was a great teacher and leader but not the Son of God who died for our sins.
- that we can become acceptable to God by being good and doing good.

The list could go on and on, but Jude has just covered the traits of false teachers. The present concern is this: What can we do about the false teaching in our midst? This is the exhortation of this passage, and note: it is the final passage of the short letter of Jude. Here is Jude's strong exhortation to believers, exhortations that tell believers what to do in the face of false teaching.

1. Remember—there shall be mockers (v.17-19).
2. Build up yourselves (v.20-21).
3. Be compassionate and reclaim people (v.22-23).
4. Walk in the keeping power of God (v.24-25).

1 (17-19) **Mockers—Teachers, False**: first, remember there shall be mockers in the *last times*. We are living in the days of the *last times* now. Since Jesus Christ came to earth, history is in its last stage. Right now, the time between Christ's first coming and His second coming, is called the age of grace—the age when God's mercy and grace are flowing out to the world through His Son, the Lord Jesus Christ. The thing to remember is that this period of history is called...

- "these last times" (1 Pt.1:20).
- "the last days" (2 Pt.3:3; 2 Tim.3:1).
- "these last days" (Heb.1:2).
- "the last hour" (1 Jn.2:18).
- "the last times" (Jude 18).

Note what Jude says about these mockers or false teachers. Five significant things are said. These are the things that we are to remember about them.

1. The apostles of our Lord Jesus Christ predicted that mockers would come (v.17).

> **For such men are false apostles, deceitful workmen, masquerading as apostles of Christ. And no wonder, for Satan himself masquerades as an angel of light. It is not surprising, then, if his servants masquerade as servants of righteousness. Their end will be what their actions deserve. (2 Cor 11:13-15)**
>
> **I am astonished that you are so quickly deserting the one who called you by the grace of Christ and are turning to a different gospel— which is really no gospel at all. Evidently some people are throwing you into confusion and are trying to pervert the gospel of Christ. But even if we or an angel from heaven should preach a gospel other than the one we preached to you, let him be eternally condemned! As we have already said, so now I say again: If anybody is preaching to you a gospel other than what you accepted, let him be eternally condemned! (Gal 1:6-9)**
>
> **For, as I have often told you before and now say again even with tears, many live as enemies of the cross of Christ. Their destiny is destruction, their god is their stomach, and their glory is in their shame. Their mind is on earthly things. (Phil 3:18-19)**
>
> **But mark this: There will be terrible times in the last days. People will be lovers of themselves, lovers of money, boastful, proud, abusive, disobedient to their parents, ungrateful, unholy, without love, unforgiving, slanderous, without self-control, brutal, not lovers of the good, treacherous, rash, conceited, lovers of pleasure rather than lovers of God— having a form of god-**

liness but denying its power. Have nothing to do with them. (2 Tim 3:1-5)

While evil men and impostors will go from bad to worse, deceiving and being deceived. (2 Tim 3:13)

They claim to know God, but by their actions they deny him. They are detestable, disobedient and unfit for doing anything good. (Titus 1:16)

But there were also false prophets among the people, just as there will be false teachers among you. They will secretly introduce destructive heresies, even denying the sovereign Lord who bought them—bringing swift destruction on themselves. (2 Pet 2:1)

Many deceivers, who do not acknowledge Jesus Christ as coming in the flesh, have gone out into the world. Any such person is the deceiver and the antichrist. (2 John 1:7)

2. False teachers follow their own ungodly lusts or desires (v.18. See note—Jude 16 for discussion.)

3. False teachers cause division among God's people within the church (v.19). There are three ways that they cause division.

a. Their false teaching presents a divided Christianity to the world. God will always have His true teachers who proclaim the truth of His Son and of His Word. When false teachers deny the deity of Jesus Christ and the Word of God, they show a divided church to the world. They show that within the church there are those who say that the church is primarily a social service for man; it is not primarily not a sanctuary where man worships and praises God for His great salvation in His Son, the Lord Jesus Christ. (See note—2 Jn.7 for more discussion.)

b. False teachers divide the church; they cause hurt and pain in the hearts of true believers because their Lord and His church are being shamed. In addition, false teachers cause cleavage between mature believers and the followers of the false teacher. True believers cannot go along with false teaching. In fact, Christ and the apostles declared emphatically that true believers must oppose false teaching and do all they can to rid the church of false teachers. Therefore, false teachers always cause division between those who follow their teaching and mature believers who are grounded in the truth of Christ and of God's Word.

But whoever disowns me before men, I will disown him before my Father in heaven. (Mat 10:33)

If anyone is ashamed of me and my words in this adulterous and sinful generation, the Son of Man will be ashamed of him when he comes in his Father's glory with the holy angels." (Mark 8:38)

That all may honor the Son just as they honor the Father. He who does not honor the Son does not honor the Father, who sent him. (John 5:23)

I have come in my Father's name, and you do not accept me; but if someone else comes in his own name, you will accept him. (John 5:43)

But there were also false prophets among the people, just as there will be false teachers among you. They will secretly introduce destructive heresies, even denying the sovereign Lord who bought them—bringing swift destruction on themselves. (2 Pet 2:1)

Who is the liar? It is the man who denies that Jesus is the Christ. Such a man is the antichrist—he denies the Father and the Son. (1 John 2:22)

Many deceivers, who do not acknowledge Jesus Christ as coming in the flesh, have gone out into the world. Any such person is the deceiver and the antichrist. Watch out that you do not lose what you have worked for, but that you may be rewarded fully. Anyone who runs ahead and does not continue in the teaching of Christ does not have God; whoever continues in the teaching has both the Father and the Son. If anyone comes to you and does not bring this teaching, do not take him into your house or welcome him. Anyone who welcomes him shares in his wicked work. (2 John 1:7-11)

c. False teachers divide people by showing partiality and favoritism. A false teacher's service, ministry, position, acceptance, approval, livelihood—everything about him—is dependent upon how well he gets along with the people to whom he ministers. Therefore, he must pay close attention to and flatter those who are influential and try not to offend them. This partiality and favoritism usually causes feelings of neglect and division among some. (See note, *Teachers, False—Preaching*—Jude 16.)

My brothers, as believers in our glorious Lord Jesus Christ, don't show favoritism. Suppose a man comes into your meeting wearing a gold ring and fine clothes, and a poor man in shabby clothes also comes in. If you show special attention to the man wearing fine clothes and say, "Here's a good seat for you," but say to the poor man, "You stand there" or "Sit on the floor by my feet," have you not discriminated among yourselves and become judges with evil thoughts? (James 2:1-4)

4. False teachers are worldly minded; they follow mere natural instincts. They are sensual and carnal (v.19). They are worldly minded in two senses.

a. False teachers believe that man is to work his way into God's acceptance. They teach that man is to be good and do good; to keep certain rituals and ordinances, rules and regulations of the church. If man does this, then he is acceptable to God. But note: this teaching is centered in man and this world, in what man can do to become acceptable to God. It honors man instead of God and His love. Therefore, the false teacher reaches out to man by participating in the pleasures of man. He sees nothing wrong with seeking the pleasures and possessions of the world.

⇒ He sees nothing wrong with joining in with people in their worldly behavior, worldly socials, and worldly talk.

⇒ He sees nothing wrong with seeking the things of this world: possessions, recognition, honor, position, influence, money, wealth, houses, and lands.

b. The false teacher believes that man is saved and becomes acceptable to God by keeping the rituals and rules of the church (such as baptism, circumcision, confirmation, the Lord's Supper), and by attending services when possible. False teachers believe that a person is acceptable to God if he has done these things no matter what kind of life he lives. False teachers think that the important thing is what a man does with his spirit—that a man take his spirit and believe in Jesus Christ and be baptized. If he does this, then God understands if he slips into sin here and there. The man is eternally secure because he believes and has been baptized. The kind of life the man lives can be worldly just so he has done these two things.

Note how natural; how sensual and carnal; how worldly this kind of teaching is. It says little about repentance and holy and separate living.

If you belonged to the world, it would love you as its own. As it is, you do not belong to the world, but I have chosen you out of the world. That is why the world hates you. (John 15:19)

With many other words he warned them; and he pleaded with them, "Save yourselves from this corrupt generation." (Acts 2:40)

Therefore, I urge you, brothers, in view of God's mercy, to offer your bodies as living sacrifices, holy and pleasing to God—this is your spiritual act of worship. Do not conform any longer to the pattern of this world, but be transformed by the renewing of your mind. Then you will be able to test and approve what God's will is—his good, pleasing and perfect will. (Rom 12:1-2)

"Therefore come out from them and be separate, says the Lord. Touch no unclean thing, and I will receive you." "I will be a Father to you, and you will be my sons and daughters, says the Lord Almighty." (2 Cor 6:17-18)

Have nothing to do with the fruitless deeds of darkness, but rather expose them. (Eph 5:11)

In the name of the Lord Jesus Christ, we command you, brothers, to keep away from every brother who is idle and does not live according to the teaching you received from us. (2 Th 3:6)

Do not love the world or anything in the world. If anyone loves the world, the love of the Father is not in him. For everything in the world—the cravings of sinful man, the lust of his eyes and the boasting of what he has and does—comes not from the Father but from the world. (1 John 2:15-16)

5. False teachers do not have the Spirit of God. No matter what they think or say, the spirit they have is not the Spirit of God. The true Spirit of God acknowledges that Jesus Christ has come in the flesh, that the incarnation is true. If a teacher has the Spirit of God dwelling in him, then he acknowledges the incarnation, the wonderful truth that God did become Man and did come to earth to save man. The Spirit of God *cannot acknowledge* anything other than the truth; therefore, every teacher who has the Spirit of God will acknowledge the same truth. He cannot acknowledge anything else because the Spirit of God Himself dwells within him. If he acknowledges anything else, then the spirit within him is not the Spirit of God. (See notes—1 Jn.4:1; 4:2-3 for more discussion.)

The Spirit of truth. The world cannot accept him, because it neither sees him nor knows him. But you know him, for he lives with you and will be in you. (John 14:17)

But the Counselor, the Holy Spirit, whom the Father will send in my name, will teach you all things and will remind you of everything I have said to you. (John 14:26)

But when he, the Spirit of truth, comes, he will guide you into all truth. He will not speak on his own; he will speak only what he hears, and he will tell you what is yet to come. (John 16:13)

You, however, are controlled not by the sinful nature but by the Spirit, if the Spirit of God lives in you. And if anyone does not have the Spirit of Christ, he does not belong to Christ. (Rom 8:9)

Because those who are led by the Spirit of God are sons of God. (Rom 8:14)

We have not received the spirit of the world but the Spirit who is from God, that we may understand what God has freely given us. This is what we speak, not in words taught us by human wisdom but in words taught by the Spirit, expressing spiritual truths in spiritual words. (1 Cor 2:12-13)

Don't you know that you yourselves are God's temple and that God's Spirit lives in you? (1 Cor 3:16)

As for you, the anointing you received from him remains in you, and you do not need anyone to teach you. But as his anointing teaches you about all things and as that anointing is real, not counterfeit—just as it has taught you, remain in him. (1 John 2:27)

Those who obey his commands live in him, and he in them. And this is how we know that he lives in us: We know it by the Spirit he gave us. (1 John 3:24)

We know that we live in him and he in us, because he has given us of his Spirit. (1 John 4:13)

2 (20-21) **Believer, Duty—Prayer**: second, build up yourselves. There are four ways that a believer builds himself up.

1. The believer builds upon the foundation of *holy faith*. What does this mean? By *faith* is meant our beliefs, the body of truth that we have learned from Scripture. It is the *Holy Scripture* that tells us about God and His Son, the Lord Jesus Christ, and about man and his world. This is

significant, for it means that our beliefs are not our own opinions nor the opinions of any other man. Our beliefs come directly from Jesus Christ and the Holy Spirit of God as they inspired prophets to write the Holy Scripture (see outlines and notes—2 Tim.3:16; 2 Pt.1:19-21 for more discussion). This is probably what Jude meant by *holy*. Remember *holy* means separate, set apart, different. Our holy faith is far different from all other faiths. It is a faith that is not based upon opinion, speculation, and imaginations of men. It is faith that has been separated and set apart from man's ideas about God and life. It is a faith that is separated and set apart by God Himself, that has come from God. It is the "most holy faith" of God, His Son, and His Spirit—the *holy faith* that is to be held by all the people of the earth.

The point is this: believers are to build up their lives upon their *holy faith*. They are to study, meditate, learn, memorize, and live out the Scripture. They are to build upon what they have learned and then continue to build more and more. The only way believers can do this is to study and study the *holy faith*, the living Word of God.

"Therefore everyone who hears these words of mine and puts them into practice is like a wise man who built his house on the rock. The rain came down, the streams rose, and the winds blew and beat against that house; yet it did not fall, because it had its foundation on the rock. But everyone who hears these words of mine and does not put them into practice is like a foolish man who built his house on sand. The rain came down, the streams rose, and the winds blew and beat against that house, and it fell with a great crash." (Mat 7:24-27)

Now the Bereans were of more noble character than the Thessalonians, for they received the message with great eagerness and examined the Scriptures every day to see if what Paul said was true. (Acts 17:11)

"Now I commit you to God and to the word of his grace, which can build you up and give you an inheritance among all those who are sanctified. (Acts 20:32)

For no one can lay any foundation other than the one already laid, which is Jesus Christ. (1 Cor 3:11)

Do your best to present yourself to God as one approved, a workman who does not need to be ashamed and who correctly handles the word of truth. (2 Tim 2:15)

Nevertheless, God's solid foundation stands firm, sealed with this inscription: "The Lord knows those who are his," and, "Everyone who confesses the name of the Lord must turn away from wickedness." (2 Tim 2:19)

All Scripture is God-breathed and is useful for teaching, rebuking, correcting and training in righteousness, (2 Tim 3:16)

Like newborn babies, crave pure spiritual milk, so that by it you may grow up in your salvation, now that you have tasted that the Lord is good. (1 Pet 2:2-3)

How sweet are your words to my taste, sweeter than honey to my mouth! (Psa 119:103)

When your words came, I ate them; they were my joy and my heart's delight,

for I bear your name, O LORD God Almighty. (Jer 15:16)

2. The believer builds by praying in the Spirit. This is the Holy Spirit. To pray in the Spirit means...

- that we pray under His guidance and influence, under His energy and power.
- that we seek and ask His help as we approach the throne of grace.
- that we focus our minds and concentrate upon the Holy Spirit helping us to pray, and depend upon Him to help us.
- that we ask and depend upon the Holy Spirit to cleanse our requests and make sure that what we ask is according to the will of God.
- that we walk in the Spirit day by day and offer unbroken prayer to God all day long.
- that we set time aside every day and wrestle in prayer before God for the needs of loved ones and for the needs of God's people and for the world—all in the Spirit.

In the same way, the Spirit helps us in our weakness. We do not know what we ought to pray for, but the Spirit himself intercedes for us with groans that words cannot express. And he who searches our hearts knows the mind of the Spirit, because the Spirit intercedes for the saints in accordance with God's will. (Rom 8:26-27)

I urge you, brothers, by our Lord Jesus Christ and by the love of the Spirit, to join me in my struggle by praying to God for me. (Rom 15:30)

For this reason, ever since I heard about your faith in the Lord Jesus and your love for all the saints, I have not stopped giving thanks for you, remembering you in my prayers. (Eph 1:15-16)

And pray in the Spirit on all occasions with all kinds of prayers and requests. With this in mind, be alert and always keep on praying for all the saints. (Eph 6:18)

Devote yourselves to prayer, being watchful and thankful. (Col 4:2)

Pray continually; (1 Th 5:17)

Look to the LORD and his strength; seek his face always. (1 Chr 16:11)

3. The believer builds himself up by keeping himself in the love of God (see note—1 Jn.3:10; 3:14; DEEPER STUDY # 1—5:16 for discussion).

4. The believer builds himself up by waiting for the mercy of our Lord Jesus Christ, by waiting for that glorious day of His return. Jesus Christ has made it possible for God to have mercy upon us *now*: God has forgiven our sins. But the day of redemption, the glorious day when God's mercy will be fully known, will not take place until the return of Christ. It is at His return that we will be transformed into His image of perfection and glory. Therefore, the way to build ourselves up is to keep our eyes upon the mercy of Jesus Christ and the glorious day of His return. (See note—1 Jn.2:28 for more discussion.)

For the Son of Man is going to come in his Father's glory with his angels, and then he will reward each person according to what he has done. (Mat 16:27)

"When the Son of Man comes in his glory, and all the angels with him, he will sit on his throne in heavenly glory. All the nations will be gathered before him, and he will separate the people one from another as a shepherd separates the sheep from the goats. (Mat 25:31-32)

Moreover, the Father judges no one, but has entrusted all judgment to the Son, "Do not be amazed at this, for a time is coming when all who are in their graves will hear his voice and come out—those who have done good will rise to live, and those who have done evil will rise to be condemned. (John 5:22, 28-29)

Therefore judge nothing before the appointed time; wait till the Lord comes. He will bring to light what is hidden in darkness and will expose the motives of men's hearts. At that time each will receive his praise from God. (1 Cor 4:5)

For we must all appear before the judgment seat of Christ, that each one may receive what is due him for the things done while in the body, whether good or bad. (2 Cor 5:10)

In the presence of God and of Christ Jesus, who will judge the living and the dead, and in view of his appearing and his kingdom, I give you this charge: (2 Tim 4:1)

Since you call on a Father who judges each man's work impartially, live your lives as strangers here in reverent fear. (1 Pet 1:17)

Enoch, the seventh from Adam, prophesied about these men: "See, the Lord is coming with thousands upon thousands of his holy ones to judge everyone, and to convict all the ungodly of all the ungodly acts they have done in the ungodly way, and of all the harsh words ungodly sinners have spoken against him." (Jude 1:14-15)

And I saw the dead, great and small, standing before the throne, and books were opened. Another book was opened, which is the book of life. The dead were judged according to what they had done as recorded in the books. (Rev 20:12)

"Behold, I am coming soon! My reward is with me, and I will give to everyone according to what he has done. (Rev 22:12)

3 (22-23) **Witnessing**: third, be compassionate and reclaim people. Verse 22 is a difficult verse to translate from the Greek. This is clearly seen by anyone who looks at several English translations. The outline follows the New American Standard: "And have mercy on some, who are doubting." Note three points.

1. Believers are to be compassionate and reclaim those who are doubting. A false teacher causes people to doubt the faith, especially those who are attracted to his charisma, appearance, beliefs, and to his preaching and teaching style. In addition to these, there are many young and immature and carnal believers who are easily led to doubt the truth. It is the duty of mature believers to reach

out to those who begin to doubt, and note how: in compassion. We are *not to reach* out in...

- censorship
- judgment
- criticism
- harshness
- severity
- haughtiness
- superiority
- spiritual pride

True, we are not the ones who began to doubt; we stood fast. But our spirit must be compassionate and loving; we must seek to restore them to the Lord Jesus Christ.

2. Believers are to be compassionate and reclaim those who are lost in the false teaching. Note how: by striking fear in them. We must warn them of God's judgment and of the danger of eternal doom if they reject and turn against and deny God's Son (see notes—1 Jn.4:2-3; 2:18; 2:22-23 for discussion).

3. Believers must guard themselves when reaching out to help others. The language used is descriptive: believers must hate "even the clothing stained [polluted] by corrupted flesh." They hate everything about false teaching that defiles people, hate it so much that they would never be deceived by its appealing ways. Believers must guard against becoming polluted themselves when they get along side those...

- who follow their own sinful desires.
- who are backslidden.
- who are deceived.
- who are teaching error.

Believers must hate the world and its false teaching and worldly lifestyle, hate them so much that they even hate the clothing stained by corrupted flesh. Believers must guard and protect themselves from all defilement of the world and its false teaching.

4 (24-25) **Power, of God—Security**: fourth, walk in the keeping power of God. This is the conclusion of Jude's short letter. Note that this is a benediction upon believers. It is one of the most well known benedictions by Christians all over the world. Note the great message on the source of the believer's security. What is the source of the believer's security? Who is it that keeps the believer secure while he walks upon the earth? It is God—God's *keeping power*.

1. God is *able to keep us from falling*. In verse 21 we are told that we are to keep ourselves in the *love of God*. Here we are told that God *keeps us*. What is the difference? "We must watch that we *stay close* to the Lord, but only He can guard us so that we do not stumble" (Michael Green. *The Second Epistle of Peter and The Epistle of Jude.* "The Tyndale New Testament Commentaries," p.190). God alone has the power to keep us from falling in a world that has so much corruption and false teaching. But for God to keep us, we must draw near Him and stay in touch with Him. How? By daily Bible study and prayer, and by walking righteously. By learning to walk moment by moment in open and unbroken prayer, communion, and fellowship with Him.

2. God is *able to make us blameless* when we come face to face with Him. The word "without fault" (amomos) means to be spotless and pure, without any defilement whatsoever. God is able to accept us in Jesus Christ, the spotless Lamb of God. If we will continue to approach God in Christ—in the name of Christ and His death—then God will accept us and count our faith as righteousness. He will accept us in the righteousness of His Son, the Lord Jesus Christ. God is able to do this, and He will do it if we will draw near Him *in Christ*.

3. God is able to infuse us with triumphant joy in the glorious day that we meet Him face to face. There will be so much to excite and cause our hearts to joy and rejoice:

⇒ the glory of God's presence and of heaven
⇒ the glory of Christ and of seeing Him face to face
⇒ the transformation of our bodies into perfection
⇒ the joy of being reunited with our deceased loved ones
⇒ the unbelievable exaltation of being made kings and priests to rule and reign with Christ
⇒ the unbelievable exaltation of being assigned the duty of serving God and Christ forever and ever.

All of this and so much more will stir our hearts to greatly rejoice in Christ for ever and ever. (See note, *Rewards*—1 Pt.1:4 for a complete list of the rewards to be given to the believer.)

4. God is the only God and He is our Savior. The idea is that He is the only living and true God—the only God who could ever plan and create the world and man, the only God who could bring about the salvation of man after man had made such a mess of things. God is the Savior. He alone has the wisdom and power to save man from this corruptible world of sin and evil, disease and accident, death and judgment.

5. God alone is the God who dwells in glory, majesty, power and authority.

⇒ He alone is the Supreme Glory and Majesty of the universe.
⇒ He alone is the Supreme Authority and Power of the universe.

Therefore, the only thing left for believers to do is to shout the praises of Him who alone can save them:

To him who is able to keep you from falling and to present you before his glorious presence without fault and with great joy— to the only God our Savior be glory, majesty, power and authority, through Jesus Christ our Lord, before all ages, now and forevermore! Amen. (Jude 1:24-25)

THE

OUTLINE & SUBJECT INDEX

REMEMBER: When you look up a subject and turn to the Scripture reference, you have not only the Scripture, you have *an outline and a discussion* (commentary) of the Scripture and subject.

This is one of the *GREAT VALUES* of **The Preacher's Outline & Sermon Bible**®. Once you have all the volumes, you will have not only what all other Bible indexes give you, that is, a list of all the subjects and their Scripture references, *BUT* you will also have…

- An outline of *every* Scripture and subject in the Bible.
- A discussion (commentary) on every Scripture and subject.
- Every subject supported by other Scriptures or cross references.

DISCOVER THE GREAT VALUE for yourself. Quickly glance below to the very first subject of the Index of Jude. It is:

ANGELS
Position in creation.
Less power than Satan. 8-9

Turn to the reference. Glance at the Scripture and outline of the Scripture, then read the commentary. You will immediately see the GREAT VALUE of the INDEX of **The Preacher's Outline & Sermon Bible**®.

OUTLINE AND SUBJECT INDEX

INDEX

PURPOSE STATEMENT

LEADERSHIP MINISTRIES WORLDWIDE

exists to equip ministers, teachers, and laymen in their
understanding, preaching, and teaching of God's Word
by publishing and distributing worldwide
The Preacher's Outline & Sermon Bible®
and related *Outline* Bible materials,
to reach & disciple men, women, boys, and girls for Jesus Christ.

•MISSION STATEMENT•

1. To make the Bible so understandable - its truth so clear and plain - that men
   and women everywhere, whether teacher or student, preacher or hearer,
   can grasp its Message and receive Jesus Christ as Savior; and...
2. To place the Bible in the hands of all who will preach and teach God's Holy
   Word, verse by verse, precept by precept, regardless of the individual's
   ability to purchase it.

The **Outline** Bible materials have been given to LMW for printing and especially
distribution worldwide at/below cost, by those who remain anonymous. One fact,
however, is as true today as it was in the time of Christ:

• The Gospel is free, but the cost of taking it is not •

LMW depends on the generous gifts of Believers with a heart for Him and a love and
burden for the lost. They help pay for the printing, translating, and placing **Outline**
Bible materials in the hands and hearts of those worldwide who will present God's
message with clarity, authority and understanding beyond their own.

LMW was incorporated in the state of Tennessee in July 1992 and received IRS 501(c) 3 nonprofit status in March 1994. LMW is an international, nondenominational mission organization.
All proceeds from USA sales, along with donations from donor partners, go 100% into under-
writing our translation and distribution projects of **Outline** Bible materials to preachers,
church & lay leaders, and Bible students around the world.

9/98

© 1998. Leadership Ministries Worldwide

Box 21310 - Chattanooga, TN 37424 • (423) 855-2181 • FAX (423) 855-8616
• E-Mail - outlinebible@compuserve.com — www.outlinebible.org •

Equipping God's Servants Worldwide

1. **PAYMENT PLANS.** Convenient and affordable ways to get/use your FullSet with easy payments.

2. **NEW TESTAMENT**. In 14 volumes. Deluxe version 3-ring binders. Also: SoftBound Set, 3 volume set, and NIV edition. All on 1 CD-ROM disc.

3. **OLD TESTAMENT**. In process; 1 volume releases about every 6-8 months, in sequence.

4. **THE MINISTERS HANDBOOK.** Acclaimed as a "must-have" for every minister or Christian worker. Outlines more than 400 verses into topics like Power, Victory, Encouragement, Security, Restoration, etc. Discount for quantities.

5. **THE TEACHER'S OUTLINE & STUDY BIBLE™**. Verse-by-verse study & teaching; 45 minute lesson or session. Ideal for study, small groups, classes, even home schooling. Each book also offers a STUDENT JOURNAL for study members.

6. **OUTLINE BIBLE CD-ROM.** Includes all current volumes and books; Preacher, Teacher, and Minister Handbook. 1 disc. WORDsearch STEP format. Also 50+ Bible study tools unlockable on same disc. **FREE Downloads - www.outlinebible.org**

7. THE **OUTLINE**. Quarterly newsletter to all users and owners of *POSB*. Complimentary.

8. **LMW AGENT PLAN.** An exciting way any user sells *OUTLINE* materials & earns a second income.

9. **DISTRIBUTION.** Our ultimate mission is to provide *POSB* volumes & materials to preachers, pastors, national church leaders around the world. This is especially for those unable to purchase at U.S. price. USA sales gain goes 100% to provide volumes at affordable prices within the local economy.

10. **TRANSLATIONS.** Korean, Russian, & Spanish are shipping first volumes — Others in-process: Hindi, Tamil, Telugu, Chinese, French, German, Finnish.

11. **FUNDING PARTNERS.** To cover the cost of all the translations, plus print, publish, and distribute around the world is a multi million dollar project.

    Church-to-Church Partners send *Outline* Bible books to their missionaries, overseas church leaders, Bible Institues and seminaries...at special prices.

12. **REFERRALS.** Literally thousands (perhaps even you!) first heard of *POSB* from a friend. Now Referral Credit pays $16.00 for each new person who orders from a customer's Referral.

13. **CURRICULUM & COPYRIGHT.** Permission may be given to copy specific portions of *POSB* for special group situations. Write/FAX for details.

9/98

For Information about any of the above, kindly FAX, E-Mail, Call, or Write

Please PRAY 1 Minute/Day for LMW!

PO Box 21310, Chattanooga, TN 37424 • (423) 855-2181 • FAX (423) 855-8616
• E-Mail - outlinebible@compuserve.com — www.outlinebible.org •

Sharing

The OUTLINED BIBLE

With the World!